Foul Bodies

FOUL BODIES

Cleanliness in Early America

Kathleen M. Brown

CABRINI COLLEGE LIBRARY
610 KING OF PRUSSIA ROAD
RADNOR, PA 19087

Yale University Press
New Haven & London

 # 150536396

Society and the Sexes in the Modern World
Christine Stansell, Series Editor

Published with assistance from the foundation established in memory of
Philip Hamilton McMillan of the Class of 1894, Yale College.

Copyright © 2009 by Yale University.
All rights reserved.
This book may not be reproduced, in whole or in part, including illustrations,
in any form (beyond that copying permitted by Sections 107 and 108 of the
U.S. Copyright Law and except by reviewers for the public press),
without written permission from the publishers.

Set in Postscript Electra type by The Composing Room of Michigan, Inc.
Printed in the United States of America.

Library of Congress Cataloging-in-Publication Data

Brown, Kathleen M., 1960–
Foul bodies : cleanliness in early America / Kathleen M. Brown.
p.   cm. — (Society and the sexes in the modern world)
Includes bibliographical references and index.
ISBN 978-0-300-10618-3 (cloth : alk. paper).   1. Hygiene — United States —
History — 18th century.   2. Hygiene — United States — History — 19th century.
I. Title. II. Series.
[DNLM: 1. Hygiene — history — United States.   2. Cultural Evolution —
United States.   3. History, 17th Century — United States.   4. History, 18th Century —
United States.   5. History, 19th Century — United States.   6. Human Body —
United States.   QT 11 AA1 B878f 2008]
RA780.B76 2008
613'.40973 — dc22
2008022131

A catalogue record for this book is available from the British Library.

This paper meets the requirements of ANSI/NISO Z39.48 –1992 (Permanence of Paper).
It contains 30 percent postconsumer waste (PCW) and is certified by the
Forest Stewardship Council (FSC).

10   9   8   7   6   5   4   3   2   1

For Ted, William, Owen, and Emily

Jaques: Invest me in my motley; give me leave
　　　　To speak my mind, and I will through and through
　　　　Cleanse the foul body of th' infected world,
　　　　If they will patiently receive my medicine.

　　　　　　　　William Shakespeare, *As You Like It*

CONTENTS

ILLUSTRATIONS

ACKNOWLEDGMENTS

Many agencies and institutions have supported my work on this book. A year-long Andrew W. Mellon Postdoctoral Fellowship at the American Antiquarian Society launched the research. A Berkshire Fellowship from the Mary Ingraham Bunting Institute of Radcliffe College provided summer support. A grant to junior faculty from the University of Pennsylvania Women's Studies Program enabled me to purchase a laptop. A National Endowment for the Humanities Fellowship for University Teachers funded a year of writing. The University of Pennsylvania School of Arts and Sciences and the Department of History supported the leave that made it possible to complete the book. I thank all of these institutions and my department chair, Walter Licht, for their support.

Numerous librarians, curators, and administrators helped me learn more about my sources and facilitated my search for appropriate images. At the American Antiquarian Society, Tom Knoles, Jaclyn Penney, Joanne Chaison, Caroline Sloat, Su Wolfe, and John Hench; Emily Guthrie, Melissa Naulin, and Jeanne Solensky at Winterthur Library; John Pollack at Van Pelt Library Rare Books; Kimberly M. Toney at the Newport Historical Society; Sylvia Inwood at the Detroit Institute of Arts; Glen Lisenbardt at the New York State Historical Association; and Elise Calvi at the State University of New York Upstate Medical Library.

Every time I presented a paper, people generously shared personal stories and citations that enriched my understanding of this topic. Thanks to audiences at the University of Connecticut, Brandeis University, Gettysburg College, the American Antiquarian Society, the History of Science, Medicine, and Technology Department at Johns Hopkins, Columbia University's Early American History Seminar, Wesleyan University's Center for Humanities, the University of

Michigan, the University of California at Los Angeles, the University of Florida, the University of Wisconsin, Harvard University's Charles Warren Center and Atlantic Seminar, the Gendered Spaces Conference at the University of California at Irvine, the McNeil Center for Early American Studies, and the University of Pennsylvania's Atlantic Studies Seminar, Department of History, Department of History and Sociology of Science, and the Women's Studies Program. I also benefited from presenting portions of this work at several meetings of the Organization of American Historians.

Thanks to the following presses for permission to reproduce material that has appeared previously: "Native Americans and Early Modern Concepts of Race," in Martin Daunton and Rick Halpern, eds., *Empire and Others: British Encounters with Indigenous Peoples*, 79–100, © 1999 Martin Daunton and Rich Halpern and contributors, portions reprinted by permission of the University of Pennsylvania Press; "Murderous Uncleanness," in Janet Moore Lindman and Michele Lise Tartar, eds., *A Centre of Wonders: The Body in Early America*, 77–94, © 2001 and portions reprinted by permission of Cornell University Press; "The Maternal Physician: Teaching American Women to Put the Baby in the Bathwater," in Charles Rosenberg, ed., *Right Living: An Anglo-American Tradition of Self-Help Medicine and Hygiene*, 88–111, © 2003 and portions reprinted by permission of the Johns Hopkins University Press; "Body Work in the Antebellum United States," in Ann Stoler, ed., *Haunted by Empire: Geographies of Intimacy in North American History*, 213–232, © 2006 and portions reprinted by permission of Duke University Press.

I could not have finished this book without lots of assistance. Jill Allison, Katherine Paugh, Jennifer Schaaf, and Lauren Smith helped me with preliminary research. Jennifer Reiss ably investigated several topics later in the project. Rachel Moskowitz proved to be a thorough and talented researcher who helped me answer questions others had found unanswerable. My neighbor and friend Beth Attig helped me to reorganize parts of the manuscript. Numerous colleagues, friends, and fellow researchers generously shared citations about cleanliness: Kon Dierks, Renee Sentilles, Walt Woodward, Sally Mason, Steven Bullock, Lucia Knoles, Mike Zuckerman, Wayne Franklin, Nicole Eustace, Dan Richter, Robert DuPlessis, John Smolenski, Harvey Greene, Fredricka Teute, Caroline Sloat, Janet Theophanos, and Harry Marks. Charles Rosenberg provided early encouragement and allowed me to work with his amazing collection of medical advice books. Angus Corbett reminded me of an unfinished conversation about Mary Wollstonecraft. My writing and life support group—Barbara Stengel, Tracey Weis, Carol Counihan, and Theresa Russell-Loretz—came to my rescue at several crucial moments and never failed to inspire me. Tracey and

Tom Ryan, Keri and Josh Cohen, Jon and Beverly Sensbach, Leslie Reagan, Maureen Fitzgerald and Leisa Meyer, Amy and Patrick Hopkins, Bill Katz and Jan Swenson, Lisa Sonneborn (proofreader extraordinaire), and Jeannine Alvaré also provided much needed friendship. For nearly ten years, Penny Rager has given me peace of mind by caring for my children when I needed to work. I also thank Diane Levin Gall, Marilyn Luber, and Steven Secunda for their assistance.

Special thanks go to Penn colleagues Dan Richter, Bruce Kuklick, and Murray Murphey, for reading the entire manuscript. Kathy Peiss's close readings and insightful comments made it a better book. Ann Moyer shared an important early modern source and guided me to a Latin translation. Roget Chartier enriched my perspective on early modern body care and shared several valuable citations. Barbara Savage, Antonio Feros, and Beth Linker offered helpful comments at a late stage in the project. Several other colleagues helped me to get back on track when this book threatened to drive me crazy. I am grateful to Barbara Savage, Deborah Broadnax, Ann Farnsworth-Alvear, and Kristen Stromberg Childers for support and friendship above and beyond the call of duty.

At Yale University Press, series editor Chris Stansell provided detailed comments that reflected a careful and rigorous reading. As outside readers, Mary Fissell caught numerous errors and generously agreed to share the term *body work* with me, and Laurel Ulrich offered sage advice that prevented this from becoming a multivolume work. I thank editor Chris Rogers for his patience and support of the project, Laura Davulis for her expert advice and goodwill, and Dan Heaton for his eagle eye and sharp wit.

My family is happy to hear that the book is finished. My mother, Sheila Brown, assisted me with some of the Boston-area research when I first began the project, never guessing I would still be at it nearly a decade later, and helped out during the copyediting. For as long as my children can remember, Mommy has been working on her book. Along with their dad, Ted Pearson, they are looking forward to life after its completion. Ted has helped the effort along in innumerable practical ways, by reading the manuscript, tracking down citations, and organizing the correspondence about illustrations. On many occasions he has taken the children on little jaunts so I could squeeze in another couple of hours work. Without his support and their cooperation, I simply could not have finished.

A Note on the Text

The archaic thorn has been changed to "th" throughout the text to reflect modern orthography.

[*Sic*] has been used sparingly to indicate only those highly irregular spellings that might be mistaken for errors in transcription.

INTRODUCTION

When Olaudah Equiano sat for his portrait sometime during the 1780s, the self-identified African and antislavery advocate appeared every bit the English gentleman. He wore his hair unpowdered and tied back in a style increasingly popular with gentlemen on both sides of the Atlantic. A pristine white neck cloth covered his skin from chin to collarbone, offsetting his dark skin and garnet-red waistcoat and jacket. The white ruffles of his linen shirt were so fine that they appeared to be nearly translucent.

Yet despite this willingness to conform to a genteel European idiom, Equiano elsewhere pointedly challenged European claims to embody civility. In *The Interesting Narrative of the Life of Olaudah Equiano, or Gustavus Vassa the African*, his powerful 1789 testimonial against the slave trade, he blamed Europeans for spreading moral and physical corruption to Africans. In contrast, the West African Ibo society about which he wrote instilled the virtues of cleanliness in children. Ritual hand washing, including a purification before mealtime, was both a "necessary habit of decency" and "a part of religion" among the Ibo, Equiano explained. "Before we taste food we always wash our hands," he noted, adding that "our cleanliness on all occasions is extreme; but on this it is an indispensable ceremony." Equiano's Ibo also had a refined aesthetics of smell. Perfume was the principal luxury of the people he described as plain living. Bodily cleanliness, achieved through ritual purification and mundane body care, marked the Ibo as civilized.[1]

Claiming to have been abducted from his idyllic West African village at the age of eleven and eventually sold to Atlantic slave traders, Equiano was appalled by what he witnessed during his forced march. The closer he got to the coast, the stronger were the cultural influences of Europeans and the dirtier people's habits. In sharp contrast to his own people, the West Africans he encountered "did not circumcise, and ate without washing their hands." Not coincidentally, he noted, these unclean people had also lost touch with indigenous spiritual traditions. Equiano's growing discomfort with the uncleanness around him only worsened with his Middle Passage across the Atlantic. Forced below decks, where the airless compartments reeked of human waste, he received "such a salutation in my nostrils as I had never experienced in my life." Sickened by the loathsome stench as well as by grief, Equiano recovered only to witness the deaths of many fellow captives, whose demise he attributed in part to the unwholesome air. Equiano employed such vivid sensory imagery to signal his pointed rejection of the idea that European commerce was simply a vector of civilization. Rather, Europeans could also be corrupt, physically and morally, and could perpetrate incalculable damage upon West Africans. It was no accident that he emphasized the strength of West African traditions of cleanliness, lest careless European readers too quickly associate slaves with the "pestilential stench" of the ships that carried them across the Atlantic.[2]

Equiano's story appeared in print at a critical historical moment. By 1789 colonial relationships, the political authority of monarchs, and the trade in African slaves were all being questioned. For three centuries, the Atlantic economy had been bringing people with different traditions of body care into contact. Europeans, Native Americans, and West Africans had different explanations for the workings of the human body: its essential qualities, boundaries, and needs, its relationship to the spiritual world, its susceptibility to disease, and the best methods for healing it. Contact among these different populations left impressions upon bodies as well as upon cultures. Raised with different standards for the body, Atlantic peoples witnessed diverse practices and adapted their own habits to new circumstances. Confronted with this "New World," Europeans, too, adjusted longstanding traditions. Equiano's challenge to beliefs in European cultural superiority and his condemnation of the slave trade as a gross violation of nature and humanity came in the midst of this disruption and reinvention. His narrative evoked several timely topics: the potentially destructive impact of new cultures upon traditions of caring for the body; the importance of genteel appearance as a mark of male refinement; the close relationship of disease, disgust, and moral corruption in the eighteenth-century imagination; and the significance of intimate domestic habits for public assessments of civilization and humanity. Taking our cues from Equiano, we ask, can a historical approach to the body reframe our fundamental assumptions about the past—about the ways in which health, domestic life, and empire are entangled—and recast our understanding of what it means to be civilized?

We often think of the body as the physical housing of an intangible self—the soul, the spirit, or the intellect—implicated in but not reducible to who we really are. The body's materiality makes it an agent in our pleasure and desire, a central player in our aging, sickness, and death. Throughout history, people have devoted themselves to beautifying, comforting, healing, and preserving their bodies. In certain contexts, care of the body can be leisurely and playful. In others, cognizance of mortality or the desire to be beautiful infuses these efforts with urgency. All of these approaches to our material selves are steeped in culture. Religion, art, medicine, fashion, literature, and manners help us to interpret and navigate the body's materiality and imbue it with meaning. But culture is hardly confined to such a reactive role. Political and economic institutions leave their imprint on our bodies, as Norbert Elias demonstrated so convincingly in *The Civilizing Process*, and delimit the formation of our desires, our modes of emotional and sexual expression, and our intellectual orientation. Indeed, we know that popular wisdom about how the body works infiltrates our interpretations of bodily sensation. Traditions of body care, as well as ideas about pain, sickness, and health, influence actual experiences of suffering and wellness. Patterns of sociability, commerce, and habitation, moreover, shape cycles of disease and mortality. Yet although it is saturated in culture, the body is also subject to the dictates of its own logic: that of a physical being, vulnerable to sickness and death despite human efforts at intervention and interpretation.[3]

I situate the history of the body—a product of culture as well as a material entity in its own right—in the context of the early modern Atlantic and the major upheavals that followed in the eighteenth and nineteenth centuries. I trace transformations in popular knowledge before the late-nineteenth-century reception of the germ theory, a period when Europeans first expanded their reach across the Atlantic basin, transported millions of Africans to work on plantations, and destroyed the lives of millions of Native Americans. Throughout the study, I try to assess body care historically on its own terms, rather than as the quaint habits of an unenlightened, bygone age. Reconstructing the major transformations in Western body care creates a new perspective from which to analyze many other crucial changes: in the social order, in the rise of Atlantic commerce, in the definitions of subject and citizen, and in the techniques of "civilizing" that became available during the nineteenth century. Writing the history of cleanliness requires careful focus on the relationship between household practices and public expectations for a civilized body, calling attention to the impact of shifting standards for appearance, smell, and privacy on the allocation of domestic labor. Perhaps most important, *Foul Bodies* illuminates the consequences of new habits of body care on sensibilities, emotions, and desires—the repository of culture that cues seemingly natural responses to others.

It is not simply a matter of reconstructing these transformations, however, but of approaching them differently than did earlier scholars. My account differs from most other studies of bodily refinement not only in its use of an Atlantic framework but in its attention to the very different historical trajectories of male and female bodies and the impact of disease on body care. Whereas most previous studies explain the rise of the civilized, refined, or mannerly body as a consequence of changing internal social and political dynamics—in Europe, England, or North America—I argue that the Atlantic aspirations of English explorers and adventurers created a crucial context for judgments about civility. A second important departure concerns gender. During the early modern period, women were typically depicted as having the foulest of human bodies. How, in the space of three centuries, were some women able to transcend reputations for disgusting physicality to become standard bearers and enforcers of a new ethos of bodily refinement and domestic purity, both in their own households and in those of people too poor to claim the protections of privacy? Why did middle-class women embrace this role with such zeal and work so hard to instill it in their children, who would become key players in the late-nineteenth-century urban sanitary reforms and imperial "civilizing" projects? Finally, given that early modern care of the skin reflected concerns about preserving the health as well as about refining and beautifying, how can we recognize the dynamic role of the body's physical reality—its vulnerability to sickness and death—as we trace the historical trajectory of the cultured body?

Weaving a tale of Atlantic contact, changing standards of cleanliness, and new perceptions of women, *Foul Bodies* is an account of the deployment of aesthetics, health fears, and purity concerns that resulted in a culture of individual responsibility for the body. Yet in fact, as I show, behind nearly every refined body was the labor of a woman—a wife, a mother, or a domestic servant. Laundering clothes has always been women's work, and there was nothing genteel about it. But producing the bathed modern body was the work of a discerning, refined woman, sensitive to the opinions of others, who took on the task of enforcing standards. This study joins several others that challenge the notion that significant historical change takes place mainly in public arenas—the realms of politics, the economy, and the law—and that domestic life presents only a grim record of endless repetition: the daily preparations of bodies for their interactions with others; the birthing, clothing, feeding, healing, sexual pleasuring, and coercion that occurs in the decentralized venues of particular households. Domestic life—always in dynamic relationship with public culture—is also a site of cultural production that undergoes profound historical transformation.[4]

Care of the body has changed dramatically over the past five centuries. Historically, such care was likely to take place in a public facility, such as a public bathhouse. Today, in contrast, the setting and resources for bodily cleanliness are usually domestic, although other types of care take place at gyms and spas. No matter where it is performed, however, and no matter how intimate the technique, body care is never entirely private but engages a society's standards for spiritual purity, health, manners, and decency. Indeed, it is not simply the end product—the groomed, cared for body—but the organization of labor necessary to producing it that articulates a culture's deepest convictions about what it means to be civilized.

My account begins with one of the signal transformations in Western body care—the turn away from bathing the body to changing its linen as a means of achieving cleanliness—which occurred during the sixteenth century. I examine this change historically, but I also plot the reemergence of the familiar, water-based regime that we think of as modern, made possible by the medicalization and secularization of water. Throughout the period I discuss here, water figured as a potent substance, capable of strengthening or weakening bodies, depending upon its temperature. Indeed, by the nineteenth century, water had once again become indispensable to body care, marking an important transformation in cleanliness. As the historian Jean-Pierre Goubert notes, water's ubiquitous use by the late nineteenth century changed landscapes, transformed domestic labor and household architecture, and created new standards of pleasure and comfort that would lead to reimagining the body itself.[5]

The history of the body reveals a crucial and largely unexplored link between domestic life and public culture; the enormous role played by female domestic labor across four centuries to produce both the "civilized" European body and its heir, the refined "modern" body. Throughout the text, I refer to this collection of cleaning, healing, and caring labors as *body work*. I also investigate how, as this work became more skewed toward cleanliness, it became more clearly a female responsibility. Ironically, although renewed interest in bathing in the nineteenth century sparked a growing desire for privacy, in keeping with the trend toward refinement, the condition of bodies was hardly a "private" matter. Increasingly graphic discussions of the body's loathsomeness and more detailed prescriptions for its refinement reflected public concerns about disease, appearance, and moral fitness. In contrast to their early modern counterparts, modern bodies depended on these so-called private methods of body care to withstand crowded cities, endure the stresses of industrial capitalist society, and participate in public life. Child rearing, medical treatment, housekeeping practices, and domestic services all rooted modern class identities in the body. But this new, seemingly hardy body remained vulnerable to a host of invisible dangers that could be detected only by smell or through assessments of other people's private habits. Bathing eventually became a requirement for sustaining the body of the hardy and socially respectable nineteenth-century citizen.[6]

Cleanliness is an ideal for body care that reflects a culture's various representations of the body—spiritual, social, medical, and economic—expresses its fears for the consequences of interactions with other bodies, and mediates the body's relationship with the environment. Strategies for cleaning the body and keeping habitations free of filth vary widely, even within a single culture, along with fears about the body's vulnerability to pollution. Yet dominant ideals for a clean body nonetheless expose the deep structures of beliefs about the individual's relation to the larger society and the meaning of civility. Maintaining bodily frontiers —the mouth, nose, hands, feet, and genitalia—where contact with other people and the larger world takes place, cleanliness practices prepare people for those interactions and respond to the pollution that inevitably results.

A host of dramatic changes—the African and European diasporas, the rapid collapse of indigenous American populations, the growing influences of markets, cities, and print, and the rise of a literate and self-conscious middle class—transformed knowledge about the body as well as the labor required to maintain it. Epidemics, in particular, were events that sparked extraordinary public debate about cleanliness and the body. During such episodes, Western cultures drew upon medical science, religion, and manners to revise the individual's responsibilities to self and society, provoking changes in cleanliness practices. Ideas about and care of the body did not simply mirror changes in deep social structures, however, for bodies were implicated in those very transformations. Indeed, it was through their bodies—the site of seemingly indisputable, unfiltered, sensory experience—that people perceived vast historical change as natural fact. This was as true for transoceanic migrations as for the habits of healing, consumption, and social discipline that subsequently reframed people's sensibilities about their physical selves. New ways of imagining and inhabiting the body fundamentally influenced how people experienced the transformations that redefined racial and ethnic difference, urban life and sociability, and expectations for domestic labor and motherhood. Investigating cleanliness as concept and practice, strenuous labor and spiritual ideal, helps us to understand the historical significance of these processes, revealing motives as varied as the fear of mortality and the desire for respectability.[7]

Approaching the history of the body from the perspective of cleanliness permits a view of a historical rather than a natural body. Considering that body in an Atlantic rather than a narrowly European context, we find people assessing different forms of self-care in a multicultural and imperial landscape. The clothed Western body, for example, became an important symbol of civility during the era of Atlantic encounters. At the height of European contact with other Atlantic peoples who bared shoulders, arms, and torsos, linen shirts served as proxies for European bodies, demarcating eligibility for membership in the civilized world. As several scholars have noted, imperial contexts also produced new expressions of sexual desire, a product of cross-cultural contact within a skewed grid of power. But the assignment of body work to women was in some senses even more fundamental to defining the Western body, essentially delegating to women the labor of producing the civilized bodies through which imperial power would be articulated. Female responsibility for this work not only embedded Western identity in the body but also tied it to a particular domestic arrangement. Over time, this package of duties and the appearance it supported acquired an aura of timeless, natural fact. Examining cleanliness historically permits us to question the process by which women gained authority over body care and appearance (put somewhat differently—how women got stuck with the responsibility for these standards) to such a degree that they, more than others, were expected to embody these ideals. It also allows us to approach the body as a historical entity and a site of cultural production in its own right. In this account of cleanliness, some bodies appear to achieve modernity sooner than others; old ideas about body care reappear under the guise of new standards; and power inequities among different groups reveal modernity's ironies—its borrowed, stolen, repressed, and superstitious nature. Public scrutiny focused on certain bodies, even as others claimed new needs for privacy.[8]

Several questions guide the discussion that follows: What form did cleanliness take, and what motivated people to pursue it: decency, refinement, health, comfort, or spiritual purity? What prompted nineteenth-century Americans to overcome nearly three centuries of European reluctance in order to immerse their bodies in water? What can the history of the body teach us about the relationship between domestic and public life and the politics of privacy?

There are several ways to gain access to the history of unarticulated bodily sensations, practices, and self-awareness. First, although not always revealing of subjective sensation, evidence of cleanliness labors abound. When such practices as laundry, killing vermin, washing hands, and airing bedchambers are examined in the deep context of the other repetitive tasks of daily life, contemporary motivations behind cleanliness begin to emerge. Second, artifacts—the close stools (early modern toilets), toothpick cases, shirts, and bathing tubs—help the historian to reconstruct the lost arts of caring for the body by people who left no written record of their experiences. Third, although sensory lives may be hard to recover, we can plumb the language used to describe body work in the past, much of which remains in contemporary use to describe character, personal attributes, and the arduousness of effort. Take, for example, the terms describing lice removal: *nitpicking*, *fine-tooth comb*, and *lousy* are all still commonly used as metaphors by people who have never needed to rid themselves of lice. Other phrases—"throwing cold water on it," "throwing the baby out with the bathwater," "washing my hands of it," "a new broom sweeps cleaner"—hark back to the cleanliness concerns of the past even as they continue to resonate with daily life in the present. Finally, assessments of printed advice across the *longue duré* permit an Olympian view of changing ideals that might otherwise disappear in thickets of idiosyncratic practice.

Together, these lines of inquiry compose a textured, albeit partial, account of what normative cleanliness practices might have meant to those who engaged in them. Such practices also reveal the politics of daily life at its most foundational: the different preparations and assessments of bodies that imparted meaning to the distinctions between slave and citizen, man and woman, respectable middle-class matron and uncouth servant.

Any effort to compile a history of the body must begin by taking stock of the various venues in which knowledge about the body was produced. Early modern European medicine, theology, literature, and social commentary all defined the body as the ultimate source of the most dangerous and defiling pollution. Models based on the ideas of two Greek physicians, Hippocrates and Galen, which dominated medical thinking until the late seventeenth century, posited the existence of a humoral body for which equilibrium or balance signified good health. Extreme temperatures, internal blockages, and obstructed evacuations of sweat, blood, and feces could disrupt this equilibrium, increasing the body's susceptibility to corruption. Women's moister bodies, with their excess of blood, were always more prone to putrefaction. The body's own evacuative processes countered tendencies to corruption, but when they failed, certain medicines and techniques had the potential to heal by flushing out impurities. Thus the evacuating body was a polluting body. It left traces of itself everywhere, and anything with which it came in contact—people, clothing, even the air of the chamber—needed to be cleansed.[9] Medical prescriptions for preserving health overlapped in crucial ways with these tasks of maintaining the body and its habitat—the primary responsibilities of the housewife—saddling women with the burden of healing along with other domestic duties.

In the early modern approach to medicine, cleanliness was often listed along with the so-called non-naturals: air, food and drink, exercise and rest, sleep and waking, retentions and evacuations, and the passions. Most popular medical guides advised adjusting the non-naturals to achieve the internal balance necessary for health. Diet and evacuations determined the body's tendency to become corrupt, while bathing, classified as an exercise, was believed to have a stimulating effect on the body's processes. In contrast, the "natural" components of human physiology—heat, cold, dryness, and moistness—were associated with the four elements: fire, air, earth, and water. These elements had the power to purify, but in the form of dampness, heat, and stagnant air, they could also hasten corruption. When England made its Atlantic debut in the sixteenth century, humoral theory held sway, calling attention to the effect of climate upon humoral balance. But English observers were also attentive to the culturally produced non-naturals: the habits of sleep, diet, exercise, domicile, clothing, grooming, and emotional expression that characterized their own customs and those of the peoples they met during their imperial forays. By the seventeenth century, body care began to incorporate the principle of "insensible respiration," an invisible but detectable evacuation of matter through the skin's pores demonstrated by the Italian physiologist Sanctorius in 1614. Under his influence and that of subsequent anatomists, who emphasized the body's solid structures, the skin's proper function assumed new importance in health recommendations.[10]

In contrast to this medical tradition, with its emphasis on the elements of health that could be adjusted by human beings, spiritual concepts of cleanliness and filth recognized a more limited role for human agency. Aversion to the body's dangerous and disgusting physicality and belief in its capacity to reveal God's will dominated Christian tradition. Without the benefits of Christian virtue, human beings became mere animals, trapped in bodies that produced loathsome smells and toxic waste. A godly person, in contrast, restrained body and behavior to efface all connections to animals. Christian teaching compared the embodied soul, situated in corrupt housing, to a vessel or garment that required scrupulous care to remain clean. Early modern Europeans used this religious framework to interpret the body and behavior. Writers documenting contact with Native Americans and West Africans evoked *civility* in exclusive ways, conjuring fears of animal natures unmitigated by Christian virtue and foreshadowing the meanings attached to *civilization* a century later.[11]

Religious and medical concepts were mutually constitutive of explanations for the body's functions and its vulnerability to disease. In humoral and religious terms, the European body of the sixteenth and the early seventeenth centuries was porous and easily thrown out of balance. When it entered a state of grace with God, it did so quietly, with little outward physical manifestation of spiritual rebirth. By the eighteenth century, Enlightenment thinkers imagined a more solid, less porous body, which operated mechanically. Pierced by the spirit, it entered the climatic moment of religious conversion with noisy convulsions, writhing, and sobbing. The boundaries between religion and medicine continued to be blurred during the nineteenth century as people embraced with religious zeal health reforms like the water cure, and spiritual leaders like Mary Baker Eddy offered guidance to followers both bewildered and seduced by medical "quackery."[12]

Yet the physical body was always at odds with the social and religious constraints placed upon it. In its earliest appearance in European courtesy books and in novels such as Rabelais's *Pantagruel* (1532), the early modern social body was depicted as a grotesque container of noxious air, fluids, and solids that were always threatening to escape. Good manners required people to minimize visible reminders of the grotesque body while in polite company, at the very least, by retaining gas, urine, feces, vomit, and mucous until they might evacuate the body discreetly. More ambitiously, polite behavior meant hiding the lower body with clothing and carefully regulating that other unruly orifice, the mouth. These were acts of bodily discipline as well as goodwill that were seemingly at odds with the body's medical need to evacuate toxins to remain in good health. The civilized body of the early modern period was, in short, a clothed body, constantly struggling to contain itself.

Smell was the common denominator of filth, disease, corruption, and disgust. As the historian Mark Jenner has noted, fear of the health hazards presented by stenches guided nuisance laws in early modern cities. Before the germ theory attributed disease to particular agents, miasmic and contagion theories explained epidemics. Fermenting organic material—vegetable or animal—emitted noxious particles, creating miasmas that were identifiable by their terrible smells. Disease spontaneously generated in these clouds of pollution, creating a contagion that could pass from person to person through processes of respiration, perspiration, and evacuation. Motivated by the fear of disease, a person tried to avoid miasmic air or contact with the bedding of the plague-stricken. But a desire to be pleasing to others might motivate similar efforts to minimize offensive odor: a change of clothes, the use of perfume, or the fumigation of a chamber. Discerning the degree to which people perceived bad smells as disgusting rather than life threatening depended on the context. During ordinary times, another person's breath might be simply disagreeable, but during the plague years, bad breath might be fatal.[13]

Civility expressed in the body began to supplant courtesy—the code of conduct based on the performance of deference to superiors—at a key moment in the history of European cleanliness habits. Transatlantic encounters reinforced the importance of bodily habits, manners, and methods of body care for this emerging Western ideal. Some of the earliest sixteenth-century uses of *civility* came in accounts of Europeans struggling to depict their own practices as superior to those of West Africans and Native Americans. "By the end of the sixteenth century," the historian Anna Bryson concludes, "the opposition between the 'civil' and the 'barbarous' clearly involved not only questions of political organization, but also a whole spectrum of what we would call social and cultural issues, such as forms of marriage, the level of arts and trade, and religious practice."[14] Manners, the guide to civil behavior, provided rules of conduct for participants in the social and political order. Commentators described civic virtue—the state of contributing to the common good—as analogous to physical cleanliness. But cleanliness was not merely a metaphor. Mannerly, self-contained bodies became necessary not just in the presence of superiors but at all times; their outer appearance revealed the virtue within, making the body's condition a matter of public scrutiny.[15]

The ideal of political virtue for male citizens and the informal designation of sexual and moral virtue to certain groups of women—white, possessed of privacy, and living in domestic respectability—led to changes in manners as well as in the responsibility for cleanliness by the late eighteenth century. As the historian C. Dallett Hemphill has observed, the middling people of British North America adapted the Renaissance code of manners—aimed at distinguishing aristocratic bodies from common bodies—to a corpus of etiquette for smoothing the social relations between equals. New attention to manners and grooming reassured members of this emerging class of their own claims to gentility and coincided with their growing political importance in the early United States.[16]

By the nineteenth century, the ungroomed, unwashed body appeared to be even more loathsome to contemporaries than it had been two centuries earlier. Advice about cleanliness now proliferated across several different fields, appearing in guides to manners and in health and domestic management books, as well as in didactic religious fiction. Interest in bodily refinement spread across a broad socioeconomic spectrum, supported by reformers of different stripes. Most depicted bodily cleanliness as a matter of moral choice and held individuals fully responsible for the state of their own bodies. Some accounted it a matter of sensibility and doubted that all people possessed it. None acknowledged that assumptions about body care and standards of cleanliness had also changed, making decency an even more elusive goal for the urban poor and the enslaved, the people most commonly faulted for their innate uncleanness. As Equiano had discerned more than sixty years earlier and as nineteenth-century moral reformers, antislavery activists, and health advocates would rediscover, judgments passed on the body were not incidental but fundamental to larger debates about who could claim the rights and privileges of civilized humanity.

Part I

ATLANTIC CROSSINGS

European traditions of body care and manners emerged during three centuries of trade, conquest, and migration in the Atlantic basin, spreading a concept of civility rooted in the body. From the earliest Portuguese voyages along the West African coast during the fifteenth century, Europeans came in contact with other Atlantic peoples who cared for the body in distinct ways. European, Native American, and West African habits of dress, grooming, and adornment differed greatly in practice and purpose, although there was some common ground. All three Atlantic cultures embraced traditions of body care intended to transform the physical body into a social person prepared to meet the expectations of society. Not surprisingly, ideals for the body varied from culture to culture and reflected different and often internally contested standards for sociability, appropriate gender behavior, and beauty. The social body was clearly a culturally contingent body, reflective of what was shared within a culture and an important site for its fractures and dissent.

Atlantic expansion coincided with the growing European aversion to bathing as a dangerous practice. This rejection of bathing enhanced the significance of the shirt for European concepts of civility, collapsing distinctions between clothing and the body. Atlantic travelers frequently invoked shirts and skins when contrasting the bodies of Europeans with those of West Africans and indigenous Americans. Worn next to the skin, the shirt or shift had the most intimate relationship with the body of all early modern apparel. Clothing not only made the man or the woman but became conflated with the social bodies it created; linen undergarments became the body's visible "skin."

Witnessing diverse Atlantic practices of body care, Europeans questioned their own theories about the body's natural capacities. The social persons produced by unfamiliar methods of body care appeared at once wondrous and disconcerting. Their unfamiliarity disturbed the seemingly natural basis of habitual bodily practices, shaking the common sense that supported European habits, and exposing their version of the physical body to be interpreted and culturally specific. Yet cultural differences cannot be made fully to account for the ferment in European thinking about the body and civility. African and Native American methods of body care sometimes included familiar practices. Viewing culture from the outside, foreign observers throughout the Atlantic basin keenly felt the conflict between the body's seemingly natural and obviously cultural manifestations. They deemed certain effects beautiful while others filled them with repugnance.

Fueled by commercial and imperial ambition, transatlantic encounters eventually helped to transform the ways all parties imagined and groomed themselves. While Europeans developed a more self-conscious concern with whiteness and the meaning of clothing after their encounters with other Atlantic basin peoples, Native Americans worried that adopting European-style clothing might compromise their beauty and comfort. West Africans, meanwhile, integrated European textiles into their thriving trade in fabric, but continued to view the skin as the body's most significant canvas. This contrast in appearances and practices contributed to emerging racial categories, consolidating a European interpretation of civility centered on the linen-clad body. European domestic practices and care of the body became emblems of Western civilization, rooting Western identity in a particular complex of self-presentation, bodily habits, and domestic arrangements. Although the origins of this body complex appear to have been internal to Europe, its importance for European concepts of civilization only intensified with Europe's expansion and encounters with other Atlantic basin cultures.[1]

1

CARING FOR THE EARLY MODERN BODY

SACRED WATERS

Religiously motivated cleanliness was perhaps the strongest formal tradition for body care in late medieval and early modern Europe. Depictions of the human body as spiritually and literally corrupt and in need of cleansing had deep roots in Greek, Roman, Jewish, and Muslim traditions. Ritual hand washing and bathing before prayer reflected long-standing folk and religious beliefs in water's power to purify an unclean body. Immersing the body in water, moreover, occurred mainly at life's dramatic transitions: at birth, before marriage, and at death.[1] Biblical metaphors drawn from both the Old and New Testaments built on this foundation to equate sin with loathsome filth. Nudity, sexual lust, and illicit sexual acts evoked the base, animal nature of corrupt humanity and located spiritual uncleanness in a foul body.

Catholicism supplied most early modern Europeans with a framework for understanding cleanliness as spiritual purity and filth as sin. Images of heaven and hell offered vivid testimony to the environments appropriate for the sanctified Christian and the lost souls of the damned; heaven's sweet scent contrasted to the foul stench of hell. Catholicism also provided a practical example of priestly ablutions and the cleansing of Eucharistic paraphernalia before and after communion. Its teachings and sacraments offered a vision of the body as the temple of the spirit, a sacred housing for the immortal soul that could be ritually purified with water. This was most evident in the sacrament of baptism, performed by dipping an infant three times in the church's baptismal font and ceremonially anointing the child. During the late medieval period, immersion by dipping was the standard, although sprinkling or affusion was becoming more common, especially if there was reason to fear that the health of the child might be compromised.[2]

Early Christian missionaries to the British Isles incorporated pre-Christian water cults to create new traditions about the miraculous healing and purifying power of water from sacred wells. Cementing the links between old and new, churches and baptismal centers were often located near wells whose special qualities derived from the lore about a saint. For centuries, rural people seeking cures for ailments, infertility, and poverty visited these sacred sites, where they might drink of the waters, sprinkle their bodies, or immerse their entire frames.[3]

Catholic monks enjoyed greater access to baths than most lay people, but the church delivered mixed messages about the spiritual value of bathing. In the post-Roman era, only monasteries, with their advanced waterworks and strict rules for communal life, preserved the ancient Roman culture of public sanitation and bathing. These traditions persisted in some orders despite the church's suspicions that bathing was a worldly indulgence that fostered immorality. It was difficult to distinguish between care of the soul's housing, motivated properly by the desire to sanctify the temple of the spirit, and the unsanctified physical comforts such cleanliness produced. Following the traditions of early Christians, ascetic Catholics renounced bodily cleanliness to demonstrate their exclusive focus on a higher form of moral purity.[4]

In contrast to monastic baths, most secular facilities for bathing were tarred with the brush of illicit sexuality, contaminated by sinful activity and the fundamental uncleanness of women. Female uncleanness was an issue for the pre-Reformation church, posing an impediment not only to a woman's spiritual purity but to that of her husband and the larger body of worshipers. The Catholic Church protected the sanctity of church spaces from contamination by insisting that new mothers be churched, wearing a white veil and carrying a lighted candle, before they could attend Mass and receive Communion. Being churched offered ritual purification rather than literal cleansing. In addition to these precautions about contact with procreating female bodies, husbands and wives were enjoined to avoid sexual intercourse during menstruation.[5]

The Jewish tradition of mikvah, or the immersion bath, grew out of a somewhat different concern for the threat posed to a husband by a wife's uncleanness. Its purpose was to ritually cleanse a woman's body, following a preliminary cleansing bath, so that she could be sexually available to her husband without compromising his spiritual purity. Waiting exactly seven days after menstruation, an observant early modern Jewish woman with access to a mikvah prayed for purity of body and soul as she immersed herself in water. The mikvah might also be used to prepare the bodies of converts and men seeking greater spiritual purity for the Sabbath or a holiday, or to render new cooking utensils and implements fit for meals.[6]

Protestants built upon the Judeo-Christian emphasis on sin as uncleanness but with several important differences: they more frequently likened the body to a vessel or garment that could be contaminated or soiled by sin, strengthening the links between the body's spiritual and physical state. Although Protestants de-emphasized the perception of the female body as particularly unclean and marital sexuality as potentially contaminating, disgust for the human body as a source of pollution persisted, especially for the bodies of the unredeemed. The Calvinist Joseph Hall, for example, described the slothful man as having "a drie [unwashed] and nastie hand, that still savors of the sheet," and shuddered at the untrimmed beard, crusty eyes and ears, and dirty linen that revealed the man's failure to wash away traces of a night's sleep.[7]

Although many radical Protestants—most notably German pietists—engaged in their own mystical practices centered on the blood and side wounds of Christ and the ritual foot washing of the brethren, mainstream Protestants drained much of the ritual content from Christian observance. In 1552 the ceremony of churching women who had recently given birth was transformed in England from a ritual purification to a thanksgiving. The shift in emphasis marked a break with Catholicism's pollution taboos. After that date, a churched woman, as she was still known, customarily offered the chrisom cloth—a length of fine linen that wrapped her newborn at its baptism—or a cash equivalent to her parish church in thanksgiving for her safe delivery. Her need for a white veil remained a source of conflict during the seventeenth century. Prohibitions on the use of "filthy" holy relics in birthing chambers and the insistence that midwives use only pure water for emergency baptisms reflected a creeping sensitivity to the physical state of previously sanctified substances. In England, Protestants streamlined the baptismal ceremony, excising the symbolic application of all substances except for water. Baptisms continued to take place in the baptismal font, although Anglicans and Puritans clashed over its appropriateness. The 1552 revised prayer book called for the child to be dipped in the font or sprinkled if its health might be endangered by immersion, and sprinkling soon became the new Protestant standard. As city officials and religious leaders, moreover, Protestants had less tolerance than Catholics for prostitution, a stance that would help to seal the fate of the public bath in early modern Europe and England.[8]

THE LOST ART OF BATHING

Early modern western Europeans knew little of ancient Roman, Egyptian, and Hebrew bathing traditions, but they eagerly greeted new opportunities for bathing, generated by contact with a wider world. During the Crusades, English

Balneator. Der Bader.

Quisquis in æstiuo malè sole viator oberras,
    Et sudore tuum corpus vbiq grauas.
Siue tuus sumptas stomachus male digerit escas,
    Siue cutem scabies impetuosa premit.

Siue tibi fusi pendent sine lege capilli,
    Nec micat artifici barba resecta manu.
Huc ades, hîc calidæ lustraberis imbribus vndæ,
    Hîc liquida poteris mergere corpus aqua.
Hîc tibi neglecti ponentur in ordine crines,
    Immunda venies & sine labe domum.

1.1. Jost Amman, *Cupping at the Stews* (1574). Bibliothèque
nationale de France

travelers returned with tales of Byzantine and Muslim baths, and public bathing again became available to the uncloistered urban dweller. In London entrepreneurs capitalized on the exotic (and erotic) appeal of the East by calling their own commercial facilities Turkish baths. Many of these establishments were brothels that provided steam baths designed to promote perspiration before the bather rinsed or plunged into a pool of water. Sixteenth-century city ordinances referred to these public baths as "hot houses," "sweating houses," or "stews," after the Anglo-French root "estuve," or stove (Figure 1.1).[9]

Throughout the medieval period, bathing had been associated with pleasure and health as much as with cleanliness. It could be done privately, by an aristocratic couple in a domestic space, semipublicly in a more festive context, or publicly in natural mineral baths or public bathhouses that served people of various ages and stations in life. German, French, and English engravings from the thirteenth through the fifteenth century depict private bathing as a central event in the culture of courtly love and the intimate relationship of an aristocratic couple. Marriage beds, roaring fires, and unguents for anointing the skin communicated the domestic and sexual intimacy of the couple's bath together. Even in those scenes of aristocratic bathing where women bathed alone, a heterosexual couple — usually a man visiting the chamber of his beloved — dominated the image.[10]

The most common medieval bathing scene was not a young couple participating in the culture of courtly love, however, but the public bathhouse, teeming with pleasurable activity. Johann Comenius, an eastern European–born author of several innovative seventeenth-century Latin grammars, described the scene. The bathhouse patron first entered a stripping room to remove clothes and don a linen apron and cap, for decency's sake. "Sitting in a Tub or going up into the Hot-house," he might be "rubbed with a Pumice Stone or a Hair Cloth." Among the benefits of "washing places, bathes and hot bathes," Comenius noted, "filth and sluttishnesse, sweat and foulnesse are washed away." But cleaning the body was only one of many pleasures of caring for the self that took place within the bathhouse walls. Preventive medical care and socializing were also integral parts of the services provided. Barbers cut hair and shaved beards, while barber-surgeons cupped and bled patrons to improve their health. Female attendants served food and drink, provided fresh towels, and massaged, manicured, and deloused clients. Bathhouses also welcomed a broad spectrum of society. Men and women, old people and children, courting couples and illicit lovers — all appear to have resorted to the bath for reasons of pleasure, health, and comfort. Urban bathhouses, moreover, doubled as brothels, providing prostitutes, clients, and illicit lovers a site for their trysts (Figure 1.2).[11]

1.2. Medieval bathhouse. Gösta F. Sandström, Olof Thunström, and Hillari Johannes
Viherjuuri, *Bad i hemmet förr och nu* (Stockholm, 1946)

The sexually charged interactions of patrons and the intimate services provided by bath maids and prostitutes ultimately compromised the propriety of all
bathhouses. Wearing very little, men and women bathed, socialized, and engaged in sex, creating a freewheeling atmosphere of bawdy pleasure. Fifteenth-
and sixteenth-century engravings depicted sensuous scenes of baths crowded
with scantily clad men and women enjoying each other's company and perhaps
a meal, wine, or music. The term *bathhouse*, as well as its many nicknames
—bagnio, stews, bordello—became synonymous with sexual ill repute. Munici-
palities licensed bathhouses and steam rooms, which lent them some legitimacy
but also made them vulnerable to regulation during periods of moral panic.
During the fifteenth century, many European cities mandated separate facilities
for men and women in an effort to stamp out illicit sexual activity. Separate
bathing days for Jews and actors also became more widespread to prevent sexual
intimacy across important social divides. By the sixteenth century, urban authorities in England and Europe prohibited the unregulated social mixing that had
given the local bathhouse its louche character.[12]

A series of deadly epidemics put a damper on fearless, recreational bathing
throughout Europe, but the effect was especially pronounced in England,
where traditions of public bathing were relatively weak. At least 10 percent of the

English population might die during a plague year. Mortality was even higher in London, reaching 25 percent in 1563 and 1603. Suspicion fell on bathhouses as sites of illicit activity linked to Europe's new disease, syphilis, which spread throughout Europe after Columbus's voyages. Although theories about the non-sexual transmission of syphilis proliferated — "the pox" was said to be transmitted by wet nurses, used sheets, or stools of easement (the early modern toilet seat) — most concurred that the greatest risk came from sexual intercourse.[13]

It no longer seemed safe to immerse bodies that could so easily be besieged by illness. Fears of immersion reflected medical theories about the dangers to a healthy body of extremes of heat, cold, wetness, and dryness. Any extreme might disturb the delicate equilibrium of the body's humors, temperature, and moisture. Steam and hot water were believed to have an especially deleterious effect, making the body vulnerable to the deadly incursions of plague and syphilis. Hot water expanded the pores of the skin, the body's natural boundary, reducing the body's defenses against "venomous air" by making it more permeable and encouraging unhealthy and excessive sweating. Cold water, which chilled the body and temporarily obstructed perspiration, had little more to recommend it. Compared to the shock of immersion in water, dirt upon the skin seemed benign; in popular traditions it even assumed a protective function by reinforcing the skin. Washing, in this view, threatened to weaken the body by removing its "relics" — the matter it evacuated. Indeed, it seemed to many that the only safe time to wash the body was after death, as a prelude to shrouding and burial.[14]

Clergy and social commentators seized upon the fears of the baneful physical consequences of bathing to intensify their attacks upon bathhouses. Beliefs in the close relationship between good health and morally virtuous living provided medical support for their regulation. Following an outbreak of syphilis, Henry VIII closed the London stews in 1546. The timing may have had as much to do with a rising population of vagrant soldiers and unemployed men, uprooted by war and declining economic opportunity, as with the fears of disease transmission in bathhouses. Many public baths continued to operate as victualing houses, the part of their service that still seemed safe. Others managed to reopen during Elizabeth's reign, despite successive waves of deadly epidemics, perhaps by convincing local authorities they were "honest stews," or by regularly paying their fines. Concerns about the dangers of bathing continued well into the seventeenth century in both England and France. Peter Chamberlain's 1648 proposal for public baths in London, in which he argued that improved personal cleanliness might help prevent the plague, was rejected on the grounds that it might compromise health and morals despite its plan for separating men and women. New sites of sociability, like the alehouse, replaced the bathhouse as a

place where ordinary people could congregate, socialize, or engage surrepti-
tiously in illicit sex without incurring punishment for blatantly sensual public
behavior. Purveyors of food and drink at alehouses also engaged in the healing
arts, a consequence of the close relationship between medicine and diet.[15]

Even during this low point in bathing's popularity, some people continued to
bathe privately or swim recreationally, and dispensers of medical advice recommended it for certain groups of people. Infants were among those believed to
need regular baths to ensure "warmenesse, clenlinesse, helth, and pleasaunt-
nesse." John Jones, a physician and the author of *The Arte and Science of Preserving Bodie and Soule in Healthe, Wisedome, and Catholike Religion,* urged midwives in 1579 to bathe newborns in a warm water concoction of cow's milk,
"mallowes," and "sallet" oil. Cold-water immersion, even for a christening, was
to be avoided. Jones took his cues from Galen, telling the story of how the Greek
physician calmed an unhappy baby whom he found to be "filthye . . . and unwashed." Once bathed and dressed in fresh clothes, the baby fell into "a most
sounde sleepe." Regular bathing made lean infant bodies "softe and moyste,"
thus facilitating growth. Indeed, compromising the boundaries of the body
could be a good thing for an infant who needed to put on weight. Adults, too,
could benefit from immersion. Thomas Brugis listed a bathing "chaire" in *The
Marrow of Physicke* (1640) as part of the equipment needed for domestic medicine, while the French midwife Louise Bourgeois recommended several different healing and cleansing baths for new mothers.[16]

Although many doctors warned that water at extreme temperatures could
jeopardize the health of a healthy person—a caution to pleasure seekers—most
agreed that it could relieve the suffering patient. During the seventeenth century, the holywells at Bath and Buxton, along with more than a dozen other natural baths, became popular spa destinations for those seeking healing or amusement. Many spagoers drank the waters for their diuretic effect, an internal
cleansing that one author compared to washing linen white. But the popularity
of the "Doctor in Physick" William Turner's guide to the healing properties of
England's natural baths testified to the continued interest in bathing; published
in 1562, it went through seven editions by 1633. Compared to their continental
counterparts, Turner found, the English baths lacked proper maintenance,
cleanliness, and propriety, yet he pointed out these flaws not to condemn but to
encourage new investment. In 1620 Tobias Venner, "Doctor of Physicke at
Bathe," promoted the benefits of warm and hot baths as cures for female complaints, including infertility and skin diseases. But he warned against resorting to
mineral waters without first consulting a doctor, a refrain that would be repeated

throughout the century. Cautions such as these reflected a genuine belief in the powerful effects of bathing and an effort to shore up the clienteles and reputations of physicians.[17]

Bathing continued to have its advocates. Later in the century, Thomas Cock enthusiastically recommended it to England's rural gentry, the population whose economic and political fortunes were on the rise, urging that they add baths to their houses. Along with a regime of modest food consumption, he claimed, baths could help prevent a buildup of corruption in the body. Cock advocated a highly medicalized routine of dry bathing or "stoving," modeled after the practices of the Turks, French, and Italians. Following half an hour's stoving in a hot chamber while drinking a special beverage, the bather washed off the "recrements, slime, mador or mud (as it were) that stoving . . . is apt to leave upon the skin," before drying himself and getting into a warm bed. The concept of the urban bathhouse, moreover, did not disappear, despite Chamberlain's failure to establish a new facility in London. Multiple editions of Comenius's grammars depicted bathhouse activities, and bathhouses themselves continued to attract wealthy and well-connected patrons; the diarist Samuel Pepys's wife, a Frenchwoman, claimed to have benefited from bathing in a London hothouse in 1665.[18]

Despite its declining practice, bathing remained a favorite subject for painters, who feminized its representation. In sharp contrast to the depictions of the medieval bathhouse, whose pleasures might be universally enjoyed, subsequent bathing scenes portrayed the bath as a moment of sensual pleasure enjoyed by a lone female bather in her boudoir or bathing chamber. Intimate acts of caring for the female body, carried out by the woman herself or her maid, took place in this voluptuous female space and offered tantalizing pleasure to a male voyeur who lurked behind a curtain or outside the chamber window. In the late sixteenth century, bathers were always depicted as nude and their skin emitted a ghostly white gleam. During the seventeenth century, however, corresponding with the nadir of bathing and the new moralism about nudity, artists often portrayed bathers fully clothed. By the eighteenth century, the trope of the naked woman, emerging from the bath with the assistance of servants, again dominated bathing scenes (Figures 1.3–1.4).[19]

Images of private bathing as an illicit indulgence provided an aristocratic counterpoint to the stigma of sexual excess and disease attached to the public bath. To Protestant reformers, these were negative associations that countered the possible physical benefits of bathing—clean skin—with the taint of the sinful body. Physical and spiritual health had long been linked: the Latin *salus*, for

1.3. Jacopo Robusti Tintoretto, *Susanna Bathing* (1530). Kunsthistorisches Museum,
Wien oder KHM, Wien

example, means salvation but also health. Although this moral language of
cleanliness appeared in many faith traditions, especially in the Judeo-Christian
traditions of western Europe, it developed a particular emphasis in the English
Puritan vocabulary of sin, deployed to condemn the sinful excesses of both high
and low cultural practices.[20]

The seeming incompatibility of bathing with good health and moral virtue
did not make the clean body irrelevant to European concepts of civility, however, but rather narrowed the ways Europeans might imagine that body. Together, medical warnings about the dangers of immersing the body, fears of the
spread of disease, and the association of moral virtue with health contributed to
an emerging concept of civility rooted in the body but not dependent on the
cleanliness achieved by bathing. Europeans turned away from water-based
cleanliness of their bodies at the precise moment that their presence in the Atlantic basin was intensifying.[21]

1.4. On the far right, a man peeks through the window. Jean-Baptiste Pater, *The Bath* (1730/1736). Founders Society Purchase, General Membership Fund. Photograph © 1997 The Detroit Institute of Arts

LINEN

The decline of bathing during the sixteenth and seventeenth centuries did not necessarily signify the erosion of personal standards of cleanliness. Cleanliness had been only one of the bather's motives, and there had always been many ways to achieve it. By the seventeenth century, wiping or rubbing the skin, a technique that had been part of bathhouse culture, replaced bathing as the main means for removing dirt from those parts of the body hidden by clothing. This "dry" cleaning, which could be achieved simply by wearing clothes, relied on the rubbing action of cloth touching the skin. Whether one deliberately buffed the skin or simply wore a linen shirt under one's outer garments, the resulting friction was believed sufficient to remove dirt and preferable to immersing the fragile body in water. Water remained necessary to cleanse the clothes that absorbed the body's toxins, but it was not to be used to clean the body itself. Even the dampness of newly washed linens could jeopardize health by chilling the body.[22]

Using linen garments for filth removal was consistent with medical theories about how the skin protected the body from putrefaction and disease. According to early modern medical texts, toxins left the body in a variety of forms, including feces, urine, perspiration, and menstrual blood. These evacuations both cleansed the blood and helped the body achieve the balance of humors necessary for good health. During perspiration, the body expelled toxins through the pores of the skin, where they accumulated dangerously. If they were not removed, they might reenter the body through these same portals and corrupt the blood or obstruct circulation, eventually causing disease or death. Linen clothing offered this porous body protection from disease by absorbing and then removing the dangerous matter it expelled. Unlike woolens, leather, and fur, which were believed to retain infection because they could not be laundered, linen could be washed, making it less hospitable to lice. It was common practice to air garments between wearings, but undergarments, especially, needed periodic laundering. Wearing a soiled or damp garment could compromise the body's own cleaning system and bring on illness. Pepys thus followed an entry about the health risk he had taken by "putting on a suit that hath lain without ayring a great while," with a fervent prayer to God that he would not become ill.[23]

The washable shirt or shift, as the woman's undergarment was known, was the key to this regime of body care. During the sixteenth century, well-dressed men and women donned fashionable jackets, bodices, and petticoats, dramatically cut away to reveal white linen undergarments. Increasingly, these underclothes

1.5. Shirt belonging to Christian IV of Denmark, c. 1648, left. Previously published in Cunnington and Cunnington, *The History of Underclothes* (London, 1951) and used by permission of the Rosenborg Castle.

1.6. Woman's linen chemise, c. 1700. Gallery of Costume, Manchester City Galleries

expressed status. The fineness of the fabric's weave, its whiteness, and the profusion of cloth at the neck and wrists—at various points taking the form of a ruff, lace, bands, or a cravat—all revealed wealth and social position. Gentlemen and women chose expensive fabrics for their shirts and shifts: cambric, garlick holland, frieze holland, and lace. As an early-seventeenth-century poet observed,

> Pure Holland is his shirt,
> which proudly faire
> seems to outface his doublet everywhere.

White linen became the standard for these foundational garments throughout western Europe during the seventeenth century (Figures 1.5–1.6).[24]

What exactly did English people mean by *linen*, a word that sometimes referred to a specific type of fabric and other times to a genre of textile goods that had intimate contact with the body (such as bed linens)? Usually they were describing raw materials and finished cloth made at least partially from processed flax or hemp. Flax and hemp had been produced domestically on a small scale in England, Ireland, and Scotland for centuries as crops compatible with dairy farming, growing grain, and producing wool. Women commonly used buttermilk to bleach fabric, and dairy maids strained milk and wrapped butter with home-manufactured linen cheesecloth. Farm households throughout England, especially in the Lincolnshire fenlands, Wiltshire, Lancashire, and Cumberland grew flax and hemp to make linen for domestic use.[25]

Linen was a tremendously labor-intensive fabric to produce, which made it a precious commodity that often outlasted its wearer. Curiously, a fabric associated with refined purity was produced through a smelly process that relied on putrefaction. Flax had to be rotted, beaten, and combed before its hard outer shell released the fibers within. Men were more likely to do the strenuous and filthy labor of retting the flax in lint dams, while women dominated the labor of beetling, scutching, and hackling. The entire process, from planting to harvest to the end of dressing, spanned at least three seasons. Only then could women spin the fibers into thread on the small wheel in preparation for weaving.[26]

Linen's capacity to be bleached white appears to have been an important factor in its appeal for fashionable Europeans. In its undyed state, linen yarn was brown. Bleaching increased its value by as much as a third and took six months. Smaller domestic producers bleached the yarn before weaving. The Dutch, who dominated the high end of the linen market during the sixteenth and seventeenth centuries, developed of a system of bleaching whole cloth that produced the fine white linen fabric known as holland. This technique was later adopted in England and Ireland (Figure 1.7).[27]

Linen not only represented a new sensibility about achieving bodily cleanliness; it also resulted from a particular organization of domestic life. It was a product of women's labor at the spinning wheel, an endless chore that became women's main contribution to textile production after artisanal weavers in many European locales successfully excluded women from their ranks late in the sixteenth century. In many places, however, women continued to manufacture linen for domestic use. Cloth production symbolized female industry and virtue; in the classical tale of Odysseus, his chaste wife, Penelope, wards off unwelcome suitors by unraveling at night the cloth she has woven during the day, vowing never to remarry until her weaving is complete. Early modern versions of the tale demoted Penelope from weaver to spinner, in keeping with guild restrictions that created a new division of domestic labor.[28]

But *linens* also had generic meaning. It denoted the textiles that dignified the body during its least dignified moments: eating, sleeping, and in death. Table

Linen Cloths.   **LXIII.**   *Lintea.*

Linen-webs | *Linteamina*
are bleached in the Sun, 1. | insolantur, 1.

1.7. This engraving by Alexander Anderson, from an early nineteenth-century edition of Comenius's Latin grammar, captures the essential tasks of linen making depicted in previous editions. *Johann Amos Comenius's Visible World* (New York, 1810). Courtesy American Antiquarian Society

linens, newly fashionable at elite tables, gentrified the untidy display of appetite during food consumption. Bed linens allowed traces of the body's nighttime effusions to be conveniently removed. But white linen's symbolic as well as literal associations with purity were nowhere more apparent than in the practice of wrapping the washed corpse in winding sheets before burial. The clean white shroud provided the deceased with a dignified send-off that both denied and hid the putrefaction that accompanied death. Even after an act of Parliament in 1678 required burial in wool, in an effort to boost the domestic woolen industry, rather than in silk, hemp, linen, flax, gold, or silver, wealthy people persisted in choosing linen as the fabric for their shrouds.[29]

Only the very wealthy could fully indulge in this new practice of bodily purity. By the late sixteenth century, people in court circles boasted large inventories of fine white linen shirts and shifts and prided themselves on frequent changes of bed linens and undergarments. As the historian Georges Vigarello notes of this trend in classical France, "fresh, white linen removed dirt by its intimate contact with the body. Its effect was comparable to that of water. . . . To the unease aroused by bathing was added the conviction that it was unnecessary. . . . Linen absorbed sweat and impurities; changing it was in effect to wash."[30] Given the expense, the habit of frequently changing linen undergarments was slow to spread beyond the aristocracy. But medical advocacy, the powerful association of clean linen with civility, and advances in cloth production that made linens more affordable helped to spread the couture of cleanliness to the upwardly mobile. As was so often the case in matters of fashion, the French took the lead in promoting this new habit. Authors of sixteenth-century French courtesy books recommended frequent changes of the shirt for comfort and health, especially after bouts of physical exertion. Laurent Joubert, the physician-author of *Popular Errors* (1578), urged ordinary people to emulate their betters by changing their linen often. Montaigne advocated hand washing and frequent changes of linen. Common laborers and seamen who could not afford fine linen wore shirts made from cheap woolen baize, hemp canvas, dowlas, flannel, lockeram, inferior domestically produced cotton, or flimsy Silesian linen, known as "sleazy."[31]

The shirt became a powerful trope of European civility and personhood, a public skin of sorts. Along with other clothing, it represented the wearer's body, declaring his place in society and helping to constitute identity. Attention to the appearance of the visible body, including the clothes that covered it, grew, even as bathing the hidden body declined. To take one example, Queen Anne, spouse to James I, was attended by a "Laundress of the Body," who washed the queen's undergarments, not her actual body (the meaning of her position is more nearly captured for the modern reader by the title "laundress of the queen's person"). Since poor people could not engage in such opulent displays of linen and lace, clean linen also erected new sensory boundaries between the rich and the poor. Wealthy people became accustomed to the bodily comfort that resulted from frequent changes of undergarments and to associate cleanliness with the fine weave and white color of cloth that only they could afford.[32]

The task of keeping these garments clean fell to women, whether servants, daughters, or housewives. Without new laundering technology to match the scythe's contributions to agricultural efficiency, clean linens could be achieved only by those households with the labor power to spare for the backbreaking work of hauling water and wood, building fires, making soap, soaking garments in lye, stirring hot kettles, wringing wet linens, ironing, and repairing damaged cloth. In the economic uncertainty of sixteenth-century England—static wages, a growing population, and spiraling inflation—many households could not afford to withdraw women from the production of cloth and food. Thus a clean linen shirt, complete with ruffs and lace at the neck and wrists, indicated not only the wearer's refinement, attention to fashion, and wealth, but his access to the services of a laundress.[33]

Already valued highly as personal property, clean white linen was fast becoming a matter of decency, creating a ready market for the labor needed to maintain it. During the late sixteenth century and especially in postplague cities like London or Norwich, laundresses might earn cash for their labor, especially if they combined it with other intimate services such as nursing, housekeeping, or prostitution. Single women who earned wages laundering the clothes of people outside their own households, however, always operated under a cloud of suspicion. The laundress's ability to be a mobile, independent, wage earner tarnished her reputation for chastity. If sexual virtue was embodied by the domestically contained industrious matron, busily employed at the spinning wheel, then her foil was the peripatetic laundress, whose labor gained her access to the intimate lives of her customers. At the end of the sixteenth century, *laundress* and *nurse* were terms rife with sexual innuendo, and connoted *whore* or *bawd*. A century later, such connotations continued to have some grounding in the realities of urban women's working lives; the Virginia planter William Byrd II discovered that London's laundresses willingly combined sex work with providing clean clothes.[34]

During the last quarter of the sixteenth century, new opportunities for wage-earning women expanded the number of settings in which the laundress labored. With the rise of poorhouses and hospitals, laboring women might combine laundry work with spinning, sewing, and nursing to earn wages in these institutions. Plague-ridden cities offered similar opportunities. In London, officials appointed plague nurses in 1578, a measure reinforced by an act of Parliament in 1604. A plague nurse's duties included dressing meat and cleaning clothes and habitations. Indeed, medical advice books of the period interpreted both forms of body work—nursing and laundering linens—as necessary for health. The need for clean shirts and bed linens spurred municipal authorities to enforce indentures requiring masters to keep servants clean and free of lice. Female attendants of poorhouses and hospitals, moreover, were charged with maintaining the health and respectability of inmates by keeping their bodies sweet and clean.[35]

Yet even the seemingly benign labors of the plague nurse or asylum matron could not quell suspicions about the laundress that stemmed from her intimate connection to the bodies she cared for and her close proximity to pollution. In addition to the questions her economic independence and geographic mobility raised about her sexual virtue, the laundress was also feared in seventeenth-century London as a spreader of plague. London's laundress-nurses worked closely with the most seriously ill people. Laying out bodies, including stripping, washing, and wrapping them in linen for burial, was also a distinctly female set of duties. High mortality among those stricken by plague gave laundresses special access to the clothing of the deceased. By law, nurses had the right to distribute the clothing of their dead charges, but this benefit only reinforced the laundress's reputation for thievery. Beliefs that contagion clung to fabric made laundresses who sought compensation in the clothing of plague victims likely targets of suspicion during epidemics, a fact reflected in a 1593 London law and reiterated throughout the seventeenth century.[36]

Opportunities for laundresses reflected the growing importance of personal linens as a manifestation of civility and English identity. English commentators claimed white linen as their own in discussions of the Anglo-Irish encounter and in the national debate about foreign fashions. Accounted by many to be "the most barbarous nacion in Christendome," the Gaelic Irish fell outside the pale of humanity because of allegedly savage customs and manners. The English traveler and writer Fynes Moryson criticized indigenous Irish both for their nakedness and for wearing linen shirts until they were ragged and infested with lice. Such practices "infected" the resident English with Irish filthiness, he contended, which he defined as "lowsie beds, foule sheets, and all linnen."[37] When yellow linens briefly became fashionable in London, critics condemned them by pointing to the uncleanness of saffron-tinted Gaelic and Spanish shirts. Yellow linens reminded English observers of the degraded lives of Spanish courtiers, who used saffron as a dye to improve their resistance to vermin, and of the fate of Europeans in hot climates, where otherwise civilized men became infested with lice and sweated profusely in shirts they could neither launder nor change. Gaelic linen dyers allegedly intensified the saffron tint by soaking the garment in urine, a practice deprecated in England, though urine was a common ingredient in English domestic manufactures. Yellow thus conjured for its detractors bodily filth, the corruption of the Spanish court, torrid climates, and lice. To its admirers, however, yellow represented an exotic fashion alternative to white.[38]

TAMING THE BODY

Frequent changes of linens reflected a growing sensitivity to unpleasant and potentially dangerous smells. Bad smells signified putrefaction, a key concept in early modern approaches to disease and understood to occur both within and outside the body. Elite people turned to perfume, powder, pomatums (scented fat placed on the head that melted slowly into the hair and scalp), and sachets or pomanders worn on the body to surround it with good smells. Perfume had been around since ancient times, but it acquired new importance during this period. Women concocted their own scents using civet, spirit of roses, musk, frankincense, and myrrh. Well-to-do people perfumed their undergarments so that clean or recycled linens refreshed the wearer with a pleasant and healthy scent. They might also follow Lady Frescheville's advice, contained in her "receipt" or recipe book of 1669, and "put a little upon a bodkin, touch the hanging or the curtain or the bed with it," to impart a clean smell to a bedchamber. Perfume did not simply mask smells, early modern people believed, but actually purged the corruption emanating from chamber pots, close stools (chairs with receptacles attached under the seat), menstrual rags, diapers, and bodies themselves. In contrast to these noxious smells, perfumed air was believed to be healthy air. Putting perfume pellets on a "burning fire shovel" to clean the household air, heating vinegar to fumigate a sickroom, and scenting the air of hospitals were all expressions of the same belief system that led French and English courtiers to daub their persons with perfume.[39]

Interest in eradicating dangerous smells did not obviate uses for water. Applied judiciously, usually without soap, water could be effective for washing the face, hands, and neck, although some advised that facial skin was too delicate for such treatment. Receipt books of the period explained how to make special washes for hands and face. Waters for the hands might be scented with oranges, cloves, rose water, or ambergris, while facial waters required more exotic ingredients, like the caul of a lamb, which had an almost magical power. In addition to washing the face in special water, like the buttermilk concoction described by Lady Frescheville, the well-groomed European lady or gentleman might apply a sear (waxed) cloth "to take out Rinckells and smoothe the face," or rub tooth powder on teeth.[40]

Hand washing before meals became a sign of civility during the early modern period. Hosts displayed friendship and good manners when they offered guests bowls of water to wash their hands. In a society in which people of all ranks ate with their fingers out of common bowls—a fact of life even for the elite until the seventeenth century—polite people performed this mealtime ritual publicly to demonstrate their civility and to put their dinner companions at ease. The Italian author Giovanni Della Casa, whose *Galateo* appeared in English translation in 1576, thus advised would-be courtiers that although one should refrain from combing hair or washing hands in public (the latter might make the assembled company mindful of a recent call of nature), "the exception to this is the washing of the hands which is done before sitting down to dinner, for then it should be done in full sight of others, even if you do not need to wash them at all, so that whoever dips into the same bowl as you will be certain of your cleanliness." The proper etiquette for this mealtime ablution, according to Erasmus, was to allow a servant to pour water over one's hands or to dip three fingers of the hand into the bowl. In polite company, one did not plunge both hands into the dish.[41]

This elaborate attention to the hands was part of the effort to suppress the body's unruly, animalistic, habits. Elite, cosmopolitan Europeans distinguished themselves from the vulgar by their apparently artless ability to achieve mastery over their own bodies. In the Renaissance court and among the literate English gentry by the seventeenth century, good manners consisted largely of repressing the body in public by hiding bodily functions. In well-to-do houses, chamber pots and close stools gentrified the process of urinating or evacuating the bowels indoors. Indeed, close stools could be rented—not unlike the modern port-a-john—for special occasions such as feasts. Tooth picking, belching, spitting, licking the fingers, and revealing genitals or buttocks—all permissible in earlier eras—were deemed the habits of the uneducated peasantry. The historian Richard Bushman describes the goals of this redefinition of polite behavior as twofold: to create a semblance of an immaculate social body for polite society, and to isolate one body from another.[42]

Guides to manners were written mainly for well-to-do men, who were expected to contain their bodies during public occasions styled as "polite." Typically these were functions organized around a meal for which proper knowledge of table etiquette was required. The overwhelming number of conduct guides explicitly written for men and the small number offering women detailed instructions on manners testified to the different contexts in which gentlefolk of each sex performed civility. Men needed to contain their bodies at formal public events like dinners, ceremonies, and in court. Women's bodily ruptures, in contrast, were typically domestic and sexual in nature, a product of the unique "leakiness" of the female body with its production of urine, breast milk, and menstrual blood, and a proper subject for medical and obstetrical texts rather than guides to manners.[43]

Yet bodily functions and emissions nonetheless threatened to intrude. Orifices and their functions—eating, digesting, and eliminating—presented a special challenge to emerging codes for proper behavior. Renaissance courtesy and court literature urged readers to avoid all behaviors that called attention to them. One of the first and most influential was Erasmus's *Manners for Children* (1530), which instructed young readers in polite bodily conduct. He urged children to clean their teeth, wash their faces, and comb their hair at the start of each day. Erasmus warned against snorting, spitting, and playing with one's teeth at the table as rude behaviors. He advised that no snot should be visible on the nose or clothing. Blowing one's nose into a handkerchief was preferable to using one's fingers, but if the latter became necessary, due care should be taken that any secretions falling to the floor should be pushed away with the foot. Unlike Baldassare Castiglione's *The Courtier* (1528), which emphasized manners as techniques for the successful courtier's seemingly artless performance of grace and charm, Erasmus encouraged manners as a form of civility everyone could achieve.[44]

Thirty years later, the Italian Della Casa dispensed similar advice, discouraging spitting, coughing, and violent sneezing as disturbing to polite company. Standing too close to another while conversing was also offensive, as "many men do not like to smell someone else's breath, even though it might not have any bad odour to it." Less blatant intrusions of the body were also bad manners. Public adjustments to the clothing could offend by reminding people of disgusting bodily functions. Peering into a handkerchief after blowing the nose, "as if pearls or rubies might have descended from your brain," was clearly forbidden, as was offering even a clean handkerchief to another: the mere thought that it might have been used previously could be disgusting. Elaborating on Erasmus, Della Casa advised that it was no longer sufficient to wipe one's greasy hands on a table napkin instead of one's own clothing, for the telltale signs of grease on the napkin were disgusting reminders of eating. Dozens of English texts appeared during the late sixteenth century and the early seventeenth offering similar advice.[45]

Recommendations to keep the body and its excrescences hidden in polite company countered folk traditions in which bodily products, like dirt itself, were believed to have magical properties. Recipes for healing and casting spells required special ingredients with extraordinary powers. Substances produced by the body, like hair and fingernails, saliva, urine, and menstrual blood, and unusual phenomena like being born with a caul, all enhanced the power of folk cures and spells. The functions of the body that embarrassed the genteel sensibilities of the etiquette authors—its oozing of fluids, its continual growth of hair and nails, its reproductive processes, and its elimination of waste—appeared to cunning men and women as magical processes of transformation and renewal.

Within folk traditions, human urine, feces, and saliva occasionally had value as magical substances, even as the etiquette authors sought to fix their negative value as polluting.[46]

The most potent and loathsome of these substances was menstrual blood, believed since ancient times to have magical qualities and the subject of numerous Judeo-Christian regulations designed to contain the defiling power of women's bodies. The proximity of menstruating women to delicate household processes could lead to their failure, resulting in sour wine, dead bees, and blunt knife edges. But menstrual blood could also spark the love of a reluctant suitor, render garments fire retardant, and remove unsightly red blemishes from the skin. Inside the womb of a pregnant woman, blood might be valued as nourishing and life giving, but outside the womb it had an unsurpassed power to pollute. Sexual partners who came in contact with it risked their health, and it increased the chance of producing monstrous offspring. Its origins in female genitalia equated it with sexual sin, while theories describing it as the periodic discharge of impurities connoted harmful toxins. The use of rags to absorb menstrual blood, moreover, guaranteed that it could not be completely hidden from view, but that it would be part of the smells and sights of the early modern household. Once saturated, menstrual cloths had to be soaked, washed, and dried. Seen as both contaminated and potentially contaminating, menstrual rags became conflated with blood itself in biblical quotations, sermons, and poems as among the most loathsome objects in the early modern material environment.[47]

A PURE AND A FRESSHE AYRE

Concerns about the cleanliness of the urban environment and domestic spaces accompanied the rise in personal fastidiousness among the elite during the sixteenth and seventeenth centuries. While the desire for sociability and distinction drove the former trend in self care, the pursuit of good health and economic vitality motivated concern for the environment. In general, most writers concurred that the countryside was healthier than the city because it was cleaner, less crowded, and better ventilated. There was an important exception to this rule, however; low-lying and marshy rural areas, like filthy urban garbage heaps, emitted excremental humors that could sicken the body.

Writing in the first half of the sixteenth century, the English physician and cleric Andrew Boorde urged readers living in the country to build houses "in a pure and a fresshe ayre to lengthen [the owner's] lyfe." Air was healthiest when in motion and dry and most dangerous when it was hot, still, and damp. Fetid air could kill healthy people by infiltrating the pores of the skin and disturbing the balance of humors, while "freshe, pure and cleane" air encouraged the production of "good blode" necessary for long life. The key to finding pure air was to avoid proximity to stagnant water, a challenge in an age in which cisterns were commonly used to store water. Boorde warned his readers that, although locating a house near water was convenient for baking, brewing, and doing the laundry—not inconsiderable virtues in the eyes of its female laborers—"standynge waters, stynking mystes, and marshes" were hazards. Gutters, canals, dunghills, and ditches also contained putrefying material that could taint the air and fill the body with excremental humors. Above all, Thomas Venner urged, the house should stand on pure and firm ground away from "low, marish or other filthy places" where the air was "impure, grosse, and intemperate."[48]

The health of a household thus depended on both its location, especially the wholesomeness of the air, and the meticulous housekeeping of its mistress and her female employees, whose habits determined the "special air of the house." The greatest health hazard resulted from the careless disposal of urine and excrement. "Beware of pyssing in drawghtes, and permytte no comon pyssing place be about the house or mansyon," Boorde instructed, "and beware of emptying of pysse pottes, and pyssinge in chymnes, so that all evyll and contagyous ayres maye be expelled, and clene ayre kepte unputryfied." He recommended that the "common howse of easement" should be located over water or at some distance from the house, advice that privileged health over convenience. It was especially important to ensure that "there be no fylthe" in food storage and preparation areas, but only "good and odyferus savoures."[49]

Boorde was not being gratuitously graphic about the manifold problems of running a household in the sixteenth century. Although most sixteenth-century European women would have been familiar with the challenges of disposing of human waste and keeping the dairy clean, it seems that the English, who were known throughout Europe as sloppy housekeepers, might have found the challenges more daunting than their French, Dutch, and Swiss counterparts.[50] When Erasmus described an English house in a 1530 letter to Cardinal Wolsey's physician, he might have been listing the contents of a gutter on a squalid lane in London: "the floors are made of clay, and covered with marsh rushes, constantly piled on one another, so that the bottom layer remains sometimes for twenty years, incubating spittle, vomit, the urine of dogs and men, the dregs of beer, the remains of fish, and other nameless filth. From this an exhalation rises to the heavens, which seems to me most unhealthy."[51] Residents of this household washed their hands before meals, but their domestic routine consisted mainly of letting filth drop to the floor where it would eventually be covered by straw.

But most early modern writers viewed the city, with its filthy streets and crowded housing, as a greater threat to the health than the rural miasmas that worried Boorde. Garbage, stagnant pools of water, urine and feces, and animal carcasses, fouled city air. Poor urban residents lived in conditions conducive to putrefaction and suffered disproportionately during epidemics. Mindful of this relationship, contemporary observers associated both the bodies of the poor and their habitations with disease. Many writers chronicling the plague recognized the greater susceptibility of poor people, whose diminished health resulted from bodies already corrupted by unclean lodgings, bad air, and unwholesome food.[52]

Streets filled with garbage also compromised water quality and flow. As the historian Mark Jenner observes, the capacity of refuse to block water flow, creating stagnant pools, was as great an issue as its power to contaminate. Analogies comparing the city's health and the body's circulation emphasized the importance of the unimpeded movement of water in ditches, rivers, and canals. Advice about how to tell good water from bad reflected similar concerns. The author of *Directions for Health, Naturall and Artificiall*, which was in its sixth London edition by 1626, included a two-page description of the qualities of wholesome drinking water. Another medical writer, Thomas Cock, presented readers with a simple rule: "that water is best, which is insipid, or without taste, clean, light and bright," but he still recommended boiling "to make bad water good, and good water better." In general, most authors agreed, wholesomeness depended upon movement.[53]

Although initially blessed with plentiful potable water supplied by three rivers, London grew rapidly, fouling these sources. By the time the Black Death killed off a third of England's population in the fourteenth century, the water in these rivers was undrinkable, thanks to the unregulated disposal of sewage and garbage. Thereafter, city ordinances prohibited the placement of latrines over the rivers and directed residents to dispose of human waste in cesspools or pits. Young children were the only exceptions to laws setting punishments for public urination. The city also began drawing additional water from suburban natural springs and wells in the effort to flush refuse and standing water out of ditches. The construction of the New River channel in 1613 provided London with a relatively pure source of water from nearly forty miles outside the city.[54]

Until the mid-eighteenth century, London's filth disgusted foreign visitors. Municipal officials tried repeatedly to protect the water supply and clear streets of rotting matter. In keeping with twelfth-century assize rules and more recent laws defining nuisances as hazards that fouled the air of otherwise wholesome districts, city officials placed much of the burden of clean streets on individual property owners. For most of the seventeenth century, residents were expected to sweep the filth from their own doorsteps into piles for the city's garbage rakers to remove. In 1655 the city briefly experimented with contracting this service out to achieve better results. Noting the dust, the "unwholsome stenches," and the mud that provoked people to jam the city with coaches on rainy days, city officials hired John Lanyon, a metalworker and mathematician who had traveled widely in the reputedly fastidious Low Countries. Among his proposals was the transportation of street soil by water rather than by cart. After Charles II himself complained of "Dirty and Noysome" streets in 1661, the city concluded that the old way of cleaning the streets was better. Conditions in the city's suburban slums, however, where collected refuse sat in storage areas, generating "a great and contagious stench," remained as bad as ever. In 1665 bubonic plague broke out in these crowded districts before sweeping into its center, eventually killing close to eighty thousand people, or one-sixth of the city's population. The plague's chroniclers attributed the disease to "contagious air"—the stenches and putrid filth associated with the poorest neighborhoods—that was believed to release plague "venom." Victims inhaled the venom, which first attacked the heart and then spread to the rest of the body.[55]

The strong odors of the early modern city signified not only unhealthfulness, however, but economic vitality, a desirable condition that might have led many to equate stench with profit. Tanners, butchers, tallow workers, and glove and hat manufacturers all worked with animal carcasses, which emitted unpleasant odors, compounded by the chemicals used in processing. Until the second half of the eighteenth century, when they were removed to the margins of the city, these establishments pumped fumes and chemical waste into London's air and waterways. On a smaller scale, market gardeners in London's suburbs contributed to the stench by hoarding organic material for fertilizer and keeping pigs and chickens. Open-air produce markets left behind rotting vegetables, which the pigs consumed and processed, producing dung. The contents of chamber pots might either be slung out the chamber window into the street below or saved for making saltpeter and soap. Then there were London's rakers, employed to remove cartloads of street soil that could then be sold as fertilizer. The very conditions that made early modern cities like London unhealthy and unpleasant for human habitation signaled the existence of a vital economy.[56]

Economic health notwithstanding, the English continued to strike fellow Europeans as dirty. Compared with the French court, where Louis XIV spent his reign installing bathrooms and bathtubs and requiring courtiers to powder their wigs and change their shirts, Charles II's retinue disgusted a local observer with their rude habits: "Though they were neat and gay in their apparell, yet they were very nasty and beastly, leaving at their departure their excrements in every corner, in chimneys, studies, colehouses, cellers."[57] German and Dutch households seem to have been both neater and cleaner, according to English travelers, while French and Italians appear to have been more diligent about changing linens, bathing, washing hands, and wearing perfume. The use of individual forks, to take another example, appears to have come into fashion among the Germans, Italians, and French before it reached England in the seventeenth century. Early in the century, English publications made little or no reference to the housewife's need to be clean in her person, moreover, except in the negative, to condemn the filthy habits of the Gaelic Irish. Gervase Markham's popular guides to rural household management, originally published in the late sixteenth century and reprinted for decades, urged housewives to keep dairies scrupulously clean and provided recipes for curing common ailments but mentioned only in passing the importance of clean food and clothing. The 1631 edition urged housewives to consider cleanliness an ornament. Richard Brathwaite's seventeenth-century advice books for English ladies and gentlemen offered detailed instructions on achieving gentility in apparel, demeanor, and character, but said nothing about personal cleanliness. Perhaps the advice dispensed by Shakespeare's Coriolanus, "Bid them wash their faces, and keepe their teeth cleane," came the closest to summing up the average English person's efforts at bodily cleanliness.[58] In their comments on Irish dairies, clothing, and houses, however, English writers positioned themselves as an outcropping of European civilization confronted with filthy savagery. The Irish, in this sense, helped to stabilize the English claim to civility rooted in the habits of the body.

On the eve of their voyages to the West African coast in the mid-sixteenth century, then, and in subsequent voyages to North America, English people made poor emissaries for European cleanliness. The condition of their houses, their bodies, and their capital city had earned them the reputation of being the dirtiest people in Europe, a stigma they deflected to the Gaelic Irish. Most Europeans had rejected the dangerous practice of bathing the whole body, although some still did so out of concerns for health and decency or for pleasure. The well-to-do focused instead on cleaning their bodies by covering them in white linen and wearing perfume and powder, practices that few ordinary Europeans could afford to emulate. White linen signified cleanliness, refinement, and most important, civility, associations that would be strengthened by European encounters with West Africans and Native Americans. Hiding the skin from view, linen cloth distanced the nude body from its uncivilized, sinful, animal essence. It also testified to the emergence of a particular domestic complex—grounded in the gendered organization of household manufacture, the exclusive sexual relation of

husband and wife, and a linen-centered regime of care for a porous, easily corrupted body. These would become the cornerstones of the concept of civilization during Europe's expansion into the Atlantic. Yet most Europeans, including
those who would not risk plunging into a tub or river, would still have viewed a
bathed body as a clean, although possibly sinful, body. Water, moreover, retained its potency as a substance that could cleanse soiled laundry and flush stagnant pools. The standard set by bathing remained enshrined in European discourse about cleanliness and in metaphors about removing the stain of sin even
as the bath began to be depicted in paintings as a sensual, feminine scene of illicit pleasure.

2

SKIN

WASHING THE ETHIOP

A well-known proverb of the Elizabethan period equated futility with efforts to "wash an Ethiop," whose immutable color was held up as an example of Nature's supremacy over mankind. The printed proverb was often accompanied by engravings of people with white skins washing a dark-complected, nearly nude African. Although the saying could have been understood to sever the association between dark skin and uncleanness—it proved that the Ethiop's complexion remained dark even after being cleaned—it presented dark skin as that which could not be washed white. Thus it supported other theories linking black skin to indecency (the curse of Ham, resulting from Ham's unclean act of looking upon his father's nakedness) or disease (syphilitic infection that discolored the skin) (Figure 2.1).

The equation of whiteness with cleanliness coincided with an emerging racial commentary on the skin of "Blackamoors" and on white skin as a manifestation of good health for born-and-bred English.[1] Hardening racial categories constituted one motive for the exaggeration of white skin in the so-called fair sex and the use of cosmetics in court. In portraits of the aristocracy, figures of black servants blending into background shadows offset the white skin of the female subjects. The emphasis on the white skin of the aristocratic lady was not simply in the mind of the portrait painter, however. Much as white linen made a person's cleanliness visible, whitening cosmetics, including powder in the hair and mercury, alum, and lead applied to the face, demonstrated refinement, at least to some. Those who discouraged the use of these potentially dangerous cosmetics—the medical writer William Vaughan mentioned Italian and Jewish skin blanchers, among other substances—described them as perversions of na-

L E A V E of with paine , the blackamore to fkowre,
With wafhinge ofte, and wipinge more then due :
For thou fhalt finde, that Nature is of powre,
Doe what thou canfte, to keepe his former hue:

2.1. Geoffrey Whitney, *Choice of emblemes*, from Henry Green, *Whitney's "Choice of emblemes,"* facsimile reprint (London, 1866). Courtesy Van Pelt Rare Book and Manuscript Library, University of Pennsylvania

ture. Critics urged instead the time-honored method of washing with water. Cold water was preferable to warm, Vaughan claimed, echoing contemporary medical explanations that "heat and drinesse are the causes of blacke-coloured." "Believe me, Ladies," he wrote in 1626, "nothing beautifies, nothing whitens more than the coldest water."[2]

Despite the deep roots of the association between black skin and uncleanness and despite Europeans' efforts to exaggerate their own whiteness, the absence of linen rather than the color of West African skin made the bigger impression upon early English chroniclers. Many of these travelers made sustained contact with West Africans during the 1550s, more than a century after the Portuguese

had established a commercial presence in the region and been granted a monopoly on trade and possessions by Pope Nicholas V. Relying on Portuguese nav-
igators and maps, the English hoped to gain a foothold on the profitable trade in
gold, spices, and slaves. But the English had little success from 1553, when
Thomas Wyndham first journeyed to Guinea and Benin, until George Fenner's
1566 voyage to Guinea.[3]

Chroniclers of these early voyages commented on West African landscapes,
the appearance of cities and villages, commercial protocol, and indigenous manners and mores. Authors borrowed wholesale from previously published texts
and echoed received wisdom about the African continent, thereby imparting authority to their accounts. They also freely passed judgment on the civility of the
West Africans they encountered. Too little or too much civility could make trade
unprofitable for Europeans; trade partners who were either savage or finicky
might impede the flow of goods. Descriptions of West African appearance thus
appeared not as ethnographic accounts of meeting new people but as showcases
of traditional knowledge and assessments of commercial possibilities.

Predisposed to believe that clothing was a prerequisite of civility and nudity a
sign of both innocence and savagery, Englishmen noted with disapproval that
West Africans wore very little. Upon traveling to the Saint Vincent (Grand Batu)
River during his first voyage to Guinea in 1555, the London merchant William
Towerson observed that the region's residents "[goe] all naked." Lacking the information conveyed by clothing, he claimed that "one cannot knowe a man
from a woman but by their breastes, which in the most part be very foule and
long." His comment joined a growing chorus of disparaging remarks by European men about the sexual attractiveness of African women. Journeying south-
east from Guinea to Mina, an area of strong Portuguese influence, Towerson
met the captain of the village of Don John, whom he described as "bare legged,
bare footed, and all bare above the loins." After his second voyage to Guinea in
1563, the poetic Robert Baker attributed West African nudity to a lack of shame.
He noted self-righteously, and perhaps with a little envy:

> They naked goe likewise,
> for shame we cannot so:
> We cannot live after their guise,
> thus naked for to go.

The following year, John Hawkins described the residents of Cape Verde as
"people who are all blacke, and are called Negroes, without any apparell saving
before their privities."[4]

Nudity rather than skin color indicated the absence of civilized humanity in these early accounts. Recalling his first voyage to Guinea in 1562, Baker described the nakedness of indigenous peoples trumping the color of their skin:

> a number of blacke soules,
> Whose likeliness seem'd men to be,
> but all as blacke as coles.
> Their Captaine comes to me
> as naked as my naile,
> Not having witte or honestie
> to cover once his taile.
> By which I doe here gesse
> and gather by the way,
> That he from man and manlinesse
> was voide and cleane astray.

As Baker described a fierce battle with these strangers, his racial rhetoric became more inflamed. But in this description of his initial meeting with Guinea natives, nudity made the greater impression. Lacking wit, honesty, manliness, and clothing, the scantily clad captain of the Guinea men fell short of the requirements for civilized manhood.[5]

The English were on shaky ground here; long voyages in hot West African climates left them with greater needs for fresh linen, soap, and female laundering skills, but with fewer resources to meet their own standards for decency. The problem usually began during the Atlantic crossing itself. Lacking a sufficient supply of linen, Europeans in West Africa commonly went weeks without washing or changing their shirts — if they were lucky enough to have them in the first place. With rhetoric about civility so focused on nudity, moreover, and with little other protection from the sun known to them, few Europeans probably voluntarily removed their decaying linen or woolen garments. As Robert Baker observed of the English after a period of acute privation, the sweat and humidity soon took its toll: "Our clothes now rot with sweat, and from our backs do fall, / Save that whom nature wils for shame, we cover not at all."[6]

Most English adventurers quickly learned that exposed bodies did not mean that West Africans were witless or innocent. Certainly they were not naked out of ignorance about cloth, but had strong indigenous traditions for manufacturing high-quality textiles. The same Guinea residents Towerson described as naked wore a "cloute about a quarter of a yarde long made of the barke of trees" spun into fine thread that reminded him of linen. This cloth might also be brightly decorated and worn on the head. The otherwise "bare" captain of the village of Don John was similarly clad in "cloth of that Country," made from tree bark.

Newcomers hoping to get in on the highly competitive West African trade soon learned that indigenous peoples prized cloth according to the quality of its fiber, weave, and design. As Towerson discovered on a return trip to Guinea, some West Africans could discern the value and variety of woven fabric as well as any European and used that knowledge to purchase only the best-quality European goods. He abandoned the effort to sell textiles at Samma after French ships undercut his trade by offering cloth that was "better, and broader than ours."[7]

If canniness in trade made it difficult to sustain ideas of West Africans as naked innocents, it did not automatically qualify them for European-style civility. Many English commentators, including the adventurer John Hawkins, persisted in seeing trade with Europeans as the main vector of civility in West Africa. The Leophares of Cape Verde were "more civill then any other," Hawkins claimed, "because of their dayly trafficke with the French-men." Almost as an afterthought he added that they were "of nature very gentle and loving." The adventurer George Fenner related the story of shipmaster William Batts to warn readers of the dangers in assuming West Africans could be civilized in the European sense of the term. Batts persuaded his crew to land unarmed at Cape Verde in 1566, telling them that "although the people were blacke and naked, yet they were civill." As a consequence of this "foolish rashness," Batts was taken captive and ultimately abandoned in Cape Verde by his traveling companions, who left responsibility for ransoming him to some French merchants.[8]

With few exceptions, early English chroniclers treated West African nudity as further evidence of the savagery and moral corruption that resulted from the absence of institutions constituting civilized society. Recounting John Lok's 1554 voyage to Guinea, Richard Eden, who had never set foot on the African continent but had steeped himself in ancient and contemporary writings on the subject, observed that the native inhabitants were "a people of beastly lyvinge, without a god, lawe, religion, or common wealth." In the midst of a lengthy lament about the harsh conditions on his second voyage to Guinea in 1563, Robert Baker condemned native inhabitants as "beastly savage people . . . farre worse than any slave," who might even be cannibals.[9]

But few of these early English chroniclers offered lengthy disquisitions on West African skin color. One exception was Baker, whose outbursts about "brutish blacke people and blacke burnt men" occurred in an account of a bloody battle during his first voyage to Guinea in 1562 in which many English and African lives were lost. Upon returning to Guinea, Baker and his men had better luck trading with Guinea natives, a success he reported in a measured account in which the African climate and paltry rations were the villains of the piece rather than savage Guinea warriors.[10] Writing in 1578, the mariner George

Best tried out two of the most popular explanations for dark West African complexions—climate and infection—and found the climatic theory wanting. Noting that American Indians, who also lived in a torrid zone, did not have black skin, Best theorized that it resulted from an infection in the descendents of Ham, who had been cursed for their father's sin of unlawful "carnall copulation" while on the Ark. His best evidence for this theory was the permanence of black skin even among the offspring of Africans born in England to Englishwomen. Observing the generational persistence of dark complexions, it seemed to Best "that blacknes proceedeth rather of some natural infection of that man, which was so strong, that neither the nature of the Clime, neither the good complexion of the mother concurring, coulde any thing alter, and therefore, wee cannot impute it to the nature of the Clime."[11] Not only did West Africans eschew the clothing Europeans deemed necessary for civility and cleanliness; their dark complexions allegedly resulted from an infection with origins in a family curse for sexual uncleanness. This topped off the evidence of so-called "beastly" living.

Beyond these theories for West African appearance, early English chronicles offered few details about how Guinea residents actually took care of their bodies. They would have been hard-pressed to do so, as their descriptions of West African peoples were based on brief commercial interactions and heated conflicts rather than on lengthier observations of manners. The emphasis on savage behavior, immorality, and blackness left little room for readers to see West Africans as a clean people who might have had their own traditions of body care. Yet hints about West African practices do appear. Several chroniclers noted that West Africans "raced," "pounced," or tattooed their skins. In his account of Lok's 1554 voyage to Guinea, Richard Eden reported hearing from the crew that "their princes and noble men use to pounce and rase their skinnes with pretie knots in divers formes, as it were branched damaske, thinking that to be a decent ornament." The intended irony of *decent* communicated European sophistication and African primitiveness. William Towerson similarly reported in 1555 that inhabitants of the Saint Vincent river had "the skinne of their bodies raced with divers workes, in maner of a leather Jerkin."[12]

Subsequent English informants elaborated on the beautiful tattoo patterns, suggesting that West Africans viewed their own skins as canvases or tapestries that could be decorated to increase the aesthetic appeal of the body. Damask, which derived its name from Damascus, was a richly patterned cloth made of cotton, linen, silk, or wool that would have been familiar to most English readers. Even more familiar was the leather jerkin, a close-fitting vest or coat that might have patterns burned or punctured onto it. Comparing tattooed and scarified West African bodies to highly decorated materials, writers employed a common strategy of likening the strange to the familiar to make newly "discovered" peoples and lands comprehensible to readers. These accounts of West African bodily aesthetics reveal the importance of the skin's appearance and the great effort expended to decorate it. They also hint tantalizingly at a key difference between Europeans and West Africans, beyond clothing, that contributed to divergent notions of civility.

Additional information about West African manners and mores would not appear in print in English for nearly seventy-five years. The lack of English success in competing with Portuguese and French commercial rivals along the West African coast discouraged English adventurers during the final decades of the sixteenth century and the first decades of the seventeenth. Then, in 1623, Richard Jobson published a pamphlet promoting exploration and investment along the Gambia River, a region in Upper Guinea that would figure prominently in the English slave trade to North America by century's end. Jobson's interest was not slaves but the gold that supplied the lucrative Moroccan trade, as the title of his pamphlet, *The Golden Trade*, suggested. He was committed to producing a comprehensive account of the region's different cultures, including information on their governments, economies, religious beliefs, manners, and mores. Unlike previous English chronicles of West Africa, therefore, *The Golden Trade* contained many details illustrative of how West Africans cared for their own bodies and suggestive of how they might have viewed the bodies of their European visitors.

Jobson drew careful distinctions between people he labeled "Blackmen," otherwise known as Mandingos or Ethiopians; the tawny complected Fulbe; and the "vagrant Portugall" and their offspring. He also devoted a special section to the Maribuckes, a self-contained village of Muslim priests whose habits of cleanliness and self-discipline impressed him. Throughout the pamphlet he took pains to minimize the danger that the recent murder of another English captain might portend, stressing instead indigenous receptiveness to trade with Europeans.

Jobson presented a mixed portrait of the civility of the Fulbe, noting both their itinerant lives as cattle herders and the scrupulous cleanliness of their women. Likening Fulbe appearance to that of gypsies, Jobson classified them as wanderers whose arduous lives had exacted a toll. Fulbe men, for instance, showed less sensitivity to the flies which stood thick upon their hands and faces than did English horses, which would at least whisk away the insects with their tails. Fulbe women, in contrast, drew nothing but praise from Jobson. Not only were they "streight, upright, and excellently well bodied, having very good features, with a long blacke haire, much more loose then the blacke women," and neatly attired, but they demonstrated superlative cleanliness as dairy maids. "In what sowever you received from them, you should have it so neate and cleane that in your milke you shold not perceive a mote, nor in her butter any uncleanliness," he reported, "nay the gourds, or dishes, they brought it in, on the very outside would shine with cleanliness, and on the inward parts, without any nastiness." Jobson claimed, moreover, that Fulbe women had completely internalized their reputation for cleanliness. "If at any time, by any mischaunce, there had beene a mote, or haire, which you had shewed unto her," he observed, "she would have seemed to blush, in defence of her cleanely meaning." He found them to be much cleaner than Irish kernes, who also raised cattle, and generally more civilized.[13]

Jobson supplied the first English accounts of West Africans washing their bodies with water. In his description of the godly Maribuckes, an exclusive Muslim priesthood that maintained itself through carefully regulated intermarriage, Jobson noted that they washed genitals, hands, and face with water contained in gourds for that purpose. No doubt many English readers would have found this a familiar, although perhaps excessive, cleanliness routine. The Maribuckes also practiced circumcision, although Jobson claimed it was done out of superstition rather than for religious or hygienic reasons. He had little else to say about bathing, although he noted the Mandingo use of the Gambia River. Mandingos took spiritual and practical precautions before entering its crocodile infested waters. When cattlemen brought their herds to the river, a priest would recite prayers and spit on the water to make it safe for human beings. Jobson's Mandingo guides apparently thought that white men in the water also offered men with black skins some protection, for they noted, "the white man, shine more in the water, then they did, and therefore if Bumbo [crocodile] come, hee would surely take us first." Jobson's guides had certainly perceived a difference between English and Mandingo complexions, although it is not at all clear that they interpreted whiteness as cleanliness the way their visitors did. In this instance, whiteness signified unwitting vulnerability to the predations of a traditional Mandingo enemy, the crocodile.[14]

The saga of Andrew Battell's imprisonment by the Portuguese in Angola during the early decades of the seventeenth century offers more details about African body care. Battell spent eighteen years as a captive of the peoples of Kongo-Angola, a region which, like Guinea and the Senegambia, would also supply slaves to North America by the end of the century. Battell was a reluctant observer of Kongo-Angolan manners and mores, a fact that explains his hostility toward the subjects of his narrative. Despite his animosity, Battell recorded several interesting practices of purity, cleanliness, and care of the body. He noted that circumcision was widespread in Angola except in the Kongo, where inhabitants had converted to Christianity. He also claimed that the most powerful man among the Gagas, Gaga Calando, anointed himself in fat taken from the bodies of his vanquished foes. Although Battell may have intended only to spin a thrilling yarn about fierce African savages, his is one of the first English accounts we have of smearing, a practice that remained widespread throughout West, West Central, and South Africa as the preferred means of cleaning the skin until twentieth-century advertising campaigns succeeded in promoting Western soap.[15] In reality, indigenous peoples were more likely to smear their skins with oil or animal fat than they were to use human fat. Inhabitants of West and West Central Africa used palm oil, mentioned frequently in English chronicles as a native-grown commodity and popular trade good, to make soap or as an unguent to protect the skin from insects and the sun. Unguents were sometimes mixed with earth or other substances to give them pigments and scents.

Other European sources provide details about West African cleanliness practices that reinforce the portrait of bathing, smearing, perfuming, and pollution taboos. The Dutch chronicler Pieter de Marees described West Africans of the Gold Coast washing their faces every morning and then smearing them with white earth. Adhering to Muslim cleanliness rules, they also circumcised their sons and refrained from spitting on the ground. He took note of the stench of coastal towns where the European presence was the greatest, which he attributed to the unregulated disposal of garbage. Marees also provided a detailed description of ritual washing after contact with the dead. "The women go waist-deep into the water and throw handfuls of water into their faces and over their bodies, washing their breasts and their entire bodies." An anonymous Dutch manuscript that described Benin in the 1640s, some forty years after Marees's account of the Gold Coast, depicted a similarly fastidious people. "No woman will enter the house in which her husband is when she had her monthly period," the source declared. "Both men and women are very inclined to physical cleanliness; for they wash at least twice a day."[16]

The exceptional instances in which English travelers commented on African women's beauty are instructive of the importance of clothing in shaping their impressions. As he passed through the Cape Verde Islands in 1647 on his way to Barbados, the English traveler Richard Ligon offered a portrait of three African women that revealed how clothing and a refined domestic context provided the backdrop necessary for perceiving African women as individuated beauties rather than as beasts of burden. Captivated by the stature and bearing of his Portuguese host's mistress, he offered a detailed description of her eyes, perfect white teeth, fine silk mantel, and linen worn beneath brightly colored petticoats.

His next encounter with twin "virgins," fetching water from a public fountain, also provoked him to effuse over the details of their costume, including the striped silk petticoats carelessly draped over their linen to reveal the natural beauty of their backs and breasts. A finely arrayed concubine, a pair of beautifully dressed innocents, carrying out a routine domestic task—both stirred Ligon's imagination in ways the enslaved field laborers of Barbados never would.[17]

As the transatlantic slave trade became a more important lens through which to view the habits of West Africans, European evaluations of African cleanliness habits changed. During the early years of European expansion throughout the Atlantic, however, English chroniclers were more likely to derogate African nudity than African filth.

NATIVE HABITS

The clean, nude skin of Indians had long caught the attention and captured the imaginations of European observers. No matter what they claimed about Native American manners or their failure to exploit natural resources, Europeans could not deny that Native Americans had smoother, cleaner skin than most Europeans. Indeed, many chroniclers candidly admired Native American appearance, particularly the women's, as embodying European ideals for clean, straight bodies, unmarked by scars or deformities. Accounts of Native Americans from the late fifteenth and the sixteenth century thus oscillated between discourses of savagery, containing pejorative comments about filthiness and beastliness, and descriptions of well-formed, graceful, bodies with the smoothest, cleanest skin Europeans had ever seen.[18]

Columbus laid the framework for all subsequent discussions by classifying Native Americans as naked innocents who bore little resemblance to West Africans. "They are not Negroes as in Guinea," he proclaimed in his *Letter to Various Persons* in 1493, "and their hair is straight" rather than curled, as it might have been had the Caribbean sun shone as harshly as it did in West Africa. He found their appearance pleasing, describing them as "well made," "strong," and "well built." But with little chance to observe their daily routines, he assumed that indigenous comeliness, as well timidity and generosity, were natural expressions of primitive innocence.[19]

Within just a few years of Columbus's letters, European chroniclers struggled to reconcile the seeming primitivism of naked Native Americans with new information about their sophisticated care of their bodies. Amerigo Vespucci's report on his voyage to the Americas in 1497, which was translated into English in 1553, linked primitive beauty, barbarity, and the sexual appeal of exotic female "others" in the European imagination. Echoing Columbus, Vespucci observed that Native Americans "goe all as naked as they came forth of their mothers wombe." Yet, as Vespucci realized, this was not a case of the impressionable nudity that had led Peter Martyr to liken Indians to unpainted tables waiting to receive a design from a painter. Vespucci offered ample evidence that Native Americans worked hard to make their skin smooth and clear. "They suffre no heare on their bodie sauing only on theyr head," he reported, "in so much that they pul of[f] heares of their browes." Hair removal was only part of the story, however, for he claimed that "theyr bodies are verye smothe and clene by reason of theyr often washinge."[20]

Indigenous skin might have been smooth and clean, but their manners and mores disgusted Vespucci and his fellow chroniclers. "They are in other thinges fylthy and withoute shame," he declared, most notably because "they use no lawful conjnunction of mariage." Unconstrained by monogamy, "every one hath as many women as him listeth, and leaveth them agayn at his pleasure." Barbarous sexual customs were the tip of an iceberg that included bad table manners and cannibalism. "At theyr meate," Vespucci claimed, "they use rude and barberous fashions, lying on the ground without any table clothe, or coverlet." Even worse, at these barbaric picnics "they eate no kynd of fleshe except mans fleshe." This collection of uncivilized behaviors was not unexpected in a people who lacked other conventions of civilization, including iron technology, government, dominion over the land, and distinct family residences, although it fit uneasily with reports of unaffected and graceful deportment, a quality Castiglione admired in *The Courtier*.[21]

Vespucci's account also hinted at the sexual attraction that would saturate subsequent European accounts of Native American women. He reported with admiration that Indian women, whom he implicitly compared favorably to West African and European women, "neyther have they theyr bellies wrimpeled, or loose, and hanginge pappes, by reason of bearing manye children."[22] Indeed, Indian women were much more likely than their African counterparts to be described as beautiful and alluring by European writers. Travelers often commented on the aesthetic and erotic appeal of Indian women's bodies and demeanor, frequently casting them as seductresses, playthings, or beautiful and virtuous allies of Europeans. In his chronicle of the decade after the first Columbian voyage, Peter Martyr described Spaniards enthralled with beautiful Indian women whose "faces, brestes, pappes, handes, and other parts of theyre bodyes, were excedynge smoothe."[23] Knowledge of Indian beauty secrets seems only to have heightened the allure of native women for European men whose sexual curiosity was stimulated by the sight of limber, naked bodies and evidence of nonmonogamous sexual practices.

Vespucci was unusually reticent compared to his fellow chroniclers about Native American skin color. Europeans who seemed unsure how to describe the skin and hair of Indians initially exaggerated their Europeanness. Often, this exaggeration occurred in the midst of a comparison of Indians to Africans, as it did in Peter Martyr's assessment: "For the Ethiopians are all blacke, having theyre heare curld more lyke wulle then heare. But these people of the Iland of Puta (being as I have sayde under the clyme of Ethiope) are whyte, with longe heare, and of yelowe colour." Like Columbus, Martyr was puzzled by the light colouring of people whose proximity to the Equator should have resulted in dark skin according to contemporary theories about the climate's effect. "They are whyte," he repeated, "even as owre men are, savynge suche as are much conversant in the sonne." The notion that Indians were born white like Europeans and became darker as a result of exposure to the sun's rays and their own grooming techniques was repeated in several English texts, along with theories linking Indian hair color to the use of cosmetics. Others insisted that Indians did not fit existing categories. Eden described natives of the West Indies as "all togyther in general eyther purpole, or tawny lyke unto sodde quynses [quinces], or of the colour of chestnuttes or olyves: which colour is to them natural and not by theyr goynge naked as many have thought: albeit theyr nakednesse have sumwhat helped therunto."[24]

Numerous chroniclers testified to the role of Native Americans in crafting their own appearance. Whereas English travelers tended to explain African appearance as the result of the hot climate ("scorched and vexed with the heat of the sunne") or infection, or to describe it as some type of deformity ("disfigured in their lippes and noses, as the Moores and Cafres of Ethiopia"), they were more likely to attribute the differences they saw between themselves and Indians to native culture.[25] Detailed descriptions of Indian cosmetic practices left little to be explained by nature. When nature was invoked, as in Eden's account, it was to compare tawny indigenous skin to the benign pastoral nature of quinces, chestnuts, or olives, rather than the deforming power of the scorching sun or syphilitic infection. John Smith, the swashbuckling chronicler of the English settlement in Virginia, echoed reports that indigenous people's bodies owed their unique appearance to native culture rather than to nature. "They are "generally tall and straight," he noted, "of a comely proportion, and of a colour browne when they are of any age, but they are borne white," an explanation that might have convinced English readers that Indians were not so different from themselves.[26]

Native Americans cared for their bodies in a variety of ways, several of which might have been familiar to Europeans from their own routines or, by the early seventeenth century, from accounts of West Africa. Vespucci noted two practices that contributed to the smooth and clean appearance of Indian skin—plucking facial and body hair and washing frequently—but there were others. Native Americans applied unguents and pigments to protect and adorn the skin. They removed lice, allegedly eating the offenders, according to one European source. They also decorated their bodies with tattoos and jewelry, treating their skins as canvases much as their West African counterparts did.[27]

Native customs for removing hair made an enormous impression on hirsute European observers for whom beards signified adult manhood. In his 1555 translation of Gonzalus Ferdinandus Oviedus's *Natural History of the West Indies*, first published in Spanish in 1526, Eden observed that despite variations in habit and appearance, "All the Indians are commonly without beardes: In so much that it is in maner a marvayle to see any of them eiyther men or women to have any downe or heare on theiyr faced or other partes of theyr boddies." Writing about Indians near Sancta Fee, in the Caribbean, in 1564, John Hawkins claimed that the men wear their hair "rounded, and without beards, neither men nor women suffering any haire to growe in any part of their body, but daily puls it off as it groweth." John Smith found that natives of the mainland had a similar aesthetic for hair removal. "Their hair is generally blacke, but few have any beards," he observed. "The men weare halfe their heads shaven, the other halfe long; for Barbers they use their women, who with two shels will grate away the hayre, of any fashion they please."[28]

European chroniclers from Vespucci to Smith took note of indigenous bathing habits, perhaps because they were already beginning to be a curiosity in mid-sixteenth-century Europe, but probably because they felt a certain admiration for a cleanliness regime most of them did not follow. Several observers noticed native customs for washing newborns. Oviedus claimed that, having delivered their children, indigenous women of the West Indies "go to the river and washe them." Smith similarly noted that "in the coldest mornings [mothers] wash them in the rivers." Along with "painting and oyntments," these cold baths "so tanne[d] their skinnes," he declared, "that after a yeare or two, no weather will hurt them." Smith believed that these practices gave indigenous peoples superior endurance, noting that "they are very strong, of an able body, and full of agilitie, able to endure to lie in the woods under a tree by the fire, in the worst of winter, or in the weedes and grasse, in Ambuscado in the Sommer."[29]

Nearly all European observers had something to say about native body painting, a practice that offers clues about body aesthetics. Oviedus described an atypically hirsute Cacique of Catarapa who painted his body with a permanent black pigment, not unlike that used by noble Moors in Barbary. He left his face un-painted so as to distinguish himself from slaves, whose faces were marked with black. John Hawkins observed that warring Florida natives "use a slighter [?] couler of painting their faces, therby to make themselves shew the more fierce: which after their warres ended they wash away againe." In Virginia, Smith de-scribed Native Americans making a red body paint from the root pocone, which they powdered and mixed with oil. The purpose of painting heads and shoulders with pocones, he claimed, was to protect from summer's heat and winter's cold. Smith himself recorded a striking instance when "thirtie young women came naked out of the woods, onely covered behind and before with a few greene leaves, their bodies all painted, some of one colour, some of another, but all dif-fering."[30]

Like Africans, Native Americans decorated their skins with tattoos. Hawkins, whose 1564 voyage took him to Guinea and the Americas, said nothing about tat-tooing in West Africa but offered a detailed explanation of Native American techniques. "They doe not omit to paint their bodies also with curious knots, or antike worke," he commented, "as every man in his owne fancy deviseth, which painting, to have it to continue the better, they use with a thorne to pricke their flesh, and dent in the same, whereby the painting may have better holde."[31] Fifty years later, Smith described similar techniques being used on the Virginia mainland. Some women "have their legs, hands, breasts and face cunningly imbrodered with divers workes," he reported, "as beasts, serpents, artificially wrought into their flesh with blacke spots."[32]

European chroniclers described a variety of other indigenous techniques for purging, cleaning, and otherwise beautifying the body. Peter Martyr supplied readers with a rare description of indigenous dental hygiene. "They keepe theyr teeth very whyte," he observed, "And for that purpose use to cary a certeine herbe betwene theyr lyppes for the most parte of the day, and to wasshe theyr mouthes when they cast it away." Others recounted Native American use of sweat lodges, not unlike the stews that were fast disappearing from Europe, and purgatives to cleanse the internal organs. The French Jesuit Paul Le Jeune described naked Montaignais men and women entering heated tents for several hours at a time, after which "they emerge completely wet and covered with their sweat."[33]

Despite their generally favorable impressions of indigenous body care, a few Europeans' claimed to be disgusted. This was especially true when they ob-served native peoples in cold northern climes, where Indians spent more time inside their houses. Comments from French Jesuits about smoky air and dirty conditions probably contain more than a grain of truth. "They are dirty in their habits, in their postures, in their homes, and in their eating," declared Le Jeune in 1634 of Montagnais people whose way of life had already suffered from a generation of contact with the French. "The entrance to their Cabins is like a pigpen," he complained, and "they never sweep their houses." In a criticism reminiscent of Erasmus, he faulted his hosts for carpeting the floors with pine branches that collected "fur, feathers, hair," and wood shavings, although Erasmus would have been thrilled to find such relatively healthful debris. Montagnais clothes were no better, according to Le Jeune, although he admitted "that this dirt and filth does not show as much upon their clothes as upon ours." The disapproving Jesuit decried native habits of sleeping naked, covered by only "a miserable strip of cloth dirtier than a dish-cloth, and blacker than an oven-mop." But his most heartfelt objections were to the unwholesomeness of native food and drink, which he found little "cleaner than the swill given to animals, and not always even as clean." In one Montagnais home, he claimed, the food preparers exhibited visible symptoms of scrofula contracted through their "filthy habits" and their indiscriminate contact with the sick. "They never wash their hands expressly before eating," he observed, and he fretted about the foreign objects like sticks, shoes, animal hairs, and ashes that made their way into the soup or fouled kettles of common drinking water. For their part, Le Jeune's Montagnais and Huron acquaintances were repulsed by certain European habits. Capturing nasal secretions in clean white linen, folding them up and putting them in one's pocket appeared to native observers to be a nonsensical way to handle nasty material. Why dignify such filthy matter with white linen and save it?[34]

On balance, however, the intensive care of body and skin by Native Americans made it difficult for early chroniclers to classify them as uncivilized primitives or savages. This may explain in part why English rhetoric about the filthiness and beastliness of indigenous sexual mores became so shrill. The attraction male adventurers felt for native women doubtless also contributed to the vehement tone. Writers struggled to distinguish between the practices of outward cleanliness, which might include washing and fasting, and those of inner or moral cleanliness, which were nearly always concerned with sexuality and manners.[35] Accounts that praised native skin for being clean and smooth were rife with pejorative comments about filthiness and beastliness, the stock language for communicating savagery.

But admiration and shrill condemnation might have been the fruits of a single tree—that of Native American nudity. European concepts of nakedness were heavily freighted with sin, guilt, sexual license, and beastliness, on the one hand, and with primitive innocence, beauty, and pleasure on the other. Native American nakedness, which most chroniclers acknowledged fell short of complete nudity, disqualified indigenous populations from being counted among the civilized—a so-called savage habit of body compounded by heathenism. Being classified among the primitives and the pagans, wearing the habit of the sexually profligate—which is to say no habit at all in the English view—and departing from European manners and mores in crucially embodied ways, Native Americans appeared to be the epitome of beastliness. If only Native Americans hadn't been so well proportioned and graceful; if only they had not taken such pains to pluck and shave hair from their faces and bodies and wash their smooth, clear skin; if only they hadn't been so diligent about removing lice and applying unguents; and if only European men hadn't found Native women's bodies, with their pert breasts, firm bellies, and comely arms and legs, so attractive, the task of dismissing them as crude savages might have been easier. Compared with their observations of European women, modestly swathed in layers of clothing, and of West African women, who appeared attractive in domestic settings but not when they were performing agricultural labor, European accounts of Native American women were saturated with sexuality.

Situating the shirt and the skin in the cultural ferment of the early modern Atlantic allows us to see more clearly the "uncivilizing process" that Native Americans and West Africans feared would follow in the wake of contact with Europeans. When we set European practices in the context of their Atlantic contacts, we can begin to reimagine the "civilizing process" as at least partly a product of imperial ambition, not simply as an outgrowth of changes internal to the European political landscape. Such an approach turns Norbert Elias's notion of a linear "civilizing process" on its head by considering the cross-cultural consequences of that process for Native Americans and West Africans. It also compels us to consider how the imperial and commercial contexts for European contact with Native Americans and West Africans spurred both the rising tide of European and North American cloth consumption and increasingly extravagant Euro-American efforts to whiten, clean, and refine the body.

3

CORRUPTION

> Beware of foul and filthy Lust
> let such things have no place
> Keep clean your Vessels in th[e trust]
> that he may you embrace

> —Benjamin Harris, *The Protestant Tutor for Children*

In a 1685 catechism, Benjamin Harris included a poem attributed to the six-teenth-century Protestant martyr John Rogers that presented a familiar concept of cleanliness. Lust was foul and filthy, capable of corrupting an individual's relationship with God, just as filth could corrupt a clean vessel. Sanctified Christians protected their vessels from such sinful pollution, rendering their bodies and souls pleasing to God. For New England's Puritans, concepts of cleanliness and filth reflected a reformist vision of the sacred and the profane. Armed with a militant definition of the profane that included many traditional features of English popular culture and offered mixed messages about those dutiful but morally empty performances of manners, Puritans protected a narrow territory of the sacred. Harris's instructional text, like many publications by Puritan ministers during the final quarter of the seventeenth century, represented a conservative effort to salvage this distinctive geography of spiritual life from an expansive ideal of politeness that was attracting well-heeled followers in New England and throughout the English Atlantic.[1]

Harris's catechism captured the most popular meaning of the word *foul* in seventeenth-century Anglo-American public culture. Early Americans were more likely to use *foul, filthy,* or *nasty* to refer to sinful acts than to describe polluted matter. In Puritan New England, which had a monopoly on North American publishing for more than a century, these synonyms for *unclean* appeared in published discussions of moral and spiritual matters. Authors of seventeenth-century catechisms and execution sermons used the language of uncleanness to warn against the polluting power of sin. Sexual wrongdoing appeared in these tracts as a particularly "foul" offense because it combined immorality with bodily filth, resulting in an uncleanness that was physically embodied and morally reprehensible. No other sin—theft, fraud, false witness, covetousness, pride, or envy—inspired ministers to such high-pitched rhetoric about filth and pollution. Even gluttony and murder, which were also sins of the body, did not provoke such excited sermonizing.[2]

Denunciations of sexual misconduct echoed in colonial courtrooms throughout the early decades of the seventeenth century. County courts from Massachusetts to the Chesapeake described the illicit sexual unions of Anglo-American men and women as "foul," "abominable," "filthy," and "odious." Those found guilty of sexual misdeeds might be sentenced to be ritually cleansed of their sins by donning a white sheet and carrying a white taper as they begged the parish's forgiveness. In the insults they hurled at each other, ordinary people revealed that they, too, saw illicit sex as a uniquely embodied form of filth.

Sin was only one of many ways of imagining corruption during the seventeenth century. In its most basic form, corruption was polluted matter that compromised the wholesomeness of everything it touched. A healthy body constantly evacuated the corruption that could jeopardize health. Sin threatened to corrupt the soul and society much like rotten matter infected the body. In all instances, corruption signified decay and referred actually or metaphorically to an organic process that remained meaningful because of continuities in ideas about filth (in contrast to purity, which no longer corresponded in practice to the bathed body). Yet distinctions between metaphors and "real" bodies might obscure more than they illuminate about a world in which people believed that magic and Providence could bring on the contagions, miasmas, and humoral imbalances that caused illness. The very words with which ministers and pamphleteers condemned sin as filth—for example, *nasty*—occupied both the moral and material realms, making it difficult to distinguish between the two. For Puritans, metaphors about cleansing the soul conjured a body whose spiritual and physical afflictions were linked to and expressive of divine will. Beliefs in the power of Christ's blood to wash away a sinner's iniquity created a new reality for saints, providing them with a spiritual foundation for concepts of cleanliness.[3]

What impact did the Atlantic crossing, new environments, and conflicts with Native Americans have upon English concepts and practices of cleanliness, both in North America and England? Lacking European-style cities, with their filthy streets, high population densities, and epidemic diseases, North America appeared at first like a wholesome paradise, conducive to long life and good health. In *The Planter's Plea* (1630), John White claimed that New England's climate and air rivaled the healthfulness of England itself for English constitutions. As the first English residents of Jamestown, Virginia, and Plymouth, Massachusetts, quickly discovered, however, life in a new settlement could be downright deadly. The absence of cities, moreover, although contributing to the healthfulness of North America, also compromised Europeans' claims to cultural superiority. Despite their filth, cities were the centers of European civilization, the mainspring of finance, technology, manners, learning, and fashion that many Europeans saw as the foundation of their own superiority over indigenous peoples. For Puritans who later spread their towns across New England, the seeming nudity, licentiousness, and seasonal itinerancy of Native Americans presented other moral dangers that imperiled the divine purpose of their mission.[4]

English speakers around the Atlantic basin inflected *corruption* with different meanings. Although they shared the conviction that the female body could be both a source of sexual filth and a potential site of domestic virtue, racial slavery and the distinctive Puritan understanding of a spiritual economy of sin created regionally specific interpretative contexts. The unhealthy conditions and skewed sex ratio in early Virginia suggested that a colony lacking female domestic labor would wallow in its own filth and sink into barbarity. In New England, ministers seeking to protect Puritan ideals for spiritual community invoked the unchaste female body as a source of sexual sin that could ultimately bring about the demise of the entire Puritan experiment. Cleanliness in the moral sense depended on female virtue, expressed in the dedicated performance of domestic labor necessary to produce civilized European bodies as well as in female sexual restraint. What would happen to civilization, as Europeans were coming to understand the term, if the link between the two was compromised by the barbaric example of Native Americans or by blatant female licentiousness, or if domestic labor, neglected or coerced through the institutions of indentured servitude or slavery, failed to meet expectations for comfort and decency?

Back in England, by the end of the seventeenth century a vanguard of evangelical Protestants responded to their nation's new prominence in the Atlantic by taking a medical perspective on corruption. Urging their countrymen to adopt healthier habits, they condemned foreign luxuries like tobacco, tea, and coffee, as well as hot baths and spicy foods, which they believed sapped the health and vigor of Englishmen. What was needed was a cooling, cleansing regimen, more appropriate to English constitutions, and a return to the wisdom of the ancients. Searching for appropriate methods of body care, turn-of-the-century health reformers repudiated the new luxuries that had come with Atlantic expansion.

NECESSITIES OF NATURE

Chesapeake residents spent their first several decades suffering from the privations of a stunted domestic economy—the mainspring of household and bodily cleanliness—including shortages of soap, linen, and women to do the work. They also suffered from diseases endemic to the semitropical climate of the region and those caused by their own lack of bodily discipline. Their response to Native American sexual mores, material culture, and care of the body was more measured than that of their northern counterparts, although by century's end, the specter of interracial sexual unions between white women and indigenous or African men provoked them to shrill denunciations of moral filth.

The Atlantic crossing presented the first ordeal, making ordinary body care difficult. Sailors and servants went weeks without changing their linen. Better-heeled passengers seized opportunities for cleanliness they might otherwise have shunned; one party took advantage of a stop in Nevis to bathe at the warm springs there and take respite from the unsavory conditions on the ship. Conditions improved very little upon arrival in Virginia. Jamestown was perhaps the unhealthiest location for a group of English men, unaccustomed to domestic or hard manual labor, to settle. The water's salinity rendered it unwholesome for drinking but perfect for microorganisms. Disease quickly became the settlers' biggest enemy as undisciplined habits combined with the estuarial conditions to turn the water into an unwholesome brew. Under Captain John Smith, the intrepid yeoman who assumed leadership of the settlement in September 1608, settlers risked Indian violence to live at a healthier distance from Jamestown. Soon after Smith went back to England in 1609 to be treated for an injury, though, the English returned to the unhealthy atmosphere of the compound, where they suffered an outbreak of disease that killed nearly one-third of the settlers.[5]

As president, Smith emphasized discipline and a fair distribution of labor among the settlers, regardless of rank. Even men unused to strenuous manual labor were expected to learn to fell trees and make clapboard, for example, an exercise that blistered their soft hands and inspired volleys of cursing. Adapting the English use of ducking to punish offenders, Smith ordered "everie mans oathes numbred, and at night, for every oath to have a can of water powred downe his sleeve." With few men able to change their linens, water down the sleeve at day's end meant sleeping in wet clothes at night, a dangerous and uncomfortable situation that most tried to avoid. "Every offender was so washed (himselfe and all)," reported Smith, "that a man should scarse heare an oath in a weeke."[6]

Soon after Smith's departure, Jamestown endured a winter of starvation and death. Deteriorating morale led Sir Thomas Gates to enact strict new laws and draconian punishments in 1610 to deal with the misconduct that compromised the settlement's survival. In an effort to reduce disease, several laws set exacting new standards to protect the purity of the Jamestown water supply: "Nor shall any one aforesaid, within lesse then a quarter of one mile from the Pallizadoes, dare to doe the necessities of nature, since by these unmanly, slothfull, and loathsome immodesties, the whole Fort may bee choaked, and poisoned with ill aires, and so corrupt (as in all reason cannot but much infect the same)." As of 1611 Jamestown residents were required to walk 450 yards beyond the bounds of the fort before performing "the necessities of nature." But continuing high death rates suggest that enforcement of this law remained partial. Another statute enjoined "every man" to "have an especiall and due care, to keepe his house sweete and cleane, as also so much of the streete, as lieth before his door." Jamestown residents probably shared the casual attitude toward housekeeping of their London counterparts, a disregard compounded by male reluctance to assume responsibility for traditionally female labor.[7]

The laundress's reputation for being a shady character crossed the Atlantic nearly intact, where it fomented conflict in the Virginia settlement, already desperate for linen and short on women's labor, honestly and carefully performed. New laws took aim at traditional practices of washing laundry and disposing of waste water: "There shall no man or woman, Launderer or Launderesse, dare to wash any uncleane Linnen, drive bucks [lye bleach], or throw out the water or suds of fowle cloathes, in the open streete, within the Pallizadoes, or within forty foote of the same, nor rench, and make cleane, any kettle, pot, or pan, or such like vessell within twenty foote of the olde well, or new Pumpe."[8] Along with carrying firewood, hauling water was the most strenuous and disliked domestic labor. In an effort to minimize this backbreaking task, Englishwomen used the same kettle of water to wash several loads of laundry. They also were accustomed to tossing waste water into streets and yards; most would have resented having to perform these labors beyond the safety of the fort. Forced to perform heavy labor they despised, many women appear to have found the access to scarce linen too tempting to resist:

> Whatever man or woman soever, Launderer or Laundresse appointed to wash
> the foule linnen of any one labourer or souldier, or any one else as it is their du-
> ties so to doe, performing little, or no other service for their allowance out of

the store, and daily provisions, and supply of other necessaries, unto the Colonie, and shall from the said labourer or souldier, or any one else, of what qualitie whatsoever, either take any thing for washing, or withhold or steale from him any such linnen committed to her charge to wash or change the same willingly and wittingly, with purpose to give him worse, old and torne linnen for his good . . . she shall be whipped for the same, and lie in prison till she make restitution for such linnen, withheld or changed.[9]

Although the law applied to "man or woman," the language throughout suggests that laundry remained a female task. Unable to rely on a sufficient population of married Englishwomen to do domestic tasks out of affection or a self-interested concern for household health and welfare, the governors of the settlement paid women an "allowance," "daily provisions," and "other necessaries," out of the store for doing laundry. If incentives did not work, whipping and prison were supposed to prevent further deterioration in Jamestown's quality of life.[10]

Filthy streets and surroundings; chronic shortages of food, fabric, clothing, bedding, household equipment and tools; and crooked laundresses, pilfering the laundry, created other problems. Some women and men ran to neighboring Native Americans to escape Jamestown's sordid conditions and strict discipline. Sir Thomas Dale threatened runaways with death, a deterrent commensurate with the harshness of ordinary servants' lives in Jamestown. But escapees may have found indigenous life more attractive than the rhetoric about savagery and beastliness would suggest. John Smith certainly found as much to admire as to disparage when he noted in December 1608, "The extreame wind, raine, frost, and snowe, caused us to keepe Christmas amongst the Salvages, where wee were never more merrie, nor fedde on more plentie of good oysters, fish, flesh, wild foule, and good bread, nor never had better fires in England then in the drie warme smokie houses of Kecoughtan."[11]

Other English observers described the cleanliness practices of Chesapeake natives in positive terms, although assessments typically included both praise and denunciation of their beastliness.[12] In addition to reports of comfortable indigenous houses and scrupulous care for their skins, several English chroniclers commented on indigenous practices of menstrual seclusion. According to Smith, women retreated to a "gynaeceum" that men took pains to avoid. Although neither Smith nor Strachey recorded women bathing at the end of their seclusion, it is likely that Powhatan, Kecoughtan, and Pamunkey women performed this ritual cleansing common among many southeastern and eastern woodland peoples. This custom, along with other facets of native life, presented a stark contrast to the filthy water and excrement that fouled the streets of Jamestown.[13]

For their part, Indians appear to have been impressed by English technology, including tools, guns, and clothing, but less impressed by English beauty and physical prowess. Native Americans deliberately removed facial and body hair to achieve the smooth skin they considered the epitome of beauty. Englishmen who obscured their faces with beards could only have been perceived as shockingly ugly. Was this one of the reasons why Native Americans tended to develop closer relationships with relatively less hirsute English boys like Henry Spelman, exchanged as a hostage with the Patawomecks? There was also the question of the odor of unwashed, unanointed English bodies, covered in layers of clothing. When Native Americans killed an Englishman, they often stripped him of his outerwear but left his shirt behind. Why? Did this garment, worn next to the skin and rarely washed, smell too much to be worn by indigenous men? Or was linen simply not valued as highly by Native Americans, who initially prized animal skins and thicker fabrics?

By 1614 Virginia Company officials and investors began to consider ways to make the colony more permanent and solve its vexing problems. Bringing over more Englishwomen, particularly those of an elevated social position, seemed to hold great promise. Women who crossed the ocean under the company's recruitment plan were expected to meet its moral standards for chastity and honesty. In turn, the company tried to ensure that they married well and supplied them with the accoutrements of English civility. Having learned what shortages of linen could do to English morale, the company provided female recruits with a complement of clothing and bedding that communicated both their respectability and the domestic nature of their labors: a petticoat, waistcoat, stockings, garters, smocks, gloves, a hat, an apron, two pairs of shoes, a towel, two head coifs, a crosscloth, a pair of sheets, and a rug.[14]

For the next several decades, the colony's promoters struggled to replace images of starvation, ragged clothing, disease, moral dissolution, and Indian attacks with ones of prosperity, good health, and domestic comfort. A major obstacle to this effort was the colony's staple crop, tobacco. James I condemned it as a filthy, stinking weed, and medical writers alleged that smoking tobacco caused ill health. Another was the colony's reputation for exploiting servant labor, making it an unattractive destination to all except the most demeaned and coerced, whom some writers described as the dregs of society. In *The Planter's Plea*, John White begged his mother country not to think of the colonies as "emunctories or sinckes of state to drayne away their filth."[15]

By 1656 the pamphleteer John Hammond claimed that the situation had improved dramatically: Virginia was not a lubberland of ease, but "wholesome, healthy and fruitfull; and a modell on which industry may as much improve it self in."[16] Twenty years later, the traveler Thomas Glover noted, "the Planters houses are built all along the sides of the Rivers for the conveniency of Shipping; they build after the English manner, whiting the inside of their houses with Mortar, made of burnt Oyster-shells instead of lime. They have pure and wholesom water, which they fetch wholly from Springs, whereof the Country is so full, that there is not a house but hath one nigh the door."[17] "Pure and wholesom" spring water right by the door would have been attractive to English readers familiar with London's fouled waterways or accustomed to the heavy labor of hauling buckets long distances.

The depiction of the colony's women as married and happily engaged in domestic labor was key to the colony's promotional campaign. In an effort to contradict rumors of women's labor in tobacco fields that promoters believed discouraged migration, Hammond claimed, "The Women are not (as is reported) put into the ground to worke, but occupie such domestique imployments and housewifery as in England, that is dressing victuals, righting up the house, milking, imployed about dayries, washing, sowing, &c." He insisted that men and women in Virginia enjoyed as much time for recreation as anyone in the world. The source of the rumors about women's fieldwork, he contended, could be traced to the treatment of morally dissolute and domestically incompetent women whose passage across the Atlantic had already been paid. "Yet som wenches that are nasty, beastly and not fit to be so imployed," Hammond acknowledged, "are put into the ground."[18]

In Hammond's Virginia industrious wives worked in a domestic paradise. "Inside" labor took place in houses with large rooms and whitelimed walls, an appearance that visually communicated cleanliness and also signified healthfulness. Abundant game and fruitful orchards enabled women to keep their larders well stocked with relatively little effort. Nature cooperated by supplying plentiful clean water and a climate that made it easy to dry laundered clothes. Backing his claim that there was little theft in the colony—a direct attempt to counter reports from the colony's first decade—Hammond observed that the hedges were typically covered with freshly laundered clothes that dried unmolested by thieves.[19]

Court records and inventories offer a considerably different view of Englishwomen's labor in the colony. Still scarce in numbers, Englishwomen found that domestic services like cooking, laundering, and sewing could generate income in a colony dominated by single men. It was not unusual for a married woman to perform such services for men other than her husband in exchange for a portion of the client's tobacco harvest, money, or goods. A Mr. Burdeck of Northampton-Accomack County, for example, sought such a woman to prepare his meals and wash his clothes. Andrew Jacob of the same county arranged for a member of Thomas Dewin's household—probably his wife, Katherine—to wash his linens. Widows—and the Chesapeake had more than its share as a consequence of the high death rate—also exploited the need for domestic labor to provide for themselves until they remarried.[20]

Women who performed domestic services for pay increased the burden of their labor in households that were often missing the essential tools of domestic production. Few if any households in the first half of the century had the equipment for spinning, weaving, or making butter, cheese, or beer. Most inventories, however, included large kettles, which could have been used for washing clothes as well as for cooking; few households, though, had irons.[21] The shortage of female labor also made it more difficult for women to assist one another with onerous tasks as they were accustomed to doing in England. Laundry was one task that Englishwomen had long preferred to do in groups, or at the very least with another woman's assistance. The demand for servant women to grind corn, hoe tobacco, and perform additional paid labor for single men meant that few women were available to assist with laundry. Margaret Barker's testimony about swooning while washing clothes is suggestive of how individual women assumed burdens that, in a more demographically balanced society with a more developed domestic economy, many women might have shared. Other evidence, however, points to persistent efforts by women to share or hire out onerous tasks like laundry whenever possible. A Mrs. Denwood of Northampton-Accomack County, for example, contracted to give Mrs. Willis a hat in exchange for doing her laundry for a year, an agreement that Willis eventually reneged on. An Englishwoman of ordinary means coming to the colony during the seventeenth century thus probably found her domestic routine to be lonely and arduous. Unless she could afford to purchase female labor over and above her household's production of tobacco, a married woman struggled to provide domestic comforts largely on her own, with few of the necessary tools.[22]

SHIFTING THE BURDEN OF UNCLEANNESS

Chesapeake residents denounced indigenous peoples as "beastly," but they reserved their most potent rhetoric—the language of filth and uncleanness—for women's tainted sexual reputations. People of both sexes insulted women's sexual honor by calling them "slut" or "jade" and by associating them with bodily filth. To take two of many examples, one William Pigg called Goody Curtis "durty face" and "slutt" in 1641. In another instance, a Mrs. Wilkins was angry with Mary Spillman over a nonsexual matter—Spillman had accused Wilkins's servant man of stealing a pot of butter—but she nonetheless reminded listeners that Spillman had recently had a narrow escape at the whipping post, probably for an alleged sexual offense. Calling her "pissa bedd Jade," she equated female incontinence with an unbridled sexual appetite.[23]

Until 1662, when English Restoration reforms reached Virginia's courts, local courts described unlawful sexual activity as "foul," "filthy," and "vile," punishing it as a sin as well as a criminal offense. After 1662 local courts cared mainly about the criminal component of sexual misdeeds and concerned themselves with the expenses generated by illegitimate births. The charged language used to denounce sexual offenses disappeared from local court records for nearly thirty years, until the colony tried to define the meaning of racial differences that underpinned its growing reliance on slave labor.[24]

Outside the courtroom, however, a potent set of metaphors linking sexual desire, bodily corruption, Africanness, and treason appeared in the political discourse of the colony's civil war, Bacon's Rebellion. Hostilities began after conflicts with Indians escalated in Virginia's frontier counties in 1676 and the wealthy newcomer Nathaniel Bacon challenged the authority of the colony's governor to handle the crisis. The bodily metaphors each side used to discredit the other revealed an emerging connection between spiritual and physical wholesomeness and political virtue. Some commentators attributed Governor Berkeley's alleged greed and political insensitivity to the distractions of being married to a significantly younger woman with an outsized sexual appetite. Unnatural sexual desires also appeared in critiques of the rebels. The author of an account of the rebellion written soon after it ended described one prominent rebel, Richard Lawrence, as having lost the "light" of his superior learning and intelligence because he not only joined the rebel side but surrendered himself to the "darke imbraces of a Blackamore, his slave: And that in so found a maner, as though Venus was chiefly to be worshiped in the Image of a Negro, or that Buty consisted all together in the Antiphety of Complections."[25] Just as Lawrence mistook his African slave for a beautiful woman, the author suggested, he confused the rebel cause with political virtue. Bacon's own fate strengthened the discursive link between political and physical bodies. Brought to his ignoble end by the bloody flux, Bacon was ultimately defeated by his body's own corruption. His enemies could not have wished for more vivid bodily testimony to the rebellion's political illegitimacy.

This example helps us to understand the way bodies could be used to communicate political meaning, but it gets us no closer to actual practices of body care and changing impressions of beauty and health across emerging racial lines. How did English and African people perceive each other's physical beings during the seventeenth century? How did enslaved Africans, in particular, care for their own bodies under the constraints of forced migration and slavery? Little information from early Virginia exists about Africans. The nearest source of an extensive early account is Barbados, where in 1647 Richard Ligon described enslaved people bathing in a pond and making use of their remarkable swimming skills to catch fish. Rather than being impressed by African fastidiousness, Ligon professed disgust at the thought that water for drinking and cooking came from the same source in which "*Negroes* wash[ed] themselves in the Ponds in hot weather." When he complained that their "bodies have none of the sweetest savours," his host reassured him that the sun's heat evaporated the "noysome vapours," rendering the water pure and wholesome again. Ligon's observations help us to imagine Virginia's small population of enslaved people, who came from societies similar to those of their Barbadian counterparts, adapting various West, West Central African, and Afro-Caribbean traditions for washing in the Tidewater's network of rivers and ponds.[26]

Racial whiteness, both as a set of legal privileges and as a meaningful concept for the ways English people imagined cleanliness, had real consequences for the condition and care of bodies in seventeenth-century Virginia. Englishwomen were more likely to escape the hot, dusty labor of tobacco cultivation than their African counterparts. Upon completing their terms of service, moreover, Anglo-American men and women received "freedom corn and clothes" according to the custom of the country. Starting their lives as free people with a new set of garments, former servants could, in theory, cast off the threadbare, stained clothes they had worn during their terms of service. Given the scarcity and expense of linens, however, it is likely that only the shabbiest and filthiest clothing was permanently retired. Still, freedom clothes constituted a privilege of completed servitude that no enslaved African enjoyed. Dependent upon the coarse blue cloth issued them by their masters and occasionally even required by law, slaves had little opportunity to don new suits of clothes that would have communicated cleanliness as well as freedom to seventeenth-century colonists.

Did Anglo-Virginians think West Africans were dirty? The frequency of sexual unions, collaborative escapes from masters, and social alliances between white servants and African slaves suggests that most white Virginians and people of West African descent lived in intimate connection. White servants probably saw West Africans as no dirtier than themselves as long as the duties of servant and slave were similar and all bound laborers endured wretched living conditions. The passage of a statute in 1691 outlawing all sexual unions between white people and Indians, Africans, or what lawmakers referred to as "mulatto" partners, however, drove a wedge into this culture of physical intimacy. Spurred into action by the "abominable mixture" that took place when white women engaged in illicit sexual activity with men of color, the authors of the law created new punishments for white female offenders and their illegitimate offspring. Indeed, the statute left no room for the children of these outlawed unions to be anything but illegitimate.

In a legal culture in which prosecutions of white men for illicit sexuality were beginning to disappear, the new concern with interracial unions signified a momentous shift in moral freight. Caught in mid-embrace of chattel slavery, colonial Virginia in the 1690s still lacked clear definitions of whiteness. The 1691 statute imparted meaning to *white* by classifying it as a set of legal privileges that could be compromised by sexual contact with people of color. White women, according to the statute, committed the gravest of sexual offenses when they crossed racial lines. They could not bequeath the privileges of whiteness to all their children, only to those who could boast white fathers. But having a white father meant little in and of itself. A child fathered by a white man and born to an enslaved African or Indian woman could look forward to no inheritance except illegitimacy and slavery.

The arrival of thousands of newly imported slaves during the final two decades of the century also eroded the earlier atmosphere of intimacy. Some white Virginians and probably some Afro-Virginians as well perceived the new arrivals as disconcertingly strange in appearance and manner, if a 1699 statute comparing Virginia "negroes" favorably to newly imported Africans is representative of wider sentiment.[27] This perception may have included disgust at the sight of weakened Africans disembarking from the putrid-smelling slave ships that docked in Virginia's ports. Most white Virginians, however, were hardly in a position to criticize anyone's habits of cleanliness, and they seem to have refrained from doing so in writing. Not until the eighteenth century did concerns for gentility, the prosperity of a rising generation of planters, and legally institutionalized concepts of race transform the aesthetics and personal habits of a class of white slaveowners.

Lacking a reliable chronicler of West African reactions, we are left to speculate about enslaved people's perceptions of their masters. Slaves had only limited ability to discourage white people from crossing the emerging color line, sexually and socially. Armed with legal statutes, militias, and the juridically sanctioned power to inflict corporal punishment, white people enjoyed greater control over black people's social mobility. Did this power influence how enslaved women interpreted the beings of white people? Did the slave's inability to fend off unwanted physical intimacies make white masters more grotesque to her? What impact did the horrors of the Middle Passage have on the sensibilities of survivors? Perhaps, like their Indian counterparts, enslaved Africans were disgusted by pale, hairy skin and the body odors that clung to English garments. Perhaps, if they hailed from Muslim regions, they were offended by the failure of white planters to bathe regularly or wash their hands before meals. Or perhaps, having had their own cleanliness sensibilities so grossly violated while at sea, West Africans had little reaction at all to the habits of their Anglo-Virginian masters. Shock, shortages of essential resources for caring for their own bodies, and resentment of those who extracted their labor might have provoked a range of responses but probably did little to make white bodies—which were usually unclean in both the European and African sense—desirable in and of themselves.

VILE HABITS

Thirteen years after the Virginia Company erected the fort at Jamestown, a group of Pilgrims disembarked in Massachusetts, expecting the worst from Native Americans. Describing indigenous peoples as cruel and barbarous, Plymouth Plantation's leader and chief chronicler, William Bradford, evoked traditions of cannibalism to underscore his point. Indians, he wrote, "not being content only to kill and take away life, . . . delight to torment men in the most bloody manner that may be; flaying some alive with the shells of fishes, cutting off the members and joints of others by piecemeal and broiling on the coals, eat the collops of their flesh in their sight whilst they live, with other cruelties horrible to be related."[28] Bradford was only repeating what countless other European texts had broadcast as the truth about Native Americans. Even before he and his band of Pilgrims had their initial meeting with actual Indians, they were committed to an image of indigenous beastliness and filth that included a legendary appetite for human flesh. The fact that some of New England's early chroniclers found much to admire in Indian culture seems only to have raised the pitch of anti-Indian rhetoric among others.[29]

Subsequent contact with Native Americans challenged the image of cannibals, smacking their lips at the thought of roasted Englishman, but did not necessarily ease English discomfort with the physical persons of Indians. Expressions of indigenous hospitality, the appearance of indigenous bodies, and the sparseness of native material culture all made Pilgrims uneasy. English rhetoric about Native American beastliness and filth expressed this visceral discomfort with Indian bodies even as other accounts suggested that the reality of indigenous life was more complex. The juxtaposition of shrill denunciation and veiled admiration revealed just how much the physicality of the human body, particularly its grosser, leakier aspects, troubled Puritans. Indians threatened to contaminate the godly communities of the New World with moral beastliness and filth, according to many of its ministers, a belief that discouraged Pilgrims and Puritans from engaging in intimate social contact with their indigenous neighbors.

But the Pilgrims were forced to acknowledge urgent bodily needs almost immediately during the starving time of the first winter at Plymouth. During January and February 1621, half of the Mayflower survivors died from a combination of poor nutrition and disease. A handful of healthy Pilgrims tended to the needs of the sick, including the distasteful tasks of cleaning their bodies and changing their bed linens: "Six or seven sound persons . . . with abundance of toil and hazard of their own health, fetched them wood, made them fires, dressed them meat, made their beds, washed their loathsome clothes, clothed and unclothed them. In a word, did all the homely and necessary offices for them which dainty and queasy stomachs cannot endure to hear named; and all this willingly and cheerfully, without any grudging in the least, showing herein their true love unto their friends and brethren."[30]

The community-mindedness of this virtuous band of nurses, however, did not mean widespread support for Bradford's plan to organize labor communally. "For this community (so far as it was) was found to breed much confusion and discontent and retard much employment that would have been to their benefit and comfort," he observed. Some Plymouth residents seemed troubled by the ways communal labor and equal compensation leveled differences in condition and rank that structured society in England. The entire community, however, appeared united in its dislike of communal labor that had traditionally been the responsibility of the conjugal couple and its household: "For the young men, that were most able and fit for labour and service, did repine that they should spend their time and strength to work for other men's wives and children without any recompense. The strong, or man of parts, had no more in division of victuals and clothes than he that was weak and not able to do a quarter the other could; this was thought injustice. The aged and graver men to be ranked and equalized in labours and victuals, clothes, etc., with the meaner and younger sort, thought it some indignity and disrespect unto them."[31]

The women were no happier with the arrangement. Bradford noted, "For men's wives to be commanded to do service for other men, as dressing their meat, washing their clothes, etc., they deemed it a kind of slavery." Much like their counterparts in Jamestown, the Englishwomen of Plymouth felt exploited by domestic labors performed not out of family interest and loyalty but out of obligation to a corporate entity. Husbands probably had their own objections. A wife's duties to prepare meals and wash laundry were supposed to be accompanied by affection and sexual intimacy. Where did a husband draw the line if a wife began to perform some of these labors for other men? But perhaps, too, the physically intimate nature of these duties was too much for Pilgrim husbands to stomach. Laundresses scrutinized garments and bedding for stains that told tales of sexual activity, menstruation, and illness. Touching the clothes worn by others, they learned about bodily functions that would ordinarily be known only within the household. The unsavory reputation of women who laundered, nursed, and kept people other than their own family might also have been too much for pious separatists to overcome.[32] By 1623 the protests of men and women alike forced the colony to abandon its efforts to make agricultural and domestic labor communal.[33] Others, disgruntled by swarms of mosquitoes and unwholesome water, provoked Bradford's scorn with their complaints. Excessive alcohol consumption had inured them to the benefits of New England's healthful waters, he retorted, and he urged those who couldn't tolerate the bites of a few mosquitoes to stay away.[34]

Meanwhile, the entire package of Indian manners, material culture, diet, clothing, and physical presence troubled many Pilgrims and Puritans who had left England to escape the evils that Indians seemed to embody. Indian customs of visiting, hospitality, and gift exchange promoted informal social contact, thereby eroding the boundaries between savage and saint and threatening the vision of an exclusive, godly community. Friendly Indians presented an especially awkward dilemma because they didn't stand at arm's length but wanted to visit and be visited by their English neighbors. Some prominent Pilgrims claimed that they avoided Native American hospitality because they could not tolerate the vermin. Invited to be the guests of Indian leader Massasoit in July 1621, during the peak of mosquito season, Edward Winslow and Stephen Hopkins endured a nearly sleepless night before refusing an invitation to spend a second night with their hosts. "We desired to keep the Sabbath at home," Winslow explained, "and feared we should either be light-headed for want of sleep, for what with bad lodging, the savages' barbarous singing (for they use to sing themselves asleep), lice and fleas within doors, and mosquitoes without, we could hardly sleep all the time of our being there; we much fearing that if we should stay any longer, we should not be able to recover for want of strength."[35] His professed reason for leaving Massasoit's house is curious given that most English chroniclers accepted lice and fleas as a staple of daily life in both England and New England. Settlers who persisted in Plymouth found ways to cope with mosquitoes. Were the vermin in Massasoit's house so different from what his English guests were accustomed to that they could not sleep?

Some of the discrepancy between English and Indians derived from a key cultural difference: rather than fearing human kinship with animals and trying to obscure it, as Europeans did, Indians emphasized it through clans named after animal ancestors.[36] Indians also acknowledged the functions of the lower body matter-of-factly, clearly troubling Puritans, who hid the body to retain their godly focus. Indian practices of keeping babies unswaddled to promote cleanliness, for example, doubtless struck many Pilgrims and Puritans as barbaric or, at the very least, rude. Whereas Puritans wrapped their own children in tight bands of linen and used a diaper "clout" to catch urine and feces, Eastern Woodland Indians let the infant's evacuations pass through openings in its garments. Nudity, even of small children, exposed genitalia to view, thus reminding godly people of shameful acts that were better banished from their hearts and minds. Inclined to view children as little vessels of depravity, Puritans were not likely to interpret infant nudity as cherubic or innocent. Indian customs for menstrual seclusion similarly called attention to a form of female uncleanness that was best kept secret. Like most radical Protestants, Puritans held up the pious ideal of helpmate for women even as they harbored fears of women's vulnerability to Satan, especially concerning sins of the flesh. Then there was the persistent Indian habit of bathing, which exposed naked adult bodies to view even as it enhanced Indian health and hardiness.[37]

When Indian bodies failed to meet their usual standards of grace and health—standards that even the most grudging critics were compelled to admire—Pilgrim leaders expressed frank disgust. During an outbreak of smallpox among Indians living near Windsor, Connecticut, in 1634, several English people risked illness to nurse the sick but did not succumb themselves. Bradford recognized their charity, which he found miraculous, but could not contain his disgust for the victims: "For usually they that have this disease have them in abundance, and for want of bedding and linen and other helps they fall into a lamentable condition as they lie on their hard mats, the pox breaking and mattering and running one into another, their skin cleaving by reason thereof to the mats they lie on. When they turn them, a whole side will flay off at once as it were, and they will be all of a gore blood, most fearful to behold. And then being very sore, what with cold and other distempers, they die like rotten sheep."[38] Lacking European-style bed linens, a necessary accoutrement of civility and bodily comfort, Indian victims suffered terrible injury to their delicate, disfigured skin.

Some English writers clearly found New England Indians and their way of life attractive. Roger Williams, for instance, encouraged Indians to admire English books and clothing as gifts from God, but he also praised indigenous people for their hardy constitutions, marital chastity, and agricultural industry. Others found the attraction to Indians to be more explicitly sexual. In 1628 Thomas

Morton allegedly hosted an evening of dancing and revelry to which Indian women were invited. Bradford, who condemned the events as nearly orgiastic, found it completely believable that Indian women might be appealing to English men, "dancing and frisking together like so many fairies, or furies, rather." The governor of Massachusetts Bay subsequently ordered the destruction of Morton's house so "that it might be no longer a roost for such unclean birds to nestle in."[39] Later in the century, the traveler and naturalist John Josslyn explained the attraction more clearly: "The Men are somewhat Horse Fac'd, and generally Faucious, *i.e.* without Beards; but the Women many of them have good Features; seldome without a *Come to me*, or *Cos Amoris*, in their Countenance; all of them black Eyed, having even short Teeth, and very white; their Hair black, thick and long, broad Breasted; handsome streight Bodies, and slender, considering their constant loose habit: Their limbs cleanly, straight, and of a convenient stature, generally, as plump as Partridges, and saving here and there one, of a modest deportment." Josselyn's list of Indian attractions included brown skin, which he found to be more beautiful than the pale skin Englishwomen needed to keep under wraps: "And such perfection here appears / It neither Wind nor Sun-shine fears."[40]

For their part, Indians of New England had mixed feelings about the persons and habits of Englishmen and -women. Clothing was a prime example. European garments, which Indians and English alike associated with Christianity, had multiple connotations for Indian wearers. They could symbolize religious or cultural conversion, polite acknowledgment of friendship with the English, or prestige.[41] In the early decades of the century, Indians displayed great interest in English clothing and might wear it for ceremony or when meeting with the English. They were disinclined to adopt it permanently, however, because they feared that it might soften their hardy bodies and compromise the comforts of clean, nude skin achieved through routines of bathing and anointing. Native people also objected to English garb for reasons of comfort, time, dependence, and labor. "They love not to be imprisoned in our English fashion," William Wood explained in *New England's Prospect*; "they love their own dog fashion better (of shaking their ears and being ready in a moment) than to spend time in dressing them, though they may as well spare it as any men I know, having little else to do. But the chief reasons they render why they will not conform to our English apparel are because their women cannot wash them when they bee soiled, and their meanes will not reach to buy new when they have done with their old." Better to "goe naked than be lousy" they told Wood, "and bring their bodies out of their old tune, making them more tender by a new acquired habit, which poverty would constrain them to leave."[42]

This passage of Wood's 1634 text offers a rare glimpse not only of New England

Indian attitudes toward the English but of distinctive native ideals and gendered responsibilities for bodily comfort. Although Wood's informants stopped short of conflating English clothing with English bodies, their reasons for rejecting English garb suggests that they, too, interpreted clothing and appearance as manifestations of a larger complex of body care and domestic labor. Their misgivings about English clothing may have stemmed from the tangible evidence of its inconveniences, its incompatibility with the protective and cosmetic use of unguents, and indigenous women's disinclination to do laundry, English style. Perhaps they had too often seen Englishwomen sweating over kettles of boiling water and lugging heavy baskets of wet clothes to find the prospect of regular laundry appealing.

Indeed, it appears that Wood's informants were politely suggesting that Englishwomen were the true squaw drudges, a fascinating reversal of the stock European denigration of Indians. Indian women and men had probably witnessed how quickly English clothing became stained, infested with lice, or worn out. The superficial attractions of English clothing were simply not worth the associated troubles of dressing, cleaning, and maintenance to a people already well served by skins. Accepting a gift of English clothes was one thing; taking on an entirely new routine of body care and the burden of laundering, mending, and replacing garments was another. Another English observer agreed with Wood's informants, stating that they looked "hansomer" in their own costumes than in English apparel because it suited their "gesture[s]" and way of life.[43]

Indian ambivalence toward English clothing and the difficulties of keeping it presentable had probably been informed by the dire situation at Plymouth, where linens were often in short supply. When Isaac Allerton was sent back to England with strict instructions not to spend more than fifty pounds for purchasing hose, shoes, and linen cloth, he went far over budget. These items were not only in great demand by English migrants; they were crucial to the daily performance of civility and Christianity. Shrewd businessman that he was, Allerton sold many of the goods on his own account and brought the rest back to the store when he returned to Plymouth in 1630.[44]

Despite these challenges to the colonists' traditional practices of body care—including disease, shortages of linen, and the example of alternative Native American methods—English standards for bodily cleanliness persisted. English people expected one another to remove soiled outergarments before climbing into bed. They also expected vessels for food preparation and the persons of the women who handled them to be clean. Anything less offended English sensibilities and undermined the precarious project of attempting to embody civilization three thousand miles from its source. Although individuals might transgress those standards out of necessity or by personal inclination, their deviance prompted reiterations of common expectations for cleanliness and decency. The Maine resident John Winter, in his 1639 letter justifying his wife's punishment of a "sluttish" servant maid, Priscilla, noted that the young woman had gone to "beed with her Cloth & stockins, & would not take the paines to pllucke of[f] her Cloths." Such disregard for the need to protect personal linens like bedding from outside dirt turned the maidservant's bed into a "doust bedd," compelling Mistress Winter to remove the sheets. Priscilla, for her part, complained in a letter home that she "was faine to Ly uppon Goates Skins," a hardship she did not connect to her own "sluttishness." In addition to this breach of cleanliness, which generated more work for his wife, Winter alleged, "Our men do not desire to have her boyle the kittle for them she is so sluttish." Indeed, Priscilla's entire body appeared implicated in her domestic ineptitude, according to Winter, who claimed that the maidservant usually required his wife to wake her. She is "so fatt & soggy she Can hardly do any worke," he declared.[45]

As relations between the English and Indians became more strained, breaking out into open warfare in 1636 and falling just short of that during the 1640s, Puritans and Indians both articulated the conflict in terms of bodily functions. In 1645, Bradford claimed, Narragansett Indians threatened to "lay the English cattle on heaps as high as their houses, and that no Englishman should stir out of his door to piss, but he should be killed." Even during such common acts as going outdoors to relieve themselves, the English would be made to feel fear. For their part, Puritan divines pondered the workings of Providence, including their own moral failures in North America. Bradford decried an outbreak of wickedness in 1642, detailing "sundry notorious sins" of "uncleanness." He was sad to report "not only incontinency between persons unmarried, for which many both men and women have been punished sharply enough, but some married persons also. But that which is worse, even sodomy and buggery (things fearful to name) have broke forth in this land oftener than once." The case that weighed on his mind was that of Thomas Granger, a sixteen-year-old servant in Duxbury accused of buggery with numerous animals. Upon being found guilty of these terrible crimes, Granger was forced to witness the killing of the animals immediately before his own execution. As Bradford explained in response to an inquiry by the governor of Massachusetts on the proper punishments for uncleanness, he had doubts about resorting to capital punishment in cases of adultery, but not in cases of sodomy and bestiality in which there had been penetration. Fears of monstrous half-human births motivated the mass execution of Granger's sex partners, but those officiating clearly believed that the implicated animals were contaminated in their very flesh. The cattle carcasses were disposed of in a pit so that no part of them could be used.[46]

In contemplating this outbreak of wickedness, Bradford struggled against interpretations of New England as morally contaminated. Rather, he laid the blame on "corrupt natures, which are so hardly bridled, subdued and mortified." Under the scrutiny of the Pilgrim community, Bradford explained, showing little self-consciousness over his choice of blatantly sexual imagery, wickedness was like a stopped-up stream that burst forth violently once it had found an opening. Stringent Pilgrim efforts to preserve holiness and to wipe out evil had enraged Satan, provoking him to carry on with "greater spite." "I would rather think thus," Bradford admitted, "than that Satan hath more power in these heathen lands, as some have thought, than in more Christian nations."[47]

Some pages later, he reasserted the purity of the Pilgrim experiment as he pondered the unprecedented longevity of the Pilgrim fathers. Despite unwholesome food, changes of air, compulsory water drinking, and the vexations of starting a new community, the Pilgrim fathers had demonstrated great endurance, with most surviving past sixty and a few reaching the advanced age of eighty. Bradford himself was sixty years old when he put the finishing touches on *Of Plymouth Plantation*. Although many English settlers had succumbed to outbreaks of wickedness, God had spared the leaders of the Puritan community from disease and early death, the usual consequences of so much geographic mobility and stress.[48]

ROWLANDSON'S REMOVES

The meaning of corruption in Puritan New England continued to evolve as the relationship between Indian skins and European shirts changed significantly in the second half of the century. The overhunting of fur-bearing animals and the interpenetration of Anglo and Indian cultures in the region meant that by the last quarter of the century Indians were less likely than before to disavow English clothing. A few high-ranking Indians even adopted garments of English-style linen and wool. But in spite of this period of transformed Anglo-Indian cultural relations, conflicts erupted in violence. Mary White Rowlandson, wife of a Puritan minister, was taken captive by Metacom's forces in 1676 during the bloody war named after the Wampanoag sachem. Her 1681 narrative of her ordeal illustrates the fever pitch of anti-Indian rhetoric. Rowlandson condemned Indian savagery and filthiness at every opportunity and attributed Indian kindness to the strange workings of Providence. Her attitudes probably drew from older accounts, including Bradford's, that had laid the foundation for racializing Anglo-Indian cultural differences. But Rowlandson's narrative also revealed how the language of cleanliness and filth was beginning to communicate the politics of

Anglo-Indian relations in new ways during a period in which European-style clothing no longer automatically distinguished Englishman from Indian.[49]

Captured by a group of Narragansett Indians from her home in Deerfield, Massachusetts, Rowlandson witnessed the killing of several relatives and friends before being forced to make a wintry march with her captors. During the course of nearly three months' captivity, Rowlandson had sufficient intimate daily contact with Indians to test the accuracy of Puritan knowledge about indigenous ways of life. If fissures in her beliefs emerged, however, Rowlandson carefully seamed them together, much as she fashioned garments for her captors from the old clothing they brought her. As she composed her narrative after being redeemed, her Providential interpretation of events rendered Indian motives irrelevant. Acts of seeming kindness and civility reflected God's mercy, not her captors' decency. If Indians fell short of their reputations for savagery, it was owing to divine intervention, not because Puritans had erred in their judgments. Even without the workings of Providence, however, Rowlandson found plenty of evidence to support interpretations of Indian beastliness.

Rowlandson indicted her Indian captors for the violence perpetrated at Deerfield and the unmerciful treatment of English captives. Although she documented several instances in which young English boys were the victims of harsh treatment, the seeming disregard of Indians for Englishwomen and children struck Rowlandson most deeply. In her account of the deaths of captive English children, Indians remained unmoved by maternal grief, considering only the practical exigencies of moving swiftly through the winter woods. With her first sustained contact with Native Americans marked by bloodshed and punctuated thereafter by the deaths of children, Rowlandson needed little else to convince her that Indians were savages.[50]

The Indian consumption of food Rowlandson deemed filthy was second in her ledger of savagery only to their spilling of innocent English blood. Echoing Smith's language comparing natives to animals, she seemed impressed by Indian industry even as she found their exigency loathsome: "Though many times they would eat that that a hog or a dog would hardly touch, yet by that God strengthened them to be a scourge to his people. . . . They would pick up old bones, and cut them in pieces at the joynts, and if they were full of worms and magots, they would scald them over the fire to make the vermine come out; and then boyle them, and drink up the Liquor, and then beat the great ends of them in a Mortar, and so eat them. They would eat Horses guts and ears, and all sorts of wild bird which they could catch." Her admiration was not for Indians who scavenged creatively in the midst of a brutal war, however, but for the God who "feeds and nourishes them up to be a scourge to the whole land."[51]

Although Rowlandson probably saw the rest of her narrative as testimony to God's mercy in allowing bloodthirsty savages to sustain the spirit of a beleaguered English captive, the details often revealed a more complex story captured in her poignant narrative of loss. In their requests for new clothing, their displays of fastidiousness, and their generally respectful treatment of her person, the Indians of Rowlandson's account became human actors in three dimensions, despite their chronicler's animus against them.

Rowlandson recorded numerous instances of Indians' desire for English clothing—a desire that had grown since the early decades of the century. At several points in her narrative she noted Indians stripping dead or captured English people of their clothes.[52] The Indians she encountered seem to have valued outer garments more highly than shirts: she observed one stripped captive who still had his shirt and a group of Indian men, dressed English-style, who wore white neck cloths rather than shirts. She also reported numerous Indian requests that she sew shirts from lengths of fabric and from old garments that needed altering. English garments clearly had prestige value for the wearer. She recounted a dance in which her Indian master donned a "Holland shirt and white stockings" and her mistress "a Kersey coat . . . Girdles of Wampom . . . fine red Stockings and white shoes, her Hair powdered, and her face painted Red."[53]

At least for werowansquas (female leaders), the time invested in dressing English-style was no longer an impediment to wearing English clothes as it might have been earlier in the century. Rowlandson wrote critically of Wettimo, the mistress with whom she had frequent angry conflicts, that she "beestow[s] every day in dressing herself near as much time as any of the Gentry of the land; powdering her hair and painting her face, going with her Neck-laces, with Jewels in her ears, and bracelets upon her hands." Comparing Wettimo to the colonial gentry was no compliment but an indictment of the werowansqua's vanity. For similar reasons, Wettimo's "work" making girdles of wampum and beads did not command the respect of Rowlandson, who saw little value in these trinkets, although she noted that Wettimo and her master wore them at a ceremonial dance, along with their English finery. In leveling such critiques against Wettimo's character, Rowlandson implicitly portrayed herself as a paragon of domestic virtue who knew better than to abandon humility and industry to play the part of a vain gentlewoman.[54]

The aesthetics of Indian cleanliness remained a mystery to Rowlandson, who found the natives' willingness to eat vile things difficult to reconcile with other expressions of fastidiousness. She criticized her Indian mistress for putting on airs because she refused to eat from a dish that contained both "pease" and "bear" together. She also related her confusion over an incident involving water:

"When I had fetcht water, and had put the Dish I dipt the water with into the Kettle of water which I brought, they would say they would knock me down; for they said it was a sluttish trick."[55] To the Indians who reprimanded her, a woman's dirty hands could contaminate a kettle of water intended for communal eating and drinking. Such standards were not so different from those of the male laborers offended by the body of the Maine maidservant. But Rowlandson was not used to thinking about her own hands as carriers of pollution and seemed surprised that her captors found her disregard "sluttish."

Rowlandson's state of uncleanness may have been offensive to her captors. Her master went out of his way to encourage her to clean and groom herself, an interest in her condition that she interpreted as kindness: "He asked me, when I washt me? I told him not this moneth; then he fetch me some water himself, and bid me wash, and give me the Glass to see how I lookt."[56] Both she and her master viewed a month without washing as an extraordinary lapse, especially when that time had been spent on the move outdoors.

As determined as she was to testify to Indian savagery and God's redeeming goodness, Rowlandson found that certain tropes of Indian beastliness simply had not proven true in her experience. She strained to fit evidence of Indian decency and civility into the dominant refrain of her narrative, that God sustained the Indians to be a scourge to New England Puritans. "I have been in the midst of those roaring Lions and Savage Bears, that feared neither God not Man, nor the Devil, by night and day, alone and in company, sleeping all sorts together," she declared, "and yet not one of them ever offered the least abuse or unchastity to me in word or action." Like most other examples of Indian humanity, Rowlandson interpreted this marvel of Indian respect for English womanhood to a merciful God who took pity on a poor captive. Yet if Indians were not the source of the filthy sins of the flesh that plagued Puritan society, Puritans would need to look within to find other vectors of contamination.

MURDEROUS UNCLEANNESS

Zech.13.1 *There shall be a Fountain Opened for Sin, and for Uncleanness.* Your *Sin* has been *Uncleanness*, Repeated *Uncleanness*, Impudent *Uncleanness*, Murderous *Uncleanness*: You must, like the *Leper*, Cry out, *Unclean! Unclean!*

—Cotton Mather, *Warnings from the Dead* (1693)

The Puritan outcry against sexual sin reached its peak at the end of the century as a generation of Puritan divines faced the reality of rising premarital pregnancy rates, a series of sensational infanticide trials, and the creeping progress of an ideal of politeness that valued privacy over guaranteeing conformity to a single moral standard. In 1693 the Puritan minister Cotton Mather used the occasion of a public execution to deliver a dramatic lecture on the fatal consequences of uncleanness. Gathered to witness the executions of two women for infanticide, the large crowd heard the thirty-year-old Mather deliver one of his most dramatic and commercially successful sermons. "The Sermon was immediately printed; with another, which I had formerly uttered on the like Occasion; (entitled, *Warnings From the Dead.*)," Mather recorded proudly in his diary, "and it was greedily bought up; I hope, to the Attainment of the Ends, which I had so long desired. T'was afterwards reprinted at London."[57]

Mather's diatribe against sexual uncleanness was occasioned by the executions of a twenty-eight-year-old white woman, Elizabeth Emerson, and an unnamed "Black Fellow-Sufferer," who was listed in other records as "Elisabeth Negro." Barely mentioning that a second woman also awaited the hangman's noose, Mather focused his comments on Emerson, incorporating her gallows statement into *Warnings from the Dead* and subsequent publications. Convicted of killing her illegitimate twins in 1691, Emerson sealed her fate by attempting to hide the evidence; she stuffed the bodies into a cloth bag and then buried them behind the house she shared with her parents. More than two years elapsed between the crime and Mather's lecture on uncleanness, which Emerson listened to in its entirety before proceeding to the gallows and her death.

Emerson's crime marked an important shift in the legal prosecution of infanticide. The sensational case provoked Massachusetts legislators to change the law under which infanticide was prosecuted at a time when many laws in the colony were being revised under its new charter of 1691. Adopting a 1624 English statute, Massachusetts no longer implicitly defined infanticide as a species of common-law murder. Under the provisions of the new law, the mere concealment of the birth of a dead illegitimate child became sufficient evidence for convicting the mother of infanticide. Although formal reception of this law took four years and another sensational case, the impact on conviction rates was striking: only one of ten accused under the guidelines of the 1624 law was acquitted during the 1690s, giving that decade both the highest rate and highest total number of infanticide convictions between 1670 and 1780.[58] This trend, then, distinguished the final decade of the seventeenth century in Massachusetts as the least forgiving of mothers convicted of killing their illegitimate infants.

The publication of Mather's sermon also marked the beginning of a new pattern in which influential ministers invoked the bodies of sexually transgressive women to symbolize the colony's spiritual degradation. Other Puritan ministers had previously published on the subject of uncleanness, most notably Samuel Danforth, who used the occasion of a seventeen-year-old boy's execution for sodomy to denounce all types of illicit sexual activities in *Cry of Sodom* (1674). But Mather gave this denunciation a new target, which apparently resonated with his fellow ministers and their readers. *Warnings from the Dead* was the first of five books published during the 1690s devoted to the cases of women executed for infanticide. In this context, Mather's choice of Emerson's execution to publicize his warning about uncleanness is significant. Emerson's alleged double infanticide not only provoked a legal redefinition but sparked a wave of publications in which readers followed convicted women to the hangman's noose. Biographies of decline into evildoing, sensational crimes, and gallows drama resonated with the Puritan etiology of sin and death and connected them powerfully to long-standing beliefs in female bodily impurity. The body of the female infanticide thus became an emblem of the colony's uncleanness and one means by which ministers could attempt to reclaim authority tarnished by complicity in the Salem proceedings.[59] This was especially the case for Cotton Mather, who had played a leading role in shaping public approval for the prosecutions and only belatedly spoke out against them.

Warnings from the Dead offers a glimpse of a fervently Protestant early modern body for which proscribed sexual acts were loathsome not simply because they sullied the purity of the soul but because of their location in the "lower" regions of the body, associated with organic filth.[60] The unclean body described by Mather was physically as well as spiritually afflicted, succumbing to disease and death as a consequence of God's wrath over its sinfulness. In a world in which disease might be providentially caused or cured, "filthy" sexual practices straddled moral and medical approaches to the body. Executions of female criminals like Elizabeth Emerson allowed ministers to minimize the abstraction in the metaphor of the unclean body and to explain graphically the danger sinners posed to the Puritan social body.[61] Even in the aftermath of Salem, Mather was unwilling to give up providentialism or the denunciation of Satan's works. Filth provided a safe way to point the finger at the devil in Puritan society with the full backing of natural philosophy. No one except the devil and his minions would contradict Mather and claim to love filth—unless, of course, he was suffering from mental derangement, the emerging Enlightenment explanation for antisocial behavior.

Mather's awareness of his own waning influence may have been a prime reason for the high pitch of his rhetoric and his focus on topics about which there had previously been little controversy: sexual sin and filth. In the colonies, ministerial influence was diminishing at century's end. The new colonial charter, which limited Puritan political and cultural influence, the post-Salem renunciation of spectral evidence, and new interest in scientific rather than providential explanations for the workings of the world all contributed to this decline. Mather had been one of the loudest proponents of beliefs in witchcraft before the outbreak at Salem. Although he subsequently married his interest in science to his belief in Providence, during the 1690s he remained focused on sin as a provocation for divine punishment.

Expanding on Job 36:14, "They dy in Youth, and their Life is among the Unclean," Mather identified uncleanness as not just an evil prerequisite for but a *cause* of premature death. "*An Early and a Woful* **Death**, *is the Fruit of an Unclean and a Wicked* **Life**," he warned, citing death and infertility as two of the punishments God visited on sinners. He distinguished two different meanings for *unclean*. Used generically, the term described many kinds of wickedness. "All our Sinfulness," Mather noted, "is call'd A *Filthiness of Flesh & Spirit*." Attempting to explain the aptness of the filth-sin metaphor, he reasoned, "a man that Lives in Sin against the God that made him, is denominated in Job 15.16. *An Abominable and Filthy man*. Why? Because the most Loathsome, Dirty, Nasty Object in the World, is not so Distastful unto us, as all *Wickedness* is unto our God, who is, *Not a God that hath pleasure in Wickedness*."[62]

Sexual sinfulness was a particularly odious form of uncleanness "because of a Special *Filthiness*, and *Ugliness*, which this Vice is attended with." Indeed, sexual uncleanness was so vile and contaminating that even public condemnations threatened to corrupt.[63] Mather catalogued sexual sins hierarchically, noting the increasing degree of uncleanness. "Cursed *Self-Pollution*" was "usually the first pit of *Uncleanness*," he noted, followed by "Odious *Fornication*, which is a further Step, of that *Uncleanness*, whereunto the Raging Lusts of men do carry them." Next came the "Inexpressible *Uncleannesses*" of "*Inordinate Affection*" in marriage, which sometimes grew into "*Adultery*." The defiling sin of incest was another, wicked for its disruption of family government. Mather found the vileness of sodomy and buggery "horrible to be Spoken!" but not too horrible for a lengthy digression, complete with an illustrative case of bestiality in New England. To this list of "*Acts* of *Uncleanness*," Mather appended unclean thoughts and words as forms of wickedness prohibited by both the Bible and "Natural *Reason* and *Conscience* in man." Although "*Looking upon a Woman to Lust after her*" and "*Filthiness & Foolish Talking*" were not bodily acts like fornication, they merited censure because they could lead to more terrible sins. The sexual nature of such thoughts and words, however, was what led to their classification among the filthiest of sins.[64]

Mather preached against strong popular trends. A growing cohort of young

New Englanders were more likely to associate sex with pleasure than with filth, even though their elders defined illicit sexuality as "profane." As early as the 1670s, the erosion of the tightly bounded and heavily guarded Puritan notion of godly conduct had prompted a group of reformist ministers to take action. Led by Increase Mather and spurred by the conviction that Metacom's War was God's judgment against New England, they pursued a general reform of manners during the 1670s and 1680s: profane living, tavern culture, the compromises of 1662 on church membership, sumptuary laws, contentious behavior, and the neglect of godly learning in private households all came under their scrutiny. Along with his son, Cotton, Increase Mather had played a prominent role not only in identifying the "Provoking Evils" that brought war to New England in 1675 but in seeking a reforming synod in 1679 and subsequent restrictions on taverns in 1681.[65] Now young Mather entered the fray against sexual sin by preaching passionately about the dangers of filthy living.

Emerson's grievous crime and subsequent execution provided Cotton Mather with a perfect opportunity to diagnose the ills of Puritan society. In Mather's text, Emerson's uncleanness became Puritan uncleanness; the unclean body of the female infanticide became the unclean social body. Denouncing her crime with potent rhetoric about uncleanness and a logical flow chart of sin, Mather revealed his own struggle to purge Puritan society—and perhaps himself—of corruption, and to reassert his authority to define moral cleanliness and filth.[66]

Born in 1665, the fifth of Michael Emerson and Hannah Webster Emerson's fifteen children, Elizabeth was punished severely at an early age for her recalcitrance. Her father's appearance in Essex County Court in 1676 to answer charges that he beat his daughter excessively suggests a clash between the stubborn eleven-year-old and her violence-prone father. According to her gallows statement, disobedience led to keeping bad company, which paved the way to uncleanness. Emerson's illicit sexual behavior became public knowledge in 1686, when she gave birth to her first illegitimate child.[67]

Following her first transgression, Emerson seems to have been watched closely by both parents and neighbors. Five years later, as her daughter grew heavier, Hannah Emerson asked her bluntly whether she was pregnant, but Elizabeth admitted nothing.[68] She later confessed to being fearful of killing her mother with the news. This fear, she claimed, also motivated her to give birth silently on the trundle bed at the foot of her parents' bed early in the morning of May 8, 1691. Never calling for help, Emerson left the twin infants amid the bedclothes. Her claim that neither baby cried was her main evidence of their stillbirth and her own innocence. Michael and Hannah Emerson corroborated their daughter's account of the babies' silence, claiming that they slept through the ordeal and noticed nothing amiss when they arose early that morning.[69]

Sharp-eyed neighbors, who might have been counting the months since Emerson's first dizzy spell at public meeting or carefully noting her size, could have become alarmed by her failure to emerge from the house. They also might have been tipped off by one Samuel Lad, the married man whom Emerson later identified as the father and the only person she had told about her pregnancy. When the group of two men and four women came to the Emerson household during the time of public meeting on Sunday, May 10, they found Emerson washing dishes but, in her own words, "unwell." While the women took Emerson into another room to search her for signs of recent childbirth, the men headed for a place in the yard where they suspected she might have buried an infant. Not one, but two dead babies, contained in a cloth bag, rewarded the searchers' efforts.[70]

The next day, the four women, "tow of us being Midwifes and the other tow acquainted amongs women," examined the bodies. All the women believed that the babies had been born alive "att thear full time." Unable to find definitive signs of murder, they nonetheless agreed that Emerson was guilty of wrongdoing: "We do certainly believe th[a]t the Children perished for want of help & Caer att time of travell."[71] Emerson initially refused to identify the father and insisted that no one, not even her parents, knew of her pregnancy, delivery, or efforts to hide the bodies. On May 11, however, she named Lad; he appears to have visited her the night before her delivery and probably knew of his lover's pregnancy. Michael and Hannah Emerson, who claimed complete ignorance not only of their daughter's condition but of the birth and burial two days later, were subsequently absolved of wrongdoing.[72]

Beyond speaking publicly about unspeakable acts of wickedness—a waiver of taboos that defined his ministerial privilege and authority—Mather hoped to diagnose the source of New England's moral corruption. Emerson was the perfect foil for this task. Her progression from bad company to bastardy and infanticide presented a powerful lesson in the etiology of uncleanness. Gradually consuming the body and soul of a woman who had once enjoyed the privileges of religious instruction, uncleanness had numbed her to her own wickedness and the certainty of divine retribution, hastening her along the path to her death. Unlike the vast majority of women convicted of infanticide—usually poor, in servitude, African, or Indian—Emerson was white and the daughter of churchgoing, if not reputable, Puritans. Only with difficulty could a witness to her execution construe her as a distant "other" to the godly community. Mather hardly needed to spell out the implication. Indeed, he seems to have assumed that his listeners would understand it; Emerson's sinful corruption was a specimen of the corruption *within* the Puritan body that would eventually kill it if not purged.

Mather sketched the relationship between sin and the body as a dynamic one of declining agency for the individual. The individual made the initial choice to sin with her will, her health, and her spiritual purity unencumbered. But having once capitulated to temptation, she rapidly succumbed to the involuntary nature of uncleanness. Weakened by pollution, disease, and the formation of evil habits, the human body lost its capacity to resist sin. What began as a struggle of the will and the spirit to avoid filthy sin ended with a degraded body, habituated to sin, and forced to capitulate to its own involuntary needs. Uncleanness thus threatened the health of the body. Mather warned ominously that it "will bloodily Disturb the Frame of our Bodies, and Exhaust and Poison the Spirits, in our Bodies, until an Incurable *Consumption* at Last, shall cut us down, *Out of Time*."[73]

Uncleanness also broke down the distinctions between humankind and brute animals, with fearful consequences for a person's relationship with God, in whose image "he" was created. Mather imagined a scene in which "it should be said, *There is a man, that is a Beast? There's a man Wallowing like a Dog, & like a Swine, in the most base Uncleanness!*" (Privately, in his diary, Mather recognized the similarity between men's and dogs' bodily functions.) In imagery redolent with Puritan hatred of Quakers, Mather also compared unclean people to "*Unclean Goats*, Quaking and Shaking, before the Tribunal of the Lord Jesus Christ, as they shall at the Last Day." Uncleanness transformed the human body from the temple of the Holy Ghost to the "*Hog-sties* of the Devil," a phrase which Danforth had also used in *The Cry of Sodom*. The young people Mather identified as being most guilty of sexual wrongdoing luxuriated in "Diabolical *Pollutions*."[74]

Mather's unclean risked not only compromising their humanity but ruining their estates, reputations, and reproductive potential. They "leave the World, with the Humiliation of seeing *None* . . . but a *Poor* Posterity rising after them. Tis a frequent Thing, for that Great Blessing of Children, to be *Deny'd* where the Guilt of much *Uncleanness* is Lying on the Soul." If any children did survive, he observed, they were likely to be cursed with sickness or destined to fight their own losing battle with uncleanness. Thus the sins of the fathers would be visited upon their sons.[75]

If godly people failed to excise corruption from the social body, Mather warned, divine curses would strip that body of its young men and thus lead to its demise: "What Multitudes among us, do we see *Dy in Youth!* . . . How many

Scores of *Young men* have sometimes been lost from one Little Town, within two of three Years, by the Disastrous *Plagues* and *Wars* that have been upon us! . . . Unto us may our God say, as He said unto *Israel* of old, *Your, Young men have I Slain.*" The reasons for the Old Testament—style decimation of young men in Massachusetts seemed clear to Mather: "Methinks, the *Wickedness,* & Especially the *Uncleanness* too rise among our Young People, should be acknowledged, among the Causes of these Calamities." With Emerson's example hovering behind his words, he identified the "two . . . most ungrateful Seasons, that *Young People* take to multiply those their Diabolical *Pollutions,*" as "the Close of *Sabbath,*" and the "Joy of the *Harvest.*" As a consequence of losing its male members, New England would be rendered weak and feminized: "So little *Joy* indeed ha's our God in our Young People, that He is every day saying over them, *Indians, Do you come; Frenchmen do you come; Fevers, do you come;* & *cut off as many of those young People, as come in your way!*"[76]

Mather offered his listeners several preventive measures for avoiding uncleanness and seeking repentance. In addition to prayer, fasting, and industrious activity, Mather recommended singing hymns. Such a remedy not only offered distracting thoughts for the mind but set the tempted body to pious activity. Mather also listed reading as one of the antidotes to a persistent unclean spirit, but cautioned the congregation to "shun all obscaene Books, as you would the Rags that had the *Plague* about them." In a specific plea to Emerson to repent, Mather recommended "vomiting" sins in confession, an act of bodily expulsion that purged uncleanness like so much bodily corruption, and shedding melting tears to wash the feet of the savior.[77]

Mather was remarkably restrained about denouncing the special dangers of female uncleanness. Most of his warnings were aimed at both men and women, although he singled out young men as the victims of divine punishments. That Emerson's execution inspired the sermon, however, and that the vast majority of people hanged for uncleanness were female, skewed Mather's message about the plague sweeping the land. Male uncleanness rarely became such a public spectacle; nor would it have resonated so deeply with Puritans whose conviction that women had a special vulnerability to diabolical temptations and sins of the flesh had led to the debacle at Salem.[78] Seventeenth-century ideas about personal cleanliness and the metaphoric emphasis on the physical manifestations of sin, exemplified in this case by a condemned woman, brought together ideas about sexuality, sin, the body, and death in ways that made the female body the standard for most kinds of bodily and social corruption.

Linens assumed special significance in the details of the Emerson case and provided a graphic exemplar of the bodily manifestations of filth that so exercised Mather. Like chemises, bed linens were the repositories of bodily filth that included the sweat emitted by the skin and bodily fluids like menstrual blood and semen. It was not uncommon for women to reserve special linens for use during childbirth. These coverings for bedding and the garments worn by the birthing woman and her infant had great emotional significance and were often passed down from mother to daughter. When they were newly made or purchased for a particular birth, they might also be invoked as a legal defense against infanticide under English law in cases where a child subsequently died. But they were also ritually significant; they protected bedding used in ordinary life from the potent bodily fluids produced during childbirth. Those fluids were filthy only when, as the anthropologist Mary Douglas has noted, they were "matter out of place." Although a laundered but stained set of childbirth linens might not be considered dirty when used at a birth, the bloody material produced at birth would have been deemed filthy if it remained on everyday bed linens.[79]

In contrast, Puritan ministerial garb was the ultimate sartorial emblem of moral and literal purity. Set off dramatically by his black coat, the minister's distinctive display of white linen marked him as not only a man of God but also a gentleman. He wore this linen around his neck, overlaid by a long white collar. The gauzy material for this collar was always pure white, although it might be either opaque or sheer.[80] It was expected that a minister would provide an example of moral cleanliness, but if he hoped to preside over wealthy and cosmopolitan congregations like those in late-seventeenth-century Boston, he also needed to affect the image of a gentleman. In an age not characterized by regular full-body bathing, no gentleman wearing white linen at the neck could neglect to change it regularly, for a collar worn for too many days would display his skin's effusions to the world.[81]

The fact that Emerson was confronted with her crime while washing the dishes, moments after burying her dead infants, would have seemed a gruesome irony to Puritans: with metaphoric blood dripping from her hands, Emerson continued with her domestic routine like any good wife, except that it was the Sabbath, she had never been married, and she had just finished hiding the bodies of two dead babies. Second, the fact that her interrogators questioned her while she was on the very bed in which she had given birth—the same bed that her parents allegedly had stumbled past, unaware that anything was wrong—would have raised an obvious question for any New England woman who had witnessed a birth; what had Emerson done with the soiled childbed linens, which surely would have revealed her secret to her household? Had she hidden or buried them, knowing that it would be impossible to wash them covertly? Or had she simply continued to sleep on such radically soiled linens, saturated with blood and amniotic fluid? Any seventeenth-century person with doubts about Michael and Hannah Emerson's innocence would have thought skeptically about the sight and smell of blood on the bed linens. No one seems to have asked whether Emerson, who had concealed her pregnancy from her own mother, had taken the trouble to borrow special childbirth linens.[82]

Finally, there is the gesture of sewing a cloth bag for the infants before burying them. Most of Emerson's English-speaking contemporaries would have seen a similarity between her action and traditions of wrapping the corpse in white linen winding sheets before burial. These traditions appear to have crossed the Atlantic intact.[83] Although storing the bodies in a bag would have made it easier for Emerson to hide and move the babies, convenience does not appear to have been her only motive. Rather, it seems that she sewed the bag *after* she stowed the babies in the chamber chest, in preparation for burying them in the ground. Emerson honored taboos about placing unprotected corpses directly in the soil; her own respect for filth avoidance thus made an unexpected appearance in a crime that Mather depicted as the epitome of uncleanness.[84]

ENGLISH BODIES

Even as Virginia lawmakers and Puritan divines struggled to enforce sexual regulations that would support the social order of their colonies, several turn-of-the century Protestant reformers in England charted a course for health in a world in which new ingredients, practices, and wealth threatened to corrupt English bodies. The resurgence of bathing in warm natural baths was one of many "nice and effeminate" habits that had taken hold among the wealthy during the first century of England's colonial presence in the Atlantic. How best to determine the proper regimen for English people if they resided all around the Atlantic basin and their diets testified to the exotic luxuries that world afforded? What could be done if newfound prosperity and new interest in politeness inspired civilized behaviors that were downright unhealthy? The hobbyhorses of these pious reformers varied—vegetable diets, bedbug prevention, and cold bathing—but the common concern was the rise in harmful vices that made English bodies prone to corruption. Decrying the popular uses of foreign ingredients was an old refrain, but the commodities these writers condemned were of new significance in an age of Atlantic expansion: coffee, tea, tobacco, imported brandies, and spices. Condemning the softening effects of new luxuries—overheated rooms, featherbeds, and hot baths—writers like Thomas Tryon and John Floyer, as well as their better-known contemporaries Thomas Sydenham and John Locke, advised their readers to exchange effeminate habits for an invigorating cool regimen of bracing air, a diet dominated by vegetables, and cold water—which was to be drunk as well as applied externally.

Tryon was a prolific English Puritan writer who had lived in Barbados during the 1660s. By the 1690s he had published on a variety of reformist topics—temperance, spirituality, education, health, dreams, mental illness, and trade—and had also produced an instructional manual for planters. He urged readers to preserve their health through internal purification, achieved by changing their diets, adopting new habits of exercise (including bathing), and embracing cleanliness of household and person. Women were central to Tryon's vision. "The Whole Preservation of Mens Health and Strength does chiefly reside in the Wisdom and Temperance of women," he claimed, criticizing mothers for intemperance during pregnancy and for overheating their children with inappropriate foods, tight swaddling, and warmed beds. "The Food of most Children, of late Years, is so enriched with West and East-India Ingredients, that is, with Sugar and Spices," he reasoned, that "it heats the Body . . . infecting the Blood with a sharp fretting Humour, which in some Complexions and Constitutions causeth Languishing Diseases . . . so that the Joynts and Nerves become weak and feeble." Spicy food, in combination with other uncleanness, also led to blotches, boils, and leprous diseases.[85]

Complaining that most people valued their health "no more than the silly *Indians* of old did their *Wealth*, when they contentedly parted with *Gold* and *Pearl*, for *Toys* and *Baubles*, and *Knives*, and *Beaugles*, and *Looking-Glasses*," Tryon offered simple Mosaic rules for good health: a diet rich in vegetables and spare in meat, bathing, exercise, and household cleanliness.[86] But he faulted housewives especially for neglecting bedding. Nestled deep in hot featherbeds (often made of imported feathers), a person generated unhealthy steams and stenches that caused disease. "They lie on Beds that do really stink worse than the Common Houses of Office [privy]," Tryon declared, "tho' being us'd to them, they do not smell it, nor can they, so great is the power of Evil Nature and Custom."[87] Most households failed to replace feathers or change bed linens regularly, creating ideal conditions for lice and other vermin. "The Original of these Creatures Called Bugs is from Putrefaction," explained Tryon, "occasioned by Stinking Scents and Vapours which do proceed from the Bodies and Nature of Men and Women." Tryon urged readers to replace featherbeds with straw mattresses. Beds of all sorts "ought to be changed, driven, or washed, at the least three or four times in a Year; or else it is impossible to keep them sweet and clean."[88] Tryon recommended exposing bedding to "good air," to remove unhealthy moisture, but he also believed cool air could benefit the body itself by purifying the blood, opening the passages of joints and nerves, and stimulating the appetite. Moderate clothing, hard beds, and unimpeded breezes would improve health and prevent infestations of bugs, while self-denial, sobriety, and cleanness in diet would slow down the body's innate tendency to putrefy. A regimen of such measures, claimed Tryon, unites "our Souls to God, and our Neighbours; and keeps our Bodies in Health, and our minds in serenity; rendering us unpolluted Temples, for the Holy Spirit and God to communicate with."[89]

Writing some fifteen years after Tryon, John Floyer, a doctor from Litchfield, England, took aim at the growing effeminacy that threatened to undermine the collective moral and physical health of the nation. Floyer, who took over the practice as well as much of the library of his University of Padua–trained predecessor, advocated a return to the wisdom of the ancients, especially on the question of bathing. In an *Enquiry into the right use and abuses of the Hot, Cold, and Temperate BATHS in England* (1697), he sought to intervene in the indiscriminate recourse to watering holes like Bath, for pleasure or on the advice of quacks, without considering the different effects of specific temperatures of water on the body. His *Enquiry* offered a detailed analysis of the consequences of bathing in and drinking waters with different properties. The detergent effect of water received only a brief mention, although he noted its uses for curing all kinds of nasty skin ailments.[90]

English vigor could be restored, Floyer claimed, if people would replace hot baths, hot clothes, spicy foods, and stimulating beverages with cold water, air, and food. "Cold Water Strengthens the natural Heat, Spirits, and Vigor or Tone of our Bodies," he explained, which is why "*Northern* Nations rub their Frozen Parts with Ice, and have always harden'd their Bodies by bathing in Cold Water." Floyer denounced tobacco, tea, and coffee for heating the body unhealthily and damaging the head and spirits. He also warned against hot liquors and sauces, quoting Hippocrates: "The frequent use of hot things, makes the Mind effeminate, the Nerves weak, the Spirits torpid." Sitting by the fire in a warm house or wearing flannels made a person perspire unnaturally (and visibly). Although he recounted the use of sweating ovens by Native Americans, Floyer remained skeptical that such practices could be healthy for English bodies, "this Practice being against the Reason of our Philosophy, and the Inclination of our tender Patient." He urged his countrymen to reject the hot regimen—brandy and spirits, strong ale and wines, tobacco, flannel garments, warming fires, excessive coffee and tea, and intemperate sex—and advocated instead that they harden their bodies by bathing in and drinking cold water. For Floyer, as for several other reformers at the turn of the century, it was the wealthy, not the poor, whose way of life seemed incompatible with good health.[91]

Hardened, vigorous bodies that could sleep comfortably on hard straw mattresses, endure submersion in cold water, and be braced by the sting of cold air—these were the Englishmen Tryon and Floyer imagined. Had nearly a century of contact with Native Americans convinced them that Indians, rather than their own wealthy classes, provided the best model of health? Some of the regimen they recommended certainly suggested admiration for indigenous hardiness. But they also eyed products and habits from the Americas with suspicion, giving a new spin to an age-old complaint about the inappropriateness of foreign ways. The cooling program they advocated became increasingly popular on both sides of the Atlantic during the eighteenth century, although cold bathing remained the peculiar passion of the English.[92]

Initially uneasy in the company of Native Americans, who struck them as being endowed with grace and health but without other trappings of civility, New England Puritans latched onto rhetoric about Native American beastliness and filth. Others simply expressed discomfort in the company of Indians and discouraged further social intimacy. During periods of conflict with Native Americans over land and trade, most notably during Metacom's War, Puritan fears about the contamination of illicit sexuality in their own midst intensified. Denunciations of uncleanness within the Puritan social body gathered momentum throughout the century, culminating in a series of high-profile accusations and executions during the 1690s. Although fears of women's corrupt bodies had long had resonance in Catholic Europe and continued to be successfully mobilized for political purposes in Anglo-America, this decade represented a high-water mark in the public denunciation of female sexual sin as dangerous to collective well-being.

Over the next thirty years, much would change. The female propensity to sexual sin became less central to public discussions of morality as privacy and politeness—the cornerstones of gentility—became more central to Euro-American concepts of civilization. Mather, his fellow ministers, and many New England courts were beginning to embrace an entirely new concept of female bodies and sensibility, one that emphasized innate piety and maternal tenderness. Seventeenth-century notions of female moral depravity and bodily corruption did not disappear with this new view of womanhood, however, but continued to justify public punishments of women of color and white servants. With uncleanness signifying race and poverty as well as illicit sex and infanticide, the condemned women of the eighteenth century were depicted as deviant outsiders whose criminality made their excision from the social body necessary.[93] The concept of filthy sin Mather denounced so shrilly thus protected a vision of Puritan community that was already on the wane.

In Virginia, the redemptive path open to white women was to be explicitly racial, paved by shifting the stigma of the "nasty wench" onto the bodies of enslaved African women. By century's end, public discussions of sexual uncleanness consisted of the Anglican Church's tempered injunctions against private sins and the legal sanctions against white women who violated the foundations of racial slavery. Transgressors forfeited their claim to the privileges of white womanhood—the edifice of the English claim to civilization in the southern colonies. The early privations and sordid living conditions of early Anglo-Virginians were gentrified along with the sexual reputations and laboring lives of the colony's white women. Conceptualizing a white woman's sexual liaison with a man of African or Indian descent as a foul sin protected the racial foundations for separate categories of master and slave in a colony on the brink of becoming a slave society.

Eighteenth-century Anglo-Americans continued to think of sexual sin as the ultimate form of filth, but certain bodies would assume more of that burden than others. Meanwhile, the ascendant polite culture privileged privacy over the public confessional, at least for white women; people were less likely to believe that individual acts of uncleanness could provoke the hand of Providence. Commentary on the body in the eighteenth century was more likely to focus on an individual's manners, breeding, and refinement than on sexual uncleanness as that body became a more important site of the work of social distinction.

Meanwhile, in England, the wisdom about bathing was changing thanks to fashion and medical advocacy. Tryon and Floyer touted self-restraint in a world of rediscovered water spas, a newly prosperous class of merchants and planters, and rising Atlantic trade. For Tryon, as for most of his predecessors, women bore the ultimate responsibility for the household cleanliness needed to keep people healthy. For Floyer, the medical man, the newfangled habits of an effeminate age threatened to weaken English bodies by overheating and softening them. Both feared that physical and moral corruption seemed to be on the rise as a consequence of overly civilized habits. Yet each advocated more scrupulous attention to body, bed, and board—not coddling the body, but restraining it and more carefully regulating the consumption of luxuries that accompanied England's rise as an Atlantic power.

Part II

GENTEEL BODIES

On May 25, 1767, Harvard student Stephen Peabody and his school chums made the first of several trips to the Watertown springs, west of Boston, to investigate "the fine conveniences for drinking & Bathing." Peabody and his friends had heard of the springs' reputation as a place where people with chronic complaints might go to "get cured of their Diseases." That night they simply observed the activity. After consulting with Colonel Brattle about the healthfulness of drinking spring water, Peabody and his friend Webster returned three days later for some sociable purging. "Mulliken, Webster & Chadwick set of[f] with me a little after sunrise up to Watertown Spring," he noted in his diary. "We drank of the Water & vomited a little & stay'd there some Time."

Soon after Peabody's visit to the springs but unrelated to it, he contracted "the itch," caused by the scabies mite whose saliva irritated the skin. Typical treatment involved smearing the body with a foul-smelling sulfur-based ointment that many deemed as filthy as the vermin themselves. During the course of his infestation, Peabody required the assistance of three doctors, a school friend, and the president of Harvard. On June 8 Peabody and his friend visited Doctor Kneeland and "got him to give the President a Note that he had the Itch, so it is probably when they meet Tomorrow they will give us leave to go Home." He surmised correctly and returned home, where he procured an ointment from his hometown physician, Dr. Kittridge. After they got the medicine, his chum "concluded to tarry & oint with me." They donned old clothes, Peabody reported, "ointed, look'd & felt very Bad." Ointing continued for five more nights, despite Peabody's optimistic declaration that they were done after only three. On June 17 Peabody wrote, "We ware getting ready to wosh up, I worsh'd a Pare of Breeches & Gloves & got all Things prepar'd & about three o Clock we clean'd up." The sensation of removing vermin, stinking ointment, and foul clothes made

Peabody rapturous: "I felt in another World," he gushed. He went out that evening and drank a glass of wine, noting with some satisfaction that he "lodg'd in a cleanly Manner." The next day, however, he found it necessary to visit another doctor to get "some Physick to take to cary off the Itch." After taking it, he declared that it "work'd cleverly."[1]

Only with the onset of warm weather, having finally defeated the itch, did Peabody consider immersing his own body. On July 1 he and his friends returned to the Watertown spring, where "we all Drank of the Water & some of us went in to the Bath." Reluctant to linger in the water, Peabody reported that he "only div'd in & made no stop but after I came out I felt very Worm." His brief immersion in the springs was the only time he recorded taking the plunge, whether for recreational or healing purposes. Imbibing water trumped immersion; when he left the springs that evening, he "brought a Bottle of the Water with me," presumably for future drinking and purging.

Laundry presented a more prosaic challenge, one for which Peabody felt only partially responsible. On rare occasions, he actually did the work himself. Peabody washed out his own shirt and breeches the day before traveling home to Andover to see his family and friends. On at least one occasion, he washed out his father's leather breeches as well as his own. He also took care to have new clothes made to replace worn garments. When Peabody needed a new greatcoat, for example, he was involved in every step of the process: piecing out the wool and trim, having the material soaked and brushed, being measured and having the pieces cut, and transporting the shrunken cloth to the tailor.[2]

Although he took the initiative for getting new clothes made, cleaning his room, and making emergency repairs to his wardrobe (he sewed a seam in his leather breeches to win a bet), Peabody regularly sent certain items of laundry home to his mother and sisters. On August 29, 1767, after visiting with his father, he "got all [his] dirty Linin by him." He recorded sending home "dirty Things" on February 27, 1768, and again on March 12 of that year. On March 23 his shirts and stockings came back clean. Peabody was willing to take on the less intensive work of washing out his breeches, and on rare occasions, his shirt, but he was content to let the women of his household wash woven and knitted items like shirts and stockings that endured more wear and required careful attention and possible mending. Shifts and shirts protected outerwear from picking up the body's odors and were laundered more frequently than breeches and petticoats, which might be brushed, aired, or more rarely washed when visibly soiled. Once Peabody married, he no longer bothered recording the details of how his laundry got done.[3]

Peabody's youthful record of caring for his body provides an interesting point of departure for examining changes in cleanliness practices during the eighteenth century. Peabody's priorities—his preference for drinking Watertown spring water rather than bathing in it—locate him within an older set of Anglo-American bodily habits that were just beginning to give way to new practices during the eighteenth century. His caution about immersion revealed both provincialism about body care—an attitude that prevailed throughout most of North America, England, and Europe during the early modern period—and a willingness to experiment. Educated and fashionable Britons in both England and the Caribbean had begun making their way to the healing waters of Bath, and other so-called "natural baths," for about a century before Peabody's brief plunge. Yet even these well-heeled patrons of the natural bath were generally more interested in drinking healing mineral waters and inhaling vapors than in immersing their bodies. In British North America, meanwhile, the craze for mineral baths had just begun with the discovery of the springs in Stafford, Connecticut, in 1765. Peabody may have ventured into the water at Watertown because he had heard about Stafford's healing waters. Significantly, however, proprietors of colonial mineral springs expected patrons to drink water as well as bathe in it.[4]

Another aspect of Peabody's habits of cleanliness—his dependence upon female labor for laundering his clothing—is unsurprising. But his investment in his own appearance and his interest in acquiring new garments and getting worn clothes laundered point subtly to important changes in the cultural context for body care. Provincial though he was, Peabody was a consumer of textiles who attended college in a cosmopolitan colonial city. Even the son of an Andover, Massachusetts, farmer who feared plunging into a mineral springs thought it important to have a supply of clean linens and a new winter coat.

4

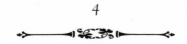

EMPIRE'S NEW CLOTHES

Linen is a thing universally worn and wanted.

—Daniel Defoe, *A Plan of English Commerce*, 1728

No perfumes, but very fine linen, plenty of it, and country washing.

—Beau Brummell, quoted in William Jesse, *Life of Brummell*, 1844

New circumstances for the production and commercial exchange of linens
at the end of the seventeenth century wrought important changes in body care,
the consumption of textiles, and the allocation of domestic labor. Exports of
linen—a crucial prop in the European performance of civility—became subject
to imperial regulation, turning the shirt into an imperial commodity. When England opened its Atlantic trade to Irish cloth, Irish linens began to circulate
around the Atlantic basin, challenging the dominance of high-end Dutch "hol-
lands." The resulting linen trade made empire wearable; belonging to the
British empire could be experienced sensually through the fabric that rubbed
against the skin. But the spread of linen shirts to North America and the Caribbean was not a simple consequence of mercantilist policy; rather, it was a form of
cultural imperialism. Europeans, Africans, and Indians in the Americas all incorporated linens into their wardrobes in increasing quantities during the eighteenth century. The shirt's penetration into new markets pointed to larger patterns of disruption and adaptation as Indians and Africans integrated and
reinterpreted it within cultural traditions that were rapidly adjusting to new
geopolitical realities.[1]

The spread of the linen shirt was the cornerstone of a new interest in gentility,
performed through material objects as well as through manners by cosmopoli-

tan people on both sides of the Atlantic during the eighteenth century. I examine gentility's spread in detail in Chapter 5. Here we will investigate a cluster of turn-of-the century developments that contributed to that shift in aesthetics, consumption, and manners, with important consequences for imperial economies and domestic labor.

An 1696 act of Parliament that gave Irish linen producers duty-free access to English markets marked the end of one imperial commercial pattern and the beginning of another. This law and the one that followed in 1704 permitted Irish linen manufacturers to ship "white or brown Linen Cloth" directly to the colonies and to avoid both transshipping and foreign export duties. Together, these two acts transformed England's textile exports, the Irish linen industry, and the consumption habits of thousands of Anglo–North Americans and Anglo-Caribbeans.[2] The resulting trade supplied textiles to Native Americans doing business with British traders, clothed enslaved laborers on plantations in the southern colonies and the Caribbean, and provided the Royal African Company with linens to trade with their West African contacts. It also represented a watershed in mercantile policy, creating a presumptive British imperial identity even before the Act of Union with Scotland in 1707 and with Northern Ireland in 1800 formally established it. This was especially striking in the Irish case: the Scottish linen industry received little or no encouragement until 1707.[3]

By the late seventeenth century, cloth had become the material lingua franca of Atlantic commerce. This role intensified as various Atlantic cultures came in contact and woolens, linens, and other fabrics crossed the Atlantic in the holds of European ships. West African traders, migrants from the British Isles to the colonies, Native Americans doing business with the Hudson's Bay Company, and enslaved Africans all needed to be supplied. But England had a peculiarly imbalanced position in this Atlantic textile trade: during the seventeenth century, it imported vast quantities of linen from the Continent and exported vast quantities of woolens. Even with supplies of linen yarn from Ireland, England produced little linen for domestic use and relied mainly on imports, especially from France, Holland, and the German states. By the beginning of the eighteenth century, however, England's position as a linen importer and woolen exporter began to change. The decade of the 1690s was pivotal for this longer-term change and its significance for empire and bodies in the century that followed.[4]

CLOTHING AN EMPIRE IN LINEN: SUPPLY-SIDE ISSUES

England's economic strength in the late-seventeenth-century Atlantic world derived in large measure from nearly two centuries of dominance in the woolens trade. England had been a major player in the sixteenth-century textile trade with the manufacture of broadcloths, heavy woolens of large dimensions. Scholars debate just how much foreign assistance the English textile industry received from refugee weavers as it responded to consumer preference for lighter, cheaper woolens. But there is no question that England successfully made the transition from broadcloths to the much-vaunted "new draperies": competitively priced, lighter-weight, woolen fabrics produced by new spinning and weaving techniques. In 1697 more that half of England's total exports of textiles other than silks and linens consisted of these lighter fabrics: baizes, rashes, says, serges, perpetuanas, flannels, and stuffs. Traditional heavy woolens made up much of the balance. The woolens industry remained oriented toward production for export, and it continued to dominate England's export trade: England exported one-third of its total textile production at the close of the seventeenth century, at a time when textiles made up four-fifths of all English exports.[5]

For Englishmen, the dominance of English woolens was a source of national pride. "We cloath half of Europe by our English cloth," a man boasted in 1657, claiming that English industry allowed the "whole man" to be made "fine and neate" in English made "cloth, stockins, and shooes." Daniel Defoe's claims seventy years later were even more extravagant and imperial in tone: "Let no man wonder, that the woollen manufacture of England is arriv'd to such a magnitude, when in a word it may be said to cloathe the world." As English textiles reached more overseas markets, the population of the kingdom directly or indirectly engaged in the textile or hosiery trades also grew—and such estimates don't include the countless farm households engaged in flax and hemp production or yarn spinning for household use.[6]

The woolens trade nourished England's budding sense of nationalism and global influence. Certainly, there were many other early manifestations of national and imperial identity, including Richard Hakluyt's collection of English travel accounts to celebrate and inspire English accomplishments overseas, and the enactment of empire through the seventeenth-century Navigation Acts. But unlike the literary proclamation of nation or the presumptive empire embodied in mercantilist policy, the production of textiles for export brought the industriousness and skill of England's manufacturers to thousands of consumers in the Baltic, Russia, the Iberian Peninsula, and eventually the Atlantic basin. Producing the fabric and garments that a growing Atlantic population would use to cover their bodies, England laid the material foundations for a form of cultural imperialism that made civilization synonymous with wearing English clothes.

For most of the seventeenth century, nearly all state efforts to protect England's domestic textile production focused on the wool trade. By the end of the century, foreign competition had begun whittling away at the English market advantage, which had been based on its ability to undersell its competitors while matching or surpassing their quality. The English Civil War (1641–1649) dealt the first blow by provoking the emigration of textile workers and weavers, but the decline continued during the Restoration (1660) and into the eighteenth century. The Woolen Act of 1699—an attempt to stanch the flow of English wool from Scotland to France, discourage colonial manufacture, and prevent the relocation of English manufacture to Ireland—failed in its first goal (Scottish exports to France ceased only with the Act of Union in 1707) but succeeded at least partially in the other two (it successfully blocked the removal of West Country serge manufacture to Ireland, and it prevented the rise of a North American woolens industry). The emergence of North American markets temporarily slowed the decline of the English woolens industry, allowing it to retain the top market position until the middle of the eighteenth century. Carded cloths, druggets, serges, and stuffs found eager consumers in the colonies.[7]

Efforts to protect domestic linen manufactures, in contrast to the woolens industry, were sporadic and mainly ineffectual. An act to restrict competition from foreign linens after 1650, for example, offered little benefit to English and Huguenot immigrant weavers. Well into the 1690s England continued to import linens in large quantities. Indeed, in 1700 linen cloth (mainly from Holland and the German principalities) was the leading import into England, accounting for 15 percent of total imports, a mark which was to fall to 5 percent by 1800.[8]

The 1696 act marked a sea change in English policy toward Ireland and its domestic linen industry. Titled "An Act for encouraging the Linen Manufacture of *Ireland,* and bringing Flax and Hemp into, and the making of Sail Cloth in this Kingdom," it aimed at reducing England's dependence on foreign linen. The act's preamble defined the problem as the "great Sums of Money and Bullion yearly exported out of this Kingdom, for the purchasing of Hemp, Flax and Linen, and the Productions thereof"; this outflow of capital, the drafters of the act reasoned, "might in great measure be prevented by being supplied from *Ireland*" if "proper Encouragement" were given to draw "foreign Protestants into the Kingdom to settle."[9] A subsequent act in 1704 expanded Ireland's privileged access to colonial markets by permitting linens to be shipped directly to colonial ports.

The act of 1696 set in motion several changes that became significant only over the course of many decades, but it also had an immediate impact. The dynamics of textile import-export and domestic production begin to shift immediately. Irish linen shipped to English ports no longer incurred the 10 percent duty on foreign textiles. The 1696 act effectively gave Irish and Scottish linens duty-free access to British and North American colonial markets at a time when shipments from continental Europe were subject to rising duties; these duties doubled between 1690 and 1704 and again between 1748 and 1779. English manufacturers of coarse linens, which competed with continental products, also gained de facto protection, an inadvertent encouragement to the domestic linen industry. During this period, English linen production increased.[10]

The initial motives for the 1696 act were fiscal, according to its main historian, and Parliament made no efforts to encourage import substitution. Duties on Dutch and Flemish linens, which had initially doubled and disadvantaged those producers, were reduced in 1707 in response to mercantile pressure from those groups. The architects of the policy only belatedly recognized and embraced its protectionist function. A 5 percent export duty on English linen, for example, was not abolished until 1717, the same year that the duty on imported linseed—the seed that produced flax—was ended. Duties on foreign (but not Irish and Scottish) raw materials—linseed and linen yarn—which rose between 1690 and 1705, only began to be reduced by 1717. A system of credits that refunded duties on linen imports reexported to the colonies also militated against protecting domestic manufactures. The mercantile policy represented by the 1696 act became truly protectionist only in 1743, with the creation of a bounty system that established monetary incentives for the production of Irish and English linens for export.[11]

Even the Crown's recruitment of Huguenot linen weavers to establish manufacturies in northern Ireland seems less important than the protection offered by the act. The French Huguenot weaver Louis Crommelin arrived in 1698 under contract from William III and Queen Anne, having spent some years in Holland, where he presumably learned the Dutch method of bleaching linen in the piece. Some five hundred Huguenot settlers subsequently came to northern Ireland. But Crommelin himself had only limited success and influence, getting credit for the industry's expansion because his arrival coincided with it. Other factors, including the large proportion of Irish farm households already involved in flax production, facilitated rapid growth. Flax processing, spinning, and weaving were by-employments of farming in many rural Irish areas. Farmers wove flax during the winter, when there was little outdoor work. None of these rural northern Irish regions was heavily invested in wool, moreover, because they lacked fallow wool and fuller's earth, a type of clay used in woolen cloth production. All of these factors enabled the industry's rapid expansion once the act of 1696 effectively opened a formerly protected market to Irish linens. By the 1750s Ireland and Scotland together were supplying England with more linen than it was receiving from the Continent. By the end of the 1760s Irish linen alone was out-stripping continental imports.[12]

The phenomenal rise of the Irish linen industry was one facet of growing English and Atlantic demand for linens and other types of textiles. During the eighteenth century, sales of Irish, Scottish, Silesian, and Saxon linens increased as part of the English colonial trade. The Caribbean was an important market for these textiles. Colonial demand for coarse-linen cloth, used to clothe slaves, stirred linen production in England, Scotland, and North America. From 1740 to 1790 the English linen industry underwent a remarkable period of growth. It doubled its output during the second quarter of the century and almost did so again in the third quarter. English demand for linen rose dramatically, too, at a rate greater than that of population growth. Demand for the fabric widened and deepened, a fact that reflected linen's status as a "decency," tied to notions of civilization. Linen was also more versatile than other textiles, finding use on beds and tables as well as on bodies. Per capita consumption of linen grew markedly throughout the Atlantic basin during the eighteenth century, a trend made possible by linen's increasing affordability.[13]

The manufacture and trade in linen products created commercial networks that would eventually support the emerging cotton trade. In southern Lancashire, a region that had produced linens for centuries, weavers combined cotton warps with linen wefts to make fabrics known as fustians. By the 1730s fustian producers were a powerful and specialized subsection of the linen trade. Some Lancashire weavers had already moved from these linen unions to pure cotton by the end of the seventeenth century. During the eighteenth century, cotton produced in these same sites superceded linen production, as calico—often printed with bold patterns and bright colors—became a popular fabric.[14]

THE STATE CREATES NEW MARKETS

Although much of the increased demand for linens can be traced to new standards for fashion and refinement, imperial ambitions also contributed to demand. Imperial expansion provided European linen producers with new markets whose defense necessitated a larger navy and army. Contracts with clothiers for shirts and drawers to outfit sailors and soldiers laid the infrastructure for the ready-made garment industry, which expanded throughout the eighteenth century. Government investment in the navy and in empire encouraged the growth of this sector of the clothing industry, transforming the clothing trade in the process. The increase in overseas trade, meanwhile, compelled the government to expand its investment in the navy. As the supplier of the Royal Navy, the government became an important consumer of textiles in its own right, thus providing yet another stimulus to the linen industry. The military needed this clothing in unprecedented quantities, and it soon overshadowed other markets. As the historian Beverly Lemire notes, "The injection of ever-larger measures of government funding compelled alterations in production; the expanding economies of scale ensured that cheap utilitarian garments were widely available to an ever-wider range of customers, both military and civilian, overseas and domestic."[15]

This transformation of the clothing trade through the impetus of military expansion occurred much earlier than many have realized. Between 1688 and 1697, eighty-two ships were built, ordered, or rebuilt, adding significantly to the existing fleet. New ships required sailcloth, mentioned specifically as a motive for the 1696 act. Although clothing represented but a small fraction of the cost of construction and maintenance, it was essential for the health of sailors, whose numbers were also growing: twelve thousand in 1688, up to forty-eight thousand by 1695. Seamen's "slops," as they were known, were defined as early as 1663 to include blue shirts, white shirts, blue neck cloths, and cotton drawers. By 1705 a full set of slop clothes included linen shirts and drawers and cost about one pound, thirteen shillings. The need for thousands of sailors to man naval ships created a demand for thousands of low-cost garments. "Shirts were replaced far more frequently than garments made of heavier materials," Lemire observes, and thus ships were stocked "with many more blue or white linen shirts, costing about 3s." As the numbers of sailors increased during the eighteenth century, the government became a market unto itself, consuming hundreds of thousands of linen garments. The size of the army, moreover, regularly surpassed that of the navy; Britain had ninety-two thousand soldiers fighting during War of Spanish Succession.[16]

The state's purchase of huge quantities of linens put those garments into circulation in the Atlantic world, where they became valued items of exchange that stimulated many other markets, including the secondhand clothing market. These recycled outfits were especially valuable to soldiers, sailors, and other itinerant men, who often could not sew their own clothes. In addition to stimulating demand for ready-made garments, the state's consumption of linens transformed the garment industry, making it ready to supply Atlantic migrants headed to the colonies. Slop seller George Risdon, for example, claimed on his trade card, "Gentlemen fitted out in the neatest Manner, for the East or West Indies."[17]

The military certainly wasn't the only institution stimulating demand for cheap linens. Beginning in the late sixteenth century, domestic institutions like

charity schools, workhouses, and foundling hospitals also needed cheap garments in large quantities. But the demand created by these institutions does not
explain the timing and the imperial dimensions of the Atlantic linen trade during the eighteenth century. For that, we need to consider not only the supply-
side issues transformed by the 1696 act but the individual consumer's interest in
fashion.[18]

NORTH AMERICAN AND CARIBBEAN CONSUMER DEMAND

If the rise of the Irish linen industry and the growing demand of the English
state for cheap garments to clothe their soldiers and sailors were two factors that
Atlanticized the linen trade, the third was the rise of American markets for linens
exported from England. This growth in American markets was dramatic, but it
did not disrupt England's continuing trade relationship with the Continent.
Continental Europe remained Britain's most important market between 1707
and the Seven Years' War, buying four-fifths of its domestic exports and reexports
and supplying most of its imports. European markets were growing slowly, however, while those across the Atlantic and in India exploded. Trade with North
America increased fourfold in the first half of the century, while total exports to
colonial markets increased just as dramatically—95 percent of the increase in
British commodity exports that occurred between 1707 and 1767 went to markets
outside Europe.[19]

Linens became increasingly important in North American markets during
the first half of the eighteenth century and thereafter, although they were gradually supplanted by calicoes. Long lists of imported specialty fabrics abounded in
colonial newspapers, testifying not simply to a growing consumer culture but to
an investment in a cosmopolitan, linen-centered standard of refinement. As
early as the 1720s merchants tried to tempt customers by listing the imported fabrics and fashion accessories available at their shops. Bostonian William Blair
took the opportunity created by a change of address to inform customers that he
was selling "all sorts of silks, Sooseys, Callicoes, Garlix, Gloves with Silver or
Gold open Lace, Velvets; and all sorts of Silver Triming." An unusual advertisement for domestic printed cloth in the *Boston Gazette* hints at one reason why
printed imports might have been preferred to domestic productions by genteelly
minded consumers even at this early date. A fabric printer boasted that he
printed "Linens, Callicoes, Silks, &c in good Figures, very lively and durable
Colours," noting that they were "without the offensive smell which commonly
attends the Linens printed here."[20]

The varieties and quality of imported cloth grew until it accounted for more than half of all imported manufactured goods in the North American colonies. The aptly named Bostonian William Merchant took out ads more than half a newspaper column long to list imported wares including "Tammies & Prunelloes, Bath & common Flannels, striped Linseys, German Serges, Fear Nothings . . . mill'd Linseys . . . black Alapenes & Bombazines . . . black Allamode . . . colour'd Chiney Taffityes, colour'd Persian Taffities, black Padusoys, India Damasks." Despite the proliferation of imports, the Scottish physician Alexander Hamilton found both imported fabrics and domestic linens, woolens, and leather to be "extravagantly dear" in Philadelphia, suggesting the limited number of consumers in that city who could afford to buy cloth.[21]

At least some of this rise in demand for textiles can be explained by examining the history of men's fashion. A new style in men's clothing began around 1700, although it took more than a century to become the standard. The gentleman's kit of a white linen shirt, breeches, stockings and shoes, a coat, waistcoat, and cravat became basic elements of male costume in the West and spread rapidly in colonized regions.[22] The major shift in patterns of the Atlantic linen trade coincided with this new fashion, which defined the upper reaches of gentility as access to the symbolic colors and fine fabrics of the aristocracy: rich-hued blues and reds, velvets, satins, and silks for breeches and waistcoat, and fine linens for shirts. Although a seventeenth-century courtier or an eighteenth-century arriviste might adopt flamboyant colors, fabrics, and jewelry to signal his passage out of society's lower order, a true gentleman didn't push the envelope of this aesthetic. Indeed, Anglo-Americans, particularly those in the Puritan tradition, also signaled gentility by wearing jackets in subdued colors, paired with white linen shirts. As this aesthetic spread through the ranks of aspiring gentlemen, influencing their consumer choices, a standard wardrobe for European men's clothing emerged. When indigenous peoples adopted shirts and coats, Euro-Americans in contested frontier zones sometimes suspected that the garments had been stolen or stripped from victims. The dominant interpretation, however, was that this change of clothes represented a step toward civilization.[23]

Traders with Indians throughout North America saw opportunity in the perceived discrepancy between their own civilized habits of body and the barbaric habits of native peoples. Hudson's Bay Company traders, for example, tried to widen demand for European goods among their Indian trade partners by weaning native people away from skins into linen or calico shirts and red kersey coats. They succeeded to a surprising degree in creating a limited market for textiles and clothing when they supplied products that appealed to indigenous consumers. In 1684 a Hudson's Bay Company list of trade goods resembled the contract for slops needed to supply a naval vessel. There was one important exception, however: traders stocked Irish stockings and linen shirts for their Indian customers, but they also supplied calico shirts. Calico was less expensive than linen and more popular with consumers because it was usually colorful. The Hudson's Bay Company relied on slops providers to supply many of these cheap garments, but problems with quality occasionally caused embarrassment and strained relationships with indigenous consumers.[24]

Another explanation lies in the household use of linen, cotton, and calico for refinement and comfort. Analyses of merchant inventories in two North American regions at two points during the long eighteenth century reveal important trends in consumption patterns among Anglo and Indian consumers. The historian Robert DuPlessis argues that after 1700 the initially distinct consumption patterns in the commercial areas centered in Philadelphia and Montreal began to break down as consumers turned toward linens, cottons, and calicoes. The export trade in linens, he argues, initially supplied North American consumers with ready-made shirts or the fabric to make them. By the 1770s, however, linen, cotton, and calico fabrics were as likely to be put to use as tablecloths, napkins, bedding, or draperies as to be worn on the body. But the climate of each commercial center continued to motivate distinct patterns of consumer preference—hot summers in Philadelphia made linen desirable, much as they shaped Caribbean consumer preferences. Frigid winters in New France helped to keep woolens popular long after the rest of the North American market had turned to linens and cottons.[25]

DuPlessis also discovered interesting differences in urban-rural and Euro-native consumption patterns. Linens found more favor among urban merchants and their customers in Montreal, but rural people, especially those involved in agriculture, favored woolens. Merchants involved in the Native American trade at the end of the seventeenth century tended to stock woolens. Linen had a different significance in the trade of each region, but in both places coarser weaves predominated. In Pennsylvania, for example, coarse ozenbriggs, dowlas, huckabucks, and garlix were plentiful in merchant stocks, with Lancashire linens the only English manufacture distinguished by a place name. Holland was the main high-end linen Philadelphia merchants supplied. Consumption patterns converged in Philadelphia and Montreal as the market share of cottons and calicoes expanded. Although the percentage of linens and woolens declined in Philadelphia merchant stocks, linens continued to dominate textile imports. Thanks to rising populations and per capita incomes, moreover, the actual amounts of all fabrics sold—linen, woolens, and cottons—increased by the 1770s.[26]

The biggest change for Philadelphia was the new appearance of Irish linens in merchant stocks, in households, and on the persons of colonists. Pennsylvania

flax producers (and flaxseed suppliers) provided raw material for local cloth production, earning cash to pay for the consumption of fine Irish linen. This fabric
for shirts appeared in the stocks for the Indian trade at Pittsburgh in 1761, a fact
that reflects both Native American consumer taste and the cheaper cost of linen.
In general, however, Pennsylvania Indian traders continued to supply three to
four times more woolens than linens to their Native American customers. In
Canada imported linen shirts and bolts of linen fabric assumed a larger share of
shipments to the frontier. Already by the 1730s linens accounted for 30 percent of
the cargoes Montreal merchants sent to Detroit. The share for linens continued
to grow until the late 1750s, while the share of woolens fell. Irish linens even
made an appearance in Montreal.[27]

This was a matter not simply of shifting consumer taste and growing population but of increased per capita ownership of linen garments and household
items that had become more affordable, a trend that spoke to the cultural meanings as well as the material role of linen. Linens could be changed and laundered more frequently than woolens, thus enabling people to meet standards for
cleanliness and comfort. By the eighteenth century, in Pennsylvania as well as in
New France, domestic manufacture competed with imports at the low end of
the market. Homespun yarn, hempen, flaxen, and linsey-woolsey also spoke to
new ways of defining the body's needs for cloth. These low-end domestic manufactures were driven less by fashion, as was the case with popular printed calicoes
and cottons, than by a growing sensibility about decency. High-end, bleached
holland linens, however, that were visible in the collars and cuffs of the well-to-
do, spoke to the desire to display bodily refinement and refined taste.[28]

Meanwhile, slaveowners throughout the Atlantic basin issued clothing of inferior appearance and quality to their slaves, thus reinforcing the notion of their
diminished refinement and cleanliness. Newly purchased slaves received a
"Coarse Shirt," according to William Hugh Grove, and afterward, "Drawers."
He described the annual allotment of cloth given to slaves as "broun Linnen,"
which carried none of white linen's associations. The servant John Harrower
recorded the first efforts at linen manufacture on the Daingerfield plantation in
Virginia in 1775 as making "coarse linnen for Shirts to the Nigers." The planter
Joseph Ball requested that his overseer issue coats of "Virginia cloth," for slave
children, summer shirts of "brown Rolls" for workers, and shirts or shifts of ozen-
brigs to the others. In South Carolina, where a black majority emerged early in
the century, the merchant Robert Pringle took pains to remind his London factors to send "white, Blue and green pla[i]ns for Negro clothing," as well as
"coarse" linens, stockings, and leather shoes.[29]

European linens not only created new standards of cleanliness and beauty but contributed to standardizing the market in goods for metropolitan residents and aspiring colonials. By the mid-eighteenth century, imported linen faced strong challenges in colonial markets from imported cottons and locally woven fabrics. Yet imported linens remained significant economically and culturally in an Atlantic defined by imperial rivalries and mercantilist policy. Shortly before the outbreak of the American Revolution, 79 percent of all linen exported from England went to British America.[30] This was the practical, day-to-day, lived experience of empire, palpable in the texture of a fine holland shirt on one's back and in the coarse weave of blue or brown linen, rough to the touch and untidy to the eye, that served as the linen allotment for the enslaved throughout the Atlantic basin.[31]

THE LAUNDRESS'S LABOR: CLEANLINESS, DECENCY, AND CIVILIZATION

The spread of the linen shirt was the cornerstone of a new interest in gentility, performed through material objects as well as through manners, by cosmopolitan people on both sides of the Atlantic. The shirt's ability to symbolize refinement made it a necessity for both English and Anglo-American consumers. As linen became more widely available during the eighteenth century — with fine linens becoming more affordable and even bound and laboring populations gaining access to coarse linens — the color and cleanliness of the shirt distinguished the wearer as much as the quality of the weave. Gentlemen and gentlewomen expected the linens that touched their skins to be "snow white" and freshly laundered. Joseph Gilman, a young New Englander, articulated this shift to his mother, explaining that his need for a clean shirt "when I want it" trumped the size and quality of his shirt wardrobe. He was willing to compromise on the fineness of the weave — even "bag Holland" was acceptable — but not on its potential to "wash white."[32]

Medical authors like Robert Wallace Johnson warned against wearing linens more than once between washings. Clean linen, Johnson instructed, was *not* "such as has once been used, of which some have a might notion, but such as is well dried." Wearing soiled linens, especially when one was ill, risked enveloping the body in humidity, which would encourage disease. Although few colonial people mentioned body odor in terms the modern reader would recognize, they were mindful that the garments worn next to the skin were also the ones most likely to pick up the body's scent.[33]

Colonial men and women appear to have taken seriously the idea of changing and washing their linens, even if they did not hew to Johnson's strict definition of *clean.* With the exception of those in dire poverty, men and women of all means owned more shirts and shifts than other items of clothing, except perhaps stockings. When Joseph Read Jr. died in 1778, for example, he left several trunks full of clothes, which included only two pair of leather drawers and one pair of linen drawers but a total of thirty-four shirts, plain and ruffled. Colonial people laundered these linens more frequently than their outerwear. Linen or calico aprons and frocks worn as an outer layer protected woolen and leather garments from dust, mud, and grease.[34]

Standards for changing linen varied, depending upon the individual's situation, circumstances, and resources. Daniel Defoe claimed that "nicer" English gentlemen changed their shirts twice a day. For men like the Virginia planter William Byrd II, living the life of a gentleman meant being able to put on a clean shirt nearly every day and owning a separate nightgown to wear to bed. Byrd's access to the labor of female slaves and a wife made this fastidious regime possible. These standards had to be relaxed out of necessity during Byrd's excursion along the dividing line between North Carolina and Virginia. Byrd noted in his tongue-in-cheek account of this expedition that he and his men "cou'd afford to drink [an excellent Cherry Brandy] no oftener than to put on a clean shirt, which was once a Week." Colonial men with meager fortunes resorted to other strategies. The fifteen-year-old Gilman cared less about the size of his wardrobe of shirts than about the availability of clean garments. One shirt per week was not sufficient, he explained to his mother, nor could he wear his stockings for more than three or four days because his sweat made them stiff and uncomfortable.[35]

As the garb of the righteous in Christian imagery and the final covering for the dead, white linen continued to connote purity and piety. Clerics thus took pains to be painted with their white collars visible. Lay people honored this religious association by making special efforts to be clean in their persons on Sunday, although they did not ordinarily labor to produce cleanliness on the Sabbath. Byrd thus noted in 1728 while on his expedition along the dividing line, "This being Sunday, I wash't off all my weeks Dirt, & refresht myself with clean Linnen." His men "thought it no Breach of the Sabbath to wash their Linnen, & put themselves in Repair, being a Matter of indispensable necessity."[36] The concern to be clean on the Sabbath transcended differences in regional cultures, appearing not only in the accounts of gentlemen surveyors like Byrd but in the diaries of aspiring ministers like New Englander Joseph Sewall, who noted the conjunction of Sabbath observance and changes of linen.[37]

Linen's capacity to be washed does not explain the dramatic expansion in demand during the eighteenth century. Rather, the growing number of shirts in wardrobes and the intensity and frequency of laundering point to a new coalescence of desire. White linen shirts had become emblems of urban sophistication, a key prop in the embodiment of civitas. White linen also symbolized the social "whiteness" of the wearer, no matter what his complexion, a sleight of hand made possible by the conflation of the shirt with the skin. So closely associated was the shirt with the skin that, for many, to be clothed only in one's shirt was to be "naked."[38] For Europeans in North America and the Caribbean, moreover, the shirt was material evidence of Atlantic cosmopolitanism, a tangible connection to European civilization worn on the back. The freshly laundered white shirt helped a European gentleman to identify his peers by revealing the wearer's good taste, refinement, and membership in a global community defined by civility. Imperial supports for Atlantic migrations, mercantilism, European contact with African and Native American cultures, and the turn to linen-centered methods of caring for the body all played a part in creating this desire for embodied gentility.

If manufacturing or purchasing fabric was one part of the equation of linen-centered cleanliness, the other most certainly was laundering soiled clothes and linens—and there was nothing genteel about this labor. Soap sellers profited from the proliferation of fabrics, the status conferred by English imports, and the desire to appear, at least from a distance, like a gentleman or woman. Their advertisements for soap and other cleaning agents confirm that consumers were more interested in laundering fabric than in washing bodies. Cosmetic benefits appeared as a secondary concern, if at all. An advertisement in 1758 for "Fine Crown Soap," for instance, boasted of its utility as a multifabric laundry soap as well as its value to barbers, presumably to prepare the face before a shave. The advertisement made no other mention of cosmetic uses. Other soap ads from the period offered lengthy descriptions of the product's usefulness in restoring softness and fullness to clothes, allowing them to "have a nearer Resemblance of the English Manufacture." As an afterthought, the advertiser mentioned that "Ladies will find great Advantage in washing their Hands with this Soap," but did not specify what that advantage might be. Presumably, the soap would do to the hands what the manufacturer promised it would do to the clothing—soften and refine their appearance.[39]

In New England and Philadelphia by the middle of the century, home producers of linen as well as those seeking to whiten or remove stains from imported cloth might seek the services of bleachers and dyers who promised to scour, dye, and whiten cloth. James Rogers, who described himself as a "Linnen bleacher," announced to *Pennsylvania Gazette* readers in 1747 that he "continues to whiten broun linnen, clean and wash white linnen, and take stains out of garments." John Brown of Boston similarly notified customers in 1763 "that the Bleaching or

Whiting of Linens is carried on as usual at the North Side of *Jamaica* Pond, in *Roxbury* . . . where any Persons may have their Cloth or Yarn whitened with the utmost Safety and Expedition." Removing or masking stains in hard-to-clean fabrics like silk, velvet, and wool was also part of refined appearance. James Vincent thus promised Boston readers in 1729 that he "Dyes and Scowers all sorts of Womens wearing Apparel," including "rich Brocades, flower'd and plain Silks . . . fine Chints and Calicoes; all sorts of Imbroidery or Needle Work," and "wet and dry Scowers Men Cloaths; Silk and worsted Stockings and Gloves."[40]

Eighteenth-century cookbooks and recipe books suggest the determination with which early American housewives did battle with stained fabrics. Elizabeth Smith's *Compleat Housewife* (1742), the first cookbook published in North America, offered detailed instructions for washing gloves with egg yolk, white lead, and a vegetable resin called gum dragant (tragacanth). She recommended soap and chalk to "take Mildew out of Linen."[41] Among the few nonmedical recipes the Quaker healer Elizabeth Coates Paschall recorded in her "receipt" book were those for removing stubborn paint and fruit stains out of linen cloth.[42]

The frequency of doing laundry seems to have varied from region to region and household to household. By the final quarter of the eighteenth century, most North American households appear to have dedicated several weeks throughout the year to doing laundry. The terrors of "washing week" inspired poets to lament the decline in domestic comforts when women were doing the wash. In 1778 a poem in the *Norwich Packet* acknowledged that "clean linen's a reviving thing" for both beggar and king but claimed that neither man suffered as much as the long-suffering husband of a wife engaged in washing week. The poet concluded,

> I hate, I must confess, all dirt,
> And truly love a well wash'd shirt;
> but once a month this reek
> Is more than flesh and blood can bear.

The poem's conclusion, "And him I hate — O make his share / A washing every week," hinted that the frequency of laundering might already have been increasing. A similarly titled poem published in the New Jersey *Sentinel of Freedom* in 1800 dramatized the hubbub with the claim,

> Sooner I a shirt would lack,
> Sooner wear one e'er to black,
> Than be doom'd with mind so meek,
> To undergo one Washing Week.[43]

When hosting guests, the mistress of the household or her daughter might also do laundry on demand, although such labor made her unavailable for other services, like cooking or conversing, that were part of her hospitality. Rachel Speight, whose indifferent cooking the traveling Byrd ate only out of fear of giving offense, instilled this sense of obligation in her guest by "offer[ing] her Service to wash my Linnen."[44]

If they were lucky, eighteenth-century women could count on male and female relatives, children, and hired girls to share the heavy physical burden of washing week. Abner Sanger's sister Rhoda called upon her unmarried and underemployed brother to borrow soap from their New Hampshire neighbors, fetch water, and assist with the wash. In 1775 Sanger recorded in his journal, "I wait on Rhoda to help wash. I back and cut wood at the door. Put brush in garden to hang clothes on and get hoop poles." But it was more common that unmarried daughters would help or that other single young women in the neighborhood would hire themselves out for pay.[45]

Access to labor enabled white slaveholders to achieve high standards for laundry. The indentured servant John Harrower, tutor to the white children of the Daingerfield plantation, noticed a difference soon after arriving in Virginia from Scotland in 1774. He marveled to his wife, "They wash here the whitest that ever I seed for they first Boyle all the Cloaths with soap, and then wash them, and I may put on clean linen every day if I please." This remarkable cleanliness may have resulted not from the technique Harrower lauded but from the ready supply of slave labor, making it typical only of a small group of elite white southerners. Harrower reported that the Daingerfield household consisted of a white housekeeper, an overseer, and himself, as well as countless slaves, including cooks, a washer and dresser, a "sewster," and a waiting girl. Every morning, a "bonny black bairn" came to Harrower's schoolhouse to "clean it out and makes my bed," a "very fine feather bed under me, and a pair of sheets, a thin fold of a Blanket and a Cotton bed spread." As for his own clothes, Harrower noted to his wife, "You wou'd scarce know me now, there being nothing either brown, blew, or black about me but the head and feet, I being Dressed in short cloath Coat, vest Coat, and britches, all made of white cotton without any lyning."[46]

The Scotswoman Janet Schaw took a dimmer view of southern laundry practices. Staying with her brother and sister-in-law in 1775, she praised North Carolina soap, made from "the finest ashes in the world" (although she observed that rather than make soap for themselves, many housewives made do with an inferior-quality Irish soap "at a monstrous price"). But laundresses were another matter entirely. "They are the worst washers of linen I ever saw," Schaw declared, attributing the mediocre results to mixing different colors and fabrics "promiscuously" into a single kettle and neglecting to "blue" white garments (a process that counteracted yellowing) or make use of the sun's rays. Unlike Harrower, she was impressed by neither the boiling technique nor the "Negro wench turn[ing] them over with a stick." Schaw's sister-in-law was affronted when Schaw's British maid Mrs. Miller offered to teach her hostess "the British method of treating linens." According to Schaw, when Mrs. Miller treated the fabrics and made use of the bleaching power of the sun, several bed and table linens were restored to their original white.[47]

The changing importance of linens for eighteenth-century households did little in and of itself to transform the stigma attached to laundresses' work. The circumstances under which an English laundress might have traveled to North America and the fate of her counterparts who remained in England did little to uplift the occupational category. Would she have been transported to the colonies as a consequence of felony conviction—stealing, or perhaps prostitution? Little about her labor would have connoted female virtue. But the context for domestic labor in many of the northern colonies reduced this stigma to some degree. Although the laundress's tainted reputation may have crossed the Atlantic nearly intact during the early years of English migration, the rural character of most North American settlements and the importance of the family as a source of household labor had, by the eighteenth century, removed much of the suspicion that surrounded her. The nature of rural communities and the youth of girls hired to do laundry limited their sexual and economic freedom, thus removing doubts about their morality.

ATLANTIC BODY CARE

What impact did new wearing habits and new demands for clean shirts have on people's perceptions of bodies? Did the white shirt symbolize civility for Native Americans and enslaved Africans as it did for Europeans? By the eighteenth century the European linen-laundry complex was beginning to transform indigenous methods of caring for the body. The overhunting of fur-bearing mammals and the introduction of English apparel changed habits of dress among those indigenous peoples in close contact with Europeans. This combination of exigency and choice eroded native traditions of skin care based on bathing, applying ointment, and wearing skins. But Indians appear to have incorporated linens into their wardrobes according to a different logic. As we have seen, linen shirts and broadcloths in bright colors had already become prestige items for powerful werowances (male leaders) and werowansquas by the 1670s. Rather than becoming staples of elite Indian wardrobes, however, as they might have been for Europeans at this time, they appear to have been treated more like accessories.

By the eighteenth century, as DuPlessis found, Indians from the mid-Atlantic to Montreal sought linens and calicoes from traders, although in Pennsylvania, the popularity of woolens persisted. Was this an indication of native resistance to high-maintenance fabrics with indisputable imperial connotations? Anecdotal evidence offers only tantalizing glimpses of how indigenous divisions of labor might have transformed in the wake of new consumption and wearing habits. The trader George Morgan, writing from the Ohio Valley in 1768, requested more soap to satisfy the demands of his Indian customers. Having invested in imported fabrics, most notably fine Irish linens, eighteenth-century Indian consumers needed greater quantities of fine, high-performance soap. Castile soap was apparently not sufficient, Morgan noted, putting in a special request for "1500 more than you have sent of the best Soap wch we sell at 6/ &," which had already sold out.[48]

Did the linen shirt signify civilization European style for Native Americans? Or did it lose some of that meaning when Indians incorporated it into their own dynamic traditions of dress and ceremony? Depending on the context, the shirt could have multiple and conflicting meanings. For an Indian bargaining with a European trader, a new linen shirt might stand for prestige among indigenous people or an improved chance of being treated respectfully by Euro-Americans. If it was fashioned from brightly colored calico, it might have represented beauty. For a Native American stripping the body of a Euro-American enemy, the repossessed shirt might signify empire thwarted. For the Indian woman who laundered it, the shirt could have represented the breakdown of culturally distinct patterns of labor, doubts about future relationships with Euro-Americans, or burdensome labor that revealed the weakness of the shirt's seams and the weave. But perhaps, too, she appreciated its beauty and comfort.

If some Indians incorporated the trappings of European civilization into their wardrobes and transformed their labor to maintain their new clothes, the situation on the West African coast is less clear. During the final quarter of the seventeenth century, the Royal African Company systematically replaced Dutch trade goods with those of English manufacture, filling outgoing ships with light woolens, fustians, silks, African-style annabasses (mantles or covers made of holland linen that wrap around the body), checked cloth, guns, knives, iron bars, pots and pans, basins, glass beads, and other trade goods. By the eighteenth century, the list of goods included a variety of linen and cotton fabrics, caps and hats, and fashionably ruffled linen shirts. West Africans incorporated these products into cultures that already placed great value on textiles, treating foreign fabrics as prestige goods. They also showed interest in substituting white, blue, and striped linens of English make for domestic textile manufactures. Did they also begin doing laundry, Western style? If so, did they use palm oil products rather than European soap?[49]

Enslaved Africans throughout the Atlantic basin revealed that, in the clothes they chose to wear for special occasions, they, too, valued finely woven white linens and bright calicos. Slaves donned special outfits for worship, community celebrations, and trips to public markets. Despite slaveowners' efforts to dress slaves in inferior-quality fabric, white observers marveled at scenes like the one Janet Schaw witnessed in Antigua, where slaves heading to market "were universally clad in white Muslin," creating one of the "most beautiful sights." Finely woven white garments not only helped enslaved people cope with the Caribbean heat but signaled a release from field labor.[50]

The proliferation of textiles around the Atlantic basin and the corresponding need for domestic labor might even have affected the trade in African slaves. A potential slave's qualifications for domestic work factored little in the slave trader's calculations between 1550, when the demand for plantation labor began to overwhelm all other uses of slave labor, and 1700, when the market for domestic laborers began to grow incrementally. This interest in domestic labor, which was never large in any plantation society, seems to have emerged sooner in the Caribbean than in the Chesapeake or the Carolinas, where few slaves were diverted to domestic work until the last quarter of the eighteenth century. However small, the new demand appears to have affected slave traders' assessments of West African ethnic differences. Traders like the Frenchman Jean Barbot, who wrote approvingly of Senegalese body care in 1732, began looking at some ethnic groups with an eye for cleanly habits. Linen consumption and the cultural significance of the shirt seems to have played some small part in creating new domestic labor needs on eighteenth-century Atlantic plantations, diverting the slave trader's attention to habits of personal and domestic cleanliness.

It is tempting to interpret the commercial boom in linens as part of what the historian Jan de Vries labels "the industrious revolution." Indeed, the consumption of linens is a good example of the expanding desire for variety and comfort achieved through the purchase of material goods. The intensification of laundry and the association of clean white shirts with cosmopolitan identity, however, suggests that the linen trade, if not the trade in other British manufactures, might have been one expression of an emerging Atlantic sensibility about refinement and civilization. Native American, West African, Anglo-Caribbean, and French colonials participated in this boom in the Atlantic linen trade, although they probably imparted different meanings to the shirt and the labor of maintaining it.

Understanding the shirt's emergence as an Atlantic commodity and an expression of empire brings us back to the shirt's peculiar, conflated relationship with the body itself and to the charged meanings connected to laundering—sexual virtue or sexual vice, depending upon whether the laborer was a wife or a wage earner. More so than other imported goods, the shirt symbolized two core assumptions upon which European empires rested: that civilized people covered their skins, and that civilized women had been rewarded with lighter domestic duties in exchange for marital chastity.[51] The shirt was the product of a particular organization of domestic life, in which civilized women produced the thread from which cloth was woven, and perpetually labored to remove traces of the body's pollution. The details of its manufacture and maintenance, its key role in European methods of body care, and the imperial context for its spread around the Atlantic—all made the shirt a proxy for the civilized body. This was an epistemology of the body informed by traditions of household labor, medicine, commerce, and empire. Unlike the consumption of other imports, the Euro-American consumption of linens appears to have strengthened a transatlantic sense of belonging to a community whose aesthetics and care of the body were captured by the laundered white shirt. Perhaps this is why homespun, a product that signified the rejection of finely textured linen imports, became such a powerful symbol of nascent American national identity on the eve of revolution.

5

GENTILITY

In 1744 the Maryland physician Alexander Hamilton left his home in Balti-more on an extended journey through the northern colonies to recover his health. When he reached the Susquehanna River, he stopped at the home of a ferry keeper, who was "att vittles" with his wife and family. The hospitable family offered to share their "homely dish of fish without any kind of sauce," but Hamil-ton refused, telling them he had "no stomach." The scene at the ferryman's table struck Hamilton as one of "primitive simplicity," reminiscent of the days "before the mechanic arts had supplied them with instruments for the luxury and ele-gance of life." A simple diet, as the English physician and popular author George Cheyne noted, was more healthful than the luxurious spreads at aristocratic ta-bles. Yet too much simplicity, absent refinement, could be disgusting. Indeed, the ferrykeeper's table took Hamilton's appetite away. "They had no cloth upon the table, and the mess was in a dirty, deep, wooden dish which they evacuated with their hands, cramming down skins, scales, and all," he reported with dis-taste. "They used neither knife, fork, spoon, plate, or napkin because, I suppose, they had none to use."[1]

Travel provided ladies and gentlemen like Dr. Hamilton with the opportunity to take the measure of their own gentility. Traveling through the British North American colonies with his black servant Dromo, the Scottish-born and -bred doctor displayed the manners and costume of a gentleman. Like many eigh-teenth-century travelers, he kept a journal in which he recorded the details of his journey. Humorous anecdotes about rustic manners, inattention to fashion, or ignorance studded these travel accounts, highlighting the author's cosmopolitan sophistication and refined sensibility. Withering judgments and disparaging wit were de rigeur. Graciousness and gratitude were appropriate only upon receipt of hospitality consonant with the traveler's sense of his own quality. Even a host's best effort might be described in condescending or patronizing terms.

Accounts like Hamilton's enable us to focus on the daily practices of caring for the body at precisely the moment in which those practices began to show significant variation by class. Scholars of manners, Enlightenment social networks, and consumption have described the eighteenth century as a watershed in the lives of Europeans on both sides of the Atlantic. Changing forms and expectations for sociability, new uses for distinction by the middling order, and the affordability of items formerly deemed luxuries by this same group all supported the pursuit of gentility, which in turn encouraged a more scrupulous attention to the body. Indeed, the effort to embody class position through grooming and the domestic environment was behind much of the commentary by genteel travelers. The emergence of a genteel aesthetic among wealthy Anglo-Americans set men like Hamilton apart from less well-to-do countrymen even as it broadcast their membership in the upper echelon of colonial society.[2]

Although slower than their English counterparts to embrace metropolitan architectural styles, fashions, and manners, wealthy colonists had begun by the middle of the eighteenth century to display cosmopolitan sensibilities about matters ranging from the proper topics of polite conversation, to bodily deportment, to care of the body. Carefully selecting imported goods for purchase, North Americans of means displayed their taste, a crucial component of gentility that resulted from unprecedented consumer choice. Demand for luxury goods like tea, china, fancy imported cloth, and fine furnishings increased dramatically during this century, setting the stage for the performance of gentility. New and freshly laundered garments, clean and comfortable bedding, wholesome food and drink, and individual table settings were all important ingredients of the genteel colonist's world.[3]

The genteel took great pains to contain their bodies through an elaborate combination of manners and refinement. Eighteenth-century conduct literature no longer aimed exclusively at providing elite readers with a distinct code of behavior or at instilling deference for superiors. Instead, it offered advice to people from the upper-middling ranks of society about controlling the body and achieving a graceful, civilized demeanor. Historians disagree about whether this represented aristocratic refinement percolating down to the middling orders, who eagerly emulated their betters, or an early bourgeois cultural formation coming from a group attempting to stake its social and political claims. But there is little disagreement that the publication of Lord Chesterfield's letters to his son Philip Stanhope in 1774 was an important articulation of the performative and instrumental nature of this genteel ideal.[4]

Cleanliness of person was a crucial part of this genteel aesthetic. Chesterfield urged his son to be "accurately clean" in his person, with "superlatively" clean teeth, hands, and nails. He issued special instructions for washing the mouth to prevent "stink" and keeping fingernails "smooth and clean." Occasionally, he thought his son's health as well as his cleanliness might benefit from a visit to the Paris bagnios.[5] Aspirants to gentility considered true embodiment of this standard and distinction from their inferiors as part of the same project. Falling between their aristocratic superiors and the lower orders created a perpetual dilemma for the middling order on both sides of the Atlantic, but in North America two unique conditions inflected their quest for distinction: the absence of a true aristocracy and the stigma of being a colonial, often depicted from a metropolitan perspective as a crude rustic. In a society in which so much important business took place face to face, people valued sweet breath and white teeth, and strove to meet this standard for their own persons. Yet clothing remained the trump card of personal cleanliness for ambitious, cosmopolitan-minded colonials. Greasy or patched clothes could undermine the appearance of civility created through rational conversation or a beautiful house.

Cleanliness, eighteenth-century style, was an emerging aesthetic of class—an expression of taste and bodily refinement—that both mobilized and strove to eliminate distinct gender practices. The pursuit of genteel standards placed new burdens upon female domestic labor, intensifying that most ungenteel of tasks, laundry, but women themselves were criticized for paying insufficient attention to their own bodies. Indeed, decrying female filth became a stock rhetorical means of articulating gentility, a reminder that a complex gender dynamic lurked beneath the surface of the aesthetic. As long as conduct literature urged women to be pleasing to men, their status as inferior persons, expected to meet a higher standard of bodily restraint in the company of superiors, determined their reputations for uncleanness. The emergence during the eighteenth century of "polite" society—manifested in forms of sociability that brought men and women together in semipublic venues—helped to foster a new expectation for women to achieve the civilized bodily comportment first articulated by and for men during the sixteenth century. The genteel style that travelers held up as the sine qua non of civility still served as the means of distinguishing the rich from the poor, the cosmopolitan sophisticate from the rude rustic. But it also enabled the genteel to identify their peers, a crucial skill in a century that placed new importance on sociability for the learned and politically ambitious. This was especially true after Chesterfield's letters linked disciplined bodily self-presentation—a performance sometimes at odds with a person's true character—with political and social success.[6]

Gentlemen and gentlewomen expressed gentility through their grooming, manners, and criticism of others—male and female—for a lack of fastidiousness. Their repeated efforts to embody these distinctions began to produce new sensibilities of disgust and attraction. At the same time, the burden of deference that had traditionally obliged servants, women, and children to make an extra effort at personal cleanliness in the presence of superiors seems to have been eroding. As cleanliness of person became a more important index of class, those excluded from membership in polite society by virtue of their race began to be defined as dirty by nature. Travelers and social commentators generalized candidly about ethnic tendencies in housekeeping and personal cleanliness, while others noted the influence of religious observance on personal appearance and conduct.

The reason for Hamilton's journey—to recover his health by visiting a more salutary climate—reminds us that the desire for gentility alone cannot account for the new interest in cleanliness. Attention to the body and upkeep of its habitations were also motivated by new patterns of epidemic disease and a new impulse to manage the environment. Following a century of unprecedented good health for English migrants and their offspring, New England began to exhibit disease patterns that resembled those in England. Medical authors on both sides of the Atlantic warned of the dangers of miasmas and urged environmental intervention, especially in cities. Belief that the environment could be made more wholesome raised the stakes of individual and collective responsibility, paving the way for judgments about those who failed to keep themselves and their habitations clean.[7]

Linen-centered cleanliness reached its heyday during the eighteenth century, but the social divisions it supported were never unmediated by other codes of civility, including politeness, and by the basic needs of travelers for food and shelter. As disgusted as Hamilton might have been by watching a rustic family eat fish with their fingers from a common bowl, his adherence to a code of polite behavior and his own need for sustenance made him mindful of his manners. Although he refused to eat, he accepted the ferryboat operator's offer of cider, the staple drink of the Anglo-American colonies, and found it to be "very good." When one was at the beginning of a long journey in which endurance as well as gentility would be put to the test, there might be virtue in primitive simplicity.

SWEET AND CLEAN

References to organic filth took on new meaning as urban dirt and epidemic disease became regular features of eighteenth-century life. Anglo-Americans still used words synonymous with corruption to refer to matters moral, sexual, and spiritual; the Virginia planter William Byrd's numerous secret diary references to autoeroticism as "uncleanness" represent one well-known example of this. But interest in the actual state of public streets, bodies, and domestic spaces became more common.[8]

The language of pollution and disease became more powerful as weapons to communicate moral corruption and to denigrate others. In 1729, just a month before Benjamin Franklin took over the newspaper, the *Pennsylvania Gazette* used references to bad smells and foul disease to offer a humorous condemnation of an unmerciful creditor named Tom Shad for his harsh treatment of an honest debtor. Hoping that Shad would repent "before his polluted Soul leaves its rotten Carcass," the editor left him this ominous poetic prediction that played on the associations between the shelf life of fish, Shad's unfortunate name, and rotten smells:

> Alas poor Shad,
> Thy Case is bad,
> Thy Soul seems all canker'd with Evil,
> Such Pranks as these
> (Like Foul Disease)
> Will make thy Name stink like the D---l.[9]

Rooted in the flesh as well as in the spirit, sexual uncleanness remained a provocative source of filth that inspired moral condemnation. But the waning of church authority, the rise of new congregations during the Great Awakening, and a century of legal reform made it less likely that the wages of sexual sin would be corporal punishment. Rather, accusations of sexual uncleanness pointed more broadly to moral corruption. An anti-Quaker pamphlet, *News of a Strumpet Co-habiting the Wilderness*, published in 1701, for example, compared Quakers to unchaste women. The author, a former Quaker turned Anglican, offered twenty examples of Quaker acts of uncleanness drawn from his "Cage of Unclean Birds."[10] An anti-Masonic poem published in a Boston newspaper in 1751 conflated the moral filth of sodomy, which the author claimed to be the predilection of the Masons, with fecal matter. Sodomitical innuendo might have besmirched Masonic reputations, but that was a far cry from public executions: only three alleged sodomites were put to death in eighteenth-century New England compared with fifteen the century before.[11] If anything, less terrifying punishments for illicit sexuality sparked greater moral vigilance, with eighteenth-century ministers leading the charge from the pulpit and press. Such vigilance seemed especially necessary in light of the proliferation of immoral reading material. Some clergy condemned books containing sexual information as filthy. In what has become known to historians as the "dirty book" incident, the Puritan divine Jonathan Edwards denounced the circulation of *Aristotle's Masterpiece*, an early modern how-to book on procreation and sexual pleasure, when a copy was found in the possession of some of the young men of his parish.[12]

With increasing frequency during the eighteenth century, people employed terms like *filth* to mean a blot on a person's reputation or to refer to a scurrilous rumor. Being "clean," in contrast, meant having an uncorrupted reputation. With the establishment of local newspapers in Boston in 1704 and in New York and Philadelphia by the 1720s, local political battles and personal rivalries could be expressed in print. Typically this involved publishing remarks damaging to a person's reputation for honesty. The target of the criticism usually felt compelled to respond publicly to avenge his reputation. One such target, Samuel Chew of Philadelphia, refrained from answering the specific points of a "scurrilous abusive Paper" in 1742, noting that he "should be very unwilling to wade thro' Dirt and Filth, as a Man must do who undertakes to answer these Remarks as they are called." Five years later, the mayor of Philadelphia, William Atwood, published a tribute in the *Pennsylvania Gazette* to the colony's departing lieutenant governor, George Thomas, noting that among his other virtues, he had "clean hands" while in office, neither skimming funds nor selling appointments as colonial administrators often did.[13]

In their most common usage, however, *clean, neat,* and *sweet* signified good order, tidiness, pleasant smells, and the wholesomeness of food, air, and water. These terms had been used for centuries to describe persons, households, and towns. During his 1704 journey to Holland and the German city of Hanover, for example, Massachusetts Governor Jonathan Belcher observed that Delft was a "very neat town, Much Sweeter and pleasanter than the City of Rotterd'm." Belcher found both the people and houses of Hanover to lack the "cleanliness of Holland," observing that "neither men nor women comb their hair among the common people but are Nasty, [and] go without shoes or Stockings." Hanoverian houses had "nothing of the neatness of Holland," he added, "by reason of the horses daily going thro' their houses" and the flies this attracted.[14] Descriptions like Belcher's often contained a moral subtext, sliding easily into judgments of character, piety, and prosperity because of a growing presumption of responsibility for environments and care of the self. Benjamin Franklin thus listed cleanliness as one of his thirteen virtues, along with chastity, justice, and temperance, to be achieved by "tolerat[ing] no Uncleanness in Body, Cloaths or Habitation."[15]

Fears of disease and the desire to improve business sparked public discussion about the healthfulness and wholesomeness of urban streets, air, and water.

Early in the eighteenth century, colonists recognized that the weather aggravated filth, making cities unpleasant as well as unhealthy. In May 1704 the *Boston Newsletter* described the weather in New York as "very rainy, dirty, and cold." Summer's heat could also turn annoying conditions into lethal ones, by generating the unwholesome stenches and mists believed to cause illness.[16] In 1739 petitioners to Philadelphia's city fathers objected to the location of tanneries, sources of "many offensive and unwholesome Smells." Tenants complained that "the Smoak arising from the burning Tan fills all the neighbouring Houses." Hatters and shoemakers, too, made it "a common practice to cast the pelts, tails and offals of the furrs, into the principle streets and alleys, and the shoemakers their ends of leather, where the same corrupt and become vermin."[17]

Manufacturing certainly contributed to urban filth, but the struggle to keep city streets clean mainly pitted residents, who disposed of garbage in nearby streets, against city councils, who reiterated versions of London's seventeenth-century street cleaning acts. In New York measures to keep the streets clean were initially crafted in 1731 and repeated verbatim for decades with little effect. The 1744 text of a law for "Cleansing the Streets, Lanes and Alleys" located on the "South side of the Fresh water" was typical of these measures. Every Friday, under penalty of fine, each citizen was to "Rake and Sweep together all the Dirt, Filth and Soil lying in the Street before their respective dwelling Houses" into "Heaps," which were to be "thrown into the River, or some other convenient Place" the next day. People caught emptying tubs, "Close Stools, or Pots of Ordure and Nastiness," into the streets rather than directly into the river were subject to stiff fines—forty shillings per offence, compared with only six shillings for failing to sweep. This resort to dumping garbage contributed to the "very bad water," which Hamilton described as "hard and brackish," and to the thriving business of bringing water in "from the best springs about the city." The council also prohibited citizens from emptying "Ordures" until after 11 P.M. between April and October, the prime season for disease. To cap its effort, the council subjected the city's cartmen to fines for failing to remove "Carrion, Guts, Garbiage, Oyster shells, Dunghills, Ashes, Dirt, Soil and Filth" gathered by inhabitants for disposal.[18]

Muck-filled streets, which obstructed foot traffic and business, were the main villains in Philadelphia. Traveling through the city in 1744, Hamilton described its streets as "unpaved, and therefor full of rubbish and mire." As Franklin recalled in his *Autobiography*, "in wet Weather the Wheels of heavy Carriages plough'd them into a Quagmire, so that it was difficult to cross them. And in dry Weather the Dust was offensive." The mayor of Philadelphia noted the "heaping great piles of filth near the gutters, so that the same is raised two and three foot above them, therby stopping the water courses" and causing "intollerable stench" and "distemper." Franklin, who resided near Jersey Market, succeeded in getting the streets near the market paved, but this measure did not solve the problem caused by filth. He subsequently called for employing scavengers or sweepers, noting among the material advantages such cleanliness might bring "the greater Ease in keeping our Houses clean, so much Dirt not being brought in by People's Feet; the Benefit to the Shops by more Custom, as Buyer's could more easily get at them, and by not having in windy Weather the Dust blown in upon their Goods." After hired sweepers cleaned the paved area around the market, "all the Inhabitants of the City were delighted with the Cleanliness of the Pavement that surrounded the Market," he exulted. The Assembly eventually agreed to pave the entire city.[19]

Despite this measure, for the next three decades, Philadelphia's city streets continued to be filthy enough to discourage foot traffic. The genteel Quaker diarist Elizabeth Sandwith Drinker decided on January 20, 1760, to skip the Sabbath meeting, "it being very dark & the Streets dirty." Darkness compounded the difficulties for a woman on foot who might not notice a mound of filth until she had already trodden upon it. Perhaps this was part of the reason why, as Hamilton observed, "the ladies, for the most part, keep att home and seldom appear in the streets, never in publick assemblies except att the churches or meetings." The *Pennsylvania Gazette*'s humorous claim in 1783 that "dead dogs, cats, fowls, and the offals of the market, are among the cleanest articles" found in the streets, reminds us that despite the continual efforts of city councils, eighteenth-century cities remained ripe with the odors of rotting carcasses, food, human excrement, and the ever-present horse manure.[20]

In the southern colonies, meanwhile, where cities were smaller and fewer in number, the climate, not dense human habitation, was the main culprit in illness. A naval officer who in 1769 recorded in rhyme his view of Charleston, South Carolina, implicitly connected the unwholesome climate to other instances of intemperate living:

> Black and white all mix'd together
> Inconstant, strange, unhealthful weather
> Burning heat and chilling cold
> Dangerous both to young and old
> Boisterous winds and heavy rains
> Fevers and rheumatic pains
> Agues plenty without doubt
> Sores, boils, the prickling heat and gout.

Topping off the list of Charleston's health hazards, the poet found the water "bad, past all drinking."[21] Travelers to the southern colonies complained about being eaten alive by mosquitoes or marveled at the sparse material lives rural people endured, often conflating these hardships with poverty and filth. None of these colonies, however, faced the same hazards of man-made filth that had threatened the Jamestown settlement upon its founding and that kept northern city councils busy.

SEEDS OF CONTAGION

Periodic smallpox epidemics reminded urban residents of the fatal consequences of filth and demonstrated the connectedness of the lives of all people in the city and, indeed, of the entire Atlantic basin. Under threat of contagion, moreover, the conceptual divide between indoor and outdoor filth broke down at least partially. City councils effected quarantines to block transatlantic pathways of disease into colonial ports and pondered the dangers of imports like cloth that were normally part of efforts to promote health and cleanliness. They also struggled to enforce strict measures for cleaning both public and domestic spaces during the crisis to stem the tide of disease.

Smallpox—categorized today as an infectious disease, spread by face-to-face contact, infected bodily fluids, and contaminated objects like bedding or clothing—epitomized eighteenth-century fears of contagious filth, literally oozing from the surface of the skin. Medical writers described the characteristic skin eruptions as the result of impurities in the blood being driven out of the body. They instructed caregivers in the importance of changing linens during this critical period, and of keeping domestic spaces clean. In July 1721, several months after the disease had began to cut a grisly swath through the population of Boston, the *Boston Newsletter* printed excerpts from the British physician and Royal Society Fellow Richard Mead's "A Short Discourse Concerning Pestilential Contagion, and the Methods to be used to prevent it." Mead, an advocate of the cool regimen who attended George II and Queen Caroline, had been solicited by the government to publish his advice in the face of an impending smallpox epidemic. Using language accessible to the lay reader, Dr. Mead explained the nature of contagion. Although much of his text echoed explanations provided by other authors, its appearance in a colonial newspaper ensured that it would reach a wide reading public.[22]

Mead identified three causes of contagion: "the Air, Diseased Persons, and Goods transported from infected Places." The constitution of the air, or the presence of miasma, was the first factor disposing a place to an outbreak of disease. "Great Heats, attended with much Rain and Southerly Winds," nearly always preceded pestilential fevers, he observed. People of all times have noted "that the stinks of stagnating Waters in hot Weather, putrid Exalations from the Earth; and above all, the Corruption of dead Carcasses lying unburied, have occasioned infectious Diseases." Once putrid, the air acted upon the human body by altering the blood in a manner favorable to pestilential disease.[23]

Diseased people could also be sources of contagion. Like a fermenting liquor, diseased blood emitted "a great Quantity of active Particles upon the several Glands of the Body, particularly upon those of the Mouth and Skin, from which the Secretions are naturally the most constant and large." Ordinarily, these particles infected mainly those in close proximity to the diseased person, but in putrid air, "they become much more active and powerful, and likewise more durable and lasting, so as to form an Infectious Matter, capable of conveying the Mischief to a great Distance from the Diseased Body, out of which it was produced." A diseased person's emissions were a necessary condition for an epidemic outbreak, entering healthy people's airways, where they subsequently invaded the blood through inspiration by the lungs, and tainted saliva.[24]

Contagion's third pathway was perhaps the most frightening and spoke to metropolitan fears provoked by the geopolitics of mercantilism. Mead identified "Goods transported from infected Places" as a source of epidemics. It happened this way: "Eastern and Southern Parts of the World, where the Heats are very great" transmitted plagues to healthier northern climates by means of commerce. "The Plague is a real Poison," he declared, "which being bred in the Eastern or Southern parts of the World, maintains it self there, by circulating from Infected Persons to Goods which is chiefly owing to the Negligence of the People of those Countries, who are stupidly careless in this affair." (He was probably referring to South Asians and Turks, although he did not mention them by name.) After generating in corrupt human bodies, contagion "lodged and preserved" itself in the "soft porous Bodies" of commodities, shipped "pressed close together." Commerce caused the contagious air to diffuse and spread over a great distance, a hazard that could be avoided if "Intercouse [sic] and Commerce with the Place infected be strictly prevented." Although substances prone to receive and communicate infection tended to be of the animal kind—fur, feathers, hair, and wool—Mead also mentioned silk, cotton, and flax. Indeed, cloth presented particular dangers because its "loose and soft Texture" readily carried the "Seeds of Contagion." The flip side of linen's role in cleanliness, then, was its suspected role in transmitting disease over great distances.[25]

Mead's pamphlet appeared in a Boston newspaper just a month before that city became embroiled in a controversy over inoculation, a preventive measure that Mead himself supported. As New England left behind its century of good health—the product of a dispersed population, a cold climate, and relative commercial isolation—and entered a new century of epidemic disease, public health became a much more pressing concern. If readers took Mead seriously, they would have had to quarantine arriving vessels and treat imported fabrics not just as sources of cleanliness but as potential repositories for the "seeds of contagion." Indeed, Mead proposed practical measures, implicitly mobilizing the labor of women, to deal with the contagion carried by ships and spread throughout the city, advising, "If there has been any Contagious Distemper in the Ship, the Sound Men should leave their Cloaths, which should be burnt; the Men Washed and Shaved; and having fresh Cloaths, should stay in the Laziretto [quarantine] Thirty or Forty Days." Sick people already within the city should be treated similarly: washed and shaved, provided with fresh cloaths, and their garments burned. Mead recommended that the houses of the healthy should be purified by freshening and cooling—washing household interiors with water and vinegar and sprinkling them with such cooling herbs as roses, violets, and water lilies—rather than by setting fires.[26]

Healthy people should avoid infected people and bury the dead far from dwellings, Mead wrote. Those tending the sick should avoid swallowing their spittle or drawing in their breath in contaminated air. Reducing the numbers of the poor, sending them to better lodgings, and encouraging them to be "more cleanly and sweet" also advanced public health. "It is of more Consequence to be observed, that as Nastiness is a great Source of Infection so Cleanliness is the greatest Preservative," Mead reasoned, "which is the true Reason, why the Poor are most obnoxious to Disasters of this Kind."[27]

Even before Mead's first essay appeared, Boston officials had taken steps to check the smallpox outbreak by assigning tasks based on commonly held assumptions about vulnerability: people of African descent were considered both less susceptible to disease and more expendable. After smallpox was reported among the passengers of the *Seahorse*, the Boston selectmen sent twenty-six "free Negroes" to clean the streets. The belief in African immunity to smallpox may have been strengthened by Cotton Mather's story of having learned of traditional West African inoculation practices from Onesimus, an enslaved Cormanti. It is doubtful that the free blacks assigned to this undesirable task had such sanguine views of their immunity, or that they undertook the labor willingly. In other contexts of illness, people of African descent sensibly tried to avoid scenes of infection.[28]

But the disease continued to spread. As the death toll rose, Boston's physicians, clergy, and press hotly debated the benefits and morality of inoculation. Meanwhile, Governor Samuel Shute proclaimed a forty-day quarantine on vessels coming from France or the Mediterranean, where populations were "Sorely visited with the Plague." None of these measures, including Mead's recommendations and the experiments with inoculation, appear to have had any affect on mortality, which reached 15 percent of all cases. Only the exodus of people from the city, along with winter weather, brought the epidemic to an end.[29]

Subsequent outbreaks of disease in other North American cities prompted similar efforts to eradicate suspected environmental sources. The Scottish-born physician Cadwallader Colden theorized that stagnant water had been behind the 1741 outbreak of malignant fever in New York City. Thoroughly engaged with environmental approaches to disease prevention, Colden had written an essay during the 1720s that analyzed the impact of sweltering summers and frigid winters on the health of New York residents. Like his Boston counterpart, the physician William Douglass, Colden opposed inoculation because it introduced gross matter into a body whose ability to throw it off would subsequently be compromised by fever. Unlike Douglass's Boston, however, New York until 1760 had no pest house to quarantine the ill. Colden thus concentrated his efforts on improving sanitary conditions in the city as a means of improving public health.[30]

When smallpox again hit the eastern seaboard in 1764–1765, Boston officials enacted a broader range of measures designed to prevent its spread. The houses of infected people were shut up, flags put out to signal illness, and barricades erected to keep passersby away from sites of infection. The selectmen called for the thorough cleaning of items in the homes of the infected that could retain contagion, such as beds, clothes, and linens. (If there had been any doubt about the potency of these contaminated items, it had been laid to rest by the deliberate communication of the disease by distributing infected blankets and handkerchiefs to enemy Native Americans near Fort Pitt in 1763.) If the smallpox patient should die, as so many did, the body was to be placed in a tarred sheet and buried in the middle of the night to avoid contaminating the air. The deceased's room was to be "washed two or three Times, and well smoked with Brimstone and Frankincense both before and after washing," a recourse to purification through heat that Mead had rejected as dangerous. Bedding and clothes were sent to a quarantine island for smoking and cleaning. The selectmen took no chances with the inoculated, insisting that they be "washed all over" and given fresh clothing in place of the "Garments worn while the Distemper was upon them."[31]

African Americans suffered disproportionately during the 1764–1765 outbreak, a fact reflected in both the numbers exposed to disease and their greater mortality once infected. Although African Americans were only a tiny percentage of Boston's population in 1764, they represented one-third of the infected. Once infected, an African American with smallpox was three times as likely to die as a white sufferer. Traveling to South Carolina while smallpox still raged in Charleston, the New Englander Pelatiah Webster was struck by the racially divided and imbalanced scenes of quarantine in that colony. On Sullivan's Island, just east of the city, he saw two to three hundred African slaves quarantined in a "pest house here with pretty good conveniences." He was more moved by the plight of "a poor white man performing quarantine alone in a boat at anchor ten rods from shore with an awning and pretty poor accomodations." Ineffective as eighteenth-century medical care might have been to stop the progress of the epidemic, it was worse in this instance to be without it.[32]

North American epidemics—in 1721–1722, 1741, and 1764–1765—provoked public discussions of the need for improving individual and collective cleanliness. The English physician George Cheyne promoted a simple diet and frequent cold-water bathing as part of a broader critique of unhealthy luxury. Robert Wallace Johnson offered advice to those attending the sick, stressing the importance of fresh air in the sick chamber. He warned against tainting it with "any smoke, dust, putrid or offensive smell," recommending instead that the floor be sprinkled with "lavendar water every now and then or vinegar, especially before it is swept." Johnson preferred supplying the sick with linen and cotton rather than silk or worsted because of the ease of cleaning these fabrics when they were soiled. Frequent changes of linens were of the ultimate importance: "It is of great moment to the sick, to have their linen shifted as often as it becomes foul or offensive; that which is used should be perfectly dry and clean, and not such as hath been used once or twice since the time it was washed, as the vulgar error is, for by this it will contract a humidity of that nature, which is to be avoided as much as possible." Other eighteenth-century authors, including Hugh Smith, shared Johnson's standards for clean linen.[33]

Johnson anticipated the shifting focus of public health, from the indulged bodies of the well-to-do who so concerned Thomas Tryon and John Floyer to the deficient lives of the poor. He speculated about the reasons for poor people's greater susceptibility to disease. "It is a misfortune to the Poor, that the Cielings of their houses are generally very low, and that they are often obliged to have several beds in the same room," Johnson observed, "but what is worse, (though usually owing to their own sloth and dirty disposition) their linen being foul, and other filth, being suffered to remain in the Room, the air becomes tainted with the putrid streams." The intensity of this filth combined with the inappropriate use of "Heartshorn-Spirits, or Venice-Treacle, &c in order to force sweats" often caused the disease to transform into "putrid or malignant and frequently infectious fever." Johnson concluded that "the sick person's room should be kept very clean, and as few sleep in it as possible. People surely may be cleanly though ever so poor."[34]

Possibly the most popular medical book read by late-eighteenth- and nineteenth-century Americans and a pioneer of the home health manual, William Buchan's *Domestic Medicine* stressed the importance of cleanliness for public as well as individual health. The nonconformist Edinburgh doctor did not mince words. "The want of cleanliness is a fault which admits of no excuse where water can be had for nothing," Buchan admonished readers; "it is surely in the power of every person to be clean." He laid a special burden upon readers with aspirations to gentility. "Whatever pretentions people may make to learning, politeness, or civilization," he declared, "we will venture to affirm, that so long as they neglect cleanliness, they are in a state of barbarity." Buchan's advice to readers picked up the long tradition of dismay at the uncleanly poor and reinforced the growing concerns of prosperous colonials to distance themselves by stressing the dangers to health. "It is not sufficient that I be clean myself, while the want of it in my neighbour affects my health as well as his own," he observed. "If dirty people cannot be removed as a common nuisance," he continued, invoking centuries of law, "they ought at least to be avoided as infections. All who regard their health should keep at a distance even from their habitations." Ships, hospitals, and military camps were as dangerous as cities, in Buchan's view. Jews became his model for cleanliness in densely populated locations because bathing and washing to produce inner purity also had the effect of preserving health. Buchan extolled cleanliness as a virtue, a way of life consonant with human nature, and a source of true gentility. Cleanliness, he claimed, "sooner attracts our regard than even finery itself, and often gains esteem where that fails. It is an ornament to the highest as well as the lowest station, and cannot be dispensed with in either." Perhaps most important, Buchan identified its practical value, noting that "few virtues are of more importance to society than real cleanliness."[35]

BODIES AND PERSONS

Surrounded by filthy city streets if they were urban dwellers, by the pungent smells and the dust of farms if they were country folk, and by potentially smelly chamber pots, diapers, and vermin no matter where they lived, eighteenth-century people engaged in an unending struggle to keep their persons and their households clean. Efforts to minimize the smells of the body and its products as well as to eliminate the sources of stench in the urban environment reveal a growing sensitivity to smell that, in turn, motivated new efforts.[36] We catch a glimpse of this struggle and of the standards of cleanliness at stake in women's cookbooks and receipt books. Elizabeth Smith's *Compleat Housewife* was the first and most popular cookbook of the day. Originally published in London in 1727, it was reprinted in two North American editions produced in Williamsburg, suggesting that her advice struck a chord with the educated white readers of that region, whose situations as managers of large households resembled those of England's rural gentry.[37]

Treating the number and purpose of Smith's entries as a rough gauge of the reader's interest in cleanliness, we gain a portrait of eighteenth-century people who cared mainly about the visible surfaces and public appearance of the body. Of the recipes targeting the body, the majority focused on the complexion, hands, teeth, and breath. There were somewhat fewer recipes for stain removers, with most of these designed to clean gloves. Even the sole recipe aimed at the household environment—a "Receipt for destroying Buggs"—had the comfort of human bodies rather than household aesthetics in view. Resorting to special washes, pastes, and powders, Smith's female readers struggled to whiten their skin and teeth, sweeten their breath, refine the appearance of their hands, remove spots from their clothing, and kill the vermin that kept them awake at night.[38]

For washing their skin, most colonial Americans resorted to a variety of home remedies and specialty washes rather than soap. Whiteners, including concoctions that purported to remove freckles, pimples, and sunburn, were among the most common skin care products. They appeared frequently in advertisements in southern newspapers and in cookbooks popular with southern readers, although they could be found in northern receipt books, too. Smith's *Compleat Housewife*, for example, contained recipes for a cleansing almond hand paste, a freckle remover, a "water to cure red or pimpled Faces," face and neck washes, a remedy for skin spots caused by morphew, ointment to efface the traces of small-pox, and a soap to "whiten and clean the hands." Numerous merchants, meanwhile, took advantage of white women's desires to look as different as possible from those who worked in the fields by marketing products like the "very good water to prevent ladies faces from tanning and to keep them smooth and white." Such products may have had special appeal for southern white women, upon whom the burden of embodying white racial characteristics increasingly fell by the middle of the eighteenth century.[39]

Even women outside southern slave societies, however, found white, smooth skin highly desirable. Most of the published cookbook recipes originated in England, where complexions were coming to distinguish white from black, the leisured from the laborer, and to symbolize British imperial ambition in South

Asia and North America. Perhaps conscious of their position at the margins of that empire or fearful themselves of "going native," mid-Atlantic and northern women also took pains to keep their skin white. The Quaker healer and receipt book author Elizabeth Coates Paschall, for example, recorded few recipes for cosmetics but included one for a freckle remover. A medical guidebook that appeared in many colonial libraries, Nicholas Culpeper's *English Physician*, offered recipes for removing freckles and sunburn from the face, neck, arms, and hands. For those concerned with the smoothness of their skin, the merchant John Julius Sorge, who boasted of having been "very much noted among the nobility in Germany," promised Philadelphia readers that he had a product that would "take the hair out of ladies foreheads and hands, without any pain."[40]

Most well-to-do, cosmopolitan colonials and many ordinary folk appear to have washed hands and face as part of a daily routine that was more scrupulous than that of their ancestors. In rural and poor urban households, washing the body consisted of immersing hands and splashing the face with water from a bucket or skillet. Eighteenth-century people would have seen the cleaning process as complete only after rubbing soil off with a towel or cloth. In the most prosperous households, especially those in the city, an imported porcelain lavabo, also known as a wall cistern, or a chamber set, consisting of a pitcher and basin arranged on a wooden stand, made it possible for household members and their guests to wash hands and face privately in their bedchambers. In Franklin's chart accounting for each hour of the day, the early morning ablutions likely took place in his chamber in this manner. At the most fashionable dinner tables, such as those frequented by Scottish traveler Janet Schaw in Antigua, dinner guests were expected to wash hands between courses and receive fresh table linens (Figure 5.1).[41]

Interest in full-body immersion, resulting in part from the chorus of medical writers after 1700 who recommended bathing, slowly rekindled throughout the century. Notable among them was Tobias Smollett, whose "Essay on the External Use of Water" in 1752 discounted mineral content and proclaimed pure water's healthfulness for bathing. Men appear to have been more willing to immerse their entire bodies in water than women, although this seems to have been motivated more by a desire for recreation, relief from the heat, and concerns for health than by the goal of cleanliness. Men of ordinary means who grew up in New England learned to swim early in life, an activity that accustomed them to the sensation of being immersed in water. "Living near the water, I was much in and about it," Franklin reported in his autobiography, and "learnt early to swim well, & to manage Boats." Stephen Peabody several times recorded walking down to the Charles River to watch others swim during the summer months.

5.1. New England wash basin, in *Instructive Hints in easy lessons for children* (Philadelphia, 1808). Courtesy American Antiquarian Society

North American women, in contrast, appear to have been reluctant to bathe, an aversion that their well-to-do British counterparts seem not to have shared. Janet Schaw bathed daily abovedeck during her Atlantic crossing in 1774 and lamented that the Anglo residents of St. Johns failed to make use of a seawater bathing facility.[42]

A few unusual men took the advice of cold bathing advocates like John Smith, whose *Curiosities of Common Water* (1723) recommended it for keeping children's lower parts clean, treating injuries, calming angry people, and curing madness, and George Cheyne, who prescribed it as a health preservative.[43] Byrd described an encounter with cold bathing at the Virginia home of Colonel Harvey Harrison: "There we took a turn to the Cold Bath, where the Colo refreshes himself every Morning. This is about 5 Feet Square, & as many deep, thro which a pure Stream continually passes, & is cover'd with a little House just big enough for the Bath & a Fireing Room. Our Landlord who us'd formerly to be troubled both with the Gripes & the Gout, fancies he receives benefit by plunging every day in cold Water."[44] As Harrison's testimonial to the curative powers of the cold bath suggests, practitioners believed that its benefits came from stimulating the circulation more than from cleaning the skin, although the two were not mutually exclusive.[45]

Cleanliness motivated some men to bathe outdoors, perhaps a reflection of the new interest in river bathing that was taking hold in Britain. Dr. James Halkerston of Boston, an immigrant from Great Britain, drowned at age thirty-six after going "to the Foot of the Common to wash himself in Swiming" in 1721. A Philadelphia attorney only recently arrived from London met a similar end in 1725. "As he was washing himself in the River," the *Boston Gazette* reported, he "went beyond his Depth and was unfortunately Drowned." It took unusual exposure to filth, as when Abner Sanger burned leaves and Byrd roughed it along the Dividing Line, for an Anglo-American man to wash more than his extremities. Sanger thus washed his "legs, hands, face and shoes," while Byrd removed a "weeks Dirt."[46]

Most eighteenth-century Anglo-Americans were more comfortable drinking water than bathing in it. Although Smith's *Curiosities* advocated bathing, most of the book was devoted to the benefits of consuming water. Franklin claimed to have learned of the benefits of drinking water while trying to cure a fever. He compared his own healthful consumption of water with the constant beer swilling of his fellow print shop workers in London, who found it hard to fathom that abstention from strong drink would not lead to physical weakness. When Elizabeth Drinker and her husband traveled to Monmouth, New Jersey, in 1776, she remained on dry land to drink seawater for its emetic effect while her husband went sea bathing, a not uncommon difference in men's and women's practices.[47]

People unused to the sensation of full-body immersion drank water and bathed cautiously, especially if the water was cold. Knowing that they were flouting popular wisdom about the hazards of submerging their bodies heightened the drama. Elizabeth Drinker's account of her family's visit to Bristol Springs, Pennsylvania, in 1771, reveals how unpleasant the first experiences of bathing could be. On Sunday, June 30, upon entering the water for the first time, she reported, "I found the shock much greater than I expected." The next day she "had no courage to go in" and the following day she drank "6 half pints of water" instead of bathing. Not until July 4, with considerable fear and trembling, did she again try bathing, but this time she "felt cleaver after it." Drinker's "3d plunge" was easier, and thereafter she simply noted that "she went in." For the rest of July and the first two weeks of August, Drinker bathed almost every day with only one mishap—she "found a difficulty of Breathing" after a morning dip on July 29.[48] During one short month, Drinker had managed to accustom her body to the sensations of full immersion, but this habit did not immediately carry over to her life in Philadelphia, where bathing the entire body would have been considerably less convenient.

Sweet breath and clean teeth were more important than bathing in a society in which so much business, socializing, and politics took place face to face. This would have been an especially difficult ideal to achieve for a population in which insufficient vitamin C left many suffering from low-level scurvy, whose symptoms included rotting gums and tooth loss. Merchants selling tooth powder, the only other cleanliness product besides laundry soap frequently featured in newspaper advertisements, promised that it "cleanses the teeth and gums from all foulness, preserves them sound and free of pain, prevents those decaying from growing worse, renders them clean and white as ivory, and the breath perfectly sweet and agreeable." Cookbook and receipt book entries for "mouth-water" or mouthwash reflected the desire to "cure the stinking breath," prevent tooth and gum decay, and whiten the teeth. One such potion in Smith's *Compleat Housewife* contained alum, cloves, sage, rosemary, and Seville oranges and allegedly would cure "scurvey in the gums" if one "wash[ed] and gargle[d] . . . with it two or three Times a Day." Smith's cookbook also listed recipes for toothpastes and powders, which she recommended rubbing on the teeth with a rag rather than with a brush. Similar recipes for tooth powder appeared in eighteenth-century receipt books, including that of Elizabeth Coultas, probably of Pennsylvania, who recommending rubbing teeth with the powder two or three times a week. The southern colonies appear to have developed a regional solution for oral hygiene. The Virginia traveler William Hugh Grove reported in 1732 that among the virtues of tobacco and its byproducts, its ashes were "Excellent to Clean teeth."[49]

Until 1800 most people who regularly cleaned their mouths would have rinsed or rubbed their teeth with a rag. Toothbrushes began to appear in merchant's advertisements only during the last quarter of the eighteenth century. One of the early mentions came in Peter Goelet's advertisement in the *New York Gazette* in 1768. Goelet's enormous list of goods recently imported from London and Bristol included exotic items like "scissars" and "twezers" for ladies' pocketbooks, tweezer cases, shaving paraphernalia, "fine dandriff combs," toothpick cases, "nail nippers," pumice stones, and flesh brushes. Toothbrushes were one of many specialized grooming aids, most of which far exceeded the ordinary person's arsenal for body care.[50]

The toothpick was another tool in the gentleman's oral hygiene kit. Indeed, its use revealed a man's genteel sensibilities. Although European and American writers had for several centuries discouraged public toothpicking as impolite, embarrassment clearly did not stop a Mr. Brooker of Boston from placing a public advertisement in the *Boston Gazette* in 1720 for his lost "Picktooth Case with a Cypher thereon."[51] Rather, the notice suggested that the case's owner viewed it as a valuable object that might even confer distinction. The Philadelphian Benjamin Chew was similarly untroubled by his toothpicking habit. His correspondent, L. Ourry, mentioned the habit with affection rather than with disgust, "I see you evry Day after Dinner, picking your Teeth in my Parlour, as if you had dined with me—I wish it was the substance instead of the Shade of."[52]

Dealing with people with bad breath was extremely unpleasant, especially if the interaction was intimate. Hamilton noted with distaste, "In the morning my barber came to shave me and almost made me sick with his Irish brogue and stinking breath." Not simply a matter of fastidiousness or ethnic prejudice, Hamilton's comment tapped into the common wisdom about barbers. The bad breath of the barber figured in Franklin's frugal suggestion that young men be taught to shave themselves, thus allowing them to escape "the frequent Vexation of waiting for Barbers, & of their sometimes, dirty Fingers, offensive Breaths and dull Razors."[53]

Hamilton conflated the barber's accent and his bad breath, treating speech as if it expanded the physical boundaries of the speaker's body, much as cartoons of the period depicted words emanating from the speaker's body in large, unwieldy bubbles.[54] To have stinking breath was not only to reveal the foulness of one's body in public but literally to poison the atmosphere in which one conducted one's business. That these smells came from the mouth, the site of speech and food consumption, and a gateway to the lower body, raised fears about bodily containment and intimate social interaction.

Early Americans may not have thought it important to bathe regularly (or at all), but most believed that dirty clothing, foul breath, and blackened teeth could give offense. The widespread self-consciousness about public appearance, especially the body's visible, clothed surfaces, is especially striking. The Atlantic traveler William Moraley, destined to become an indentured servant in the North American colonies, understood that in addition to causing discomfort, odd, shabby, or dirty clothing had a social cost. After meeting an American recruiter at the Royal Exchange, where ships bound for America placed their advertisements, he reflected on his appearance. "I was dress'd at that Time in a very odd Manner," he recalled. "I had on a Red Rug [coarse woolen] Coat, with Black Lining, Black buttons and Button Holes, and Black Lace upon the Pockets and Facing; and old worn out Tye Wig, which had not been comb'd out for above a Fortnight; an unshaven Beard; a torn Shirt, that had not been wash'd for above a Month; bad Shoes; and Stockings full of Holes." His recruiter friend took the quickest means to improving Moraley's appearance—he shaved his face—before helping to arrange for his transportation to America. When his ship was ready to sail, Moraley received new apparel, including "two coarse chequ'd Shirts, a Woollen Waistcoat . . . one Pair of Hose . . . and a pair of bad new Shoes."[55]

The failure to appear clean could have serious consequences. Concerns for appearing respectable as well as for honoring the Sabbath may have been the motives of the visiting Quaker, noted by the diarist Elizabeth Drinker in 1759, who "could not go to Meeting, for want of Clean Cloaths." The Scottish servant John Harrower, a well-educated man who eventually found work as a tutor on a Virginia plantation, set off for the colonies with a large store of clothes to avoid such an eventuality. He brought greater quantities of those items that would need more frequent washing: eleven white shirts, ruffled and plain, eleven pairs of stockings, seven muslin stocks (cloths worn below the collar), and five pocket napkins. Despite this wardrobe, he hoarded clean clothing, perhaps anticipating difficulties in getting it washed. He thus wore the same jacket, big coat, and shirt each day during his trip to London in 1774. Once in London, he reported, "I shifted my cloaths and put on a clean Ruffled Shirt, clean Britches and waistcoat & my Brown Coat." Only then did he call on Captain Peery to arrange for transportation to North America. During his Atlantic crossing, he occasionally shifted from long trousers to short to allow one pair to be washed. His employer, a Mr. Daingerfield, greeted him with orders to gather "all my dirty Cloaths of every kind" to have them "washed at his expence in Toun." With evident satisfaction, Harrower recorded that the next day he received his "Linens &ca. all clean washed."[56]

No one wished to share close quarters with people who failed to adhere to basic standards for personal cleanliness. A 1729 newspaper reported on a Court of Admiralty trial of a ship's captain for murdering a passenger, Tom Flory. The reporter described the deceased as "an odious filthy Fellow," whose distemper and laziness "rendered him extremely uncleanly." As the court subsequently discovered, Flory's death may have been at least partially a consequence of his filth, which was so intolerable that his fellow passengers locked him out of the passenger's berth, leaving him to die on deck.[57]

Vermin infestations were a special case of uncleanness and called for decisive action. "I have reason to belive that some of the Oswins Family has got the Itch," Drinker recorded in her diary for September 1763, "at which I am alarm'd [and] design for home tomorrow." Drinker's concern stemmed from knowing the ease with which the condition could spread. Lice infestations, more than the itch, connoted poverty and uncleanness, most notably the failure to change clothes or comb hair. The physician John Pechey, whose *General Treatise of the Diseases of Infants and Children* was published in London in 1697, recommended bathing and frequent linen changes for infants. He devoted an entire chapter to "the Lowsie Disease," noting that although "this nasty disease is most familiar to Children," even striking "Gentlemen's children," grown people who "live nastily and wear foul Cloaths, and do not change often their Woolen, as well as their Linnen, are subject to lice." Pechey described lice as breeding in the head and "occasioned by putrifaction." "It is a troublesome and nasty disease," he concluded, adding that infestations of lice had killed people with chilling consequences: "Lice forsake people when they are dying, and run away in Troops; they being offended with the ill vapours that arise from dying bodies." Yet remedies for lice infestations did not count on offending the lice as much as killing them. The Quaker healer Paschall recorded a recipe drawn from *Poor Richard's Almanack* of 1759 that involved rubbing powdered sassafras bark into the hair and wrapping it up in a handkerchief.[58]

Vermin plagued every region of the Atlantic basin. A recipe from Smith's cookbook for destroying bugs reinforces the impression of their omnipresence. Readers were to take a mixture of "Lamp Spirits," turpentine, and camphor and apply the fast-drying liquid to all parts of the bed linens and furniture "wherein those Vermin harbour or breed." Failure to rid the bed of vermin indicated improper use of the concoction, an admonition that gives us a sense of the ubiquity of the problem and the enormity of the task: "If any Bug or Bugs should happen to appear after once using it, it will only be for want of well wetting the Lacing, &c Of the bed, or the Foldings of the Linings or Curtains near the Rings, or the Joints of Holes in and about the Bed, Head-Board, &c wherein the Bugs and Nits nestle and breed." Smith assured her readers that though the mixture was powerful enough to kill a live bug on contact, it would not damage even the finest silk or damask bed. It also had a powerful smell, which would be gone in two or three days, although she claimed that the odor was "very wholesome, and to many People agreeable." For those who found the camphor smell and the risk of setting the bed on fire too great, there was always scalding—pouring boiling water over the entirety. After suffering for several nights with bugs in his bed at Harvard, Peabody reported, "I found so may Inhabitants in my Bed Sted, I was oblig'd to take it down & get it scalt by Mrs Pierce."[59]

Despite Pechey's warnings about the universal vulnerability to lice, many gentlemen associated vermin with poverty. The young George Washington complained about bugs when he was forced to stay in vermin-ridden beds in 1748 while traveling over the Virginia mountains. Gentleman that he was, Washington "striped myself very orderly" before crawling into bed, although he noted

that the rest of his company did not. The bed was not his usual fare: "To my Sur-
prize I found it to be nothing but a Little Straw-Matted together without Sheets
or any thing else but only one thread Bear blanket with double its Weight of Vermin such as Lice Fleas &c." Washington noted that he "was glad to get up (as
soon as th[e] Light was carried from us)" and "put on my Cloths and Lay as my
Companions." Rather than sleep in such conditions, he decided "to sleep in
th[e] Open Air before a fire." He took note when, the next night, the accommodations improved, consisting of "a good Feather bed with clean sheets."[60]

GENDER

Eighteenth-century standards for cleanliness accentuated distinctions between public and domestic life and between men and women. Although older associations of women with sexual lust continued to appear in commentaries on
promiscuous (usually poor, single, and shamefully public) women as sinks of vice
and disease, new trends—women's engagement in the market as consumers and
their participation in religious revivals—strengthened the potential for their domestic labor to refine and redeem by producing the material and moral conditions of cleanliness. As the people responsible for maintaining both the tidiness
and respectability of households, married women became closely linked with the
details of personal appearance and domestic life that signified cleanliness.

The focus of married women's labors was quite different from that of their
nineteenth- and twentieth-century counterparts, who were centrally concerned
with producing the hygienic body. Yet we might still describe the majority of
their household labors—focused on removing the polluting traces left by bodies—as "body work." Whether they delegated the work to servants or performed
it themselves, married women were the providers of clean and pressed clothing,
aired featherbeds, and clean bed linens. They were expected to maintain orderly
pantries stocked with wholesome food and drink. They were also charged with
keeping the physical space of the house and the people in it free from vermin
and disease. In their moral roles, married women were increasingly depicted as
the guardians of private virtue, the people who nurtured the spiritual lives of
adult members of the household, and, through careful scrutiny of their own
conduct, protected the house from sexual contagion and dishonor. Although responsible for the discipline necessary to maintain the cleanliness of the household in all the various meanings of the term, married women were not invested
in making men and children wash their bodies.[61]

Domestic spaces were held to a higher standard than the outdoors or public
spaces; they were not supposed to have the bugs, dung, and other organic gar-

bage of city streets and farmers' fields. Yet the household was where food was prepared, consumed, and digested, creating problems of how to dispose of waste. In
an age before refrigeration, keeping meat, vegetables, and dairy products from
spoiling was no mean feat. Cooking in and of itself was a dirty process, requiring
direct contact with uncooked (sometimes live!) substances and generating
smoke and heat. Indeed, smoke and flies were the calling cards of the colonial
domestic environment. Even in households with outdoor privies, human beings
occasionally needed to relieve themselves indoors. Chamber pots, commodes,
member mugs, and menstrual rags generated odors that lent an unwholesome
atmosphere to the household. Wet diapers were often dried before the fire rather
than washed between uses. In addition to the problems of ridding the household
of the organic filth generated within its walls, there was also the problem of keeping outdoor filth outside. Sweeping and dusting, scouring floors with sand, washing chambers, and killing vermin needed to be repeated perpetually to free a
household of unwanted matter from the outdoors.[62]

Contradictions between women's social and physical beings bedeviled the
eighteenth century's inexorable movement toward refinement and its redefini-
tions of domestic spaces. Well-bred, well-mannered ladies were crucial for the
forms of sociability that made up polite society. Hamilton's observation that,
in Philadelphia, conversation was polite despite the absence of women from
the streets and public assemblies points to contemporary expectations about
women's capacity to refine sociability. A woman's physical being, in contrast, was
often judged within the context of her household. A woman with freshly laundered clothes, combed hair, clean hands and face, sweet breath, and white teeth
might be praised along with (more nearly, conflated with) "her" snowy bed
linens, polished kitchen implements, and newly scoured floors. Likewise, a
woman with her hair about her ears and her clothes in disarray symbolized the
problems of a poorly run household and the ungenteel nature of her duties.
Only with great difficulty, some eighteenth-century people seemed to believe,
could a woman conquer the natural loathsomeness of her body. This acute sensitivity to the filth of the female body reflected centuries of wisdom about its special corrupting power, only recently overlaid with a veneer of gentility. Since so
many of her household duties centered on serving the needs of the bodies in her
household—in actually touching the food and linens that others would consume and use—the state of her own body and the condition of her household often collapsed into a single impression of tidiness or squalor. That her own body
and those of her female servants were so central to making the domestic environment comfortable only tightened the links between the female body, the
bodies under her care, and the space of the household.[63]

Intimacy with women whose bodies could never meet their standards provoked elite men to some of the harshest comments on bodily filth that one finds in the eighteenth century. Elite women, in particular, bore the pressures of supporting emerging class distinctions as well as overcoming an age-old presumption of their inherent filth. Indeed, the French use of the bidet, a habit confined mainly to a small, female elite, manifested this sensibility about women's bodies, located the problem in the genitals, and represented a reemerging faith in water's power to cleanse. Advice books to daughters, which appeared in several colonial editions during the second half of the century, emphasized cleanliness as an important although frequently overlooked female virtue. To take one example, Mathew Carey's *Lady's Pocket Library*, published in Philadelphia in 1794, included several essays on the differences between men and women by popular English moralists including Hannah More, Hester Chapone, Jonathan Swift, and Dr. John Gregory, the author of *A Father's Legacy to His Daughters* (1744). These last two, in particular, harped upon the theme of a young woman's ability to disgust men should she fail to conceal or order her physical being. Thus Gregory noted the "indelicate and disgusting" habit of women engaging in the luxury of eating, and enjoined his daughters to be neat at all times, even in their "most unguarded hours." Swift went one better by chastising young women for neglecting the "cleanliness and sweetness of their persons." One has only to think of his portrait of Gulliver in the land of the Brobdingnagian giants to recognize the popularity of the trope depicting the persons of so-called ladies of quality as disgusting.[64]

Male disgust for the female body was the hobbyhorse not only of British authors but of Anglo-Americans, too, at least two of whom helped to create the new nation. In 1761 John Adams penned a lengthy piece of advice to his "Dear Nieces," on subjects ranging from female dress to conduct in mixed company. Adams's first topic was "the Delicacy of your own Persons and Houses." British ladies, he noted, were well known for having fallen short in keeping their houses and persons clean.

> The very general Complaint of british Ladies is that their Teeth, Necks, Hair, Perspiration and Respiration, Kitchens and even Parlors are no cleaner nor sweeter than they should be. And the same ground of Complaint is in America. For my own part, tho not very attentive to my own Person, nothing is so disgustful and loathsome to me, as almost all of our sex are of my mind, as this Negligence. My own Daughters, whenever they shall grow to Years of Discretion, I am determined to throw into a great Kettle and Boil till they are clean, If I ever find them half so nasty as I have seen some.[65]

Following this outburst, which one hopes was at least partly tongue in cheek, Adams recommended Swift's works to his nieces, urging them to ignore "that open Defyance and Contempt in which he held your sex."

Writing about his impending marriage, Charles Carroll of Carrollton, Maryland, included in the list of his beloved's virtues that "her person is agreeable & cleanly," qualities he evidently believed to be lacking in most women of his class. "Cleanliness in a woman," he told his correspondent, "is a strong recommendation the more so, as it is a quality very often wanting in the fair sex at least I have found it so. . . . If women who live by a certain profession are so deficient in an essential point of their calling, what are we not to apprehend from wives, who are above those little arts of pleasing: many married men have complained, that prostitutes are neater than their wives: I presume they spoke from experience."[66]

The topic of female cleanliness also provoked a warm reaction from Thomas Jefferson. In a letter to his daughter Martha, written in 1783, Jefferson echoed Chesterfield's advice. The passage is worth quoting in full for its articulation of a rigorous standard for elite women:

Above all things and at all times let your clothes be neat, whole, and properly put on. Do not fancy you must wear them till the dirt is visible to the eye. You will be the last one who is sensible of this. Some ladies think they may, under the privileges of dishabille, be loose and negligent of their dress in the morning. But be you, from the moment you rise till you got to bed, as cleanly and properly dressed as at the hours of dinner or tea. A lady who has been seen as a sloven or a slut in the morning, will never efface the impression she has made, with all the dress and pageantry she can afterwards involve herself in. Nothing is so disgusting to our sex as a want of cleanliness and delicacy in yours.

Earlier in the century, Hamilton had found it possible to distinguish between casual "deshabille" and uncleanness, but for Jefferson, the two could not be so easily separated.[67]

Disgust for the female body transcended the sex of the beholder. Indeed, expressing such disgust appears to have been a crucial component of eighteenth-century gentility. The prosperous backgrounds of most of these writers remind us that their accounts are less useful as snapshots of the ordinary travel experience than as evidence of travel's impact on the formation of gentility. Although gentility bound them to receive hospitality politely, it also required that they make unambiguous distinctions between conditions that were disgusting, dirty, and impoverished and those that were wholesome, clean, and comfortable.

For the truly genteel, such distinctions were already becoming a matter of deeply internalized response. A good housewife put her household at the disposal of the hungry, weary traveler and shared travelers' own standards for cleanliness and wholesomeness. Journeying across New England in 1701, Sarah Kemble Knight reported from the Havens' household with obvious approval. "I was very civilly Received, and courteously entertained, in a clean comfortable House and the Good woman was very active in helping off my Riding clothes, and then ask't what I would eat." An active, welcoming hostess with a clean kitchen, Mrs. Havens subsequently fixed Knight some chocolate with the help of "a little clean brass Kettle." Byrd, traveling in Virginia, attributed the quality of the hospitality at the Widow Allen's house to the widow herself: "She entertain'd us elegantly, & seem'd to pattern Solomon's Housewife if one may Judge by the neatness of her House, & the good Order of her Family." A generous landlady presiding over a clean household made the difference between a restful night and a distressed one. The difficulty of containing the odors of cooking and chamber pots so that the air in bedchambers remained sweet was one of the greatest impediments to providing appealing accommodations. Lacking separate sleeping quarters, most eighteenth-century houses subjected guests to all the smells of the household. For the well-heeled traveler, accustomed to larger houses with well-defined rooms and distinct uses of household space, the potpourri of lye, urine, smoke, cooked fish, and body odor affronted the senses.[68]

When households failed to meet the genteel traveler's standards, out of poverty, stinginess, laziness, or ignorance, overnight guests endured discomfort silently, out of politeness, or improvised creatively to minimize their suffering. After noting that at Captain Embry's, "the House keeping [was] much better than the House . . . His Castle consisting of one Dirty Room, with a dragging Door to it that will neither Open nor Shut," Byrd found himself constrained by the need to be polite. "For this reason, we chose to drink Water, and stow thick in a dirty Room, rather than to give our black-Ey'd Landlady the Trouble of making a Feast to no purpose," he explained, underscoring that his company knew the difference between good accommodations and bad. Rather than insult her, they expressed their appreciation for the hospitable intentions of a good housewife who happened to be stuck in a bad house.[69]

Unwholesome food tested a guest's manners like nothing else, except perhaps no food at all; the modern reader may be surprised by how often travelers consumed foods that disgusted them. Byrd reported choking down "a Mess of Hominy toss't up with Rank Butter & Glyster Sugar" at one house. "This I was forc't to eat," he declared in a display of his own politeness, "to shew that nothing from so fair a hand cou'd be disagreeable." Knight seemed to have fewer scruples about rejecting unwholesome food, which she explicitly connected to the unwholesome body of her hostess: "Landlady come in, with her hair about her ears, and hand at full pay scratching. Shee told us shee had some mutton wch shee would broil, wch I was glad to hear; But I supose forgot to wash her scratchers; in a little time shee brot it in; but it being pickled, and my Guide said it smelt strong of head sause, we left it." The smell combined with the image of the woman's scratching made the meal inedible for Knight. For George Washington on the Virginia frontier, much as for Hamilton in this chapter's opening episode, presentation mattered nearly as much as the food itself. He was dismayed to discover at the table of the Frederick County justice of the peace in 1748 "neither a Cloth upon the Table nor a knife to eat with." Washington and his men fortunately were spared having to use their hands, for they had brought their own knives.[70]

Travelers seem to have been less disgusted although more discomfited by dirty or in other ways substandard bedding. Byrd recognized the importance of white linen for creating a cleanly appearance. At one place "there was no more than one bed to pig into, with one Cotten Sheet and the other of Brown Ozzenbrugs made brouner by a months Persperation." Byrd's exemplary politeness again trumped the revulsion he felt at having to lie in a crowded bed against sheets already saturated with the bodily effusions of others. He contrasted his response to the reaction of his dissatisfied company; "I think they ought all to have been perfectly satisfy'd with the mans hospitality who was content to lye out of his own Bed to make room for them," he moralized. Even when a straw bed was free of bugs, however, a genteel traveler might object to its associations with animals and its unforgiving nature. After criticizing her host's poor fare, Knight complained about bedding "wch Russelled as if shee'd bin in the Barn amongst the Husks, and supose such was the contents of the tickin . . . found my Covering as scanty as my Bed was hard."[71]

Despite travelers' preoccupations with food and the quality of bedding, housewives actually devoted most of their time to other tasks: manufacturing cloth, laundering clothes, healing sick or injured bodies, and killing vermin. This suggests a distinct domestic ethic, different from the standard that genteel writers advocated. Homespun can be found throughout the eighteenth century. Advertisers like one James Vincent, who noted in 1729 that he "full'd, dy'd and press'd" homespun, and travel accounts like Hamilton's 1744 record of his meeting with an old woman dressed in homemade cloth, testify to its presence. Colonial inventories from all regions included spinning wheels: reports of coarse linen "negro" cloth being woven on Virginia plantations point to a steady if not sizable production of homespun by the second half of the eighteenth century. Historians have more to learn about the chronological ebb and flow and regional nature of such efforts—but knowing the linen-centered nature of eighteenth-century cleanliness provides an interesting new angle from which to evaluate the significance of even small outputs of cloth, part of a larger effort to enhance comfort and decency.[72] Laundering linens once they were soiled, as we have seen, was another important way a housewife cared for the bodies in her household, and the time devoted to this task increased as wardrobes and expectations for clean linen grew.

Eighteenth-century housewives cared for the bodies of household members in many ways, but not with the focused attention to cleanliness of person that would begin to take hold in the nineteenth century. Rather, they tried to keep those bodies healthy, providing wholesome food and an environment free of disease and vermin. Healing thus rounded out the housewife's duties. At least one copy of Smith's *Compleat Housewife* was bound with John Tennant's *Every man his own Doctor* (yet another Williamsburg publication), suggesting that for white southerners and probably for housewives throughout the colonies, doctoring and basic housewifery went hand in hand. Elizabeth Paschall's receipt book, containing recipes for medicines as well as for foods, and outlining detailed cures for illnesses, testifies to the prominent role women healers continued to play at midcentury.

Although married women and female servants bore the greatest responsibility for producing the moral and material conditions of cleanliness during the colonial period, male aspirants to gentility led the way on matters of personal grooming. Eighteenth-century school boys learned from books like Eleazar Moody's oft-reprinted Erasmian text, *The School of Good Manners* (1769), that good breeding required discipline over their bodies. In particular, Moody recommended washing hands and face and combing hair before meals and refraining from spitting, coughing, nose blowing and toothpicking at the table. He also warned against allowing fingers to become greasy beyond what was necessary at the dinner table. Soiling the entire napkin or any part of the table cloth with said fingers, eating and drinking noisily, scrutinizing meat excessively, and stuffing food or drink into an already full mouth were discouraged. Away from the table, Moody enjoined children to spit outside rather than in the house, but if this was not possible, to do it in the corner of the room and rub the spit into the floor with their foot. Chewing fingernails and loud nose blowing were also to be avoided.[73]

A good husband, according to qualities listed in *Poor Richard's Almanac* for 1763, was "Always clean, but not foppish in his dress," and possessed "an easy and unaffected Politeness," a widely held ideal for gentlemen. Elite men as well as educated bachelors appear to have internalized this ideal and taken responsibility for their own persons in situations where women's labor was not available. George Washington conscientiously removed his clothing before bed and struggled futilely to bring provincial recruits up to British standards of a "neat," "clean," and "soldier-like" appearance during the Seven Years' War. Up-and-coming men with scholarly and clerical ambitions also concerned themselves with cleanliness. Young Joseph Gilman requested money from his mother for new shirts and urged her to keep the clean ones coming. The Harvard student Stephen Peabody, as we have seen, occasionally washed out his own shirt and breeches before traveling home to Andover to see his family and friends. Mainly, however, prosperous and well-educated men purchased the necessary female labor while they remained single, made use of family labor when possible, and turned over responsibility for the upkeep of their clothes and households to their wives once they married.[74]

APPEARANCES

The fluidity of class identity, especially away from stationary props like houses, libraries, and extensive wardrobes, motivated travelers to scrutinize strangers' persons carefully. Dr. Hamilton's account of an incident involving a man in a greasy jacket and breeches and a dirty worsted cap captures the close link between genteel appearance and identity. Mistaken by the landlady for a cart driver or plowman, the poorly dressed man pulled out a linen cap and commented sarcastically about needing to look more like a gentleman the closer he got to Philadelphia. Mindful that most in the company would doubt him, he took pains to inform them that he could afford better than many who went finer. He boasted of good linen, silver buckles and clasps, gold sleeve buttons, two Holland shirts, some neat night caps, and his wife's habit of drinking tea twice a day. Hamilton's punch line revealed that there was rarely such a gap between actual status, appearance and behavior. The would-be gentleman let slip that he had yet to secure the title to his land, inadvertently revealing that all his claims were spurious.[75] Judging the book by its cover, however, occasionally led to error, as it did when Hamilton encountered a wealthy old bachelor dressed in "an old plaid banyan, a pair of thick worsted stockings, ungartered, a greasy worsted nightcap, and no hat." The discrepancy between the man's appearance and his worth provoked Hamilton to observe, "Tho he makes but a pitifull appearance, yet is he proprietor of most of the houses in town."[76]

The worst breach of manners Hamilton reported during his journey was what we might interpret as a violation of mealtime etiquette. It occurred in the company of a doctor who lacked refined manners and breeding. His behavior "exceeded every thing I had seen for nastiness, impudence, and rusticity," Hamilton declared. "He told us he was troubled with the open piles [hemorrhoids] and with that, from his breeches, pulled out a linnen handkercheff all stained with blood and showed it to the company just after we had eat dinner."[77] What could be more repulsive than the sight of blood that originated in the lower body? Indeed, Hamilton's disgust at the doctor's rudeness offers us a clue about attitudes toward female bodies; menstrual blood ultimately made the female body difficult for elite men to reconcile with genteel cleanliness. Filth originating within the body was more disgusting than filth that originated outside.

But cleanliness of person was becoming less a matter of gender than of class, despite a division of labor heavily skewed toward women. In prosperous households, women distanced themselves from domestic contamination by hiring servant women to perform undesirable tasks: emptying chamber pots, plucking chickens, cooking, tending fires, and washing dirty clothes.[78] To earn the wages to purchase decent food, laboring people were often compelled to perform work that compromised their ability to remain clean in their persons. Scullery maids, domestic servants, washerwomen, street cleaners, chimney sweeps, butchers, candle makers, and most enslaved people who worked in cities came in close contact with substances that more privileged people deemed dirty or contaminating. Poor people were most likely to live near the undesirable sections of the city: docks, tanneries, slaughterhouses, and tallow factories. Their crowded dwellings were situated closer to the street, with its fetid garbage and poor drainage. Wholesome food and drink were also harder to come by if one was poor in an early American city.

Genteel people expressed the emerging gap between rich and poor through material goods in the domestic environment and in their clothes, deportment, and care of the body. As early as 1720, advertisements for fine china ware and tea tables "just arrived from London" appeared in the *Boston Gazette.* Frequent changes of linens, the quality of provisions, the manners of the company, the elegance of the setting, and the forms of sociability all signified gentility. As the century progressed, certain accoutrements, like individual place settings and commodes or night chairs rather than chamber pots distinguished the homes of the genteel from those of ordinary or poor folk.[79] Women's labor was crucial for all of these material displays.

Genteel travelers often equated rusticity with filth. Knight, for example, believed that country people were irredeemably dirty and awkward. "Being at a merchants house, in comes a tall country fellow, wth his alfogeos (cheeks) full of Tobacco," she noted with disgust,

> for they seldom Loose their Cudd, but keep Chewing and Spitting as long as they'r eyes are open,—he advanc't to the midle of the Room, makes an Awkward Nodd, and spitting a Large deal of Aromatick Tincture, he gave a scrape

with his shovel like shoo, leaving a small shovel full of dirt on the floor, made a full stop. Higging his own pretty Body with his hands under his arms, Stood staring rown'd him, like a Catt let out of a Baskett. . . . I should be glad if they would leave such follies, and am sure all that Love Clean Houses (at least) would be glad on't too.[80]

Well-heeled travelers recommended cleanliness, rather than genteel living, as an appropriate goal for the poor, claiming that it cost nothing. As we have seen, this was becoming a familiar refrain of the medical literature. Some poor people seem to have shared this view. Knight described the stark poverty of an old man in Narragansett country in 1701:

This little Hutt was one of the wretchedest I ever saw a habitation for human creatures. It was suported with shores enclosed with Clapbords, laid on Length-ways, and so much asunder, that the Light come throu' every where; the doore tyed on wth a cord in the place of hinges; The floor the bear earth; no windows but such as the thin covering afforded, nor any furniture but a Bedd with a glass Bottle hanging at the head on't; an earthan cupp, a small pewter Bason, A Board wth sticks to stand on, instead of a table, and a block or two in the corner instead of chairs . . . all and every part being the picture of poverty.

But despite her distaste for such a scene, Knight could see cleanliness in the midst of poverty: "Notwithstanding both the Hutt and its Inhabitance were very clean and tydee; to the crossing the Old Proverb, that bare walls make giddy hows-wifes."[81] Cleanliness of place and person imparted a sense of order and self-respect in the absence of material goods.

Well-to-do observers believed that keeping a tidy house was not as incongruous as the efforts of the poor to own genteel possessions: this seemed a ludicrous aspiration beyond one's station. Hamilton's friend Milne took him around the "small log cottage" of a poor man and his family: "The children seemed quite wild and rustick. . . . This cottage was very clean and neat but poorly furnished. Yet Mr. M——s observed severall superfluous things which showed an inclination to finery in these poor people, such as a looking glass with a painted frame, half a dozen pewter spoons and as many plates, old and wore out but bright and clean, a set of stone tea dishes and a tea pot. These, Mr. M——sl said, were superfluous and too splendid for such a cottage." Hamilton's friend was full of helpful ideas about how the residents of the cottage could have made wiser decisions, including selling the finery to buy wool, substituting a pail of water for the looking glass, and getting rid of the tea set. Such finery was essential for his own comfort and pleasure, but his plan for the poor residents of the cottage allowed only for functionality. Their choice of furnishings testified to a different ethos in which touches of luxury embellished cleanliness to grace their otherwise spare daily lives.[82]

REPUTATIONS

Anglo-Americans drew upon evidence of distinctive cleanliness practices to frame blunt judgments about ethnic and religious difference. Philadelphia's Quakers must have been mindful of the nexus of respectable appearance and piety in cultivating their reputation for cleanliness of person, especially visible when they walked en masse to Meeting. Drinker's diary entry about a visiting Quaker who "could not go to Meeting, for want of Clean Cloaths" suggests that these standards were part of a larger Quaker aesthetic of decent appearance. It also reflected the Quaker emphasis on plainness: warmth and cleanliness of clothes took priority over fashion.[83]

The axiom for which John Wesley is most well known, uttered in 1786, "Tell them cleanliness is next to godliness," reflected widely held views on the interconnections between piety, bodily discipline, respectability, and cleanliness of person. His popular *Primitive Physic* (1747), a collection of maxims and recipes, resonated with readers who believed that simple rules of body care, including cleanliness, were the best means of preserving health. When Wesley wished to spur his Methodists to a more respectable appearance, he recommended that they adopt the plain and modest apparel for which Quakers were known. He also offered advice about personal habits and appearance, condemning tobacco and snuff as "uncleanly and unwholesome self-indulgence," and a "silly, nasty, dirty custom." To strengthen the body and prevent disease, he advocated using the flesh brush, bathing in and drinking cold water, and gaining control over the passions. Cleanliness of body and habitation revealed and inspired moral virtue. "Be cleanly . . . avoid all nastiness, dirt, slovenliness, both in your person, clothes, house, and all about you," he wrote in 1769. He urged followers not to "stink above the ground," before death produced unavoidable decay, as such inattention to cleanliness smacked of laziness. Infestations of vermin also indicated uncleanness and laziness, he claimed, and he enjoined them to "Clean yourselves of Lice. . . . Do not cut off your hair; but clean it, and keep it clean." In like fashion, Methodists were to deal immediately with the itch, rather than cultivating "sloth and uncleanness" by letting it run on. Mindful of how appearance reflected class and respectability, Wesley recommended that his followers wear clothes that were whole, without rents, tatters, or rags. "Mend your clothes," he instructed, "or I shall never expect you to mend your lives. Let none ever see a ragged Methodist." Even the poor should try to be as clean as possible, he declared, "because cleanliness is one great branch of frugality."[84]

Baptists were known more for their rejection of gentility's props and displays than for cleanliness of person: they abjured wigs, drinking, gambling, and dancing as the profane ways of provincial gentlemen and condemned the rowdy tavern culture enjoyed by ordinary New Englanders who wore their religion lightly. Indeed, early Baptists were the antithesis of polite society. Baptismal rites based on full-body immersion rather than the sprinkling of infants revitalized the link between water and bodily purification that had weakened with the decline of bathing. Baptists turned to water not to make their bodies decent for the world, however, but to signify the consecration of the soul. Known as "dipping," baptism by immersion began in North America in 1665 among a tiny cohort of New England believers some twenty years after it appeared in England. Marking the adult convert's rebirth with an experience that mimicked both death by drowning and birth, immersion reminded provincials that water healed and purified the spirit as well as the body, making the person anew.[85]

Observations of cleanliness practices helped to classify other groups of Europeans. Most Anglo-Americans were impressed by Dutch habits. During her trip to New York City in 1701, Knight commented approvingly on Dutch-American housekeepers. Inside the houses, she observed, the "Sumers and Gist are plained, and kept very white scowr'd . . . the stair cases laid all with white tile which is ever clean, and so are the walls of the Kitchen wch had a Brick floor." Hamilton similarly found that "the Dutch here keep their houses very neat and clean, both without and within. Their chamber floors are generally laid with rough plank which, in time, by constant rubbing and scrubbing becomes as smooth as if it had been plained. . . . Their kitchens are likewise very clean." Yet even with all this evidence of domestic order, he found them to lack personal refinement: "Notwithstanding all this nicety and cleanliness in their houses," he noted with disapproval, "they are in their person slovenly and dirty . . . a civil and hospitable people in their way but, att best, rustick and unpolished."[86]

Hamilton took pleasure in comparing the Dutch with the French, whose filthy habits could not be hidden by superficial attention to their appearance: "The French are generally the reverse of the Dutch in this respect. They care not how dirty their chambers and houses are but affect neatness much in their dress when they appear abroad. I cannot say cleanliness, for they are dirty in their linnen wear." The French, in other words, did not change their shirts frequently enough, although they were fastidious in their outerwear and fashionable in their manners. Accepting an invitation to dine with a Frenchman enabled Hamilton to elaborate on filthy French domestic habits. His host's casual violation of categories of filth that genteel Englishmen were beginning to recognize caught his attention: "The same individual bason served him to eat his soup out of and to shave in, and in the water, where a little before he had washed his hands

5.2. "L'Après Dinée des Anglais" (1814). The Fitzwilliam Museum, University
of Cambridge

and face, he washed likewise his cabbages. This, too, serve him for a punch-
bowl."[87] Although he appeared to be both disturbed and amused by such uncouth ways, this did not stop Hamilton from eating the soup. Eating from the
basin in which one's host had performed his toilet might not have been appealing, but Hamilton clearly did not believe it would make him sick.

In sharp contrast to the French, who had formerly enjoyed pride of place at
the top of the personal cleanliness hierarchy, the English appear to have been exchanging a reputation for uncouth filth with one for refinement—although this
was still a matter of debate early in the nineteenth century (Figure 5.2). Improvements in English plumbing and housekeeping standards, which one historian attributes to Puritanism and economic prosperity, made them the envy of
fellow Europeans and North American colonials alike. Medical advocacy of
bathing, greater access to water, and the containment of nuisances to certain city
districts probably also contributed to their climb. Living at the epicenter of empire, genteel Londoners set the standard for polite living achieved through the
accoutrements of civility: table linens, draperies, tableware, and fashionable
clothing. Provincials could only look east and try to emulate their more refined
peers. They rivaled their metropolitan counterparts only in the matters of bathing, which became the popular standard for Anglo-Caribbean body care early in
the eighteenth century, and avoiding the foulness of city life.[88]

Recognizing cleanliness in others did not necessarily lead to a sense of affinity. The German settlers of Pennsylvania, to take one example, were reputed to be cleaner and tidier than the English. Descriptions of tidy German farms and neat German households fill travelers' accounts. Yet English observers balanced their praise of higher standards of cleanliness, which would have tended to make German assimilation in Anglo-colonial society more appealing, with complaints about German clannishness and stubborn adherence to German language and customs. Men like Benjamin Franklin viewed Germans as a menace to English culture in the colonies.[89] Perhaps the persistence of ethnic Germanness, a result of efforts to maintain a healthy cultural distance, could be traced in part to German revulsion at Anglo-American filthiness.

Anglo-American judgments about Irish filth reflected attitudes toward poverty. A *Boston Gazette* report on poverty in Ireland made its relationship to dirt explicit and portrayed victims sympathetically. The contributor recounted seeing "the Swarms of Poor which crowded along the Roads, scarce able to walk, and infinite Numbers starving in every Ditch in the midst of Rags, Dirt & Nakedness, which methought was enough to move the most obdurate Heart." Along with the Scots, who many seventeenth- and eighteenth-century English commentators described as wallowing in their own filth, the Irish appeared to endure intolerable conditions. When searching for a way to communicate the abject poverty of a rural North Carolinian whose house went unroofed for want of nails, Byrd described him as being "poorer than any Highland-Scot, or Bog-trotting Irishman."[90] Uneducated, illiterate, poor, and filthy to English eyes, the Irish could not possibly meet standards for refinement. At a distance, they might be meet objects for pity and charity, but up close their bodies disgusted. Comments about the Irish epitomized gentility's aims: to identify the unclean, the uncouth, and the unmannered, who provided potent reminders of untamed physical bodies, and to avoid intimate contact with them.

As self-styled genteel Europeans around the Atlantic pursued greater refinement in their domestic lives, European writers paid closer attention to habits that might suit particular West African ethnic groups to being household slaves. In 1732 the French traveler Jean Barbot introduced this perspective in his letters about indigenous life along the Senegal River. Barbot wrote at a time when both the French and the English were increasingly invested in the transatlantic slave trade and focused on a region that was a source of North American slaves. Unlike his English counterparts of the previous century who searched for gold, he viewed Africans through the lens of the slave trade, assessing their customs and manners according to their potential value as laborers. French cleanliness aesthetics undoubtedly sharpened his observations of indigenous care of the body, but it seems more likely that the traffic in human beings defined his sensibilities.

Barbot viewed Senegalese cleanliness as evidence of their aptitude for domestic labor. Senegal blacks "have an attractive, shiny black skin, which comes from their washing and anointing it," he observed. They are, he wrote, "the cleanliest and fittest for house-hold servants, being very handy and intelligent at any thing of that kind they are put to, and will wash themselves all over three times a day." Senegalese habits of cleanliness appear to have begun early. After giving birth, women took their newborns to the nearest river to wash them, a practice Barbot mentioned to illustrate female robustness. As for Senegalese houses, Barbot described them as being only lightly furnished with flimsy but clean mats.[91]

Barbot's most sustained commentary on cleanliness, however, came not in discussing indigenous habits but in defending the reputation of French slavers. Although he conceded that the Dutch had the best ship design for transporting slaves and the Portuguese provided mats for slaves to lie on, he boasted of the measures taken by the French:

> We are very nice in keeping the places where the slaves lie clean and neat, appointing some of the ship's crew to do that office constantly, and several of the slaves themselves to be assistant to them in that employment, and thrice a week we perfume betwixt decks with a quantity of good vinegar in pails, and red-hot iron bullets in them, to expel the bad air, after the place has been well wash'd and scrubb'ed with brooms: after which, the deck is clean'd with cold vinegar, and in the day-time, in good weather, we leave all the scuttles open, and shut them again at night.

French slavers not only issued a piece of coarse cloth to each captive, Barbot claimed, but "took care they did wash from time to time, to prevent vermin, which they are very subject to; and because it look'd sweeter and more agreeable." The humanity and civility of French slave traders appeared in the distribution of wooden spoons to make eating meals "more cleanly than with their fingers, and they were well pleased with it."[92] With little elaboration on why such cleanliness measures might be needed except to note that the "poor wretches . . . are so thick crouded together," Barbot celebrated the crowning glory of enlightened French modernity: the production of cleanliness using the most approved contemporary methods. Indeed, if it were not for the word *slave*, one could mistake his passages as descriptions of hospital or military hygiene.[93]

The importation of hundreds of thousands of Africans into North American ports during the eighteenth century meant that more Anglo-Americans made their initial contact with Africans aboard slavers than ever before. William Hugh

Grove thus reported in 1732 that when he went on board two ships from Guinea and Angola, he saw men, women, and children divided into groups, wearing little clothing except "a ragg or Peice of Leather the bigness of a figg Leafe." More shocking to Grove was the presence of an Anglo-Virginian woman on board "who Examine[d] the Limbs and soundness of some she seemed to Choose."[94] Sellers took pains to prepare the bodies of the enslaved for these inspections by washing and oiling their skins so that buyers would not be put off by signs of dirt or disease.

The turn to slavery enabled the English domestic complex of household and body care gradually to reemerge in the southern colonies in a new guise. Although only a small percentage of enslaved African women would perform domestic labor until late in the eighteenth century, the wealthy white planters who owned them self-consciously began to participate in a transatlantic standard of civilized living. But even for those households where African women and men performed only agricultural work, their labor increased the possibility that the white woman of the house could avoid the tobacco fields altogether. Hot in pursuit of the gentility they would come to claim as their own by virtue of their race, white women distanced themselves from the legacy of "nasty wenches," rife with associations of sexual contamination, smelliness, and agricultural labor. An eighteenth-century white Virginia woman thus commented with distaste about her grandson's habit of hugging and kissing his African nurse, "He kisses her and runs his head in her neck, for wich he is never the sweeter nor cleaner but you know Children thrive best in durt." Such comments reflected popular wisdom about the healthfulness of a little dirt but did little to uplift the reputations of Africans. Reflecting medical thinking as well as desires for refinement, Janet Schaw described an elaborate long-handled ladle, used in a planter's house, to protect the purity of water from the contaminating breath of the slaves who served it. Others, including Thomas Jefferson, elaborated theories about racial difference rooted in the production of sweat and offensive odors, failing to embed their observations in the context of strenuous agricultural labor.[95]

For women of African descent, however, the chances of escaping the stigma of the "wench" legacy, like the chances of escaping slavery itself, were rapidly closing. In every region except New England, where standards for proper speech were slow to loosen their grip on public discourse, the growing racial exclusivity of the term *wench* signified the ineligibility of women of color for the privileges of civilization defined by the domestic virtue of white women. By century's end, even plain-style New England newspapers had adopted this racial language. Schaw repeatedly commented on the sexual mores, reproductive capacity, and domestic labor provided by black "wenches" of Antigua and North Carolina in 1774. Curiously, she referred to enslaved women as "women" only when they were splendidly arrayed in white linen on their way to market. Even before such race-specific lingo had taken hold, travelers like Knight were disgusted by intimate contact between black and white bodies. Upon witnessing an interracial supper table at a Connecticut farmer's house, Knight commented snidely, "into the dish goes the black hoof as freely as the white hand."[96]

Anglo-Americans had more conflicted feelings about Native Americans, known since the beginning of European settlements as a clean-limbed, comely people. Early in the eighteenth century, many English chroniclers were still complimentary about Indian body care. In 1705 Virginia's first historian, Robert Beverley, claimed that the Indian practice of washing their children in water and "greasing" their skins was the equivalent of an Englishwoman's undressing a child to clean it and shift its linen. Beverley's contemporary John Lawson noted that Indian men and women in the Carolinas washed themselves in river water during the summer. Although Indians' teeth were stained brown from tobacco use, Lawson admitted, "their Breaths are as sweet as the Air they breathe in." That Indians were "troubled with a multitude of Fleas" was owing not to filthiness but to their use of deerskins. The ultimate test for Lawson was that English people could not maintain such high standards for cleanliness if they were compelled to live as Indians did. "I never felt any ill, unsavory Smell in their Cabins," he claimed, "whereas, should we live in our Houses, as they do, we should be poison'd with our own Nastiness; which confirms these *Indians* to be, as they really are, some of the sweetest People in the world." In keeping with the cleanliness of their bodies, Lawson noted, Indians had no word for sodomy, thus proving the inappropriateness of the label *savage*.[97]

By many accounts, Native Americans did indeed seem to maintain standards for cleanliness that were beyond the reach of Europeans. Traders with Indians did a brisk business in the very goods that produced cleanliness for the English: cloth and soap. Wearing European-style clothing did not necessarily mean an end to Native American style bathing, however. So-called primitive cleanliness practices, including regular bathing, remained the standard recommended by European medical writers, who depicted those practices romantically as a dip in a cold stream at sunrise. Less romantic was Thomas Gist's account of being bathed by Indian captors. When Gist, the son of the Indian agent Christopher Gist, was captured at Fort Duquesne in 1758, he found, to his surprise, that his adoptive family's first concern was to strip off his tattered, dirty clothing and wash him "from head to foot." Ostensibly this was to remove decorative paint that his previous captors had applied, although one suspects that they might also have been interested in removing dirt and odors. Gist, who probably had rarely bathed before this incident, grudgingly described his Indian landlady as "the cleanliest Indian that I ever met with."[98]

But by midcentury, the old respect had begun to wane. A chorus of Anglo-colonials complained that Indians were unclean. As wealthy European settlers made a virtue of disciplining the smells and appearances of their own persons, as relations with Native Americans deteriorated, and as indigenous cultures began to show the strain of disease and warfare, Anglo-colonials commented more insistently on the offensive smell of Indian bodies and to describe their settlements as intolerably smoky and squalid. Upon attending a chapel in Boston, the ever-sensitive Hamilton claimed that the Indian congregants "stunk so that they had almost made me turn up my dinner."[99] During his Dividing Line expedition, Byrd included a lengthy discussion of his men's efforts to extract sexual favors from native women, whom he unfailingly described as unclean. "The Ladies had put on all their Ornaments to charm us," Byrd claimed, "but the whole Winter's Dirt was so crusted on their Skins, that it requir'd a strong appetite to accost them." Telltale marks on the men's white linen told the story of the previous night: "I cou'd discern by some of our Gentlemen's Linnen, discolour'd by the Soil of the Indian Ladys, that they had been convincing themselves in the point of their having no furr," he commented slyly. Following this stay with the Indians, Byrd and his men "scrubb'd off our Indian dirt, & refresht our selves with clean Linnen."[100]

Accounts of Indian filth were consistent with fears of the indigenous capacity to turn Europeans into savages. For Knight, the savagery of poor rural folk she so often noted with relish was best expressed through comparisons to Indians, whom she likened to animals. Elizabeth Trist expressed a similar view in 1783, upon meeting the "savage" descendent of an Indian and a Frenchman and after seeing French traders whose scant clothing revealed "hides quite as dark as the Indians."[101]

The Philadelphian Elizabeth Trist's commentary on hospitality and accommodations during her journey to Louisiana in 1783 is a fitting conclusion to our excursion through the intimate lives of eighteenth-century North Americans. As travelers and writers, gentlewomen shared ideals of refinement that were increasingly part of a transcendent cosmopolitan sensibility. Trist, an intimate of Thomas Jefferson's who helped to raise his daughter, judged her rural hosts harshly at the beginning of the journey: "We were obliged to push on for want of a place to stop at that was fit for a christian. At one House we stayed to feed our horses . . . but every thing was so dirty that I would rather have slept out of doors. I dont believe any of the children had been washed since they were born; one of the Girls was allmost a woman. I had no Idea that there were such beings upon this earth." The hospitality did not improve much upon reaching the banks of Pennsylvania's Juniata River. "Our entertainment the worst we had met with, notwithstanding the Man was a Colonel in the Militia," she reported. "The whole House consisted of two rooms: the private room was occupied by the Colonel, his lady and children. The other, which serv'd as kitchen, cellar, and Hall, had two dirty beds. The one occupied by Polly and my self was up in a dark corner surrounded by pickling tubs which did not yield the most agreeable smell in the world. . . . A Hog driver, his Son and daughter, a Negro wench, and two or three children had the floor for their birth." Like Washington, Trist took extreme measures to keep herself from becoming contaminated, treating her clothes as a barrier against the filth that surrounded her: "For my part, I kept my cloaths on, to keep my self from the dirt off the bed cloaths." The "self" she protected included her undergarments as well as her body.[102]

Normally, Trist removed her clothes at night to sleep in her shift and donned them again in the morning. She took great pains to avoid being seen in a state of undress, especially by the men who shared the same room. Her scruples about keeping her body and underclothes hidden from the rest of the company set her apart from the other women:

> I made it a rule to get up before day light that I might not see anybody nor they [see] me dress. It is so customary for the Men and Women to sleep in the same room that some of the Women look upon a Woman as affected that makes any objection to it. One told me that I talk'd to upon the subject that she thought a Woman must be very insecure in her self that was afraid to sleep in the room with a strange man. For her part, she saw nothing indelicate in the matter, and no man wou'd take a liberty with a woman unless he saw a disposition in her to encourage him.[103]

Trist's scruples make it clear that, like other wealthy, urban Americans, she was already living in a different world from the vast majority of her countrymen and women. That genteel world was characterized by more privacy, greater bodily comfort, and higher standards of cleanliness. And yet, too often the histories of this new elite represent them as living in a sealed world, a class apart. The humor, contempt, and revulsion they deployed around these "rustics" betrayed that colonial gentlefolk were not as far removed as they liked to believe. Despite her shock at discovering "beings upon this earth" like the young woman who appeared never to have washed, Trist dined and slept with people whose circumstances otherwise repelled her. Indeed, although new expectations for personal cleanliness among Trist's set were helping to transform the relationship between society and the body, the travel accounts and diary entries we have examined here suggest that intimate contact across those social divides still made up the fabric of daily life in eighteenth-century North America.

6

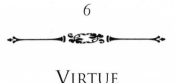

VIRTUE

In 1783 the American sailor Andrew Sherburne and his uncle took their first shaky steps as free men on the shores of Rhode Island. Weakened from months spent aboard the *Jersey*, a British prison ship that Sherburne described as "extremely filthy," "loathsome," and full of vermin, Sherburne and his uncle had finally been released with the coming of peace. Detention in British prison ships—little more than floating dungeons—was a horrible experience and became, in postwar narratives, the touchstone of British brutality and American suffering. After being ferried by hospital ship to Rhode Island, the two began their journey by land to Sherburne's home in Portsmouth, New Hampshire. Many years later, as he wrote his memoirs, Sherburne remembered that first momentous day of freedom as being marked by an incident that left "an indelible impression" on his mind.[1]

Having entered a bake house to warm themselves, the two ragged, weak men encountered the owner, a friendly man who invited them upstairs for something to eat. There they "discovered a beautiful young lady" with a baby in a well-appointed room, attended by a female servant. The baker (who had, by this point in Sherburne's narrative, turned into a gentleman) invited the men to sit down while the servant prepared them breakfast. Although he was famished, Sherburne hesitated to accept the invitation. He considered the great contrasts—between the baker's genteel home and the filth of the prison ship, between the neat apparel of his hosts and his own ragged condition—before replying, "Sir, we are not fit to be where clean people are." Unfazed by the filthy condition of the two men, the gentleman-baker repeated his invitation to sit down. But Sherburne remained uneasy about accepting his hosts' hospitality. "To tell you the truth, Sir," he admitted, "we are lousy!" Giving no indication (at least in Sherburne's account) that he wished to retract the invitation, the gentleman-baker replied philosophically, "'O well,' said he, 'if you should drop a few of them we shall not be so bad off as you are; sit down, sit down.'"

The baker's wife, whom Sherburne described several times as a "lady," behaved with similar charity and generosity toward her two vermin-ridden guests. "Instead of shewing a haughty, disdainful temper, which some would on a husband's introducing a couple of dirty, lousy fellows," Sherburne recalled, "her deportment was the most amiable." When Sherburne saw that his hostess's eyes were filled with tears, presumably at the sad condition of her two guests and not at the thought of the infestation that might follow their visit, he could not forbear crying at the kindness she had shown them.

Sherburne's account of his meeting with the baker and his wife points to the complex of eighteenth-century ideas that linked cleanliness to gentility and morality, and the way these ideas framed the meaning of citizenship, society, and nation during and after the Revolutionary War. The eighteenth-century rise of a cosmopolitan urban culture, new health concerns about densely populated armies and prisons, and genteel Americans' tendency to defer to European taste and fashion had intensified the desire for cleanliness, a shift manifested by the new emphasis on gentility. The war's mobilization of large numbers of men into military service provoked an unprecedented public discussion of the importance of cleanliness for the health and morale of the troops, and by implication, the nation. Sherburne's memoir suggests how bodily cleanliness could figure in the ways people experienced and remembered the war and, more abstractly, the way it might be used to construct national virtue.

The soldier's need for cleanliness had been articulated before, most notably in the conflicts between provincial New England soldiers and British regulars when they fought together during the Seven Years' War. It was during this war that British doctors first turned their attention to military hygiene. General James Wolfe described provincial recruits as "the dirtiest, most contemptible, cowardly dogs you can conceive." Lieutenant Colonel Ralph Burton attributed the staggering provincial mortality at Fort William Henry in 1756 to the fact that New Englanders were "extremely indolent and dirty to a degree [that] the fort stinks enough to cause an infection. . . . The camp [is] nastier than anything I could conceive. Their necessary houses, kitchens, graves, and places for slaughtering cattle, [are] all mixed through the encampment." British officers' attempts to impose order on provincial military encampments by using harsh punishments for infringements of discipline had only mixed success. They came away from the war with an impression of Yankee sloth and ineffectiveness, a distorted assessment based on the circumstances of the young men recruited to fight alongside British regulars rather than of the more prosperous and well-established members of the state militias who remained near hearth and home.[2]

Context was everything. During the Revolutionary War, elite officers had similar complaints about the cleanliness and discipline of troops, but in this war the imposition of bodily discipline came not from British officers, whom New Englanders had come to identify as cruel and profane, but from fellow North American independence seekers with whom soldiers were supposed to be making common cause. Growing personal fastidiousness heightened the importance of appearance, an indication of gentility and political virtue. Lamentations about soldiers' unclean habits were less stigmatizing judgments, as they had been during the previous conflict, than desperate efforts to sustain the military force necessary to secure political independence. In this revolutionary context, public discourse about cleanliness began an important shift that would continue for decades after the war ended. Relationships between freedom and discipline, manhood and gentility, were all realigned as a consequence of war and nation making.

Revolutionary era sources illuminate the unique ways Americans employed both the moral and hygienic meanings of cleanliness to distinguish themselves from the British enemy and to reinforce the notion that their cause was virtuous and divinely sanctioned, even in the face of evidence to the contrary. These sources also contain clues about how the link between cleanliness and morality shaped the concepts of nationhood and male citizenship that emerged during the postwar period. Political commentators and architects of the American government created a disembodied ideal for the white male citizen, whose qualifications for citizenship included his freedom from the bodily constraints that limited the intellects and public-mindedness of his white female, African-American, and Indian counterparts. But these assumptions stood in tension with the paeans to the suffering bodies of Revolutionary War soldiers. Published during the war and in subsequent decades, these memoirs focused national sentiment on the bodies of citizens who were otherwise depicted as rational and nearly disembodied. Sherburne's narrative is but one example of this genre, which reached fullest expression during the early 1830s, as Congress debated whether to give pensions to veterans. Such discussions constituted a process of Americanizing cleanliness, through which the memory of wartime suffering became part of the narrative of national virtue.[3]

MOBILIZING A CITIZEN ARMY

The outbreak of hostilities in 1775 and the resulting mobilization of a citizen army disrupted and temporarily transformed practices of cleanliness. New populations of rural dwellers experienced crowded, dirty, and disease-ridden camps that encapsulated the worst of eighteenth-century urban life. Some of these men became subject to the discipline of their social superiors for the first time in their lives. Individuals accustomed to making decisions about their own bodily needs found themselves chafing under military strictures designed for the collective good. Efforts to get soldiers to wash their shirts, change their straw bedding, and use a common latrine fell to the better-dressed and better-fed officers, who often appeared to enlisted men to be exacting punitive disciplines upon their social inferiors. The officers' attempts to instill morality and discipline in the troops — by issuing punishments for uttering oaths, for example — were in keeping with the model for order set out in military guidebooks.[4] But they also reflected the officers' own sensibilities, which differed significantly from those of both ordinary enlisted men and noncommissioned officers. In other words, there was a conflict between the standards of many ordinary soldiers, for whom rural life had never required such a degree of body discipline, and the cream of the officer corps, for whom the absence of such discipline signified sloth and incivility.

The gap between officers and enlisted men was smallest during the first year of the war, when New England's militia companies were actively engaged in combat, but became greater in later years when Continental Army troops did most of the fighting. Militia companies typically elected their officers, often choosing leading men from their communities. Although these men tended to be wealthier than the rank and file, they were not a class apart, as was the case with high-ranking Continental Army officers. Indeed, Washington indirectly diagnosed the problem with New England's fighting force as too little distinction between officers and privates; he decried New England's commanding officers as "indifferent" leaders and the troops as "an exceeding dirty and nasty people."[5]

Almost as soon as the war began, the Continental Army began to suffer from problems with supplies of tents, clothing, shoes, soap, food, and drink. Officers complained about unlicensed liquor sales and the availability of contaminated cider and unwholesome oysters that made their troops sick during the summer of 1775; the men, for their part, complained about sour bread. Cloth, normally imported from England, was also in short supply during these early months of the war, and it remained an expensive and rare commodity for the duration. Such shortages discouraged the men from washing their own shirts, since many would have been forced to don damp clothing or go shirtless while they waited for laundered garments to dry. Within weeks of his enlistment in the Continental Army, Captain Nathan Peters of Preston, Connecticut, began requesting that his wife send him shirts and stockings, a refrain he continued for the entire nineteen months of his service, while she, in turn, requested fabric and money.[6]

The Provincial Congress of Massachusetts was initially more worried about keeping order among the troops than about cleanliness, although it soon became apparent that the two were linked. Cursing and disregard for authority sparked concerns about the troops' morality and their receptiveness to discipline, reflected in *The Rules and Regulations for the Massachusetts Army*, compiled in April 1775. Officers repeatedly reminded the troops "that all Prophane Cursing & Swearing and all Ind[ecent] Language & Behaviour Will Not be tolerated in Camp." They also prohibited "Lewd Wimen" from frequenting the camps.[7]

Restrictions issued by Army Headquarters in November 1775 against certain types of enlistees reveal the Massachusetts lawmakers' vision of the ideal soldier—the kind of man most receptive to military discipline—as mature, white, and property owning. Prohibitions against enlisting vagabonds, African Americans, boys, and old men point to the commanders' conviction that these were the most unruly as well as the least able men. Dunmore's Proclamation, issued the same month and promising freedom to any enslaved person who reached British lines, deepened fears about African Americans. Indeed, Massachusetts officers not only reflected the Continental Congress's disinclination to enlist them but exhibited an outright suspicion of their presence near the camps: "Any Negro that is found stroling about the Camp — or Road — or Villages — near Roxbury or Cambridge" was to be "seazed and confined tell sun rise." Having excluded black men from service as soldiers, white officers feared their activities as spies or smugglers. In setting the criteria for the sensitive position of camp sentinel, they described a man whose nature and interest they saw as most tractable to military discipline and the patriot cause: one who was a "Native of this Country or has a Wife or family in it or is known to be ateached to it," a definition that implicitly limited the pool to white colonials of good community standing.[8]

On the ground in Massachusetts, and thereafter in most Continental Army camps, officers quickly perceived enlisted men's lack of cleanliness as a threat to the collective health of the troops and part of a more widespread discipline problem. Colonel Ephraim Doolittle, veteran of the Seven Years' War and a native of Worcester, Massachusetts, repeatedly noted the efforts of his superiors to bring the camp up to military standards in 1775. In late April headquarters ordered latrine vaults to be dug for the use of the troops. Within days, that order had become more specific: the parade and camp needed to be cleaned daily and "all the filth buried." The troops were reminded on June 1 to clean their own barracks and tents, and their officers were enjoined on July 4 to keep their men "neat and clean." In addition, the general orders specified that the men should have "straw to Lye on" if possible and that "Necessaries" be "frequently Cle'nsed to prev[en]t Being Offencive, and Unhealthy." Regimental orders called for drafting three men to dig a third latrine vault and threatened a court-martial for men "found Easing themselves" too close to the regiment. If needed, a fourth vault might be dug to receive the dirty water, pot liquor, and bones that threatened to contaminate the encampment. Company officers were further instructed to have "their Men Wash their Linnen and Keep it as Clean as possible."[9]

Smallpox was one of the threats motivating the efforts at cleanliness. As the historian Elizabeth Fenn has noted, "it was no coincidence that smallpox and independence fever erupted together or that contemporaries wrote of republicanism itself spreading 'l[i]ke Contagion, into all the other colonies.'" Incubating quietly in the towns near Boston in early 1774, smallpox erupted with the beginning of troop mobilizations and armed conflict during the summer of 1775, taking a steady toll of illness and death in the city. Officers struggled to combat it by cleaning up the camps, quarantining the infected, and limiting the possible avenues for the contagion to spread. Once the havoc wreaked by the epidemic became clear, the Continental Army took steps to prevent the deliberate transmission of smallpox by the enemy. Colonel Ebenezer Learned, a company commander during the Seven Years' War and a battalion and regimental commander during the Revolution, recorded on December 4, 1775, that all letters coming from Boston were to be dipped in vinegar. In addition, only men who had survived smallpox were to go to the lines with the flag of truce for fear that the disease might be communicated during interactions with the enemy. Meanwhile, in Boston, residents underwent a general inoculation for the disease in an effort to stem the spread of infection. But inoculation was impractical for American troops, since most had no acquired immunity; if inoculated, they would become ill with a mild form of the disease, making them temporarily unavailable for combat. After the British evacuated Boston and Bunker Hill in March 1776, only soldiers who had already had smallpox were permitted to enter the city. Despite this precaution, the disease continued to spread.[10]

On July 14, 1775, headquarters created a schedule for digging new necessaries and disposing of garbage, declaring, "The Health of an army principally Depends upon Cleanness." The order also mandated camp kitchen inspections to ensure the provision of wholesome food, which, next to cleanliness, was most "Condusive to Soldr Health."[11] Throughout the August heat, the quartermaster continued to try to procure "Shirts, Shoes & Stockings, Briches & wescots" from the Massachusetts Committee of Safety. Meanwhile, problems with discipline and provisions abounded. Residents of Watertown complained that their gardens had been plundered. An enlisted man convicted of stealing a cheese was punished with thirty-nine lashes on the bare back. In one brigade, officers furloughed large numbers of men for illness, allowing them to return "home to

Work Upon their farms for their own private" gain. Irregular pay and paltry provisions made it nearly impossible to regulate the quality of the food being given to the sick and wounded. Even worse, visitors feeding sick soldiers might contract diseases and spread them throughout the camp. Mindful of the disgraceful appearance of the troops and the genuine fears of illness their presence raised, headquarters reiterated the command to quartermasters to stop up old latrines and dig new ones, reasoning optimistically that "by perserverence in the constant and unremitted execution thereof," they might "remove that odious Reputation which with too much Reason has stigmatised the American troops." Colonels James Frye and Ebenezer Learned each copied a slightly different version of this command into his orderly book, specifically mentioning that the stigma compromised "the Character" of American troops.[12]

The term *character* hinted at the clash of values, behaviors, and habits of self-discipline that would emerge during the first year of the war. Officers struggled to get poorly paid soldiers, many of whom owned little besides the clothes on their backs, to conceive of gleaning from gardens, removing boards and bricks from houses, and stripping tree bark as destroying private property. General Washington condemned such behavior as "unmanly" and not befitting the "Dignity of the Great Cause in Which We are all Engaged." To the dismay of officers and the detriment of camp security, ordinary men unaccustomed to owning a working weapon found it hard to resist the temptation to fire their guns, especially if they saw the enemy camp in the distance.[13]

Officers viewed the recognition of authority as crucial to forging a successful fighting force, yet they despaired of achieving it. This was a particular challenge in egalitarian New England, where officers often violated Washington's orders to leave all manual labor to the enlisted men and pitched in themselves. After enduring weeks of humiliation at being stopped by sentries and after innumerable instances of soldiers confusing commissioned and noncommissioned officers, Washington established colored cockades to distinguish among ranks. As soon as it could, the army also attempted to provide uniforms for soldiers, in the hope that uniformity of dress might inspire better-regulated behavior.[14] When clothing was distributed to Massachusetts troops early in 1776, the commanding officer noted, "Nothing more adds to the appearance of a man than Dress and proper Degree of Cleanliness in his Person," adding that he hoped each regiment would contend for the most "Soldier Like appearance."[15]

Military discipline aimed at recasting the soldier's basic bodily habits and postures. Officers sought to make civilian behavior and appearance "soldier-like," a term that appears often in Washington's orders. Embedded in this term were a host of assumptions about how a man's class, race, and marital status (signifying his access to domestic services) affected his chances of achieving the soldierly ideal. Officers were ordered to inspect soldiers' quarters regularly "to impress on them the Necessity of frequently changing their Linen[,] cleaning their Rooms and when it Can be avoided not to Cook their victuals in the Rooms where they sleep." The concerns with the cleanliness of quarters, garments, and air reflect the effort to improve the health of the troops. Yet all these injunctions imposed alien habits of dress, housekeeping, and food preparation upon young soldiers from rural communities, where low population density made such health precautions seem unnecessary, and where mothers and sisters took responsibility for producing basic comforts. The bodily postures required for marching in formation and ceremonial parades were similarly unfamiliar impositions. Colonel Learned tackled the challenge of teaching novice civilian soldiers to march properly to the music that accompanied them. He ordered regimental drummers and fifers to practice for two hours every day "so that they may attain the knowledge of some of the best Musick in Voge now in Camp—that by their good Musick the Regt may March with greater Ease and more Correct."[16]

The Continental Army's attention to the men's appearance and demeanor also reflected beliefs that in addition to improving health and discipline, maintaining well-regulated, neatly dressed troops would have a positive impact on morale and win divine support for the American cause. New bylaws in 1776 challenged American soldiers to look the part of men fighting for a worthy cause. "If a soldier cannot be indused to take Pride in his Person he soon becomes a sloven and Inconsiderate to Every thing Else," one of the articles reasoned, "whilst we have men thereof in every respect superior to Mersinary troops that are fiteing for 2d or 3d a Day only why cannot we in appearance be Equal to them when we Fight for our life—Liberty—Property and our Country." Noting that heavenly blessings were especially necessary during times of "Publick Danger and Distress," Brigade orders for New York troops on July 12, 1776, urged the "officers and Soldiers [to] Pay a Steady Reverent & Devout attention on Publick worship and that they be Perticulary Carefull to keep their Cloaths Clean and Neat that Every one may appear With a becoming Decency on Such occasions." A week and half later, Washington communicated to the same Brigade his "Pleasure" at seeing "the Soldiers appearing in the house of God on Sundays with Clean linnen as it is not only Decent but will Greatly contribute to their helth."[17] Bodies dressed in clean linen that maintained erect postures and marched in time to the music not only served the purposes of the military, but might ensure the divine favor needed to triumph over the better-equipped and -trained British.

During 1776 and 1777 shortages of clothing and food became acute. In a variant on Washington's usage, correspondents pejoratively described their sparse existence to their families as "soldier-like." In Pennsylvania, Lieutenant Colonel Francis Johnston wrote to his commanding officer Anthony Wayne to report a mutiny in February 1776 that he believed was connected to soldiers' grievances over short supplies. "In short, D[ea]r Sir, unless you bring with you a considerable quantity of Cash, Shirts, breeches, Stockings, Shoes, Hats &c," Johnston noted, "there will not remain the most distant prospect of tranquility or discipline among them." In New York the "Difficulty of Providing Cloath of almost any kind for the Troops" prompted Washington to issue orders on July 24, 1776, for the men to don hunting shirts and long breeches of the same material. Writing to his father in Connecticut, the private soldier Jedediah Huntington reported, "Almost all the Goods of all kinds are moved into the Country—White Linnens such as you yourself wear cannot be had under two Dollars or two & half p[er] yard." Wayne wrote from Fort Ticonderoga on April 14, 1777, "We are totally Destitute of Shoe's Sockings, Blankets and almost every Other Article in the Clothing way."[18]

Contaminated water plagued many regiments. In July 1776 regimental orders warned soldiers in New York to "be very careful not to Drink any Warten [*sic*] that comes out of the Pumps in this City as it will Prove very Dangerous to their Helth." The Massachusetts private Elijah Fisher observed in his journal in December 1777 at Valley Forge, "The warter we had to Drink and to mix our flower with was out of a brook that run along by the Camps and so many a dippin and washin it which maid it very Dirty and muddy." Officers encouraged soldiers' "dippin and washin," but an entire camp's efforts at cleanliness could foul the water supply. Washington ordered his officers to clean out the springs from which the soldiers had been supplying themselves and to take precautions "to prevent any accumulation of Filth."[19]

Although some of the problems with the men's cleanliness and health could be traced to problems with the army's supply lines, others clearly lay with the inability of commanders to impose the discipline necessary to keep such a large population of disgruntled men clean. It was not that ordinary enlisted men, particularly those from Massachusetts, feared water. On the contrary, both Washington and General Nathanael Greene of Rhode Island had to issue orders forbidding men who had been swimming from strutting about stark naked on public bridges and in plain view of "Ladies of the best Fashion." Swimming clearly remained popular even if it inspired mixed feelings among officers. Although neither general wished to discourage bathing, both men worried about the impact of prolonged swimming upon the health of troops as well as the loss of "all sense of Modesty & common Decency."[20]

The distinctive sensibilities of the army's top officers contributed to the gap between commanders and troops. Many elite officers had the expectation and means to continue grooming themselves as they might have done in civilian life. General officers of the Massachusetts Army urged "Any Young Man of good Character who can Shave and dress hare well" to apply to the brigade major for employment. When the Woburn, Massachusetts, native Loammi Baldwin, Colonel of the 26th Regiment of the Continental Army, returned an inventory of his possessions to his wife, Mary Baldwin, it reflected the comforts of clean and fashionable dress enjoyed by a man of his rank: seventeen shirts, several coats and jackets, eleven pairs of stockings, including silk, and silver buckles and buttons. The Connecticut surgeon Albigence Waldo noted the importance of genteel dress for advancing the career of an ambitious officer. "An Officer frequently fails of being duly noticed, mearely from the want of a genteel Dress"; he observed critically, "and if joined to this, he has a bungling Address, — his situation is render'd very disagreeable." Waldo decried that custom dictated the necessity of "superfluous Dress," when simple neatness would do. "Neatness of Dress, void of unnecessary superfluities is very becoming — and discovers a man at least to have some Ambition — without which he will never make any figure in life."[21]

Anthony Wayne, whose fastidiousness earned him the nickname "Dandy Wayne," embodied the ideals for genteel appearance. From May 1775 to April 1776, while he commanded a militia company and served as colonel of the 4th Regiment of Pennsylvania, he had his hair professionally dressed at least once a month. In all his posts, he continually sought to improve the cleanliness and neatness of his troops. Wayne procured new uniforms for his men, insisting that they be well groomed for parade. "For God's sake give us — if you can't give us anything else — give us linnen," he demanded in an effort to defeat what he saw as the troops' worst enemy: vermin. He regularly issued orders requiring his men to appear shaved, with powdered hair and clean clothes, and was angry when troops appeared in dirty linen. His attention to grooming and health was not lost on his subordinates. Colonel Nicholas Hansseger, commander of the German battalion of the 1st Pennsylvania Regiment, wrote to Wayne with pride about the appearance of men he paraded before the general quarter; "They Look Exceedingly well," he boasted, "as I Make them put on Clean Shirts." Upon learning that Wayne planned to reassign him, a Major Ryan wondered what he had done to offend his commander: "I am Generally as Clean dress'd as my Situation will admit of, I know of Nothing in my Mann[e]r which Makes Me Despicable If I did I would Rectify it."[22]

Most Continental Army soldiers had never lived in such large concentrations of people and were unused to even the most rudimentary cleanliness disciplines practiced by the elite officer corps. A Massachusetts soldier, George Norton of

Ipswich, reported an egregious case in 1778 of a man who seemed almost proud of his unbroken record of filth. Norton wrote, "This day the old Carter, Brown, washed his face & handes he Desired to have it seat down in the Journal the first time since he come in." What were the circumstances of Brown's hiatus from washing? Did he consider himself liberated from the constraints of a domestic routine in which a wife or adult daughter might have reminded him to wash at a well or washstand before entering the house for dinner? Or had he simply not had the opportunity to wash? Was it the act of washing or the long abstention that Brown thought worthy of being recorded in a literate man's military journal?[23]

LAUNDRY

Laundry created an important flash point in the conflict between officers and soldiers, one that provoked the Continental Army's concerns about the moral virtue of the men and women on its payroll. The skewed sex ratio of the military camp forced adaptations to customary divisions of labor, commonly understood to be rooted in tradition and nature and necessary for standards of decency and comfort. Separated from their households, the men could no longer count on women to produce and maintain their cleanliness for free. Instead, soldiers had to pay "camp women" to do laundry or to assume responsibility for their dirty clothes and lice-infested bodies. *Camp follower*—a derisive nineteenth-century term that tarred all women accompanying the troops with the brush of prostitution—was not in common use during the Revolution. Instead, specific labels defined the legitimate purposes of women who accompanied the Continental Army—wives, washerwomen, nurses, or matrons—but they might also be more generally known as camp women or "women of the Army." Depending upon the context, even these designations could connote ill repute. Distinguishing honestly employed women from "lewd women" was important for army morale and discipline, but not always easy to achieve in practice. As we have seen, women who laundered for pay had long been suspected of engaging in illicit sex. Living in the midst of hundreds of troops for whom they provided domestic services, such women were often assumed to be of dubious character. But the Continental Army was desperate for women's labor. Bodily filth not only threatened the health of the troops but also made them unappealing heroes in a war in which the colonies staked their victory on superior virtue. When women did perform vital services for the army as payrolled employees, they ameliorated the sanitary problems to some degree but made it more difficult for the troops to appear virtuous.[24]

Ordinary soldiers were reluctant to cross the line demarcating women's work

to wash their own clothes. The soldiers' filth resulted in large part from this disinclination, but fears that the dampness of newly washed clothes could cause illness also discouraged them. Soldiers who had no other source of clean clothes
simply continued to wear dirty clothing until it disintegrated. Men with more resources dealt with this problem by paying a washerwoman attached to the army.
As we know from the frequency of citations issued to washerwomen for violating
rules about fouling drinking water or tent sites, the women of the army provided
this vital service throughout the war. More rarely, a soldier might delegate laundry duty to another he outranked. James Anderson, an African-American soldier
serving in a Virginia regiment, was assigned such duty, but he stole the leather
breeches he had been ordered to wash when he deserted in 1780. Others sent
laundry home to be washed and repaired by women. Still others relied on
women for new socks and shirts to replace clothing worn day and night. Better-
heeled officers seem to have had steadier supplies of new and laundered clothing from the women of their households, a crucial reason why they enjoyed
greater bodily comfort than the average enlisted man.[25]

The women of the Continental Army—paid employees who provided material support to the troops—would have been likely candidates for the labor of
washing clothes, but insufficient numbers and the army's mixed feelings about
their presence prevented them from solving the problem early in the war. Driven
by poverty or entrepreneurial ambition, women on the army's payroll received
rations—usually a third to a half of a man's, although valuable labor might earn
them a full measure—in exchange for cooking, caring for the sick and wounded,
washing and mending clothes, scavenging the battlefield for abandoned goods,
and burying the dead. As the war progressed, certain of these duties proved essential. One was nursing the sick and wounded, a task Congress delegated to
hospital matrons in April 1777 when it reorganized the army. As Washington explained in 1776, hospital nurses were needed to wash patients' entire bodies
upon admission and their faces and hands thereafter, empty close stools and
chamber pots, and fumigate and sweep the wards. Laundry was another essential
task, needed to maintain healthy soldiers, and it occupied more women even
than cooking. The availability of women to wash clothes varied greatly from
company to company. A 1776 return for the Delaware company of Captain
Joseph Bloomfield listed three washerwomen along with seventy-two soldiers,
two officers, and one volunteer. But in other companies, the numbers of women
and children swelled. On average, the Continental Army gave 3 percent of its rations to women, who were then encouraged to labor, compared with the official
6 percent figure used by the British army to distribute provisions. One woman
was supposed to receive half rations to wash for ten men.[26]

Wives who laundered clothes for their husbands might have been viewed as the paragons of domestic virtue, but as hangers-on who gained sustenance informally in exchange for vaguely defined "services," they conjured the worst of female vices: the sale of sex. Women's visibility in the garrisons embarrassed some officers, including George Washington, who believed that they undermined the army's virtue and military effectiveness. He struggled to hide women and children from public view, requiring them to walk next to the baggage wagon when the army was on the move. Issuing rations to those formally designated as camp women helped to draw the distinction more clearly, as did punishments of "bad women." From the earliest days of the war, officers warned recalcitrant men that "no Lewd Wimen" should come into the camp. Those that did were to be reported so that they could be punished and the camp "rid . . . of all such Nuisances." When a young woman in William Barton's Elizabethtown unit was discovered masquerading as a young man, allegedly to search for her fiancé, he ordered her to be taken out of town accompanied by drums beating the whore's march.[27]

As the historian Richard Godbeer has argued, this fear of the corrupting influence of camp life was not merely the product of overworked rural imaginations but was rooted in the reality of many men's first exposure to casual and commercial sex. Ordinary soldiers and civilians interpreted the presence of women in military camps as ambiguous, even compromised. Perhaps it was the poverty of many of these women and the fact that, for many rural men, military service represented their first opportunity for a sexual encounter away from the surveillance of families and communities. Reports of the heckling that women endured reveal soldiers' assumptions about sexual availability. "Madam you shoew your Peruke wigg," a soldier shouted at a "Camp Lady" who walked by a tent, to which "the pretty creature" retorted, "Then damn ye throw your hat at it." Were the address "Madam" and the term "Camp Lady" ironic references to a woman suspected of being a prostitute? Her spicy language suggests as much, revealing the rough and tumble nature of men's interactions with women in an army camp. Alexander Hamilton (the statesman, not the traveling doctor) suggested that a somewhat higher standard prevailed among the officers. In a letter to his wife about "a pretty little Dutch girl of fifteen" who was most obliging in her service to the quarters, he claimed that her innocence and simplicity shielded her from the machinations of even the most determined rake. Captain Nathan Peters's wife confronted him directly with the rumor in 1776 that every soldier had a lady and that "allmost the whole of our army was under the Salivation," a symptom of the mercury-based treatment for venereal disease.[28]

Officers took strong measures to exploit this paradox of women's potential both to contaminate and to clean. Suspected prostitutes were ritually punished and banished from camp, as in the case of one "bad woman" who, Caleb Haskell reported, was "taken up . . . doused in the river and drummed out of town." General Wayne issued strict orders that any woman "who shall refuse to wash for the Men" be "drumm'd out of the Regt, as they are not found in Victuals to distress and render the Men unfit for Duty, but to keep them clean and decent." Wayne's treatment of those who shirked their laundry duties echoed the treatment of prostitutes and suggested that a woman's goodness depended on her willingness to perform domestic duties; she might prove her own moral worth by cheerfully taking on the labor of laundering men's clothing. In the case of enterprising women too eager to profit from the desperate need for their laundry services, however, the army responded by limiting the fee they could charge.[29]

Small numbers of women and the ability of some to avoid laundry duty might have meant that the burden of washing clothes fell on the men. Yet military journals and orderly books from the first two years of the war make little mention of men actually washing clothes, despite numerous orders to do so.[30] Donning new clothes while waiting for someone to launder the dirty ones became more difficult as cloth became more scarce. The universally filthy and ragged condition of enlisted men's clothing suggests that laundry was done only infrequently. Early in the war the Massachusetts Legislature warned George Washington that the state's young recruits had not learned "the absolute necessity of cleanliness in their dress and lodging, continual exercise, and strict temperance, to preserve them from diseases." A few years later, Colonel Israel Angell, a militia captain who assumed leadership of the 2nd Rhode Island Regiment, complained about the terrible condition of the men's clothes, describing it as "scandallous."[31] The surgeon Albigence Waldo described a suffering soldier at Gulph Mills, Pennsylvania, in a pitiful state: "His bare feet are seen thro' his worn out Shoes, his legs nearly naked from the tatter'd remains of an only pair of stockings, his Breeches not sufficient to cover his Nakedness, his Shirt hanging in Strings, his hair dishevell'd."[32] By February 1, 1778, almost four thousand Continental Army soldiers had been reported unfit for duty mainly as a result of inadequate clothing. One month later, Benjamin Rush described the men at the encampment at Valley Forge as "dirty and ragged.[33]

Shortages of vital supplies, large concentrations of soldiers, and the failure of individual men to take responsibility for their own cleanliness resulted in many soldiers succumbing to "the itch" and to infestations of lice. Colonel Winds reported to General Gates from Ticonderoga in October 1776 that the troops were "severely afflicted" by the itch, which many believed to have been communicated through their inoculation for smallpox the previous June. The foul-smelling remedy only added to the stench of camps and the filthy appearance of the men. Entire camps were also overrun with lice. General Wayne reported to the secretary of war that he would "cheerfully agree to enter into action once every week in place of visiting each hut of my encampment. . . . The whole Army is sick and crawling with vermin."[34]

This was a particularly dramatic expression of filth in a society whose definitions of personal cleanliness centered on clothing. It demanded a readjustment in standards and practices. In the absence of military discipline compelling men to wash their clothing with regularity or sufficient numbers of women to do the work for them, some simply endured their dirtiness, their choices constrained by hunger, fatigue, illness, and a lack of soap or spare clothes. Wayne worried about the morale of his poorly supplied Pennsylvania soldiers in 1777. "They never Recd any uniform except hunting Shirts which are worn out," he lamented, "and Altho a body of fine men — yet from being in Raggs and badly armed — they are viewed with Contempt by the Other Troops, and begin to Dispise themselves." The result of such discontent, he warned, would be desertion.[35]

How did civilian observers understand this suspension of civilian standards for cleanliness? As a patriotic sacrifice in pursuit of the larger goal of liberty? As a forgivable negligence when men were separated from women? Neither patriotism nor the maleness of the camps was enough to silence civilian condemnation of the soldiers' appearance. Ordinary people showed little restraint in making known their disgust for particularly dirty regiments of soldiers. In an effort to procure additional supplies for his troops, Colonel Angell reported to Rhode Island's governor on August 27, 1777, that his regiment was "scandallous in its appearance in the view of everyone and has because of this incurred from surrounding regiments from the inhabitants of Towns thro which they have lately passed, the disagreeable and provoking Epithets of the Ragged Lousey Naked Regiment."[36]

This critique of the soldiers' appearance is in keeping with what we know about the class dimensions of revolutionary service; by 1777, in the face of veteran unwillingness to reenlist, the economic wherewithal of the average soldier declined, leading better-heeled civilians to disdain the Continental Army. As conditions deteriorated, the army found it more difficult to retain mature, white, native-born enlistees and depended more heavily on recruits it deemed less desirable: the old, the young, African Americans, Indians, and the poor. Indeed, these were precisely the men Washington believed to be less "soldierlike" by nature. By 1777 Massachusetts and Rhode Island were enlisting African Americans, slave and free. In other states, after Congress recommended the draft, many black men were substituted for white draftees. General Wayne complained to a correspondent in April 1777 that his troops were now mainly "Negroes, Indians, and Children."[37]

Some of the citizen hostility also stemmed from the diseases following in the wake of the army. It was common, particularly during the dog days of late summer, for entire regiments to succumb to fevers and diarrhea. The cause was usually typhus, borne by lice and also carried by ticks and fleas. Known to civilians as "camp distemper," typhus spread quickly throughout densely populated camps and surrounding neighborhoods.[38] "Sickness is in the neighborhood," Lois Peters of Connecticut noted ominously to her husband in August 1776. A month later Peters was still blaming "Camp distemper" for the illness that had struck her own family. Like many other civilians, she associated the unprecedented cluster of deaths with the proximity of the army: "This Neighberhood is allmost Stript of men and women since I wrote To you before Miss Rosseter is dead . . . there wa[s] Six funerals here in Eight days." Another diarist, who observed eighteen thousand troops encamped near his neighborhood in August 1777, soon recorded the deaths of several women and children who had been ill with dysentery. "The flux seems very Mortal," he commented, "I think I never knew so many people Die in so short a time, in this Neighbourhood."[39]

Smallpox continued to affect North American–born soldiers in larger numbers and to a much greater degree than it did the inoculated and immune British troops. It struck fear in the hearts of soldiers, who probably had heard stories about the ghastly deaths of its American victims in the Quebec, Boston, and Virginia outbreaks of 1775. Suspected cases were enough to make some men consider desertion, while others viewed with suspicion preventive measures like inoculation. Having considered mass inoculation too risky during the opening months of the conflict, Washington reversed his position several times before deciding in January 1777 to inoculate all new recruits. The decision was to be kept secret from the enemy, who might see opportunity even in the relatively mild illness of recently inoculated men. Washington struggled with the practical consequences of the policy. Men suffering from the milder version of smallpox still developed fevers and skin eruptions. They needed attendants to help them through the illness and clean linens to replace those soiled when pus-filled sores burst. These were exactly the resources Washington could least spare, the ones most needed to prevent filth among the healthy and to cope with the suffering of the sick and wounded. The inoculation policy heightened the need for strict camp hygiene and the quarantine of new recruits to counteract the ability of the dread disease to decimate the ranks of fresh troops.[40]

LATRINES

A second flash point in the conflict between officers and soldiers concerned the use of common latrines. Latrines had been a bone of contention during the Seven Years' War, when New England provincials had chafed under orders to dig them at the edge of the camp. From the first days of the Revolutionary War, officers repeatedly reminded the men to confine themselves to "necessaries," which were, for health reasons, to be located at least one hundred yards from the tents — just far enough, apparently, for some men to consider alternative sites. Camp colormen — soldiers assigned to maintain the camp — had the unenviable duty of stopping up old latrines, digging new ones, and removing filth and trash. Soldiers were instructed to sweep "filth and nastiness" from their barracks into camp streets, much as city residents were regularly reminded to do, so that these piles of garbage could be removed by the colormen. During the hot, unhealthy summer months, officers might require latrines to be located even farther away from the lines, which made the temptation to go elsewhere even greater. Men who failed to abide by the rules incurred severe penalties, including being taken prisoner and court-martialed for offenses to health and decency.[41]

The camp's health may have been the main concern, but commanders were also hoping to maintain good relations with local residents, who feared the consequences of having so many soldiers quartered nearby. Orders from headquarters on August 12, 1777, condemned "the neglect" of the rules for erecting and using latrines and burying offal at the camp near the falls of the Schuylkill River, warning that it threatened not only the health of troops but their "reputation by such uncleanness & offensive Smells." Indeed, the damage to the army's reputation was integrally connected to the public's fears of the diseases carried by the camp's fetid water and foul smells. Division orders a few weeks later for the same troublesome Pennsylvania camp called for using vinegar, the all-purpose purifier, to prevent disease. But the failure of the same troops to erect latrines contributed to the public relations problem, leading headquarters to note that the "Necessaries" were to be covered with "Boughs and Bushes," placed in the rear of the encampment, and not located "indecently" where every passerby could see them.[42]

During the long winter at Valley Forge (1777–1778), when the numbers of women caring for soldiers reached its all-time low of one for every forty-four men, the unwillingness of soldiers to use latrines became a particularly serious problem. Colonel Henry Bicker of the Second Pennsylvania Line dutifully recorded orders that "Centinels from the Qr. Guards are to . . . make prisoner of any Soldier who shall attempt to ease himself at any where; but at the proper necessary and five lashes are to be immediately order'd." In addition, Bicker noted, new necessaries, or latrine pits, were to be "immediately dug" and fresh earth to be thrown in them every day. The orders should be read "frequently," moreover, and "New Commers" apprised of the punishment for disobedience. Despite new measures and warnings to the men about the health hazard presented by the approaching warm season, soldiers still refused to confine themselves to the latrine pits. General George Weedon's orderly book reported still harsher punishments, including this almost unbelievable measure: "Major Claiborne will in Future mount a Brigade Guard to afford three Sentinels with *orders to Fire on any man* who shall be found easing himself elsewhere than in the Vaults."[43] Yet faced with sanctions prohibiting such behavior, the men nonetheless continued to avoid designated latrines.

Why? The enlisted men's persistence in viewing the entire camp as a latrine probably reflected the considerable freedoms of the agrarian communities from which most came. Many of these men had spent their entire lives relieving themselves outdoors in privies, fields, or woods as soon as they felt the urge. Known as "shit houses," privies were usually small but well ventilated buildings located behind the house. When a privy hole filled, the men of the family or their male servants stopped it up and changed the location. During the day, rural people made use of privies that they shared with members of their household. In cities, two or more households might share a privy. At night, when men and women might be reluctant to venture outdoors, they used chamber pots, bedpans, close stools, or "member mugs." In all of these instances, men and women limited their exposure to the unpleasant smells emanating from human waste, sharing that exposure with a limited circle of household members or neighbors, the people about whose health they were well informed. The smaller than usual presence of women in the Valley Forge camp did little to inhibit men already predisposed to avoid latrines.[44]

The unpopularity of the army's "necessaries," then, probably had as much to do with their offensive smell as with the men's libertarian convictions. Looking more closely at Weedon's orderly book, we notice the orders to quartermasters to make latrine pits cleaner: more new pits should be dug, and the old pits be covered with fresh earth *twice* daily rather than once, as in the original order. Rural men apparently preferred to relieve themselves in a place cleaner than a collective latrine. The men had not abandoned civilian standards of cleanliness, as they had done out of necessity with their laundry. Rather, they continued to adhere selectively to certain standards, such as avoiding the stench of a latrine pit, because it offended their sensibilities and threatened to spread disease.

MORALE

Although most soldiers did not respond to filth by voluntarily changing their cleanliness habits, this did not mean that they found their squalor tolerable. Some ordinary soldiers and, one suspects, a large proportion of the better-heeled officer corps, found camp life unhealthy and dispiriting. Colonel Angell reported that the ragged condition of his Rhode Island troops provoked public ridicule and resulted in low morale. As Angell saw it, "such treatment . . . is discouraging dispiriting in its tendency: it does effectually unman the Man and render them almost useless in the Army." Men who protected their manhood by refusing to do their own laundry ultimately became unmanned, in Angell's analysis, by the shame of their own filth. But by refusing to change their habits, enlisted men were also conveying their disregard for the complex of soldier-like behavior, refined manhood, and patriotic virtue that commanders insisted upon. No ordinary soldier probably enjoyed physical discomfort, but he might not have found his commanding officers' ideals for bodily discipline a compelling remedy.[45]

The damage that being dirty could effect on morale was especially pronounced for those men with vivid memories of domestic comforts. The surgeon Waldo, a prosperous married man, found his filthy, uncomfortable circumstances in the camp at Gulph Mills, Pennsylvania, during the horrible winter of 1777–1778 hardest to endure when he compared them to his life with his family: "Poor food—hard lodging—Cold Weather—fatigue—Nasty Cloaths—nasty Cookery—Vomit half my time—smoak'd out of my senses—The Devil's in't—I can't Endure it—Why are we sent here to starve and Freeze—What sweet Felicities have I left at home; A charming Wife—pretty Children—Good Beds—good food—good Cookery—all agreeable, all harmonious. Here, all Confusion—smoke & Cold—hunger & filthyness."[46] Supporting the Continental Army required that Waldo sacrifice bodily comfort. He dealt with his suffering by recording his hardships in his diary and learning from a soldier "how to Darn stockings to make them look like knit work."[47] Other soldiers simply endured their discomfort or voiced their unhappiness by "Immitating the noise of Crows and Owls," on a cold December night when there was no meat for dinner. More seriously, as Anthony Wayne noted, they raised mutinies in an effort to get needed supplies. Yet for most of these men, remedies for the problem of ragged, rotting clothing came only when they crossed the threshold of their own homes. In this respect, they shared with Waldo the identification of domestic life as the source of physical comfort and decency, manifested in the availability of a clean change of clothes.[48]

At Ticonderoga during the winter of 1776–1777, Wayne met his match in short supplies, disease, and filthy conditions. Shortly after the American defeat at nearby Valcour Island in October, he had ordered the men in the Fourth Pennsylvania, recruited from Chester, Lancaster, and Bucks Counties, to shave — and deducted the barber's fee from their wages — the night before they were to be on parade. As conditions worsened with the coming of cold weather, he directed officers to set their own tailors to repair the men's clothing. He also excused the troops from duty the next Sunday so that they could appear bearing arms, "fresh shav'd, clean, and well powder'd at Troop beating." Officers were also to provide the men with newly issued white waistcoats, stockings, leggings, and shirts. In December 1776, as winter set in, Wayne "observ'd with a good deal of Pain that some of the Regts have sent their Men to the Parade with unpowder'd Hair, long Beards, dirty Shirts and rusty Arms," and ordered soap to be issued to the men on the spot.[49]

Such was Wayne's faith in the power of the clean uniform that, he claimed, he would rather have the fate of the country rest on five thousand men in neat uniforms than on an army one third larger and equally well armed but "covered with raggs & crawling with vermen."[50] In June 1777, having suffered through the winter at Ticonderoga, he wrote to an unnamed correspondent about the merits of tidiness. A neat uniform that made a soldier appear as a gentleman would, he reasoned, inspire him to act like one. Out of pride, well-dressed men would keep themselves clean, which would save more lives than a doctor's nostrums ever could. In subsequent orders, Wayne described a cleanly appearance as masculine and patriotic.[51] But Wayne's troops may have had a different view. The nickname "Dandy Wayne" suggests that his men might have had their own critique of their general's impeccable grooming.

PUBLIC DEBATE

Public discussion of the filth of the Continental Army began to appear in newspapers even before the nadir of conditions and collapse of morale at Valley Forge. On April 22, 1777, just one week after Congress approved a military draft, the *Pennsylvania Packet*, an intensely patriotic paper, published a lengthy article. "Directions for preserving the HEALTH of SOLDIERS: Recommended to the consideration of the OFFICERS in the ARMY of the UNITED STATES" was later acknowledged to be the work of Benjamin Rush, who was in the midst of a dispute with George Washington over the condition of army hospitals. The piece began with an emotional appeal to the people of America to consider the tragedy of losing patriotic young men not to enemy fire but to fever and languishing illness in a hospital. Arguing against the fatalistic idea that mortal illnesses were part and parcel of military life, Rush urged officers to enforce the disciplines that would preserve the health of soldiers.[52]

Rush's directives included prescriptions for dress, diet, and cleanliness in the camps, but personal hygiene was a dominant theme. Precedents for linking health and bodily cleanliness abounded in both military hygiene guides and his own writings. "Too much cannot be said in favour of CLEANLINESS," he noted, instructing officers to concentrate efforts on the body, clothes, and food of the soldier. The soldier "should be obliged to wash his hands and face at least once every day, and his whole body twice or three times a week, especially in the summer." Rush cited the Romans, noting that cold baths were part of the military discipline of their soldiers. Frequent changes of clothing were crucial, but flannel shirts were preferable to absorbent linens that became overloaded with toxins and generated miasmas.[53] He also enjoined officers to ensure that soldiers cooked their meals in vessels carefully washed after every use. In addition to these three principles of cleanliness, Rush advised that soldiers avoid sleeping in wet clothes or on damp ground and be required to change straw bedding and air blankets to avoid a morbid buildup of perspiration. The camp itself, Rush noted, "should be kept perfectly clean of the offals of animals and of filth of all kinds."

Rush held up the model of the ancient Greeks and Romans, with only a few offhand references to the superior military discipline of the British troops. He had earlier sung the praises of British General Howe's encampment, noting to John Adams that "they pay a supreme regard to the cleanliness and health of their men," but he de-emphasized this theme in his published essay. It would not do to look to the cruel and corrupt British enemy for an example of military virtue, especially if Rush hoped to change the attitudes of patriot officers. Rush also drew no examples from the domestic routines of women or the bathing traditions of Native Americans, praised for cleanliness in popular medical guides of the period, including his own. If the point of improving the cleanliness of the men was to improve their readiness for battle, their health, and their morale, it would do little good to point out women and heathens as models to follow.[54] Rush's ideal soldier thus washed his own body and did his own laundry as an exercise in military virtue that did not entail any loss of manliness.

A week after the publication of Rush's "Directives to Officers," the *Pennsylvania Packet* published another discussion of the Continental Army's cleanliness, this time directed to soldiers. The author, identified only as W., was probably George Washington himself or his aide-de-camp, Alexander Hamilton. W. hoped to reach an audience who had "no acquaintance with medicine." He reasoned that, if the common soldier had more knowledge of the subject of his own health and the need for military discipline, he would more readily submit to infringements on his liberty and comply with military regulations.[55]

W. devoted his essay to the need for ordinary soldiers to be more attentive to cleanliness. "It is extremely difficult to persuade soldiers that cleanliness is absolutely necessary to the health of an army," he observed. "They can hardly believe that in a military state it becomes one of the necessaries of life." Ordinary soldiers suffered from disease because they continued to practice poor hygiene as they had always done in civilian life in the mistaken belief that "they shall continue to enjoy an equal degree of health under the like degree of negligence." The problem with this reasoning, W. explained, was that "they do not consider the prodigious difference there is in the circumstances of five or six people who live by themselves on a farm, and of thirty or forty thousand men who live together in a camp." The filthy state of enlisted men was a commentary not on their moral condition but on their rural origins.

W.'s explanation for ordinary men's poor hygiene focused on education. Soldiers "are not supposed to be acquainted with the art of preserving health," he claimed, because "they are little versed in books." But he refused to consider such a state of ignorance a lost cause. "To the honor of American soldiers, it is allowed that no men in Christendom of the same occupation are so well acquainted with their bibles," he averred, and such knowledge could be of some use in instructing them in the habits of cleanliness. "Let them, once more, read the history and travels of the Children of Israel while they continued in the wilderness under the conduct of Moses; and let them consider at the same time that they are reading the history of a great army, that continued forty years in their different camps, under the guidance and regulations of the wisest General that ever lived." Using this reasoning, W. observed, Exodus became an everyman's guide to being clean:

> In the history of these people the soldier must admire the singular attention that was paid to the rules of cleanliness. They were obliged to wash their hands two or three times of a day. Foul garments were counted abominable; everything that was polluted or dirty was absolutely forbidden. . . . The utmost pains were taken to keep the air in which they breathed free from infection. They were commanded to have a place without the camp, whither they should go, and have a paddle with which they should dig, so that when they went abroad

to ease themselves, they might turn back and cover that which came from them.

In W.'s analysis, the piety of American soldiers, reflected in their familiarity with the Bible, could become the basis for camp cleanliness, with Jews serving as a model for soldiers. Although W. eschewed much of medical terminology used by Rush, his use of the Jews as an example of cleanliness had strong precedents in medical circles. It was, for example, strikingly similar to William Buchan's argument in *Domestic Medicine*, published just a few years earlier.

In addition to setting forth the Bible as a source of information about cleanliness, W. offered some tips on personal hygiene. He echoed Rush's advice about changing straw bedding and avoiding damp ground, but detailed specific instructions about clothing. "A soldier should change his shirt and stockings once every two or three days," he declared. Even if linen is in short supply, he insisted, "a shirt is soon washed." But W. stopped short of urging men to wash their own laundry. "Women are never wanting in a camp for such offices," he claimed, placing the burden of actually cleaning the soiled linen on washerwomen. Unlike Rush, W. depicted ordinary men as having no obligation to compromise their manhood by doing their own laundry.

Ultimately, Rush's directives to officers, not W.'s directives to soldiers, became the standard text on cleanliness for the Continental Army. The piece was reprinted in its entirety in on May 15, 1777, in John Gill's *Continental Journal*, whose masthead read, "The Entire Prosperity of every State depends upon the Discipline of its Armies." The essay appeared a week later in the *Connecticut Gazette*.[56] In 1778 it was published as a pamphlet attributed to Rush, *Directions for Preserving the Health of Soldiers*. That text added material on exercise and the dangers to soldiers of returning to the soft conditions of civilian life. It also detailed the horrible consequences of a soldier's death for his female dependents to persuade officers to redouble their efforts to keep the men clean. Reprinted throughout the nineteenth century, it became part of the standard guide for the United States Army, although the call for cold bathing seems to have had little effect. The pamphlet's longevity can be attributed not only to widespread respect for Rush's medical authority but to the fact that John Dunlap, publisher of the *Pennsylvania Packet*, subsequently became the official printer for Congress.[57] Meanwhile, the essay signed W. appeared as a broadside in the fall of 1777 but disappeared until a twentieth-century historian identified it as Washington's.[58]

In choosing Rush over W. and the Romans over the Jews, the army embraced a vision of manly soldiers obeying orders to launder their own stockings, remove dirt from their faces and hands, and use designated latrines, all under the watchful eye of paternalistic officers. Roman exemplars of military valor and cleanliness thus became the model for the American citizen-soldier. Jews were not held up to revolutionary-era Americans to inspire them to military discipline and national glory except in two instances: a poem by the Reverend Wheeler Case, published in the same year as the *Pennsylvania Packet* articles, that explicitly compared America with Zion, and a similar effort by Timothy Dwight in 1785. Neither of these exceptions cited the Jews as models of cleanliness for ordinary Americans, even though Rush and several other medical authors had done so in earlier writings.[59]

The cleanliness of soldiers remained at a low ebb throughout 1777. Then in May 1778 Washington appointed Baron Frederick Von Steuben, a veteran of the general staff of the Prussian army, to be inspector general of the United States. Von Steuben immediately began to work on the conditions and morale of the troops by training small model companies whose compliance with military discipline would inspire the larger brigade. Among those disciplines he successfully introduced were those related to camp sanitation, dress, cleanliness, and health.[60] Once the need for bodily discipline was instilled in men by officers who were expected to conduct themselves according to the same principles, voluntary compliance could take hold, much as W. had envisioned. Journals from the later years of the war reveal stronger military discipline and higher standards of cleanliness. Lieutenant William Feltman of the First Pennsylvania Regiment, commanded by Wayne, recorded that his men frequently "washed their clothing and furbished up their arms and accoutrements" in 1781–1782. When Wayne reviewed them, Feltman noted, they made a "very respectable appearance." Captain John Davis of Wayne's brigade recorded cleaning his own clothes on May 30, 1781.[61]

Washerwomen also appear more frequently in military records from this point in the war. By 1780 army commanders required detailed information about the women and children in camp as part of a more stringent effort to determine women's marital status and character. But the need for female labor was not always the motive for keeping women on the army's payroll. Commanding officers sometimes listed the wives of poor men as washerwomen to keep the men to their duty and to provide for families that would otherwise be destitute. In 1781 the army allotted rations to one woman for every fifteen men. This ratio was drawn from British army guidelines but resisted by Washington, who felt that it tied the hands of commanders who might need more flexibility to provision the wives and children of enlisted men. From this point to the war's end, evidence of women washing appears in soldier's diaries. In mid-1781, for example, a group of women were washing clothes when the Appomatock River bridge collapsed upon them. In another instance, Private Elijah Fisher, who served with Pennsylvania troops, reported on April 29, 1782, that he brought pails of water for "the young women to wash with." By the final year of the war, as the historian Holly Mayer notes, conditions of troops in winter quarters were better than they had ever been.[62]

Despite real improvements in camp health and discipline, the American army continued to suffer from shortages of clothing. Correspondence throughout the remainder of the war features complaints about the lack of clothing, its poor quality, and despair over how it could be procured. Wayne continued to press for additional supplies with some success. In December 1780 Washington ordered Wayne's men to receive eight hundred of two thousand shirts recently sewn by "Mrs. Blair and the Ladies." This was apparently the same batch of shirts reluctantly produced by Esther de Berdt Reed and her Ladies Association after Washington urged them to donate clothing rather than cash to the patriot cause.[63]

SUFFERING BODIES

After the American Revolution, cleanliness—both as a form of bodily care and as an ideal for civilized living—continued to take on new meanings.[64] If before the war cleanliness had signified gentility and health, by war's end it had become a mark of humanity whose abrogation or disregard was considered barbarous. Horrific conditions of filth and disease among American troops prompted interventions in historical memory-making following the war. Americans ritually cleansed the soldier's body by asserting their own virtue, humanity, and civility and by emphasizing British cruelty. Men like Andrew Sherburne, whose account opens this chapter, illustrated the barbarity of their British captors by documenting squalid conditions and unspeakable filth. Writing his memoir in the 1820s, Sherburne must have been aware that disease and filth were the staples of army life early in the war, before the imposition of military discipline reined in enlisted men. Yet in his narrative, as in many others, dirt signified the callous inhumanity of his British captors. This had been a familiar theme during the war and the subject of numerous newspaper accounts.[65] Evil and filth could thus be attributed to the British while a discourse of suffering victimhood cast Americans as pure innocents.

Postwar interpretations of cleanliness as a basic privilege of humanity reflected a new moral language that moved readers by depicting the plight of suffering human bodies. Although there were many ways to stir readers to feel empathy for suffering humanity, evoking the disgust and discomfort of people compelled to endure filth imposed on them by brutal others had become a powerful rhetorical tool. Olaudah Equiano employed this set of meanings to good effect to create a graphic condemnation of the slave trade in his autobiographical tale of 1789, describing the violated humanity of West Africans transported against their wills. He insisted on historical and cultural reasons for enslaved people's degraded condition, claiming that they, too, possessed sensitive human bodies that suffered through exposure to filth, bad smells, and prison conditions. The implication of Equiano's memoir was that all people shared a basic vulnerability to pain and suffering if they were denied access to domestic comforts, including clean clothing, the ability to clean their bodies, and clean air. Such an argument represented a significant intervention in the hardening racial categories that excluded Africans from a genteel sensibility. It was a radical view of a common humanity, rooted in the feeling body.[66]

Although Sherburne's experience as a prisoner of war was distinct from that of both the transported slave and the ordinary Continental Army soldier, representations in his memoir of innocence and cleanliness, evil and filth, reflected a similar depiction of suffering humanity. Sherburne deflected discussions of cleanliness and virtue from the conditions of military camps, where the conclusion was politically troubling — their filth could signify either the corruption of the troops or the barbarity of their officers — to the scene in British prisons, where the moral message was unambiguous. Thus the condemnation of British cruelty paved the way for readmitting dirty Americans into civilian society as virtuous victims. Sherburne's tale of the hospitable baker might seem initially to suggest the unimportance of cleanliness for the right-thinking civilian; but it also points to a different meaning. The baker could emerge as singularly charitable and generous only in a society where people were beginning to draw sharp distinctions between the clean and the dirty. Willingness to overlook the filth of two lousy fellows translates into a supreme act of kindness, particularly in the case of the baker's wife who, Sherburne suggests, would be naturally less inclined to do so. Cleanliness, as embodied by the baker and his wife, was also associated with morality and refinement, reflected in their sympathy for the physical suffering of their guests. Their acceptance of the ragged Sherburne into their genteel home symbolized the republican values of democracy and equality, the readmission of the dirty to civilian life, and the recognition of the men's military service.

Despite these new meanings, however, the war does not seem to have transformed most Americans' fundamental practices of cleanliness or their understandings of the workings of the human body. Continental Army officers' efforts to instill habits of order and hygiene among their troops had no lasting effect on men returning to civilian life. For rural men who served in the Continental

Army, the strict discipline imposed by military superiors might have its place in an army camp but was useless back on the farm. The fact that provisioned women might have been behind the improved conditions meant that enlisted men's habits had changed very little. The army rejected the one approach that might have worked with ordinary men — the example of Jewish cleanliness rituals, detailed in the Old Testament and familiar even to illiterate men — for a top-down model of cleanliness as a discipline imposed by officers on the unwashed rabble and carried out, in large measure, by paid washerwomen. Injunctions to clean one's clothing and one's person thus remained unpleasant strictures on personal freedom that could be abandoned upon returning to civilian life, where women once again assumed responsibility for cleanliness.

Yet the war did have an impact on the meanings North Americans ascribed to cleanliness and its place in the new political landscape. At a critical moment of nation making, it strengthened the associations of cleanliness, both moral and physical, with the domestic realm. In the public memory of the war, cleanliness was persistently portrayed as domestic and connected to the labor of women. Sherburne's memoir is a prime example of this trope: filthy, starving men shed lice-infested rags for clean clothes and slept in comfortable featherbeds only after they crossed the thresholds of their own houses. Forced to make do with only the ragged clothes on their backs upon their release, Sherburne and his uncle depended on the hospitality of strangers for food and shelter, but they did not attempt to clean their bodies or don fresh clothes. Indeed, fearful of contaminating their hosts' clean bedding, they scrupled to sleep only with the dirty blankets they carried.

Returning to his family's household, Sherburne elicited tears from his mother and affectionate attentions from his sisters, who provided him with fresh garments. His brother, however, bore the initial responsibility for helping him clean his body. "My brother Samuel took me into another room to divest me of my filthy garments, wash and dress me," he reported. But Samuel was overcome when he saw Sherburne's emaciated body and was unable to assist further. "I was able to wash myself and put on my clothes," Sherburne noted, before collapsing in his bed. Here he remained for weeks, suffering from a relapse of his fever.[67] In this, as in several other narratives, the return to civilian life was described as a return to cleanliness, morality, and decency, symbolized by exchanging lousy rags for clean linen.

Not all postwar assessments shared this view of the inherent healthfulness of the domestic scene. Looking back on the war in 1785, Benjamin Rush, who had once advocated improving conditions in camps, offered a more ambivalent reading of the soldier's return home as a potentially dangerous transition from the rigors of camp life. Although Rush had been a vocal critic of the pitiful conditions of the army throughout much of the war, once it was over, he argued, the men's return to domestic comforts could have fatal consequences for their now hardened constitutions. Sherburne's description of his relapse after his homecoming presented an extreme example of the dangers of this transition. In light of Rush's other published concerns about the legacy of the Revolution and the proper course for citizenship, it seems that he feared the physical as well as moral consequences for men as they returned to a softer life.[68]

This concern with distinguishing hardy masculinity from domestic comfort was not new — we caught an early glimpse in John Floyer and Thomas Tryon's recommendations for health — but it nonetheless reflected the ambiguous legacy of the Revolution for American masculinity. Autonomy and discipline competed to define an ideal American manhood that remained fractured along lines of class and race. An emerging American sensibility, rooted in the experience of rural farmers' sons and the urban poor, opposed European affectation and genteel regimes of body care as indulgent, effete, and corrupt. Popular plays, poems, songs, and pamphlets mocked aristocratic pretension. From as early as the 1770s, cartoons, rhymes, and satiric plays made fun of men who appeared to be overly focused on their own persons. Lampooning macaronis, fops, dandies, mollies, and men of fashion, authors and engravers questioned the manhood of men devoted to grooming and fine clothing. Cartoon dandies became feminized, exhibiting swollen hips and breasts and tiny waists. Ridiculing men of fashion for their gender transgression became a way of voicing disapproval of men who transgressed class boundaries (Figure 6.1).[69]

While not the lone source of shifts in attitudes toward cleanliness — one can find examples of many of these ideas about cleanliness in England and France — the American reaction against genteel habits became an expression of patriotism and incipient national identity that competed with the interest in gentility. Pride in honest and wholesome rural ways, which were idealized as quintessentially American during the early republic, suffused the critiques of urban artifice, including the fussy manners and fastidiousness of city dwellers. Fashion-conscious urban women as well as rural women who put on airs were as subject to these criticisms as their menfolk, but with an important difference. Women were supposed to attend to the neatness of their households and persons — if they did not, they might be branded sluts or slovens. Men, in contrast, were expected to get a little grimy as they pursued farming and public life. In this version of the American Revolution, hardy sons of the soil returned to their labors in the fields after the conclusion of the war, sustained by the same virtue — in this case, dirt accumulated through honest toil — that had enabled them to triumph over the British enemy.

6.1. William Charles, *Modern Dandy's* (1807). Courtesy American
Antiquarian Society

Rush participated in important ways in the postwar refiguring of the implicit racial meanings linking cleanliness and citizenship. Before the war, Rush had held up Indian practices—for example, the habit of moderate eating—as a healthy alternative to gluttony at elite European tables. This use of Indians as a primitive foil for overly civilized European habits commonly appeared in eighteenth-century medical texts, both before and after the war, with specific reference to Indian bathing.[70] In contrast, in "An Account of the Vices Peculiar to the Indians of North America" (1798), Rush linked the alleged moral and sexual uncleanness of Native Americans to poor hygiene. He faulted Indians for uncleanness—the absence of "morality and decency, as far as they relate to the marriage bed," a refrain that dated back to Vespucci—and nastiness, as revealed by their "food—drinks—dress—persons—and above all, in their total disregard to decency in the *time—place—*and *manner* of their natural evacuations."[71] He argued, in essence, that the natural tendencies of the native inhabitants of the continent—namely, their incontinence—rendered them unfit for possessing the land. Indians, rather than unruly Continental Army soldiers, failed to live up to the standards of cleanliness, civility, and citizenship. Had he applied the same criteria to combatants during the war, however, he would have been compelled to predict victory by highly disciplined British troops rather than by the Americans, with their disregard for camp hygiene.

The Continental Army was neither the first nor the last army to suffer from sanitary problems or from the discrepancy between the cleanliness habits of enlisted men and officers. Rather, it was the extremity of these problems, the fact that they occurred during a war for independence in which a national identity had yet to take hold, and the American hope that virtue would enable them to triumph over the British enemy that made the problems with filth significant. In the wartime discussions, at least two models for cleanliness appeared, although they were not always distinct. In one, advocated by elite, cosmopolitan men like Benjamin Rush, cleanliness was a body discipline imposed by elite officers on their social inferiors. According to this model, the demands of nationhood and the interests of public health justified the imposition of discipline upon the individual's body. Such discipline enabled the individual, who might otherwise pose a threat to the nation or the public good, to become a valuable citizen, capable of serving the nation. Elite commanding officers revealed that they saw certain bodies—clean, well fed, and sufficiently clothed, but also white, mature, property owning—as most able to achieve this feat of discipline.

The second model of cleanliness embraced virtuous voluntarism. Ordinary soldiers need only be persuaded of the necessity of cleanliness for health and military success for higher standards of personal cleanliness to take hold. Rather than imposed discipline and nationhood, this second model relied upon persuasion, religious belief, and individual responsibility—although it ultimately delegated much of the work of cleanliness to women. Noncommissioned officers, commissioned officers of lower rank, and especially militia officers, who often came from the same communities as the men under their command, were caught in the middle of this conflict. The war also pitted military exigencies against civilian mores and gentlemen's standards against those of laboring men, leaving a mixed legacy for ideals of American manhood.

The war also contributed to a new sensibility about basic expectations for humane conditions, one that realigned eighteenth-century meanings of gentility. Publicity about atrocities in British prisons stressed the enemy's barbarity and the innocent suffering of American prisoners, subjected against their will to filthy conditions. Such concepts—of human suffering inflicted by denying people the ability to combat the filth of their bodies and their surroundings—created a foundation for postwar humanitarian reform. True gentility could not be assessed simply by judging appearances but rather by considering how one endured suffering and attempted to ameliorate the bodily misery of others.

Part III

TRANSFORMING BODY WORK

By the early nineteenth century, the domestic sources of cleanliness had become more prominent in public discussion and explicitly connected to the important task of nation making. Having been presented as a matter of male military success and pride during the war, bodily cleanliness retained its patriotic associations, appearing in American medical advice books as a prerequisite for a successful democracy because it promised to protect the state from the burden of "weak" and "effeminate" citizens. Increasingly, the individuals charged with disciplining the bodies of male citizens were neither generals nor quartermasters but mothers, upon whose shoulders the fate of the nation rested. When this happened, a new chapter began in the history of cleanliness, featuring mothers, social reformers, and methods of body care that are more familiar to the modern reader. A signal part of this transformation was the changing view of certain female bodies; under certain circumstances, mothers might be sources of refinement and cleanliness.

One of the opening salvos of this new regime of body care came in 1811, when the New York publisher Isaac Riley released a pocket-sized volume of medical advice dedicated to the care of infants and young children. *The Maternal Physician: A Treatise on the Nurture and Management of Infants, from the Birth until Two Years Old* claims the dual distinction of being the first child-care manual written and published in the United States and one of the earliest American health guides of any kind. It was also the first book of medical advice written by an American woman, who identified herself on the title page as "an American matron." Offering extracts from "the most approved medical authors" as well as the fruits of her "sixteen years' experience in the nursery," the anonymous author hoped to provide readers "with a concise and simple statement of the characteristic symptoms of the various complaints to which children are subject, in so small a compass that it may become a pocket companion." Although much about the book's publishing history remains unknown, its New York edition sold well enough to justify the publication of a second edition in Philadelphia in 1818. Nineteen years later, when Lydia Maria Child completed *The Family Nurse*, her own volume of popular advice, *The Maternal Physician* was among the works cited. Only recently have scholars identified its author as Mary Hunt Palmer Tyler, wife of the playwright Royall Tyler, whose popular play *The Contrast* urged Americans to redefine ideals of manhood and whose scandalous sexual conduct has now come to light.[1]

Tyler responded to shifts in medical and maternal authority at a time when physicians were still struggling to prove their legitimacy and the concept of republican motherhood connected the domestic labors of a privileged group of mothers to the needs of the fledgling nation. Her advice to American mothers included recommendations for diet, clothing, the domestic environment, and care of babies' bodies. Tackling suspicions about bathing that were only beginning to give way to beliefs in its importance for health, Tyler urged mothers to wash infants daily with cold water. The combination of her gender and the genre of her published advice make her an interesting outlier: male doctors wrote most of the popular medical advice books in Britain and North America before 1850. Before Tyler, moreover, male doctors had monopolized the publication of advice on the care of infants and children. Women's books, in contrast, focused on midwifery, the household, cookery, or tales for children. Tyler entered the field of popular medical advice, basing her claims not only on book knowledge but on her experience as a mother.[2]

Tyler joined a chorus of popular medical authors articulating a new vision of domestic healing. Many literate Americans knew of William Buchan's popular advice book *Domestic Medicine*, in print in North America since 1772 and still circulating in the early nineteenth century. Buchan, his Swiss counterpart S. A. Tissot, and the German Bernhard Christoph Faust all emphasized the importance of domestic resources like cleanliness, diet, fresh air, and clean water for the health of ordinary people. Indeed, they shared a vision of public health, built upon the wholesomeness of each household, in which the mistress of the house played a vital role as steward.[3]

Even as these European writers and numerous lesser-known Americans stressed the role of the domestic environment for good health, authority for health care had begun to shift subtly to the public realm. In part, this shift reflected efforts at professionalization by academically trained doctors, but it was also a product of the debates surrounding North American epidemics between 1790 and 1820. Following the smallpox outbreaks of the revolutionary and early national years, North America's cities were periodically devastated by yellow fever and typhoid. Growing urban areas and commercial networks created new venues for disease. Yellow fever, a viral disease transmitted to humans by mosquitoes, hit Philadelphia several times during the 1790s, prompting city officials to enact new policies to promote cleaner air, streets, and water. Faced with an epidemic whose origins they did not fully understand, doctors debated the likely sources and possible cures, generating an unprecedented public conversation about disease, urban life, poverty, and cleanliness. The stakes were high: credibility for a fledgling profession that had not yet standardized training and practice or overcome the skepticism of ordinary people.[4] Despite the lack of consensus, city and state officials mobilized to clean urban spaces — indeed, these early sanitary measures were often the only thing everyone could agree on.

As turn-of-the-century epidemics brought the diseased body into sharp public focus, domestic body work began a long and gradual transformation. During the first four decades of the nineteenth century, northern housewives renewed their efforts to produce bodily comfort by manufacturing cloth, laundering linens, and cleaning the household with greater intensity than they had in the past. Women still practiced the healing arts, but they were more likely to focus on providing bodily comfort through cleanliness and less likely to become healing specialists. A veritable marketplace of doctors, advice books, medical theories, and medicines offered housewives the chance to become health care consumers. Maintaining the domestic environment and producing clean bodies became a primary part of the housewife's responsibility for her household's health. But it also left somewhat vague the division of labor between the mistress of the house, in her role as housewife and mother, and the doctor, whose public visibility became greater with each epidemic even if his medical credibility did not.

More curious still was the new prominence of the maternal body in medical advice books, children's literature, and household management books. Diagnoses of the female body as inherently diseased and filthy intensified, yet popular medical guides and advice books charted the path to redemption. If sexual activity and reproductive capacity lay at the root of the female body's putrid state, redemption came with increased vigilance over that body's cleanliness and new responsibility for the health and appearance of children. This revised package of female duties marked a northern departure from the older ethos of refinement jointly embraced by prosperous southerners and northerners. In its early expression, bourgeois motherhood resembled this older ideal for female refinement.

Redeemed from Eve's filth and expected to protect her husband, children, and her household from disease and moral decay, the antebellum mother lost some of her authority to heal. In its place came the burden of new expectations for the mother's literal embodiment of cleanliness and new health and class-driven imperatives to provide scrupulous and intimate care for children's bodies.[5]

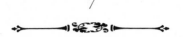

7

REIMAGINING SICKNESS AND HEALTH

BODY WORK IN THE URBAN ENVIRONMENT

Mary Tyler's effort to stake out terrain for maternal healers came in the wake of debates about public health that featured competing theories about disease transmission and the rising influence, if not actual legitimacy, of university-trained physicians (still only a small minority of doctors). These debates continued the slow but inexorable shift in healing authority from its roots in domestic practice to a growing interest in public health. Philadelphia's 1793 epidemic was the city's sixth episode of yellow fever in the eighteenth century and the first of four outbreaks during the 1790s. It was also North America's first major urban yellow fever epidemic. The intensity of the public response, however, was not simply a consequence of the epidemic's severity. Rather, as the historian Susan Klepp has argued, both the context of declining death rates immediately before the outbreak and the political ramifications of its spread to what was then the nation's capital, the heart of the republican body politic, made the sudden onset of this deadly disease more dramatic. As the first urban epidemic after the Revolutionary War to test the assumptions linking the political health of the new nation with the health of its citizens, yellow fever unnerved political observers when it spread to the seat of government. Doctors like Benjamin Rush, who had for many years commented on the analogous workings of physical bodies and the body politic, saw the crisis as a political as well as a medical test of the credibility of doctors.[1]

Philadelphia's yellow fever epidemic foreshadowed the public nature of nineteenth-century debates about competing medical explanations — none of them capable of accounting for all the patterns of disease transmission, mortality, and cure — and the struggles of municipal authorities to respond effectively to health crises by cleaning streets, purifying sick chambers, and relocating hospitals and cemeteries. In Philadelphia, doctors who embraced environmental theories of disease transmission followed Rush in arguing that the combination of weather, local conditions, and a shipment of rotting coffee beans created unhealthy air that overstimulated the victims' blood vessels, causing fever. The theory that the characteristics of a site determined its pattern of epidemic disease — an environmental view supported by William Currie's *Historical Account of Climates and Diseases of the United States* (1792), among other works — enabled doctors to explain large epidemics even if it failed to explain the spread of disease from victim to victim. Both older humoral and newer theories about the body's solid structures were deployed to explain the outcomes of individual cases — why some people suffered death while others recovered or never sickened at all. Rush's opponents, in contrast, advocated a model of contagion, arguing that sick refugees from Saint-Domingue (now Haiti) carried the disease to the city. Although they criticized the inefficacy of Rush's heroic methods of bloodletting and medication, his opponents could not explain why Rush, who had been exposed to hundreds of sick patients, had not been infected himself.[2]

The body that emerged during these public discussions was vulnerable, according to Rush, to unwholesome stenches and putrefaction of the air; and, according to his opponents, to the contagious effluvium of diseased West Indian bodies. In either scenario, large numbers of people could become ill, falling victim to the putrid piles of refuse on city streets or docks, to the damp air blowing east from millponds, or from the presence of sick people. The body susceptible to yellow fever was practically defenseless against airborne hazards, whether local, inanimate, imported, or human. Whether one blamed the environment or contagion, moreover, it was clear that these threats were greatest in the city — especially in the damp and filth of its poorer neighborhoods near the waterfront — and less dangerous in the countryside.[3]

Environmental and contagion theories for yellow fever transmission overlapped, making it possible for both arguments to be used in support of improving city sanitation efforts. City officials responded to the crisis in 1793 much as their counterparts in North American and European cities had done for centuries. They called for draining stagnant water, removing filth from the streets, increasing the wholesomeness and capacity of hospitals, and ventilating the closed quarters of sick chambers and households. Rush, who had made his debut in the city's public life during the 1762 yellow fever epidemic as Doctor Thomas Bond's assistant, had decades of experience supporting urban health efforts. His medical analysis of the causes of yellow fever pointed to the importance of street cleaning and challenged the need for quarantine. This latter measure had little support from the business community, which feared its effects upon commerce.[4]

Mayor Matthew Clarkson fell in line with the environmental approach, which was almost the only feasible response to disease for an eighteenth-century municipal authority. He reacted to initial reports of yellow fever by reissuing an old law requiring householders to clean out their walks and gutters and pile trash in street for scavengers. He also ordered the city's three major markets, especially the butcher shops, to be cleared of filth and rotting matter and washed with water. Water Street, the first site of infection and the closest to the stenches of the Delaware River, was his first priority for cleaning, to be followed by the other streets, where the air seemed healthier. The city fell short in most of its early cleanup efforts, including those calling for the immediate establishment of a hospital in an airy and healthy place. Yet the call-and-response pattern of physician advice to clean the city and municipal efforts to implement new sanitation measures created a powerful, if still clearly fallible, partnership to protect the health of the city.[5]

As news of the fever spread, Philadelphia's denizens dispensed advice that revealed widespread and popular belief in the miasmic transmission of disease. Contributors to local newspapers urged readers to purify the air of their houses with tobacco smoke, vinegar, fresh earth on the floor, or lengths of tarred rope. Reflecting beliefs in fire's purifying qualities, others urged citizens to light bonfires in the streets. Inadvertently stumbling on the main vector for transmission, disease-carrying mosquitoes—even if his concern was probably rooted in beliefs that contagious air caused the proliferation of pests—one author suggested that each household top off its water barrels with a small quantity of oil to kill mosquito larvae. To protect against infection, contributors recommended using strong-smelling substances such as camphor, vinegar, tobacco, and garlic to create individual pockets of purified air around the persons of those compelled to venture outdoors or interact with the sick. These remedies might be worn around the neck in linen bags, soaked into a sponge, snorted up the nostrils, chewed, or smoked. Most derived from apocryphal stories of survival from previous plagues but all were grounded in popular beliefs that disease could be spread by breathing infected air.[6]

Efforts to improve the wholesomeness of the urban habitat sparked new domestic practices. Households transformed their routines through precautions to protect themselves from contagious agents and to reassure others that they posed no danger of infection. Some tried to make household air healthier by whitewashing their walls with lime, burning gunpowder, nitre, or tobacco, sprinkling vinegar, or scouring kitchens, walls, and floors. The College of Physicians endorsed most of these measures as effective means of improving indoor air quality. They also urged that sickrooms be well ventilated, their beds stripped of curtains, and all fouled linens and chamber pots removed. Before it could be used again, moreover, the bedding and clothing of the deceased needed to be purified with smoke and their chambers thoroughly cleansed of infection. During the epidemic, these labors, along with care of the sick, traditionally performed by women, increased exponentially.[7]

Contagion theories grounded the practices of Philadelphians who hoped to take refuge from the disease in other locales. Upon learning that the residents of Albany, New York, were opposed to his visit in September 1793, at the height of the epidemic, the Federalist Alexander Hamilton wrote to Abraham Yates and General Philip Schuyler, his host and father-in-law, to reassure them that he was free of contagion. Both Hamilton and his wife had been attacked by the disease but had recovered and were now, according to their physicians, disease free. They had taken other precautions to avoid reinfection. In addition to residing two and half miles outside of Philadelphia, at their summer house, and avoiding all trips into the city for nearly three weeks, they had left their servants in an informal quarantine across the river from Albany. Hamilton struggled to reassure Yates that they were "particularly careful in leaving behind us every article of cloathing which had been on us or near us from the earliest approach of the complaint." The exception to this rule was their personal "linnen which was first thoroughly washed." Hamilton invoked the widespread belief that laundering destroyed the contagion in the linens of diseased people, noting "with regard to washed articles, common sense will at once pronounce that there can be no possibility of danger."[8]

Climbing death rates and the exodus of nearly one-quarter of Philadelphia's white population created labor shortages that reinforced racial and environmental assumptions about the disease. White women seem to have been more likely than their menfolk to escape the city with children, causing acute shortages of female labor. Women were normally responsible for nursing the sick, preparing shrouds, and washing and laying out the dead. Their death work transcended class to some degree—all women were expected to have intimate contact with the sick and dying, although wealthy women were more likely to hire nurses or watchers—but male death work was distinctly lower class: cleaning streets, building coffins, transporting bodies, and digging graves. Obliged by their much-touted hardiness and the unending need to prove their worth as citizens, Philadelphia's black population was expected to fill in as nurses, transporters of the sick and deceased, and graveyard diggers—in short, any hazardous occupation that white people's vulnerability made them unable to do. Depending upon their sex, then, black people entered the scenes of white illness in domestic settings or as part of the public response to widespread mortality.[9]

Lifetimes spent in Philadelphia's unhealthy miasmas—the confluence of deadly environmental and contagious factors theorized by medical authorities to be so deadly for white people—were assumed by contemporaries to have little effect on black people. The bodies of black people remained defined by their skin pigment and their alleged immunity to the disease, two linked characteristics that initially were not complicated by place of birth. Eventually it became clear that black people died from yellow fever at significant rates, although not as high as those for white people: roughly 9 to 11 percent of black victims succumbed compared with 14 percent of white victims. Only after black people revealed vulnerability to yellow fever did the College of Physicians conclude in 1797 that natives of Africa, rather than black people generally, carried the immunity. Yet racial models of the vulnerable white body, sickened by the very air it breathed, and the hardy, constitutionally invulnerable black body were not immediately revised. Doctors could not explain conflicting evidence of immunity among migrants, white and black, who had been exposed to the disease in the Caribbean or the South. The initial refusal to acknowledge the black death rate persisted, owing not only to the labor shortage created by disease but also to the tenacity of racial models and the tendency of white city officials and chroniclers of the disaster to value black life less than white.[10]

Subsequent yellow fever outbreaks heightened the importance of household cleanliness for public health.[11] The physician John Vaughan, who had attended medical lectures at the University of Pennsylvania in 1793 and 1794, viewed the disease patterns of his patients in Wilmington, Delaware, through the lenses of both the environment and contagion. He sought to stem the tide of infection by cleaning the city's public spaces and private properties. During that city's yellow fever episode of 1802, Vaughan kept detailed notes, which ultimately became the basis for an American Philosophical Society pamphlet on yellow fever. He identified the first patient as Ann Davidson, who lived next door to Hadley's cellar, a basement that had long been a sink for stagnant water and the most offensive filth, "of hogpens & Cloacinian ordure." The city's physicians responded to inquiries from the Board of Health by "*laying aside* technical differences" and recommending the "necessity of cleansing the lower parts of the town and removing all putrefactious materials from the streets, cellars, yards &c without further delay." They affirmed their conviction that, whether contagious or not, the strength of the "bilious fever" would likely be influenced by "the sensible qualities of the atmosphere." In his own notes on the epidemic, Vaughan recorded the unwholesome smell of bilge water poisoning the air downtown and the thick clouds of mosquitoes uptown. No one in Wilmington could remember so many pesky insects for at least a generation.[12]

Vaughan's colleague, Dr. Joseph Bailey, noted that the flight of residents from the lower parts of town in the neighborhood surrounding Hadley's cellar might actually heighten the threat to public health by increasing the environmental hazards in the now-abandoned households. Bailey urged that all "alleys, cellars, yards, sinks, rain-water-casks, and hog-styes" be examined and cleansed. He also worried about decaying green wood and other vegetable matter, left to rot in deserted cellars and outhouses, emitting "noxious air." All deserted enclosures should be examined, he urged, and all houses must be "regularly opened & ventilated once in every twenty four hours." He recommended that particularly filthy or suspicious places might be strewn with lime to lessen the danger.

Vaughan worried that many of these measures stirred up unwholesome effluvia and might actually aggravate the conditions of disease. "If the filth of the prescribed cellars &c w[e]re now stirred up, and set afloat in the air, it would not be generally diffused in the atmosphere, but hover about us in the disguised shape of fog, until dissipated by a fortuitous change of weather or disarmed by frost," he warned his friend Isaac Dixon on September 23. "There are many instances of embedded filth being disengaged at improper seasons, to the great injury and destruction of mankind," he noted, urging caution in dealing with toxic sites like Hadley's cellar. Best to "cover it over, until frost," he thought, or "hastily drain it off during a strong northerly wind, into a well dug for the purpose, & correct the remaining ordure with lime."[13]

By the early nineteenth century, cleanliness of place had become synonymous with disease prevention. Urban public health seemed to depend upon how people managed their households: the way they disposed of garbage, cared for livestock, ventilated their chambers, and constructed and maintained their outhouses. Yellow fever spurred city residents to such collective measures as street cleaning, efficient garbage collection, and the provision of hospitals, a process that helped to medicalize public authority. But it also sparked discussion about domestic practices, including those that focused on the body.[14]

BATHING

Bathing enthusiasts and new installations of baths and showers appeared in nearly every eastern city during the early nineteenth century, but the turn to bathing had already begun in Philadelphia, where public debates about the connections between disease prevention and cleanliness reached their apogee in the 1790s. That decade also marked the arrival of refugees from Saint-Domingue, who established several public facilities known to customers as French baths. Seized with the spirit of perfectionism that infused the activities of turn-of-the-century moral reformers, evangelicals, and patriotic supporters of the republican experiment, the health-conscious turned to new hygienic practices out of the desire to improve their own and their community's health. Public discussions about disease prevention and urban sanitation convinced Philadelphians that a plentiful supply of pure water was necessary for the health of city residents. Such discussions raised the awareness not only of the dangers of polluted water, with its noxious miasmic vapors and potential to poison, but of the positive good of wholesome water. By 1800 the city supported several plans to improve access to pure water, including the purchase of the Delaware and Schuylkill canal and sponsorship of a steam-powered waterworks, the nation's first large-scale watering system. By January 1801 the municipal waterworks had begun supplying the city with water, giving rise to its nineteenth-century reputation for cleanliness.[15]

These measures coincided with a resurgence of interest in water's powers to revitalize the body. Benjamin Rush's *Directions for the Use of the Mineral Water and Cold Bath* (1786) echoed an older generation of physicians in England and on the Continent, who saw cold bathing not just as a means of removing filth but as a healthful stimulant to the circulation that enhanced organ function and ultimately warmed the body. Cold baths improved the health by allowing a person to "wash off impurities of all kinds from the skin . . . thereby promot[ing] a free and equal perspiration." Water also created healthful pressure on the body's fluids, braced the animal fibers, and stimulated the entire nervous system in ways that strengthened and revitalized the body. Rush recommended the use of the cold bath every day for patients seeking to restore their health, and at least three times a week for those seeking to preserve it.[16]

But across the Atlantic the trend was clearly moving toward acceptance of warm water bathing. William Falconer, the reigning doctor at Bath, extolled warm water's virtues as a stimulant and skin cleanser in *Essay on the Bath Waters* (1772). Echoing Tobias Smollett, he distinguished between mineral waters and "simple water" for domestic use and urged the use of the latter in shower baths, tubs, and vapor baths.[17] In his 1803 *Advice to Mothers*, William Buchan modified his call for cold bathing, citing the danger to infants, and urged instead that bathwater initially be lukewarm. A. F. M. Willich, Christian Struve, and others heralded cleanliness as both a moral virtue and a key means of safeguarding health. Both recommended frequent warm-water baths to maintain the skin's health. Meanwhile, refurbished facilities in Bath and new bathhouses in London contributed to a peak in bathing—in both cold and warm water—during the 1790s.[18]

7.1. Amos Doolittle, *David and Bath-Sheba*, in *The Self-Interpreting Bible* (New York, 1792). Courtesy American Antiquarian Society

These positive associations of bathing with cleanliness and health were at odds with familiar depictions of bathing as morally suspect and dangerous. American hostility to bathing had intensified after the American and French Revolutions as part of the larger reaction against European corruption and the embrace of rural wholesomeness as quintessentially American. Most American engravers' representations of bathing connoted vice, seduction, and vulnerability, none of which was compatible with virtuous citizenship in the new nation. Tainted by associations with French moral corruption and the sexual license suggested by nudity, bathing raised issues of questionable morals and vulnerability, as in an American engraving of David spying upon Bathsheba from the *Self-Interpreting Bible* (1792; Figure 7.1).

Artists typically depicted women and children at the bath, preparing to immerse their naked bodies in water. In these scenes, they were implicitly or explicitly subject to the gaze of a male onlooker, a trope common to bathing scenes from sixteenth-, seventeenth-, and eighteenth-century European paintings. While appropriate when fixed upon social dependents and inferiors, as in the engraving of young boys swimming from the Philadelphia edition of Johan Guts-Muths *Gymnastics for Youth* (1802; Figure 7.2), such a gaze upon naked adult men clashed with ideals of independent male virtue and departed from the usual depictions of bathing as a feminine indulgence. It just wasn't done.

In American depictions of bathing, female virtue seemed to be at risk. To take one example from a Boston edition of an English work on adultery and divorce, *The Cuckold's Chronicle* (1798), the engraving showed a man (presumably an adulterous lover) peeping at an aristocratic woman through a window in the bathhouse as she is about to take her bath (Figure 7.3). Lacking a male onlooker, amateur poet John M. Breese anthropomorphized the wooden planks of the bathhouse:

> Oh! Had these senseless boards but eyes,
> How they would gaze in pleas'd surprise,
> At each fair form that's here displayed!
> Pleasure to great for mortal sight,
> to Jove himself 'twould give delight,
> Unseen to view each naked maid.[19]

Most ordinary Americans lived in rural areas, where moral suspicion surrounding bathing only reinforced the disincentives: the belief that it was unnecessary for health in the wholesome atmosphere of the countryside, and the practical difficulties of procuring and heating water. The author Charles Brockden Brown probably did not exaggerate when he claimed in 1804 that most Ameri-

Bathing & Swimming

7.2. "Bathing and Swimming," in Johann C. Guts-Muths, *Gymnastics for Youth* (Philadelphia, 1802). Courtesy American Antiquarian Society

7.3. "Lady Worsley Dressing in the Bathing House." *The Cuckold's Chronicle* (Boston, 1798)

cans passed through life without bathing more than once a year. This was probably truer of the average northerner, with whom Brown was more familiar, than of wealthy white southerners who continued to define themselves as genteel.[20] His comment points not to the unrepentant filth of most Americans, as several modern historians have assumed, but to the changing sensibilities of elite city residents like himself who had begun to integrate water-based cleanliness of the entire body into older practices based on linen.

Mainly, then, the association of bathing with sinful pleasures remained strong during this period, but there were two exceptions: the moral injunctions to water-based cleanliness in children's literature, a topic to which we will return, and the tiny but growing number of well-to-do urban dwellers, interested in warm rather than cold bathing, who invested in bathtubs and showers. As the historians Richard and Claudia Bushman have suggested, this interest in the bath reflected several late-Enlightenment trends, including the religious emphasis on individual responsibility and reform, the growing concern with gentility, and the chorus of medical authors who advocated cleanliness.[21]

By the last two decades of the eighteenth century, shower baths and bathtubs had begun to appear in a handful of elite homes, especially in Philadelphia, where wealth, a large Quaker population, and the city's cosmopolitan character encouraged elite residents to care for their bodies. During the colonial period, few households would have boasted more than a washstand for each bedroom and a commode, but by 1790 the wealthy were ready to try new gadgets. The advertised inventory of John Penn Jr., for example, published in May 1788, listed both a washing stand and a tin shower bath. The Philadelphia merchant John Carson had a shower bath in his home in 1790. Bathtubs installed in Rose Hill Manor, home of Maryland Governor Thomas Johnson between 1794 and 1819, and in the Williamsburg home of St. George Tucker in 1796 suggest that bathing's appeal extended well beyond Philadelphia. Bathing equipment continued to be viewed as newfangled and unusual, however, as Thomas Sandeford's reply to the Philadelphian Samuel Meridai's request to fix his shower bath suggests — neither party knew what the fee for such a repair should be.[22]

The Drinker household marked the new turn to bathing with the purchase of a shower bath in 1798. Elizabeth Drinker's husband, Henry, her daughter Nancy Skyrin, and Nancy's maid Patience each showered many times that summer. Elizabeth felt poorly during much of July and waited until the next summer to "pull the string." When she finally got up her courage to use it, she noted that it was the first time she had immersed her entire body in twenty-eight years.[23] In 1803 the Drinkers bought a bathing tub, an expensive wooden model lined with tin, but William continued to visit the public bath at 3rd and Arch Streets, to use up bath tickets and because it was less trouble than filling, heating, and emptying water for the tub at home. Public discussions about body care combined with the city's growing conviction of the healthfulness of pure water to enable wealthy Philadelphians like the Drinkers to let go of their reluctance to bathe. In their case, the link between public works and private practice was direct. Their son Henry served on the city's Watering Commission during the time when his family installed their shower and then their bathtub.[24]

But the Drinkers were certainly not the only ones to make this connection. Seizing on the new interest in cleanliness and health, the scientist Charles Wilson Peale urged readers of his *Epistle to a Friend on the Means of Preserving Health* (1803) to consider cleaning the body inside and out by means of clysters (purgative enemas) and bathing. Whereas clysters, he claimed, presented "the most ready and effectual means to cleanse away filth" inside the body, "frequent *bathing* is good through all seasons, but more especially in Summer."[25] Cleanliness, he wrote, had helped him to avoid yellow fever during the recent epidemics: "When I was exposed to the infection of yellow fever, it was my practice to take a pail of cold water to my bed-room and wash from head to foot either in the morning or evening." Reassuring the anxious reader, he insisted that the practice was not "the least dangerous, even to those of a delicate habit, taking the precaution to begin with washing and rubbing the hands and feet: and after completely cleaning the whole frame, to rub till perfectly dry with a *coarse* linen towel." "*Cleanliness* is commendable," he declared, a comment that appears in his text juxtaposed with his regimen against yellow fever, thus linking health and virtue.[26]

Of the bathing methods available to his readers, Peale rated the luxurious plunging bath as safer than the shower bath and better for the health. But he conceded the difficulty of filling a plunging tub and heating the water on a regular basis, an inconvenience the Drinkers had discovered firsthand. The virtue of the pail method, in contrast, was that it was "simple, and so easy as to be in the reach of every one at all times." Water-based cleanliness depended, of course, on the availability of pure water. Peale noted in a postscript that putrid water could now be purified with a filter, a feat his son had recently demonstrated at City Tavern. But this achievement was not repeated on a grand scale in most eastern cities until late in the century.[27]

Peale's endorsement of bodily cleanliness testifies to the transatlantic bathing revival that was finding a receptive audience among wealthy and reform-minded Americans. Robert Wallace Johnson's *Friendly Cautions*, published first in London in 1767 and in Philadelphia in 1804, joined the growing list of medical works urging people to clean the surface of their bodies with water. The newly established Pennsylvania Hospital installed a shower bath for residents in 1799. Other communities built public baths by subscription. Henry Drinker went to investigate one in Downingtown, Pennsylvania, where a large German population had reinvented Old World traditions of public bathing. In New York, Nicholas Denise announced the completion of a bathhouse with eight rooms in 1792. The public bathhouse that William Drinker patronized was one of Philadelphia's first, constructed in 1801. By 1823 Philadelphia's Watering Commission reported

401 baths in private households, a number that suggests that, for a small number of Americans, bathing had become an essential method of caring for the body.[28]

It is tempting to assume that this early-nineteenth-century bathing boom presaged practices of bodily cleanliness familiar today. But there were important differences: the emphasis upon bathing's health benefits, rather than upon what a twenty-first-century person would define as cleanliness per se; and the expansive notion of bathing as immersion of the body, not just in water but in steam vapor and air, for the purpose of stimulating and invigorating the constitution.[29] Thus Henry Wilson Lockette's thesis, "An Inaugural Dissertation on the Warm Bath" (1801), submitted to the University of Pennsylvania for the degree of doctor of medicine, concerned itself only with the consequences of immersion for the body's constitution rather than on the impact of cleanliness upon health. Conducting experiments on himself and his friends, Lockette tested the benefits of water baths of different temperatures and different durations. In each instance he measured the effects of bathing by gathering data on the subject's pulse rate, his reports of strength and weakness, and his digestion. Although he warned that excessive bathing at high temperatures was injurious to health and recommended it only in cases of inflammatory disease or fever, he concluded that the warm bath might be used "as a preventive of all those diseases which so frequently originate in crowded hospitals, jails, &c." Lockette theorized that the benefits were twofold: promoting perspiration, which cleared obstructions from the skin that set the stage for disease, and stimulating the body's constitution much like fresh air or exercise. Although the first of these benefits overlapped with contemporary claims for the benefits of cleanliness, Lockette saw the bath as a means to provoke a bodily process—perspiration—rather than as a way of removing obstructions from the skin's pores. Nor was Lockette wedded to the water bath as the only form of healthful bathing. He included a diagram of Peale's steam bath and cited the benefits of bathing enjoyed by Native Americans, Russians, and Siberians, all of whom resorted to vapor baths to cure illness.[30]

Lockette's endorsement of Peale's steam bath pointed to the entrepreneurial component of renewed interest in health and bathing. Early-nineteenth-century inventors seized upon the concept of bodily immersion and medical theories about the environmental causes of disease to promote patent bath machines. In essence, these machines created temporary environments for the body. Often, these patent baths had little or nothing to do with cleanliness, as we would define it today, but like Lockette's experiments, focused on stimulating and invigorating the body's constitution. The inventor Samuel K. Jennings, to take one example, issued a pamphlet advertising his patent warm and hot bath in 1814. Its two selling points, as Jennings saw it, were its portability and its heat. A cold body was not simply caused by being exposed to cold air, according to Jennings, but was a symptom of being insufficiently vigorous, a consequence of being raised effeminately. Jennings's bath counteracted these chills by sending heated air, produced by setting fire to ardent spirits, through a pipe. Using a different logic from cold-bathing advocates, Jennings promised to make patients hardier and less effeminate by heating them in his bath, a much-touted benefit of water and steam vapor baths as well.[31]

Even with uses of the bath that initially appear familiar to the modern reader, we find small discordances. When the Drinker family used their bathtub, several people bathed in the same water; once, during the summer of 1806, six people dipped in the warm water in succession. Recycling bathwater made sense from the standpoint of the labor invested in heating the water and filling the tub. It also made sense if one believed the salutary effects of the water bath derived from immersion rather than from pure water's powers to cleanse the skin. Yet, one wonders, were early-nineteenth-century bathers so untroubled by the accumulation of sweat and dirt in the used bathwater that they did they not perceive the sixth bath as a dangerous immersion in dirty water? How could water remove bodily filth and still retain its healthful properties?

Indeed, the succession of bathers in the Drinker household followed a pattern that suggests an awareness both of the dirt collecting in the water and of the family pecking order. When Henry Drinker Sr. bathed, he was nearly always the first person in the tub. Elizabeth, his wife, entered after her husband and son William had taken their turns. Servants bathed last. "I have no objection to going into it after my husband or son &c," the unassuming Elizabeth noted, but her children objected to dipping in dirty water: "William and Nancy chooses to be the first," she reported, "or not to go into it at all." On the day that record numbers made use of the Drinker tub, three of the bathers seem to have been servants, moving Elizabeth to comment, "If so many bodies were clensed, I think the water must have been foul enough."[32]

At least some of the healing powers attributed to water came from the romantic associations of natural springs and baths with nature—a particularly appealing thought for city dwellers seeking to recover their health. An 1811 article touting the benefits of Pennsylvania's Bristol Springs and Bedford Springs emphasized the healing inherent in the natural setting. For the Bristol Springs patient "with fevered frame," recovery would come from immersion in the rapturous beauties of nature as much as from the waters (Figure 7.4). Bedford's reputation as a medicinal springs, in contrast, was based on the healing properties of the water. Located in the oxygen-rich atmosphere of a mountain forest, Bedford Medicinal Springs came to the attention of health seekers in 1804 when

7.4. "Baths Near Bristol, Pennsylvania," in *The Portfolio*, n.s., vol. 5 (Philadelphia, 1811).
Courtesy American Antiquarian Society

a local mechanic drank and bathed in the waters and was relieved of his rheumatism and skin ulcers. The article detailed specific diseases for which the waters were particularly effective when ingested. Indeed, the flavorless quality of these springs was key to their appeal. Yet once the author had completed his discussion of the water's medicinal qualities, he fell back on a romantic ideal of health associated with nature: "Here amid the mazy forest, or rugged landscape, they steal the roses of youth from the zephyrs of the mountains and vallies, and purify their feelings, whilst they lave their bodies in the translucid streams, sparkling with the richest gems of Hygeia."[33]

Hopes for avoiding disease and beliefs in the virtues of cleanliness overlapped in personal practices of body care as well as in the larger urban sanitation and public health efforts of the period. In both instances, people evinced dissatisfaction with older filth removal techniques and experimented with new measures believed to improve individual and collective health. Still, suspicion of bathing remained great, as in this caveat issued by the University of Pennsylvania physician William Dewees in 1825: "We have employed the words bathing and washing synonymously in our present chapter. We think it necessary to explain this; as in no instance have we wished to be understood submersion by the term bathing; and when we have spoken of washing, it always had reference to the whole body undergoing this discipline, in distinction to the partial cleansing of the hands and face." Even the term *bathing* continued to have multiple and contested meanings that reflected widespread caution about immersing the body. The numbers of washtubs in estate inventories suggests that Dewees's careful parsing resonated with people willing to wash their bodies while they stood in a basin but unwilling to immerse themselves fully. Yet, as we have seen, for those well-to-do and self-consciously enlightened Americans who installed shower baths and bathtubs, as well as for those who supported subscriptions for new public baths or who purchased portable vapor baths, immersion of the body was key to the meaning of bathing.[34]

8

HEALING HOUSEWORK

How did the new interest in bathing affect the responsibilities of northern housewives for the health of their households? Did concerns about health hazards in cities recast housewives' priorities? Answering these questions requires that we take stock of domestic practices during the early nineteenth century and examine the relationship between healing and other housekeeping duties.

IS THERE A HEALER IN THE HOUSE?

Northern cities like Philadelphia and Wilmington confronted yellow fever earlier than their southern counterparts during the formative decade in nation making, a fact that was to have a lasting impact on northern domestic life. During the same decades, literate white northern women were receiving British bourgeois texts on manners, child rearing, and health, actively applying them to their own circumstances in North America. Indeed, the much-touted republican motherhood of northern women arose in part from the circumstances of their reception and translation of bourgeois values: in the midst of recurrent public health crises, northern women consumed texts that offered strategies for protecting the health of children. In contrast, urban health crises triggered by yellow fever did not become a feature of southern life until later in the nineteenth century, when the disease struck repeatedly in New Orleans, Charleston, Memphis, and Mobile and prompted efforts at public sanitation. Southern women, moreover, did not embrace republican motherhood with the enthusiasm of their northern counterparts; the hierarchical and highly ritualized nature of public culture in the south encouraged the emulation of aristocratic ways rather than the reception of the emerging bourgeois form. It is not surprising, then, that although southern women might have read and adopted the health advice of northerners like Mary Tyler, they did so for different reasons, from a commitment to an older interest in bodily refinement, and in the absence of public debate about the role of filth in disease transmission.[1]

Motivated by the desire to protect the family's health and its reputation for decency and morality, northern housewives invested considerable energy in body work: maintaining the bodies of household members while they were alive, caring for them during illnesses, and preparing their corpses for burial. The labor involved ranged from tasks we might classify as housework—manufacturing and washing clothes, preparing meals, killing vermin, sweeping dirt, making soap—to others we might consider part of the healing arts—alleviating the pain of sufferers and attempting to cure their ailments. The New Englander Elizabeth Cranch Norton's record of labor for 1797 was typical of the housewife's endless and extensive range of chores: in addition to laundering, mending, and making shirts for her husband, she scoured chambers, cleaned the buttery and kitchen, mended carpets, made butter, cheese, and soap, watched over a sick child, and assisted an ill neighbor with a clyster.[2]

Although popular medical literature increasingly saw women's role in disease prevention as stewardship over a healthy home, vulnerable to many of the same threats as the city itself, an older generation of female healers continued to be an important resource. They reacted to the growing public influence of doctors by integrating new resources into their arsenal. We might think of them as consumers, situated in a medical marketplace, as well as healers in their own right. This integrative response was in keeping with the methodology of traditional housewifery, exemplified by the receipt book, but we can also find this pattern in women's adaptation of household production to new consumer choices to purchase cloth and food. Choosing in certain instances to consume rather than produce or to call a doctor rather than to rely on receipt book remedies, women began to transform "body work."

For centuries, receipt books—the accumulated knowledge of the housewife's craft collected in recipes—had testified to the domestic medical wisdom of the housewife and local healer. Gathering conflicting advice derived from contradictory first principles and methods, receipt book authors retained a strong connection to folk traditions for healing, even though they included remedies and methods from academically trained doctors. Claims to efficacy—subsequently dismissed as rank empiricism by regular physicians—were the ultimate test of all remedies. A recipe from an unschooled person might thus present itself in such a book as equal in value to a wealthy landowner's or doctor's cure. This was the leveling potential of the receipt book.[3] Well into the nineteenth century, collections of receipts remained the most common textual sources for traditions of female healing (although men occasionally kept them, too) and our best evidence for how they constructed their authority as healers.

One particularly rich early American example of this tradition, the receipt book of Elizabeth Coates Paschall, provides a useful baseline for assessing the changing nature of body work. The daughter of a prominent Philadelphia Quaker and wife of the merchant Joseph Paschall, Elizabeth was born in 1702 and began keeping a receipt book sometime in her early adulthood, probably after she was married in the 1720s. Like other receipt books, hers is an eclectic collection containing recipes for pickled oysters and potted venison, directions for an ointment to relieve sore nipples, and a cure for "Pissing a Bed." This smorgasbord quality captures the porous nature of eighteenth-century domestic responsibilities, ranging from stain removal to making sausages to curing cancerous tumors.[4]

Paschall's recipes came from a variety of sources. She included recipes given to her by itinerant strangers as well as by neighbors, carefully noting the anecdotal evidence of efficacy in each case. As time passed, she included a growing number of remedies gleaned from newspapers and magazines—the *Pennsylvania Gazette* and the *London Magazine,* for example—and from medical texts. Indeed, the integration of print sources into the compilation distinguishes it from earlier receipt books. It reminds us, moreover, that even women healers who appear "traditional" by the standards of modern professional medicine actually ranged widely in their search for cures, more like hunter-gatherers than folk practitioners bound by custom. Their nineteenth-century counterparts built on this hunter-gatherer tradition and might be described as medical consumers who assessed competing cures and healers pragmatically rather than with a predisposition to consider only certain possibilities.[5]

Paschall's eclectic healing methods both competed with and complemented those of trained doctors, whom she regarded skeptically. She included some recipes because she believed they would make a physician's intervention unnecessary. Other recipes appear in her book because she had occasion to recommend them to grateful doctors, whose own remedies were failing. In still other cases, a remedy's efficacy became clear only after doctors had pronounced a case hopeless.[6]

When her book contained several remedies for a single ailment, Paschall gave no indication that one method or theory of healing was more trustworthy than another. Deciding which remedy to try first in situations of serious illness would have been an analytic process of the utmost importance, but her book offered few clues about how it happened. Empiricism—the trial-and-error method and the "experiential" data it yielded—accorded little inherent authority to a remedy because of its source or method, but it also provided little guidance for sifting through competing claims to efficacy. Her system for deciding among remedies may lie in the innumerable recorded details of patient symptoms, the administration of medicine, and the road to recovery—details available to female healers who took responsibility not only for curing the patient but for providing bodily comfort. But it is also likely that the availability of ingredients influenced her choice of remedy.

Paschall's book only hints at the relationship between her work as a healer and her other responsibilities as a housewife. She commented systematically on recipes designed to heal but rarely evaluated the efficacy of recipes for stain removers or mince pie. Did Paschall, like the Maine midwife Martha Ballard, invest more time and effort in her healing work because she found it more rewarding than her other labors? Or did the life-or-death consequences of healing give those recipes greater value?

By the early nineteenth century, housewives were less likely to be healing specialists like Paschall. For most white women, the work of healing, like the circumstances of most illness and injury, was embedded in rather than extractable from a domestic life in which expectations for bodily comfort and refined appearance were rising. The New Englander Hannah Heath's diary for a busy Monday in March 1808 testifies to the range of body work, including healing and laundry, that might take place on any given day: "a cloudy day we had hard work to get through with washing Mrs King does not improve upon acquaintance she is affraid of hard work, I tired my self out in trying to help[.] aunt White came over a little while to see how Charles was who swallowed a brass button, he did not appear to mind it much but we were anxious about."[7]

The child's mischief—swallowing a button that might have been deliberately removed from an item of clothing awaiting the wringer—reflected the task absorbing the attention of the adult women. Monday was laundry day for the Heath household, as it would have been in most nineteenth-century households. Cloudy weather meant that wet clothes would benefit little from drying and bleaching in the sun. In large households, women often hired other women, usually young and single, to help with the backbreaking work. Heath focused on the laundry and had little energy to look after her children.[8]

Doing laundry weekly rather than seasonally reflected the new intensity of domestic body work in the early nineteenth century. Sometime around the turn of the century, Monday became the universal day for laundry, replacing the old practice of a "washing week" every month or two. Numerous diaries from this period testify to the emergence of a designated day for this essential domestic chore. Women used this regular laundry day to wash shirts, shifts, aprons, stockings, bedding, household cloths, and diapers in the effort to keep bodies comfortable, healthy, and respectable. Every week, then, amid her other labors, Heath mobilized her household and hired help to do the wash.[9]

Why had the frequency of laundry increased? By the nineteenth century, many households boasted larger quantities of personal linens in their quest to keep up with rising expectations for the white garments associated with health, refinement, and national virtue. In October 1811, for example, Heath recorded washing "sixteen dozen" items in her Monday wash, a quantity that she noted on several other occasions.[10] Linen remained the standard for undergarments and household textiles on both sides of the Atlantic, but nineteenth-century consumers increasingly chose to wear white cottons and muslins next to their skins. Cheap cotton textiles required more frequent washing (and mending) to maintain their clean, white appearance. "D[oing] up muslins"—the curtains, sheets, and garments that took their name from the eastern origins of cotton—was particularly time-consuming and labor intensive. Gauzy white garments had come into fashion during the 1790s as a symbol of female purity, and they appeared prominently in the iconography of American national virtue. Respectable gentlemen, for their part, continued to wear shirts with white stocks, neck cloths, or cravats that could be laundered separately from the shirt itself (Figure 8.1).[11]

The labor of washday intensified at the turn of the century, owing to the increasing numbers of these fine garments and higher standards for their cleanliness. Rhymes lamenting the terrors of washing week gave way to those bemoaning "The Washing Day," although the sentiment expressed was nearly the same:

> The sky with clouds was overcast,
> The rain began to fall,
> My wife she beat the children,
> And raised a pretty squall;
> She bade me with a frowning look
> To get out of the way;
> The de'il a bit of comfort is there
> Upon a washing day.
> For its thump, thump, scold scold.
> Thump, thump away,
> The de'il a bit of comfort is there,
> Upon a washing day.

Washing day turned good-natured women into shrews who scolded their long-suffering husbands. On washday, a woman's family prayed for clear skies and hoped that no "gown or handkerchief" would accidentally be laid in a ditch. It

8.1. "Liberty and Washington" (ca. 1805). Courtesy Fenimore Art
Museum, Cooperstown, New York. Photo: Richard Walker

was certainly not the time for a man to invite a friend to dine, for there was no telling what might be served for supper.[12]

Monday laundering, like many other household tasks, reflected a growing convergence of the rhythms of housework and religious observance. Designating one day of the week for laundry reflected not only the material demand for clean, white garments but the need to prepare both body and spirit for the weekly Sabbath. The house needed to be put in order, baking done, and laundered clothes available so that Sunday might be a day of rest and attendance at public worship. Monday laundry day ensured a supply of clean, pressed, and mended clothes by week's end, allowing household laborers five days to complete the tasks of washing, drying, sewing, and ironing. Although putting on one's Sunday best had yet to become a national habit, among churchgoing people the need for neat Sunday attire was already dictating the housewife's schedule for laundering clothes. Doing laundry on Monday also permitted women to schedule their most strenuous day of labor immediately after a day of rest.[13]

Decades later, the antebellum house advice maven Eliza Leslie described weekly laundry as a distinctly American phenomenon and implied that it spoke well of American cleanliness: "In America most families have their washing done once a week. This is much better, in some respects, than the European custom of monthly or quarterly washes, as the clothes derive great injury from lying in their dirt; and also a quantity of clothing, often inconveniently large, is requisite when the intervals between the washes are so very long."[14] In fact, the shift to weekly laundry had also occurred in England by the early nineteenth century, although it may have become standard practice in some North American households sooner than it did for their British counterparts. American consumption habits—which, in turn, spurred the need for more laundering—reflected the pressure on Americans to represent their class position through personal appearance in a fluid society where social mobility (both upward and downward) was still possible.[15] The greater availability of female family members to assist with laundry in many rural American households probably also influenced its early transformation into a weekly chore.

Weekly laundry was easily the most consistent and strenuous type of body work performed in the household. Washing itself took nearly a full day and was accomplished much as it had been for centuries: with scrub brushes, washboards, and mangles, although occasionally a prosperous household might own a washing machine. Drying wet clothes might also take a full day, depending on the weather. Once dried, clothes needed to be ironed, a labor-intensive task that required a clean, flat surface for pressing and folding. Mending might precede or follow ironing, depending on the garment, and required close work to repair

8.2. Michele Felice Corne, *Hanging Out the Wash* (1800). Newport Historical Society

items damaged by the rigors of being washed.[16] Housewives disliked these other chores nearly as much as laundry but dutifully tackled them every week, less for health reasons (though vermin continued to be a concern) than out of the desire for a neat appearance that reflected positively on the family (Figures 8.2–8.4).

Once the ironing had been done and clean clothes returned to dresser drawers, attention turned to the house itself, with sweeping, beating carpets, dusting and "straightening up" as the main activities. Some of these chores inevitably spilled over into Saturday. As Anna Cushing, wife of a Brookline, Massachusetts, physician, put it after a day of polishing silver and "sweeping &c &c," "Saturday is an important day to housekeepers" that might be reserved for baking and other preparations for the Sabbath meal.[17] Monday laundry also diverted labor from meal preparation following the day when many households enjoyed a larger-than-normal spread for dinner.

8.3. Abel Bowen or Alonzo Hartwell, *Mending*, in *Rhymes for the Nursery* (Boston, 1837). Courtesy American Antiquarian Society

8.4. *Woman Ironing*, Pennsylvania (ca. 1819–1820), John Lewis Krimmel, sketchbooks, 1809–1821. Courtesy The Winterthur Library: Joseph Downs Collection of Manuscripts and Printed Ephemera

Weekly wash necessitated the regular performance of several other tasks to maintain a healthy household. Housewives needed to manufacture or purchase soap, still reserved mainly for laundering and washing objects rather than for use on bodies. Heath made her own soap from the by-products of other household labor—lye or potash and grease—which she assembled to make a leach. Despite her experience, the finished product varied in quality from the "very good soap" she made in February 1805 to the "pleasant soap" she attributed to "good luck" in April 1806 to a poor soap in February 1812. In other households, concerns about pump water being "hard" led to the search for better soap. *Freemason's Magazine* boasted of an Asian soap used by seamen that made it possible to use hard water rather than rain or river water for laundering.[18]

Cloth production was part of the effort to assure decency and health in many rural households. Like many of her fellow New Englanders, Heath spun, twisted yarn, and manufactured diaper web. Ruth Henshaw Bascom, who spent her life in small Massachusetts towns, recorded an ambitious schedule for cloth production that included spinning linen, cotton, and wool, carding, and weaving. She recorded her output from the late 1780s, when she was still a teenager, through the 1810s, when she was in her early forties and the mistress of her own household. Bascom's daily record of her cloth output was part of her calculation of productivity, an exercise that allowed her to estimate her own domestic virtue.[19]

Assessing female value in the tangible products of labor was a traditional, even reactionary, perspective at a time when many American women were beginning to pursue genteel occupations. George Wright, author of *The Lady's Miscellany; or, Pleasing Essays, Poems, Stories, and Examples, for the Instruction and Entertainment of the Female Sex in General, in Every Station of Life* (1797), pontificated on the importance of teaching girls useful skills: "I do not mean trailing of silk upon muslin, flouncing of gauze, and crimping of wires: but making my shirts, and the houshold linen, and now and then mixing a pudding, and tossing a pancake, when the maid is doing the drudgery of the house, or when we have no maid at all, which is often the case." Wright had a specific grievance prompting his recommendation: "My wife spends so much time in dressing," he complained, "that she cannot be of the least service in the kitchen."[20] Heath's rural routine made her the antithesis of Wright's fine lady, although her husband, like Wright, believed she spent too much and produced too little.

In their stewardship over their households, Heath and her contemporaries marked the beginning of a trend in which the housewife's responsibility for preventing disease grew and her authority as a healer declined. Her numerous labors were domestic expressions of medical environmentalism, evident in the calls for cleansing cities of filth. They found support among popular medical authors who saw themselves as defining a new role for housewives as caretakers of healthy households rather than as medical healers in their own right. On Wednesday, September 17, 1805, and again on Tuesday, October 9, Heath "clean[ed] house," a task that included airing chambers, washing windows, sweeping, dusting, cleaning carpets, scouring floors and pans, and removing candle wax drippings. These were familiar duties to all New England housewives and many southern mistresses, although in the South, women in well-appointed homes would have been more likely to assign the tasks to enslaved women. All of these chores would have been motivated as much by the desire to keep domestic spaces free of contagion and vermin as by the pursuit of a tidy appearance. On August 6, 1805, Heath noted "a tedious time cleaning bedstead," a reference to the labor-intensive work of killing vermin living in the joints of the bed frame. In May 1807 Heath arranged for a mason to whitewash the house, a chore that not only created a neat appearance but was also believed to provide some protection from smallpox and yellow fever because of the wash's lime content.[21]

In addition to these basic domestic chores, aimed at keeping bodies healthy and comfortable and prepared for their business in the larger world, Heath and her contemporaries actively attempted to heal sick and injured bodies. She reported on Wednesday, September 4, 1805, that she feared she had "killed" Miss Sawer, a young woman working for her, with "the dose she had yesterday." When her young nephew Frances fell ill, she "gave him antimony, made him puke three times, [and] carried a bed downstairs to lay by the fire with him." After her seven-year-old daughter Hannah became sick, she administered a "dose of rheubarb." At age ten, an ill Hannah received "two great spoons full of Antimony and two little spoonsfull," along with a dose of physic. The next day Heath followed up with blackberry root to relieve her daughter's pain, and then, in some desperation, she "borrowed Mr Lucas's syring," most likely in an effort to counteract constipation. Laudanum, procured from a doctor, helped Hannah through her pain during the next several days. When Heath's husband returned home sick from drinking beer with relatives, she reported an act that combined wifely tenderness, a remedy for a cold body, and an effort to make him more comfortable: "I got up and made a fire to heat him some water to put to his feet."[22]

Heath's recipe book, like those of generations of women before her in both England and North America, appears to have been her first resort when faced with common illness and injury. Although much less extensive than Paschall's and without commentary about the efficacy of particular remedies, Heath's book covered most of the ailments likely to occur in a nineteenth-century household filled with children: a recipe for curing colds and croup, a remedy for a sore throat (salt, vinegar, and water), and a "good salve for burns or any other sore." It also included a wash to alleviate the toothache, two cures for dysentery, a chicken broth remedy for "coleramorbus," a cure for a cough, and an ointment for the itch. Heath's duty to maintain a healthy domestic environment appears in the instructions "for cleansin a sick room." Inserting a hot poker into a pan of vinegar and saltpeter every four hours, she noted, would fumigate "the contagion of the distemper."[23]

Heath's store of recipes did not qualify her to be the local wise woman in the manner of Paschall, however. Heath used these remedies only for members of her own household, including people working there. In Heath's world the only nonacademically trained healers whose reputations extended beyond the walls of their own households were Mrs. Jackson, the local midwife, and Aunt Susannah White. Heath called in Jackson when she was about to give birth or was experiencing gynecological problems—frequent occurrences in the life of a woman who eventually bore nine living and one stillborn child. In contrast, White was her first consultant if a trusted recipe failed or if the problem seemed serious.[24]

White appeared to be somewhere between a local wise woman like Paschall and a family resource whose specialized domestic authority was limited to cases that did not require a midwife.[25] She is an intriguing historical protagonist: her ability as a healer was one of several special domestic skills she drew on to help the younger Heath at points of great stress in her family's life cycle. Her healing work reinforces the impression given by the Heath diary that care provided by domestic healers was part of a larger household effort to mobilize family labor. White's experience enabled Heath to delegate certain patients to her aunt so she could return her attention to other pressing household tasks. White's expertise was also highly valued by a household that could little spare female labor for nursing a chronically ill patient back to health. This is not to suggest that Heath viewed White's healing powers only instrumentally as a means of restoring household labor. Her terse diary entries clearly indicate the fear that accompanied the illness of any member of her household. But as Heath herself put it so elegantly after her sister was successfully brought to bed with a son, she hoped that her sister would "soon be restored to health and usefulness again." Health enabled one to be useful; sickness vitiated usefulness. Hannah Heath approached the task of healing as one of many domestic duties that contributed to her household's well-being and her own sense of purpose.

THE MATERNAL PHYSICIAN

The housewife and medical writer Mary Hunt Palmer Tyler tried to address the dilemma of the overlapping responsibility and competing medical authority of physicians and housewives with a unique intervention into debates about health care. One of the first women to write in the burgeoning genre of efforts to improve the health of citizens, Tyler translated these concerns into a regime of child care that could be practiced by republican mothers. Her advice, compiled in *The Maternal Physician* (1811), deferred to the superior medical training of academic physicians even as it delineated the special authority of mothers over the bodies of their young children. One part receipt book, one part popular medical guide, and a step removed from women's traditional expertise in midwifery, Tyler's book broke new ground for female healers, adapting it to their situation in a new nation. She also left a record of her domestic labor, allowing us to place her advocacy of women's maternal healing authority in the broader context of her housekeeping and child-rearing practice.

Tyler proposed a program of domestic healing that was at once more nationalistic, more cosmopolitan, more narrowly maternal, and more openly competitive with academic medical authority than that of her female contemporaries. She also embraced Enlightenment medical advice and adapted it to child rearing. Born in Boston in 1775, just a month before the clashes at Lexington and Concord, she identified her own coming of age with that of the nation and participated in self-conscious efforts to fashion intellectual and cultural independence.[26] Tyler eventually married her father's friend and her mother's erstwhile lover, the lawyer Royall Tyler, author of the novel *The Algerine Captive* and the play *The Contrast*.[27] Soon after, the Tylers moved to Vermont, where Royall assumed responsibilities as attorney general, judge, and, eventually, a state Supreme Court justice. In 1811, the year that Mary Tyler completed work on the *Maternal Physician*, she was thirty-five years old, living in rural Vermont, and the mother of eight children. In many ways, she seemed to emulate the ideal reader of medical guide books that the authors S. A. Tissot and William Buchan had envisioned: an educated rural matron, maintaining her own wholesome household, and dispensing medical knowledge to an uneducated peasantry.

In addition to her avant-garde medical ideas and pioneering role as a female medical author, Tyler engaged in extensive domestic textile production. Producing homespun was part of a trend in New England that overlapped with the rise of textile factories and commercial manufacture.[28] With the help of an unmarried sister, her daughters, and hired girls, she embarked on an ambitious plan for producing homespun cloth. Initially learning to spin flax and cotton during a period of unstable family finances in her youth, Tyler put these skills to use in her own household to produce fiber that she then gave to a neighbor to weave. This initial reliance on networks of neighbors and relatives to produce cloth might also have made it possible for information about child care to pass among several generations of women, a circumstance elided in Tyler's textual representation of her maternal authority as based mainly on her own experience. In the decade before she wrote *The Maternal Physician*, Tyler decided it was more cost effective to purchase a loom and use the labor within her household, supplemented by additional hired help. She used this home-produced cloth for the household as well as for the children's everyday clothing.

Tyler took the idea of republican motherhood to its literal and logical conclusion—the physical nurture of potential citizens—and integrated it into a New England framework for women's usefulness. In so doing she provided an American translation of the British imperial concern to improve maternal care for infants, what one scholar has described as "colonizing the breast."[29] As imperial power increasingly depended upon legions of able-bodied men to stake its claim, child nurture became yoked to empire. Thus Tyler claimed to have been provoked to write her guide for reasons similar to the imperial concerns that motivated the English physician-authors Hugh Smith and Michael Underwood: when reading some "old" newspapers, she was struck by the fact that so many children died before reaching the age of two. She laid the blame for this mortality squarely at the door of ill-informed mothers and nurses, who she believed mismanaged children to death, either directly, through bad care, or indirectly, by too quickly consigning them to the care of physicians. This was an interesting twist on the receipt book's skepticism of doctors who were as likely to kill as to cure. In contrast, when Tyler considered the blooming health of her own growing brood of children (who, her reasoning implied, had not been mismanaged), she could only look heavenward and give thanks. With her fellow American matrons as her intended audience, Tyler proposed to "take the babe from birth, and attend it through every stage until it is two years old; after which period children . . . will increase in health and strength without any attention except the ordinary care conducive to cleanliness and exercise, two points never to be dispensed with through life" (17–18).

Tyler organized her book around the assumption "Every Mother her Child's best Physician," a clever play on the stock claim of several popular medical manuals, "Every man his own physician." In the early pages of her book, she modestly distanced herself from her own advice, noting that her frequent summons of a doctor for the minor illnesses of her first child had provoked him to counsel her, "You may yourself be your child's best physician . . . if you only will attend to a few general directions." Thus Tyler wrote under a medical man's mandate. But she transformed her intellectual debt to him into something all her own: "Why then may I not show my gratitude by presenting to the matrons of my country the fruits of *my* experience, in the pleasing hope that I may be instrumental in directing them in the all-important and delightful task of nursing those sweet pledges of connubial love" (5–6; emphasis mine).

Tyler carefully maintained her intellectual independence from the other toilers in the advice book genre, all of whom happened to be male. This combination of seeming deference to medical authority and confident self-assertion—a variant of the independent judgment we saw in the colloquial receipt book—was repeated throughout the volume. Although she acknowledged that she had learned "many useful hints" from the writings of "the most able" gentlemen physicians, she insisted that in most ordinary circumstances a mother knew her child's body—and cared about it—better than anyone: "Who but a mother can possibly feel interest enough in a helpless new born babe to pay it that unwearied, uninterrupted attention necessary to detect in season any latent symptoms of disease lurking in its tender frame, and which, if neglected, or injudiciously treated at first, might in a few hours baffle the physician's skill, and consign it to the grave" (7).

Tyler's claims might seem to have sprung from a prevailing belief in women's innate aptitude for taking care of children, which was to become the pillar of nineteenth-century domesticity. But Tyler's concept of maternal authority rested on the collection of empirical data, and was thus contingent upon the mother's ability to "observe all the minutiae of her child's state of health"—for example, body temperature, appetite, and coloring, as well as the early signs of illness—while breast-feeding. In this she called upon the growing body of advice literature, most of it British in origin, urging women to nurse their own infants. If women cast off this "sweet privilege of nature," Tyler averred, "my system must fall to the ground" (9). But seeing breast-feeding as an opportunity for mothers to gather data on healthy children represented a significant departure from male advice book authors, who described nursing mothers passively offering the breast to infants and noting details about the child's health only when it was sick.

In emphasizing the mother's relationship with her child and in eschewing customary methods of childrearing, Tyler endorsed Enlightenment theories of child development. Advocating greater physical freedom for the baby so that it might follow the path dictated by nature rather than by wrong-headed custom, doctors such as William Cadogan, Bernard Faust, A. F. M. Willich, William Buchan, Christian Struve, and Hugh Smith advised dispensing with the confining clothes, swaddling bands, and stays, all in common use during the eighteenth century.[30] In keeping with this back-to-nature, rational approach to child rearing, Tyler rejected the traditional explanations and confining devices resorted to by "great grandmothers," a move that highlighted her own modernity. For example, she classified left-handedness as a naturally occurring defect rather than as the fault of the mother. She also disputed that early walking indicated superior health, urging parents not to use artificial means to force children to walk before they were ready (125–126, 128–132).

In keeping with Enlightenment medical advice, Tyler's system centered on a regimen of cleanliness: daily cold water washes for newborns, frequent changes of clothes and bed linens, and fresh air. Tyler advocated applying water from a cold basin with a warm hand rather than immersing the child, after which the "nurse" should wipe it "perfectly dry" with a "warm soft cloth." "This washing I would have repeated every morning," she instructed. The point of this daily wash was to keep the baby's skin healthy and prevent "excoriation," or sores and chafing. Anticipating her readers' fears that cold bathing was unnecessarily cruel or unnatural for infants, she wrote, "Now I would ask, which is the most cruel or unnatural; to lave its little limbs with the pure element designed by a beneficient Creator for our purification, and consequent health, and beauty," or to treat the skin "already perhaps in many places excoriated" with ardent spirits which "must occasion intolerable smarting and pain." Tyler urged her readers to experiment with both methods to see which one made the child cry less. In suggesting that mothers experiment, she parted company with Underwood, who condemned the regime of cold-water immersion that so discomfited tenderhearted mothers. Hers was a practical assessment in which infant suffering might be rationally calculated by mothers and weighed against the benefits of the treatment (22).[31]

Throughout the daily bathing and changing of the young, Tyler emphasized the mother's or nurse's hands-on opportunities to observe children's bodies. Women removed children's clothing, exposing their bodies to scrutiny. They used their hands to apply water all over the child's body, including the genitals, then dried the entire body with towels. Although nothing in Tyler's recommendations suggested that such practices could be sensual, her directives encouraged physical intimacy and tactile bonds between mother and child, laying the groundwork for the bourgeois supervision of children's bodies that the philosopher Michel Foucault claims gave rise to modern sexuality.[32]

Tyler's *Maternal Physician* joined Faust's much-copied *Catechism of Health* in urging American readers to adopt daily washing for their children as the best protection for their health. Although friction remained an important part of the cleanliness regimes that these books advocated—Tyler warned that soiled linens would allow the "little frame, already loaded with disease, to imbibe again the bad humours kind nature is struggling to expel from the innumerable pores of the skin"—water had become increasingly important as a means of both stimulating circulation and cleansing skin. Both books also stressed the tactile, sensual presence of the mother or nurse at bath time. For Tyler, washing and frequent changing of clothing provided the mother with additional information about her child's body while it was *healthy*, an important departure from previous medical guides and the receipt book emphasis on gathering data about sick bodies (180). This knowledge, combined with the information gathered during breast-feeding, was the foundation of American matron's medical authority and strong support for her claim to be her child's best physician.[33]

Tyler appealed to the American reader's interest in the American mother's experience. This was an important attraction in a new nation that claimed cultural distinction and rested its hopes for a republican form of government on the unparalleled virtue of mothers. In parting company with the popular advice literature, much of which was English, Tyler occasionally positioned herself as a cultural translator who could help the American reader find native medicines and remedies equivalent to those recommended in European texts. But she also called upon prominent medical authors for corroboration, which allowed her to embrace the popular health manual's tactic of recommending a regimen that readers were predisposed to accept as common sense.[34]

Tyler was not an uncritical advocate of academic medicine. She viewed the distinction between medical theory and folk belief skeptically, as in her lengthy defense of the claim that a woman's breast would run dry if her milk was thrown away rather than fed to a baby. The connection between unused milk and the cessation of lactation could not be accounted for by "any known principles," she admitted, but she derided the medical theorists who would discount such occurrences as the superstitious beliefs of the ignorant vulgar. Although Tyler's own experience led her to side with the ignorant vulgar, even without a satisfactory explanation for the phenomenon, she still sought the approval of regular physicians, whom she invited to read her book and offer corrections, reassuring them that any errors were the result of ignorance and inexperience, not vanity or empiricism (283).

Tyler recognized limits to maternal medical authority, however, and cautioned her readers not to make the mistake of assuming that they could cure all their children's ills. She enjoined "every intelligent mother to improve her judgment by consulting the most approved medical books on the treatment of children, but more especially by observation and attention to their constitutions and complaints." This combination of book learning and observation would enable them "to judge when nature really requires assistance, and how to administer it with propriety, in all *common complaints.*" Thus she delineated the boundaries between domestic healing and professional medicine: "If your infants are really ill, so that their complaints will not readily yield to the common palliatives, or the often greater efficacy of good nursing, let me entreat you not to delay calling in professional aid until your children are too far gone to admit relief. Thousands of helpless little innocents suffer greatly from the too prevalent opinion (especially among the lower classes of society) that a physician cannot tell what to do for such young children" (73).

Tyler also envisioned her female readers being able to minister to the needs of poor neighbors: "Every lady who has a family, or who wishes to impart the blessings of her medical knowledge to her poor neighbours, should furnish herself with a medicine chest, containing every drug of known and established efficacy, and a set of scales and weights for the purpose; for no one but a regularly bred physician should ever venture to give any potent drug, especially opium, calomel, or emetic tartar, unless weighed with scrupulous exactness, according to the above-mentioned rules" (175). Her advice, like that of Tissot and Buchan before her, imagined charitably minded, educated matrons acting as physicians to the poor. But educated women did not escape unscathed. She condemned fashionable women for failing to breast-feed and leaving their children to untrained nurses. Tyler admitted only the strictly supervised nurse and defined the mother's role as one of continuous connection to her child's body both in sickness and in health.

Comparing Tyler with Paschall and Heath, we discover several significant differences. Tyler's indebtedness to the receipt book tradition appears to have grounded her confidence in domestic experience as a basis for medical authority. Yet clearly, Tyler inhabited a world in which medical knowledge was increasingly disseminated through the printed word. Thus, in the very act of publishing her advice, Tyler sought to capture some public authority for women to heal. But in entering the fray, she narrowed her claims on behalf of maternal medical authority. It was as if her attempt to challenge the growing influence of academically trained doctors had come at the cost of a dramatic reduction in the range of a woman's ability to heal: Tyler claimed a special authority for mothers, but only over the bodies of children two years and younger.

Finally, we catch a glimpse in Tyler's account of the widening rift between household duties, broadly construed, and healing. Her regime of infant health care required the presence of a diligent mother with few other domestic duties competing for her attention. Although Tyler herself successfully juggled cloth production and the management of a large rural household with scrupulous watchfulness over her children's bodies, one finds it hard to imagine Hannah

Heath or many other early-nineteenth-century housewives with the time or the energy to devote to *healthy* children. Amid Heath's perpetual labors of launder-ing clothes, cooking, sewing, and cleaning, there was barely time to attend to sick children, whose care she once described as "troublesome," never mind to scrutinize the bodies of those who were healthy. Indeed, Tyler and Heath re-sponded to somewhat different problems. Tyler aimed to help children live until their second birthday, but Heath's energies were dispersed by the serious ill-nesses that could still threaten the health of older children, laborers, or her hus-band. Few women burdened by routine domestic chores could sustain the do-mestic help and resources necessary to live up to Tyler's ideal of the maternal physician.

FROM PHYSICIAN TO NURSE

Tyler would have been disappointed to see that her own faith in maternal healing did not spread widely. Perhaps nothing illustrates this point so poig-nantly as the speed with which Tyler herself faded from the collective memory of even those New Englanders who had read her book, including Lydia Maria Child. Child's *Family Nurse* (1837) illustrates the decline in maternal authority to heal. Reformer, antislavery agitator, and author of domestic advice books, Child envisioned the mother as nurse rather than as physician, a change that pointed to shifts not only in the relationship between domestic and academically trained healers but in the substance and meaning of women's household labor. By 1837, when *The Family Nurse* was published, a small but significant cohort of white New England women were already leading lives we might describe as bourgeois. They consumed more and produced less than their mothers or their grandmothers. They were likely to see themselves as more responsible for bodily comfort than for healing per se, although in their minds, as in our own, the two were certainly linked. They also saw the state of their households as a direct re-flection of their own character and felt more compelled than their grandmothers to keep it "clean" rather than simply tidy. This was less a question of usefulness, as it had been with Hannah Heath, than one of respectability and morality. Most important, they assumed primary responsibility for the cleanliness, good behav-ior, and well-being of their children, a set of tasks that dramatically increased the potential physical intimacy of mother and child.[35]

Child articulated an approach to health care that emphasized nursing as something distinct from healing. She assumed that her female reader would be caring for patients in three main capacities: providing bodily comfort to those al-ready receiving medical care from physicians, responding to emergencies, and attending to mundane ailments for which a physician was not required. She established clear limits for the female healers who read her advice: "This book merely contains the elements of nursing, and is by no means intended to supersede the advice of a physician. It is simply a household friend, which the inexperienced may consult on common occasions, or sudden emergencies, when medical advice is either unnecessary or cannot be obtained."[36]

Child still embraced an holistic view of healing that included keeping the patient clean, freshening the air of the sick chamber, and providing a special diet, but most of these measures had been drained of authority. Specific instructions for patient care and medical authority came from the doctor alone. Indeed, Child found the possibility of a domestic healer's independent judgment and authority dangerous for the patient:

> The first and most important duty of the nurse is to follow scrupulously and exactly the directions of the physician. Let no facts be concealed from him, or half told. Let no entreaties of the patient, or faith in your own experience, induce you to counteract his orders. If a person be trusted at all in this capacity, he must be trusted entirely; for health, and even life, may be sacrificed by different individuals trying experiments unknown to each other. If you think of anything which seems an improvement upon his practice, suggest it to him, and mention your reasons.[37]

Child's attitude toward domestic healers is almost too easy to caricature as a retrenchment. Indeed, we know that despite their efforts at professional consolidation during the first half of the nineteenth century, regular physicians continued to compete with a host of other healing traditions, including botanical medicine and the water cure. Alternative practitioners, moreover, still touted women's authority to heal. The water curist and health reformer Mary Gove Nichols, for example, marked the opening of a new hydropathic medical school in 1851 in New York with a lecture, "Woman the Physician," that went beyond Tyler's own claims for female healing. Even female midwifery, which revealed most dramatically the ability of male doctors to encroach on medical terrain claimed by women, had a brief resurgence during the 1840s.[38]

Child's *Family Nurse* probably exaggerated the rise of the professional doctor and the demise of the domestic healer. We should expect this, despite Child's reformist temperament, for she had "submitted [her manuscript] to the examination" of a member of the Massachusetts Medical Society. But it is difficult to ignore Child's deliberate effort to rein in domestic healers' reliance on their own experience—the source of confidence we find in Paschall, Heath, and Tyler—just as it is impossible to gloss over Child's backhanded recognition of

Tyler's *Maternal Physician*. Although Child cited numerous popular medical authors, she referred to Tyler's anonymous text only once. Curiously, this reference pointed to the least academic portion of Tyler's text; her discussion of the mysterious phenomenon of unused breast milk causing the supply in the breast to dry up. Why did Child cite this unscientific explanation in a text that otherwise castigated folk wisdom and old wives' tales? Apparently, Child believed that the anonymous author of *The Maternal Physician* was a male doctor with credentials in regular medicine rather than in the patchwork traditions of domestic healers. Little of Child's own credibility would be risked if she cited a male doctor's discussion of a superstitious belief. It seems that she never considered that the author of *The Maternal Physician* might be a woman.

Paschall, Heath, Tyler, and Child provide us with a view of how the desire for bodily and household cleanliness began to encroach on women's responsibility for healing. Early in the nineteenth century, domestic healing could be described as doctoring, aimed at promoting the household's health and well-being. Certain women, including older relatives and midwives, were still recognized as having special knowledge. Gradually, female healing began to transform from the first line of defense in the case of illness, to the special province of a mother responsible for the health of young children, to the duties of a nurse who followed the orders of a physician. The female healer shifted her focus from curing to providing bodily comfort, although the two always overlapped. The labor of cleanliness was the common denominator between the new and old rosters of her duties, but standards and practices underwent their own changes, as we will see, intensifying the housewife's responsibility to maintain a healthy and respectable home environment.

9

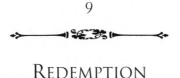

REDEMPTION

THE BOURGEOIS MOTHER'S HOUSEHOLD

Mary Tyler's effort to carve out some healing authority for women might at first glance seem to have defied emerging trends in medicine, domestic labor, and motherhood — all the harbingers of a coalescing bourgeoisie. But in fact, her vision of increased maternal scrutiny over children's bodies was in keeping with new expectations for body work that transformed both motherhood and female bodies during the nineteenth century. Presiding over a household that reflected her own character, the ideal mother was defined less by the amount of cloth she produced — the traditional measure of the goodwife's virtue — than by the appearance and health of her family, the cleanliness of her domestic environment, and her own refinement. More consumer, domestic manager, and provider of bodily comfort than producer or healer, as Tyler might have imagined her, the bourgeois mother assumed new responsibility for the air her family breathed, the cleanliness of the carpets, walls and windows, and the state of her children's hair, teeth, and shirt collars. Meeting these standards required her to domesticate her own body and maintain her person in a clean and wholesome state. This was no mean feat at a time when conduct book authors were beginning to condemn the dominant form of body care — linen changes — as insufficient to combat the body's normal effusion of odor.

Conflating the state of a woman's body with the tidiness of her household was not new to the nineteenth century, as we have seen. But by the 1830s a host of domestic advice authors had given the association new emphasis by placing advice about health, household management, and personal cleanliness between the same two covers. Thus the health reformer and prolific author William Alcott linked a wife's disregard for her household with disregard for her own person in

The Young Wife (1836), urging her to maintain high standards for cleanliness in both cases for the sake of her marriage. In *The House I Live In* (1837) Alcott used the metaphor of the body as the soul's housing to advocate for cleanliness in the home as a means of improving the health of its tenants. Catherine Beecher's *Treatise on Domestic Economy* (1841) followed this approach of treating household management, personal cleanliness, and health as related topics. The domestic advice guru Eliza Leslie, however, kept care of the body and health separate from domestic management in *The House Book* (1840), one of the era's best-selling household advice books, as did Lydia Maria Child in separate publications of *The Frugal Housewife* (1830), dedicated to effective cost cutting measures for running a household, and *The Family Nurse* (1837), which outlined protocol for nursing the sick.

Whether they approached household management from the perspective of medicine or that of domestic advice—and often the two overlapped—authors from the late eighteenth century on agreed on the importance of clean, wholesome air. Fears of unwholesome, damp, or corrupt air had been around for centuries, but several factors revived them: the medical turn to environmentalism during the eighteenth century, the highly publicized horrors of the Black Hole of Calcutta (1756), and narratives of American prisoners suffering in British prisons during the War of 1812. In 1781 the Edinburgh obstetrics professor Alexander Hamilton (no relation to either the traveler or the statesman) had warned against crowded, unventilated rooms and the dangers of impure air for children in *The Family Female Physician*. Numerous popular medical advice books, including William Dewees's *Mother's Own Book* (1825), William Horner's *Home Book of Health* (1835), and William Alcott's *Young Mother* (1836), joined the chorus proclaiming the dangers of damp, unwholesome air and small confined spaces.[1]

All of these authors addressed their advice to the lay reader and advocated reforming daily household routines. One of the major tenets of this advice, that fresh air was purer and more wholesome than fumigated air and necessary for good health, dated back to John Floyer and advocates of the cooling regimen. Dewees, for example, recommended daily airings of children's rooms to disperse the foulness that accumulated overnight. He also claimed, six years before the 1832 cholera epidemic, that while cities were less wholesome than the countryside, in the United States "the evils of cities are more limited than in those of Europe," owing to less dense populations, wider, better-ventilated streets, fewer factories to pollute the air, and less poverty.[2] Horner elaborated on this point, noting that the air in cities and small confined spaces became unhealthy because of the respiration of too many bodies without adequate ventilation. Depleted oxygen and dangerous levels of carbonic acid gave the air in small rooms, hospitals, jails, and ships an "unwholesome and pernicious quality" that also threatened the health of city residents. In contrast, Horner noted, "in the open country there are few causes to contaminate the atmosphere, and the vegetable productions continually tend to make it more pure." The winds, moreover, "waft the pure country air to the inhabitants of the cities, and dissipate that from which the oxygen has been in a great measure extracted." Alcott amplified the warnings about carbonic acid build up and the superiority of fresh air over vinegar or camphor fumigations. He took specific aim at the practice of mothers sleeping with their babies, which made them vulnerable not only to being crushed or smothered but to "inhaling impure air." Already predisposed to be disgusted by bad breath and acute body odors, a nineteenth-century reader—especially one who had experienced the cholera epidemic of 1832—might have needed little convincing that stuffy or malodorous air was dangerously impure or that cities were less healthy than the countryside."[3]

How, exactly, was the housewife to ensure the wholesomeness of the air her family breathed? Most of the suggestions were simple to implement, although they contradicted older advice about health and eighteenth-century intuition about bodily comfort. Proper ventilation was as easy as opening the doors or the windows regularly, many writers urged, so that people could avoid inhaling already breathed (thus spoiled) air. This was especially important for American houses, which tended to be made "close and almost air-tight" and heated by charcoal fires.[4] During the day, according to the experts, bedchambers and bedding should be aired to ensure that pure air replaced the stale air that accumulated over night and to prevent any damp bedding from contributing noxious exhalations into the chamber. Echoing Thomas Tryon and other critics of hot regimen, Horner inveighed against featherbeds, which many of his readers might have considered to be the most comfortable, for being "too hot and injurious to the health." He also recommended removing bed curtains, used to keep out drafts, because they inhibited the circulation of air and increased the amount of dust children breathed in.[5] Dewees warned against washing, ironing, or performing any other domestic task in the nursery—a separate chamber for children that had begun to appear in wealthy households—as these processes filled the air with unwholesome vapors. Dewees also urged women not to strew sand on the nursery floor, a popular method for cleaning, as breathing in the dust would be injurious to the children's health.[6] Most writers made special mention of the need to keep cellars clean and dry because those filled with filth and stagnant water could compromise the health not just of the household but of the entire neighborhood.[7]

Fresh air, open bedsteads, the separation of work and sleeping spaces, and rig-

9.1. The small boy on the right holds his nose in the presence of the farmer, who has kept his boots on. Alexander Anderson, *The Sideboard*, from M. Berquin, *The Looking-glass for the mind* (New York, 1804). Courtesy American Antiquarian Society

orous measures to remove dust and grime were part of a gradual shift in housekeeping standards, from a simpler, less labor-intensive ethos aimed at achieving neatness to an ideal aimed at achieving gentility as well as health. Household cleanliness became integral to notions of refinement as housewives did battle with flies, tobacco spittoons, and the smells of food and chamber pots. But contemporaries who observed the changes in housekeeping practices during the late 1820s and 1830s had mixed feelings. In 1828, *The Ladies Magazine*, later *Godey's Lady's Book,* published a story that compared the rustic simplicity of the Grants, a Yankee family who inhabited a small cottage, with their snooty neighbors' misguided pursuit of elegance. Preparing to host a beloved family member, the Grants "cleaned" the parlor floor with fresh sand and decorated the mantelpiece with green boughs. In contrast, in the house where taste had been dictated not by simplicity but by greed and fashion, the mistress scolded her husband and sons if ever they dared tread on her new carpet.[8] In *The Housekeeper's Book*

(1837), Frances Green criticized "pretenders to gentility" who purchased heavy curtains and draperies and replaced the high-backed chairs of their forefathers with fashionable but vulgar furnishings. Yet Green was relentless about the need for spring and fall cleanings and daily polishing, dusting, and sweeping in between, especially for those nouveau genteel who had succumbed to the temptation to clutter their homes with showy ornaments (Figure 9.1).[9]

An older generation of housekeepers regarded the shift from tidiness to cleanliness with skepticism as being at cross purposes with the ethos that valued the housewife's health and usefulness above the cleanliness of her house. As a young woman and housewife, the New Englander Ruth Bascom occupied her days with cloth manufacturing and fashioning hats for special occasions. By 1840 she was a tart sixty-one-year-old with little patience for the obsession with cleanliness that she observed among younger women, particularly those living in the city. She recorded her May visit to a Mrs. Captain Stratton, who was "quite low & confined after a spell of 'cleaning house,' when in a very weak state of body, & of *mind too*, one would *suppose*. This 'cleaning house' fall & spring being *indispensable* with *some* 'more nice than wise' ladies—*sick* or *well*. Well it is Sabbath but, I must record this piece of agredious [*sic*] Folly & pride—& wish the case might be warning to all *house wives.*"[10] Bascom found the pursuit of cleanliness foolish when it came at the expense of the housewife's own health and compromised her ability to be useful.

THE MATERNAL BODY

Changes in the way women cared for bodies—their own as well as their children's—accompanied the new approaches to housework. By the 1830s women wore shifts that were no longer as visible beneath their dresses, and therefore much plainer. Women on both sides of the Atlantic were also more likely to wear underdrawers, a French habit that spread to the English speaking world. Their adoption cannot be explained fully by fashion, however, as they were supposed to remain hidden from view. Rather, they represented a new way to signify female refinement using an old technique: covering the body in white fabric.[11]

Northern mothers intervened more actively in their children's appearance during the nineteenth century. Take the example of Stephen Salisbury, son of Stephen and Elizabeth Tuckerman Salisbury of Worcester, Massachusetts. Correspondence and clothing passed between parents and son during Stephen's years at Harvard between 1812 and 1817. But while Stephen senior sent messages about the contents of arriving bundles and issued instructions about the correct way to pack dirty laundry for the return journey, Elizabeth wrote with intimate reference to her son's body, prodding him to keep himself well groomed. Reminders to send home dirty clothes and advice about how frequently to change his shirts — Mrs. Salisbury thought three shirts a week was reasonable — came every couple of months. "I hope you had your hair cut some of these fine warm days we have had," she wrote her son in November 1813, and "that you don't fail to comb and brush your hair every day." She also urged him not to neglect his teeth, reminding him to "clean them every day." In addition to instructing him to care for his own body, she requested his dirty laundry and sent him new and clean items in exchange. "How do you like your new neck cloths?" she inquired. "You had better send home all the white ones you had before & your cotton stockings," along with dirty bedsheets, she enjoined him. A few months later, she scolded him for failing to heed her advice to be clean. "I am afraid from the appearance of your collars that you do not wash your neck," she accused. "I charge you my son if you *have been* negligent, to be so no more." Salisbury viewed the dirty neck cloths as evidence of a larger failure to groom. "Wash and comb every day, and do not by any means neglect to keep your teeth clean," she added.[12]

Southern parents wrote to sons and daughters attending boarding school with similar concerns. This overlap in parental advice from regions that were embarked on diverging cultural, economic, and political paths reminds us of the close relationship between genteel and bourgeois regimes of caring for the body. Indeed, in many respects it is difficult to discern differences between northern and southern standards for body care before 1840. Yet even before that date, southern correspondence shows fathers to be as invested as mothers in urging their children to greater diligence, revealing that responsibility for the appearance of children had not yet devolved upon southern mothers to the same degree as in the North.[13]

Tooth care remained important to fashionable people, North and South, who wanted "a regular and white set of teeth" and hoped to avoid the disagreeable smell of decay. Adding to these aesthetic incentives, popular medical guides urged readers to keep their teeth clean for health reasons. In the North, toothbrushes could be purchased at a range of establishments, including pharmacies and brush shops. In the South during the same period, it was more difficult to procure a toothbrush, but parents nonetheless wrote urging children who were away at school to brush their teeth. Despite differences in access to toothbrushes, people who considered themselves genteel aspired to clean, white, odor-free teeth and wished their children to achieve this mark of physical refinement as effortlessly as possible. The South Carolinian Caroline Laurens reported her mother-in-law's efforts to encourage two-year-old John in his toothbrushing in the hope that it would become a lifelong habit. The widowed Reverend Drury

Lacey urged his daughter, who attended school in Greensboro, North Carolina, to make her teeth look "pure and white as monumental alabaster."[14]

Salisbury's struggles to spur her son to greater effort with his person reflects one side of a larger debate about how much dirt was healthy for children. This became especially fraught in the case of sons, who were urged to attend to their persons but warned not to exchange the sweat and dirt of honest labor for the affectations of the dandy. Several early-nineteenth-century essays and pamphlets criticized men who devoted too much time to their own persons.[15] In Tyler's *Maternal Physician*, for example, she rhetorically asked her readers at the end of the book, "As for your sons, let me entreat you to reflect upon what manner of men you will wish to see them in after life. . . . Do you wish to see them effeminate and pusillanimous, then be it your care to guard their complexions, to instil in their tender minds the love of dress and show, to lead their attention to the best drest guest and most splendid equipage. . . . But if, on the other hand, you wish to rear the hero and the sage, teach them betimes to set no more than their just value on the trappings of fashion" (280–281). Tyler's own plan of daily baths, clean clothes, and close scrutiny of the young child's body, she implied, in no way compromised his hardy masculinity. Indeed, she contended that the use of water strengthened rather than weakened the body—that it combatted effeminacy. Yet to many readers, as perhaps to Tyler herself, this must have seemed like walking a fine line between scrupulous care of the body and succumbing to the follies of fashion. Alcott still found it necessary in *The Young Mother* (1836) to dispute the adage that dirt was healthful and cleanliness of person an immoral self-indulgence.[16]

Medical advice authors challenged fears that bodily cleanliness would debilitate boys by depicting bathing as part of a program of child care necessary to produce useful, healthy citizens, a new version of a much older argument about the benefits of cold bathing. Mothers were represented in this literature as uniquely positioned to enforce habits of cleanliness that would not only protect the child's health and strengthen its constitution but contribute to the health of the state and *its* constitution. The burdens and responsibilities of caring for the little bodies of children were clearly those of the mother because, as the authors circularly reasoned, "the attendance and nursing, the tender and affectionate treatment which a child stands in need of, can only be expected from a mother." Failure to bathe a child regularly, the anonymous author of the *New Guide to Health* (1810) noted emphatically, was one of several causes of weakness and effeminacy that brought harm not only to the individual child but to the state. Even if there were no public baths to speak of, Dewees averred, bathing was still possible.[17] Mrs. William Parkes, the British author of *Domestic Duties* (1825), which appeared in several editions in the United States, provided explicit directions for sponge bathing infants daily and washing young children in a standing tub once a week. "No children could look more wholesome and healthy," she insisted.[18]

Ambivalence about male cleanliness and its potential to undermine both masculinity and male citizenship appeared in children's stories and nursery rhymes. Didactic tales of premature death, many borrowed from English texts, employed a maternal narrator to instruct children in the importance of literacy, morality, and habits of cleanliness. *Instructive Hints in Easy Lessons for Children*, reprinted in Philadelphia in 1808, contained a graphic image of a dog attacking a tattered young boy, and the author's note that dogs disliked dirty and ragged people. The child's tattered clothing and grubby face evoked beggars, who lacked the benefits of an established home where cleanliness could be produced. An American edition of Ann Taylor Gilbert's *Rhymes for the Nursery* (1810), featured two poems with messages about cleanliness. In "For a Little Girl that did not Like to be Washed," a maternal voice warned children that if they didn't wash, they would be unfit to be seen and unworthy of a "sweet kiss from papa." The engraving, probably done by an American, showed a mother, armed with wash basin and towel, holding up a looking glass to her daughter's dirty face. The second poem complicated this message by depicting a smug, overly fastidious, young gentleman who never

> Need do any thing but play,
> Nor even soil my little hand,
> Because I am so very grand,

thus presenting a sharp contrast to his laboring counterpart.[19] By the 1830s messages to children about the importance of cleanliness had intensified. In the 1837 edition of *Rhymes for the Nursery*, the poem about the girl who would not wash had been supplemented by several others, including "Dizzy Girl," about a child who spun around outside until she fell to the ground and soiled her dress, and "Dirty Hands," an admonition to children who thought clean hands were necessary only when there was company (Figures 9.2–9.3).[20]

The maternal voice in these children's books belonged to women who both embodied and enforced the rules of cleanliness, but in other genres, women were depicted as needing careful instruction to overcome the filth of their persons. In the instructive novel *The Farmer's Friend* (1793), the author and Presbyterian minister Enos Hitchcock created personifications of the female ideal and its foil, praising Mrs. Charles Worthy for "carry[ing] cleanliness to its highest pitch" and condemning Mrs. Straton (her name a convenient near rhyme with *slattern*) both for allowing her house to be "up in arms" and for growing "very

9.2. A ragged boy, in *Instructive Hints in easy lessons for children* (Philadelphia, 1808).
Courtesy American Antiquarian Society

careless about her person, and from that to downright sluttishness." British advice book literature for women, frequently reprinted in the United States, noted
that neatness and cleanliness enabled women to earn the good opinion of men.
In *The Lady's Miscellany* (1797) the author George Wright lambasted married
women for neglecting their persons:

> Let me now proceed to recommend *neatness*, which cannot be cultivated with
> too much attention. I would press it on every female, as strongly if possible, as
> Lord Chesterfield did the graces on his son. The want of it is unpardonable in
> a man, but in a *woman* it is shocking. It disgusts all her friends and intimates;
> has estranged the affections of many an husband, and made him seek that sat-
> isfaction abroad, which he found not at home. Some ladies, who were remark-
> ably attentive to their persons before marriage, neglect them afterwards in an
> egregious manner. They cannot pay a worse compliment to their own deli-
> cacy, or to their husbands. If they conceived some efforts necessary to gain the
> prize, more, I am sare [*sic*], are required to preserve it.

For a little girl that did not like to be washed.

9.3. "For a little girl that did not like to be washed," in *Rhymes for the Nursery*
(Philadelphia, 1810). Courtesy American Antiquarian Society

An essay on female sluttishness that appeared in *Freemason's Magazine* in 1811 tempered Wright's message by acknowledging that married men's neglect of their wives was often at the root of women's failures to care for their own persons, but still treated uncleanness as a special challenge for married women.[21]

This trope of the disgusting female body continued to appear in nineteenth-century medical advice and social commentary, accompanied by ever more elaborate remedies. Bathing was usually recommended as the key to treating the unpleasant diseases afflicting women's reproductive organs. Indeed, disease appeared in these texts as a normative condition of female anatomy. In 1793 the obstetrician Hamilton urged adult women to use the bidet to prevent excoriations near their genitals and douches to cure "the whites," a female malady.[22] The Virginia physician Thomas Ewell, who had studied under Philadelphia's Benjamin Rush and Washington's John Weems, recommended bathing to alleviate the disgusting odors and condition of the female body. "You are spoken of, in the most disgusting manner, particularly by the lower classes of society, on discovering that you may be smelt as themselves," he warned in 1818, and ruminated on the possible reasons for female body odor: "Indeed, it would be difficult to imagine the reason why females were so constituted as to become offensive to the nose, unless for the purpose of suppressing too ardent devotion in males. One might suppose, that nature designed this quality as a defensive weapon; agreeably to which, I would suggest, to those apprehending a rape, to insure protection, by rendering themselves as disgusting as possible." Stench offensive enough to deter a would-be rapist had little value in polite company, Ewell observed, and he reminded his readers that female odor reflected badly on all women. As was true for all body odor, moreover, it "shocked" the "finest, most tender excitements of love."[23] Citing the examples of Roman, French, and even southern women for their admirable habits of regular bathing, Ewell urged the rest of the nation's women to bathe regularly even during menstruation to improve their health and combat female diseases. Dewees recommended bathing to reduce female odor, while Alcott echoed Ewell's praise for the cleanliness of the Romans and urged women to bathe regularly and attend to their persons.[24]

By the 1830s body odor had begun its gradual transformation from a consequence of the innately diseased state of female anatomy to a normative condition, offensive to genteel aesthetics, that women especially needed to guard against. Drawing ever finer distinctions, middle-class women evaluated odors to assess their would-be social peers, distinguishing the truly genteel from mere pretenders. In 1833 Eliza W. Farrar, the French-born wife of a Harvard professor and intimate of Elizabeth Peabody's intellectual circle, provided a detailed discussion of the origins of this odor. Rather than focus on female reproductive organs, as many medical writers did, Farrar tried to nudge young ladies into greater self-awareness of odor of a less explicitly sexual origin. "It may shock the feelings of a young lady," she warned, "to be told that this large quantity of matter, in the shape of insensible perspiration, which is constantly passing off through the skin, has an individual odor, more or less disagreeable in different persons." The offensiveness of such odors needed to be taken on faith, she argued, since "each person is so accustomed to his own atmosphere, that he is no judge of its odor; but since most persons can recollect some one of their friends who affects them disagreeably in this way, all should bear in mind the possibility of so offending others." "Though none of us can change the nature of the atmosphere which we are always creating around us," Farrar conceded, "we can prevent its becoming a nuisance by the accumulation of excreted matter on the skin or in the clothing."[25]

The body described by Farrar was newly loathsome in its normal state. Laundering and changing linen were no longer sufficient to combat its odors. Only regular washing could contain its innate offensiveness. Departing from previous advice, Farrar recommended "washing every part of the skin once in twenty-four hours," to be sure of "sending off only fresh exhalations." This was especially important for those parts of the body that produced stronger smells, like armpits, that needed "a thorough washing with soap and water every day." In urging her readers to use soap, Farrar parted company with two centuries of bathing advocates, who emphasized the use of water alone, except for babies. Her approach to body care represented a new fastidiousness about body odor that increased the labor required to achieve decency, raising the bar far beyond the reach of the urban poor, whose access to running water already limited their ability to meet standards for clean linens. It also challenged the long-standing belief that the friction of linen against the skin could effectively clean the body.[26]

Farrar saw this new standard of cleanliness as a national issue for Americans and a question of time and privacy for young women. There had been no American golden age of cleanliness, she claimed, only a haphazard attention to the rudiments of bodily cleanliness that persisted to the present day. She condemned American women for their lax practices compared with their European sisters, but acknowledged that many were prevented from bathing by the lack of privacy. Indeed, during the 1830s most Americans lived in houses that lacked separate sleeping chambers and bathing facilities. "The primitive manners of our forefathers (and of the back country at the present day), which required that every one should wash at the pump in the yard, or at the sink in the kitchen, were not favorable to cleanliness and health," Farrar concluded. But body care was also a matter of priorities: "In the most civilized nations of Europe, great attention is paid to the health of the skin, and all the arrangements of domestic life include the means of copious and constant bathing. There, it is thought more essential to happiness to have a warm and cold bath at command, than to own spacious apartments and costly furniture. Large provision is made for washing in the sleeping-rooms of the English; and travellers are not thought unreasonable if they require more than a quart of water for their morning toilet."[27]

Rustic traditions made privacy difficult, a particularly delicate issue for young women aspiring to a genteel life. Farrar urged young women to overcome their reticence by thinking of gentility not simply as the refinement of the material objects that surrounded them but as scrupulous care of their persons. According to Farrar, young women needed at least half an hour "to wash themselves thoroughly, and attend properly to their hair, teeth, and nails, and put on the simplest dress," a claim that struck at one of the time-honored criticisms of ladies, that they spent too much time dressing. Individual indoor washing made privacy necessary: a washstand, pitcher, and basin must be provided for each person in the family rather than the old standby of the kitchen sink or backyard pump. Recent evidence of female gentility, reflected in education, domestic goods, and a release of some women from some of the rigors of domestic labor, did not ease Farrar's mind about the care people lavished on their own bodies. Although Farrar believed daily bathing was less necessary for laborers than for "children of ease and luxury," she feared that "many a young lady who treads on Brussels carpeting, and wipes her hands on damask towelling, does not more daily washing in her china wash-bowl than does the farmer's daughter at the sink."[28]

Other authors followed Farrar's lead. Emily Thornwell, author of *The Lady's Guide to Perfect Gentility, Manners, Dress, and Conversation,* published in 1856 and reprinted for three decades, provided a gruesomely detailed account of how the skin actually generated odor: "The skin is everywhere . . . pierced by innumerable little holes . . . which pour out upon its surface an unctuous or oily fluid, which lubricates it, and renders it soft and shining. . . . Unless removed from the surface from time to time, it accumulates, and causes light dust to adhere to it, and if long neglected, obstructs its healthy function." These oily effusions caused other problems that Thornwell saw as particularly disagreeable to ladies: "When there is not sufficient attention paid to cleanliness, the matters accumulated on it become rancid, and impart a peculiarly disagreeable odor." Thornwell prescribed a cleanliness regime similar to Farrar's, but placed even more stress on the importance of soap. She observed the "impossibility of cleansing any part of the body by mere wiping or rubbing, and as plain water makes little or no impression on anything greasy . . . without a frequent application of soap and water to every part of the skin, it cannot be kept clean."[29]

Thornwell provided damning evidence that the time-honored practice of changing linen did not constitute real cleanliness and suggested that it persisted among readers during the 1850s:

> By changing the linen often, much of the impurities which accumulate on the skin may be rubbed off, but enough will be left to clog its pores, and debilitate its minute vessels. Now what must we think of those genteel people who never use the bath, or only once or twice a year wash themselves all over, though they change their linen daily? Why, that, in plain English, they are nothing more or less than very filthy gentry; and you will find, if your olefactories are at all sensitive, whenever you happen to be near them, and their perspiration is a little excited by exercise, that they have a something about them which lavender water and bergamot do not entirely conceal. And what is this something? Why, it is simply the odor, occasioned by the fluids which are naturally poured out upon the surface having become rancid. . . . Those persons who have enough

of this odor about them to be perceptible to other when very near them, are often unconscious of it themselves, and this, above all things, should put ladies on their guard.

Like many of her contemporaries, Thornwell tried to convince her readers of a dangerous condition that none could see and only the refined could detect with their noses. True gentility required an almost ritual effort at personal cleanliness to prevent such body odors from occurring. Only regular bathing with soap could achieve true cleanliness; changes of linen were no longer enough.[30]

Farrar's and Thornwell's focus on bathing to prevent body odor added a new twist—the desire for refinement—to recommendations in popular household advice books and health journals to wash the entire body daily for reasons of health. Catharine Beecher's 1841 discussion of bodily cleanliness, in contrast to Farrar's and Thornwell's, emphasized the health benefits of washing the skin.[31] In *The Skillful Housewife's Book* (1852), which also contained recipes for soap and stain removers, Mrs. L. G. Abell urged readers to wash children twice and adults once a day followed by a vigorous rubdown with a coarse towel, but included an ambiguously worded suggestion about using a flesh brush for fifteen minutes—was it a substitute for the bath or the towel? Elsewhere Abell suggested that such ablutions merely had to be frequent. Feet, moreover, "should be bathed as often as once or twice a week." *The Family Manual* (1856), a household compendium of wisdom about cooking, nursing the sick, and cleaning house, contained identically worded advice, supposedly excerpted from Sir R. Philips's rules for "Preserving Life and Health," to wash the whole body.[32]

Recommendations to bathe increasingly appeared in all published domestic advice by the 1850s, although the motivations for doing so differed depending on the audience. For young ladies aspiring to gentility, social fears, including the embarrassment of exuding offensive odors, spurred new attention to grooming and demands for greater privacy. For those with less social ambition, washing the body was part of a regime of healthful living that included moderate intake of food and nonalcoholic drink, regular sleep, well-ventilated chambers, and clean cellars and storage bins. Only the injunctions to bathe the feet "as often as once or twice a week" betrayed the family advice book's concern with body odor.[33]

Children's stories, in contrast to the advice manuals and medical guidebooks directed at women, featured an already refined and authoritative maternal body, the source of bourgeois morality and respectability, whose relation to the child consisted of a combination of discipline and love. Washing a child's face, bathing its body, and dressing it in clean clothes were physical disciplines, imposed by a mother on the body of her child and expressive of love and protection.

Mothers who attended to their own persons but not those of their children acted selfishly. Children who refused to submit to these disciplines by letting mothers wash their faces were naughty. The mother in these texts was not only the agent of cleanliness discipline but a product of it, with the condition of her own person absolutely essential to making the representation of maternal intimacy palatable to the reader. By attending to her person and inculcating proper cleanliness habits in the child, a woman not only performed her duties as a mother but served the interests of her class.

Changing representations of the mother's role in the practices and meanings of cleanliness are not terribly surprising in light of what we know about the history of motherhood during this period—especially the mother's growing investment of emotion in her child—although understanding precisely how this process unfolded merits further attention. More surprising is the emotionally freighted position of daughters in depictions of the new importance of cleanliness. Unlike sons, whose masculinity depended upon achieving a balance between honestly acquired dirt and a program of bathing designed to strengthen their constitutions, there was little ambivalence about the importance of cleanliness for little girls. In fact, most of the images of recalcitrant children in need of bathing featured girls. If they did not submit to their mother's cleanliness disciplines, daughters risked disgusting their loved ones. The stories spelled out in graphic terms the consequences for girls who did not let their faces and hands be washed or who failed to keep their frocks clean. Unfit to be seen, unworthy of papa's kiss, denied a place at the family dining table, those girls were left to wonder at the reasons for the withdrawal of affection until they learned this difficult lesson: that their persons were essentially disgusting until they were cleansed. Injunctions to be clean thus appear to have converged on daughters during the early decades of the nineteenth century, even as their mothers found respectability.

This emphasis on the potential filthiness of girls' bodies built on an older theme of men's disgust at reminders of women's physicality. Continued mixed feelings about the compatibility of masculinity and refinement made boys less useful than girls as the subjects of lessons about personal hygiene. In addition, the person denouncing girls for their filth and disciplining them into cleanliness was no longer the father, offering advice to his daughter—the format of so much published advice in the eighteenth century—but the mother, who had succeeded in taming her own physicality. In children's rhymes, she enjoyed the most unambiguous authority when she was disciplining her daughter, a trope that points to the important role of women in creating the new standard of cleanliness and the ways it exacerbated the emotionally fraught relationship between mothers and daughters. Submitting to having her face washed, the fictive naughty daughter offered readers reassurance of discipline, respectability, and gentility produced at home by virtuous mothers.

The figure of the mother as guardian of cleanly respectability quickly became a touchstone of middle-class decency. In 1846 *Godey's Lady's Book* published the poem "Saturday Evening," by J. Ross Dix, accompanied by a comic engraving. Dix's verse began with the nostalgia of an older man for the carefree days of his youth. Deciding to focus on these happy memories rather than on the disappointments of his adult life, Dix adopted a humorous tone:

> Think of the scrub
> Just when the day began to fail;
> Ponder o'er soap, and brush, and pail,
> And *swiftly* tell, like Swift, a tale —
> "Tale of a Tub"

Dix's tale of the tub was of the weekly ordeal of being washed by his mother at the pump at the back of the house:

> My heart beats to my mother's thump
>   When from the street,
> She quietly enticed me in,
> Then tucked a cloth beneath my chin,
> And soaped me till she vowed my skin
>   Was clean and sweet.

As Dix recalled, being washed was a bruising experience, complete with blows, painful rubs, and the punishing roughness of the towel. After the physical ordeal came the reward of being enveloped in mother love, which in Dix's recollections inspired youthful feelings of piety.

> Well, I remember now with pride
> How mother drew me to her side —
> The scrubbing o'er — (let none deride
>   With foolish airs) —
> How I was nestled on her breast —
> Earth's dearest, holiest place of rest! —
> And on that sanctuary blest
>   Said childish prayers.

After noting with humor that money now bought the cleanliness that his mother used to supply for free, he reflected on how cleanliness revealed god's grace and maternal love:

9.4. "Saturday Evening," *Godey's Lady's Book* (November 1846). Courtesy
American Antiquarian Society

Remember her who made your face
Twist into many a queer grimace —
Remember cleanliness is grace.
   It may sound oddly
To ears polite, but there's no doubt —
And they who've sense will find it out —
He who's a clean face is about
   The next to godly.

Last but not least, remember this —
Thy mother's care, thy mother's kiss,
Her prayers for thee and for thy bliss;
   And often trace
Through after life, the heart which bled,
The eyes which living lustre shed
On yours — the hand, cloth-covered,
Which wiped your face.

In Dix's sentimental ode, the scrubbing at the pump enveloped him in mother love and divine grace. A mother's tears mingled with the water from the pump. The bruising physicality of the scrubbing transformed into an intimate and sacred expression of love for a child. Washing a child's body had become a way of loving it (Figure 9.4).[34]

10

LABORERS

In 1827 a butler in the household of the prominent Massachusetts Federalist Christopher Gore published a book of advice for men entering domestic service. Appearing a decade before the best-selling household management guides by Lydia Maria Child, Catharine Beecher, and Eliza Leslie, Robert Roberts's *House Servant's Directory* found a receptive audience, prompting two subsequent editions. In addition to being in the vanguard of the American house books, Roberts's manual stood out among antebellum advice manuals for its author's social and racial position. Roberts was not the master of the house, writing to assist other masters and mistresses in the task of running a household full of servants, but was himself a domestic servant. He was, moreover, not a woman, as was the case with most domestic servants and the authors of most household guides, but a man. He was, most exceptionally, a free African American who had experienced the workings of a prominent northern household in a nation where his closest counterparts, racially speaking, were overwhelmingly enslaved and living in the South. Taking advantage of his employer's status and his own literacy, Roberts dispensed household advice that depicted a disciplined and sanitized servant body navigating the intimate spaces of an upper-class white household. Translating Old World taste, manners, and standards into an American idiom, Roberts aimed at capturing the aura of elegance associated with European aristocracy for an audience of newly prosperous Americans who needed to know how to burn Lehigh coal as well as to clean a japanned tea urn.[1]

Roberts was a fastidious man who found bodily filth distasteful, especially if it broadcast social differences. Urging his imagined audience of young male readers to heed his advice, he warned, "How many have we seen going about a city, like vagabonds, diseased in mind and body, and mere outcasts from all respectable society, and a burthen to themselves."[2] According to Roberts's interpretation of the urban scene, vagabonds threatened all who entered public spaces, but he might have considered them especially damaging to the integrity and respectability of working-class people, particularly those who made up the servant class and needed to be seen as fit and trustworthy to enter middle- and upper-class homes.

This would have been a particular concern for African Americans in the north by the 1820s. The alchemy of southern slavery—the strong desire of white southerners to believe that they knew and could trust their enslaved domestics and the equally intoxicating belief that purchasing human property enabled an owner to refashion both his own and his new slave's identity—technically did not exist in northern states that had abolished slavery in the decades following the American Revolution. But the North had its own regional version of this alchemy nonetheless. The domestic employment of free African Americans gave wealthy northern households an exotic cachet, enabling masters and mistresses to associate their own social standing with that of a planter aristocracy. This cachet was available only to a handful of households—a northern aristocracy of sorts—and depended in large measure on the seeming exceptional character of their hired domestics. Racial divisions hardened in the North following the abolition of slavery there, virtually complete by the 1820s, manifested and reinforced by discouragements to intimate contact across racial lines. African Americans in the North increasingly bore the stigma of racial difference. In contrast to their white laboring counterparts, who rejected demeaning labels and insisted on being considered "help," moreover, African-American domestics found it hard to distance themselves from the term *servant*. As the case of Robert Roberts suggests, however, certain black domestics might still, at least until the 1820s, produce that alchemy by marking wealthy households as aristocratic spaces, akin to the large plantation households of the South and the great houses of Europe.[3]

How did prosperous white northerners and their hired domestic laborers negotiate the physical proximity of bodies, distinguished by inequities of wealth, power, and cultivation, within intimate domestic spaces that served simultaneously as workplaces and domestic sanctuaries? Thinking about the physical interactions of employer and employee bodies as cartographies, or culturally meaningful patterns, of domestic labor rather than as merely pragmatic routine helps us to understand their importance and the attention of both parties to tiny details. Both employers and employees helped to produce cartographies that reinforced the division of labor into zones—upper and lower, public and private—and mapped them onto different domestic spaces. It followed that the bodies of entire groups of people might be similarly classified based on the location and nature of their work. Analyzing domestic labor helps us to appreciate the mundane ways bodies acquired meaning as well as how those meanings contributed to changing perceptions of the body and its implication in concepts of racial, ethnic, and class difference.[4]

Bemoaning the difficulty of finding good domestic labor became a defining preoccupation of the American middle class during the period between the late-eighteenth-century intensification of cloth production, which according to the historian Laurel Ulrich lasted until the 1820s in New England, and the mid-nineteenth-century industrialization of textile manufacture. But this was as much a way of talking about class in the changing economic and aesthetic landscape of the northern United States as it was an actual problem. Roberts's book appeared in the midst of the labor crunch caused by rising domestic standards and diminishing native-born sources of domestic labor. If women in prosperous urban households were to attend more to their own persons and those of their children; if they were to express their refinement in the material goods that decorated their parlors and protect their families' health with improved standards for housekeeping, arrangements for domestic labor would need to change. The historian Faye Dudden describes this period as one of transition from a concept of hiring "help" (usually neighbors or relatives) to enhance household production for the market to one of hiring "domestics" (more likely to be strangers and of a different class, religion, or ethnicity) to perform household services like laundry, cooking, and cleaning. As other scholars have shown, however, young native-born women sought to retain independence and autonomy and balked at being treated like servants. When the work or the wages didn't suit, they turned to dressmaking, a different employer, or marriage.[5]

Domestic laborers in the antebellum North—including parlor maids, cooks, laundresses, nurses, and hired men—were increasingly likely to be Irish or African American rather than native-born white by the 1840s, a trend that began during the 1820s. They brought what many middle-class people saw as the most distasteful feature of democratic society—the disorderly mingling in public spaces of people of different races, classes, religions, and ethnicities—into the sacralized private spaces of the emerging white middle class. Yet servants also provided the labor indispensable to differentiating those domestic spaces from the public and imbuing them with the meanings that anchored the privileged social identities of their inhabitants. For middle-class women and children, in particular, domestic spaces consolidated refined social identities defined by privacy, purity, and a partial release from manual labor. Although Roberts wrote about running an aristocratic home, both his book and the goals of gentility and privacy it advanced typified the central tenets of bourgeois domestic agendas during the antebellum period.[6]

By the 1850s native-born white employers viewed not only the work but the persons of their domestic laborers with a critical eye and nose. Irish immigrant women, in particular, had a sensibility about body care and housekeeping that was at odds with that of their genteel employers.[7] The rise of a domestic labor market provided employers with new opportunities to define the physical beings of the people they employed. Those like Roberts, who were able to put their own stamp on standards for self-care, prospered under this new regime of domestic labor, while others found judgments of their deficiency projected onto their bodies rather than based on the work they performed.

Taken together with other sources, Roberts's book gives us a glimpse of the complex negotiations over the aesthetic and metaphysical dimensions of waged domestic work as well as its better known physical dimensions. What comes into view are struggles over the cleanliness of servant bodies—especially feet, hands, and clothes—that inevitably became soiled as they labored to meet (or occasionally to challenge) elite and bourgeois domestic standards. This was a matter not simply of domestic laborers' appearance but of how they contributed to the smells, tastes, sounds, and appearance of the household, providing elite and middle-class men and women with unwelcome reminders of their place in a larger world of unruly bodies. Some employers dealt with this challenge less by scrutinizing each servant's appearance and deportment than by organizing labor to give certain trusted employees greater access to the bodies of the family while keeping others at a farther remove.[8] Others tried to prevent fatal diseases from crossing class lines: they attempted to cleanse the bodies and homes of working-class people whose odors and habits threatened the purity and healthfulness of the middle class. Native-born perceptions of Irish and African-American differences sprang as much from these relationships within households as from those in more public sites. Through careful choreography and a distinctive ethos for household cleanliness, middle-class homes became crucibles of ethnic and racial differences.[9]

THE REFINED SERVANT

Roberts's guide reflected new concerns for the body, reflected in grooming and dress, and found in the diaries of well-to-do Americans throughout the country. Roberts capitalized on this desire for refinement as well as on the emerging crisis in domestic standards and labor. The details of his early life, although sketchy, help to explain his appeal to his wealthy northern employers. Born around 1780 in South Carolina and raised in close proximity to slavery if not actually enslaved himself, Roberts acquired domestic skills and literacy before

moving north. He may well have symbolized the exoticism and aristocratic privilege of southern slavery to his first northern employer, Nathan Appleton, who
visited Charleston between 1802–1803. Whether Roberts joined Appleton's household during that trip or after traveling to Boston a few years later is not known. By
1805, however, he was living in New England, married to the daughter of an
African-American Revolutionary War veteran, and probably employed in Appleton's household.[10] In 1825, at about age forty-five, he left Appleton to work for former Massachusetts governor and senator Christopher Gore, an ailing man in his
sixties who presided over a large country estate in Waltham. As butler, Roberts
enabled the Gore family to live comfortably amid the material objects that
broadcast their refinement and good taste.

Elite Federalists like Gore and Appleton mourned the passing of a hierarchical social order that justified their own brand of paternalism—a world that had
certainly disappeared with the abolition of slavery in Massachusetts, if it had ever
truly existed—even as they engaged in the commercial activities that had
wrought its demise. In Roberts both men found the combination of experience,
competence, and seeming deference that many elite New Englanders believed
no longer existed among native-born whites. In different ways, both men also
probably found Roberts's associations with the slave South soothing to their political sensibilities, and useful to their projects of aristocratic self-fashioning. For
Appleton, who supported slavery throughout his political career, Roberts might
have embodied the alchemy of slavery so seductive to wealthy northern men for
whom southern planters represented the nearest model of aristocratic life. In
contrast, Roberts's presence might have allowed the antislavery Gore to mimic
certain privileges of slave ownership without complicity in its evils. Literacy,
freedom, and wages distinguished Roberts from the debased southern slave of
the northern antislavery imagination. Yet he might still have enabled Gore to indulge in a fantasy of aristocratic life.[11]

The House Servant's Directory reflected Roberts's experience as a servant in
aristocratic European households—he boasted of service in England and
France as well as in the United States—and thus anticipated the concerns of an
upwardly mobile middle class, eager to gentrify their domestic lives. The book's
subtitle suggested that, although "chiefly compiled for the use of house servants," the text was "identically made to suit the manners and customs of families
in the United States," many of whom could not procure the domestic labor to
live in the style of Christopher Gore. Roberts's warnings about diseased vagabonds wandering city streets echoed similar refrains in cities throughout Europe and spoke to fears of an unruly and potentially dependent underclass.

Let us, then, consider Roberts on the subject of dirt. His admonitions to manservants to keep their persons free of dirt—including that honestly acquired through their domestic labors—were ostensibly designed to protect the genteel inhabitants of upper-class domestic spaces from distasteful spectacles. Much of his advice thus echoed the content of conduct books that urged wives to keep their own persons presentable. To accomplish this sleight of hand, servants needed to discipline themselves to rise early and immediately take on the dirtiest chores before ladies and gentlemen arose for breakfast. "There is nothing more disagreeable than to run about with dirty hands and dirty clothes," Roberts wrote, "and this must inevitably be the case if you defer this part of your work until every body is stirring and bustling about." *Disagreeable*, as Roberts used the term, captured the sentiments of genteel employers at the sight of filth on the body and clothes of manservants, but not the views of manservants themselves: "There is not a class of people to whom cleanliness of person and attire is of more importance to servants in genteel families. There are many servants, whom I have been eye witness to, through negligence as I must call it, who are a disgrace to the family that they live with, as well as to themselves, but appearing in their dirty clothes at a time of day that they should have all the dirtiest part of their work done."[12]

Designating different clothes for different kinds of work was another strategy to spare the sensibilities of the affluent. Roberts recommended a separate outfit for dirty work, made of dark-colored fabric, so as to minimize the appearance of soil. Accessories such as vests, caps ("to keep the dust from your hair"), and aprons were essential. Having completed the dirty work of cleaning boots, shoes, knives, and lamps, and in winter, taking up ashes, cleaning grates, tidying up the hearth, and making fires, a good manservant carefully washed his hands before touching window shutters or breakfast place settings, where dirty fingers were likely to leave unsightly smudges. Never, Roberts warned, should a manservant "attempt to wait on the family in the clothes" worn during this dirty morning labor. Rather, "before your family come down to breakfast," he advised, "you should have on a clean shirt collar and cravat, with a clean round jacket, white linen apron and clean shoes, with your hair neatly combed out."[13]

Roberts urged servants to labor as silently as possible. Wearing slippers minimized the noise from running about to accomplish morning tasks. Even after the family was awake, Roberts warned against wearing thick shoes or boots, suitable for navigating city streets and muddy country lanes but inappropriate for attending guests in the parlor or waiting on dinner. His advice throughout maximized the distinctions between the refined spaces of the middle-class family and the hurly-burly of city streets. Domestic laborers needed to take pains to efface any visual or auditory links between their own laboring bodies and those of uncouth vagabonds who contributed to the squalor and noise of public life.[14]

Roberts was painfully aware of the need for domestic laborers to efface traces of their own physicality to minimize the conflict between who they were and where they worked. Washing was an important part of this effort, as it had been for respectable people for several centuries. "You must always be very clean in your person, and wash your face and comb your hair, &c," he admonished. Yet more attention to the body was necessary for people performing strenuous physical labor: "Wash your feet at least three times per week, as in summer time your feet generally perspire; a little weak vinegar and water, or a little rum is very good for this use, as it is a stimulant, and there is not danger of taking cold after washing in either. Servants being generally on foot throughout the day, it must cause perspiration, which makes a bad smell, which would be a very disagreeable thing to yourself and the company on whom you wait."[15]

Mindful of the servant's vulnerability to the judgments of fastidious masters, Roberts did not aim simply at distancing employers from distasteful smells and sights. He also sought to protect servants from having their bodies used in evidence against them. Thus, for example, although he warned servants not to drink, he provided a remedy "to prevent the breath from smelling after drink" so that "no person can discover by your breath whether you have been drinking or not." Recipes also allowed servants to make their appearances more appealing to employers: for instance, a wash "to give a luster to the face," a wash for the hair, an "an excellent paste for the skin to firm it," and a hair dye to turn red hair black.[16]

Roberts painted a portrait of the dutiful, accomplished manservant, who had mastered the challenges of his occupation through a combination of bodily discipline (rise early, wash the body, and tread softly), strategy (do the dirty work before anyone wakes up), and subterfuge (don't drink, but if you do, efface the traces from your breath). Was Roberts perhaps more scrupulous about the state of his clothes, hands, feet, hair, and breath than a white writer might have been? There is not much in the text to identify him as African American except perhaps this careful attention to areas of the body that represented the body's frontiers—the smells emanating from its mouth and its feet, the appearance of clothing that revealed the labor it engaged in, and the condition of the hair and skin on the visible body. Although such efforts reflected Roberts's immediate concerns with the impression he made, they also suggested more abstract concerns about social contact across race and class lines, and the ways people understood cities, the social order, and the state through the metaphor of the human body. In a climate increasingly hostile to black people and more committed to views of race as an innate, embodied condition, Roberts may have been more self-conscious of his own physical presence in a middle-class household than his white servant counterparts.[17]

One tiny detail in his advice manual suggests that Roberts did indeed have a heightened sensitivity about his close proximity to middle-class female bodies. In the midst of instructions about how to black shoes, Roberts reminded readers that ladies' shoes required special treatment. As in other instances in which direct contact with the bodies of the white family necessitated that the manservant wash his hands (for example, when waiting on them at the breakfast table), a domestic laborer who had been blacking men's shoes—shoes that were worn outside—needed to wash his hands before touching the shoes of the lady of the house. Ladies' shoes were not blacked but literally "whitened" with milk or egg whites. The linings of such shoes were also usually white, Roberts explained, and so only clean hands should touch the inside of the shoe to hold it while polishing the exterior. To do otherwise would soil the white linings with dark finger smudges, destroying the illusion that the wearer's feet were as pure and clean as the lining of her shoes and reminding her of her manservant's intimate access to accessories that were part of her social person.

One could read race into Roberts's advice to servants to defer to employers in their speech. But how could such a seemingly deferential text be written by a man who devoted the rest of his life to fighting racial injustice? A closer look at his text reveals a more complicated view of the master-servant relationship, one that provided a religious context for deference and eschewed any association between domestic service and slavery. A few circumscribed examples showcasing the virtue of long-suffering Old Testament "servants," Joseph and Jacob, suggest that Roberts deliberately employed this euphemism for slavery as part of his project to redeem domestic labor as an honorable and dignified occupation for free African Americans. In a pointed double entendre, moreover, he warned his readers "never to be a slave to passion." In addition, Roberts's advice to would-be servants departed from injunctions to be deferential and delivered a subtle moral indictment of their masters. Endowing the domestic laborer with the dignified obligations of the true Christian, he reminded readers to bestow charity upon those less fortunate than themselves, to love their enemies, no matter how unjustly they behaved, to choose honesty over flattery, and to resist the desire for riches, glory, and pleasure as a disease of the mind. "It is much better to be the oppressed than to stand in the place of the oppressor," Roberts observed, "for patience is ever acceptable in the sight of God, and in due time will be rewarded, for God hath promised that it shall be so; and when have his promises failed?"[18]

Roberts remained silent about his race, his place of birth, and his possible former connection to slavery. Indeed, the message of his text appears to be that those biographical details were irrelevant to the corpus of advice he dispensed. Did he fear that his race would hurt sales of his book in a region where racism against African Americans was on the rise? Perhaps. But it seems more likely that he hoped to protect his brand of domestic professionalism and competence from both the stigma of slavery and white fantasies about slave deference. His silence about his own life was an assertion of the irrelevance of race to professional standards for domestic service. For a man who made a career out of disciplining his body into silence and invisibility, dignity cohered in the refusal to expose the struggles of his inner life to the white gaze and in the patient endurance of injustice and oppression.[19]

SETTING STANDARDS

Roberts's dignified domestic competence ensured the success of his household advice. *The Household Servant's Directory* (1827) set the standard for American house books for the next twenty years and appeared in two subsequent editions. Although later manuals borrowed from Roberts's text and imitated its combination of practical advice on cleaning, dining etiquette, and household management, none was authored by either a servant or a man. Rather, successful household guides came from the pens of women, American and English, whose claims to expertise derived from their experience running their own households and creating labor-saving systems of management. On occasion, such women directed their advice to servants or urged mistresses to have greater sympathy for the difficulties of a domestic's life. But after Roberts's text, most domestic advice targeted housewives who hoped to remain pleasing in their persons even if they had to perform housework themselves. Even middle-class housewives with hired help could benefit from advice that had originally been aimed at helping servants achieve efficiency, decency, and dignity.

The burgeoning American household management literature differed from its English counterpart on two main topics: distinctive American manners and negotiation of the class relationship between mistress and servant. Indeed, when publishers produced American editions of popular English guides, they often provided additional commentary to address the unique aspects of American households. In Frances Byerley Parkes's *Domestic Duties*, originally published in London in 1825, most of the advice needed no translation. But the 1829 American edition included asterisked material contradicting the author's suggestion that it was acceptable for the mistress to tell a white lie when refusing a social call. Such falsehoods were not harmless euphemisms, the editor of the American version warned, but could have a baneful effect on the honesty of servants, who would surely see this for what it was—a lie.[20]

As this instance of the socially acceptable falsehood suggests, not all features of European polite society were readily embraced across the Atlantic. Advice book authors walked a fine line between explaining European practices, which had an inherent appeal for American social climbers, and selecting only certain ones for Americans to emulate. They also passed judgment on home-grown habits. Eliza Leslie, whose best-selling *House Book; or, a Manual of Domestic Economy* first appeared in 1840, offered advice ranging from fashionable furniture to table manners for Americans who sought a perch in polite society. They must rid their homes of rocking chairs, she declared, which represented an unrefined rural habit and a noisy, undisciplined movement of the body that was by nature ungenteel.[21]

Perhaps the greatest social distinctions appeared at the dining table, where knowledge of the proper placement and use of paraphernalia revealed comfort with genteel practices. "There are few genteel families who are not in the practice of using napkins at table," Leslie explained, "to spread on the lap while eating, and for wiping the mouth and the fingers." Clearly she believed at least some of her readers needed instruction in the basic use of the napkin. In addition to its placement and use, napkin color reflected the status of hosts, with "coloured borders . . . less genteel than those that are all white." True gentility required that there be "a sufficiency of knives, forks, &c.," not merely to afford each diner with his or her own utensils, as would have been de rigueur at a genteel table, but to avoid ever having to use a utensil more than once between washings. She also found it necessary to explain the purpose and proper use of finger glasses (the English actress Frances Kemble noted their absence at the dinner table of her New York hotel in September 1832, along with the disorderly service of food and a dirty tablecloth).[22] Leslie decried the European practice of using them as mini-spittoons. "The disgusting European custom of taking a mouthful or two of the water, and after washing the mouth, spitting it back again into the finger glass, has not become fashionable in America," she declared with obvious relief. "Neither is it usual in our country to place tooth-picks on the table for the benefit of the company," she observed, commenting pointedly, "most *gentlemen* preferring to pick their teeth and wash their mouths in private." Catharine Sedgwick agreed that "hawking" or spitting and using a toothpick at the table revealed as much coarseness as the failure to use a toothpick or the habit of sitting on only two legs of a chair.[23]

Addressing their guides to mistresses, nearly all authors of household management books assumed that readers shared some blame for the shortage of good domestic labor. The Rhode Island reformer Frances Green, whose *The Housekeeper's Book* appeared in 1837, warned mistresses not to overstep themselves by trying to follow the latest fashions in food, furniture, and hospitality. Rather, they should aim to run households that were within their means. Debunking the received wisdom about the servant problem, Green commented drily, "That 'servants are great plagues' may be the fact; but I am, nevertheless, bold enough to assert that it is a greater plague to be without them." She also urged mistresses to be more sympathetic to the servant's plight, a note that had been missing from Roberts's text for servants but that marked many of the American home books. "When all the hardships which belong to the life of a maid-servant are taken into consideration (which I am afraid they very rarely are)," she chided, "the wonder is, that the greater part of this class of persons are not rendered less obliging and less obedient to the will of their employers, and more callous to their displeasure, than we really find them."[24]

In trying to explain why American women faced unique difficulties, many authors alluded to the dilemma of female education in a republic, which pitted cultivation and upward mobility—the accoutrements of ladies—against the practical education in domestic skills needed for hands-on housewifery.[25] As the historian Catherine Kelly has shown, this critical discussion of fashion was part of a larger provincial project of drawing social boundaries and preserving rural identities in the face of (and occasionally in league with) market encroachments. Leslie, too, placed the blame for the domestic labor problem squarely on the shoulders of ignorant mistresses. "Complaints are incessantly heard of the deterioration of servants," she observed, "but may not one source of this growing evil be traced to the deterioration of *mistresses* in the knowledge and practice of all that is necessary to a well-ordered household?" Lacking domestic skills, the novice mistress could neither instruct her domestics nor do the work herself in "emergencies," Leslie noted, making advice books necessary. Leslie condemned the emphasis on "the cultivation of showy accomplishments, or the unavailing pursuit of studies that to females are always abstruse." She hoped that her book would not only provide practical advice and useful receipts but give women a more substantial way to promote marital happiness than "showy accomplishments."[26]

Writing in 1841, Catharine Beecher agreed with Leslie that American girls were being poorly prepared for their futures as housekeepers. She defined the problem as improper practical and physical education, which left them unfit to deal with their inevitable exposure "to a far greater amount of intellectual and moral excitement, than those of any other land." Beecher proposed a coherent educational plan that would give women's domestic calling greater dignity and improved efficiency. She borrowed heavily from Leslie, but she incorporated this advice into a larger body of knowledge that included fields we might dub domestic medicine, domestic sociology, domestic philosophy, and domestic religion. To prepare American women to master these various branches of the domestic arts, Beecher recommended, "much less time should be given to school, and much more time to domestic employments, especially in the wealthier classes." But Beecher doubted that her domestic reforms would take hold if the rich failed to set good examples of housekeeping. "Whatever ladies in the wealthier classes decide shall be fashionable, will be followed by all the rest," she observed, denouncing the persistence of "aristocratic habits" that left women physically as well as practically unfit to be housewives. What all American women needed was the regular exercise and experience that came with domestic labor: "It is, therefore, the peculiar duty of ladies who have wealth, to set a proper example, in this respect, and make it their first aim to secure a strong and healthful constitution for their daughters, by active domestic employments. All sweeping, dusting, care of furniture and beds, the clear starching, and the nice cooking, should be done by the daughters of a family, and not by hired service."[27] Beecher's advice echoed the refrains of a broom sellers' jingle, "And what better exercise pray can employ you/Than to sweep all vexatious intruders away."[28]

These standards for domestic cleanliness, elaborated in excruciating detail by Leslie, Beecher, Green, and others, created a daunting prospect for those who would manage without hired help. Indeed, both Leslie and Beecher presumed the assistance of some paid help to accomplish daily and weekly housecleaning. To make a good initial impression on visitors, Leslie recommended that "white marble door-steps should be washed every morning (except in freezing weather) with cold water and soap." "This is the custom in Philadelphia," she added, alluding to the city's reputation for cleanliness (Figure 10.1).

She also urged her readers to sweep the kitchen floor every morning after the fire was made. A clean, well-swept hearth imparted an "air of cleanness, neatness, and gentility to a room of very moderate pretensions," she noted, while a dirty hearth and a grate choked with cinders and ashes is "infallible evidence of bad housekeeping." Washing unpainted hearths daily and the entire kitchen floor once a week in winter (twice in summer) helped to maintain this clean appearance.[29]

Inside the house, American women needed special measures to deal with two problems that had long been features of the American environment: the abundance of bedbugs and the effects of summer's heat. Indeed, as a contemporary cartoon suggests, the presence of bedbugs could no longer be accepted as a discomfort to be endured (Figure 10.2). In the American climate, Leslie declared, no bed or bedding that was shut up during the day would remain free of bedbugs. Bedstead joints, particularly those of servants, required a weekly dousing with water to keep the bugs at bay. Carpets should be swept frequently with a corn

10.1. Thomas Nast, Philadelphia street scene. Charles Dickens, *Scenes from Italy, Sketches by Boz, and American Notes* (1877)

broom, with damp tea leaves facilitating the collection of tiny debris. Other tips dealt more generally with preventing filth. Don't put rugs in the kitchen, where they were likely to soak up grease and dirt, Leslie urged, and avoid white carpets, which rarely look clean for long. Remove old wallpaper, which harbored bed-bugs, she advised, and purify walls with whitewash or paint. In addition to these special measures, house books were filled with chores American women shared with their European sisters.[30]

Cooking utensils and tableware, objects intimately connected with ingestion, demanded special care to minimize the dangers of pollution. All authors mentioned specially designed tools, such as the Shaker "cup-swab or mop" recommended by Leslie for "tea things," to ensure that all traces of food or drink could be removed from items that touched the lips. But none of the antebellum advice book authors found the final appearance of the dish an adequate indication of its cleanliness. Beecher expanded the need for scrutiny from the dishes and utensils themselves to everything that touched them. "The sink should be thoroughly washed every day, and often scalded with ley or hot suds," she warned. She also

10.2. D. C. Johnston, *Great Cry and Little Wool* (1832), *Scraps*, no. 3 (Boston, 1849).
Courtesy The Winterthur Library: Printed Book and Periodical Collection

advised the housewife to "keep a supply of *nice* dish-cloths hanging near the sink, hemmed and furnished with loops." These were not to be used indiscriminately, however, but according to an elaborate hierarchy: "There should be one for the dishes that are not greasy, one for the greasy dishes, and one for pots and kettles." Furthermore, having been used, "these should all be put in the wash every wash-ing day. If the mistress of the family will insist on this, she will be less annoyed by having her dishes washed with black, dirty, and musty rags."[31]

As Beecher's comment suggested, the purification accomplished by washing dishes was jeopardized if the dishcloth was itself a filthy, smelly rag. But there were other dangers too. Leslie stressed the importance of clean hands for keep-ing mealtime paraphernalia free of pollution, urging mistresses to keep a soap cup and towel near the kitchen sink to encourage frequent hand washing. Frances Green elaborated a hierarchy for drying towels that had less to do with minimizing pollution per se than with avoiding traces of lint on glasses. "There are four kinds of cloths which ought to be provided for the use of the kit-chen—knife-cloths, dusters, tea, and glass-cloths," she observed, distinguished by their harsh feel (used for knives), their ability to pick up dust (cotton and flax dusters), and their lint-free nap (tea and glass cloths made from old bedsheeting). In addition, Green noted, a good housewife kept supplies of other cloths with special functions: knife tray cloths, house cloths for cleaning, pudding cloths, cheesecloths for protecting food from flies, round towels, and the linens used at the table itself: tablecloths, finger napkins, and place mats. Although their taxonomies differed somewhat from Green's, both Leslie and Beecher recommended multiple drying cloths and cleaning tools, distinguished both by the kind of filth they came in contact with and by their design. These elaborate hierarchies for removing dirt and dealing with the body's pollution contrasted sharply with representations of the way non-Anglos lived; in 1840 *The Pennsylvania Inquirer* claimed that Indians used a dog's tongue as a dishcloth.[32]

By the 1840s the need had intensified for household cleanliness to define domestic spaces as cleaner, purer enclaves, separate from the dirt of the outside world. Housework thus assumed some of the ritually protective functions of religious faith. Laundering, sweeping, reordering closets, seasonal cleaning of carpets and floors, airing chambers—each of these tasks so obsessively detailed by the advice books was supposed to have its own day or season. In addition to providing order and structure to the domestic environment, these chores offered the possibility of preventing disease and making the home environment safe, much as prayers and days of fasting and thanksgiving might have done in the seventeenth century. Middle-class women were increasingly responsible for both cleanliness of person and preparation of the spirit. Spiritual and domestic exercises, moreover, had in common their vulnerability to pollution (sin and filth), their need to be endlessly repeated, and the belief that their ritual performance might offer some protection from the dangers of life. Both labors were at once strenuous and ephemeral. Self-conscious housekeepers such as Anna Thaxter Cushing of Boston evaluated themselves against these standards. Cushing noted with evident satisfaction in her diary when she achieved her goals: "I did the work which belongs to me on Monday," she wrote on Monday, February 28, 1848, and, on the following Friday, "I did my Friday sweeping and dusting." Accomplishing Saturday's tasks at the end of a long week was a unusual achievement, which received special emphasis. She remarked self-critically about a night during which she stayed up late to finish mending, "A good housekeeper would have the mending done before Saturday evening."[33]

Despite Cushing's self-conscious efforts to adhere to a strict schedule, the actual labor of completing household tasks necessitated flexibility. Other than a designated day for laundry, the ritual nature of housework appears more in the sequence of chores and the larger pattern of weekly and seasonal labor than in rigid conformity to a daily assignment. In several diaries, for example, women noted they were just getting around to folding clothes on Thursday and Friday and replacing them in dressers and wardrobes. The weather, sudden changes in the health of a hired laborer or a family member, and other shifts in the availability of domestic help required that housewives be flexible about when they accomplished their labors. During one particularly rainy week, the Worcester housewife Emeline Rice reported to her sister on a Friday that the clothes had been soaking since Monday with no prospect of drying them in sight.[34]

Standards for clothing and appearance, like standards for the household itself, had become more rigorous by the late 1830s. By that decade, if not before, people were donning their Sunday best—special garments and freshly laundered, ironed, and mended clothes. Commenting on this practice, Leslie argued for a Tuesday washday, reasoning that "some articles, which were put on quite clean on Sunday, might very well be worn one day more." Attempting to extricate housekeeping from tradition and organize it scientifically, Leslie and Beecher both suggested that Tuesday made more sense for laundry because it allowed a full day for softening hard water, sorting clothes, soaking whites, and preparing the day's meals in advance. But there is little evidence that they succeeded in budging laundry day from its Monday spot, a tradition since the 1790s.[35]

All house book authors offered advice on two challenges of doing laundry that had become more significant by the 1830s: whitening or stain removal, and procuring good labor. Achieving whiteness had taken on new importance. All fabric originally colored white—whether it be shirting, bedding, or dish towels—had to be white to be considered clean. Contact with bodily products, including the skin's effusions and animal fat from meals, resulted in contamination that could be removed only by restoring whiteness. This fetishized value of whiteness, based on its symbolism of purity, transcended sectional cultures; it was also potent in the South. Thus Mildred Coles Cameron effused upon staying at the house of her fellow North Carolinian Mrs. Boylan in 1839, "The chamber prepared for us looked as if it had been prepared for a bride, every thing snowy white."[36]

Leslie and Beecher reiterated time-honored techniques for achieving whiteness by soaking items overnight, boiling, and blueing (a dye process that combated yellowing). The most crucial ingredient for keeping white clothes white, however, as Leslie and Beecher reminded readers, was an adequate supply of water, so that soiled water could be changed frequently. "Washing in dirty suds is of very little avail," Leslie instructed, advice that put a premium on the labor and technology for supplying households with water. For best results, all authors recommended doing laundry according to a system that differentiated and ranked items to be washed. Whites needed to be laundered first, while the water was the hottest and cleanest. Colors could be safely washed in water that had already been used. Nearly all authors also offered special instructions for cleaning blankets, colored dresses, gold and silver muslins, black silk, and bed feathers. Leslie also described special soaps and recipes for whiteners containing milk, egg whites, white rice starch, and onions. After being treated with these special solutions, white garments and linens should be laid in the grass and exposed to the bleaching power of the sun, much as they had been for centuries.[37]

Of course, stain removal and whitening, although crucial to producing clean laundry, was only one part of the process. Getting washed items through drying, mending, and ironing without contaminating them required considerable care. Clothes hung outside, as most were, became targets for birds and could be soiled by dust on dry windy days, spattered by mud if an unexpected rainstorm occurred, or stained by the grass. If they dried incompletely, moreover, they were subject to mold and mildew, which were difficult to remove. Worse, once brought inside to be mended or ironed, clean clothing might absorb the odors of the kitchen. Leslie advised that foods with a powerful smell not be cooked on ironing day, so that clothes would not become saturated with the odors. This required the housewife to coordinate the schedule for laundry with the week's dinner menus not just on washday itself but also on ironing day, a difficult feat when so many variables such as drying time were unknown.[38]

Women of means dealt with the strenuous labor of laundry in a number of ways. To save labor as well as soap, Frances Green recommended soaking washables overnight. Cushing experimented with a new washing fluid, touted as a way to save labor, and "found it quite successful—scarcely any rubbing to be done to the clothes." Other women tried washing "jinnys" and other machines to speed up the process and lessen their dependence on hired or slave labor. Institutions like the New York poorhouse also purchased washing machines to maximize laundry output with a minimum of human labor.[39]

The invention of the detachable collar was one of many efforts to reduce the enormous burden laundry placed upon household resources. It also reflected the continued importance of a cleanly appearance in the visible body and less concern for hidden parts of the body and clothing. In 1827 the Troy, New York, housewife Hannah Lord Montague allegedly cut off her husband's shirt collar to wash it without having to launder the entire shirt. Once it was washed, starched, dried, and ironed, she sewed it back on the shirt. When a local shopkeeper got wind of her invention, he started manufacturing them, giving rise to a brisk trade in detachable collars. These soon became standard; along with neck cloths, they allowed a man to appear to be clothed in a freshly laundered shirt even if the only clean garment was around his neck.[40]

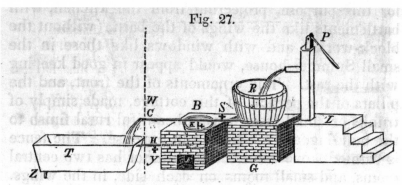

P, Pump. L, Steps to use when pumping. R, Reservoir. G, Brickwork to raise the Reservoir. B, A large Boiler. F, Furnace, beneath the Boiler. C, Conductor of cold water. H, Conductor of hot water. K, Cock for letting cold water into the Boiler. S, Pipe to conduct cold water to a cock over the kitchen sink. T, Bathing-tub, which receives cold water from the Conductor C, and hot water from the Conductor H. W, Partition separating the Bathing-room from the Wash-room. Y, Cock to draw off hot water. Z, Plug to let off the water from the Bathing-tub into a drain.

10.3. Household plumbing, from Catharine Beecher, A *Treatise on Domestic Economy* (1841). Courtesy American Antiquarian Society

The boom during the 1840s and 1850s in plumbing supplies, including pipes, cisterns, faucets, and tubs, reflected the housewife's effort to meet new demands for clean clothes by employing new conveniences. Hauling water had long been despised as a backbreaking, time-consuming chore that limited the cleanliness that could be achieved. Public water systems, established in many cities by mid-century, made water available at a price to a tiny minority of elite city dwellers; but privately engineered cisterns, wells, pumps, and pipelines brought running water to thousands of others. The desire for greater convenience sparked the sale of plumbing fixtures to provide running water for laundry and, as we will see, bathing (Figure 10.3).[41]

Yet despite these convergences and the symbolic meanings of clean clothes, middle-class women had little investment in doing the wash themselves. Clearly, if snowy white linens in middle-class homes and on middle-class backs symbolized moral purity, they did so because of indirect associations with domestic virtue rather than through some mystical process directly involving middle-class women's labor.[42] No nineteenth-century middle-class woman who has left any written account of her domestic life ever described doing laundry as spiritually uplifting, edifying, or purifying. Quite the contrary. Women described washday as leaving them fit for little else. Fourteen-year-old Louisa Jane Trumbell thus observed in her diary in 1836, "I have been washing all this morning and my fingers feel rather unlike writing."[43]

Indeed, domestic servants seemed necessary to the production of the clean clothes that symbolized refinement. As the household management gurus Eliza Leslie and Catharine Beecher reminded their readers, with proper supervision servants would be unlikely to damage the delicate and intricate materials that made up middle-class wardrobes and household linen chests. By performing the most strenuous tasks of the workweek and the ones that reflected least personally on middle-class woman's character, domestic servants enabled the transformation of middle-class women from potentially disgusting slatterns into morally pure mothers. In addition to attending more carefully to their own persons, mothers could devote themselves to children precisely because the expanding responsibility for washing an ever-diversifying collection of fabrics could be turned over to other women, who could perform the work as well as their employers even if they failed to imbue it with moral or spiritual feeling.

So as soon as a northern white woman of any class had the means, she hired a woman to do her laundry. This presents an interesting comparison with the white yeoman households of the South, where a woman with access to slave labor would first replace herself in the fields. A wife's or daughter's field labor remained the first impediment to gentility in the yeoman South, whereas in the North, it was the physical exertion, sweat, and muscle required to do laundry. Most household management books assumed that a laborer might be hired to do the laundry in house, although they conceded the difficulty. "It is a common complaint, in all parts of the Country, that *good* washers are very rare," Beecher noted, but she believed that half of the problem could be attributed to poor organization of the washerwoman's work environment and inadequate supplies. Eliza Leslie, however, suggested a solution that potentially avoided the problems of securing a steady employee for the most distasteful work of the household and the disruption of washday. "In Philadelphia it is very customary for families, as well as single persons, to put out their washing," she observed. "There are many excellent washerwomen who take it by the month or quarter, at a very reasonable price; and if the *washing only* is put out, and the clothes brought rough-dried to be ironed at home, the expense will be found scarcely, if at all, to exceed that of having it done in your own house; and you are relieved from the trouble and inconvenience of washing-day."[44]

Even if they hired out the labor, the house book authors urged their readers to attend to the minute details of domestic tasks. At least in Philadelphia, readers

10.4. D. C. Johnston, *Height of Cleanliness* (1835), *Scraps*, no. 6 (Boston, 1849).
Courtesy The Winterthur Library: Printed Book and Periodical Collection

appear to have taken the daunting domestic advice in stride. A series of cartoons penned in 1835 lampooned the fastidiousness of the city's matrons (Figure 10.4). Was it possible to be too clean, the cartoons asked satirically, to lose one's common sense so thoroughly that one engaged in ludicrous labors to meet ridiculous standards? Beecher addressed this question by condemning blind subservience to the hierarchies of filth and dirt laid out in books like her own. "*System, economy,* and *neatness,* are valuable only so far as they tend to promote comfort and the well-being of those affected," she reminded her readers. "Some women seem to act under the impression, that these advantages must be secured, at all events, even if the comfort of the family be the sacrifice. True, it is very important that children grow up in habits of system, neatness, and order . . . but it is more important, that they grow up with amiable tempers, that they learn to meet the crosses of life with patience and cheerfulness; and nothing has a greater influence to obscure this than a mother's example."[45]

Somehow, a housewife needed to achieve the rigorous new standards of cleanliness without forsaking the new expectations for her family's emotional life. Beecher offered detailed advice to help servantless women manage the laundry, establish order, and care for the bodies in her household. But clearly, a mother stood a better chance of conforming to elaborate cleanliness hierarchies and remaining cheerful if she could procure extra labor. Yet as their diaries and correspondence about their households reveal, middle-class women often found that these very standards became a major source of conflict between mistress and servant.[46]

DOMESTIC POLITICS

Most of the influential house book authors writing in the 1840s traced the domestic labor problem not only to poorly educated mistresses but to the uneasy fit between the egalitarian strains of a republicanism and the hierarchical nature of the mistress-servant relation: the source of the problem, in common parlance, of "uppity" servants. American domestics "are not willing to be called *servants*," Sedgwick and Beecher warned.[47] Theirs was a common complaint. Indeed, Beecher noted, this refusal by domestics to accept a label they regarded as degrading was accompanied by a host of behaviors that denied or undermined the social distance between employers and their employees. The insistence on being treated as an equal reflected the unique evolution of American domestic labor in the North from "help" to "domestics," with the former persisting in rural areas and the latter emerging more quickly in cities. "In some places," Beecher observed, "they claim a seat, at meals, with the family; they imitate a style of dress unbecoming their condition; and their manners and address are rude and disrespectful." Beecher urged forbearance, observing that the label *servant* stung not because of overweening pride but as "a consequence of that noble and generous spirit of freedom, which every American draws from his mother's breast, and which ought to be respected, rather than despised. In order to be respected by others, we must respect ourselves; and sometimes the ruder classes of society make claims, deemed forward and offensive, when, with their views, such a position seems indispensable to preserve a proper self-respect."[48]

The fact that most domestics were unmarried obviated some of the potential conflict for a hired woman at the beck and call of her employer: usually she did not have to struggle to keep up with the cooking, cleaning, and laundry required by her own family. But it also made her more vulnerable to her mistress's demands. Ethnic and racial differences also strained the relationship. Irish women made up a large proportion of the pool of domestic laborers and free African

Americans but a small portion of that pool. Yet these two groups had in common the fact that domestic service led the list of the occupations their populations entered.[49]

Increasingly, American house book authors negotiated the awkward politics of the mistress-servant relation—the close proximity of people occupying different stations in life—by attempting to minimize the physical traces left by servant bodies in domestic spaces. Even if one could draw firm social boundaries between the persons of mistress and servant, one could not prevent the servant's physical body from penetrating the most intimate spaces of the household. In this respect, we can describe the American house book literature as undergoing a process of Anglicization, with Robert Roberts's manual providing a precocious example. Like Roberts, British house book authors revealed concern over the contact between servants and the middle-class families they served. Intimately connected to the domestic environment they labored to maintain and in which middle-class people anchored their own gentility, servants communicated the household's status with their bodies, both in the impression they made on visitors and in the physical traces they left on domestic accoutrements. If servants were undisciplined in their grooming—visibly dirty, smelly, or vermin-ridden—the household would suffer from like unpleasantness.

Employers were discomfited by reminders of the physical proximity of servants, particularly of their hands, the part of their bodies that touched articles that were then used by middle-class people. The British author Parkes instructed that "those who are called from other household work to assist in making the beds . . . should previously wash their hands, as nothing looks more untidy or disgusting, than the marks of dirty fingers upon the bedhangings, sheets or counterpanes. With cleanly servants, this can seldom occur." A nursemaid who cared for children "should be particularly cleanly in her person, washing herself almost as frequently as she washes the children." Parkes suggested issuing a footman a towel, bowl, and piece of soap so that he could wash his hands frequently. "A good steady servant will keep his clothes and person clean and neat," she declared; "he will be particularly careful in washing his hands, being called upon constantly to wait and hand about so many things." To avoid touching the hands of his middle-class employers, moreover, the footman should always use a waiter's tray to deliver messages, calling cards, or other objects.[50]

With the exception of Roberts, who anticipated much of the later concern with intimate contact between bodies from different stations, American authors were slower than their British counterparts to show concern for the aesthetics of physical proximity and initially focused more on morality and orderliness. Writing in 1837, Green acknowledged the importance of a servant's appearance for broadcasting the character of the household and its mistress: "Well dressed, that is to say, neatly dressed, clean looking, and well mannered servants always impress a visiter with a favourable idea of the house; while, on the contrary, there is no one so free from hasty judgment, as not to be more or less prejudiced against the mistress of the house, by the untidy appearance or the awkward behaviour of her domestics." But this was all Green had to say on the question of servants' physical bodies. The remainder of her text focused on servant honesty and the mistress's responsibility to establish punctual habits and lock up supplies.[51]

By the 1840s popular American house books had begun representing the servant's physical body as intrusive and at odds with middle-class sensibilities. This view reflected two phenomena: the growing influence of the market on domestic hiring practices (as well as the depiction of this influence as an "intrusion" into middle-class domestic sanctuaries) and the shift to Irish laborers, whose differences in grooming practices, real or imagined, provoked comparisons with their native-born counterparts.[52] Perhaps as a consequence of spending many of her formative years in England, where she was likely to have heard much about the need for boundaries between middle-class and servant bodies, Eliza Leslie dealt with the physicality of servants directly. She insisted that a servant waiting on table should "be clean and neatly drest," wearing clean white cotton gloves that reassured diners forced to watch servant fingers touch plates, utensils, and glasses and serve food. Urging mistresses not to put mirrors in the kitchen, she observed that in houses that had them, "hairs are frequently found in the dishes that come to the table. All the combing and dressing of the servants ought to be done in their own sleeping-rooms; and it is best to give them no facilities of performing this business in any other part of the house." Servant hair in the food was but the tip of the iceberg. Claiming that servants were less likely to be sensitive to the bites of bedbugs, Leslie warned that servants' neglect of their own bedding would lead to infestations of vermin spread via servant clothing.[53]

Beecher's advice echoed Leslie's concerns but with a more pragmatic awareness of the market for domestic labor. For households prosperous enough to have a servant waiting table, she suggested that "this domestic, male or female, wear a large clean apron, while in attendance, to be used for no other purpose, and also to require his hands and head to be put in the neatest order. It is peculiarly unpleasant to have food served by an untidy domestic." Beecher agreed with Leslie that servants couldn't be counted on to keep their own quarters and appearance up to snuff. "Domestics are very apt to neglect the care of their own chambers and clothing," she pronounced, "and such habits have a most pernicious influence on their wellbeing, and on that of their children in future domestic life." But unlike Leslie, she urged employers to add this duty to their other responsibilities, developing a paternalistic style that might both soften the inequities of the mistress-servant relationship and elevate it above the crassness of the market. Beecher was not unsympathetic to the Yankee girl who used the market to better her position, but her sympathy did not extend to the entire pool of domestic laborers. Indeed, the failure to maintain minimum standards of cleanliness and refinement separated a native-born domestic from the "coarse and dirty foreigner" with whom she might be forced to share quarters.[54]

The domestic management literature reveals the household's role as a crucible of racial and ethnic difference. Following the mass Irish migration in the 1840s, American house book authors began to describe domestics hailing from Ireland as irretrievably other, a judgment that reflected the poverty and rural origins of most migrants. Transplanted rural standards simply did not pass muster with American employers. Thus, *Harper's Weekly* dubbed the Irish "unwashed and totally ignorant of housewifery."[55] Such comments had long been part of the discourse about servants: Roberts had pointed out that most servants were unmindful of their own bodily filth, a weakness he sought to remedy by raising their awareness and offering practical advice for staying cleaner on the job. Lydia Maria Child attributed shoddy domestic practices to servant laziness and an inability to withstand minor physical discomfort. "Always have plenty of dish-water, and have it hot," she urged her readers. "There is no need of asking the character of a domestic, if you have ever seen her wash dishes in a little greasy water." Any woman who refused to make the effort to heat the water, was unwilling to stand the discomfort of washing dishes in it, or could not understand why doing dishes in cold greasy water was unacceptable did not have the requisite character to be a good domestic. Evaluations like these based on physical capacity made the designations "coarse and dirty" seem to adhere naturally to the category "Irish." In the domestic environment, where boundary-crossing contact between servants and employers was especially fraught in the intimate spaces designated for food preparation, eating, and sleep, a servant who was by nature filthy was a dangerous interloper.[56]

Evidence from New England households between 1840 and 1855 offers several different views of this politics of domestic labor. The rich material found in correspondence, diaries, and account books can be read in at least two ways: with the grain, to capture the employer's perspective on domestic labor, and against the grain, to permit speculation about hired women's own views of their situations. Closely examining four northern households with different means to employ servants—the Waterhouse, Rice, Cushing, and Lawrence households—we turn the tables on mistresses to ask, what were hired women's strategies for meeting their employers' expectations and maintaining their own households?

Where did laundry rank in a hired woman's hierarchy of waged labor? How did hired domestics evaluate the cleanliness of employers whose laundry they washed, chamber pots they emptied, and meals they prepared?[57]

The mistresses in all of the households defined their own work based on the availability of domestic help. Although all women were forced to do certain work when domestic employees were scarce, they considered several core tasks to be their own, distinguishing themselves from their hired laborers. In 1850, for example, Emeline Rice reported to her sister that by having hired a woman to do the wash, she and her eldest daughter "have got along with our work very well." *Work*, a term which usually referred to sewing clothes, produced something tangible: shirts, dresses, and other garments. Washing, in contrast, produced only temporary results. It was heavy work, too heavy for a sick woman or one in late pregnancy, and it left a legacy of painfully dry and cracked hands that might actually make other tasks, like sewing, more difficult.

In the Cambridge, Massachusetts, household of Louisa Waterhouse, domestic labor troubles erupted in 1839 when two longtime employees left after thirteen and fifteen years, respectively. Waterhouse, a well-educated doctor's wife, struggled to find replacements. The first person she hired was an older woman who wanted Dr. Waterhouse to take his tea early so that she could go out. Waterhouse looked for excuses to get rid of her but admitted to her diary that the woman was "a good Cook, good washer, good House maid, very neat, attends to the Table." Still, Waterhouse did not like her, describing her as deficient compared with her ideal domestic, "a woman who can sew & read, & who is kind & pleasant & willing to stay home."[58]

The next employee was a young woman who thought in terms of efficiency and collective responsibility rather than gentility. The new girl questioned Waterhouse's instruction that she answer the door, even if she was in the middle of a task. "She can go to the door, & open it as well as I can," she told her more experienced coworker, who responded, "Mistress doesn't like to go to the door." The new girl's rejoinder brimmed over with pragmatic objection, probably based on a cooperative rural work life in which lightly burdened people assisted those more heavily burdened. "Well, nor I neither dont like to do it," she complained, "as soon as I am about an thing, the Bell rings, & must leave what I am doing & go to the door?" The young hired girl's approach to work was based on assessments of what was needed and who was in the best position to do it. "Why she is close to the door & doing *nothing else*," she retorted to her coworker, "Im sure she might as well go herself."[59]

Employees often knew more about the labor they were expected to perform than their mistresses. Waterhouse told her young domestic Elizabeth Brown,

"Always wash the meat before you roast, it is uncleanly not to," explaining her purity concerns about the food she served: "It lays in the stall, in the cart, & the handling, it is all a notion that washing meat hurts it, wash it just before you Roast, it gets off all the loose particles of bone, & other impurities." Elizabeth gently demurred, "I will if you say so, I've heard that meat was'nt so good for washing, but I shall do as you say." Still, the finicky Waterhouse remained unsatisfied, mainly owing to her own insecurity about housekeeping. "I would'nt have you act blindly," she enjoined Brown. Indeed, Waterhouse admitted to more expertise in judging the final product than in actually producing it. The secret to domestic harmony, she confided to Elizabeth, was in having "things done every day just as I would for company, & then there is not running about in a hurry." Waterhouse explained that she wished her domestic help to "have an interest in her work, do it as they would for themselves."[60]

By the 1840s securing a female domestic who would meet the new rigorous domestic standards competently and cheerfully had become a competitive endeavor. Anna Cushing reported a trek to Boston's Jamaica Pond on behalf of her friend Lucy, to find Bridget Gately, a relative of her own domestic Mary Gately. When she got to Bridget's home, however, she learned that Bridget had already found a place for herself. Two years later, Cushing noted that her friend Susan "meets with no success in getting a good girl and is at a loss which way to turn next." Cushing herself was fortunate in her employment of Mary, an Irish Catholic who was reliable and generous with her time. However, when a second hired girl, Kate, left suddenly in spring 1853, some spring cleaning chores went undone until late July. Cushing was forced to pay a new girl, Ann Cunliff, half a dollar more per week. She seemed worth the price, however, because she was a "grown up girl" who seemed capable of helping with the children. When Ann left to be married in January 1854, Cushing engaged Margaret Gately, sister to Mary, to take Ann's place, reasoning that without a second girl, she would be forced to hire out laundry and spring and fall cleaning.[61]

For Emeline Rice, mistress of a modest Worcester, Massachusetts, household, it was hard to compete successfully for even one domestic during the early 1850s. Rice's letters to her sister Sophia White about her problems holding onto "girls" reveals how a succession of domestic employees evaluated their situations in her household. During her early childbearing years, Rice determined to do her own housework and hire a woman to wash. By the late 1840s Rice appears to have been doing her own washing and that of her son James, who brought his dirty clothes home every two weeks to be laundered (presumably to save the expense of hiring someone himself). She also did all the rest of her own housework, including the care of several young children, one still a baby, and seasonal housecleaning twice a year. In a letter to Sophia in 1847, which echoed the laments of thousands of other northern housewives, she complained of being "hurried all the time." In between baking, scalding preserves, and doing the routine house-work that "takes a good part of my time," she salvaged enough time over the course of two days to complete her letter. It was not uncommon, Rice noted in several other letters to her sister, for her to complete her day's work in the evening, as she did on February 27, 1850: "It is now 8 clock, and I have but just got my dishes washed, and baby asleep, ready to sit down."[62]

Rice found conflicts over cleaning methods, standards, and wages so stressful that she wished at all costs, even if it required that she lead a reclusive existence, to avoid hiring a girl for more general purposes: "Any way to get along without hiring a girl I say . . . it strikes *dread* all over me to *think* of it." By 1850 Rice had begun keeping her daughter Lucy at home from school to help with the house-work, a practice at odds with the national trend toward withdrawing daughters from domestic chores; Rice thought it "the most *profitable* school she has at-tended for a long time." She also began to pay a woman to come in to do her laundry as she had first done during her early childbearing years to enable her to focus on sewing and other housekeeping tasks.[63]

Yet, like many other mistresses, Rice found it necessary to hire Irish women despite reservations about their suitability for domestic labor. In February 1853, soon after learning that her diseased lung was tubercular, Rice hired Bridget to do the wash while she concentrated her own energies on the other housework: sweeping, baking, washing dishes and sewing. By July 1853 Rice was preparing herself for the departure of yet another girl who seems to have been doing more than just the laundry. "How is Sarah," she inquired after her sister's domestic. "You are not bothered with changing help[?]" she wondered. Her own situation was quite different: "Our girl is going to leave Sat. Night, to go into a shop to work, down street, where her sisters husband works, she thinks it a very good chance, & a week ago, told me she was so *tired* doing housework thought she should not do it much longer, and finally told what was in her head, told her ex-pected her to stay until Oct, she knew it, but wanted much to go, thought it of no use to refuse."[64] Fatigue, a dislike for housework, a better opportunity, a chance to work with kin—all these factors led this unnamed domestic laborer to termi-nate her informal contract with Rice.

Rice noted that she found it hard to "boss" Irish women. Less consciously, she was repelled by their personal hygiene and manners, exactly the situation about which Roberts had tried to warn his fellow domestics. No surprise then that the next "girl," an Irish woman, did not live up to Rice's expectations. As before, Rice dealt with the shortage of labor by periodically withdrawing her daughter from school to do most of the housework except for the washing. Her other strategy was to "try to take things *calm* and *easy,* and let the dirt in a measure go." Although she vowed to hire an American replacement, Rice found herself having to engage an Irish woman to do the wash in the basement kitchen. Whether she was referring to a specific woman, the same one who had washed for her in the past, or was simply referring to Irish domestics generically, she noted, "Bridget will wash tomorrow."[65]

Even when she snared a desirable native-born domestic—Esther, who had been laid off during the "dull" season of a dressmaker's shop—Rice still found fault. Esther took on most of the housework her sick employer could no longer do, baking pies and ironing, while Rice washed the dishes and swept up the sitting room. In a letter she noted, "Esther is very kind and willing, not very swift but *thorough,* Has just got her work done after washing, 15 minutes past 3 o'clock." A month later, Rice again commented on her domestic's slowness: "Esther is washing to day. It takes her until the middle of the afternoon to finish, she is slow and thorough, charges 2.00 pr week." This wage was higher than the $1.50 Rice would have paid an Irish woman, she acknowledged, but she claimed that she would rather pay $10.00 a week to keep Esther than have to resort to an Irish domestic.

What Rice's description of Esther can't capture for us is the reason for Esther's slowness. Was she a methodical worker who couldn't meet her employer's expectations for speed? Was she working slowly because working more quickly meant that more would be expected? Did Rice's comment about Esther's getting her work done after washing mean that even on washday Esther was expected to cook? Rice's letter does reveal that Esther had devised her own system of rewards for doing work that most native-born women tried to avoid. After finishing her work (and presumably being paid, perhaps a quarterly wage like those recorded in the family account book), she went down the street to buy herself a new dress. Perhaps this system of incentives allowed her to remain "kind and willing" even with an obsessive employer looking over her shoulder.[66] Perhaps, too, her "good" attitude came from knowing how much her employer valued her "thorough" work.

In contrast to the Waterhouse and Rice households, domestic laborers abounded in the affluent Brookline, Massachusetts, household of Sarah Appleton Lawrence. In the records Lawrence kept, we find few overt references to employee bodies but complex calculations of wages, physical strength, and character. She showed little concern for the bodily deportment and containment that had absorbed Robert Roberts. Indeed, her most pointed commentary about the bodies inhabiting her domestic space concerned her own and her children's bodies. Yet Lawrence's journal and her book of wages also revealed a geography of intimacy created by her allocation of labor to different household spaces.[67]

From the moment she became the mistress of her own household in 1842, Lawrence was fortunate to be able to employ a full complement of servants to perform a wide range of domestic tasks. Her ledger listed "chamber maids" and "parlor girls," who were paid the least, as well as "trusty and industrious" men, who usually earned three times as much and were paid monthly rather than weekly. For twenty-two years, until she was forty-two, she kept a journal describing household and family events, and a book of wages, in which she recorded employment tenures, dates and amounts of payment, and miscellaneous comments about ability and character. Through these documents we learn how Lawrence created bodily zones for her household as well as evaluated her domestic laborers.

Lawrence adhered to a gender division of labor in which women filled differentiated slots, notable for their different degrees of intimate contact with the bodies of the Lawrence family. Chambermaids and parlor girls, for instance, were defined by their responsibility for spaces that emphasized different regions of the body: the sleeping chambers, the province of the lower body, where one might encounter filled chamber pots, soiled sheets and undergarments, and the semidressed bodies of occupants; and the parlor, the most public room in the house, where codes of formal dress and social behavior emphasized the social "upper" body. Lawrence expected the chambermaid to do the family's laundry—yet another indication of the undesirable and strenuous nature of the job and its focus on the family's intimate, lower bodies. The parlor girl, in contrast, would have been expected to display great discipline over her own body, much as Roberts recommended in his book. Cooks and nursery women also cared for the Lawrence family's bodies in intimate ways by preparing food and looking after the health and welfare of the children. The greater the employee's access to and responsibility for actual bodies, the more trust Lawrence had to place in the employee herself.[68]

The wages Lawrence paid her employees reveal an agenda at odds with the larger currents of the labor market and the smaller struggles of laborers to improve their situations. Although chambermaids performed the most strenuous female work in the household—weekly laundry—they were paid the least of Lawrence's employees. Lawrence's chambermaids made $1.75 per week until late 1853, when Lawrence contracted to pay Margaret Amos—probably a distant relative of her husband—$2.00. The turnover in chambermaids may have been one of the reasons Lawrence finally decided to raise wages. During the twelve years she kept accounts, Lawrence recorded employing twelve women for this job. Two of the women, Abby Foster and Mary Gutterson, left on account of "not being strong enough to wash." Mary Anne Dorety left to take up dressmaking, Laura returned home to continue her schooling, and Mary Ann Coburn and Maria Coburn, possibly sisters, each left paid domestic labor to perform work for their own households as married women (Maria returned briefly twice after her marriage). More than half of her chambermaids, in short, revealed an agenda at odds with Lawrence's own, or they placed priority on education or marriage over earning wages.[69]

Lawrence employed even more cooks than chambermaids—fourteen—over the course of twelve years, but comparatively few parlor girls. Parlor girls and cooks made at least $2.00 per week, with cooks earning an additional fifty cents if they provided the household with fresh butter. The reasons for the turnover of cooks were similar to those for the chambermaids. Jane Walter was too old to continue the work, while Susan Hayden found it too hard. Dorothea Lord and Julia Quinn each left to marry. Barbara Gifford was unwilling, after two years' service, to continue accompanying the family to the north shore for the summer. Eliza Dimond gave up on going out to work. Betsy Chase left for Nauvoo, Illinois, in June 1843, where the Mormon leader Joseph Smith had recently dictated his revelation on "Celestial Marriage." Sarah Roberts proved to be an "excellent" cook despite her "peculiar disposition," but wanted to return home. Mary Ann Pickett left in haste for more wages.

In contrast to the Lawrence household's female employees, the men were paid better and tended to stay longer. They performed seemingly generic male labor, undifferentiated in Lawrence's account book and at least partially located out of doors. Upon leaving Lawrence's employ, at least one of these men took up farming, returning for seasonal employment during the slow winter months. The only exception to this divide between men and women occurred in 1853, when Lawrence noted that her parlor maid, Phebe M. Coombs, left after Lawrence "took a man," most likely a manservant to perform indoor work, because Coombs "prefered to do chamber work—& live in town."

Lawrence's comments about the men and women in her employ suggest that she was carefully sifting through evidence of morals and character as much as she was evaluating their work. Her positive judgments of the women tended to be more generous than those of the men—perhaps a consequence of greater opportunity to observe and converse with them—and equally dismissive when they were negative. Successful female employees were "good," "clever," "neat," and "obliging," while the unsuccessful ones had "bad character[s]," were "lazy" or "shiftless," or "tired of work." One exceptional young woman left her employ because the washing was too hard but subsequently benefited from the good impression she had made; in 1851 she traveled to Europe as a lady's companion to Lawrence's younger sister Nancy. Another "very good woman" left to keep Lawrence's mother's house when she no longer wished to cook.

It is difficult to ascertain how much race and ethnicity entered into these judgments. Lawrence never made disparaging remarks about dirty "Bridgets" or lazy "Negroes," as some of her white New England contemporaries did. Was this a dimension of her own performance of elite authority, that it transcended the particularities of region or the race of local laborers? Or was she simply striving to make her daily dealings with laborers live up to her charitable ideals? In the absence of clear ethnic or racial labels in her account book, we guess about the ethnic-racial identities of her laborers at our peril. Julia Quinn and Mary Dorety probably were Irish. When we correlate Lawrence's comments on morals and character with our guesses about ethnic backgrounds, we find Lawrence slightly more likely to judge as "good" and "clever" girls with Yankee-sounding names and plans for marriage and education than their Irish-named counterparts or those leaving her employ for other reasons—dislike of hard work or desire for higher wages.[70]

But women from ethnic backgrounds similar to Lawrence's own may also have had some advantage in gaining and keeping the most intimate jobs in the household—those that involved care for the Lawrence children. Mrs. Moulton, the children's nurse, was one of the best-paid women and the one with the longest tenure. Her duties revolved around relieving Sarah of child care. She remained in the household from 1843 to 1854 at the wage of $2.50 per week plus a quarterly bonus of $5.00. Lawrence also seemed more inclined to become involved in the lives of intimately employed laborers, such as wet nurses, than those of other employees. Examining the employment records of Lawrence's nurses and wet nurses reveals a subtle pattern of bringing Anglo-American women rather than Irish or African-American women into the inner sanctum of labor centered on caring for the children's bodies as well as greater personal involvement in the lives of these trusted employees.[71]

Indeed, comparing Lawrence's diary with the account book, we get the impression of a household that revolved around her own reproducing body and those of her children. During the first sixteen years of her marriage, she recorded the births of seven children: Mary Ann in 1843, when her journal begins, Sally in 1845, Amory in 1848, Willie in 1850, Susan in 1852, Hetty in 1855, and Harriet in 1858. In addition, Lawrence assumed responsibility for her deceased sister's twins, born in 1844, and an orphaned relative. Lawrence's experience of running her own household was thus punctuated by multiple pregnancies, lyings-in, breast-feeding (which she seems to have done on her own for the most part for at least eighteen months after each birth), teething crises, weaning, and the inevitable bouts of illness. This cycle of childbearing lent a distinctive rhythm to the household's needs for midwives, doctors, the occasional wet nurse, nursery women, and cooks.

Lawrence's graceful performance as wife and mother, despite the growing size of her family, was made possible by the extensive labor provided by her domestic staff. Her cheerful demeanor confirmed the righteousness of the paths chosen by the men in her life. Men such as William Appleton, her father, and Amos Lawrence, her husband, situated at the cutting edge of global commerce and national politics, required seemingly endless affirmation that they were living Christian lives. In addition to the material and familial comforts she provided, Sarah made them feel like they were good men. "Dear Sarah is as loving & lovable as ever," her father observed in 1851. "All agree she is a worthy pattern for her sex." Ten years later, he was still struck by his daughter's wonderful qualities: "Sarah is one of the best of wives, Mothers, friends & housekeepers," he noted approvingly, "all order & not fuss." After forty years of marriage, her husband, Amos, effused, "Dear, good wife she has been to me, the light of my life and my chief worldly support. May we live together in the hereafter forever!"[72] Seen in the context of Beecher's admonition to be cheerful as well as systematic, Lawrence's careful accounts of employees and the records she kept of care for her own and her children's bodies reflect a corpus of bourgeois body work that marked her domestic life as modern.

The presence of a free market in domestic labor and the ethnic cleavages resulting from the influx of rural Irish migrants to urban areas set the domestic politics of northern households on a distinctive regional path. In southern slave-owning households, in contrast, domestic politics revolved around struggles between mistresses and enslaved women. Most instructive of these regional differences are the occasions in which elite southern women traveled north and attempted to replicate southern domestic standards using hired rather than enslaved labor. Like Lawrence, the Cameron women of North Carolina were used to delegating housework to others. Traveling north without their enslaved laborers in 1855, they relied on a hired woman until she proved incompetent. The sisters "went to work as if they were accustomed to it," with brushes and brooms until Bridget, a "remarkable cleanly and very obliging" woman, took over. "She made a grand cleaning up," Margaret Cameron noted, but she feared that Bridget's disgust "with the proceedings in the kitchen" might provoke her to leave. "She is a *real* old maid," observed Margaret, who had herself remained single until the age of forty-two. Attributing Bridget's skills to cranial structure, she reasoned, "she seems to have the bump of order very fully developed."[73] Craniology—the popular antebellum "science" of how skull shape revealed intelligence, character, and ability—enabled the Cameron sisters to appreciate their Irish employee's domestic skills. But keeping house in the North forced them to confront two new circumstances absent from the slave South: the desirability of spinsterhood in a hired woman to minimize conflicts with an employer's demands upon her, and the possibility that the labor would be so difficult or dirty that she might leave in disgust.

BOUNDARIES

Middle- and upper-class households enacted much of their power and privilege through judgments of other people's filth, moral turpitude, and disorder. Articulations of the boundary-defining functions of cleanliness appear in middle-class women's comments about the Irish, African Americans, the poor, and even other middle-class people. These judgments were often passed against the same groups of people whose domestic labor made them witnesses to genteel people's filth—the backstage grooming, dressing, eating, and cleaning that allowed for public presentations of refined, disciplined bodies. Ultimately, servants' intimate access made middle-class people vulnerable, not just to the unblinking judgments of their domestic employees—who were, after all, unlikely to print denunciations of their employers' true condition—but to contact with people who hailed from domestic environments tainted by poverty, disease, and vice. Increasingly, the message of didactic tracts and religious pamphlets aimed at the poor emphasized that these three characteristics of their domestic lives need not be linked. Although poverty might not be easily remedied, both disease and vice could be quelled by habits of discipline and cleanliness. In embracing cleanliness, poor people might also demonstrate their morality and respectability.[74]

The use of filth to warn genteel people of the dangers of crossing social boundaries—including the subtle divide separating the truly genteel from mere pretenders to gentility—appeared in countless fictional accounts of the fatal consequences of these transgressions. The victims were often young, hailing from genteel families, but poorly versed in the need to respect the gulfs of taste and education that separated them from the vulgar. Eliza Leslie's "The Truant," which appeared in her collection of juvenile tales *The Mirror* (1828), depicted the near fatal consequences of Selina Colville's decision to visit the uncouth Pringle girls on a day when the school they attended was closed unexpectedly. The main room of the Pringle house was small, dark, hot, and redolent with the odor of cockroaches. Located behind their store, this all-purpose living space offered a sharp contrast to the ostentatiously furnished tea room they opened only once a year for a party. After suffering the Pringles' bad food (greasy corned beef, hot corn, smoked herrings, bad butter) and poor table manners, Selina began to pine for home but was delayed by a severe thunderstorm. Setting out alone from the Pringles' house with an old umbrella, Selina was soaked and taken in by an old huckster woman to the garret she inhabited with her two children. The garret room was hot and airless, and the children with whom Selina shared a bed were dirty and restless. As her discomfort turned into a nearly fatal illness, she longed for "her own nice bed and cool airy chamber."[75]

Suspicions that Irish, African-American, and poor white women were inherently dirty coalesced around reports following epidemics of high death rates and squalor in poor urban neighborhoods. The convergence of moral judgments with beliefs about the preventive health value of cleanliness appeared in a flurry of pieces in *Godey's Lady's Book* during the 1830s, soon after the first cholera epidemics hit northern cities. Between 1832, when the magazine published a "Letter on Cholera" about the disease's origins in the sinful habits of the poor, and 1836, when an article appeared connecting infant mortality to stale air, bad food, and filth, *Godey's* departed from its strictly moral fare to give advice on bathing (to improve health and beauty) and preventing tooth decay. Thereafter, articles discussing the care of the body, including physical exercise, appeared more frequently. Significantly, the initial "Letter on Cholera" rejected the notion that the disease might be a natural phenomenon and concluded that higher death rates among the poor revealed God's judgment. The author identified a special role for middle-class women, who could help sinful poor women by educating them about temperance, cleanliness, and prudence.[76]

As the *Godey's* piece on cholera suggests, a mother who pursued cleanliness not only protected her household from organic and social dangers but implicitly delineated social boundaries and passed judgments on those lacking clean, moral, and healthy habits. These judgments, which were medical and moral as well as social, might focus on a home space or another woman's body. During the 1830s and 1840s the unhealthful consequences of filth were increasingly attributed not to poverty or the lack of clean water but to sin, laziness, a failure of the will, or, somewhat more benignly, to ignorance.

After a second devastating cholera epidemic and new waves of Irish and German immigration in 1849, diatribes against the intemperance and filth of the poor sharpened. Cleanliness of body, abode, and city streets reflected morality, many commentators noted, which manifested itself empirically in a lower death rate from the disease.[77] Illustrating the links among moral virtue, cleanliness, and health, an American Sunday School Union (ASSU) tract, *The Two Homes Compared; or, the Advantages of Cleanliness* (1850), argued that cleanliness and order might defeat moral decay even among the poor. In this fictional account of a visit to two homes of equal income, but with vastly different states of cleanliness, the reader encountered cleanliness as a literal manifestation of morality. In the first home, the visitor found a squalid hovel situated next to a "sort of pool, into which were thrown ashes, cabbage leaves, potato peelings, meat and fish bones, and refuse of almost every kind." A pig "grubbed" at this cesspool, next to which two dirty children played. "It was plain," the visitor noted, "that the poor children had not been washed or combed for a long time." The interior of the cottage was no less disgusting. Filth obscured the floor, and free-ranging rabbits, pigeons, and dogs gave off a terrible stench. Dirty linen, greasy plates, and a pan of dirty soap suds sat together in a pile. A dirty man (with "dirty face and hands and dirty clothes, smoking a short dirty pipe") sat in the corner, spitting on the floor. No one washed hands before the dinner of potatoes and fried herring, which was served inelegantly on plates the visitor suspected the dog had licked (Figure 10.5a). Although this description contained no ethnic labels, the cabbage, potatoes, and pipe would have tipped readers off that the hovel's inhabitants were immigrants, probably Irish.[78]

The clean and orderly home presented a stunning contrast. Even the doorway, the cottage's most liminal space, was perfectly clean. The windows "were as bright as crystal" and the curtains and table linens perfectly smooth and clean. Freshly washed linen hung on a drying rack before the fire, waiting to be ironed. Clean dishes sat "in regular rows on dresser shelves." As the little girl in the family returned with her infant brother from his daily airing, she wiped her feet out of habit on the doormat provided for that purpose. In an analysis that would have pleased the sociologist Pierre Bourdieu, the author of the tract noted, "The habit of doing so had, no doubt, been so early instilled into her, that she could not enter the house without doing it; and *habits* of cleanliness form the only security for *acts* of cleanliness." In this model dwelling, "there was no dust, no litter, no dirty fingermarks on the door, no grease on the floor, no slops on the table" (Figure 10.5b).[79]

The growing sensitivity to the physical presence of domestic laborers inside the sanctuary of middle- and upper-class homes manifested itself in a new sensibility about servant body odor.[80] Concern about bad smells had become a hallmark of middle-class life during the antebellum period. As we have seen, sensitivity to household odors and the bodily "exhalations" of family members, especially women, were de rigueur by the 1850s. As Roberts had anticipated, white women who had become more fastidious about their own bodies began to complain that their Irish or African-American laborers were not clean. For these women, ethnic, racial and class differences resided in the bodily habits of hired

10.5. *Two Homes Compared; or, The Advantages of Cleanliness* (Philadelphia, 1850).
Courtesy American Antiquarian Society

help. Newly attuned to the need to wash the entire body, especially the feet, employers objected to the odor of employees who failed to do the same. An 1849 edition of *The Family Messenger and National Gleaner* exploited the potential for humor in this clash of standards. In a section titled "Humorous Brevities," the paper recounted the story of a "maid servant [who] was dismissed on account of a lack of cleanliness." Honoring the fired woman's request to gloss over the reasons for her dismissal in a letter of reference, her employer mentioned only "that the main cause of her dismissal" was her "tendency to *hydrophobia!*"[81]

The ASSU saw little humor in the conflict in an 1860 pamphlet in which it approached the body politics of the employer-employee relationship as a struggle over domestic laborers' grooming habits. Formed in 1827 from the Philadelphia Sunday School Union, this interdenominational national network of ministers, teachers, missionaries, and writers hoped to bring gradual improvement to American society through the spread of Christian beliefs and ideals.[82] The anonymous author of *Parlour and Kitchen* (1860) aimed to ameliorate the relationship between mistress and servant, which many mistresses felt had deteriorated as a consequence of wage work opportunities, the influx of immigrants, and the market's erosion of servant deference and loyalty. "If the suggestions made in these pages were generally regarded by persons at service, as well as by their employers," the author predicted, "a great deal of misery and guilt would be saved, and every class of society would feel the happy change." Bringing about this "happy change" was mainly a matter of making servants more agreeable to their employers.

Parlour and Kitchen presented the story of Ann Connover, an orphan left in the care of her Aunt Jane, a career domestic who freely dispensed advice about how to succeed at a life in service. Significantly, Ann was her Aunt Jane's only family connection. Having devoted herself to her employer, Jane had never married or had children. Much of Jane's advice echoed that of Roberts but was directed instead at female domestics whose choices as laborers and consumers so disturbed their mistresses. Jane warned Ann against switching employers, borrowing her mistress's clothing, or eating food without her employer's permission. She also urged the servant not to socialize with gentlemen above her station, especially those who insisted on secrecy. Above all, she pointed to the folly of purchasing flimsy, expensive, muslin dresses and light shoes, like those worn by women in the mistress class, rather than the sensible calicoes and sturdy shoes more suitable for servants.

According to Aunt Jane, the servant's duty to discipline her body went far deeper than Roberts would have considered advisable. She taught Ann, "If we are to please our employers well *in all things*, besides *doing* as they like, we must *be* as they like." Roberts's mindfulness of racial politics made him wary of such a thorough internalization of white employer expectations and cautious about racial self-revelation. Jane, whose character was ventriloquized by the master class, saw such an internalization as necessary for employee success. In response to Ann's inquiry about how a servant should be pleasing to her employer, Aunt Jane stressed the need to be "clean and tidy": "If a girl goes about the house with an old torn frock, with holes in her stockings, and her shoes down at the heels; with hair all flying about her face; and leaving the marks of her fingers on the doors, shutters, and every thing she touches. Can her appearance 'please' the lady of the house?" she asked rhetorically. "So far from it, a slatternly, dirty person is one of the most disagreeable things that can be met with."

Overcome by her own distaste for such frank discussion, Jane resorted to reading to Ann from a book she received from her employer, saying, "I read it, because I cannot bear to talk about such things, and yet I am sure you ought to be told of them." This confidential information concerned servant bodies. Now completely and openly ventriloquized by her mistress, Aunt Jane read of the importance of wearing clean, mended clothing, well-maintained shoes, and clean aprons; of grooming the hair; and of having clean hands that leave no telltale smudges and prints. But the greatest concerns were clearly servant feet and the smell of servant bodies: "As to the *feet*. These are not to be *seen*; but I beg you will pay particular attention to their cleanliness. Wash them often; and even this will be of little service, unless your stockings are kept nice and clean too," she instructed.

Jane then read the following illustrative account of a generous mistress who decided to hire a servant maid who had been sent away from her seventh job in seven years:

> I thought it so hard a case that I would try her myself [.] I did so; but soon the secret was discovered; she would not keep her feet and body clean. Whenever she came near, you could perceive that however clean she appeared, she was not clean herself. I thought much what I must do. She was an honest, diligent, good creature; did all her work well; and yet I must send her away from me. I determined at last to tell her, which I did. She was at first, mortified and distressed. At last she shed tears, and said, She never could account for why all her mistresses had sent her away, and yet always spoke well of her character, as if they were satisfied with her. "Indeed," she said, "I have always desired to please, and it was my earnest desire to keep my place. What shall I do! Will *you* too send me away? Cannot I do any thing to remove it?"

The mistress replied, "'Yes, I think you can; but then you must be regular and attentive to do it. Wash your self frequently and thoroughly in hot water, from head to foot[.]' If ever she neglected this rule, I could perceive it in a day or two; but when I reminded her of it, she would wash herself thoroughly, and then she was as agreeable a servant, in all respects, as I could wish. And she stayed with me, a faithful, and good, and valuable servant, till she went to take care of her old father." The moral of the story was "be then mindful of what I call *bodily cleanliness*."[83]

In the world of servants and mistresses conjured by the author of *Parlour and Kitchen*, success in domestic service required discipline over one's person, much as Robert Roberts had noted nearly thirty years earlier. Yet here is where the similarity ended. Being an agreeable servant like the one described in Aunt Jane's story was not sufficient to integrate a young woman successfully into her employer's household. Despite her tears—a ritual cleansing that indicated her heartfelt desire to please and be pleasing—the young maidservant consistently revealed her difference from her employer with her body's bad smells. Concern about body odor had, by 1860, become an important component of bourgeois sensibilities. The hapless servant girl proved the class-specific nature of this sensibility. Even after she was told of the reason for all the dismissals and taught how to remedy the problem, she failed to internalize the lesson in body discipline. She had no self-consciousness of her odor and had to be reminded to wash her body by her mistress. Aunt Jane, in contrast, had so thoroughly imbibed the gospel of cleanliness that she, like the delicate women of the mistress class, could not bear to speak aloud of bodily filth and odor. The crucial information necessary for a domestic thus came in the form of a book, passed from mistress to servant and read aloud by the loyal Aunt Jane. Aunt Jane, moreover, believed that it was possible for a servant to transform herself, to embody her employer's desire for a laborer who leaves no traces of her corporeality. The text does not resolve this conflict between employer desire for a more thoroughgoing transformation of servant bodies and the stubborn traces of difference—the servant woman's failure to conform to her employer's expectation in her habits of caring for her body.

The rise of a domestic labor market provided employers with new opportunities to define the physical beings of the people they employed. Concern about social mixing manifested itself in ever more precise domestic classification, distinction, and separation: of clean from dirty, of different kinds of filth defined by its origin and proximity to the human body, of good and bad smells, and of cleansing agents of varying strength. Advice on laundry and housecleaning proliferated, revealing that concerns for tidiness had given way to near obsessiveness over cleanliness by the 1840s. This was certainly true for prosperous urban households but also increasingly true for provincial households as well. Whiteness—long valued as the ideal state of refined skin, clean teeth, and freshly laundered linen—became newly important as evidence of the respectability and purity of the domestic environment. The quest for white shirts, snowy table linens, and whitewashed walls, along with the effacement of bodily odors—for aesthetic reasons rather than simply to protect the health—reflected new ways of imagining contamination in the domestic environment and new practices of combating it. As the historian Christine Stansell has noted about New York's mistress class, ultimately "it was the mistress alone who was the judge of what was dirty and what was clean," although, as we have seen, asserting her will often engaged her in a struggle with domestic laborers.[84]

Cleanliness had long provided a vocabulary for assessing civility, gentility, and humanity, but by the antebellum period, northern writers used it as evidence of the morality of individuals and ethnic groups (when they turned their gaze on the South, as we will see, they indicted southern society and the slave economy). Reformers described households as unclean to condemn the immorality and laziness of inhabitants. Employing servants made for a regular breach of the boundary between the morally pure and clean and the habitually immoral and unclean. In antebellum tracts and fiction, disease became a moral consequence, triggered by the failure to respect or maintain class boundaries. If a person lived badly or took up with the wrong associates, he or she became vulnerable to contracting a disease generated by poverty and vice. Middle-class northerners needed hired laborers to meet rigorous new standards of cleanliness—yet bringing servants into their households exposed them to the very risks they were trying to avoid.

Part IV

─◆─────◄◄ ≋≋ ►─────◆─

CRUSADES

By the mid-nineteenth century, cleanliness did not simply signify moral good but had become an important means of achieving it. Reformers of various kinds depicted the imposition of filth on innocents (schoolchildren, enslaved people) as subjection to unnatural conditions and violations of humanity. Advocates for the water cure, meanwhile, claimed that by drinking pure water and immersing the body regularly, an individual could combat disease, chronic pain, nervous disorders, and reproductive afflictions, many of which had become staples of nineteenth-century life. Although not motivated solely by the desire to clean the body, the water cure habituated its devotees to the sensations of daily washing and regular immersion, thus laying the foundation for the subsequent popularity of bathing. Even those not convinced by the more radical claims of hydropathy, however, found reason to seek alternatives to allopathy in mineral springs, warm baths, cold compresses, and saltwater bathing.

Warnings about the dangers of bad air accompanied the advocacy of the water cure. Indeed, regular exercise and exposure to fresh air were part of the healing regimen at water cure establishments. Popular medical guides had long advocated the benefits of fresh air and blamed disease on stagnant, overheated, or already breathed air. The movement to reform school architecture, which first appeared in the North during the late 1830s, reflected this older knowledge about the body's respiration of poisonous vapors as well as new fears about the proximity of students from different ethnic and class backgrounds. Reformers applied contemporary medical wisdom to a peculiarly northern institution — the public school — at a time when epidemic disease and immigration were heightening northerners' awareness of class and ethnic differences.

New beliefs in human agency left less room for thinking about certain people as naturally dirty and popularized the notion that all people could be taught to be clean, a step toward achieving spiritual awakening and claiming their human birthright of good health and bodily comfort. This democratic view of the human capacity for cleanliness and morality emphasized access to water (spas, mineral springs, public baths, private tubs) and taking responsibility for one's own health through diet and reformed habits of body care. Transforming the outer man had become a means of transforming the inner man, one soul at a time.

But resistance remained strong to the environmental approach to the squalid lives of children, slaves, and the poor. White southerners and conservative northerners still clung to the notion that some people were dirty by nature. Meanwhile, a new phalanx of health reformers, originating in the North, were beginning to articulate differences in regional approaches to the body. People from throughout the nation still traveled to mineral springs and seaside resorts, and bathed their bodies, but the philosophic and habitual commitment to the water cure as a species of personal reformation was a northern phenomenon. The tension between these two views — the environmental and the essentialist explanations for the filth of the poor and the enslaved — defined the dynamic pitting health and social reformers against their detractors. It also reflected different beliefs about the human body and its inherent capacity for decency.

11

IMMERSION

On July 8, 1840, the *Pennsylvania Inquirer* printed a report from Cape May, New Jersey, about the beginning of "the season" for travelers to seaside resorts. Noting that three boarding houses were already accepting guests, the reporter commented, "With reference to the pleasures of sea bathing and the invigorating influence of the sea air, it is not necessary to say much. A large number of our citizens had tried them, and in most instances, with the happiest results." Four-fifths of first-time visitors "are anxious for a second" visit, he claimed, "not so much on account of the 'fashion and frolic' . . . but because of the beneficial effects upon the general health." The reporter included a striking testimonial to the salubrious climate at the resort: "Our informant . . . was surprised to find, strolling along the beach, an old couple from Philadelphia, who had just arrived on their FORTIETH annual visit, — and both in the apparent enjoyment of excellent health. They expressed the opinion that they would have been dead long ago but for the happy influence of the sea breeze and the sea bath."[1]

By the date of this report, Americans of means from every region were flocking to seaside resorts to enjoy brisk ocean breezes and saltwater bathing. This impulse to head for the shore, which gathered momentum during the 1840s and 1850s, traced its roots to many long-standing traditions, including the annual migration of urban dwellers to the wholesome air of the country to avoid summer epidemics and the gathering of well-to-do women and men at the healing waters of mineral springs, where they socialized, drank water, immersed their bodies, and consulted with doctors. Unlike these other recourses to travel and bathing, however, seaside recreation featured immersion in water as a central pleasurable activity, justified as much by the bather's enjoyment as by the health benefits. It was one expression of the new enthusiasm for bathing the body that was changing the habits of middle- and upper-class people throughout the United States, and, more broadly, in England and Europe.[2]

In the northern United States, however, bathing was not simply a new and fashionable form of summer recreation but one of several health reforms to emerge there. The water cure, based upon a turn to the natural healing powers of pure water, was part of a larger set of reforms attempted by northerners who, along with their European peers, doubted traditional wisdom about diet, bathing, and medicine in an age in which city life, new disease vectors, and rising consumer choices about food and clothing seemed to be undermining rather than improving health. Hydropaths criticized the heroic medicine of regular physicians (allopaths), insisting on bathing and imbibing pure water to preserve good health and cure debilitating illness.

Public baths and private ownership of bathtubs had surged during the first two decades of the century, as we have seen, reflecting a change in habits of body care by a small but influential urban elite. Bodily immersion by a broader public had yet to take hold, however, and followed a different path. By midcentury, well-to-do men and women traveled to seaside resorts or mineral springs, subjected themselves to the rigors of daily cold baths, or bathed in the warm waters of a public bath or their own tubs. This new relationship with their bodies contributed to a profound change in contemporary attitudes about the healthfulness of immersion in water, and established new thresholds of physical sensation and lay intervention in the body's processes.

PRESERVING HEALTH

The middle-class man's encounter with the city stood at the core of an emerging antebellum sensibility about the importance of self-restraint and a wholesome environment for good health. Much about this sensibility is familiar to us: the focus on diet, the sensitivity to bad smells, and the appreciation of genteel manners. But city life and the growing emphasis on individual responsibility gave it a new direction at midcentury. We see this ethos at work in the writings of the twenty-five-year-old printer David Clapp, a native of Dorchester, Massachusetts, who documented a journey to New York in August 1831, more than ten years before Charles Dickens's published account of his trip to that city. He recorded his adventures—a lost letter to a bookseller, a trip to Peale's Museum, a visit to Castle Garden—as well as his sensory impressions. Like many visitors before him, Clapp was convinced that urban filth caused disease. New York's size and diversity provoked observations on health hazards and efforts at healthful restraint.

Clapp was astonished to see hogs in the streets. "Hardly a peculiarity was observed until a huge hog was seen wallowing in the mire before me," he reported. "This was a most forcible appeal to my sense of sight, and at once convinced me so strongly that it could be no other place than New York that I had alighted upon, that I did not again imagine myself in the good, though swineless city of Boston." Usually ranked as one of the nation's cleanest and healthiest cities, Boston had given Clapp a lofty perspective from which to evaluate New York.[3] He adopted a tone of amused superiority, based in part on an assumption about northern sophistication, as he considered the city's approach to street cleaning:

> Hogs, of all ages, shapes and sizes, were busily engaged in all the streets we entered, in doing the business which in Boston is entrusted to another and more faithful class of workmen. It does excite a smile of surprise in a Northerner, as well as a sensation of disgust, that the authorities of New York should let loose, to *cleanse* their city, a swarm of beasts which are proverbially the *dirtiest* of all cattle. They doubtless eat up much of the vegetable matter that is thrown out into the streets; but they leave something in its place as much worse than decayed vegetables, as New York economy in this instance is in the end less beneficial than Boston prodigality in regard to the same subject.[4]

Disgusted by pig feces in the street, Clapp remained on his guard about other stenches. Stumbling upon a Catholic graveyard at the Battery, Clapp and his companion "were assailed by a very offensive smell from the corpse." They immediately "commenced a hasty retreat; for in addition to the odor being unpleasant we were fearful we might derive from it as we know not the disease of which the person died, — the seeds of some contagious disorder." Certain parts of the city struck him as especially dangerous to the health. After leaving Peale's Broadway museum to walk the city, he observed "many dirty and confined places, where, if any where, disease would be expected to prevail."[5]

Although Clapp traveled to New York for business purposes, health preservation often entered his thoughts in such a menacing place. A temperance man who talked openly with sailors about the virtues of abstaining from alcohol, Clapp drank water during his stay at the Franklin Hotel. He carefully shaved and washed (probably his face, hands, and neck) before changing his clothes and setting out to explore the city. He noted with interest the presence of a "great number of men and boys . . . bathing at the wharves, and swimming off at various distances from the shore." Was he also a swimmer? He also thought carefully about his intake of food, although this did not spoil his enjoyment of the ample meals served at his hotel. He refrained from spirits and cigars at Castle Garden, a pleasure spot, choosing soda and cake instead. After seeing an anaconda on display at

Peale's museum, Clapp mused that if humans could adopt eating habits like the snake's, forgoing condiments or conserves, gravies, sauces, brandies, and liquors, they would likely improve their health. At one hundred and eighteen pounds, Clapp was a model of restraint.[6]

The seasonal exodus of wealthy white families from the hot city left Clapp with the impression that New York was less genteel than Boston, a judgment based on the numbers of African Americans and prostitutes he saw. The "spectacle" of New York's African-American laboring population struck him most forcefully in the evening; people walking home from work or taking their evening strolls presented a sharp contrast to a typical evening scene in Boston, where most of the faces would have been white. Clapp admitted to having seen modest and beautiful faces among both races in New York, but he remained discomfited by women casting wanton looks as well as by the numbers of African Americans, who "are marked out to you by their color as cooks or house servants; and you are irresistibly reminded, while the thermometer is ranging between 80 and 90, of hot kitchen fires, cooking stoves, and smoking dishes of all kinds of flesh and fowl." Thoughts of the strenuous domestic employment of New York's African Americans disrupted Clapp's reverie. Imagining people disconnected from their physical bodies was necessary for romanticizing female beauty and, indeed, for the entire project of gentility.[7]

Clapp recorded his prescient comments about pigs, temperance, and the seasonal exodus the summer before cholera struck New York, an event that temporarily shifted the relationship between public health concerns and domestic cleanliness practices and heightened concerns about the unhealthiness of the urban environment. As the historian Charles Rosenberg has noted, "the cholera pandemics" that swept across the Atlantic during the nineteenth century marked a particular moment "during which public health and medical science were catching up with urbanization and the transportation revolution." The presence of cholera bacteria in water, food, or the feces of an infected person, scientists now believe, spreads the disease, which is characterized by severe diarrhea. Reluctant to acknowledge the likelihood of cholera's spreading from Europe to New York and baffled by how best to combat it, city officials reiterated street cleaning measures and tried to eradicate the menace of its many "dirty and confined spaces." In early July 1832, as the epidemic became evident, the city's newspaper editors offered sharp critiques of public health measures. The *New York Evening Post* reprinted a suggestion from a correspondent that "the sewers of the city should be extended to the ends of the piers which reach far out into the river," so that the "filth which they discharge may be carried away by the tide, and not, as now, suffered to collect and form an intolerable nuisance in the slips." Two weeks later, the *Evening Post*'s editors observed that "the cleansing of the city is as yet imperfectly performed. The filth taken from one part of the city has in some instances only been deposited in another. There are many places yet to be disinfected and purified."[8]

Cholera provoked wealthy white residents to flee the heat in greater than usual numbers during the summer of 1832. The *Evening Post* reported roads clogged with stagecoaches just days after the first cases became public knowledge. Seeking to stem the tide in the hopes of minimizing the disaster for city businesses, the paper denied the presence of Asiatic cholera for as long as it could, insisting that the summer was no deadlier than previous ones, and proclaimed the immunity of virtuous private citizens from a disease that initially struck the hardest in crowded public buildings and the poorest neighborhoods.[9]

Imperfect understanding of cholera's transmission spurred speculation about why it struck New York more severely than Boston or Philadelphia, and certain neighborhoods harder than others. Building on an argument made by a British nobleman, who claimed that London owed its less devastating epidemic to the "abundance of water and water closets" compared with Paris, the *Evening Post* editors wondered, "May not the comparative exemption of Philadelphia from the epidemic be owing, in some measure, to the same cause[?]" Visitors to Philadelphia often commented on its abundant water, so plentiful that servants applied it generously to steps and sidewalks to clean them. Public officials in New York could do little to match London's or Philadelphia's use of water to combat filth. But New York's City Board of Health nonetheless attempted to stop cholera at what they believed to be its source: they called for the regular purification of all dwelling houses and out buildings with chloride of lime and, if possible, whitewash, with special attention given to privies. They also urged citizens to bathe in either warm or cold water, noting that "cleanliness is allowed by all to be an excellent and efficacious preventive of the cholera, as well as of many other distempers."[10]

As journalists, public officials, and doctors struggled to make sense of the pattern of death, they blamed intemperate and slothful habits for increasing individual susceptibility to disease. In the medical community, some considered again the possibility of live agents of contagion, but most public health measures reflected continued belief in a zymotic theory of disease—that it spontaneously generated in fermenting filth—making the poor targets of regulations designed to prevent its spread. New York newspapers repeatedly claimed that no person of temperate habits need fear cholera. "Not one single instance can be pointed to of a person of correct habits having died under such circumstances as would at all justify the ascribing his fate to Asiatic Cholera," the editors insisted on July 3.

Background reports on victims included information about excessive consumption of alcohol or food, or other vices. "If only the imprudent and intemperate in drink and diet are to fall victims to Cholera," they argued reassuringly, "surely no great apprehension need prevail, since then every one has it in his own power to avoid the attack of the dreaded scourge." *Godey's Lady's Book* echoed such sentiments by pointing to the disproportionate number of the poor struck down as a sign of God's judgment. Only temperance, cleanliness, and prudence could save the poor. Seventeen years later, as cholera struck the city a second time, the New Yorker Philip Hone observed the concentration of cases in the impoverished Orange Street district, "where water never was used internally or externally, and the pigs were contaminated by the contact of the children."[11]

But as the *Evening Post* defined them, temperate habits meant avoiding extremes, including the strictures of a reformed diet. On July 1, as news of the outbreak hit the stands, that paper condemned Grahamites—a new movement committed to reducing unhealthy stimulation by reforming dietary and sexual habits—as well as the more conventionally intemperate for inviting cholera to New York. Sylvester Graham had lectured in several northeastern venues before the outbreak, including New York's Clinton Hall in March and the Mercantile Library in May. The editors indicted as "intemperate" those who drank malt and spirits, ate full meals of beef, spread rumors, read newspapers avidly, or, out of Grahamite convictions, consumed only arrowroot and barley water: "It is these six classes that supply the Cholera Morbus with victims and terrors; and when we get free from them, we shall see an end to the epidemic."[12]

Cholera epidemics in 1832 and 1849 across the North and regular appearances by yellow fever in the South spurred awareness of regional differences in disease and national interest in the new approaches to health preservation. Philadelphia, for example, reissued seasonal restrictions on emptying privies in 1840 in an effort to cut down on the spread of disease during the hot, stagnant days of summer.[13] Few of the measures proposed were actually new; calls for improved street cleaning and restrictions on dumping sewage were nearly identical to eighteenth-century proposals to improve the healthfulness of the city. They became the mantra of municipal officials nationwide as epidemics struck repeatedly during the nineteenth century. Concerns about protecting health from the hazards of the urban environment, already in evidence before cholera struck, only intensified as the century progressed.

But while the city was a breeding ground for filth and disease, it was also a marketplace for commodities to preserve health. Most of the advertised remedies presented alternatives to allopathy, the conventional use of drugs to counteract symptoms. Bold claims during the 1840s and 1850s to have harnessed nature's healing powers gained wider circulation, appearing in advertisements that promised to cure ailments ranging from venereal disease to hair loss. In New Orleans, readers of the *Daily Picayune* encountered advertisements for "Indian's Panacea," which featured an engraving of an Indian armed with a bow and arrow shooting a many-headed serpent labeled "cancer," "scrofula," and "syphilis." Another ad for Wright's Indian Vegetable Pills exploited the associations between Indians and nature even more boldly. Comparing the body's discharge of impurities through "natural drains"—the lungs, skin, kidneys, and bowels—to the workings of a mighty river's channels, a powerful image for New Orleans residents, the advertisement crudely asserted that "the Red Men of the Wilderness have been taught by Nature true medical knowledge."[14]

Advertisements promising protection from the hazards of city vices, particularly the sexual transmission of disease, proliferated during this period. Sarah Yeo, a New York leather goods dealer, listed condoms under the rubric "HEALTH PRESERVER, too well known to the public, and too strenuously recommended by the Faculty to need further eulogium." Her Philadelphia counterpart, George Wright, posted a notice of his receipt of dressed lambskins—condoms—suitable for the druggist's use.[15] Philadelphia readers learned of Minerva pills, an antisyphilitic. New Orleans boasted a much more openly advertised roster of goods and services for the infected. In addition to the Orleans Infirmary and Private Chambers for Sick Gentleman, a victim of venereal disease could seek treatment from Dr. Huet, "late of Philadelphia," who "cures secret diseases in a very short time, by a new system without the use of mercury, copevia, or any decoction." An advertisement for Levison's Hunter's Red Drop claimed that it cured without noticeable side effects, so that the most intimate friend could not detect its use. The high mercury content of most antivenereal disease treatments spawned a market for such antidotes as Carpenter's Extract of Sarsaparillo, which claimed to purify the blood and cleanse it of excess mercury.[16]

Advertisements for skin whiteners, hair washes, and depilatories filled the pages of newspapers with promises of a natural appearance, newly important during the nineteenth century as a sign of health, an expression of sincerity, and a benchmark of beauty. Atkinson's depilatory promised to remove superfluous hair from the face, neck, or arms, "leaving the skin softer and whiter than before the application." Halford's Pearl Water claimed to render the skin white and blooming. Grooming aids for the hair emphasized natural appearance and cleanliness over wigs and greasy pomatums. Falon's Hair Invigorator promised a "cleansing and purifying wash ... beautifully blended with a most delicate, silky, and glossy moisture for the hair, never before attained." Roussel's Eau Lustrale Odorante combined the fragrance of a pomatum with the healthful benefits of a shampoo that would remove "scurf and dandruff." Even better, it imparted a "soft and natural lustre, entirely devoid of greasiness."[17]

Discernibly more technical in their claims than in the eighteenth century, dental product advertisements exploited concerns about health in general and tooth decay specifically as a widespread problem among Americans. Characteristic of animals, invalids, and the uncouth, "strong, sickening breath," a telltale sign of unhealthy teeth and gums, was to be avoided at all costs. Advertisements for a chlorine tooth wash boasted, "This popular wash for cleansing the mouth and purifying foul breath occasioned either by carious teeth, disordered stomach, or from the use of tobacco, has of late met with an extensive demand."[18] Dr. Wright's Asiatic Tooth Wash, marketed to "the Ladies" as "a new and important discovery for cleaning the mouth and teeth," offered detailed information about its benefits: "This liquid has the properties of dissolving and removing from the teeth all the deposites from the saliva, without injury to the enamel, which it leaves white and smooth. It cures the scurvy, strengthening and hardening the gums, causing them to adhere closely to the teeth, whereby the latter are retained firmly in their sockets and imparts to the breath an agreeable odor." Warning of the role of "septic acid" in promoting tooth decay, one advertisement urged readers to brush regularly with Orris Tooth Powder and get professional dental help. Advertisements for Snook's Dentrifice, a tooth powder imported from England, even included a quotation from the *Journal of Health* and claimed to produce a "delicate whiteness on the teeth" and relieve the gums of disease.[19]

Behind the new interests in disease prevention and natural beauty lay a growing belief in the efficacy of individual and collective intervention. Convinced that their efforts might improve their health, families altered their diets and tried different medical remedies. If these failed, a family of means might resort to travel to escape the deleterious effects of a particular climate on an individual's constitution. These were not Clapp's reasons for travel, although he shared many of these sensibilities. Like the nineteenth-century traveler in pursuit of health who remained mindful of air, water, and diet as he searched for the climate that would allow him to rid himself of his cough or chronic indigestion, Clapp sized up the pigs, sniffed the air, and scrutinized the faces of the locals to take the measure of the city. His fears about the its lack of cleanliness overlapped with his assessment of its lack of healthfulness, the validity of which New Yorkers were to discover to their sorrow in the summer of 1832.

TRAVEL

Northerners and southerners shared the belief that a change of scene could promote physiological improvement as well as lift spirits depressed by illness. Faith in the impact of climate upon the body's constitution, a long-standing belief that was rejuvenated by environmental intervention in the eighteenth century, persisted in nineteenth-century medical teaching and treatment and motivated much of the travel by wealthy invalids. Healthy people migrated seasonally to avoid illness, and the desperately ill with the wherewithal traveled to forestall further decline. In May 1850 Sarah Ker of Louisiana, daughter of the Philadelphia-trained physician John Ker, urged her mother, Mary, to relocate to their summer residence by a river as soon as possible, before it was too late to benefit her health. But even normally unhealthy climates, such as the malarial swamps Ker hoped to avoid, were believed to have some healing potential for certain diseases, such as acute pulmonary cases. Thus the homeopathic doctor William Holcombe searched the New Orleans area for such a swamp to help cure his brother Johnny's lung condition.[20]

In contrast to modern health assessments in which travel might be discouraged as too stressful for the seriously ill, acutely sick people in the nineteenth century who had the means set off on long journeys to regain their health. Yet even for those wealthy enough to insulate themselves from rude accommodations and rough company, travel itself involved numerous difficulties that could compromise health. All travelers experienced the need to alter their plans in response to inclement weather, sudden mishaps, or the onset of a more acute phase of illness. They were also subject to prosaic annoyances of poor roads, broken coaches and steamboats, and substandard accommodations. En route to London to further his education as an engraver, the healthy Massachusetts native Joseph Andrews found the smell of bilgewater in his cabin almost too much to bear. Even worse was the food prepared by the ship's African cook, "the dirtiest fellow I have ever met with. . . . The patches of white pork spattered on to his dark visage during his culinary labours were frequently obvious." Forced to economize on his way home, Andrews traveled steerage, where he was subjected to vomiting women, sheep feces, and an airless compartment. Once the weather cleared, however, the situation improved, thanks in part to the "excellent, cleanly cook," Mrs. Fagan, who also agreed to wash some of his clothes.[21]

At its most basic, bodily comfort meant finding facilities for washing faces and clothes along the journey and being able to answer the call of nature conveniently. For male travelers in good health, maintaining decency on the road was not that difficult. For genteel female travelers, the portable porcelain bord-delieu, which resembled a large gravy boat, could be discreetly carried among personal effects in a stagecoach and slipped under the skirts to provide relief when making a brief stop. When invalids became acutely ill, incontinence sometimes required them to remain secluded from company and brought an end to the hopes that travel would induce a recovery. Travelers scrutinized each other's appearance, taking note of the telltale neglect of grooming that signified illness.[22]

Travelers usually sought to benefit from healthier air or to escape a particular hazard, such as a city's summer season of sickness. For northerners, this often meant traveling south; for urban residents of any region, it meant escaping to the countryside. On his third tour of the southern states in November 1853, the author and landscape architect Frederick Law Olmstead escorted his tubercular brother John, noting, "As the number of northerners, and especially of invalids, who come hither in winter, is every year increasing, more comfortable accommodations along the line of travel must soon be provided." Thomas Bennehan, a student at Chapel Hill, North Carolina, urged his sister Rebecca to "escape the noxious fall vapours, that are still to come" in their hometown of Petersburg, Virginia, in October 1800. Bennehan thought Petersburg "the most nois[y], dirty place I ever saw." Small wonder that one resident of that city, Margaret Cameron Anderson, wrote to her brother Duncan Cameron in Hillsborough, North Carolina, that their sister Jean hoped to be restored to health after her trip to Duncan's home, "where it is so healthy."[23] Mary Phillips wrote her mother, Rebecca Cameron, from Mount Prospect, North Carolina, that her health had improved as soon as she left on her journey. As the sickly season was nearly over, she hoped to return home completely recovered in time for the upcoming camp meeting.[24]

Northern men of means interpreted ill health as both a cultural and a regional phenomenon that could be traced to the stresses of overwork. Travel meant enforced leisure and an escape from the cares that they believed contributed to their physical decline. Men like William Appleton, a successful New England merchant and father to Sarah Lawrence, suffered from chronic dyspepsia, a common complaint among businessmen who worried about matters they could not control: the safe passage of ships laden with expensive goods, global commodity prices, the health and happiness of children, and their progress on their own spiritual journeys, which they feared had been compromised by worldly success. Soon after his marriage in 1815, Appleton went to Charleston, South Carolina, to combat his dyspepsia. After the condition worsened, William, his wife, Mary Anne Cutler, and his physician, Dr. James, traveled to the Mediterranean. Their pursuit of health took them to Sicily, Rome, Paris, and London before they returned. In autumn 1817 Appleton headed again for Charleston. This time, his health improved sufficiently for him to return north to his pursuit of wealth.[25]

Business-related health problems were less common among southern men, whose sufferings doctors traced to the region's climate. For different reasons, southern doctors also prescribed travel. When John B. Laurens was taken with a "violent spitting of blood" in April 1827 following a day of deer hunting and a hearty meal, a doctor came and bled him until he was out of danger. Health problems continued to plague Laurens, however, and he embarked on a boat trip with his physician. By late May, Laurens's declining health led him to plan a trip to Europe with his wife. This was no frivolous decision, but one that required much forethought about the risks of travel. Caroline Laurens wrote letters directing how the children should be educated in case the couple died before returning from Europe.[26]

When life-threatening illness struck more than one family member, wealthy families became expert in traveling to seek medical advice and a more salubrious climate. William Appleton confided to his diary that he was among the wealthiest and most successful men of his generation, yet that success could not protect his family from illness and premature death. Together, he and his wife had ten children, six of whom predeceased them. Five of these had reached adulthood and four left offspring. Following his own triumph over dyspepsia, William Appleton sent his ailing son to Europe, but young William died before his return home. With his faith unshaken in the healing power of travel, Appleton sent his chronically ill daughter Mary Anne to the springs in Virginia, accompanied by two physician friends. When his own health began to decline again in 1839, Appleton headed for England. Upon learning that Mary Anne's now acute illness might be cured by the sea air, he outfitted his ship *The Cygnet* to take her and her family to the Mediterranean, but she died before she could make the trip.[27]

Although the Camerons of North Carolina were perhaps the wealthiest family in the state, they, too, were devastated by illness and premature death. Of the eight children born to Rebecca Bennehan Cameron and Duncan Cameron, one was mentally impaired, four died of tuberculosis in their twenties or early thirties, and one became paralyzed by her mid-thirties, remaining an invalid for the rest of her life. One of the few healthy children, Margaret Bain Cameron (Mordecai) spent most of her early life caring for her siblings and parents and managing the household. She married at age forty-two, only to suffer a single pregnancy that ended in stillbirth, after which she resigned herself to childlessness.

When Anne Cameron, Margaret's sister, became ill with tuberculosis in 1839, she had been preceded in death by three older sisters, and her family was willing to go to extraordinary lengths to save her life. The entire white family, accompanied by at least two enslaved domestics, embarked on the journey. Nineteen-year-old Mildred, the baby of the family, kept a diary of their travels from North Carolina to Charleston, Savannah, and Saint Augustine, and their eventual return to Wilmington. They were spurred on their journey by the belief that salubrious air and a change of scene might arrest the progress of Anne's disease and allow her to regain some of the weight and strength she had lost. When they reached a destination on their itinerary, they stopped for several days to see the sights, visit with old friends, and walk or ride for exercise. From time to time, various members of the family took advantage of opportunities to weigh themselves. Two months into the journey, as they waited for a steamboat to take them to Saint Augustine, Anne and her parents were delighted to discover that she had gained five pounds since her last weigh-in. This gain suggested that the trip had enabled Anne to turn the tables on the flesh-wasting disease, even though she appeared to be declining in health.[28]

As the Camerons discovered, travel had pitfalls that could undermine as well as bolster an invalid's health. Staying in private homes, boarding houses, and hotels, a well-heeled traveler was forced to cope with indifferent or even offensive food, dirty accommodations, and noisy neighbors. For the wealthy white southerner, the inconveniences of a long journey included trying to maintain authority over enslaved domestics who saw opportunity for self-assertion in the ever-changing routine. The perils of the journey sometimes made it necessary to put up with these conditions until it was possible to move on. Setting off for Saint Augustine in the steamboat *The Southerner,* the Cameron women were stuffed into an overcrowded ladies' cabin that was so hot they could hardly breathe, a common problem with berths belowdecks. After an unfortunate collision with another boat incapacitated *The Southerner*'s rudder, the Camerons decided to disembark and start again.[29] Anne's health took a turn for the worse during this delay and never rebounded.

Sometime before May 30, 1840, Anne joined her three sisters in death. Mildred recorded her religious confirmation on that day with the note that "the stern hand of death" had taken *"three beloved sisters* & with my beloved Anne who took her departure last."[30] The extended trip along the southern seaboard had not saved Anne's life, although this failure does not seem to have shaken the family's faith in the curative powers of travel. Anne would be the last Cameron child to die of consumption, the disease whose incurability made travel the remedy of last resort; it stirred the hopes of invalids that the body might become new and whole with a change of climate.

TAKING THE WATERS

Warm mineral springs became a set piece of the elite southern social scene during the nineteenth century and constitutive of a sectional network of wealth and gentility. Sociability was a major draw. Wealthy white southerners flocked to mineral springs and spas as much for the refined and sociable atmosphere as for the access to fashionable medical treatment, which included bathing in and drinking healing mineral water. Such resorts provided the traditional benefits of travel — escape from an injurious climate and recourse to physicians — but allowed the seeker of health to remain among his or her own peers in a posh setting. Combining the promise of physical and psychic relief with the aesthetic appeal of a rural retreat, springs and spas grew in popularity during the 1840s and 1850s as an all-purpose cure for wealthy invalids.[31] The popularity of mineral springs and spas, however, was not simply a southern phenomenon. Northern springs such as those in Saratoga, New York, became a popular destination by the 1830s, especially after it became accessible by railroad. Wealthy northerners, moreover, frequented southern springs until the eve of the Civil War, for reasons of health and fashion.

Well-to-do white southerners had been seeking relief in the healing waters of southern springs since the early eighteenth century and continued to do so throughout the nineteenth century. Regular visits to the springs had been a Cameron family tradition since the early decades of the century. Writing from Petersburg, Virginia, where he had recently concluded a tour of duty as a soldier, William Cameron reported in 1813 that he would not be able to make it to the warm springs in his home state of North Carolina. Continued lameness and weakness, perhaps a consequence of disease or injury contracted during his military service, threatened to restrict him to his current quarters all summer. Four years later, William mentioned that rheumatism kept him confined to his house and yard in Stagville, North Carolina, but that he was beginning to feel more supple. Whenever he was able to get on horseback to cross the mountain and plunge into the warm baths, they never failed to provide relief.[32]

Warm springs continued to be a popular destination throughout the antebellum period, especially for white southerners. Ann Stanley wrote in 1801 to her friend Mary Hollock of Elizabethtown, New Jersey, "Your last letter my dear Mary, found me at Stafford [Connecticut] a journey I performed for the purpose of accompanying my Aunt, and her Daughter Betsey who were both unwell and expected the Waters would prove benificial to their healths." Davis Ker concluded a letter to his mother in 1850 about his declining health with the hope that he would be able to visit White Sulphur Springs in Green Brier County, Virginia, that summer. His sister Sarah recommended the Arkansas Springs for her ailing aunt. Margaret Bain Cameron reported to her brother Paul that Mildred's bout of dysentery had weakened her, making a trip to White Sulphur Springs necessary. Awaiting the arrival of Aunt Mildred in Brooklyn, New York, Lizzie Jones reported to her Cousin Becca that she had "not heard lately from Miss Patty and Sallie at the Springs — but I hope that the water is as beneficial to them, as it is to most persons, and that both of them will return home perfectly well."[33]

By the 1830s travel to southern mineral springs and spas defined high society in the South, with their social exclusivity setting them apart from resorts in the North. As Charlene Boyer Lewis notes in her study of planter society at the Virginia Springs, "People always assumed that travelers to the Virginia Springs were of the 'better class.' Guests who sought to create or strengthen ties at the resorts knew that they would socialize only with those from their own social level. This fact alone placed the Virginia Springs ahead of Saratoga in the opinion of most southerners."[34] Indeed, although spagoers might travel by railroad to Saratoga, the Virginia Springs remained difficult to reach, a challenge that winnowed out casual or less refined visitors. Such exclusivity made it possible for white planters to drop some of their normal reticence about their bodies and indulge in the spa's focus on bodily comfort. Knowing that the people they met at the springs were like themselves, elite families like the Camerons did not hesitate to incorporate new acquaintances into their social networks. Thus Duncan and Rebecca gratefully accepted invitations from spa acquaintances as they journeyed south in pursuit of a cure for their daughter Anne.

The racial exclusivity of the springs, especially those in Virginia, went without saying. Exceptions were shocking and scandalous to white southerners who counted on the whiteness of the spa clientele. Mary Ker reported to her mother her surprise when an old "'lady of colour' as black as the ace of spades: without a tooth in her head, & decked out in silks, laces & jewelry of every description," turned out to be the wife of Uncle Jake Flower and a patron of the springs. Ker had condescendingly addressed the woman as "Auntie" and was amused to learn later of her marriage to Flower and that "he was taking her to the Virginia Springs for *her health*."[35]

Northern spas may have been less exclusive and, from the white southern perspective, less congenial socially, but they continued to be popular with northerners as health resorts where pleasure—physical, social, gastronomic, and aesthetic—was part of the cure. Some northerners preferred southern watering spots, however, drawn by the promise of a more exotic cure and greater exclusivity. When William Appleton sent his daughter to a spa accompanied by physicians, he chose the Warm Springs in Virginia rather than a northern resort.

Boasting a somewhat less exclusive atmosphere, Yellow Springs in Pennsylvania and Saratoga Springs nonetheless drew visitors who hoped to benefit from the change of scene, the focus on bodily pleasure, and the healing properties of the waters, taken internally and externally. Sarah Weeks Custis reported in 1858 that her brother "Charles had returned from the [Saratoga] springs, after spending a very pleasant time and drinking plenty of the celebrated Congrys water."[36]

Mineral spring and spa resorts competed fiercely for new clients, trying to lure travelers out of their own regions to sample the benefits of different healing waters and settings. In an effort to compete with better-heeled and better-reputed southern competitors, northern springs compared themselves to those in the South. As an advertisement for the Pavilion in Sharon Springs, New York, suggests, Virginia's springs set the standard. "The clear, pure, waters of these Springs, greatly resembling White Sulpher Springs of Virginia, have been proven to be highly efficacious in Rheumatic, Cutaneous, Billious, and Dyspeptic complaints," the text proclaimed, as well as for liver ailments, scrofula, and other maladies. The springs themselves offered romantic scenery, including caves and villages. The Pavilion also boasted "Warm, Cold and Shower Baths furnished at all times, either of the mineral or fresh water; and every attention given to render the stay of visitors agreeable." On the eve of New York's 1832 cholera epidemic, which one might have expected to heighten fears about travel to popular destinations, Saratoga Springs reassured readers that they counted even more visitors to their facilities than in past summers. This fact likely did not impress southern spagoers who already found Saratoga too plebeian.[37]

Amid rising competition and higher expectations for elegant surroundings, spa resorts boasted of their investments in new buildings and bathing facilities. An article in the *New Orleans Daily Picayune* on summer retreats included information about Kentucky's Harrodsburg springs, which had recently erected a new $30,000 edifice. In an 1840 advertisement for Pennsylvania's Yellow Springs, the new owner detailed improvements to the facilities that "she flatters herself will be found to gratify the taste of the most cultivated eye. The grounds, which have always been admired for their natural beauty, have been embellished by the buildings which she has erected for the use of the waters. They consist of a pavilion of a hundred feet height, in which, besides the ancient and celebrated Cold Plunging Bath, are contained Hot and Shower Baths of the same water."[38] Reflecting the rising expectation that bathing as well as drinking would be part of the spa treatment, owners renovated bathing facilities that often dated back to the late eighteenth century.

The healing properties of the ingested waters were even more important than the rural setting and the physical plant of the resort for attracting visitors. A testimonial appended to the advertisement announcing new facilities at Yellow Springs declared that the medicinal springs "are situated in one of the most healthy portions of the State, the waters of them are intensely cold and strongly chalybeate [filled with iron salts], and at the same time supplying the various modes of bathing." An advertisement for the Dardanelles Chekely Springs in Arkansas promoted the benefits of white and black sulfur water, claiming that it would "increase the appetite, purify the blood, and renovate the system." Such claims emphasized the benefits of drinking water rather than of bathing, in keeping with older spa practices and the new emphasis on internal medicine. William Appleton's report in July 1855 that he and his wife were taking the waters freely and with pleasant effect probably referred to imbibing rather than immersing. The market for bottled mineral water testified to its popularity as a drink. *Pennsylvania Inquirer* readers learned that they could purchase bottled water from Blue Lick Sulphur Spring in Maysville, Kentucky, and the Louisiana resident Sarah Ker Butler consumed Saratoga water as an antidote to the bad blood she believed made her popular with mosquitoes. The *New Orleans Daily Picayune* advertised Saratoga Union Spring water. Health-conscious consumers could even purchase water that its bottlers claimed had come from White Sulphur Springs.[39]

Mineral springs, spas, and bottled spring water continued to have a devoted following throughout the antebellum period, although important sectional differences had emerged. Northern spas tended to be less exclusive and less renowned for the healing properties of the waters, although like their southern counterparts they had an exotic cachet for those from other parts of the country, drawing the occasional southern visitor. More serious for the emerging sectional cultural difference was the critique of the pleasurable excess of southern spa culture by northern health reformers who were dismayed by the sight of spagoers wolfing down their food and the suspension of genteel demeanor. An anonymous "Boston Traveller," whose observations were quoted in the *Picayune*, was affronted by the table manners of guests at the springs: "To be serious, I regard this hasty, piggish manner of eating as one of the worst Americanisms. Even the very savages do better. Nothing like it is seen in all Europe and Asia, and probably not among the Hottentots themselves. It is one of the principal causes of all those dyspepsias, diseases of the liver, inflammations of the brain, and prostrations of strength and life, which are with us in such peculiar haste for their victims. I have no doubt but the beneficial influence of these waters is by it often more than counteracted."[40] Excessive eating threatened to negate the benefits of the setting, especially the healing qualities of the waters, and flew in the face of the gentility that southern spas were supposed to embody.

SALUBRIOUS SEASIDES

The unrestrained consumption of food at southern spas exposed one of the many emerging cultural fault lines distinguishing North from South. But regional differences seem less clear when one considers the lure of the ocean for antebellum people. Northerners and southerners alike traveled to seaside resorts as they did to mineral springs in search of relaxation and improved health. Some of these migrations were seasonal efforts to take advantage of hot days and temperate oceans. Others occurred with greater urgency in response to doctors' orders for sick patients who had shown little improvement during more conventional courses of treatment. In general, northerners appear to have placed greater priority on the pleasures of ocean bathing and did so sooner than their southern counterparts.[41]

Epitomizing nature's curative power, the ocean combined the stimulation of fresh, moving air with the efficacy of bathing and the healing properties of the mineral waters — in this case, salt. Immersion in saltwater had long been believed to obviate the dangers of freshwater immersion: taking a chill or compromising the body's constitution. As Susan Burns recounted of her sea voyage from Philadelphia to Charleston, seeking fresh air on deck subjected her to being soaked by seawater, but she took no illness from it. Had it been freshwater, she believed, such a soaking might have killed her. Sarah Ker Butler's ailing family friend Dr. Young headed with Sarah's husband for the seashore, where Sarah "trust[ed] the bathing will quite restore him."[42] Beliefs in the superior healing powers of saltwater and fears of freshwater do not appear to have deterred people from swimming in rivers and ponds, however, a deliberate immersion of the body that could be followed by briskly rubbing the skin and dressing in dry clothes to prevent a postbath chill.

The family of Louisa Clapp Trumbull of Worcester, Massachusetts, used the seaside to intervene in her sister Jane's poor health. When Jane "became very feeble & we were exceedingly anxious for her," a family friend "assisted us to obtain a situation at Nahant in the hope a residence near the sea might benefit her." In June 1839, after preparing "bathing garments &c&c," Jane left for an eight-week stay in Nahant, Massachusetts, after which she returned "much improved in appearance." The good consequences continued long after the visit to the seaside had ended, Louisa noted, for Jane "continued to gain & now enjoys better health & spirits than for many years past." Two years later, the young Trumbull women embarked on a visit to the ocean for less urgent reasons. "Yesterday Caroline & Jane left home to enjoy the luxury of sea air & bathing," Louisa noted in her diary. "They are at Nantasket beach for a fortnight with a pleasant party[;] both needed a change."[43]

By 1840 many places along the northern seaboard could be described as having a summer "season" of travelers in search of healthful recreation at resort
hotels. Nahant and Nantasket in Massachusetts, Cape May, New Jersey, and
Coney Island, New York, all drew crowds of eager bathers and curious onlookers.
The public notice given to such places emphasized health benefits. Beachgoers
enjoyed leisure activities such as strolling along the beach and the pleasures of
saltwater bathing. Donning special costumes to enter the water, bathers created
a spectacle most unlike that of the exclusive spa.[44] Sarah Appleton Lawrence
was aware of the entertainment her family provided onlookers by ocean bathing.
Each summer, beginning in May or June, the Lawrences relocated to Nahant on
Boston's North Shore, where visitors to the family might divert themselves by
watching their hosts bathe.[45]

Much like the spa experience, ocean bathing dissolved the reticence of
bathers to divulge the intimate effects of bathing on their bodies. In July 1854
Sarah Ker Butler visited the seaside resort of Last Island, a barrier island on the
Louisiana coast. After donning bathing dresses and turkish trousers — wide
legged pants that permitted greater mobility than a dress — she and a female
friend went down to the surf to enjoy the water. "Since that bath — I have not
been the same person," she reported to her mother, "it certainly is the most en-
chanting thing I ever felt." About ten days later, Butler followed up with more
personal reflections. Instructing her mother, in large letters at the top of the
page, "Don't read this aloud," Sarah again sang the praises of bathing: "I cannot
express how delightful the Bathing is & indeed one must enjoy it to know what a
pleasure it is. It seemed to act like magic with me & I had such an appetite, that
I was ashamed to go to Table." Indeed, Butler's appetite was not the only physical
process stimulated by bathing: "It seems to have a remarkable effect in one
way — for Nannie Ellis who had been unwell [menstruated] not 2 weeks before,
had only bathed 2 or 3 days when she was taken so again. She was not much so —
& after 2 or 3 days bathed again — & was again taken — I think because it had
been checked the first time I had not bathed quite a week when I was taken — the
first time for 5 months." Plagued by amenorrhea before her visit to the resort,
Sarah soon recovered her regular cycle, a fact she believed "shewed the great
benefit I had received — I was 20 as usual & the usual time & after 5 days." She re-
sumed bathing only after her menstrual period ended, observing to her mother,
"I was sorry to miss bathing during the time I was sick . . . tho I was told that many
who resided on the Island all summer did not allow it to make any difference."[46]

Sarah's sister Mary still found saltwater bathing a novelty when her family sent
her north in 1855 to get over her infatuation with a drunkard. There she encountered the ocean resort. Mary reported from Brooklyn about the bathing at Coney

Island. "It is a delightful place to bathe," she wrote to her mother on July 15. "It is about 6 miles from here, and a great many persons go down there from the city every evening to bathe." Ker and two female travel companions watched with amusement "at the *pretty figure* every one cut in the water." The spectacle aroused her own interest in bathing, which she thought she might enjoy were she not so afraid. One month later, she reported from the Atlantic Hotel in a letter to her brother that she had taken the plunge. "I went in bathing this morning for the first-time and found it so delightful, I think I shall go in every day here after, as long as I stay." She bathed daily until cold weather brought an end to this recreation on August 28. She also believed she had benefited from the "bracing & delightful air," which left her wondering how a person "could feel any think [*sic*] but well" at the seaside.[47]

Sarah Ker Butler and Mary Ker were just two of the thousands of recreational bathers during the antebellum period who discovered to their surprise that bathing was an enjoyable experience that stimulated rather than debilitated the body. The craze for the ocean spurred interest in saltwater bathing in hotels and in private homes and encouraged the burgeoning interest in private baths to promote health and comfort.

BATHS

It was unusual in 1822 for an American man to experience a Turkish bath, and William Swift knew it. He recorded in great detail his visit to a bathhouse in the North African city of Tunis during his service to the U.S. consul there, describing the sensations in eschatological terms of heaven and hell. Although the heat of the flagstones made him think of hell, the vapor that surrounded him and the cistern of water by his side made "this highly heated place far more temperate." "Bathed in vapour & perspiration, the system relieved from all oppressions & breathing freely at every pore"; while a masseur freed his body from "every particle of . . . defilement[,] purity prevail[ed]" in his thoughts and his sensations were "those of happiness." Watching the "filth which the man at work upon you rolls from your skin . . . forcibly reminds you that notwithstanding the calm delight and most grateful enjoyment you experience, you cannot yet be in heaven." The bodily suffering that accompanied the "perfect purification," and the massage that followed made Swift think purgatory was a more apt description for the Turkish bath than heaven.[48]

Although few of Swift's American contemporaries had the opportunity to experience a Turkish bath, during the forty years following his purification in Tunis the number of public and private bathing facilities and the demand for plumbing equipment increased dramatically, a trend that coincided with the legislation across the Atlantic establishing public baths in England in 1846. Motivated by the need for sufficient supplies of water to extinguish fires and clean streets, cities throughout the nation built water systems that gradually increased the supply of water available for bathing in private households. By the mid 1850s the Croton Aqueduct provided water to nearly fourteen thousand baths and more than ten thousand water closets in New York. In 1853 the Cochituate water supplier to Boston recorded serving eighteen hundred bathtubs, many with attached showers. By 1858 that figure had risen to thirty-three hundred. Many households, unable to afford water from these suppliers, used private wells, pumps, or cisterns to deliver it conveniently, although none of these substitutes worked well for the urban poor.[49] Despite the prevalence of smaller water systems during the 1840s and 1850s, most poor urban households lacked running water on the eve of the Civil War and had to transport it if they wished to bathe — a major obstacle to meeting new standards for decency. But privately owned bathtubs were becoming less rare by the 1850s; bathtub owners even became the target of scams. The *Pennsylvania Inquirer* ran a story about a man posing as a plumber who instructed a domestic to fill the tub and remain in the room until it was two-thirds full, apparently hoping to create an opportunity to steal the family silver.[50]

The growing numbers of private households that boasted bathtubs and shower baths reflected how immersion of the body had become habit for a significant minority. The novelist Catharine Sedgwick's fictional representation of bathing reflected both this rising popularity and the sense of its newness for Americans who still associated fastidious bathing habits with the English. In her novel *Home* (1835), Sedgwick described a tidy, respectable household that contained "as nice an apparatus for ablutions as a disciple of Combe could wish, jugs, basins, and tubs large enough, if not to silence, to drown a traveling Englishman." The reference was to Andrew Combe, the English advocate of warm bathing, whose *Principles of Physiology Applied to the Preservation of Health* (1833) stressed the need for greater English attention to a practice taken for granted in continental Europe. The bath of choice was neither hot, like Swift's Turkish experience, nor cold, like that subsequently recommended by water cure advocates, although people might resort to either one to affect a cure. Rather, in keeping with beliefs in natural healing properties and the avoidance of extremes, it was warm. *Godey's Lady's Book*, too, extolled the virtues of the warm bath in 1833, while condemning hot baths as harmful and cold baths as pointless. The same piece reminded readers that baths were not used as frequently as health, cleanliness, and the preservation of beauty required.[51]

A cross-section of wealthy and middle-class Americans resorted to the bath. The textile worker Lucy Larcom's sister braved a full cold bath every morning. The Cortland, New York, native Frances Burgess "took a *bathe*" in her room after completing the Monday wash. The ailing Boston Brahmin Mrs. Lowell struggled to wash herself daily, and when she could not, relied on her servant to help her. The southerner Mary Bethel followed the message of her dream, that the cold bath would restore her health, and bathed in cold water for several weeks in 1863 with good results. The South Carolinian Keziah Brevard's neighbor and friend Mr. R. treated his own illness, brought on by a trip to Columbia, by bathing and going to bed.[52]

The rising availability of public facilities indicates that bathing had become popular for a population larger than that of bathtub owners. Although one still needed means to purchase a shampoo or a season's bathing tickets, one did not need to purchase a bathtub, pay a plumber to install it, or hire the labor to fill it. The luxury of a deep tub was also more possible in a public facility, where the cost of the equipment was shared with hundreds of bathers, than in a private home. Visiting Philadelphia in 1834, George Shattuck commented that the tubs at the public bath were "quite deep." Five years later, that city boasted at least five different bathing establishments, including medicated vapor and sulphur baths. Served by only three public baths in 1832, New York could claim nearly twenty facilities by the 1850s. An advertisement from 1853 noted that the Rabineau Bath at Castle Garden Bridge had been fitted with a "Ladies Bath." The city directory from that year listed baths of four types: medicated, swimming, warm, and cold. In Boston bath patrons could choose from fourteen establishments, including the facilities at the Tremont House, the American House, and the rear of the Marlboro Hotel. Public bathing facilities expanded access to regular bathing in ways that are difficult to quantify as precisely as bathtub ownership, but that were probably more significant as an indication of the shift in popular attitudes toward bathing and the changes in actual practice.[53]

Interest in erecting public baths stirred in response to disease. Newspaper editors and city officials in 1832 emphasized the importance of public baths to improve the health of the poor. As news of the first cholera cases broke, the *New York Post* claimed that bathing could actually prevent cholera and described various facilities in the city. When trustees for the Philadelphia Peel testimonial, named after the recently deceased Sir Robert Peel, debated how best to use the funds in October 1850, soon after the 1849 cholera outbreak, they concluded that baths and wash houses would provide "the greatest amount of public good."[54]

Queasy about coming into close contact with the poor and the sick, the genteel traveler probably found little appealing in the democratization of bathing for public health reasons. By the 1840s public bathing establishments struggled to assert their gentility, tastefulness, and distance from scenes of urban vice. In Philadelphia, Harmer's Hot and Cold Baths, on 3rd Street opposite the City Hotel, boasted single baths for twenty-five cents, five tickets for a dollar, and the availability of season tickets. Harmer stressed luxury, convenience, and the upstanding character of his baths. The advertisement noted that "he has just fitted up the most extensive and convenient BATHING ESTABLISHMENT in Philadelphia, and in a situation where such a luxury has been long needed." What's more, the facility was "on the most liberal scale, and are calculated at once to save time, afford pleasure, and promote health." To that end, "The Bathing Rooms will be kept open from 5 o'clock in the morning to 12 o'clock at night; and the plan of the baths is on a principle that will ensure a constant supply of warm water at every hour." To reassure the prospective bather anxious about the tastefulness and morality of the operation, Harmer added, "The Proprietor has incurred considerable expense, in the machinery employed, the materials of which the baths are constructed, the furniture of the rooms, and the character of the attendants. His ambition is to afford entire satisfaction and with this object, he is determined to exert himself to the utmost." Reassurances like these seem to have succeeded in allaying the suspicions of genteel customers who patronized public baths. In 1856, during her stay in Philadelphia, Margaret Bain Cameron (by then, going by her married name, Mordecai), regularly used them. Clearly, elite white southern women who frequented the Virginia Springs found nothing ungenteel about purchasing bath tickets. By that date, the city also boasted a combination shaving and bathing establishment for gentlemen.[55]

In New Orleans proprietors of public baths reminded prospective clients of the convenience, the healthfulness, and the scriptural support for cleanliness. Kirkpatrick's floating bath on the Mississippi at the head of Gravier Street boasted, "The Bath for bathing and swimming is 60 feet long by 22 feet in width—with from 3 feet 9 inches to 7 feet depth of water, which is continually flowing through all its parts. Dressing rooms are arranged on each side of the Bath, with suitable appurtenances for bathers, and every attention will be made to render this luxury, which is so conducive to health, a most desirable pleasure Bath." Eager to compete for clients on their day of leisure, the proprietor reassured readers, "take a dive before you go to church and you will be but complying with a command of scripture." Meanwhile, African-American barbering establishments, many of them designated "French," hoped to win the business of men who sought regular shaves, shampoos, and baths. William Holcombe availed himself of facilities like these to get a proper shampoo once a month.[56]

Public baths did not so much compete against as capitalize upon the growing popularity of private bathing facilities. Once bathing became a habit at home, a traveler so habituated would have a greater desire to bath while on the road. Model house designs increasingly included space for bathrooms, which housed bathtubs, and for water closets, the indoor alternative to outdoor privies.[57] Household advice gurus like Catharine Beecher urged her readers to make this investment in household plumbing for the health and welfare of their families. Advertisements for plumbing services and plumbing supplies abounded. The pages of the Pennsylvania Inquirer were filled with advertisements featuring bathtubs, shower baths, and water closets. By the 1850s in most major cities, a property owner wishing to install a bathtub could find a reputable and well-stocked plumber to do the job.[58]

But interest in what William Holcombe described as "tee-total" bathing seems to have been only a small part of the growing dedication to washing the body. The health reformer William Alcott claimed in 1850 that 25 percent of New Englanders never bathed during the course of the year; among the regular bathers, men washed while swimming, and women and children limited themselves to a weekly bath on Saturday night or Sunday morning. Short of immersing the body in a tub or shower, many Americans described themselves as engaging in "customary ablutions." The editor of the *Tobacco and Health Almanac for 1849*, a water cure journal, declared that "those who wish to keep the body clean, and free from colds, would do well to bathe themselves with cold water, every morning," and gave an explicit description of his own routine, which he insisted would "not occupy more than one minute": "As soon as you rise, turn two or three quarts of water into your wash-bowl," he instructed. "First wet your head, neck, and shoulders, thoroughly, and let it trickle down your body; then rub yourself briskly with a coarse towel."[59] As a young woman, Sarah Ker described taking her "usual bath," in the morning before she dressed. William Holcombe required soap and towels for his ablutions, which he performed at night before he retired. He distinguished these nightly cleansings from the "tee-total bath" he hoped to take on May 1, 1855, and from the monthly shampoos and bathing operations he purchased in New Orleans.[60]

With increasing pressure to provide facilities comparable to mineral spas and public baths, American hotels scrambled to improve their accommodations and advertise them to best advantage. The Tremont House Hotel in Boston put soap in guest rooms for the first time in 1829, along with tubs. In 1836 the Astor Hotel led the way for New York with a bathtub for each floor. The Madisonville Hotel, listed in the *Picayune* as a summer retreat, boasted a "good Bathing-house for the convenience of his boarders" and was reputed to be a generally healthful place. An advertisement for Florida House in Pensacola mentioned extensive bathhouses that would be kept "constantly in good order." Foreign travelers, used to better-furnished hotels and beginning to consider bathing facilities a necessity rather than a luxury, commented upon hotels' failure to provide such amenities. By midcentury, however, more American hotels featured private baths for guests in response to the growing expectation that such facilities would be available.[61]

WATER CURE

Water cure devotees shared with the patrons of mineral spring spas and ocean resorts the belief in water's natural healing properties. At spas, seaside resorts, and water cure establishments, an adventurous bather might enjoy the stimulating tingle of water on skin. But here the similarities ended. Spa culture was the centerpiece of elite sociability that required little discipline or denial of the pleasures of food, drink, or company. In contrast, the water cure was the latest incarnation of a medical regimen of renunciation: of alcohol, tobacco, caffeine, and excessive consumption of food, particularly meat. Not least of these renunciations was the rejection of conventional allopathic remedies like mercury, which many practitioners of alternative medicine deemed harmful. Unlike both the spa and the seaside resort, where bathing was as much social and recreational as it was healthful, the water cure privileged the healthful reasons for immersion and made play incidental. It provided certainty about treatment, moreover, at a time when regular physicians and their rivals could be frustratingly indecisive or inconsistent. Water cure enthusiasts adopted an almost religious devotion to their health-maintenance and healing methods. Spagoers and ocean bathers may have become devotees of their practices, but their adherence to bathing remained casual and playful, even when it became habitual. The water cure, in contrast, combined a transformation of the individual's sensory thresholds with faith in the ability to intervene in the body's processes. "One peculiarity of the treatment is, that it is intended to call out the courage and active exertions of the patient," the *New Graefenberg Water-Cure Reporter* noted, with the express purpose of "banish[ing] the *tone* of the sick-room."[62]

Water cure purists believed in hydropathy's powers to cure most common and acute ailments when combined with fresh air, a reformed diet, and exercise. They constructed a vigorous regime of daily habits consistent with nature's laws that rejected the effeminate excesses of modern life. "Temperance and moderation are no less useful in the water-cure than everywhere else," a water cure journal noted somewhat defensively, mindful of the charge that they recommended extreme measures. "He who comes to it only to gain fresh licence for bad habits and unhealthy tastes, had better not come at all," the editor warned; "it is only those who desire to return to the purity of Nature's ways, to renounce the vitiated habits of civilized effeminacy, and to make themselves strong for good work and a useful life, who desire to be cured, and it is only they who will be." The *Tobacco and Health Almanac for 1849* advised readers, "Never hurry or retard nature; only remove obstructions which may be in her way. She never errs, neither asks advice, but pursues her own course; and those who will observe her laws will grow wiser and wiser."[63]

Such a philosophy required abandoning other harmful types of medical treatment. Water cure testimonials typically featured an invalid's last-ditch effort to combat a serious illness by visiting a water cure resort, where health underwent a miraculous restoration. An important part of that recovery occurred as a result of the daily physical stimulation of the body by cold water. Washing the skin "stopp[ed] all nonsense from entering the body . . . and invited the blood from the part where it is causing obstruction, to the surface and extremities, where it belongs," the *New Graefenberg Water-Cure Reporter* explained. In addition, clean skin meant that the "ten thousand little doors" in the skin would be open to allow waste matter to be thrown off. The healthy individual as well as the invalid could benefit. "When from almost any cause, one rises from his bed in the morning, languid and dull, and perhaps with a heavy feeling of the head and foul taste of the mouth," a water cure journal suggested, a bath followed by brisk rubbing with a towel "refreshes him astonishingly." Tooth brushing completed the morning toilet and wrought the transformation in sensation from sluggishness and symptoms of incipient illness to brisk alertness.[64]

Converted to the wisdom of hydropathy, the individual altered daily habits to incorporate hydropathic principles of health, making return visits to water cure centers as needed and resorting to special medicalized baths: sitz baths, head baths, leg baths, shower baths, and plunge baths. Although militant devotion to the water cure required more than the washstands increasingly found in people's homes and advertised in newspapers, water cure journals pointed out that "an ordinary washstand and bowl, or even a pail of water, with a good sponge or coarse towel, will answer the purpose." Better still was "a tub to stand in, surrounded by a screen made of cheap cotton cloth, nailed upon a frame like a clothes horse." Even a traveler might enjoy the benefits of a daily bath by packing an oil cloth to serve as a bathing mat and sponging the body with water. The consequence of daily attention to bodily cleanliness by bathing was the conditioning of the body's sensations to create a lifelong habit: "Let a child wash himself all over every morning for sixteen years, and he will as soon go without his breakfast as his bath," a water cure journal predicted. Once established, habits of regular bathing became a physical necessity like food (Figure 11.1).[65]

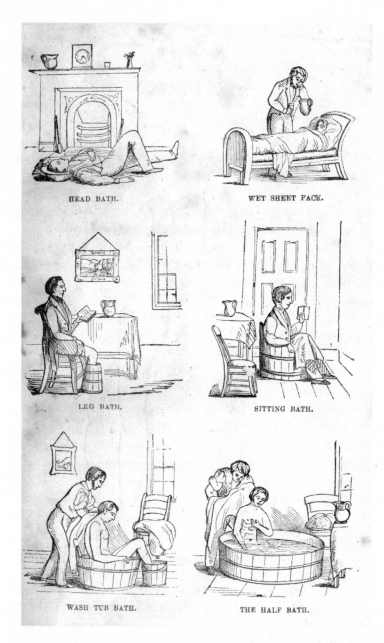

HEAD BATH.

WET SHEET PACK.

LEG BATH.

SITTING BATH.

WASH TUB BATH.

THE HALF BATH.

11.1. Water cure processes, from Joel Shew, *The Hydropathic Family Physician* (New York, 1854). Department of Historical Collections, Health Sciences Library, SUNY Upstate Medical University

Hydropaths valued the bodily cleanliness that came with bathing in water for both medical and moral reasons. They found support for their methods in the health reforms of William Alcott, the traditional bathing practices of Native Americans, and the precepts of cleanliness expounded by Dr. Combe and John Wesley.[66] The motto "Wash and be Healed" communicated the essential medical principle of hydropathy. The moral consequences of bathing included the reduction in pauperism and crime. If public baths could be established to place regular bathing within reach of even the poorest citizen, the editors of the *Water-Cure Journal* reasoned, they would contribute to "habits of personal cleanliness and comfort, so indispensable to self-respect, and so essential to the preservation of virtuous habits generally. A free use of water in this way would tend in no small degree to prevent the moral as well as physical atmosphere from becoming tainted." Quoting the *Boston Bee*, the same journal observed, "Filthiness of person engenders filthiness of mind, and dishonesty and crime are the spontaneous growth of a soil thus manured."[67]

Cold, pure water, taken internally and applied externally, was the foundation of the water cure. "Those who drink water have much whiter and sounder teeth than others," the *Water-Cure Journal and Teacher of Health* reported in 1844, and they were also "brisker and more alert" than those who drank "malt liquors." For the purposes of bathing, cold water was also superior, although by 1850 many hydropaths were willing to concede that each patient needed to find his or her own appropriate temperature for daily washing, especially during the winter. Cold water cured disease by "strengthening the general health and fortifying the system" and by bringing "'bad stuff' out of the system."[68] Yet the editors conceded that the shock of cold water deterred many. "The supposed *chilling* effect of the treatment is a great obstacle to the advancement of water-cure," one admitted. "What a hydrophobic dread of cold water do most persons have. Many for years dare not touch water so far as any thing like a general bath is concerned. But this supposed *uncomfortableness* of the treatment is altogether a mistake."[69] The same journal warned that "the direct effect of warm baths is to weaken" and prescribed that if a warm bath were used, it should be short and followed immediately by a plunge or shower in cold water. Corroborating evidence for the harmful effects of warm water could be found in the mundane duties of housework: "It is well known by some housekeepers that 'washing day' can be much less fatigue if most of the water used be cool or cold," the editor noted.[70]

For those not converted to hydropathy, water cure principles seemed easy to incorporate into existing tactics for combating ill health. Many health-conscious families adopted water cure techniques or made use of the healing properties of warm water. Sarah Lawrence's family were avid seaside bathers but also willing to experiment with the water cure when a case seemed easily treated at home or if a more conventional treatment failed. As her brother Frank's mental illness worsened, despite treatment by the family's longtime physician, Sarah noted in her diary the decision to try the water cure. Holcombe, the homeopathic physician, applied cold water to his own body after a fall from a horse in June 1855, a simple enough adaptation of the water cure that he saw as perfectly compatible with his homeopathic methods. Ann Cushing, a physician's wife, put her ill daughter in a warm bath in February 1854 to alleviate her suffering.[71]

The extended correspondence of Sophia Draper White of New York and her sister Emeline Rice during the 1850s illustrates the water cure's place in the spectrum of medical treatments as well as its jarring physical sensation for nineteenth-century Americans unused to immersion. It reveals, moreover, the faith of purists and the difficulty for nonbelievers in accepting the claims for the water cure's efficacy. Sophia was a recent convert who had received treatments from the water cure guru Mary Gove Nichols, but her sister Emeline remained skeptical about the use of cold water. Despite this difference between them, both women appear to have considered it standard practice to bathe babies, the linchpin of Mary Tyler's system of child care. About their childless sister Lucy's report that she bathed her dog, Emeline commented, "What a pity that she hadn't a *baby* to *wash* as you and I have, her *dog* would receive *less* attention."[72]

Emeline's objections to her sister Sophia's use of water are instructive of the American middle-class consumer's skepticism about medical claims in a dynamic medical marketplace. She objected more to the temperature of the water than to the frequency of its application. Upon learning that Sophia had used hydropathy to treat her son Albert when he contracted measles, she commented sharply, "I do not wonder he *screamed* when they poured the cold water over him." When her pregnant sister turned to hydropathy to prepare herself for giving birth, Emeline wrote skeptically, "[I] should think you had to suffer enough in preserving your health, without suffering from sickness. I think cold water useful in its place, but I do think there is such a thing as carrying it too far, all new measures run into *extremes*, and hydropathists I believe are as faulty in this respect, as other classes of Physicians." She concluded that she would "rather suffer more pain wen [*sic*] sick, than to go through so many different water applications every day." She hoped Sophia would "be compensated for your trouble in the end," by having an easy confinement.[73]

Sophia testified to the positive effects of regular bathing on her postpartum recovery and her newborn's health in a letter written soon after the birth of her daughter. Although she confessed to leaving off hydropathic treatments for much of her pregnancy, she continued to have "a bath every morning." "It was a deal of work to use it as much as I did all winter," she admitted, "but I think it did me good." Hoping to convince her skeptical sister of the benefits she had gained, she testified, "I never got up so soon after my confinement as I did this time, was *dressed* and *through* all my rooms in less than a week, and to see Mrs. Nichols in two weeks. I felt well enough to go out in a week." When her newborn contracted whooping cough, Sophia put her faith in the water cure. She "*packed* the little thing for it" by putting a soft wet linen cloth across her chest underneath dry flannels and then bathing her all over in cold water. The cough improved in three or four weeks. "She was hardly over *that* before she had a *sore mouth*, which went completely *through her*," she reported to Emeline. With the baby's "*bottom* in a *dreadful state*," Sophia "was obliged to keep a bowl of water and Castile soap standing by me all the time, and *wash* her every time I changed her towel, which was pretty often."[74]

The appeal of hydropathy may have resided partly in its alleged whitening effects on the skin. Sophia observed about her daughter's complexion, "She is very *white*, and always has been, so much I suppose for *water*, as Mrs. Nichols babe was just so white at first."[75] Although Sophia was not certain that hydropathy could be directly linked to whiteness, she saw no harm in a treatment that made a baby's skin whiter. Water's likely agency in whitening already white skin was a positive side effect of bathing.

Emeline remained curious about Sophia's daily application of water. She seemed to pity Sophia's daughter for having "to take cold water every morning" and wondered whether Sophia herself "bathe[d] in the morning yet." Sophia responded with a detailed account that revealed how hydropathy changed the lexicon of terms for water as well as the practitioner's relationship to her own body and the bodies under her care. Of her daughter, Sophia wrote, "I wash her every morning in what you would call cold water," noting the inaccuracy of this moniker, for "I take the *least bit* of the *chill* off." She admitted that she did not "bathe myself *every* morning all over." On the off mornings, "I wash myself down to my waist, put on my shirts and let my unclean clothes fall over them." Her manservant, Moors, however, "baths *all over* every morning," a habit of which she approved.[76]

Sophia White's efforts to persuade her sister to try the water cure took on a new urgency after Emeline was diagnosed with tuberculosis. Emeline initially declined her sister's invitation to come to New York for hydropathic treatment, claiming that her own worsening condition was actually in remission. Indeed, although she was willing to try the unproven remedies of many different doctors, she resisted the testimonials to the water cure as so much propaganda. The January 1853 issue of the *Water Cure-Journal* struck her as having "too much *Slung* in" it, with the case for the water cure being made with inaccurate claims about the methods of regular physicians. "Let Hydropathy rise on its own merits not by misrepresenting Allopathy," she lectured her sister. She did ask Sophia to have her husband inquire after a Brooklyn physician who claimed to be able to cure consumption but added pessimistically that she presumed him to be a quack.[77]

Despite her suspicions about inflated claims and quackery, Emeline traveled to New York in the late spring and availed herself of several different treatments, including a visit to a bath and daily applications of water to her body. Weeks after Emeline's departure, as Sophia described a recent visit to a bathing facility, she compared it with the bathing experience they had shared. Even though Sophia was a practitioner of the water cure, both sisters had been shocked by the sensation of full-body immersion in cold water; they laughed convulsively, they were "noisy" (shrieks? gasps?), and Emeline only reluctantly submerged her body. "How I wish you were there, there was no *fun* in being alone," Sophia lamented of the visit she made by herself:

> You would have thought I had *improved* some I *guess*, for I could swim *both limbs* and only my *head* out of water, but I did not dare *let go the rope*, as you were not there to *assist* me in case I *could not get my feet down again*. What made me *improve* as much, while waiting for my bath I watched the young Ladies in the *swimming* bath, there were nearly a *dozen* there, and they made more noise than *we ever did*. I wanted *you* to see them too, it was equal to the *museum:* those who were *used* to it, would *give* a *leap* from the platform into the *midst* of the bath, and go under the water *out of sight.* . . . Others were more *timid*, just *learning*, and would be about as long as *you* were getting in the water.

For her part, Emeline had apparently acquiesced to her sister's persistent efforts to apply water directly to the diseased parts of her body. Sophia inquired, "do you wear a wett cloth at night across your lungs and shoulder? I am afraid not always, as you have not got *me* to *make* you, I still have great *faith* in *water*, and could you have been *willing* would rather you would have gone to a great *water cure* than to have done any thing else."[78] Emeline stopped short of attempting a water cure, however, a decision over which Sophia later expressed regret.

Emeline's objections to the water cure seem to have stemmed less from the actual treatment than from the insistence of practitioners that using other treatments would compromise its efficacy. Yet some of the hydropathic precepts she had learned seem to have impressed her, for when she succumbed to a gastrointestinal ailment after her trip, she "abstained from eating 24 hours, used sitz baths, cold water on the bowels, and did take some rhubarb syrup and havequrie."

Her attitude toward the range of possible treatments reflected her position as a layperson navigating a confusing medical landscape: "Hardly know whether it did any good or not," she admitted, but "was thankful to get well by any means."[79]

Rendered desperate by the terminal nature of consumption, by December she allowed her sister to bring a lock of her hair to a New York clairvoyant, Mrs. Briggs—probably Sarah Briggs of Chrystie Street—who prescribed a medicine. Briggs had made an initial diagnosis of sickness in the throat rather than the lungs based on holding one of Emeline's letters. Emeline claimed, rather, that it was the "nauseating" lobelia prescribed by Briggs that irritated her throat. She returned to the care of a regular physician, Dr. Sargeant, who insisted the problem lay in her ulcerated right lung, not her throat, and who dismissed the efficacy of clairvoyance. His cod liver oil medicines struck her as "not half as bad as that *lobelia.*" A few months later, she was visiting another regular physician, Dr. Richardson from Ware, Massachusetts, who also had little regard for clairvoyance and doubted that Emeline's cough would have been cured by lobelia. But in other respects, his diagnosis agreed well with Briggs's, which Emeline found comforting. Indeed, six months later, in June 1854, she permitted Sophia to visit Mrs. Briggs again to secure another prescription for a different medicine.[80]

Ultimately, neither clairvoyance nor the treatment of allopaths could protect Emeline from the death sentence of tuberculosis, then an incurable disease. Sophia remained convinced that the water cure could have saved her sister and continued to be a devotee of health reform. A decade after Emeline's death, she and her husband traveled to a health resort at the springs in Poland, Maine, where she hoped to cure her persistent cough by drinking the healing waters and eating a healthful diet of whole grain bread, crackers, and fruit and vegetables.[81]

SECTIONAL CULTURES

Sectional divides did not compromise the genuinely national enthusiasm for healing waters. Wealthy white northerners and southerners shared a culture of travel, spagoing, seaside resorts, and daily ablutions, but a newly moralistic and individualistic approach had emerged in the North. Southerners continued to be motivated by medical consumerism, traveling north when necessary to investigate the more expansive range of cures available in that region. After Mildred Coles Cameron, the diarist, developed a paralysis that could not be cured by a trip to White Sulphur Springs, her recently married sister Margaret accompanied her to Brooklyn to seek treatment from a Dr. Barnes, who offered an eclectic therapy that included electricity, applications of mineral and herb water compresses, and the immersion of affected limbs in small and full-body baths. "For several mornings past she has had her arms immersed in warm water," Margaret reported, "but for a morning or two the Dr. has had salt added to it." Three weeks later Dr. Barnes planned to apply electricity to Millie, but he soon returned to baths, ointments, compresses, and wet wraps. On January 25, 1856, Margaret observed that Mildred's failure to improve prompted the doctor to try an aromatic iron warm bath to strengthen and give tone to the nervous system. The efficacy of Barnes's treatments appeared in Mildred's weight gain: four pounds since her arrival in Brooklyn, up to ninety-one pounds. Eventually, although she clung to signs of improvement, Margaret Bain Cameron Mordecai concluded that she could not "perceive the slightest good" resulting from the daily use of warm baths. By May 1856 Margaret and Mildred had given up on the northern treatments and soon paid another visit to White Sulphur Springs, where Millie might at least be comforted by old acquaintances, southern manners, and familiar scenery.[82]

Elite southern women might still go north in search of a cure, but the newly moralistic and individualistic approach of the water cure remained a mainly northern phenomenon. Although wealthy white people from both sections of the country had in common the beliefs in nature's healing properties, in the North the immersion of the body in pure water as a means of effecting an all-purpose cure pointed to new convictions about the individual's responsibility for his own health. By 1847, twenty-one water cure establishments served patients in nine states. Over the next eight years, nearly a dozen journals spread the word of the water cure's miraculous healing properties to thousands of other sufferers. Its advocates saw the water cure as the body's best ally against disease spread when people of different ethnic, racial, religious, and material circumstances crossed paths, and against the many other hazards of modern life.

12

MISSION

I earnestly believe that the day is not far distant when water, hygiene, and obedience to physical law will be deemed as essential and prove as effectual for the regeneration of mankind, physically, as faith, baptism, and obedience to moral law are for his regeneration spiritually.

— E. P. Miller, *How to Bathe*, 1869

By 1850 the American Sunday School Union (ASSU) had a booming business publishing and distributing pamphlets among the poor to induce conversion to Christianity. *Little Bill at the Pump*, published in that year, expressed how mainstream Protestants in the North had come to see the relationship between cleanliness of body and purity of spirit. The pamphlet told the tale of a minister's successful efforts to save the soul of Little Bill, a ragged and dirty boy discovered playing marbles with some other boys by the public pump. All the other children fled, but Bill remained behind. When invited by the minister to attend Sunday school, Bill declined, looking with shame on his person and saying, "I am too dirty and ragged, it will not do." Undeterred, the pastor tried another tactic. "Never mind—just stop here. I will pump the water, and you can wash your hands and face, and that will do."[1]

Bill expressed astonishment, "You pump water for me to wash!" before accepting the pastor's help, but he declined his offer of a clean, white handkerchief, as it was too much for Bill to contemplate dirtying such a clean and refined object. "Oh, no! It is so white—not, not with that." But the pastor reassured him that he used it "when I am out of doors and want to wash, and can get nothing else to wipe with—it will not hurt it." After convincing the boy that the other children would not laugh at his clothes, the pastor persuaded him to attend a class. Thus began Bill's wholesale transformation to a life of piety, respectability and prosperity. Years later, when the pastor happened to cross paths with Bill, he saw a "young and well-dressed gentleman, of tall and elegant stature, and in all respects exceedingly fair to look upon." What's more, Bill had become a Sunday school teacher, thus completing the cycle begun at the pump.[2]

During the nineteenth century, reformers increasingly began to define their goals for changing the lives of the poor in spiritual terms. Male and female reformers alike initially saw their task as combining moral enlightenment with the amelioration of the suffering caused by poverty. The conviction that the poor were the agents of their own poverty as a consequence of their moral failings entered public discourse during the second decade of the century. By the 1820s, as the historian Bruce Dorsey demonstrates for Philadelphia, evangelical organizations that aimed at uplifting the spiritual lives of the poor—defined as the "poor in heart"—were outpacing the fund-raising and membership of charitable associations that provided material relief like food, fuel, and clothing. Male-led reform groups, especially, suggested that relief might actually make the situation worse by encouraging idleness, one of the vices believed to cause poverty, instead of motivating the poor to action. Their emphasis on instilling traits in the poor that allegedly enabled the prosperity of able-bodied workingmen—industriousness, independence, and a robust vitality—implicitly endorsed a reformed model of health and body care even as it failed to address the problems facing the growing ranks of impoverished women.[3]

By the mid-nineteenth century, cleanliness had become nearly synonymous with respectability and moral virtue in northern religious reform circles. Closely tied to similar reforms among the middle class in England and mirroring the political uses it was acquiring in a wider world, this northern reform culture spread throughout American cities and their hinterlands. In conversion narratives, the convert ritualistically shed rags and filth, bathed, and donned clean new garments before beginning a new life of morality and industry. Reformer, missionary, and imperialist alike used the language of cleanliness to articulate moral ideals and urge people to adopt new habits. Armed with a worldview that linked morality and cleanliness and encouraged greater discernment over the practices of others, reform-minded northerners found fault with the habits of immigrants, the urban poor, ignorant rural dwellers, and the vast majority of southerners, black and white, with little attention to their limited access to water for bathing or laundry. Efforts to ameliorate urban poverty thus focused more on the moral failings of the poor for refusing to strive for cleanliness than on the material impediments making such goals impractical. When an exceptional reformer like John H. Griscom tried during the 1840s to establish that poverty rather than vice was the root cause of disease, his findings were largely ignored. His *Sanitary Conditions of the Laboring Population of New York* (1845) yielded no new approaches to combating disease in American cities.[4]

Children's bodies assumed a new importance in this northern reform culture, owing in part to their visibility in city streets, as Christine Stansell has shown, their susceptibility to being missionized separately from their parents, and their entry into a new arena—the public school. A child attending school placed a family's intimate habits on display for all to see. Poorly groomed, unclean, or diseased children created a risk of contamination for others. Ultimately, the condition of a child's body reflected her mother's respectability and the moral and physical order of the household. Reformers attempted to influence how mothers cared for their children and to improve the design and healthfulness of public schools as a means of lowering the risk of disease.[5]

The diverse cluster of meanings attached to the concept of cleanliness by the 1840s fitted it for multiple purposes and endowed it with moral force. Attention to cleanliness signified not only refinement and health but empowerment and responsibility for oneself. The clean person who took care to live in a clean environment displayed agency, decency, and virtue and could claim humanity in full. In contrast, filth connoted vice, disease, and degradation, or, more benignly, exploitation and victimization. Few considered that city squalor and southern rural poverty made such standards impossible for the nation's poorest citizens, many of whom would not gain access to running water until after 1900.[6]

Those who made it their mission to transform the bodily habits and living conditions of the allegedly unclean engaged in a dynamic process that was at once an act of distinction, humanitarian intervention, cultural imperialism, and intimate intrusion into the lives of others. By making cleanliness their mission, they announced their own bodily refinement and claimed the authority to set standards. Privacy was the privilege of the indisputably clean who peered at the bed linens, dinner tables, and scalps of those they aimed to transform. The desire to end the bodily suffering caused by filth—the fate of those who did not know the physical comforts of being clean—was the humanitarian motive for their intervention. This was less tactic than genuine impulse for those who believed that nature's laws and God's laws converged in the practices of washing the body and achieving an orderly and clean domestic life. However genuine the impulse, the missionary zeal to bring godly, civilized cleanliness to the unclean constituted an effort to transform the intimate bodily practices of others—indeed, in some cases, to pluck them from allegedly contaminated families and homes—bringing them into conformity with a standard imposed by those with legal and economic power. As in Dutch Java, British South Africa, and Quaker missions to

Native Americans, this was cultural imperialism of a most intimate variety, and it furthered a political agenda even if it was not accompanied by the formal structures of empire.[7]

The quest to reform the habits of the poor may have had mixed motives, but as Olaudah Equiano had early recognized, the moral language of cleanliness provided an important way to denounce the corruption of slavery. Although the privilege symbolized by white skin still mattered to white northerners, some were putting more emphasis on purity of spirit, as reflected in behavior and character. For these reformers, cleanliness of person and place signified a person's inner moral state. White southerners, in contrast, interpreted cleanliness according to an older logic; it was a racially exclusive mark of southern gentility, especially evident among the aristocracy of the planter class. To the degree that they subscribed to cleanliness as a reform, southern planters did so for medical and economic reasons. An enslaved person's cleanly habits were mainly seen as a manifestation of his value — measured in estimates of health and longevity — or less frequently as evidence of his owner's progressive thinking and humanitarianism.[8]

For antislavery activists, the plantation was a site of moral and physical contagion. Sullied by the moral wrong of slavery, the whiteness of slaveowners no longer indicated superior character. Opponents of slavery worked to disrupt cherished associations between "spotless" moral character, refinement, and whiteness by claiming that skin color could not be trusted as a reliable sign of a person's moral interior. Indeed, it could not be so interpreted in the North. The urban poor, especially Irish immigrants, and unsophisticated rural folks appeared to live in ways that violated the reform tenets of individual responsibility and respectability, morality, and good health.

THE CHILD'S BODY

By the 1830s the state of the child's body had become newly important in the North as a consequence of the movement to establish public schools. Although nursery rhymes had for decades condemned children as "naughty" for their failure to wash obediently, now the child's body became the site of new concerns about cleanliness that identified the dangers as a public rather than a domestic matter of obeying parents. If children were to be required to attend public school or even Sunday school, their bodies would be on display and in contact with other children's bodies. Cleanliness practices at home suddenly acquired new significance for public health, and the child's body became the focus of attention.

In the poem "Untidiness" (1857), the ASSU took pains to distinguish between poverty — manifested in worn clothing — and filth, which resulted from a neglect of "common" decency:

> To come uncombed, unwashed, to school,
> Is breaking every decent rule;
> A worn-out dress we may permit,
> But dirty children can't admit.

Failure to attend to one's person — revealed in "rough and tangled hair" and unclean face and fingernails — created a disgraceful situation in which dirty children might sit next to clean ones. The ASSU poet likened their filthy condition to that of homeless vagabonds, who clearly should not be the associates of decent children:

> Such dirty children are not fit
> Beside the others e'en to sit;
> They're like poor vagabonds, who roam
> About the streets, without a home.

Neglect of one's person reflected other disorders at home, including a failure to say prayers or honor the Sabbath:

> Back to your home you now must go,
> We never can receive you so:
> Come back well washed and dressed with care
> Say also your neglected prayer.[9]

For the ASSU as for other native-born Protestants, proper care of the self included attention to body as well as spirit. A child who went off to school — especially Sunday school — with a dirty face and untidy clothes was probably not receiving the proper spiritual training at home. The model child, in contrast, was a well-mannered, industrious, dutiful girl whose appearance reflected an orderly moral interior. The title of one didactic poem, "The Good Example," made the point clearly:

> See, there is a nice little girl;
> How neat and how pretty she looks!
> She is going to school, I have not the least doubt,
> For you see she walks on, without looking about.

The girl's neat appearance and concentration on her walk to school reflected a well-ordered, clean, well attended domestic life:

> She lives at that house where the steps are so white,
> The garden so clean and the windows so bright,
> And her name is, I'm told, Susan Bell.

Among Susan's virtues were her prompt attention to chores that affected her appearance:

> She never is idle, they say,
> But attentive to every duty;
> She keeps things in order, mends all her own clothes,
> Is never untidy, for Susan Bell knows
> That neatness is better than beauty.[10]

In addition to the messages about bodily cleanliness and tidiness, both of these poems reveal how, by attending school, a child displayed the household's intimate habits. School had become the showcase for grooming and moral training. It also turned the child's body into a matter of public concern. Carrying unhealthy and immoral habits into the public space of the school, vagabonds might sicken children from better homes, spreading the diseases and afflictions of vice and poverty beyond their usual bounds. As Henry Barnard, secretary for the Board of Commissioners for Connecticut, noted about public schools, the average scholar tended not to be as clean as his adult counterparts, thus increasing the danger of contamination.[11] Faced with this public connection between the otherwise private domestic lives of people of vastly different circumstances, school reformers tackled the unpleasant consequences of democracy by attempting to cleanse the air of taint.

SCHOOL ARCHITECTURE

The belief that fresh air was necessary to good health could still be characterized as a reformist view by the mid-nineteenth century, but it had gained new adherents. A poem from the *New Graefenberg Water-Cure Reporter* gave exuberant testimony to the benefits of fresh air:

> Throw open your window and fasten it there!
> Fling the curtain aside and the blind,
> And give a free entrance to heaven's pure air —
> 'Tis the life and the health of mankind
>
> Are you fond of coughs, colds, dyspepsia and rheums?
> Of headaches, and fevers, and chills?
> Of bitters, hot drops, and fumes?
> And bleeding, and blisters, and pills?

Then shut yourselves up like a monk in his cave,
Till nature grows weary and sad,
And imagine yourself on the brink of the grave,
Where nothing is cheerful and glad.[12]

The *Tobacco and Health Almanac for 1849* urged readers to "keep your windows open during sleeping hours, for the lungs require wholesome air, as well as the stomach requires wholesome food, whether they get it or not." Using an analogy that would not be lost on even the most resistant reader, the editor reasoned, "The stomach would not willingly receive the same food the second time, therefore be consistent, and treat the lungs accordingly."[13]

Foreign travelers were under the impression that most Americans ignored the body's need for fresh air. The English actress Frances Kemble complained about the American proclivity for traveling in crowded, overheated carriages and railway cars in 1839: "No words can describe the foulness of the atmosphere, thus robbed of all vitality by the vicious properties of that dreadful combustible [anthracite coal], and tainted besides with the poison emitted at every respiration from so many pairs of human lungs." "The utter disregard" for air quality "renders them the amazement of every traveler from countries where the preservation of health is considered worth the care of a rational creature," she wrote with disgust to her friend, the Irish aristocrat Harriet St. Leger.[14]

Popular medical advice books had long been concerned with bad air in crowded urban housing and in institutions, first established at the end of the eighteenth century, for the poor, criminals, and the insane. The want of pure air was one of several dangers, including the lack of cleanliness, bad food, and the abuse of medicine, popularly believed to contribute to infant mortality. The public school was new among these institutions in the antebellum United States, and it was a different type of institution, intended to train citizens rather than to warehouse them or reform the marginal. Only pure wholesome air would do for innocent children, sentenced to spend long days in the schoolroom not as a result of poverty, unfitness, or criminality, but because the state saw value in educating them.[15]

By the early 1830s health reformers were applying data from new studies about the dangers of foul air to public institutions such as schools, which were increasing in size and number in the North. Some of these ideas found receptive audiences through popular medical advice books on child rearing and domestic medicine or the Lyceum lecture circuit. The Worcester resident Louisa Clapp Trumbull attended a lecture on physical education by the phrenologist Dr. George Combe, older brother of Andrew, in which he compared a feeble constitution to an unsettled account, a sensitive subject for Louisa, who had suffered through several of her husband's business failures. She noted in her diary, "He showed by forcible argument that no one can enjoy perfect health without having well ventilated sleeping apartments." After traveling to New York from the South, Susan Weeks Curtis diagnosed her mother's illness as a consequence of the unwholesome "furnace-heated air" that was common during northern winters. Her doctor prescribed an immediate trip south as a remedy. Sarah Ker Butler refused to spend a night on a steamboat docked in New Orleans in 1853 that was full of passengers fleeing the city's latest outbreak of yellow fever. She feared exposure to both respirated air and night air, the latter of which was believed to cause malaria.[16]

Findings about the hazards of bad air tested northern commitments to provide educational opportunities to students from a variety of ethnic, religious, and economic backgrounds. William Alcott, yet to make his reputation as a popular author, published *Essay on the Construction of School-Houses* in 1832; the piece had won a prize from the American Institute of Instruction the previous year. The publication coincided with the first cholera epidemic to strike American cities, an event that dramatically illustrated the power of disease to cross class and ethnic lines. Attempting to convince taxpayers that stinting on school construction was a foolish economy, he quipped, "*Health*, as well as *time*, is *money*." The biggest problem with most school buildings, as Alcott saw it, was the unwholesome quality of the air resulting from too many bodies and other sources of uncleanness crowded into a small, unventilated space. "It is a most mistaken economy which confines a child to those arrangements, and to that atmospheric impurity," he warned, which "render him unfit for vigorous effort, and thus slowly, though surely, impair his constitution." Alcott explained the dangers with reference to a recent study of air quality in solitary-confinement cells in the Philadelphia prison. Respirated air, which scientists knew as carbonic acid, sank to the floor, where it rapidly accumulated to reach the height of a schoolchild, who would be forced to inhale it. Inadequate facilities for washing hands and face, dirty walls, ceilings, floors, and furniture, as well as the vapors from coats and hats, also added contaminants to the air. Alcott proposed better ventilation, separate entrances for boys and girls, new seating arrangements, improved washing facilities, a separate room for coats and food, and frequent scouring, washing, and brushing of school interiors. He also thought students should be out in the open air at least once every hour.[17]

Alcott's ideas were incorporated into a more detailed discussion by Henry Barnard in 1838 and subsequently published as *School Architecture; or, Contributions to the Improvement of School-Houses in the United States* (1848). Barnard addressed the status and condition of school buildings throughout New England, providing dramatic examples drawn from prisons and hospitals around the world of the consequences of bad air and the beneficial effects of pure air. The essay included excerpts from a study of London's public buildings and an address given in 1840 at the American Institute of Instruction. Barnard saw the problem with school ventilation as unique, resulting from the small size of the schoolhouse in relation to the number of scholars, the duration of the school day, and the fact that young students "are less cleanly in their personal habits than adults."[18]

Claiming that the "heat and stifling air and nauseating effluvia" found their equal only in the biblical dilemma of Jonah, trapped in the belly of a whale, Barnard condemned the average schoolhouse as a "miserable abode of accumulated dirt and filth, deprived of wholesome air." Apt comparisons included the Black Hole of Calcutta and factories, both of which brought untimely death to their unfortunate inmates. "The languor, debility, loss of appetite, difficulty of breathing, coughs, distortion of the frame . . . nervous irritability, and chronic affections of various kinds, so common among females in factories, even in our own healthy New England," resulted from contaminated, already respirated air not unlike that found in public schools. Barnard included a compelling excerpt from a work of architectural hygiene that compared the problem to manners at mealtime: "People, who would revolt at the idea of drinking out of the same cup or glass with a stranger, or even with a guest," explained William Hosking, the author of the quoted text, "suffer no annoyance from, and feel no disgust at, inhaling what has already passed through the lungs of those who may be shut up in a room with them, however close the room may be, and whether the room be an apartment of a dwelling-house, a shop, a chapel, a church, or a theatre."[19]

Subjected to these conditions, Barnard argued, students became weary and confused, developed headaches, and became unnaturally thirsty. Teachers, too, became victims of the "close, stagnant, offensive atmosphere." Little wonder that so many teachers suffered disease or untimely death. Substandard privy and washing facilities exacerbated problems caused by bad air. Forced to answer the call of nature outdoors or in filthy privies that lacked separate stalls for boys and girls, students either abandoned modesty or retained their feces, an unnatural habit that Barnard claimed was "the foundation for chronic diseases, and the principal cause of permanent ill health, resulting not infrequently in premature death."[20]

At the heart of these concerns about air quality was the class mixing inherent in the classroom. Barnard quoted the principal of the high school for girls in Newburyport, Massachusetts, about the social mixing that took place and the reassurance that a well-ventilated, clean schoolhouse might provide:

We have had in our number many from the best families, in all respects, in the place. They sit side by side, they recite, and they associate most freely with those of the humblest parentage, whose widowed mothers, perhaps, toil day after day, at a wash-tub, without fear of contamination, or, as I honestly believe, a thought of the differences which exist. I have, at present, both extremes under my charge — the child of affluence and the child of low parentage and deep poverty. As my arrangements of pupils in divisions, &c., are, most of them, alphabetical, it often happens, that the two extremes are brought together. This never causes a murmur, or look of dislike.

Reforming school architecture, in other words, could make public schools palatable to the wealthy. The problem, as the Natchez, Mississippi, homeopath William Holcombe admitted, was the physical intimacies that resulted from democratic access to public spaces and conveyances. "I am a Democrat, I love Democracy, but it is Democracy in the abstract," the Philadelphia-trained native son of Lynchburg, Virginia, confessed to his diary during a steamship trip in the South in 1855. The democracy he embraced, he admitted, was "beyond the sphere of olfaction or the possibility of cutaneous infection." For those northerners who shared Holcombe's love of democracy but were revolted by being near people whose smell or appearance they found distasteful, the effort to prevent students from breathing secondhand air represented an important intervention in the physical intimacies resulting from institutions such as the public school.[21]

CONVERSION

Long the site of civilization's and etiquette's borderlands, childhood became newly politicized in the North by the 1830s. Public schools trained children to assume the responsibilities of citizens; yet this very training created undesirable links between households of varying domestic practices and exposed children to the airborne diseases believed to result from immoral and sinful habits. Reforming school architecture could make such contact safer, but as the tale of Little Bill suggests, a more effective remedy would be to convert deficient households to the moral practices that would prevent vice and disease.

Reform-minded northerners of different stripes shared the belief that bodily cleanliness manifested moral character. During the nineteenth century, however, cleanliness was no longer depicted simply as an expression of spiritual purity but had become a key instrument to achieve it. Tales of spiritual conversion, physical renewal, and moral regeneracy often featured a cataclysmic moment in which the unwashed became clean, thus awakening to the possibilities of a "new" life of spiritual grace, good health, or morality. ASSU writers described wholesale spiritual and moral conversions beginning with cleaning the body. Just as Little Bill began his new life with the application of water at the pump — a baptism of sorts — the unregenerate, especially the young victims of parental vice, might cleanse themselves of the traces of sin manifested in their rags and dirt and start anew.

As the ASSU saw it, bodily cleanliness was part and parcel of the larger fabric of domestic habits that determined a family's health and respectability. As part of this larger social unit, there was just so much that an individual, particularly a child, could do to overcome a filthy and unhealthy home. In *Two Homes Compared* (1850), the tract that contrasted clean and dirty ways of life, the author depicted domestic habits as the foundation of bodily and moral sensibilities and the health of a larger public. Efforts to reform habits would have better success if the household, rather than the individual, were targeted. Tragic consequences illustrated the problem. A daughter who had previously been taken from the filthy home to learn "notions of cleanliness" had returned to her parents' home and "had in vain endeavoured to introduce them there." Almost immediately, she contracted a "violent fever," a consequence of "sleeping in a close apartment, and being surrounded with impure air." Two other children in the household and an aunt had already fallen victim to cholera, which provoked municipal authorities to have the house thoroughly cleansed. "But the dirty habits of the family were so fixed," the narrator observed grimly, "that they were now as bad as ever."[22]

Throwing open the window of the sick room cleared the foul air and brought the patient temporary relief. A clean cup and basin of fresh water allowed her to rinse her mouth and wash her face and hands, also bringing some comfort. In addition, two visitors — her fictive clean family — conversed with her, prayed, and read the Scriptures. The narrator rejoiced that the poor girl, "surrounded as she was by those who seemed to disregard both cleanliness and godliness, was not herself indifferent to either." The invalid had embraced the lessons of cleanliness, but they were not enough for her to overcome the hazards of her filthy home or to enable her to convert her family to more healthful practices. Ultimately, she died, another victim of filthy domestic habits. "In all probability those habits had occasioned the sickness and death of four persons in their family," the narrator concluded, and "could not fail to produce hurtful effects on all the rest."[23]

One of the tract's main messages concerned the importance of childhood training for establishing lifelong habits that determined health and prosperity. Indeed, this conviction justified intrusions into the homes of the poor and interventions that ruptured family and neighborhood ties. If the two families had swapped abodes, the narrator speculated, the filthy cottage would soon be clean and the clean cottage filthy. Reasoning that "comfort depends much more on disposition and habits than on circumstances," the author offered advice on how to form habits of cleanliness and order during childhood. Although children's habits depended largely on parental practices, the children of vicious parents were not hopeless cases. The narrator instructed those unfortunates that "it is quite time for you to begin forming a character for yourselves in these respects. Do not give way to the indolent practice of excusing dirt and negligence by saying, 'It did well enough for our parents, and surely it may do for us.'" In essence, the ASSU was urging young readers to reject the standards of slothful parents and to assume responsibility for themselves: "You do know that you ought to be as much cleaner and better, and as much more respectable as you possibly can." With the caveat "You need not, on this account, despise them; you ought not to do so," the author urged young readers to "adopt better habits" than those of their parents. At the very least, this meant achieving cleanliness in their persons by taking advantage of the allegedly abundant supply of water and the minimal expense of soap, towels, brushes, and basins. The pamphlet writer urged readers to go beyond the superficial wiping of face and hands with a wet towel, to engage in a "thorough washing" every day; "The nearer it can be to a complete bathing, the better." Frequent changes of apparel could be "truly refreshing," and those who could not afford this luxury could try to protect outer clothes from dirt and to use aprons, collars, and cuffs judiciously to maintain "a respectable appearance of cleanliness."[24]

Cleanliness, once achieved, brought numerous benefits. The first was good health. "It tends to prevent disease and promote recovery," the pamphlet's author instructed, warning that "many lives are every year lost for want of attention to cleanliness." Cleanliness also promoted activity and enjoyment. "Dirty people are generally slothful and indolent, but those who are cleanly move about with briskness and cheerfulness," motivated by the desire to be clean. In addition to these benefits, the author claimed, "cleanliness is conducive to wealth." A clean appearance and work habits would lead to being valued and promoted by one's employer. But the link to prosperity was even more direct. The author reasoned, "dirtiness is generally connected with waste, and waste leads to poverty." "A cleanly person," moreover, "is likely to earn more money than a dirty person, and to make money go further." All things being equal, "he is a richer person." Placed in a narrowly economic frame, "cleanliness makes things look better and last longer, and therefore it is a gain or saving of property."[25]

The narrator also touted advantages of cleanliness that had little to do with actual self-respect and more to do with securing the respect of others. The first impression of clean people was always favorable, the author claimed, but those of filthy persons were nearly always unfavorable. Even good deeds might not redeem the respectability of a filthy person, because of the close association between filth and vice. "When we see a person notoriously and shamefully dirty," the author vouchsafed, "we involuntarily, and seldom mistakenly, fear that he is a vicious person." Impressions of character varied "in proportion to the degree of cleanliness and neatness exhibited." The author did not try to press the point that cleanliness signified actual virtue or self-respect, but rather extolled the benefits of the *appearance* of respectability when one was seeking employment.[26]

The ASSU writer found the lack of cleanliness to be at the root even of domestic discord. "Cleanliness is favourable to *family harmony*," he declared, noting that "dirty people always look discontented, and generally are so; and a great many family broils arise from dirt and negligence, or the inconvenient consequences they involve." Providing a somewhat different perspective from Catharine Beecher's about how the pursuit of cleanliness might sap the cheerfulness of a housewife, the author emphasized how the failure of individual family members to maintain their own persons increased irritation and annoyance, ultimately eroding family harmony. "Let it not be said, that cleanliness is a small and insignificant virtue, if the neglect of it leads to great sin."[27]

In the pamphlet's final pages, its author considered the relationship between cleanliness, religion, and virtue. Going beyond the maxim "cleanliness is next to godliness," the author provided a detailed biblical exegesis to support the religious roots of cleanliness. Not only did Christians have an obligation to practice those things that are "lovely and of good report," but they were bound to pursue every virtue and employ their time properly. The author debunked the excuse of ragged clothing as a reason not to attend church, praising the decent poor who "make themselves and family clean and tidy to enjoy the privileges of public worship and the Sabbath-school."[28]

The author's most sophisticated argument was his exploration of the biblical use of cleanliness metaphors to signify spiritual purity. Sin was represented in the Bible as defilement and pollution of the soul, while the Holy Spirit was represented as cleansing the sinful heart of man and restoring it to a pure and holy state. Biblical cleansing metaphors likened the purification from sin to washing the body and its filthy garments in water. The "atoning blood of Christ," moreover, was a "pure and living water to wash away our guilty stains." The metaphor echoed centuries of Christian tradition; a substance that ordinarily stained —blood—became capable of removing the stain of sin from the soul.[29]

The tract writer deduced the spiritual significance of bodily cleanliness from its use in biblical metaphors. "If, then, outward cleanliness is worthy to be made in Holy Scripture an emblem of the restoration and purification of the soul," the author reasoned, "it must deserve to be highly esteemed by all." Yet he was at pains to distinguish between spiritual and bodily cleanliness. Although they were linked by their metaphorical association in the Bible and the close tie between virtuous behavior and cleanly appearance, bodily cleanliness "is but an emblem of that which is greater, and to that greater thing it is of chief importance that all should attend. The great purpose and end of salvation, as it regards mankind, is the cleansing and purifying of the soul for God's use."[30]

For some evangelical Protestants, such an analysis was not mere propaganda but reflected personal experience. The transplanted northerner Dolly Lunt Burge, a hot Methodist from Maine who made her living as a schoolteacher in Georgia after being widowed, frequently prayed to God to give her a "clean heart." She also took pains to prepare for the Sabbath by "perform[ing] some Saturday night ablutions." For Burge, the linguistic and sensual links between bodily and spiritual cleanliness were so tight that one practice stirred feelings about the other. On Sunday, April 1, 1849, Burge recorded that she "arose & took [her] bath," adding the supplication, "O that the Good One would cleanse my heart even as I cleanse outwardly." But it went even deeper. Just as a Sabbath rain inspired her to wish for "the showers of Divine Grace" to be "sent down upon us a dry & thirsty people," her Sunday morning shower bath in preparation for church turned into a spiritual experience. "Took my usual bath," she recorded on January 13, 1850. "Felt while the liquid shower was pouring over me—that the Holy Spirit might . . . in like manner be bestowed." Yet Burge knew that spiritual purity was the more difficult state to achieve. "Sometimes I think could I as easily cleanse myself from Sin & impurity how holy I should be," she mused, but concluded "poor human nature cannot do it & it is hard to look up by Faith & claim it."[31]

The act of bathing may have excited heady spiritual as well as physical sensations for some hot Protestants, but few women seemed to have risen to such lofty heights while doing domestic chores. Removing filth from clothing, carpets, and floors apparently reminded nobody of the Holy Spirit bestowing God's grace. Yet in the weekly struggle to accomplish domestic tasks by the Sabbath and to spend the day with one's own body clean, in a clean and tidy house, dressed in fresh clothes, in the company of well-scrubbed children, antebellum women gave silent testimony to the validity of the ASSU author's exegesis of cleanliness. Along with other motives for housecleaning, the desire for spiritual purity, untainted by the imperfections of life on earth, still factored into women's motives for performing housework.

Infused with morality and linked to spiritual purity, personal cleanliness took on new importance as evidence of a person's inner life and personal habits, and as an entrée to establishing a new social identity. As in the story of Little Bill, success in removing grime from a poor child's skin—a northern class-based version of washing the Ethiop white—might open the heart of the disbeliever headed down the road toward a dissolute, unhappy life of immorality and poverty. But as in the case of the water cure, instilling new habits of cleanliness also created conditions under which new thresholds of bodily sensation might be established. Cleaning the skin and donning new clothes might come to feel necessary, as they did for the dying girl in the unclean cottage. Creating new needs required that one establish new habits of body, spirit, and domestic life. Ultimately, this shift in habits paved the way for forming new ties to like-minded, cleanly people whose personal appearance broadcast their elevated moral condition.

The class implications of the relationship between cleanliness and moral character appeared in many other mid-nineteenth century texts. In Horatio Alger's popular *Ragged Dick* (1868), Dick's honest demeanor and open manner inspired trust and made him appealing, despite his dirt and rags, even to those from higher social positions:

> Washing the face and hands is usually considered proper in commencing the day, but Dick was above such refinement. He had no particular dislike to dirt, and did not think it necessary to remove several dark streaks on his face and hands. But in spite of his dirt and rags there was something about Dick that was attractive. It was easy to see that if he had been clean and well dressed he would have been decidedly good-looking. Some of his companions were sly, and their faces inspired distrust; But Dick had a frank, straight-forward manner that made him a favorite.

Dick's good character shone through the dirt and grime. But even with this promising foundation, washing and a change of clothes were necessary to begin his transformation into a gentleman. Mr. Whiting, a gentleman who took Dick under his wing and gave him his nephew's gray suit, instructed his protégé, "before you put them on, my lad, you must wash yourself. Clean clothes and a dirty skin don't go very well together."[32] Bodily cleanliness was such an important marker of class that men as well as the women most expected to embody its ideals might exercise cultural authority through its enforcement.

Frank, Whitney's nephew, helped his new friend clean his body. Did Dick take a bath? Alger did not provide details, although Whitney and his nephew were staying in a New York hotel that probably had a bath by 1866. At the very least, Frank assisted Dick in cleaning his grimy hands and face and brushing his hair. Alger's comments on Dick's receptiveness to this unfamiliar practice of cleaning his body again spoke to his promising character and future success:

"The process of cleansing commenced. To tell the truth, Dick needed it, and the sensation of cleanliness he found both new and pleasant."[33]

Washing his body and donning a fresh shirt, Dick completed his outward transformation. "When Dick was dressed in his new attire, with his face and hands clean, and his hair brushed, it was difficult to imagine that he was the same boy," the omniscient narrator commented. Removing dirt erased nearly all traces of Dick's class position, except for the telltale appearance of his hands, which did not look like those of a scholar. "He now looked quite handsome, and might readily have been taken for a young gentleman, except that his hands were red and grimy."[34]

Although many publications emphasized cleaning the body as a first step in saving the soul it housed, there were limits to the transformative power of cleanliness. In a few tracts, washing the body had only limited ability to penetrate the skin to remake the habits and character of the person within. Often this limitation illustrated the diminished capacity of people from certain ethnic, class, and racial backgrounds to accomplish the moral transformation cleanliness made possible. In the ASSU tract *Parlor and Kitchen* the servant with offensive foot odor willingly accepted her employer's diagnosis of her problem but needed constant prodding to alter her habits of bodily care. Cleanliness remained a superficial remedy in her case and failed to bring about the deep conversion in manners and grooming that would have made her sensible of her body's offensiveness. Unlike Dick, who, in addition to being handsome, immediately felt the pleasure of clean skin, the hapless servant from *Parlor and Kitchen* resembled the animal-like inhabitants of the squalid cottage in *Two Homes Compared*, who lived in subhuman conditions because they were inured to their own filth.

ANTISLAVERY CHALLENGES

A broad spectrum of reformers accepted the notion of bodily cleanliness as the leading edge of larger transformations of body and soul. Yet some ambivalence remained about the link between the outer appearance of the body and the process of instilling new habits and manners. This became a particularly fraught issue for popular conceptions of race, which continued to rely upon centuries-old associations between fair complexions and cleanliness, and between dark complexions and dirt. As habits of regular washing and bathing became more widespread, eventually to become ritualized in the practice of a weekly bath featuring soap and hot water, white skin, the white porcelain of the bathtub, and white soap acquired some of the symbolic freight previously borne by white linen. By the second half of the nineteenth century, soap advertisers seized upon these associations and those between cleanliness and civility to depict soap as an imperial agent, capable of civilizing the brown peoples of the world when it came in contact with their skin and culturally, if not actually, whitening them. Ivory Soap and Imperial Leather were just two of the products that symbolized this power by the last quarter of the nineteenth century. Although not fully articulated as a strategy of commodification during the first half of the century, the link between white skin and cleanliness remained strong and lurked beneath popular depictions of enslaved people, and the continued significance of white linen as a marker of a refined body.[35]

The minstrel show, an emerging antebellum entertainment for white northerners, both disrupted and reinforced this association. White people changed their racial appearance at will by applying burnt cork to their faces and impersonating African Americans on stage. In one sense, such a transformation spoke to the superficial and skin-deep qualities of racial identity even as it reinforced the boundaries of whiteness for the white audience that was so entertained by such displays. George Shattuck spoke in glowing terms of a minstrel show held in Philadelphia on Christmas Day 1834. "We had quite a laugh," he reported, "every thing was done perfectly naturally, & I have seldom seen people enjoy themselves more." But in another, perhaps more significant sense, the application of burnt cork reinforced the trope of racial blackness as a stain that could not be washed off. White entertainers removed the burnt cork at the end of a performance, but real African Americans remained black, unable to wash off their racial markers. In this context, white skin continued to signify a body that had been carefully cleansed of dirt.[36]

Following in the footsteps of Equiano, who had used the stench of the slave trader's vessel to disrupt the connection between Europeans and bodily refinement, nineteenth-century antislavery writers called into question the alleged links between bodily cleanliness, symbolized by white skin, and spiritual purity. Such a focus on the outer person — particularly the superficial characteristic of skin color — often missed more important evidence of moral character visible in habits and manners or contained in the hidden terrain of the soul. These writers consciously disrupted associations between white skin and refinement that white southerners and racist white northerners counted on to support their own privilege. Claiming that it was more a matter of spirit than of skin color, they advanced a notion of sin as completely internal and disconnected from the external appearance of race.

One antislavery poet gave a fresh twist to the old chestnut of washing the Ethiop white in "The Little Colored Boy," which began with a young enslaved boy's sorrow at being unable to wash his skin white with water:

> "I cannot, cannot wash it off,"
> Said the little colored boy,
> Whose countenance ne'er shone
> With the beaming light of joy —
> "I went down to the river's side,
> While master's people slept,
> But I could not, could not wash it off,"
> Said the colored boy, and wept.
>
> He looked upon his master's childe,
> And thought with what delight
> 'Twould fill his little breaking heart,
> were his brow so pure and white;
> And softly to the river's brink
> At early dawn he crept,
> "I cannot, cannot wash it off,"
> Said the colored boy, and wept.

The poet intervened in this conventional association between dark complexion and dirt to offer a deeper meaning for purity, one rooted in the heart and mind. Of what significance was complexion, the poet asked, compared with the state of the soul?

> Though dark his brow as ebony,
> And sable was his skin,
> The gentle *mind* that he possessed
> Was pure and fair within:
> But the Ethiop dyes which guilt and *sin*
> Have spread o'er human clay,
> There is not any earthly stream
> Can cleanse or wash away.

True purity could be found not in the complexion but in God's grace, which would wash away the stain of sin:

> O no! But there's a fountain pure,
> Whose sacred source is Heaven;
> Whose ever-living waters
> To a sinful world are given —
> Wash in *that* fountain and be clean,"
> Faith hears the spirit say —
> "Go to *that* pure and holy stream,
>
> And wash thy stains away."[37]

In the poet's revisionist rendering, the dark-complected enslaved boy who was pure of heart might be clean in a more significant sense than his light-skinned master, who persisted in his sinful ways. Skin color was but a poor index of the kind of cleanliness that really mattered.

SLAVERY'S CORRUPTION

The standards of bodily and domestic cleanliness commonly used to define class and ethnicity proved to be well suited to articulating sectional differences. The concept of cleanliness as a set of bodily practices to which one converted as part of the reception of Christian values did not appear to many northerners to have taken hold in the South. Reform-minded northerners who denigrated southern filth had trouble understanding white southerners' moral framework for cleanliness.

In the South, bodily cleanliness remained defined by an ideal of civility whose expression was largely made possible by slave labor. For white southerners, cleanliness was a form of distinction that articulated important class and racial divisions. More commonly, white southerners defined cleanliness spiritually in terms of moral purity, which referred opaquely to resisting ordinary temptations to commit sin and respecting taboos on enacting sexual desire across the color line. Thus cleanliness in the South remained a matter of morality as well as a marker of civility but did not acquire the moral association with disciplined bodily habits and individual responsibility for health that it did in the North.

Indeed, motives for cleanliness in the South were based less on Christian responsibility for self-care or mission to the less fortunate than on the desire to preserve human chattel and mitigate the regular outbreaks of yellow fever in southern port cities. Guides to plantation medicine instructed planters in the construction of slave housing, the provision of indoor privies, and the benefits of cold baths to maximize population growth and longevity. The American author J. Hume Simons, for example, recommended raising structures above ground level and making flooring airtight to counteract the slave's tendency to dump slops out the door or through the cracks in the floor. Planters were also urged to provide an indoor privy hole with a seat and a cover (Simons frowned on porcelain chamber pots, which he claimed enslaved people would only break) to discourage enslaved people from relieving themselves outdoors in inclement weather and when ill. Simons and others also recommended keeping slave clothing clean and distributing combs to help combat the diseases of the scalp that arose from vermin and constant scratching.[38]

Yellow fever, which had spurred northern cities to greater vigilance over street cleaning, garbage disposal, and access to pure water at the end of the eighteenth century, had become almost exclusively southern in its range after 1820. Although southern physicians disagreed whether the disease could be spread from port to port and debated the role of contagion and home-grown miasmic agents, by the 1850s, when New Orleans suffered its most devastating series of epidemics, many were convinced that the South had a peculiar disease climate that required specialized medical study. This does not seem to have diminished the numbers of southern medical students trained in Philadelphia, however, who accounted for more than two-thirds of the students enrolled in the city's two medical schools in 1858.[39]

For slaveholding women, alleged by at least one medical author to be more scrupulous in caring for their own bodies than their northern sisters, cleanliness retained religious meaning consistent with usages from the seventeenth and eighteenth centuries in which sin was often the most vivid manifestation of filth. The South Carolina planter Keziah Brevard reflected in October 1860, "I do try to avoid commiting those sins God plainly forbids — anger & unpleasant thoughts often rise in this breast of mine — but all that is filthy I immediatley call on God to help me put down." Soon after South Carolina's secession, she articulated a "live and let live" attitude toward sin that stood in stark contrast to the stance of reform-minded northerners, seeking to cleanse the nation of the moral stain of slavery. "We of the South have no desire to interfere with others," she observed; "we try to wash out our own sins — & leave each one to answer to God for *their own sins*." Grieving over the dissolution of the Union and the impending conflict, she prayed, "Lord watch over our once favoured country — but above all give us clean hearts."[40]

The prototypical southern sin, in both the northern imagination and the southern confession, was not slavery per se, but race mixing. Frances Kemble observed the hypocrisy of white claims of a natural repugnance toward black people in the face of the notorious fact "that almost every Southern planter has a family more or less numerous of illegitimate colored children."[41] "Many white faces in this land of light sin high in the presence of God[,] sitting our poor negroes degraded examples," Brevard confessed. "I thank the Heavenly Father I have never had a son to mix my blood with *negro* blood," she declared, noting that "such a sin would [be] & is disheartening to Christian Mothers." She saw salvation for the South in a moral reformation that would reaffirm slavery's hierarchy: "Oh God preserve us to the end & make us all thy true followers," she supplicated; "let us all try to do good & be contented with our lot here on earth — '*Cleanse thou me*' is my prayer *now & Oh may it ever be*."[42]

Travelers to the South deployed the moral language of cleanliness to articulate the sectional differences that were increasingly dividing the nation. The northern insistence on cleanliness as an index of character gave added moral and political weight to descriptions of southern dirt. A system of labor that produced people inured to their own filth, in addition to other moral outrages, could never become the basis for enlightened citizenship, public virtue, prosperity, or good health. What travelers to the South described as a regional propensity to filthiness was attributed, explicitly or implicitly, to the great corruption of slavery. Often comparing poor whites and enslaved blacks with the most prosperous northerners rather than with the immigrant and rural poor who served as foils for native-born bodily refinement, travel writers fingered the easy culprit, slavery, when they might have indicted the larger inequities of class.

Slave ownership and the material culture of white people's homes distinguished different classes of white southerners. Susan Burns, a woman who claimed to be a "native daughter" of North Carolina but who found much that was unfamiliar on her trip from Philadelphia to Charleston, ranked the dwellings according to their airtightness and appearance:

> The grades of civilization and enlightenment (judging from the domiciles) appear to run thus — first log-cabins with a hole in the roof, to let the smoke out, and the glory in, — next ditto with daubed chimneys, — next weather-boarded houses, minus window sashes, — still higher, frame tenements with glass windows — and finally painted dwellings, which are like "Angels" visits few and far between, and if my memmory serves me, I did not see a single one in the country, which had arrived at the period of painted window-shutters. And in all probability will not, for ten future generations.[43]

Glass windows and paint stood at the top of Burns's hierarchy of dwellings but did not guarantee that the accommodations would be satisfactory or the meals wholesome. Of her host in Lancaster, South Carolina, Burns wrote, "I can say with certainty, that he has the most indifferent set of servants, and the dirtiest worst kept house in this, or any district that I have ever visited." She also found the entertainment provided by her host boring beyond measure. Burns and her companions visited another house, "a fine, well furnished house, — glassed, painted, yea, even skittered, — with scarlet & white curtains, handsome piano, zephyr work in profusion." Despite the genteel appearance, the food and service turned her stomach: "We are now asked into the breakfasting room, where were spread all manner of greasy eatables on the table, and dirty little negroes all round, who invited us to partake of each and every article, among which was a dish of what appeared to be new light-colored leather straps, rolled up in curls, and then dipped in molasses[.] I asked what they were and the negro replied, Frizzles, so not thinking that I could either chew, swallow, or digest Frizzles, I declined."[44]

White northerners and foreigners were more likely than white southerners to find the proximity of black bodies disruptive to notions of wholesomeness and cleanliness based on elaborate articulations of domestic hierarchies of dirt. Kemble described with disgust a scene in Roanoke, North Carolina, as she and her traveling companions waited for their train. "Of the horrible dirt of everything at this meal, from the eatables themselves to the tablecloth, and the clothes of the Negroes who waited upon us, it would be impossible to give any idea," she reported to her friend Harriet St. Leger. She was dismayed to be served tea by a "black girl of most disgustingly dirty appearance." Although Burns claimed roots in North Carolina, her ties to Pennsylvania may have influenced her view of enslaved people as "dirty negroes," a standard northern perspective. She denigrated Lancaster, South Carolina, for its racial demographic: "population 195 white folks, and lots of dirty negroes." She also found the appearance of enslaved African Americans worthy of note, as in the case of one driver, whom she described as the "blackest negro . . . you can imagine, charcoal, I am confident, would look very ashy if not chalky, on his blackest of faces."[45]

Given this distinctive moral and racial landscape, what were white southern women's housekeeping motives and priorities? What was the relationship between morality, as they defined it, and domestic cleanliness? In what ways, if at all, did their bodily practices and housekeeping depart from northern standards?

Fear of disease motivated housecleaning in southern slaveholding households. The Louisiana mistress Eliza Marsh Robertson recorded in November 1854 that "the yellow fever is still dreadful in Franklin over 35 persons have died already." For the next few days, Robertson's slaves cleaned the garret, taking up the straw matting in her room and putting down carpet, as well as cleaning the parlor and children's rooms. Relying heavily on the labor of her enslaved domestic Ann, Robertson routinely cleaned her house in the spring. The South Carolinian Keziah Brevard, who supervised a large plantation, rarely described housecleaning but frequently recorded her efforts to contain the stench of a nearby poultry house. She ordered enslaved men to scald, clean, and whitewash it. For good measure, she had the south door of the kitchen sprinkled with lime, presumably to ward off any contamination.[46]

Cleanliness of person in white southern households centered around killing vermin and manufacturing clothes, much as it had in the eighteenth century. Robertson's diary is punctuated with these efforts. She washed and deloused all the children's heads on Good Friday 1856, the day before a birthday party. She also sewed clothes by hand, including pillowcases, baby garments, and clothes for slaves. A new sewing machine, purchased in 1855, made this labor more efficient. In an effort to keep her household clean and healthy and to protect her provisions, Robertson recorded stopping up rat holes and killing rats. On occasion she still made her own soap, although she usually recorded buying it. Her diary also mentioned washing dishes and filling in for enslaved women who had been hired out.[47]

The main differences between Robertson's work routine and that of a rural northern woman of the same period was readily available relief from the grueling labor of laundry: enslaved women performed this task. Whereas most northern women's diaries of the period include a weekly record of laundry day, followed by details of drying conditions, mending, ironing, and putting clothes away, Robertson recorded only her orders to Ann to mend the clothes that had been washed earlier in the week. This freedom from the tyranny of the weekly laundry most resembles the privileged existence of Sarah Lawrence, who employed more servants than any other northern woman examined here. Having lost the labor of her enslaved washerwoman after the Civil War began, the Virginia mistress Cornelia Peake McDonald salvaged "a long forgotten old washing machine from the cellar" to help her cope with the backlog of soiled clothes.[48]

The privileges of owning slave labor enabled Robertson to focus her manufacturing energies on her own family. Unlike Maria Fifield, who spent her days in New Hampshire braiding hats; Sarah Bixby, who invested in her education so that she could earn money teaching; or less well-off southern white women, who might have engaged in agricultural labor to produce for their families or the market, Eliza Robertson sewed garments for children, slaves, and herself. Ella Clanton Thomas's diary reveals a similar focus to her labors, although she admitted an "aversion" to sewing. Throughout most of her prewar life as a plantation mistress, Thomas relied on the labor of slaves and friends to make household linens and dresses for herself.[49]

In the households of slaveholding women like Robertson, there was little of the concern about black women's bodies that we find elicited in the North by female servants' body odors. The persistent challenge to white gentility was not body odor per se, but dirty clothing and vermin, as it had been for most Americans before 1800. The renowned gynecological surgeon J. Marion Sims of Lancaster, South Carolina, thus remembered learning about the meaning of racial difference from his mother, who drummed home the dangers of contracting head lice from black people, among whom the infestations were allegedly endemic. In a diary with little mention of cleaning the bodies in her household, Robertson twice recorded removing lice from the children's heads. But she and most other white southern female diarists had little else to say about the bodies of the enslaved. Visitors to the South, however, commented at length. During her first stay at her husband's Georgian plantations, Frances Kemble interpreted the vermin that infested the bodies and garments of her husband's enslaved laborers as evidence of their miserable and wretched condition. "The swarms of fleas that cohabit with these sable dependents of ours are — well — incredible," she reported to her friend Elizabeth Sedgwick, sister to the author Catharine Sedgwick. "Moreover, they are by no means the only or most objectionable companions one borrows from them," she added. "I never go to the infirmary, where I not infrequently am requested to look at very dirty limbs and bodies in very dirty draperies, without coming away with a strong inclination to throw myself into the water, and my clothes into the fire." The enslaved people's chronic suffering from infestations of their homes and their persons thus became for Kemble a manifestation of the gulf that separated her from them.[50]

Unlike many southern white people, Kemble interpreted vermin infestations from a global as well as a local perspective. She admitted "that these hateful consequences of dirt and disorder" were probably no worse among enslaved people than "among the poor and neglected human creatures who swarm in the lower parts of European cities." But having only rarely "penetrated into fearfully foul and filthy abodes of misery in London," and then without much contact with the residents, Kemble had not "incurred the same amount of entomological inconvenience." Her personal attendant, Jack, an enslaved man, disputed her charge that the presence of vermin signified the "want of decent cleanliness generally among the people," pointing out that the island itself swarmed with fleas, especially in the sand. Rather than attracting vermin, he contended, slave cabins actually contained fewer of the insects than the surrounding woods.[51]

Kemble viewed the American South through the fastidious lenses of an Englishwoman whose standards of cleanliness generally surpassed those of her northern American hosts. During her stay in the United States, she frequently railed against the shortage of clean towels, the lack of private sleeping and dressing accommodations, the nearly universal habit of chewing tobacco, and the general deficiency of politeness. After marrying Pierce Butler, whose rice and cotton plantations she visited during the winter and spring of 1838–1839, she admitted candidly that she was "prejudiced against slavery, for I am an Englishwoman, in whom the absence of such a prejudice would be a disgrace." Antislavery sentiments, English fastidiousness, and guilt combined during her stay in Georgia to create a missionary zeal to "civilize" her husband's slaves and alleviate their suffering. With attempts to wash the allegedly unwashed as the leading edge of her reform efforts, Kemble articulated a form of imperial domesticity similar to northern plans to convert the poor, missionary efforts to transform the lives of Native Americans, and English endeavors throughout the world to Anglicize the indigenous peoples they had colonized.[52]

Kemble claimed to have laid eyes on slaves for the first time in Portsmouth, Virginia, as she and her family traveled to Georgia in 1838. "They were poorly clothed; looked horribly dirty, and had a lazy recklessness in their air and manner," she noted in her journal, which she later organized for publication as a series of letters to her friends Elizabeth and Catharine Sedgwick of western Massachusetts and Harriet St. Leger. Upon her arrival at her husband's rice plantation on Butler Island, she had her first prolonged contact with African Americans who had spent their lives enslaved. She complained to Elizabeth Sedgwick that the dairymaid, laundress, housemaid, and footmen "are perfectly filthy in their persons and clothes — their faces, hands, and naked feet being literally incrusted with dirt." Kemble claimed that their filth led her to dispense with their attendance upon meals as much as she could. She also found her chambermaid, Mary, to be "so intolerably offensive in her person that it is impossible to endure her proximity," which resulted in her "wait[ing] upon herself more than I have ever done in my life before."[53]

Kemble's perception of the bodies of the enslaved as offensive embroiled her in a nature-nurture question about the suitability of African Americans for slavery. White southerners, she claimed, insisted that the offense given by black bodies was "inherent with the race" and "one of their most cogent reasons for keeping them as slaves." Yet Kemble found this difficult to believe. Not only did white southern sensibility to bodily odors and filth not square with her perception of slaveowners' moral degradation — she could not imagine refined senses being compatible with putrid morals — but her observations of white intimacies with black bodies suggested that white southerners could not have been so offended. "Hanging their infants at the breasts of Negresses . . . having one or more little pet blacks sleeping like puppy dogs in their very bedchamber, nor almost every planter . . . admitting one or several of his female slaves to the still closer intimacy of his bed" made Kemble suspicious of the claim that slavery was the just reward for bodily uncleanness.[54]

Indeed, believing that bodily and domestic cleanliness were signs of enlightened self-care, health, and civility, Kemble was hard-pressed to accept an argument for bodily filth as being the "nature" of African Americans. Rather, "that peculiar ignorance of the laws of health and the habits of decent cleanliness are the real and only causes of this disagreeable characteristic of the race," she contended, noting that "thorough ablutions and change of linen, when tried, having been perfectly successful in removing all such objections." The unassailable evidence against filth as a manifestation of race came from Kemble's global experience. Poverty rather than race accounted for many of the offensive bodies she had encountered around the world. "If ever you have come into anything like neighborly proximity with a low Irishman or woman," she contended, referring to an ethnic type that would have been more familiar to her New England friend, "I think you will allow that the same causes produce very nearly the same effects." Indeed, Kemble found it impossible to distinguish between different ethnic manifestations of filth bred by poverty: "The stench in an Irish, Scotch, Italian, or French hovel is quite as intolerable as any I ever found in our Negro houses," she insisted, "and the filth and vermin which abound about the clothes and persons of the lower peasantry of any of those countries as abominable as the same conditions in the black population of the United States." Rather than seeking the answer in race, she laid slave uncleanness at the door of slavery, noting "a total absence of self-respect begets these hateful physical results, and in proportion as moral influences are remote, physical evils will abound." Self-respect flourished where there was "well-being, freedom, and industry," and in turn "induce[d] cleanliness and personal attention, so that slavery is answerable for all the evils that exhibit themselves where it exists — from lying, thieving, and adultery, to dirty houses, ragged clothes, and foul smells."[55]

Kemble thus interpreted slave filth not as intrinsic to the body but as evidence of abject exploitation, a source of physical suffering, and a danger to health. Cherishing her own privacy, she was horrified to discover that often more than one family inhabited a slave cabin, where the only bed covering was a "filthy, pestilential-looking blanket." Her description of slave dwellings, "filthy and wretched in the extreme" — written in 1839, but not published until 1863 — echoed ASSU depictions of filthy northern cottages:

> Instead of the order, neatness, and ingenuity which might convert even these miserable hovels into tolerable residences, there was the careless, reckless, filthy indolence which even the brutes do not exhibit in their lairs and nests. . . . Firewood and shavings lay littered about the floors, while the half-naked children were cowering round two or three smouldering cinders. . . . The back door of the huts, opening upon a most unsightly ditch, was left wide open for the fowls and ducks, which they are allowed to raise, to travel in and out, increasing the filth of the cabin by what they brought and left in every direction.[56]

Cleanliness seemed to offer Kemble one tangible way to alleviate the suffering and exploitation of her husband's slaves. She saw it as a means of elevating their condition, improving their health and physical well-being, and introducing them to civility. Although she despaired that by attempting to "awaken a new perception, that of cleanliness," she was starting at the end of a process that rightly should begin with moral awakening, she still believed that any improvement in their condition might yet "expel slavery."[57]

Kemble focused her efforts on convincing enslaved people in the infirmary "that they should keep their room swept, and as tidy as possible." Toward that end, she marched into slave cabins and began sweeping the floor. Attempting to persuade some young enslaved girls to clean their cabin, she told them that "it was a shame for any woman to live in so dirty a place and so beastly a condition." The young women's retort was telling: "They said they had seen buckree (white) women's houses just as dirty, and they could not be expected to be cleaner than white women."[58]

She also exhorted enslaved women "to go home and wash their children and clean their houses and themselves," offering a penny to those who presented themselves and their babies with clean faces and hands. She ordered that "little babies" should have a warm bath, to their mothers' apparent amazement. Kemble's assessment of the children's filth was not reducible to their failure to wash with water, however, but included her negative view of bare feet and swaddling, the latter an approach to caring for young children that had been condemned as hopelessly old-fashioned more than twenty-five years earlier by Mary Tyler, who, like Kemble, embraced Enlightenment precepts. Kemble described as a "stupid Negro practice . . . keeping the babies with their feet bare, and their heads, already well capped by nature with their woolly hair, wrapped in a half a dozen hot, filthy coverings."[59]

Kemble treated enslaved women who practiced cleanliness with an extra measure of sympathy and attention. Of the enslaved woman Psyche, whose interest in remaining with her husband became one of Kemble's causes, she recorded, "She has two nice little children under six years old, whom she keeps as clean and tidy, and who are sad and as silent as herself." Kemble reported proudly to Elizabeth Sedgwick in February 1839, "You cannot imagine how great a triumph the virtue next to godliness is making under my auspices and a judicious system of small bribery. I can hardly stir now without being assailed with cries of 'Missis, missis, me mind childe, me bery clean,' or the additional gratifying fact, 'and chile too, him bery clean.'"[60]

Part of Kemble's sense of her own success was the fact that she had convinced many of the enslaved women to remove the filthy coverings from their babies' heads, "the poor little woolly heads now, in most instances, stripped of their additional filthy artificial envelopes." Upon visiting slave quarters on Butler Island, she "confiscated sundry refractory baby caps among shrieks and outcries, partly of laughter and partly of real ignorant alarm for the consequences. I think, if this infatuation for hot headdresses continues, I shall make shaving the children's heads the only condition upon which they shall be allowed to wear caps."[61]

Although Kemble carefully eschewed arguments that would have collapsed uncleanness and African descent into a single racial profile, she herself embraced a concept of cultural racism in which slaves became "whiter," or as she described it, more civilized, as a result of their contact with white people. Cleanliness of body and abode provided important data for Kemble's interpretation and a crucial criterion for ranking enslaved people of different regions and plantation regimes. Finding the slaves on the cotton plantations of St. Simons Island generally cleaner and better off than their Butler Island rice plantation counterparts, Kemble attributed much of the difference to the "influence of the resident lady proprietors of the various plantations, and the propensity to imitate in their black dependents: the people that I see all seem to me much tidier, cleaner, and less fantastically dressed than those on the rice plantation, where no such influences reach them." Had she known more about southern slavery, she might also have attributed differences in bodily cleanliness to the filth of "mudwork" on rice plantations, and the relatively cleaner labor of cultivating and harvesting cotton.[62]

Despite Kemble's efforts to interpret the evil consequences of slavery or enslaved people's standard of living within a global context, she and other travelers to the South lost sight of these larger frames and fell back on explanations closer at hand that held slavery or sectional difference responsible. Kemble noted that Georgia's pinelanders, for example, represented "the most degraded race of human beings claiming an Anglo-Saxon origin that can be found on the face of the earth — filthy, lazy, ignorant, brutal, proud, penniless savages." Their lack of civility provided a pointed example that undermined racist arguments about the superiority of Anglo-Saxons over other peoples of the world. Yet Kemble occasionally seemed overwhelmed by the contrasts between North and South and unable to go beyond them to establish causes. She grasped for a vaguely sectional explanation when comparing an enslaved engineer to a northern artisan: "Think of the rows of tidy tiny houses in the long suburbs of Boston and Philadelphia, inhabited by artisans of just the same grades as this poor Ned," the head engineer on Mr. Butler's plantation, "with their white doors and steps, their hydrants of inexhaustible fresh flowing water, the innumerable appliances for decent comfort of their cheerful rooms, the gay wardrobe of the wife, her cotton prints for daily use, her silk for Sunday churchgoing; the careful comfort of the children's clothing." In contrast, she lamented the fate of Ned, "whose sole wages are his coarse food and raiment and miserable hovel, and whose wife, covered with one filthy garment of ragged texture and dingy color, barefooted and bareheaded, is daily driven afield to labor with aching pain-racked joints, under the lash of a driver, or lies languishing on the earthen floor of the dismal plantation hospital."[63]

Georgia's pinelanders and the similarity of the degradations suffered by enslaved Africans and poor Irish anchored Kemble's argument against the racial defense of slavery. She found it ironic that Irish laborers in America despised African slaves when both groups had been victimized by spurious racial explanations for their condition. "The fact is, that a condition in their own country nearly similar has made the poor Irish almost as degraded a class of beings as the Negroes are here," she mused, "and their insolence toward them, and hatred of them, are precisely in proportion to the resemblance between them." In Ireland, Kemble noted, "nothing can be more savage, brutish, filthy, idle, and incorrigibly and hopelessly helpless and incapable than the Irish appear," and yet, "transplanted to your northern states, freed from the evil influences that surround them at home, they and their children become industrious, thrifty, willing to learn, able to improve, and forming, in the course of two generations, a most valuable accession to your laboring population." She asked rhetorically, "How is it that it never occurs to these emphatical denouncers of the whole Negro race that the Irish at home are esteemed much as they esteem their slaves."[64]

Most American-born partisans of the North reflected little of Kemble's awareness of global patterns of poverty. The celebrated landscape architect and author Frederick Law Olmstead clung to a narrow sectional perspective in *The Cotton Kingdom* (1861), which featured accounts of his travels to the South previously published in serial form during the late 1850s. His overdetermined sectional analysis allowed him to gloss over similarities between well-to-do white southerners and northerners and to emphasize instead the ways that poor whites in the South led lives of harsh poverty bordering on barbarity. He sang the praises of a Georgia plantation where, during February 1853, he had enjoyed comfortable accommodations and fine warm weather. Happy with the stable full of well-maintained thoroughbred horses, the clean and efficient servants, and the excellent table fare, he wrote enthusiastically, "Nowhere in the world could a man, with a sound body and a quiet conscience, live more pleasantly, at least as a guest, it seems to me, than here where I am." Such a situation was exceptional, however, and Olmsted made it his personal crusade to debunk the myth of southern hospitality. He offered a hypothetical comparison between a northerner's house, recommended to the weary traveler as uncommonly good and worth riding an extra five miles, and a similarly recommended house in the southern states. In the North, Olmsted argued, he could expect genteel accommodations: "a private room, where I could, in the first place, wash off the dust of the road, and make some change of clothing before being admitted to a family apartment. This family room would be curtained and carpeted, and glowing softly with the light of sperm candles or a shaded lamp. When I entered it, I could expect that a couch or an arm-chair, and a fragrant cup of tea, with refined sugar, and wholesome bread of wheaten flour, leavened, would be offered me."[65]

Olmsted's imagined northern home included cultural amenities such as piano music ("the snatch of 'Tannhauser' or 'Trovatore' which had been running faintly" in his head), and a library with volumes of Shakespeare, Longfellow, and Dickens. At bedtime, he observed, "I should expect, as a matter of course, a clean, sweet bed, where I could sleep alone and undisturbed, until possibly in the morning a jug of hot water should be placed at my door, to aid the removal of a traveller's rigid beard. I should expect to draw a curtain from before a window, to lift the sash without effort, to look into a garden and fill my lungs with fragrant air; and I should be certain when I came down of a royal breakfast." A host of this caliber, "cannot exist in the country without ladies, and ladies cannot exist in the country without flowers," he noted. Olmsted not only expected breakfast to be a "meal as well as a feed—an institution of mental and moral sustenance as well as of palatable nourishment to the body," but he wanted flowers to grace a refined table.[66]

Southern hospitality could not hope to measure up to Olmsted's lofty expectations. Although he was careful to blunt the harshness of his sectional comparison by noting that he had found "a dozen" homes as good as that of his fictional northern host, he had been disappointed in nearly a hundred cases where the accommodations did not live up to their billing:

> Nine times out of ten, at least, after such a promise, I slept in a room with others, in a bed which stank, supplied with but one sheet, if with any; I washed with utensils, common to the whole household; I found no garden, no flowers, no fruit, no tea, no cream, no sugar, no bread (for corn pone . . . is not bread) . . . no curtains, no lifting windows (three times out of four absolutely no windows), no couch — if one reclined in the family room it was on the bare floor — for there were no carpets or mats. For all that, the house swarmed with vermin.[67]

What Olmsted and Kemble both seemed to be missing in the South was the influence of the well-to-do — measured in comforts, accoutrements, and expressions of familiarity with high culture — upon the taste of an ambitious middle class. A significant population of these prospering and aspiring classes, clustered in northern towns and cities, protected travelers from direct encounters with the region's rural poverty. In the predominantly rural South, however, a traveler could not hope to organize each day's journey from showcase plantation to showcase plantation and was instead forced to seek hospitality from lesser households. Never having spent the night in the home of a poor farmer in New York or in his native Connecticut, Olmsted was ill prepared for rural poverty in the South.

In the accounts of both writers, free labor implicitly, and sometimes explicitly, became the root of all that was comfortable, virtuous, and healthy about life in the North. In contrast, slavery was the source of moral corruption, which, in turn, led to physical dissipation and material degradation. Decency, as the North defined its own standard of cleanliness, required the absence of vermin and the availability of fresh sheets, privacy, resources for grooming, and wholesome food. It was part of a larger complex of material goods and domestic labor that had spread through the northern states, where it became laden with moral value.

Kemble and Olmstead also reflected the larger set of assumptions, articulated by antislavery writers and ASSU reformers, that people could be made anew by being taught new habits of bodily care and domestic management. Although such beliefs had a progressive strand — they were grounded in the potential for every individual to acquire new sensibilities — they also fostered judgments about the moral failings of recalcitrant or "slow" learners and gave rise to increasingly ambitious civilizing missions, both within the United States and abroad. In its most radical, imperial form, the mission of bringing cleanliness to the unclean masked and justified the violence of empire — the rupture of familial and affective ties necessary to refashion people — with the rhetoric of progress and civilization.[68]

Afterword: Toward the Modern Body

Civilizing the body was not simply a process. It was an ethos of the self in society, spread and reinterpreted by many different historical actors and spurred, on occasion, by epidemiological ones. Its aesthetics and practices would become ingrained in those reared to live by its rules. Initially, its advocates were doctors and elite men, but eventually its most vociferous practitioners became middle-class mothers and social activists, interested in bringing the lives of their children, the poor, and the enslaved into conformity with its standards. Intrinsic to this civilized ideal was a new ideal for health, focused less on protecting a fragile body from imbalances and extremes, as had been the case during the sixteenth and seventeenth centuries, and more on invigorating it to meet its economic and moral obligations.

The expansion of Europeans across the Atlantic created the conditions for the transformation of early modern body care. New ways of imagining both the diseased body and the civilized body emerged from this imperial context. Even as English writers commented disparagingly about exposed indigenous skin, they praised its beauty. Syphilis, a scourge new to early modern Europe, joined the plague and other sixteenth-century social and economic upheavals to motivate sharp departures from early modern traditions of body care: public baths became subject to closure, condemnation, and suspicion. Medical theory encouraged a more cautious respect for the body's delicate boundaries. The shirt, an undergarment that increasingly became the body's public skin, acquired new meanings as a symbol of refinement, a key cleanliness resource in an era of greater caution about bathing, and a marker of the civilized body. This costume distinguishing Europeans from West Africans and Native Americans was also the product of a particular organization of domestic labor that revolved around women's manufacture of cloth and the laundering of clothing.

When they settled in North America, Englishmen and women found themselves without some of the resources necessary to produce this civilized body. Limited access to female labor and shortages of linen, especially in demand during times of illness, made it difficult to maintain decency. New concerns to distinguish English bodies from those of laboring Africans and resistant Indians increased the pressure on clothing and appearance to broadcast those differences. Religious concerns about sin's corrupting power intensified during the seventeenth century as colonists faced still new challenges: indigenous peoples wearing English clothes by the final quarter of the century and white women tainting the social body by having sex with black men and committing infanticide. Confronted by extreme climates, foreign spices, new sexual temptations, and potent new diseases, Puritans and medical men alike wondered how to chart a path for health. A few mavericks concluded that cold regimen — cold water washing, cool air, spartan bedding, and cooling foods — was the best course.

But Atlantic expansion also meant the creation of new markets. The cloth for shirts became a crucial commodity in the eighteenth-century Atlantic trade. The "foot soldiers" of empire — the British sailors and soldiers who protected British commerce and defended territorial claims — needed to be clothed. Their fellow travelers — the migrants (free and indentured), planters, and merchants — also needed cloth. So did the slave laborers who cleared plantation lands and produced staple crops. Meanwhile, the associations of certain kinds of cloth with comfort and civility fed new desires for goods and generated more work for laundresses, a traditional female occupation that had only recently been commercialized in England. Even Native Americans began to incorporate imported fabrics into their wardrobes, although according to a different logic and to a lesser degree than their Anglo counterparts. By the eighteenth century, linen had become an imperial product and the material lingua franca of the Atlantic basin.

Elite men led the race toward gentility, distancing themselves from the bodily practices of the past with a heightened fastidiousness about changing linens and lavishing new care on face, hands, and teeth. They advised sons and daughters to attend to their persons and castigated womankind for inherently loathsome bodies and habitual neglect. The bodies of women, slaves, Indians, and the poor became the repositories for outmoded customs although, especially in the case of Indians, they did not always provide simple foils for civilized bodies. But as refinement was ultimately a technology of class and status rather than of gender, elite women gradually joined the chorus, hiring domestic labor to avoid ungenteel tasks and commenting acerbically on men and women whose domestic lives and grooming failed to pass muster. The desire for gentility created new standards as certain groups of women started to claim refinement as their own. This trend was spurred, in part, by the growing association of disease with filth. The eighteenth-century smallpox epidemics led several medical advice authors and city officials to link domestic practices, carried out in private households, with the condition of public spaces, including streets and zoning, and the vulnerability of all city residents to disease. The cleanliness of the poor — their habits of body and domicile — began to be a matter of public concern. Refined people came to know their own distinction through their visceral response to the filthy state of others.

The period between the Seven Years' War and the end of the eighteenth century brought two main changes: a new European interest in military hygiene, in which medical authors depicted the strength of the nation as dependent on the condition of the soldier's body, and a new humanitarian view of cleanliness in which those who denied others its comforts and benefits were cruel. When, during the Revolutionary War, the practical challenges of keeping men clean and free of disease overwhelmed the Continental Army, a state of affairs they could not possibly interpret as separate from questions of character and virtue, officers and doctors called for more discipline, better camp hygiene, and, above all, more clothing for soldiers. Ultimately, despite all the efforts to encourage men to take more responsibility for their persons and their surroundings, it may have been increased access to female labor that improved the health and the appearance of the Continental Army in the final years of the war, a fact that reiterated the connection between bodily cleanliness and domestic life.

The devastation wrought by yellow fever in Philadelphia and Wilmington during the 1790s and the early years of the nineteenth century intensified concerns about the impact of individual domestic practices — uncovered cisterns, filthy basements, and unsecured livestock — upon public health. Philadelphia moved quickly to apply the lessons of eighteenth-century environmentalists and established the nation's first municipal water works. The avant-garde advice about bathing, moreover, reached a receptive elite audience. Fear of disease, revived beliefs in water's healthfulness, and the optimism of early national perfectionist reformers spurred interest in public baths and in the purchase of shower and plunging baths for private homes. Health reformers claimed that bathing was not an immoral indulgence if it took place in cold water; rather, it was a means to combat the effeminacy "that will ever prove the ruin of any state where it prevails."[1]

Women's place in this landscape of disease and concern for public health shifted as a consequence of a new medical marketplace, encroachments on traditional female claims to healing expertise, and rising standards for domestic life. Behind it all lay women's own interest in protecting family members from illness and preserving the household's reputation and status. Health concerns prompted new vigilance about domestic conditions and encouraged experimentation with cold regimen like cold bathing and airing bedchambers. Meanwhile, homeopaths, medical botanists, and water curists challenged the approach of regular physicians. For women, "body work" was shifting from healing the sick body to maintaining a healthy and wholesome home environment and enforcing new standards. Women might have lost some of their authority over the healing arts, but they gained a new class-based authority over setting standards for domestic life and over the bodies of children, newly subject to scrutiny and efforts to improve their hardiness.[2]

Women's own bodies were key to this transformation. Representations of mothers as the loving civilizers of dirty and recalcitrant children competed with both traditional images of female foulness and newer medical treatises about the unpleasant diseases afflicting women's reproductive bodies. The women most central to this shift — white, middle-class, and upwardly mobile if not already privileged urban northerners — debunked the old reliance upon linen and insisted that only washing and bathing could make a body clean enough for polite society. Here is where the nagging mother, the enforcer of strict standards, makes her entrance. When fastidiousness about body odor necessitated bathing rather than putting on a fresh shirt, a new era in body care began: the body had become too loathsome, its effusions too offensive, to be cleaned only by changing clothes. For young women to meet this standard, they needed not only to become more self-conscious about their own persons but to enjoy more privacy than most Americans had traditionally known.

Yet expressing refinement in the body, especially in light of women's traditional responsibilities for the health of their households, was not enough. Households needed to reflect that refinement as a matter of taste and they also needed to be wholesome. Decades before the popular reception of the germ theory, household management books, popular fiction, and Sunday school tracts warned about the hazards that might make homes unpleasant, or worse, unhealthy. Dirty kitchens, vermin, dust, and stale air all threatened the health of the family. The bodies of servants could also offend. Dirty hands, stray hairs in the food, smelly feet, and a failure to follow protocol in the kitchen sullied the purity of domestic spaces. But there were other dangers — poor hygiene could bring about lice infestations that might affect the whole household. The smells clinging to a servant's unwashed body also raised alarm about catching illnesses from people who lived in neighborhoods where diseases preyed with greater force. Honing beliefs in dangers that could, with the proper sensibility, be smelled but not always seen, middle-class women helped to create normative standards for the cleanliness and decency of bodies and households.

Although the desire for a refined, odor-free body may have motivated some to more ambitious care, the greatest factor propelling Americans back into the water appears to have been the belief that immersion might be healthy. For travelers to the seashore or to mineral springs and spas in the mid-nineteenth century, pleasure overlapped with the pursuit of health. The growing popularity of recreational and purposeful bathing served as a backdrop for the more radical message of water curists, who saw in water immersion and consumption a panacea for many of the ills of modern life. The body belonging to a nineteenth-century person who feared the social as well as medical consequences of invisible body products—body odors and skin toxins—and for whom the human body served as social capital as much as a tool of labor, needed regular immersion in water to cleanse and invigorate it. This new faith in water's efficacy, along with rising standards for clean bodies and clothes, prompted thousands to invest in plumbing devices to improve their access to water. Others, left behind by the difficulty of procuring water for bathing, found themselves excluded from the new standard for decency.

By the middle of the nineteenth century, reformers began to pair cleanliness with spiritual purity in new ways. The clean body was understood to be the product of a domestic life that featured moral instruction and access to water for washing the body and laundering clothes. But such a body did not necessarily reflect an already awakened spirit. Rather, reformers sometimes described the body itself as the key that opened the hearts of the unredeemed. Concern for public health motivated many urban reformers to target the "vicious" habits—drunkenness, laziness, and unrestrained sexual appetite, among others—that were still believed to cause disease among the urban poor. But evangelical authors and lay readers of medical advice attributed greater spiritual agency to cleanliness of body and abode, which they insisted was a matter not of privilege but of education and choice. The removal of filth, according to this view, could actually provoke a purification of the spirit by introducing the potential convert to a new, empowered relationship with his or her body.

Viewing a poor person's body as the appropriate focus of moral reforms represented a new iteration of older wisdom about the poor as health hazards and the immoral agents of their own poverty. It was a view that went beyond the long-standing belief that external appearance simply reflected inner virtue. Rather, cleaning the body might awaken body and soul, enabling a person to meet his or her economic and moral obligations with energy and persistence. This was a new epistemology of the body that reflected an interest in achieving a new kind of health, based on a renewable source of vigor, vitality, and briskness. Such a standard colored assessments of the deficiencies of the poor and licensed intimate intrusions — remedies aimed at remaking the body — that revealed the weak claim of the poor to privacy and self-determination.

Making this happen on a grand scale required interventions in the households and lives of people who for a variety of reasons had not already "converted" their bodies. Children were especially ripe for being made over in the image of godly and cleanly reformers. Instilling new habits in the young required that they renounce their old ways, often reflected in the bodies of family members and the squalor of their households. Being made anew thus entailed the rupture of existing affective bonds but created the possibility of a new social identity, defined by connections to clean and moral people. Enslaved people constituted another important test case for reformers. Antislavery activists debunked older racial lore about the permanence of skin color, broadly construed by white people as a marker of the slave's inability to achieve bodily and cultural civility. They insisted on the possibility of the slave's inner purity, in contrast to the moral corruption of the slave owner, and on his ability to acquire new habits.

In many ways, this new sensibility reflected more rigorous standards for bodily cleanliness, requiring the individual to go beyond appearance to consider the source of the body's own odors. Formally, we can trace this seeming "civilizing process" in printed medical advice, more frequent changes of clothes, the insistence that only regular bathing could eradicate body odor, and the growing pressure on hired domestic labor. Informally, and more in the guise of ingrained habit, we can find it in the growing middle-class revulsion toward bad smells, and in the rising sensitivity to stale air. The increased concern about servants' body odors, for example, suggests a new map of the human body as well as a new social map, identifying certain bodies as potentially more contaminated and contaminating than others.[3]

Certainly, cleanliness standards did become more exacting, both in an objective sense and as contemporaries perceived them. By the early nineteenth century, laundry had become a weekly rather than seasonal event. By midcentury, genteel people aspired to change their underclothes daily rather than weekly (or less frequently), as they might have done in times past. New methods were needed for a body that might unintentionally broadcast its incivility with odors, despite having a respectable appearance. It was, moreover, no longer enough to have a tidy home; households had to meet more stringent standards. Air quality, bedding, carpets, walls, lamps, dining accoutrements, kitchen utensils, and washing and drying equipment all became subject to domestic advice.

But increasing stringency was certainly not the whole story. Cleanliness standards had changed in their premises, purpose, and practice, giving rise to a new bodily self-awareness, and new thresholds of disgust. Unlike its porous, deferential, early modern counterpart, which relied on linen shirts to civilize it, the "modern" body also required bathing and a clean and tidy abode to be qualified to participate in middle-class society. The putrefaction that caused illness in the early modern body still threatened its modern heir: wealth, gluttony, and a sedentary life could still produce internal corruption. But there were new fears about the environment, not only the filthy habitations of the poor, which had long been identified as sources of disease, but even middle-class homes, and the body's own production of odors. Modernity had thus intensified the association of the unrefined body with vice and illness. The emergence of this modern sensibility about cleanliness was predicated upon a much more rigorous ranking of society into two groups — the diseased and morally dissolute and the healthy and morally wholesome — at exactly the moment when the fate of both seemed more linked than ever before.

Filth avoidance was not the main impetus for many people's decision to immerse their bodies — but it nonetheless directed the interpretation of habits, smells, and appearance that prompted mid-nineteenth-century judgments of the poor as moral and hygienic hazards. In the name of civilization and following a route mapped by new standards of cleanliness, reformers, doctors, employers, and mothers judged the bodies of others and engaged in unprecedented intimate interventions into the care of those bodies and their environs. Claiming that resources for achieving cleanliness were available to all, no matter how poor, urban reformers denied that the bar had been raised by new expectations for bathing. Refusing to acknowledge the practical impediments to obtaining water-based cleanliness, they felt free to judge.

Thus the civilized body appears both less modern and less Western than we expect. Less a product of a European civilizing process, as Norbert Elias would have it, than of contact with other Atlantic basin cultures, it emerges only after the era of intercultural conflict and exchange that began with Columbus. Bathing, moreover, was actually a feature of medieval life and so-called primitive cultures well before Americans began to see it as an important component of their own body care. Although desires to meet rising expectations for refinement motivated efforts to achieve bodily cleanliness, concerns for health were even more important for coaxing reluctant Americans into the water. Bourgeois motherhood, defined by the nexus of domestic healing, child rearing, and the nurture of class identities, intensified this dual interest in health and decency. So-called moderns took pride in their own hardiness and ability to withstand immersion in water — they hailed the brisk, invigorated body it produced — but they were threatened by contact with others, especially by the dangers of disease and the vulnerability to social judgments.

When sectional conflict erupted in war in 1861, northerners drew upon the concept of cleanliness as civilizing mission to articulate a sense of their own modernity and moral superiority over uncivilized southerners. In cartoons, newspaper articles, children's literature, and serial fiction for adults, white southerners appeared as an unwashed rabble. Their lack of civility was communicated through depictions of ragged clothing, unfamiliarity with northern domestic technology, and deficient practices of body care. A *Harper's Weekly* cartoon from September 27, 1862, featured a Maryland Quaker woman preparing to be invaded by Robert E. Lee's men. She sets out a washbasin and pitcher, the basic equipment for rudimentary washing, which the rebels mistake for an "infernal machine" of war. As the Confederate soldiers turn tail, she calls out to them, "If thou wants my House, Friend, thou may'st have it; but oh, do wash thyself before entering in."[4] The cartoon pitted the plainspoken, plainly dressed Quaker, a symbol of northern virtue, who could hardly be accused of being too modern by her contemporaries, against ragtag Confederates, to highlight southern backwardness (Figure 13.1).

The alleged southern proclivity to filth, the impoverished living conditions of enslaved people and poor whites, the incidence of sexual relationships between white masters and enslaved women — all added up to a lack of modernity and moral decency in the South. Assured of the righteousness of their cause, northerners attempted to remake the intimate habits of southern blacks and whites, most notably through the efforts of the Freedman's Bureau to teach former slaves rudimentary hygiene, northern-style. Hadn't New Orleans escaped yellow fever during the war years, when Union General Benjamin Butler enforced strict quarantine and sanitation measures? The prominence of sanitation in these northern efforts was later incorporated into federal programs to combat yellow fever. This initiative gave rise to the United States Public Health Service and dominated subsequent federal public health policy until 1905.[5]

But cleanliness of body and abode was a double-edged sword for the North. White northerners may have found it politically useful to scoff at the premodern sensibilities of their southern enemies, but poor sanitation and hygiene exacted a heavy cost on Union armies. As in earlier wars, the majority of deaths came as a result of infection or disease rather than combat. Armed with guidelines for camp discipline that had gone mainly unrevised since they were written by Benjamin Rush in 1777, the Union Army saw nearly a quarter of a million die from

THE "INVASION" OF THE NORTH.

(Old Quaker Lady of Maryland, anticipating the seizure of her House by Lee's Troops, puts out a Washing Stand as a desirable preliminary step thereto. The Rebel Scouts mistake the—to them—Strange Apparatus for an Infernal Machine, and Skedaddle.)

OLD LADY *(to retreating Rebel)*. "If thou wants my House, Friend, thou may'st have it; but, oh! *do wash thyself* before entering in."

13.1. "The 'Invasion' of the North," in *Harper's Weekly* (1862). Courtesy American Antiquarian Society

disease, many as a consequence of poor camp and hospital sanitation. The new policies of the U.S. Sanitary Commission, an organization that began as a volunteer effort by northern women before becoming a government agency in June 1861, eventually reduced the toll taken by illness. Headed by Executive Secretary Frederick Law Olmsted and supported by army nurses under the superintendence of Dorothea Dix, the Sanitary Commission created new regulations and a schedule of inspections for military camps. In its "Rule for Preserving the Health of the Soldier," the commission issued guidelines that reflected beliefs in the utility of bathing: mandatory weekly baths for all enlisted men (Rush had praised Roman bathing and advised washing the whole body as often as three times a week during the summer months, but this had never been enforced) and weekly laundering of undergarments. It also issued strict rules to limit the crowding of men and improve camp sanitation in the effort to do for the Union Army what Florence Nightingale had done for the British Army during the Crimean War.[6]

Decades would pass before the lessons learned during the Civil War helped to transform the living conditions of the urban poor. As Nancy Tomes has shown, sanitarians working to improve public health anticipated many of the measures later recommended by proponents of the germ theory of disease during the 1890s. Reforming sewage disposal, including new designs for pipes that would end the threat of breathing harmful sewer gas, drainage of puddles of stagnant water, and garbage removal, all helped to lower white infant mortality from its high of more than 217 deaths per thousand in 1850 to a new low of 120 per thousand in 1900. (Black infant mortality also declined but remained 1.5 to 2 times as high as that of white babies.) Not until the massive influx of federal money during the Great Depression did the amenities necessary for this standard of cleanliness—electricity and running water—reach the majority of rural southerners. For immigrants newly arrived from eastern and southern Europe at the turn of the century, introductions to the ideals of a bathed body, clad in clothes that were regularly changed and laundered, and living in vermin-free quarters, were critical to the process of Americanization. Immigration officials, public health nurses, settlement house workers, and social workers all helped to spread this process by teaching body care and housekeeping to new arrivals.[7]

Cleanliness practices continue to reflect older regimes of body care and protective ritual as well as to embrace new knowledge and technology. We imagine ourselves to be more sophisticated and refined than our ancestors and, to some degree, we are: the reception of the germ theory wrought a signal transformation in private behavior as well as in public health, changing the way people tended their homes and regulated their contact with other healthy people. In general, the ideals for the civilized body have triumphed, creating zones of privacy and beliefs about gender that have become second nature to us. We may frequent gyms, spas, beauty parlors, and doctor's offices, in addition to our own bathrooms, but we expect a certain degree of bodily privacy even in these institutional spaces. Flouting that privacy by revealing the body publicly—long a form of "lowbrow" entertainment—still creates a spectacle even as it becomes de rigueur on televised makeover programs and tell-all talk shows. Still, the civilized body has become so central to our standards of conduct, it is supposed to go without saying. Our lives in public—at work, on public transportation, and in school—reinforce normative grooming practices: daily showers, laundered clothes, brushed hair and teeth, the use of deodorant. The privacy that still surrounds the bathroom, if not the bedroom, informs our understanding of what is appropriate to reveal to others. Finely wrought twenty-first-century sensibilities about cleanliness, which appear to go well beyond what is necessary for health (indeed, efforts to disinfect and sanitize arguably may jeopardize our health) leach into even our most determined efforts to respond with equanimity to people who, by necessity or choice, care for their bodies according to a different logic: children, the homeless, the so-called Third World, the inhabitants of the early modern world with whom they are regularly compared, and the Greens who refuse regular showers out of concern for the environment.

Yet like the people of the past, we rely on repeated behaviors to navigate a safe path through the world. Daily showers, endless rounds of laundry, rubbing hands and surfaces with moistened wipes—all help us to believe we are protected from disease, death, and disgrace. We also place our trust in substances that appear clean because of their color and smell: citrus and pine-scented cleansers, aromatic candles, tinted toilet water, and antibacterial soaps. The germ-obsessed twenty-first-century mother, moreover, has inherited the Victorian mother's responsibility for setting and enforcing standards. Nagging, repeating, and reminding mark her role as civilizer, even if, like her Victorian forbear, she outsources the actual labor to other women. Meanwhile, modern-day infestations of lice and bedbugs reconnect us to the sensory worlds of early modern people and enrich the meaning of our linguistic heritage from that era of body work. Situating our own ways of caring for the body in the history of that care, we confront the limits of our modernity, its debts to empire, its vulnerability to disease, and its continued reliance upon the domestic labor of women.

NOTES

ABBREVIATIONS

AAS   American Antiquarian Society, Worcester, Massachusetts
BG   *Boston Gazette*
BN   *Boston Newsletter*
CP   College of Physicians Library, Philadelphia
DL   David Library of the American Revolution, Washington Crossing, Pennsylvania
HSP   Historical Society of Pennsylvania, Philadelphia
JAH   *Journal of American History*
MHS   Massachusetts Historical Society, Boston
NODP   *New Orleans Daily Picayune*
NYEP   *New York Evening Post*
PG   *Pennsylvania Gazette*
PI   *Pennsylvania Inquirer*
PMHB   *Pennsylvania Magazine of History and Biography*
SHC   Southern Historical Collection, Wilson Library, University of North Carolina, Chapel Hill
VG   *Virginia Gazette*
WL   Winterthur Library, Delaware
WMQ   *William and Mary Quarterly*

INTRODUCTION

1. Paul Edwards, ed., *The Life of Olaudah Equiano, or Gustavus Vassa, the African* (Essex, England, 1988), 11, 5.
2. Ibid., 17, 19–21, 23. Equiano's critique of European culture and his rehabilitation of West Africans' moral and physical characters constituted a unique intervention by a canny writer, who, it now seems, probably invented his West African persona. See Vincent Caretta, *Equiano, the African: Biography of a Self-Made Man* (New York, 2005).

3. Norbert Elias, *The Civilizing Process: The History of Manners and State Formation and Civilization*, trans. Edmund Jephcott (Cambridge, Mass., 1994); Michel Foucault, *The History of Sexuality*, vol. 3, *The Care of the Self*, trans. Robert Hurley (New York, 1986); Isabel Hull, *Sexuality, State, and Civil Society in Germany, 1700–1815* (Ithaca, N.Y., 1996); Laura Engelstein, *The Keys to Happiness: Sex and the Search for Modernity in Fin-de-Siècle Russia* (Ithaca, N.Y., 1992); Kathy Peiss, *Hope in a Jar: The Making of America's Beauty Culture* (New York, 1998); Nancy Rose Hunt, *A Colonial Lexicon of Birth Ritual, Medicalization, and Mobility in the Congo* (Durham, N.C., 1999); Dorothy Ko, *Cinderella's Sisters: A Revisionist History of Footbinding* (Berkeley, 2005).

4. Leonore Davidoff, "Mastered for Life: Servant and Wife in Victorian and Edwardian England," *Journal of Social History* 7 (Summer 1974), 406–428; Ruth Schwartz Cowan, *More Work for Mother: The Ironies of Household Technology from the Open Hearth to the Microwave* (New York, 1983); Jeanne Boydston, *Home and Work: Housework, Wages, and the Ideology of Labor in the Early Republic* (New York, 1990).

5. Harold Donaldson Eberlein, "When Society First Took a Bath," in Judith Walzer Leavitt and Ronald L. Numbers, eds., *Sickness and Health in America: Readings in the History of Medicine and Public Health* (Madison, Wis., 1978), 331–341; Jean-Pierre Goubert, *The Conquest of Water: The Advent of Health in the Industrial Age* (Princeton, N.J., 1986); Richard L. Bushman and Claudia L. Bushman, "The Early History of Cleanliness in America," *JAH* 74 (March 1988): 1213–1238; Jane B. Donegan, *"Hydropathic Highway to Health": Women and the Water Cure in Antebellum America* (New York, 1986); Susan E. Cayleff, *Wash and Be Healed: The Water-Cure Movement and Women's Health* (Philadelphia, 1987); Suellen Hoy, *Chasing Dirt: The American Pursuit of Cleanliness* (New York, 1995); Maureen Ogle, *All the Modern Conveniences: American Household Plumbing, 1840–1890* (Baltimore, 1996); Nancy Tomes, *The Gospel of Germs: Men, Women, and the Microbe in American Life* (Cambridge, Mass., 1998); Franìoise de Bonneville, *The Book of the Bath* (New York, 1998); Katherine Ashenburg, *The Dirt on Clean: An Unsanitized History* (New York, 2007); Virginia Smith, *Clean: A History of Personal Hygiene and Purity* (New York, 2007).

6. The term *body work* comes from a conversation with Mary Fissell, May 2004.

7. Robert Blair St. George, *Conversing in Signs: Poetics of Implication in Colonial New England Culture* (Chapel Hill, 1998).

8. Ann Laura Stoler, *Race and the Education of Desire: Foucault's "History of Sexuality and the Colonial Order of Things* (Durham, N.C., 1995); Ann Laura Stoler, *Carnal Knowledge and Imperial Power: Race and the Intimate in Colonial Rule* (Berkeley, 2002); Cowan, *More Work for Mother*; Boydston, *Home and Work*.

9. Andrew Wear, *Knowledge and Practice in English Medicine, 1550–1680* (Cambridge, 2000), 30, 89, 90, 133, 136, 137, 140.

10. On the non-naturals see Antoinette Emch-Deriaz, "The Non-Naturals Made Easy," in Roy Porter, ed., *The Popularization of Medicine, 1650–1850* (London, 1992), 134–159, esp. 134; Virginia Smith, "Cleanliness: The Development of Idea and Practice in Britain, 1770–1850," Ph.D. diss., University of London, 1985, 62–92; and Smith, *Clean*, 95–98, 121, for *non-natural* as the corruption of *neutral*.

11. Roger Chartier, *The Cultural Uses of Print in Early Modern France* (Princeton, N.J.,

1987); Anna Bryson, *From Courtesy to Civility: Changing Codes of Conduct in Early Modern England* (New York, 1998), 51. For the linked fate of enthusiastic religion, popular culture, and lay healing in the eighteenth century, see Mary Fissell, *Patients, Power, and the Poor in Eighteenth-Century Bristol* (Cambridge, 1991), esp. 171–195.

12. Charles Rosenberg, *The Cholera Years: The United States in 1832, 1849, and 1866* (Chicago, 1987); Fissell, *Patients, Power, and the Poor;* Susan Juster, "Mystical Pregnancy and Holy Bleeding," *WMQ* 3rd ser., 57 (April 2000): 249–288.

13. Mark Jenner, "Early Modern English Conceptions of 'Cleanliness' and 'Dirt' as Reflected in the Environmental Regulation of London c. 1530–c. 1700," Ph.D. diss., Oxford University, 1991. David S. Barnes, *The Great Stink of Paris and the Nineteenth-Century Struggle against Filth and Germs* (Baltimore, 2006).

14. Bryson, *From Courtesy to Civility,* 44–45, quotation on 52.

15. J. G. A. Pocock, "Virtues, Rights, and Manners: A Model for Historians of Political Thought," in *Virtue, Commerce and History: Essays on Political Thought and History, Chiefly in the Eighteenth Century* (New York, 1985), 48–50; Bryson, *From Courtesy to Civility,* 43–45; Woodruff D. Smith, *Consumption and the Making of Respectability, 1600–1800* (New York, 2002); T. H. Breen, *The Marketplace of Revolution: How Consumer Politics Shaped American Independence* (New York, 2004).

16. Karen Halttunen, *Confidence Men and Painted Women: A Study of Middle-Class Culture in America, 1830–1870* (New Haven, 1982), 92–123; Ruth Bloch, "The Gendered Meanings of Virtue," *Signs* 13 (Autumn 1987): 37–58; John F. Kasson, *Rudeness and Civility: Manners in Nineteenth-Century Urban America* (New York, 1990); Richard L. Bushman, *The Refinement of America: Persons, Houses, Cities* (New York, 1992); C. Dallett Hemphill, *Bowing to Necessities: A History of Manners in America, 1620–1860* (New York, 1999), esp. 73, 82.

PART I. ATLANTIC CROSSINGS

1. Anna Bryson, *From Courtesy to Civility: Changing Codes of Conduct in Early Modern England* (Oxford, 1998), 51–52; David Eltis, *The Rise of African Slavery in the Americas* (New York, 2000).

1. CARING FOR THE EARLY MODERN BODY

1. Jean-Pierre Goubert, *The Conquest of Water: The Advent of Health in the Industrial Age* (Princeton, N.J., 1986), 23.

2. W. Coster, *Baptism and Spiritual Kinship in Early Modern England* (Burlington, Vt., 2002), 57–71. Horton Davies, *Worship and Theology in England: From Cranmer to Hooker,* 1534–1603 (Princeton, N.J., 1970; rpt ed. combined vols. 1 and 2, Grand Rapids, Mich., 1996), 194, 217.

3. Janet Bord and Colin Bord, *Sacred Waters: Holy Wells and Water Lore in Britain and Ireland* (New York, 1985).

4. This summary draws on Keith Thomas, "Cleanliness and Godliness in Early Modern England," in Anthony Fletcher and Peter Roberts, eds., *Religion, Culture, and Society*

in Early Modern Britain (Cambridge, 1994), 60; Mark Jenner, "Bathing and Baptism," in Kevin Sharpe and Steven N. Zwicker, eds., *Refiguring Revolutions: Aesthetics and Politics from the English Revolution to the Romantic Revolution* (Berkeley, Calif., 1998); Woodruff D. Smith, *Consumption and the Making of Respectability, 1600–1800* (New York, 2002), 116; Anna Bryson, *From Courtesy to Civility: Changing Codes of Conduct in Early Modern England* (New York, 1998), 59.

5. W. Coster, "Purity, Profanity, and Puritanism: The Churching of Women, 1500–1700," in W. Sheils and D. Wood, eds., *Women in the Church* (Oxford, 1990).

6. Chava Weissler, "*Tkhines* and *Techinot*: Ancient Prayers," in Rivkah Slonim, ed., *Total Immersion: A Mikvah Anthology* (Northvale, N.J., 1996), 95–99; Chava Weissler, *Voices of the Matriarchs: Listening to the Prayers of Early Modern Jewish Women* (Boston, 1998), 72–73; Judith R. Baskin, "Women and Ritual Immersion in Medieval Ashkenaz: The Sexual Politics of Piety," in Lawrence Fine, ed., *Judaism in Practice: From the Middle Ages through the Early Modern Period* (Princeton, N.J., 2001), 131–142; Francoise de Bonneville, *The Book of the Bath* (New York, 1998), 11; Katherine Ashenburg, *The Dirt on Clean: An Unsanitized History* (New York, 2007), 67–70.

7. Joseph Hall, *Characters of Vertues and Vices*, quoted in Thomas, "Cleanliness and Godliness," 79.

8. Davies, *Worship and Theology in England*, 194, 217; Coster, *Baptism and Spiritual Kinship*, 57–71; Thomas, "Cleanliness and Godliness," 61–62; Mary Fissell, *Vernacular Bodies: The Politics of Reproduction in Early Modern England* (New York, 2004), 28–42, 44; David Cressy, "Purification, Thanksgiving, and the Churching of Women in Post-Reformation England," *Past and Present*, no. 141 (November 1993): 126; David Cressy, *Birth, Marriage, and Death: Ritual, Religion, and the Life-Cycle in Tudor and Stuart England* (New York, 1997), 197–229.

9. Lawrence Wright, *Clean and Decent: The Fascinating History of the Bathroom and Water Closet and of Sundry Habits, Fashions, and Accessories of the Toilet Principally in Great Britain, France, and America* (New York, 1960), 24–26, 58–60; Georges Vigarello, *Concepts of Cleanliness: Changing Attitudes in France since the Middle Ages* (Cambridge, 1988), 22; Phillipe Braunstein, "Toward Intimacy: The Fourteenth and Fifteenth Centuries," in Georges Duby, ed., *History of Private Life: Revelations of the Medieval World*, trans. Arthur Goldhammer (Cambridge, Mass., 1988), 600–610; Jacques Rossiaud, *Medieval Prostitution*, trans. Lydia G. Cochrane (New York, 1988), 5–7; Ruth Mazo Karras, "The Regulation of Brothels in Later Medieval England," *Signs* 14 (Winter 1989): 409; Marilyn Thornton Williams, *Washing the Great Unwashed: Public Baths in Urban America, 1840–1920* (Columbus, Ohio, 1991), 6–7.

10. Virginia Smith, *Clean: A History of Personal Hygiene and Purity* (New York, 2007), 168–178.

11. Johann Comenius, *Orbis Sensualium Pictus* (London, 1659), 152–153; Johann Comenius, *Janua Linguarum Reserata; or, A Seed-Plot of All Languages and Sciences* (London, 1636); Braunstein, "Toward Intimacy," 597–598; Wright, *Clean and Decent*, 58–61; Vigarello, *Concepts of Cleanliness*, 22, 29–34; Jacques Le Goff and Nicholas Truong, *Une histoire du corps au Moyen Age* (Paris, 2003), 158–160; Karras, "The Regulation of Brothels," 399–433. See also Lyndal Roper, *Oedipus and the Devil: Witchcraft,*

Sexuality, and Religion in Early Modern Europe (New York, 1994), 189, for examples of the bath maid's access to the body's detritus — hair and fingernail clippings — implicating her in possible magic or witchcraft in early modern Germany.

12. Vigarello, *Concept of Cleanliness*, 29, 30; Braunstein, "Toward Intimacy," 597–598, and bathing images, 597–603; Williams, *Washing the Great Unwashed*, 6–7; Wright, *Clean and Decent*, 60–61; Karras, "The Regulation of Brothels," 404; Virginia Smith, "Cleanliness: The Development of Idea and Practice in Britain, 1770–1850," Ph.D. diss., University of London, 1985, 169–170.

13. Andrew Wear, *Knowledge and Practice in English Medicine, 1550–1680* (Cambridge, 2000), 14, 268; Johannes Fabricius, *Syphilis in Shakespeare's England* (London, 1994).

14. Smith, "Cleanliness," 117; Thomas Moulton, *The Myrrour or glasse of Helth* (London, 1545), quoted in Smith, *Clean*, 199–200.

15. Wright, *Clean and Decent*, 60, 80–83; Vigarello, *Concepts of Cleanliness*, 7–27; Williams, *Washing the Great Unwashed*, 6–7; Roy Porter, *London: A Social History* (Cambridge, Mass., 1995), 56, 64. For the Proclamation of 1546 closing London's stews, see Fabricius, *Syphilis in Shakespeare's England*, 75–76; Rossiaud, *Medieval Prostitution*, 51–52. Peter Clark, *The English Alehouse: A Social History, 1200–1830* (London, 1983), 115, 137, 149; Edward Jorden, "A Discourse of Naturall Bathes, and Minerall Waters . . . Especially Bathes at Bathe in Sommersetshire (London, 1631), Houghton Library, Harvard University. Thomas, "Cleanliness and Godliness," 79. Smith, "Cleanliness," 173, 247.

16. John Jones, *The Arte and Science of Preserving Bodie and Soule in Healthe, Wisedome, and Catholike Religion Phisically, Philosophically, and Divinely* (London, 1579) 32, 35, 42, Houghton Library, Harvard University. Wear, *Knowledge and Practice*, 54. Louis Bourgeois, *The Compleat Midwifes Practice* (London, 1656), 95–101.

17. William Turner, *A Booke of the bath of Baeth in England, and of the vertues of the same with diverse other bathes, moste holsom and effectuall* in *The first and seconde partes of the herbal of William Turner Doctor in Physick* (Collen, 1568); Tobias Venner, *Via Recta Ad Via Longam, or a Plaine Philosophical discourse of the Nature, faculties, and effects of all such things, as by way of nourishments, and dieteticall observations, make for the preservation of Health, with their just applications unto every age* (London, 1620), Houghton Library, Harvard University, 12; Smith, *Clean*, 204–205.

18. Wear, *Knowledge and Practice*, 54, 184; Thomas Cock, *Miscelanea medica; Or, a Supplement to Kitchin-Physick; to which is added, A short discourse on stoving and bathing* (London, 1675), CP, 48, 32, quotation on 29. See also Samuel Pepys, *Diary of Samuel Pepys*, 4: 40, quoted in Thomas, "Cleanliness and Godliness," 59, and ibid., 74.

19. Orest Ranum, "The Refuges of Intimacy," in Roger Chartier, ed., *A History of Private Life: Passions of the Renaissance* (Cambridge, Mass., 1989), esp. images on 221–225. Bonneville, *Book of the Bath*, 82.

20. Wear, *Knowledge and Practice*, 30; Ann Jones and Peter Stallybrass, *Renaissance Clothing and the Materials of Memory* (New York, 2000), 269–270; Dyan Elliot, *Fallen Bodies: Pollution, Sexuality, and Demonology in the Middle Ages* (Philadelphia, 1999).

21. Bryson, *From Courtesy to Civility*, 43–51.

22. Vigarello, *Concepts of Cleanliness*, 27–37; Jacques Revel, "The Uses of Civility," in

Chartier, *History of Private Life*, 189. Mark Jenner, "Early Modern English Conceptions of 'Cleanliness' and 'Dirt' as Reflected in the Environmental Regulation of London c. 1530–c. 1700," Ph. D. diss., Oxford, 1991, chapter 2.

23. Pepys, *Diary*, 6: 32, cited in Andrew Wear, "Puritan Perceptions of Illness in Seventeenth-Century England," in Roy Porter, ed., *Patients and Practitioners: Lay Perceptions of Medicine in Pre-Industrial Society* (Cambridge, 1985), 83. See also Wear, *Knowledge and Practice*, 329; C. Willett Cunnington and Phillis Cunnington, *The History of Underclothes* (London, 1951), 54–55. Margaret Pelling, *The Common Lot: Sickness, Medical Occupations, and the Urban Poor in Early Modern England* (New York, 1998), 82, 129, 197; Ashenburg, *Dirt on Clean*, 97–123.

24. Eric Kerridge, *Textile Manufactures in Early Modern England* (Manchester, 1985); Cunnington and Cunnington, *History of Underclothes*, 58, quotation on 45, from Henry Fitzgeffery, *Poems*; Florence Montgomery, *Textiles in America, 1650–1870* (New York, 1984), 259.

25. Kerridge, *Textile Manufactures*, 15, 23–24, 122; W. H. Crawford, *The Impact of the Domestic Linen Industry in Ulster* (Ulster, 2005), 50–51, 119; Brenda Collins and Phillip Ollerenshaw, eds., *The European Linen Industry in Historical Perspective* (New York, 2003), 14–15.

26. Adrian Hood, *The Weaver's Craft: Cloth, Commerce, and Industry in Early Pennsylvania* (Philadelphia, 2003), 49–57; Nesta Evans, *The East Anglian Linen Industry: Rural Industry and Local Economy, 1500–1850* (Aldershot, England, 1985), 20–23, 31.

27. Kerridge, *Textile Manufactures*, 190; Vigarello, *Concept of Cleanliness*.

28. Luc Martin, "The Rise of the New Draperies in Norwich, 1550–1622," in N. B. Harte, ed., *The New Draperies in the Low Countries and England, 1300–1800* (New York, 1997), 256–257; Martha Howell, "Women's Work in the New and Light Draperies of the Low Countries," ibid., 197–216, esp. 211.

29. Cunnington and Cunnington, *History of Underclothes*, 55. For the 1677 act, see John Spurr, *England in the 1670s* (Oxford, 2000), 125–126. For the use of cotton shrouds by the poor, see John Cary, *Essay on the State of England* (1695), cited in Smith, *Consumption and the Making of Respectability*, 260 n. 110.

30. Vigarello, *Concepts of Cleanliness*, 67, quotation on 60.

31. Vigarello, *Concepts of Cleanliness*, 58–59; Kerridge, *Textile Manufactures*, 125; Montgomery, *Textiles in America*, 206–207; Arnold J. Cooley, *The Toilet in Ancient and Modern Times, with a Review of the Different Theories of Beauty and Copious Allied Information Social, Hygienic, and Medical* (1866; rpt. New York, 1970), 50.

32. *The Itinerarium of Dr. Alexander Hamilton*, in Wendy Martin, ed., *Colonial American Travel Narratives* (New York, 1994), 179; Jones and Stallybrass, *Renaissance Clothing*, 2; Anne Somerset, *Ladies in Waiting* (New York, 1984), 96; Vigarello, *Concepts of Cleanliness*, 61–77; Cunnington and Cunnington, *History of Underclothes*, 35, 56; Smith, *Consumption and the Making of Respectability*, 60–62.

33. Anne Laurence, *Women in England, 1500–1760: A Social History* (New York, 1994), 109–115; Barbara Hanawalt, "Peasant Women's Contribution to the Home Economy in Late Medieval England," in Barbara Hanawalt, ed. *Women and Work in Preindustrial Europe* (Bloomington, Ind., 1986), 4–17. Pelling, *Common Lot*, 191–192, 201–202.

34. Pelling, *Common Lot*, 192. For the place of washerwomen in Italian culture, see Douglas Biow, *The Culture of Cleanliness in Renaissance Italy* (Ithaca, N.Y., 2006).

35. Pelling, *Common Lot*, 123, 191, 194, 196–197.

36. Beverly Lemire, *Dress, Culture, and Commerce: The English Clothing Trade before the Factory, 1660–1800* (New York, 1997), 121–146; Pelling, *Common Lot*, 197.

37. Fynes Moryson, *An Itinerary containing his ten yeeres travell through Germany . . . England, Scotland and Ireland* (London, 1617; rpt. Glasgow, 1917), 236–238.

38. Jones and Stallybrass, *Renaissance Clothing*, 63–85; Bryson, *From Courtesy to Civility*, 52; Edmund Spenser, *A View of the Present State of Ireland* (London, 1596; rpt. Oxford, 1970); Cunnington and Cunnington, *History of Underclothes*, 39.

39. My Lady Frescheville's Receipt Booke, 1669, Joseph Downs Collection, Winterthur Library, 69, 80, 84. Vigarello, *Concepts of Cleanliness*, 83–89; Alain Corbin, *The Foul and the Fragrant: Odor and the French Social Imagination* (Cambridge, Mass., 1996). Cunnington and Cunnington, *History of Underclothes*, 47, 54, 62; Wear, *Knowledge and Practice*, 328, for the distinction between the special air of the house and the general air outside it. Richard Palmer, "'In Bad Odour': Smell and Its Significance in Medicine from Antiquity to the Seventeenth Century," in W. F. Bynum and Roy Porter, eds., *Medicine and the Five Senses* (Cambridge, 1993), 61–68; Constance Classen, David Howes, and Anthony Synnott, *Aroma: The Cultural History of Smell* (New York, 1994), 62–66, 70–73.

40. My Lady Frescheville's Receipt Booke, 25, 26, 75, 110, 111, 231.

41. Giovanni Della Casa, *Galateo: A Renaissance Treatise on Manners*, trans. Konrad Eisenbichler and Kenneth R. Bartlett (1628; 3d rev. ed. Toronto, 1994), 34, 95. See Bryson, *From Courtesy to Civility*, 24; Vigarello, *Concepts of Cleanliness*, 47–48; Erasmus quoted in Norbert Elias, *The Civilizing Process*, trans. Edmund Jephcott (Cambridge, Mass., 1994), 46. My Lady Frescheville's Receipt Book, 233.

42. Richard L. Bushman, *The Refinement of America: Persons, Houses, Cities* (New York, 1992), 41–42. For the concept of the grotesque body that informs my interpretation, see Mikhail Bakhtin, *Rabelais and His World*, trans. Helene Iswolsky (Bloomington, Ind., 1984); Elias, *The Civilizing Process*; Conte de Baldassare Castiglione, *The Courtier* (London, 1727); Pelling, *Common Lot*, 26.

43. Patricia Crawford, "Attitudes Towards Menstruation," *Past and Present* no. 91 (May 1981): 47–73; Gail Kern Paster, *The Body Embarrassed: Drama and the Disciplines of Shame in Early Modern England* (Ithaca, N.Y., 1993). See Roper, *Oedipus and the Devil*, 112, 153, for her distinction between the way contemporaries described the unruly male body bursting its bounds through drunkenness and violence and the dangers presented to society by a sexually unruly female body. Laura Gowing, *Common Bodies: Women, Touch, and Power in Seventeenth-Century England* (New Haven, 2003), 22–26; Bryson, *From Courtesy to Civility*, 38.

44. Elias, *The Civilizing Process*, 43–47, and 242 n. 2. *Manners for Children* appeared in English translation in a dual-language edition in 1532. Elias bases his discussion on the 1530 edition of *On Civility in Children*, although he claims that there was an edition in 1526. See Bakhtin, *Rabelais and His World*. See also Revel, "Uses of Civility," 168–182, 191–192. Roger Chartier, *The Cultural Uses of Print in Early Modern France*, trans. Ly-

dia G. Cochrane (Princeton, N.J., 1987), 77, interprets Erasmus's text as a watershed in defining European society because it established a unified code of conduct and a common foundation for child rearing. See also Peter Burke, *The Fortunes of the Courtier: The European Reception of Castiglione's Cortegiano* (University Park, Pa., 1995); Bryson, *From Courtesy to Civility*, 29–30, 47, 82.

45. Della Casa, *Galateo*, quotations on 40, 35. See also Revel, "Uses of Civility," 191–192. Bryson, *From Courtesy to Civility*, 35.

46. Keith Thomas, *Religion and the Decline of Magic: Studies in Popular Beliefs in Sixteenth and Seventeenth Century England* (London, 1971).

47. Crawford, "Attitudes Towards Menstruation"; Elliot, *Fallen Bodies*, 1–13. Fissell, *Vernacular Bodies*, 32–33.

48. Andrewe Boorde, *Here foloweth a Compedyous Regyment or a dyetary of helth* (London, 1554), Biii. Venner, *Via Recta Ad Via Longam*, 5–6. See also Wear, *Knowledge and Practice*, 191–206. Smith, "Cleanliness," 114a, for a discussion of Bartolomeao Anglicus on odor, and 115. Classen, Howes, and Synnott, *Aroma*, 62–66.

49. Boorde, *Here foloweth a Compedyous Regyment*, Bi, Cii, Ciii; "special air of the house" from Wear, *Knowledge and Practice*, 328.

50. Simon Schama, *The Embarrassment of Riches: An Interpretation of Dutch Culture in the Golden Age* (New York, 1987), 375–480.

51. Erasmus quoted in Latin in Wright, *Clean and Decent*, 68.

52. Wear, *Knowledge and Practice*, 15, 21, 191, 284. Pelling, *Common Lot*, 19–24; Jenner, "Conceptions of 'Cleanliness,' and 'Dirt.'"

53. William Vaughan *Directions for Health, Naturall and Artificiall: Derived from the best Phisitians, as well Moderne as Antient* (London, 6th ed., 1626), 13–15. Thomas Cock, *Kitchin-Physick; or, Advice to the poor* (London, 1675), CP, 47. See also Jenner, "Conceptions of 'Cleanliness' and 'Dirt,'" chapter 6. Maureen Ogle, *All the Modern Conveniences: American Household Plumbing, 1840–1890* (Baltimore, 1996), 57, observes that open drains were thus believed healthier than enclosed sewers because exposed sewage could be purified by running water, sunlight, and air.

54. Porter, *London*, 80–84, 126; Wright, *Clean and Decent*, 65; Donald Reid, *Paris Sewers and Sewermen: Realities and Representations* (Cambridge, Mass., 1991), 9–17. Pelling, *Common Lot*, 110.

55. Mark Jenner, "'Another Epocha'? Hartlib, John Lanyon and the Improvement of London in the 1650s," in Mark Greengrass, Michael Leslie, and Timothy Raylor, eds., *Samuel Hartlib and Universal Reformation: Studies in Intellectual Communication* (New York, 1994), 343–356, quotations on 344, 356. Porter, *London*, 80–84, 126; Wright, *Clean and Decent*, 65. Reid, *Paris Sewers and Sewermen*, 9–17. Wear, *Knowledge and Practice*, 163, 300. See also Jenner, "Conceptions of 'Cleanliness' and 'Dirt,'" chapter 6, for acts in 1662 and 1690. Classen, Howes, and Synnott, *Aroma*, 54–58. Emily Cockayne, *Hubbub: Filth, Noise, and Stench in England, 1600–1770* (New Haven, 2007), 183–187.

56. Reid, *Paris Sewers and Sewermen*, 9–10, Jenner, "'Another Epocha'?" 344–345.

57. Wright, *Clean and Decent*, 76.

58. Schama, *Embarrassment of Riches*. Bryson, *From Courtesy to Civility*, 79. Gervase

Markham, *Countrey Contentments, or the English Huswife. Containing the Inward and Outward Vertues which ought to be in the a compleate woman* (London, 1615). Richard Brathwaite, *The English Gentleman* (London, 1630); Richard Brathwaite, *The English Gentlewoman* (London, 1631); William Shakespeare, *Coriolanus*, II.iii.54–55 (Cambridge, 2000); Thomas, "Cleanliness and Godliness," 58, 73.

2. SKIN

1. Eldred D. Jones, *The Elizabethan Image of Africa* (Charlottesville, Va., 1971), 45–48. See Andrew Wear, *Knowledge and Practice in English Medicine, 1550–1680* (Cambridge, 2000), 188, for William Harrison's 1577 description of white complexions as healthy and natural for English natives.

2. William Vaughan, *Directions for Health, Naturall and Artificiall: Derived from the best Phisitians, as well Moderne as Antient* (London, 6th ed., 1626), 66–67; Johann Comenius, *The Gate of Tongues Unlocked and Opened; or else, A Seminarie or seed-plot of all Tongues and Sciences* (London, 1633), 147. Kim F. Hall, *Things of Darkness: Economies of Race and Gender in Early Modern England* (Ithaca, N.Y., 1995), 1–24; Georges Vigarello, *Concepts of Cleanliness: Changing Attitudes in France since the Middle Ages* (Cambridge, 1988), 83; Winthrop Jordan, *White over Black* (Chapel Hill, 1968); Kathleen Brown, *Good Wives, Nasty Wenches, and Anxious Patriarchs: Gender, Race, and Power in Colonial Virginia* (Chapel Hill, 1996); Kathleen Brown, "Native Americans and Early Modern Concepts of Race," in Martin Daunton and Rick Halpern, eds., *Empire and Others: British Encounters with Indigenous Peoples, 1600–1850* (Philadelphia, 1999), 79–100.

3. Kenneth R. Andrews, *Trade, Plunder, and Settlement: Maritime Enterprise and the Genesis of the British Empire, 1480–1630* (New York, 1984), 107. See also Michael Sturma, "Dressing, Undressing, and Early European Contact in Australia and Tahiti," *Pacific Studies* 21, no. 3 (1988): 87–104.

4. Richard Hakluyt, *The Principall Navigations, Voyages, Traffiques and Discoveries of the English Nation*, 8 vols. [London, n.d.], 1: 101, 106, 139, 141; 2: 525. See also Jennifer L. Morgan, *Laboring Women: Reproduction and Gender in New World Slavery* (Philadelphia, 2004), 12–49.

5. Hakluyt, *Principall Navigations*, 1: 132.

6. Quoted ibid., 1: 141. See Richard Ligon, *A True and Exact History of the Island of Barbados* (London, 1657), 13, on alleged sexual assault by Portuguese and Negroes upon Englishwomen sent ashore to wash linens.

7. Hakluyt, *Principall Navigations*, 1: 101, 106–107, 117. John Thornton, *Africa and Africans in the Making of the Atlantic World, 1400–1680* (Cambridge, 1992), 48–53.

8. Hakluyt, *Principall Navigations*, 2: 525; 1: 144.

9. Richard Eden, "The Second Voyage to Guinea," in Edward Arber, ed., *First Three English Books on America* (New York, 1971), 384; Hakluyt, *Principall Navigations*, 1: 94, 139.

10. Hakluyt, *Principall Navigations*, 1: 130–142. Brown, "Native Americans," esp. the discussion of Baker on 83–84.

11. Hakluyt, *Principall Navigations*, 8: 13–14; Brown, "Native Americans," 84.

12. Eden, "Second Voyage to Guinea," 386; Hakluyt, *Principall Navigations*, 1: 96, 101.

13. Richard Jobson, *The Golden Trade; or, A discovery of the River Gambra, and the Golden Trade of the Aethiopians. Also; the Commerce with a Great blacke Merchant, called Buckor Sano, and his report of the houses covered with gold, and other strange observations for the good or our owne countrey* (London, 1623), 35, 56.

14. Ibid., 18.

15. See "The Strange Adventure of Andrew Battel of Leigh in Essex," in Samuel Purchas, *Hakluytus Posthumus; or, Purchas his pilgrimes*, 20 vols. (Glasgow, 1905–1907), 6: 376, 393, 385, 395, 400. Timothy Burke, *Lifebuoy Men, Lux Women: Commodification, Consumption, and Cleanliness in Modern Zimbabwe* (Durham, N.C., 1996), 22–31.

16. Pieter de Marees, *Description and Historical Account of the Gold Kingdom of Guinea* (1602), trans. and ed. Albert van Dantzig and Adam Jones (Oxford, 1987), 68, 73, 77, quotation on 182. Marees copied entire passages on West African flora and fauna from other publications, as was common in the early modern travel genre. He was in turn copied by the anonymous English author of *The Golden Coast* (1665) and by French traveler Jean Barbot, whose commentary I discuss in chapter 5. Adam Jones, ed., *West Africa in the Mid-Seventeenth Century: An Anonymous Dutch Manuscript* (Atlanta, 1995), 53.

17. Ligon, *True and Exact History*, 12–14, 15–17.

18. Karen Ordahl Kupperman, "Presentment of Civility: English Reading of American Self-Presentation in the Early Years of Colonization," *WMQ* 3rd ser., 54 (January 1997): 193–228, analyzes the admiration for indigenous bodily comportment, which Europeans interpreted as similar to the refined and graceful presentation of elite bodies. See also Joyce Chaplin, *Subject Matter: Technology, the Body, and Science on the Anglo-American Frontier, 1500–1676* (Cambridge, Mass., 2001).

19. "Letter of Columbus to Various Persons Describing the Results of His First and Written on the Return Journey," in J. M. Cohen, ed., *The Four Voyages of Christopher Columbus* (London, 1969), 117, 121.

20. Amerigo Vespucci, "The fyrst voyage of Americaus Vesputius," in Arber, *First Three English Books*, 37.

21. *Quoted ibid.* Paul Le Jeune, *Relation of What Occurred in New France in the Year 1634*, in Reuben Gold Thwaites, ed., *Travels and Explorations of the Jesuit Missionaries in New France, 1610–1791* (Cleveland, 1897), 6: 253, claimed that "among themselves [the women's] language has the foul odor of the sewers." For a parallel between Native Americans and Castiglione's prescriptions, see the annotations of Henry Howard, later the Earl of Northumberland, in his copy of *The Courtier*, in Peter Burke, *The Fortunes of the Courtier: The European Reception of Castiglione's Cortegiano* (University Park, Pa., 1995), 80.

22. Vespucci, "The fyrst voyage," 37. Morgan, *Laboring Women*, notes the existence of a few exceptional images of Native women with hanging breasts, but such imagery appeared mainly in depictions of African women, witches, and elderly women.

23. Peter Martyr, "The First Decade," in Arber, *First Three English Books*, 83.

24. Jordan, *White over Black*, 241; Brown, "Native Americans," 89; Martyr, "First Decade," 88, 89, 91; John Smith, *A Map of Virginia: With a Description of the Countrey, the Commodities, People, Government and Religion*, in Philip L. Barbour, ed., *Complete Works of John Smith* (Chapel Hill, 1986), 1: 160; William Strachey, *The Historie of Travell into Virginia Britania*, ed. Louis B. Wright and Virginia Freund (London, 1953), 70; A. L. Rowse, ed., *The First Colonists: Hakluyt's Voyages to North America, a Modern Version* (London, 1986), 69; Francisco Lùpez, "Other notable thynges as touchynge the Indies," in Arber, *First Three English Books*, 338; Eden, "Second Voyage to Guinea," 387; Hakluyt, *Principall Navigations*, 2: 530.

25. Thomas Stevens, "A letter written from Goa," in Hakluyt, *Principall Navigations*, 1: 162.

26. Smith, *Map of Virginia*, 1: 160.

27. Le Jeune, *Relation*, 6: 245.

28. Oviedus himself noted an exception to the native lack of beards, but subsequent English adventurers found it to be true of most Native Americans they met; see Oviedus, "Hystorie of the west Indies," in Arber, *First Three English Books*, 237. Hakluyt, *Principall Navigations*, 2: 530. John Smith, *The Generall Historie of Virginia, New-England, and the Summer Isles . . .*, in Barbour, *Complete Works*, 2: 114.

29. Oviedus, "Hystorie," 237; Smith, *Generall Historie*, 2: 116, 115. See also George Percy, "A Discourse of the Plantation of the Southern Colonie in Virginia, 1606–1607," in Peter C. Mancall, ed., *Envisioning America: English Plans for the Colonization of North America, 1580–1640* (New York, 1995), 126.

30. Oviedus, "Hystorie," 237; Hakluyt, *Principall Navigations*, 2: 539; Smith, *Generall Historyie*, 2: 183.

31. Hakluyt, *Principall Navigations*, 2: 539.

32. Smith, *Generall Historie*, 2: 114–128.

33. Martyr, "First Decade," 95; Smith, *Generall Historie*, 2: 121; Le Jeune, *Relation*, 6: 191.

34. Le Jeune, *Relation*, 6: 261–265.

35. Martyr, "First Decade," 101.

3. CORRUPTION

1. Richard P. Gildrie, *The Profane, the Civil, and the Godly: The Reformation of Manners in Orthodox New England, 1679–1749* (State College, Pa., 1994), distinguishes between manners, which he considers a secular form of gentility, and the sacred. In contrast, C. Dallett Hemphill, *Bowing to Necessities: A History of Manners in America, 1620–1860* (New York, 1999), 17–31, argues that the New England elite, including magistrates, ministers, and merchants, were well versed in Renaissance courtesy books. See also Anna Bryson, *From Courtesy to Civility: Changing Codes of Conduct in Early Modern England* (Oxford, 1994) 197, 214–215. For a nuanced view of the relationship between popular culture and the sacred, see Peter Lake, "Deeds against Nature: Cheap Print, Protestantism, and Murder in Early Seventeenth-Century England," in Kevin Sharpe and Peter Lake, eds., *Culture and Politics in Early Stuart England* (Stanford, Calif., 1993), 257–283.

2. For one example, see Mary Winthrop Dudley to Margaret Tyndal Winthrop, January 1635/1636, in Sharon M. Harris, ed., *American Women Writers to 1800* (New York, 1995), 236–237.

3. Richard Godbeer, *The Devil's Dominion: Magic and Religion in Early New England* (New York, 1992); Patricia Ann Watson, *The Angelical Conjunction: The Preacher-Physicians of Colonial New England* (Knoxville, Tenn., 1991). Philip Stubbes, *Anatomy of Abuses in England*, "A Perfect Pathway to Felicite," cited in Keith Thomas, "Cleanliness and Godliness in Early Modern England," in Anthony Fletcher and Peter Roberts, eds., *Religion, Culture, and Society in Early Modern Britain* (Cambridge, 1994), 63.

4. White cited in Andrew Wear, *Knowledge and Practice in English Medicine, 1550–1680* (Cambridge, 2000), 187. See also Kathleen Donegan, "'As Dying, Yet Behold We Live': Catastrophe and Interiority in Bradford's *Of Plymouth Plantation*," *Early American Literature* 37, no. 1 (2002): 9–37.

5. George Percy, "A Discourse of the Plantation of the Southern Colonie in Virginia," in Peter Mancall, ed., *Envisioning America: English Plans for the Colonization of North America, 1580–1640* (Boston, 1995), 125; Carville V. Earle, "Environment, Disease, and Mortality in Early Virginia," in Thad W. Tate and David L. Ammerman, eds., *The Chesapeake in the Seventeenth Century: Essays on Anglo-American Society and Politics* (Chapel Hill, 1979), 96–125.

6. John Smith, *The Proceedings of the English Colonie in Virginia*, in Philip Barbour, ed., *The Complete Works of John Smith*, (Chapel Hill, 1986), 1: 238–240.

7. "Articles, Lawes, and Orders, Divine, Politique, and Martiall for the Colony of Virginia," in Peter Force, ed. *Tracts and Other Papers, Relating Principally to the Origin, Settlement, and Progress of the Colonies in North America, from the Discovery of the Country to the Year 1776*, 4 vols. (Washington, D.C., 1836; rpt. Gloucester, Mass., 1963), 3: 9–19. Earle, "Environment, Disease, and Mortality."

8. "Articles, Lawes, and Orders," 3: 15.

9. "Articles, Lawes, and Orders," 3: 9–19.

10. Kathleen M. Brown, *Good Wives, Nasty Wenches, and Anxious Patriarchs: Gender, Race, and Power in Colonial Virginia* (Chapel Hill, 1996), 85.

11. Smith, *Proceedings*, 1: 245.

12. John Smith, *The Generall Historie of Virginia, New-England, and the Summer Isles . . .* , in Barbour, *Complete Works*, 2: 116. William Strachey, *The Historie of Travell into Virginia Britania*, ed., Louis B. Wright and Virginia Freund (London, 1953), 70. See also Percy's comment on Indian bathing in his "Discourse of the Plantation," 126. These bodily habits persisted until the end of the century. The Reverend John Clayton, a clergyman in the colony during the 1680s, observed that "young people during most of the winter goe into the river if they be near one, every morning, and wash themselves for a considerable time"; Clayton quoted in Stanley Pargellis, ed., "An Account of the Indians in Virginia," *WMQ* 3rd ser., 16 (April 1959): 234. John Smith, *A True Relation of Such Occurrences and Accidents of Noate as Hath Hapned in Virginia*, in Barbour, *Complete Works*, 1: 73. Smith described an Indian who "seemed to take pride in shewing how litle he regarded that miserable cold and durty passage, though a dogge would

scarce have indured it." Joyce Chaplin, *Subject Matter: Technology, the Body, and Science on the Anglo-American Frontier, 1500–1676* (Cambridge, Mass., 2001).

13. Strachey, *Historie of Travell*, 74. See also Theda Perdue, *Cherokee Women: Gender and Culture Change, 1700–1835* (Lincoln, Neb., 1998), 27–30, 32.

14. David R. Ransome, "Wives for Virginia, 1621," WMQ 3rd ser., 58 (January 1991): 3–18.

15. John White, *The Planter's Plea; or, the grounds of Plantations Examined, and usual objections answered* (London, 1630), 33.

16. John Hammond, *Leah and Rachel; or, The Two Fruitfull Sisters* (London, 1656), 10.

17. Thomas Glover, *An Account of Virginia, its scituation, temperature, productions, inhabitants and their manner of planting and ordering tobacco &c* (London, 1676; rpt. Oxford, 1904), 30–31.

18. Hammond, *Leah and Rachel*, 12.

19. Ibid., 18, 16.

20. Susie M. Ames, ed., *County Court Records of Accomack-Northampton, Virginia, 1632–1640* (Washington, D.C., 1954), 119. Susie M. Ames, ed., *County Court Records of Accomack-Northampton, Virginia, 1640–1645* (Charlottesville, Va., 1973), 169, for Dewin's suit against Jacob for seven months' worth of soap and washing.

21. See, for examples, Ames, *County Court Records, 1640–1645*, inventory of William Burdett, 419–423, inventory of John Severne, 423–425. See also Carole Shammas, *The Pre-Industrial Consumer in England and America* (Oxford, 1990).

22. Ames, *County Court Records, 1632–1640*, 2, 12, 103, 160, 199, 269; Ames, *County Court Records, 1640–1645*, 12. York Deeds, Orders, and Wills, 6, October 24, 1682, 435, York County Project, Colonial Williamsburg Foundation, Williamsburg, Virginia.

23. Ames, *County Court Records, 1640–1645*, 104, 292.

24. Brown, *Good Wives*, 187–211.

25. "A Narrative of the Indian Civil Wars in Virginia, in the Years 1675 and 1676," in Force, *Tracts and Other Papers*, 1: 46.

26. Richard Ligon, *A True and Exact history of the Island of Barbardos* (London, 1657), 28, 52. Indeed, many of the colony's enslaved laborers during the first half of the century hailed from the Caribbean rather than directly from West Africa, making it more likely that the body care witnessed by Ligon also took place on the North American mainland.

27. Minutes of the Council, June 2, 1699, Board of Trade of Virginia, 53, quoted in Philip Alexander Bruce, *Institutional History of Virginia in the Seventeenth Century*, 2 vols. (1910; rpt. Gloucester, Mass., 1964), 1: 9.

28. William Bradford, *Of Plymouth Plantation*, ed. Samuel Eliot Morison (New York, 1952), 26.

29. Peter Hulme, *Colonial Encounters: Europe and the Native Caribbean, 1492–1797* (New York, 1992).

30. Bradford, *Of Plymouth Plantation*, 77. See also Donegan, "'As Dying, Yet Behold We Live."

31. Bradford, *Of Plymouth Plantation*, 121.

32. Ibid. Margaret Pelling, *The Common Lot: Sickness, Medical Occupations, and the Urban Poor in Early Modern England* (New York, 1998), 192.

33. As soon as they divided the land into individual plots for families to grow corn, Bradford wrote, "the women now went willingly into the field, and took their little ones with them to set corn; which before would allege weakness and inability." See Bradford, *Of Plymouth Plantation*, 120. See also Mary Beth Norton, *Founding Mothers and Fathers: Gendered Power and the Forming of American Society* (New York, 1996), 7–8.

34. Bradford, *Of Plymouth Plantation*, 143–144.

35. Winslow quoted in Neal Salisbury, *Manitou and Providence: Indians, Europeans, and the Making of New England, 1500–1643* (New York, 1982), 118. Bradford noted the journey of Winslow and Hopkins as July 2, 1621, reporting that the men found "but short commons and came both weary and hungry home"; *Of Plymouth Plantation*, 87.

36. I am grateful to Dan Richter for the conversation that resulted in this insight.

37. James Axtell, *The Indian Peoples of Eastern America: A Documentary History of the Sexes* (New York, 1981), 6, 22, 50, 57. French chroniclers described Huron hygiene as follows: "When the child is swaddled on this board, which is usually decked out with little paintings and strings of wampum beads, they leave an opening in front of its private parts through which it makes water, and if the child is a girl they arrange a leaf of Indian corn upside down which serves to carry the water outside without the child being soiled with its water; and instead of napkins [diapers], for they have non, they put under it the beautifully soft down of a kind of reed [cattail fluff] on which it lies quite comfortably, and they clean it with the same down. At night they put it to bed quite naked between the father and the mother, without any accident happening, or very seldom." For Puritan practices, see Stephanie Wolf in *As Various as Their Land* (New York, 1993), 112; William Wood, *New England's Prospect*, ed. Alden T. Vaughan (Amherst, Mass., 1977), 114. See also Perdue, *Cherokee Women*, 30. For Puritan views on women, see Carol Karlsen, *The Devil in the Shape of a Woman: Witchcraft in Colonial New England* (New York, 1987); Elizabeth Reis, *Damned Women: Sinners and Witches in Puritan New England* (Ithaca, N.Y., 1997). See also Axtell, *Indian Peoples of Eastern America*, 22, for Adriaen Van der Donck's 1656 observation: "After their children are born, and if they are males, although the weather be ever so cold and freezing, they immerse them some time in the water, which, they say, makes them strong brave men and hardy hunters."

38. Bradford, *Of Plymouth Plantation*, 270–271.

39. Ibid., 205–206, 216.

40. John Josselyn, *New England's Rarities Discovered* (London, 1672), 99–101.

41. Karen Kupperman, *Indians and English: Facing Off in Early America* (Ithaca, N.Y., 2000) chapter 2, esp. 53–55, 71–74.

42. Wood, *New England's Prospect*, 84.

43. Morton cited in Kupperman, *Indians and English*, 52–53.

44. Bradford, *Of Plymouth Plantation*, 212, 217.

45. Donegan, "As Dying, Yet Behold We Live"; Winter quoted in *Trelawney Papers: Collections of Maine Historical Society*, 3: 166–168, rpt. in Ruth Barnes Moynihan, Cynthia Russett, Laurie Crumpacker, eds., *Second to None: A Documentary History of American Women* 2 vols. (Lincoln, Neb., 1993) 1: 66–67.

46. Bradford, *Of Plymouth Plantation*, 341, 316, 320.

47. Ibid., 316–317.

48. Ibid., 328.

49. Rowlandson has received much recent scholarly treatment. See Mitchell R. Breit-wieser, *American Puritanism and the Defense of Mourning: Religion, Grief, and Ethnology in Mary White Rowlandson's Captivity Narrative* (Madison, Wis., 1990), for the narrative as an exemplar of the Puritan culture of affliction; Lisa Logan, "Mary Rowlandson's Captivity and the 'Place' of the Woman Subject," *Early American Literature* 28 (Winter, 1993): 255–277, for Rowlandson's efforts to keep her narrative within the bounds of Puritan expectations for women; Theresa A. Toulouse, "'My Own Credit': Strategies of (E)valuation in Mary Rowlandson's Captivity Narrative," *American Literature* 64 (1992): 655–676, for her efforts to account her own worth using Puritan strategies that are undermined during her captivity; Ralph Bauer, "Creole Identities in Colonial Space: The Narratives of Mary White Rowlandson and Francisco Nuñez de Piñeda y Bascunçn," *American Literature* 69 (1997): 665–695, for the creole's desire to exorcise the influence of the Indian; Dawn Henwood, "Mary Rowlandson and the Psalms: The Textuality of Survival," *Early American Literature* 32 (Spring 1996): 169–186, for Rowlandson's use of the psalms to find a culturally sanctioned, devotional, voice for expressing anger and sustaining her identity during her captivity; Margaret H. Davis, "Mary White Rowlandson's Self-Fashioning as Puritan Goodwife," *Early American Literature* 27 (Spring 1992): 49–60, for Rowlandson's combination of submission and self-assertion within the Puritan "good wife" framework. See also Christopher Castiglia, *Bound and Determined: Captivity, Culture Crossing, and White Womanhood from Mary Rowlandson to Patty Hearst* (Chicago, 1996).

50. See Davis, "Mary White Rowlandson's Self-Fashioning," 56.

51. *A True History of the Captivity and Restoration of Mrs. Mary Rowlandson,* in Wendy Martin, ed., *Colonial American Travel Narratives* (New York, 1994), 41–42.

52. The Indian practice of stripping clothes from the bodies of dead Englishmen dated to at least the 1630s. See Ann Little, "'Shoot That Rogue, for He Hath an Englishman's Coat On!': Cultural Cross-Dressing on the New England Frontier, 1620–1760," *New England Quarterly* 47 (June 2001): 238–273.

53. *Captivity and Restoration,* 29, 32, 26, 35, 37, 39.

54. Ibid., 34, 39. See also Davis, "Mary White Rowlandson's Self-Fashioning," 55.

55. *Captivity and Restoration,* 22, 31.

56. Ibid., 34.

57. Cotton Mather, *Warnings from the Dead; or, Solemn Admonitions unto All People; but Especially unto Young Persons to Beware of such EVILS as would bring them to the Dead* (Boston, 1693). Worthington Chauncey Ford, ed., *Diary of Cotton Mather,* 2 vols. (New York, 1911), 1: 164–165. See also Lake, "Deeds against Nature."

58. Peter C. Hoffer and N. E. H. Hull, *Murdering Mothers: Infanticide in England and New England, 1558–1803* (New York, 1984), 20, 33–40; Cornelia Hughes Dayton, *Women before the Bar: Gender, Law, and Society in Connecticut, 1639–1789* (Chapel Hill, 1995), 207–215, esp. 210–211.

59. Samuel Danforth, *The Cry of Sodom Enquired Into; Upon Occasion of the Arraignment and Condemnation of Benjamin Goad, for his Prodigious Villany, together with A*

Solemn Exhortation to Tremble at Gods Judgements, and to Abandon Youthful Lusts (Cambridge, Mass., 1674); Daniel A. Cohen, *Pillars of Salt, Monuments of Grace: New England Crime Literature and the Origins of American Popular Culture, 1674–1800* (New York, 1993), 55. Lake, "Deeds against Nature."

60. Mikhail Bakhtin, *Rabelais and His World*, trans. Helene Iswolsky (Bloomington, Ind., 1984), 368–436; Peter Stallybrass and Allon White, *The Politics and Poetics of Transgression* (Ithaca, N.Y., 1986), 108–109, 144–145.

61. David D. Hall, *Worlds of Wonder, Days of Judgment: Popular Religious Belief in Early New England* (Cambridge, Mass., 1989), 168–197. Mather's familiarity with seventeenth-century medicine and connection to transatlantic scientific circles reminds us that scientific and providential views of the body continued to overlap, even as they had begun to diverge. See Michael P. Winship, *Seers of God: Puritan Providentialism in the Restoration and Early Enlightenment* (Baltimore, 1996). Kenneth Silverman, *The Life and Times of Cotton Mather* (New York, 1984), 357.

62. Mather, *Warnings from the Dead*, 40.

63. Mary Douglas, *Purity and Danger: An Analysis of the Concepts of Pollution and Taboo* (New York, 1966), 159–179.

64. Stallybrass and White, *Politics and Poetics*, 108–109; Mather, *Warnings from the Dead*, 40–45.

65. Gildrie, *Profane, Civil, and Godly*, 24–40, 74–75.

66. See Douglas, *Purity and Danger*, 130; Susan Sontag, *Illness as Metaphor* (New York, 1977), 71; Silverman, *The Life and Times of Cotton Mather* (New York, 1984), 55–137; and Hall, *Worlds of Wonder*, 181.

67. Laurel Thatcher Ulrich, *Good Wives: Image and Reality in the Lives of Women in Northern New England, 1650–1750* (New York, 1980), 198; *Vital Records of Haverhill, Massachusetts, to the end of the year 1849*, 2 vols. (Salem, Mass., 1993), 1: 113. See Suffolk County Court Records, file 2636, p. 93, for the reference to the first child "which was standing by."

68. Examination of Hannah, the wife of Michael Emerson, May 11, 1691, Suffolk County Court Records, file 2636.

69. Interrogation of Elizabeth Emerson, September 25, 1691, Suffolk County Court Records, file 2636.

70. Suffolk County Court Records, file #2636, May 10, 1691, p. 93.

71. Report of the Female examiners, May 11, 1691, Suffolk County Court Records, file 2636.

72. Suffolk County Court Records, file 2636, May 11, 1691.

73. Mather, *Warnings from the Dead*, 46–47, 66.

74. Ibid., 48, 52, 53, 59. Ford, *Diary of Cotton Mather*, 1: 357; I am grateful to Murray Murphey for calling this quotation to my attention.

75. Mather, *Warnings from the Dead*, 49, 50–51.

76. Ibid., 56–57, 58–59.

77. Ibid., 46–47, 66, 64, 73, 75–76.

78. Karlsen, *Devil in the Shape of a Woman*; Reis, *Damned Women*. Mather was not the only minister to seize this opportunity during the 1690s, nor was this his last chance to

preach on this subject. The executions of Sarah Threeneedles and Sarah Smith both afforded him similar opportunities. The Reverend John Williams of Deerfield also preached at the execution of Smith, quickly publishing his sermon *Warnings to the Unclean* (1698). In addition to the thousands of spectators who flocked to these two executions, the stories of Threeneedles's and Smith's unclean lives reached untold numbers of readers through Mather's *Pillars of salt*, where, along with the confession of Elizabeth Emerson, they demonstrated how uncleanness would bring early death and, ultimately, the demise of the Puritan community. See John Williams, *Warnings to the Unclean: In a Discourse from Rev.XXI.8* (Boston, 1698); Cotton Mather, *Pillars of salt: An history of some criminals executed in this land, for capital crimes . . .* (Boston, 1699), 99–102; Edwin Powers, *Crime and Punishment in Early Massachusetts, 1620–1692: A Documentary History* (Boston, 1966), 287–294. I am indebted to Thomas Doughton for information about the large crowd that attended the Threeneedles's execution.

79. Ulrich, *Good Wives*, 126; Douglas, *Purity and Danger*, 35, 40; William K. Boyd, ed., *William Byrd's Histories of the Dividing Line Betwixt Virginia and North Carolina* (New York, 1967), 317. I am indebted to Thomas Doughton for reminding me of the "linen defense"; on this point, see Hoffer and Hull, *Murdering Mothers*, 68–69.

80. Doriece Colle, *Collars . . . Stocks . . . Cravats: A History and Costume Dating Guide to Civilian Men's Neckpieces, 1655–1900* (Emmaus, Pa., 1972), 11–17.

81. Michel Foucault, *The History of Sexuality*, vol. 3, *The Care of the Self*, trans. Robert Hurley (New York, 1986); Norbert Elias, *The Civilizing Process: The History of Manners and State Formation and Civilization*, trans. Edmund Jephcott (Cambridge, Mass., 1994); Bakhtin, *Rabelais and His World*. See also Winship, *Seers of God*, 94–95.

82. The "linen defense," noted in a 1673 English case by Hoffer and Hull, seems not to have applied here; Hoffer and Hull, *Murdering Mothers*, 68–69.

83. James Deetz and Patricia Scott Deetz, *Times of Their Lives: Life, Love, and Death in Plymouth Colony* (New York, 2000), 168–170.

84. Mather's experience of family tragedy just before the Emerson execution further illuminates his relation to providentialism, uncleanness, and guilt over his role at Salem. Just two months before Mather delivered the sermon, young Increase Mather, named for Mather's illustrious father, was born without a rectum; he died a slow, agonizing death. This tragedy, like Emerson's crime, incorporated infant death and bodily corruption, but Mather appears to have fixed upon only one possible interpretation of the workings of Providence, at least in the pages of his diary. Mather attributed the deformity to a fright his wife Abigail had experienced during pregnancy over a threat made by a witch. But as his sermon suggests, he might easily have interpreted his son's death as a divine punishment for the sins of a father who had played such an important role in the witchcraft persecutions that wracked the colony. See Ford, *Diary of Cotton Mather*, 1: 162.

85. Thomas Tryon, *A treatise of cleanness in meats and drinks of the preparation of food, the excellency of good airs and the benefits of clean sweet beds; also of the generation of bugs and their cure* (London, 1682), 13, 15; Susan Amussen, *Caribbean Exchanges: Slavery and the Transformation of English Society, 1640–1700* (Chapel Hill, 2007), 181–184.

86. Thomas Tryon, *The Good housewife made a doctor, or, Health's choice and sure friend* (London, 1685).

87. Thomas Tryon, *Some memoirs of the life of Mr. Tho. Tryon, late of London, merchant, written by himself; together with some rules and order, proper to be observed by all such as would train up and govern either familes or societies in cleanness, temperance, and innocency* (London, 1705), 29–30, cited in Virginia Smith, "Cleanliness: The Development of Idea and Practice in Britain, 1770–1850," Ph.D. diss., University of London, 1985, 69.

88. Tryon, *Cleanness in meats and drinks*, 11.

89. Tryon, *Memoirs*, 40–41, cited in Smith, "Cleanliness," 89.

90. John Floyer, *Enquiry into the right use and abuses of the Hot, Cold, and Temperate* BATHS *in England* (London, 1697), 3, 87.

91. "Preface," ibid.

92. Smith, "Cleanliness," 93.

93. Ulrich, *Good Wives*, 196; Cohen, *Pillars of Salt*, 117; Hoffer and Hull, *Murdering Mothers*, 47–48; Dayton, *Women before the Bar*, 207–215. In *Elizabeth in her Holy Retirement* (1710), Mather argued that these two qualities were linked, with the dangers and pain of childbirth motivating women's superior piety.

PART II. GENTEEL BODIES

1. Stephen Peabody diary, MHS photostat, June 8–18, 1767. For a wash to get rid of the itch advertised by Mr. Hind, goldsmith, see *Boston Gazette*, no. 491, April 21, 1729.

2. Peabody's efforts to get a coat made resulted in a comedy of errors. The tailor attempted to piece the cloth to make it fit, but in transporting it from the cutting to the sewing, Peabody dropped the smaller pieces in the street. He found them unexpectedly, although the seamstress assured him she could make the coat even without the facing. See Peabody diary, November 18–27, 1767. For other examples of men's concerns about their appearances, see Louis P. Masur, ed., *The Autobiography of Benjamin Franklin, with Related Documents* (Boston, 2003), 49; *The Itinerarium of Dr. Alexander Hamilton*, in Wendy Martin, ed., *Colonial Travel Narratives* (New York, 1994), 276; John C. Fitzpatrick, ed., *The Writings of George Washington from the Original Manuscript Sources*, 37 vols. (Washington, D.C., 1931–1944) 1: 5.

3. Peabody diary, June 16, July 9–11, 27, August 1, 29, December 1, 1767; January 5, February 27, March 12, April 12, October 22, 27, 31, November 2, 4, 11, 20, 21, 23–26, 30, December 31, 1768. See also Edward Miles Riley, ed., *The Journal of John Harrower: An Indentured Servant in the Colony of Virginia, 1773–1776* (Colonial Williamsburg, 1963), 156; Lois K. Stabler, ed., *Very Poor and of a Lo Make: The Journal of Abner Sanger* (Portsmouth, N.H., 1986), 19, 24, 71; Laurel Thatcher Ulrich, *Good Wives: Image and Reality in the Lives of Women in Northern New England, 1650–1750* (New York, 1980), 80–81; Fitzpatrick, *Writings of George Washington*, 1: 31–32, 94, 173, 395.

4. Carl Bridenbaugh, "Baths and Watering Places of Colonial America," *WMQ* 3rd ser., 3 (April 1946): 151–181.

4. EMPIRE'S NEW CLOTHES

1. Jan de Vries, "Between Purchasing Power and the World of Goods: Understanding the Household Economy in Early Modern Europe," in John Brewer and Roy Porter, eds. *Consumption and the World of Goods* (New York, 1993), 85–132, and Lorna Weatherill, "The Meaning of Consumer Behaviour in Late Seventeenth- and Early Eighteenth-Century England," ibid., 206–227, have helped me to think about the importance of the household in larger patterns of trade and consumption.

2. Owen Ruffhead, *The Statutes at large, from Magna Charta, to the end of the last Parliament, 1761* [continued to 1800], 18 vols. (London, 1768), William, 1696, chap. 39, p. 637; Anne, 1704, chap. 8, p. 179.

3. N. B. Harte, "Protection and the English Linen Trade," in N. B. Harte and K. G. Ponting, eds. *Textile History and Economic History* (Manchester, 1973), 92.

4. Beverly Lemire, *Dress, Culture, and Commerce: The English Clothing Trade before the Factory, 1660–1800* (New York, 1997), 32; Eric Kerridge, *Textile Manufactures in Early Modern England* (Manchester, 1985), 24.

5. Kerridge, *Textile Manufactures*, 219, 220.

6. Ibid., 225, 240.

7. Parliament passed legislation to stop the export of wool, woolfells, woolen yarn, and fuller's earth from leaving the British Isles to protect overseas markets for woolen cloth finished in England. French efforts to exclude British textiles led to a wool export prohibition in 1662 that was seriously enforced. See ibid., 151–152, 23.

8. Brenda Collins and Philip Ollerenshaw, eds., *The European Linen Industry in Historical Perspective* (Oxford, 2003), 15; Kerridge, *Textile Manufactures*, 122.

9. Ruffhead, *Statutes at large*, William, chap. 39, p. 637.

10. Collins and Ollerenshaw, *European Linen Industry*, 8, 15; Harte, "Protection," in 78, 80, 101. The duties, which had been established as rates in 1660 and were not revised to account for changes in the quality of foreign products, disadvantaged coarse-linen producers: the duty was disproportionate on cheaper fabrics than on more expensive cloth. This inequity gave a comparative advantage to German producers, who were making new types of finer linen but remained subject to the same rate, while disadvantaging French, Dutch, and Flemish producers, whose products had become coarser.

11. Harte, "Protection," 97–98.

12. W. H. Crawford, *The Impact of the Domestic Linen Industry in Ulster* (Ulster, 2005), 22; Kerridge, *Textile Manufactures*, 122–123; Harte, "Protection," 94.

13. Collins and Ollerenshaw, *European Linen Industry*, 9; Harte, "Protection," 107, 108.

14. Collins and Ollerenshaw, *European Linen Industry*, 16; Kerridge, *Textile Manufactures*, 125; Harte, "Protection," 111–112.

15. Collins and Ollerenshaw, *European Linen Industry*, 16; Kerridge, *Textile Manufactures*, 8; Lemire, *Dress, Culture, and Commerce*, 11, 40; Linda Colley, *Britons: Forging the Nation, 1707–1837* (New Haven, 1992), 68, 70.

16. Lemire, *Dress, Culture, and Commerce*, 10–22. Ibid., 10, for Lemire's citation of Daniel Roche on the similar impact of the French military on the French clothing trades.

17. Ibid., 21.

18. Ibid., 38; Margaret Pelling, *The Common Lot: Sickness, Medical Occupations, and the Urban Poor in Early Modern England* (New York, 1998).

19. Colley, *Britons*, 69.

20. BG, no. 461, September 23, 1728; BG, no. 19, April 25, 1720.

21. BG, no. 67, April 19, 1754. The proliferation of imported cloth is striking. See, for comparison, the relatively short list of fabrics in advertisements earlier in the century BG, no. 385, April 17, 1727; BG, no. 461, September 23, 1728; and the enormous advertisements by the 1750s and 1760s, for example, BG, no. 64, March 19, 1754. Cloth imports also increased in variety in southern colonies; see VG, no. 41, October 11, 1751. See also Priscilla Holyoke's diary, AAS, 1766; *New York Gazette*, February 23, 1747, for imported pewter plates, spoons, and teapots; March 16, 1747; May 2, 1768; *The Itinerarium of Dr. Alexander Hamilton*, in Wendy Martin, ed., *Colonial American Travel Narratives* (New York, 1994), 197. T. H. Breen, *The Marketplace of Revolution: How Consumer Politics Shaped American Independence* (New York, 2004), 62–63.

22. Karin Calvert, "The Function of Fashion in Eighteenth-Century America," in Cary Carson, Ronald Hoffman, and Peter J. Albert, eds., *Of Consuming Interests: The Style of Life in the Eighteenth Century* (Charlottesville, Va., 1994), 252–283, esp. 261.

23. Ann Little, "'Shoot That Rogue, for He Has an Englishman's Coat On!': Cultural Cross-Dressing on the New England Frontier, 1620–1760," *New England Quarterly* 47 (June 2001): 238–273; Richard L. Bushman, *The Refinement of America: Persons, Houses, Cities* (New York, 1992), 70.

24. Lemire, *Dress, Culture, and Commerce*, 36–37.

25. R. DuPlessis, "Transatlantic Textiles: European Linens in the Cloth Culture of Colonial North America," in Collins and Ollerenshaw, *European Linen Industry*, 123–137.

26. Ibid., 129.

27. Ibid., 130–131; Adrian Hood, "Flax Seed, Fibre and Cloth: Pennsylvania's Domestic Linen Manufacture and Its Irish Connection, 1700–1830," in Collins and Ollerenshaw, *European Linen Industry*, 139–158, esp. 141.

28. Leach tub and linen wheel, Inventory of Francis Bloodgood, May 20, 1746, manor of Phillipsburg, box 16, 74x370; weaving paraphernalia, Ezra Man, June 23, 1760, Wrentham, Mass., 79x121; cotton wool, cards, linen yarn, and three wheels, Estate of William Wood, January 4, 1696, Dartmouth, Mass., all in Inventories and Vendues, Joseph Downs Collection, WL.

29. Gregory A. Stiverson and Patrick H. Butler II, eds., "Virginia in 1732: The Travel Journal of William Hugh Grove," *Virginia Magazine of History and Biography* 85 (1977): 32; Edward Miles Riley, ed., *The Journal of John Harrower: An Indentured Servant in the Colony of Virginia, 1773–1776* (Colonial Williamsburg, 1963), 121; Joseph Ball letterbook, letter to Joseph Chinn, February 14, 1742, Colonial Williamsburg Library. Pringle cited in Breen, *Marketplace of Revolution*, 125.

30. John McCusker and Russell Menard, *The Economy of British North America*, (Chapel Hill, 1991), 284. Canada was a similarly big consumer of French woolens and linens.

31. Carole Shammas, "Changes in English and Anglo-American Consumption from 1550 to 1800," in Brewer and Porter, *Consumption*, 192–193; Bushman, *Refinement of America*, 71–72.

32. Gilman cited in Laurel Thatcher Ulrich, *Good Wives: Image and Reality in the Lives of Women in Northern New England, 1650–1750* (New York, 1980), 80 [original letters from Gilman in Mrs. Charles P. Noyes, *A Family History in Letters and Documents* (St. Paul, Minn., 1919), 55–65].

33. Robert Wallace Johnson, *Some Friendly Cautions to the heads of families: containing ample directions to nurses who attend the sick, and women in child-bed &c By a Physician* (London, 1767), 22. The Philadelphia edition of this text is a smaller size, prefaced by three chapters on persons, dress, and diet.

34. Contents of trunks belonging to Joseph Read Jr., July 20, 1778, box 11, 57x4.1, WL. Jane Nylander, *Our Own Snug Fireside: Images of the New England Home, 1760–1860* (New York, 1993), 132–133. Even servants customarily received "washing," as well as apparel, although if they were female, they were themselves likely to provide some of the labor needed to do laundry; see also Chester County Archives and Records, March 5, 1726/7, 11–19. I am indebted to Nicole Eustace for this citation.

35. Daniel Defoe, *The Complete English Tradesman* (Oxford, 1841), 2: 232, cited in Keith Thomas, "Cleanliness and Godliness in Early Modern England," in Anthony Fletcher and Peter Roberts, eds., *Religion, Culture, and Society in Early Modern Britain* (Cambridge, 1994), 71. See also C. Willett Cunnington and Phillis Cunnington, *The History of Underclothes* (London, 1951), 102; William K. Boyd, ed., *William Byrd's Histories of the Dividing Line Betwixt Virginia and North Carolina* (New York, 1967), 194. Byrd also learned a trick for sleeping outside in the cold: "Till this Night, I had always lain in my Night Gown, but upon Tryal, I found it much warmer to strip to my shirt, & lie in naked Bed with my gown over me. The Woodsmen put all off, if they have no more than one Blanket to lye in, & agree that 'tis much more comfortable than to lye with their Cloaths on, tho' the Weather be never so cold." Ibid., 231. Gilman cited in Ulrich, *Good Wives*, 80. Lois K. Stabler, ed., *Very Poor and of a Lo Make: The Journal of Abner Sanger* (Portsmouth, N.H., 1986), 7.

36. Boyd, *Byrd's Histories*, 217–219.

37. Clifford K. Shipton, *Sibley's Harvard Graduates: Biographical Sketches of Those Who Attended Harvard College in the Classes of 1701–1712* (Boston, 1937), 5: 379. See also Benjamin Franklin's advertisement for the sermons of Reverend Ebenezer Erskine, "God's little Remnant keeping their Garments clean in an evil day," in *PG*, July 18, 1745; *Itinerarium*, 206. The tutor John Harrower described a corpse buried in Virginia "being drest in a Calico Goun and white apron," with a sheet wrapped around it, then placed in a black walnut Coffin lined with flannel; Riley, *Journal of John Harrower*, 87.

38. Gilman, cited in Ulrich, *Good Wives*, 80; Boyd, *Byrd's Histories*, 231.

39. *PG*, July 6, 1758; *PG*, February 13, 1766. For other examples, see *BG*, no. 622, September 27, 1731, ad for Castile soap; *BN*, no. 3094, April 7, 1763; *VG*, no. 41, October 11, 1751, ad for Castile soap and other specialty items, including Lisbon lemons, ginger, capers, coffee, and chocolate.

40. *PG*, April 23, 1747; *BN*, no. 3096, April 21, 1763; *BG*, no. 523, Dec. 1, 1729.

41. Elizabeth Smith, *The Compleat Housewife* (Williamsburg, 1742), 172, 228, 214, bound with *Every Man his Own Doctor*, AAS.

42. Elizabeth Coates Paschall receipt book, College of Physicians, Philadelphia, 24. Ingre-

dients for medicines and cosmetics sometimes included substances that would otherwise be accounted foul, like excrement. Paschall thus listed a turd as a key ingredient in
one of her recipes.

43. "Washing Week," *Norwich Packet,* July 6, 1778; "Washing Week," *Sentinel of Freedom,*
Newark, N.J., April 29, 1800. Thanks to Russell Martin for these citations.

44. Anne White Diary, MHS, 1783; Boyd, *Byrd's Histories,* 77; Ulrich, *Good Wives,* 28.

45. Stabler, *Very Poor and of a Lo Make,* 71, entry for November 16, 1775; William B.
Lapham, ed., *Elijah Fisher's Journal while in the War for Independence and Continued
Two Years after he Came to Maine 1775–1784* (Augusta, Maine, 1880), 19. Mercy Seccomb recorded laundering, quilting, and washing "our little Chamber floor," July 21,
1770, Seccomb Family Diaries, 1753–1770, AAS typescript carbon.

46. Riley, *Journal of John Harrower,* 56, 57.

47. Evangeline Walker Andrews, ed., in collaboration with Charles McLean Andrews,
*Journal of a Lady of Quality; Being the Narrative of Journey from Scotland to the West In-
dies, North Carolina, and Portugal, in the years 1774 to 1776* (New Haven, 1921), 204.
Schaw also noted that North Carolina housewives did not put clothes through a "cal-
endar," a machine with rollers that smoothed and pressed the cloth as it removed water.

48. George Morgan diary, HSP, 100, 125, quotation on 207.

49. K. G. Davies, *The Royal African Company* (New York, 1960), 174–179; Eric Williams,
Capitalism and Slavery (Chapel Hill, 1994), 65–71; Timothy Burke, *Lifebuoy Men, Lux
Women: Commodification, Consumption, and Cleanliness in Modern Zimbabwe* (Durham, N.C., 1996), notes that instruction on how to wash fine linens was part of the
twentieth-century colonial curriculum.

50. Andrews, *Journal of a Lady,* 108. Schaw interpreted this scene with an imperial eye, noting that it reminded her of Indian faithful going to make a sacrifice to their gods.

51. De Vries, "Between Purchasing Power and the World of Goods"; Breen, *Marketplace of
Revolution.*

5. GENTILITY

1. *The Itinerarium of Dr. Alexander Hamilton,* in Wendy Martin, ed., *Colonial American
Travel Narratives* (New York, 1994), 181; George Cheyne, *An Essay of Health and Long
Life* (London, 1724).

2. Steven C. Bullock, *Revolutionary Brotherhood: Freemasonry and the Transformation of
the American Social Order, 1730–1840* (Chapel Hill, 1996); Dena Goodman, *The Republic of Letters: A Cultural History of the French Enlightenment* (Ithaca, N.Y., 1994);
David S. Shields, *Civil Tongues and Polite Letters in British America* (Chapel Hill,
1997); Cary Carson, Ronald Hoffman, and Peter J. Albert, eds., *Of Consuming Interests:
The Style of Life in the Eighteenth Century* (Charlottesville, Va., 1994); Woodruff D.
Smith, *Consumption and the Making of Respectability, 1600–1800* (New York, 2002).

3. Carson, Hoffman, and Albert, *Of Consuming Interests;* T. H. Breen, *The Marketplace of
Revolution: How Consumer Politics Shaped American Independence* (New York, 2004),
xvii.

4. For a discussion of Norbert Elias, *The Civilizing Process*, Anna Bryson, *From Courtesy to Civility*, Richard Bushman, *Refinement of America*, and C. Dallett Hemphill, *Bowing to Necessities*, see the Bibliographic Essay.

5. Lord Chesterfield, *Letters*, ed. David Roberts (New York, 1992), 18–19, 73, 128, 155, 158, 169, 200, 232. See also Lord Chesterfield to his son, Letter 123, November 12 o.s., 1750, at www.gutenberg.org/files/3354/3354.txt; Keith Thomas, "Cleanliness and Godliness," in Anthony Fletcher and Peter Roberts, eds., *Religion, Culture, and Society in Early Modern Britain* (Cambridge, 1994), 69.

6. C. Dallett Hemphill, *Bowing to Necessities: A History of Manners in America, 1620–1860* (New York, 1999), 72–73; Thomas, "Cleanliness and Godliness," 71–72.

7. James C. Riley, *The Eighteenth-Century Campaign to Avoid Disease* (New York, 1987), argues that European doctors embraced Hippocratic approaches to disease that encouraged environmental intervention. See also Andrew Wear, *Knowledge and Practice in English Medicine, 1550–1680* (Cambridge, 2000), for mid-seventeenth-century efforts to slow the spread of the plague in London that anticipated the trends described by Riley; Helen Brock, "North America, a Western Outpost of European Medicine," in Andrew Cunningham and Roger French, eds., *The Medical Enlightenment of the Eighteenth Century* (New York, 1990), 195–216.

8. Clifford K. Shipton, *Sibley's Harvard Graduates: Biographical Sketches of Those Who Attended Harvard College in the Classes of 1701–1712* (Boston, 1937), 5: 379. Thanks to Tom Knowles for this citation.

9. *PG*, September 4, 1729. In the satirical *Androboros*, a pamphlet that lampooned affectation in Governor Edmund Andros's New York, the characters debate the best term for the excrement that soils clerical robes in Trinity Church. They decide to call it "turdure," a combination of *turd* and *ordure*, before one declares "A T--- is a T--- all the world Over"; cited in Patricia Bonomi, *The Lord Cornbury Scandal: The Politics of Reputation in British America* (Chapel Hill, 1998), 125.

10. Cited in Bonomi, *The Lord Cornbury Scandal*, 122.

11. Thomas A. Foster, "Antimasonic Satire, Sodomy and Eighteenth-Century Masculinity in *The Boston Evening Post*," *WMQ* 3rd ser., 60 (January 2003): 171–184.

12. Mary Fissell, "Making a Masterpiece: The Aristotle Texts in Vernacular Medical Culture," in Charles Rosenberg, ed., *Right Living: An Anglo-American Tradition of Self-Help Medicine and Hygiene* (Baltimore, 2003); Otho Beal, "*Aristotle's Masterpiece* in America: A Landmark in the Folklore of Medicine," *WMQ* 3rd ser., 20 (April 1963): 207–222.

13. *PG*, March 3, 1742; *PG*, May 28, 1747. For other examples, see *BN*, no. 3090, March 10, 1763, in which the author refers to a detraction as throwing dirt, "which, contrary to their expectations, is often fuller's earth, and rather cleans than defiles." Fuller's earth was a common ingredient in spot and stain removers: see Judith Bedingfield's recipe and account book, manuscript, 1730–1744, Van Pelt Rare Books, University of Pennsylvania.

14. Jonathan Belcher, "A Journal of My intended Voyage & Journey to Holland, Hannover, &c. Beginning at London Saturday July 8th O.S. 1704," Belcher Papers, Massachusetts

Historical Society, 14, 16, 39, 54, 101, 106. My thanks to Steven Bullock for this citation. Simon Schama, *The Embarrassment of Riches: An Interpretation of Dutch Culture in the Golden Age* (New York, 1987).

15. See, for example, the advertisement in the *BG*, no. 7261, May 13, 1746, for a house "situate in a clean street, a sociable and polite neighborhood, and near a decent Church." Louis P. Masur, ed., *The Autobiography of Benjamin Franklin, with Related Documents* (Boston, 2003), 90.

16. *BN*, no. 4, May 15, 1704. See Riley, *Campaign to Avoid Disease*, for the efforts of city councils on both sides of the Atlantic to make cities healthier through a combination of drainage, lavation, and ventilation.

17. *PG*, August 30, 1739; *PG*, July 12, 1750.

18. *New York Weekly Post Boy*, reprinted in *PG*, January 11, 1744, February 2, 1744, March 15, 1744. See also *Itinerarium*, 241. See Esther Singleton, *Social New York under the Georges* (New York, 1902), 13; *New York Gazette or Weekly Post-Boy*, March 2, 1746/1747.

19. *Itinerarium*, 321; Masur, *Autobiography of Benjamin Franklin*, 122, 123; *PG*, July 12, 1750; "City of Philadelphia," March 1765, Early American Imprints, Evans 10132; and *PG*, April 24, 1766; *PG*, June 6, 1771. Once in London, Franklin wrote a proposal addressed to Dr. John Fothergill for employing poor people to sweep and cart dirt from that city's perennially muddy streets; *Autobiography*, 124.

20. *Itinerarium*, 197; "City of Philadelphia," March 1765. See *PG*, June 6, 1771; *PG*, August 27, 1783. Elaine Forman Crane, ed., *The Diary of Elizabeth Drinker* (Boston, 1991) 1: 44. See also Benjamin Rush to his wife on the muddy conditions of the streets, which kept the ladies inside, Baltimore, January 24, 1777, in L. H. Butterfield, ed., *Letters of Benjamin Rush*, 2 vols. (Philadelphia, 1951), 1: 130. For similar concerns, see *New York Weekly Post Boy*, reprinted in *PG*, January 11, 1744, February 2, 1744, March 15, 1744.

21. "A Naval Officer's View of the Metropolis," in H. Roy Merrens, ed., *The Colonial South Carolina Scene: Contemporary Views, 1697–1774* (Columbia, S.C., 1977), 230–231.

22. "A Discourse of Pestilential Contagion and Methods to Prevent It," *BN*, July 10, 1721. Mead published "A Short Discourse Concerning Pestilent Contagion and the Methods to be used to Prevent it" on November 29, 1720. See also Riley, *Campaign to Avoid Disease*; Thomas Thacher, *A Brief Rule to Guide the Common People of New England How to Order Themselves and Theirs in the Small Pocks or Measels*, 3rd ed. facsimile reprint (1722; Baltimore, 1937). Thacher's pamphlet appeared in three editions from 1678 to 1722.

23. *BN*, July 10, 1721.

24. Ibid.

25. Ibid.

26. Genevieve Miller, "Smallpox Inoculation in England and America: A Reappraisal," *WMQ*, 3rd ser., 13 (October, 1956): 476–492; Maxine de Wetering, "A Reconsideration of the Inoculation Controversy," *New England Quarterly* 58 (1985): 46–67; John B. Blake, "The Inoculation Controversy," *New England Quarterly* 25 (December 1952): 489–506; *BN*, July 10, 1721.

27. *BN*, July 10, 1721. The last two quotations in the paragraph come from a second installment of Mead's suggestions in *BN*, July 17, 1721. In it, Mead argued that shutting up

houses of the diseased was ineffective, breeding contagion that would inevitably fly out once the house was opened, no matter how long it remained shut: "The Poison will fly out, whenever the Pandora's Box is opened." He declared that "nothing approaches so near to the first Original of Contagion as Air pent up, loaded with Damps, and corrupted with the Filthiness, that proceeds from Animal Bodies."

28. Blake, "Inoculation Controversy," 491. Ralph Emmett Fall, *The Diary of Robert Rose: A View of Virginia by a Scottish Colonial Parson, 1746–1751* (Verona, Va., 1977), 45: entry for November 28, 1748.

29. *BN*, August 14, 1721. John B. Blake, *Public Health in the Town of Boston, 1630–1822* (Cambridge, Mass., 1959).

30. Alfred R. Hoermann, *Cadwallader Colden: A Figure of the American Enlightenment* (Westport, Conn., 2002), 40–49; Brock, "North America."

31. *Report of the Record Commissioners of the City of Boston containing the Selectman's Minutes from 1764 through 1768* (Boston, 1889), book 12a, p. 3; June 6, 1764, p. 76. See also Elizabeth A. Fenn, *Pox Americana: The Great Smallpox Epidemic of 1775–82* (New York, 2001), 88–89.

32. Pelatiah Webster, "Journal of a Voiage from Philadelphia to Charlestown in So. Carolina, begun May 15, 1765," in Merrens, *Colonial South Carolina Scene*, 224.

33. Cheyne, *Health and Long Life*, 84, 102, 104, 198; Robert Wallace Johnson, *Some Friendly Cautions to the heads of families: containing ample directions to nurses who attend the sick, and women in child-bed &c By a Physician* (London, 1767), quotations on 20, 31.

34. Johnson, *Friendly Cautions*, 17–18. See also Benjamin Grosvenor's *Health: An essay on its nature, value, uncertainty, preservation, and best improvement*, 3rd ed. (Boston, 1761), by an English minister of an Independent congregation who made health a question of national vigor, vitality, and prosperity.

35. Charles E. Rosenberg, "Medical Text and Social Context," in *Explaining Epidemics and Other Studies in the History of Medicine* (New York, 1992). Buchan's *Domestic Medicine* was first printed in the colonies in 1772, and regularly reissued thereafter. All citations of Buchan are to *Domestic Medicine* (London, 1784). The 1772 and 1784 editions of the manual contain identical material on cleanliness. For imported editions of Buchan, see *New York Daily Advertiser*, March 16, 1785. Buchan, *Domestic Medicine*, 95, 96, 97–98, 99. See also Mark Jenner, "The Concept of 'Cleanliness' and 'Dirt' in Early Modern England," Ph.D. diss., Oxford University, 1991, chapter 2.

36. Riley, *Campaign to Avoid Disease*, 111. See, for example, John Armstrong cited in Virginia Smith, "Cleanliness: The Development of Idea and Practice in Britain, 1770–1850," Ph.D. diss., University of London, 1985, 130.

37. Elizabeth Smith, *The Compleat Housewife* (Williamsburg, 1742), bound with *Every Man his Own Doctor*, AAS; Kevin J. Hayes, *A Colonial Woman's Bookshelf* (Knoxville, Tenn., 1996), 12, 83.

38. Nathaniel Bailey, *Dictionarium Domesticum* (London, 1736). Often, unless there is a geographic identifier or recipes are attributed to lords and ladies, it is difficult to tell from the content of a receipt book which side of the Atlantic it is from. See Codex 388, 1699–1703, anonymous manuscript, Van Pelt Library, University of Pennsylvania. See

also receipt book of E. Warren, 1743, document 120, Cookbooks and Receipt Books, Joseph Downs Collection, WL. Hannah Huthwaite receipt book, Document 193, Cookbooks and Receipt Books, Joseph Downs Collection, WL. See also Judith Bedingfield's recipe and account book, manuscript, 1730–1744, Van Pelt Library Rare Books, University of Pennsylvania.

39. Smith, *Compleat Housewife*, recipe for "The Italian Wash for the Neck," 215; Ingredients, including powder of pearl and white sugar candy, broadcast its whitening properties, ibid., 214; *VG*, December 1760, cited in Julia Cherry Spruill, *Women's Life and Work in the Southern Colonies* (New York, 1938), 283. The intrepid Scottish traveler Janet Schaw noted that creole Anglo-Antiguan women carefully covered their heads and faces to maintain their pallor; see Evangeline Walker Andrews, ed., in collaboration with Charles McLean Andrews, *Journal of a Lady of Quality; Being the Narrative of a Journey from Scotland to the West Indies, North Carolina, and Portugal, in the years 1774 to 1776* (New Haven, 1921), 113.

40. *PG*, March 4, 1755; Elizabeth Coates Paschall receipt book, College of Physicians, Philadelphia, 34; Nicholas Culpeper, *The English Physician*, (rpt. Boston, 1708), 70.

41. Porcelain lavabo bowl, object id. 19660768, dated to 1700–1730, imported, Winterthur; porcelain/brass lavabo/wall cistern, 1700–1730, object id. 19660769AB. See also Winterthur inventory from Lansdown, Pa., which includes several washstands, 55.113, no date, although the evaluation in sterling suggests it is colonial. Masur, *Autobiography of Benjamin Franklin*, 94; Andrews, *Journal of a Lady*, 97; Richard L. Bushman and Claudia L. Bushman, "The Early History of Cleanliness in America," *Journal of American History* 74 (March 1988): 1213–1238.

42. Tobias Smollett, *An Essay on the External Use of Water*, ed. Claude E. Jones (1752; Baltimore, 1935); Thomas, "Cleanliness and Godliness," 75–76. Masur, *Autobiography of Benjamin Franklin*, 33. Laurel Thatcher Ulrich, *Good Wives: Image and Reality in the Lives of Women in Northern New England, 1650–1750* (New York, 1980), 95, notes that a group of male servants were forced to put their shirts on in the water for modesty's sake because a married woman stood at the edge of the pond watching them. See also Stephen Peabody diary, MHS photostat, June 4, July 10, 1767; Andrews, *Journal of a Lady*, 69, 111; John R. Betts, "Mind and Body in Early American Thought," *Journal of American History* 54 (March 1968): 787–805.

43. John Smith, *The Curiosities of Common Water; or, The Advantages thereof in Preventing and Curing many Distempers. Gather'd from the Writings of several Eminent Physicians, and also from more than Forty Years Experience*, 4th ed. (London, 1723). Smith's work was first published in North America in 1725 and reprinted for more than 170 years. Cheyne also advocated cold-water bathing in *Health and Long Life*, 100–103.

44. William K. Boyd, ed., *William Byrd's Histories of the Dividing Line Betwixt Virginia and North Carolina* (New York, 1967), 143.

45. Warm-water bathing was a different story. One diarist, a Delaware cabinetmaker who strained his back, described his remedy: "I get my back Bath'd before the fire as worm as I can bare it." Diary of a Newcastle County, Delaware, cabinetmaker, 1785–1786, Joseph Downs Collection, Winterthur Archives, October 18, 1785.

46. *BN*, June 19, 1721: the obituary noted that Halkerston had been a master surgeon in the

Royal Navy and had practiced medicine for the previous six years in Boston. *BG*, no. 294, July 19, 1725, news from Philadelphia; Boyd, *Byrd's Histories*, 217. Virginia Smith, *Clean: A History of Personal Hygiene and Purity* (New York, 2007), 219, notes the publication of William Pearcy's *Compleat Swimmer; or, The Arte of Swimming* (London, 1658).

47. Smith, *Curiosities of Common Water*; Masur, *Autobiography of Benjamin Franklin*, 47, 61. Crane, *Diary of Elizabeth Drinker*, 1: 220.

48. Crane, *Diary of Elizabeth Drinker*, 1: 160–164.

49. Brock, "North America," 210–211; *PG*, April 27, 1769; see also Sorge's ad, *PG*, March 4, 1755; "Greenough's Tincture for the Teeth," *Connecticut Journal and New Haven Post Boy*, June 4, 1773. Smith, *Compleat Housewife*, 214, but see also 179, 186, 213, 219. Culpeper, *English Physician*, for the cure for stinking breath. Elizabeth Coultas Recipe Book, January 9, 1749/1750, Cookbooks and Recipe Books, Document 1044, Joseph Downs Collection, WL; Stiverson and Butler, "Virginia in 1732," 43.

50. Peter Goelet advertisement, *New York Gazette*, March 7, 1768. For flesh brushes and toothbrushes, see the *Connecticut Journal*, June 25, 1773; advertisement for toothbrushes, Samuel Taylor, brushmaker, November 1793, Collection 61, Inventories and Vendues, 61x47, Joseph Downs Collection, WL.

51. *BG*, no. 22, May 16, 1720. Perhaps emboldened by Mr. Booker, another toothpick user advertised for his lost silver case in the next issue. See *BG*, no. 23, May 23, 1720.

52. L. Ourry, Hammersmith to Benjamin Chew, Esqr, Philadelphia, July 10, 1766, Benjamin Chew Papers, HSP.

53. *Itinerarium*, 321; Masur, *Autobiography of Benjamin Franklin*, 125.

54. Smith, *Compleat Housewife*, 172, 173, 177, 179, 183, 186, 192, 209, 213, 214, 215, 217, 219, 220, 227–228.

55. Quoted in Susan Klepp and Billy Smith, eds., *The Infortunate: The Voyage and Adventures of William Moraley, an Indentured Servant* (University Park, Pa., 1992), 50, 54, 77. Upon arrival some weeks later, apparently having had little opportunity to wash or change his clothes, Moraley was "stripp'd of my Rags" and given a torn Shirt and an old Coat to wear temporarily. The voyage back to England took a similar toll on Moraley's appearance. As he set his foot on English ground, Moraley noted, "I was drest in the following Trim. I had a Shirt on above fourteen or fifteen Weeks, a miserable Pair of Breeches, adorn'd with many living Companions, two torn Waistcoats, no Coat, a coarse, lousy, Woolen Cap, an old Hat give me in *Ireland*, a Pair of torn Stockings, a bad Pair of Shoes supported by Packthread, no Handerchief: So I looked not unlike the Picture of Robinson Crusoe"; ibid., 133.

56. Crane, *Diary of Elizabeth Drinker*, 1: 31; Edward Miles Riley, ed. *The Journal of John Harrower: An Indentured Servant in the Colony of Virginia, 1773–1776* (Colonial Williamsburg, 1963), 45, entry for January 19, 1774, 14; 30, 40. See also Masur, *Autobiography of Benjamin Franklin*, 45–46.

57. See *PG*, December 1, 1729.

58. Crane, *Diary of Elizabeth Drinker*, 1: 108; John Pechey, *A General Treatise of the Disease of Infants and Children* (London, 1697), chapter 8; Paschall receipt book, 26.

59. Smith, *Compleat Housewife*, 227–228; Steven Peabody diary, August 13, 1767.

60. John C. Fitzpatrick, ed., *The Diaries of George Washington, 1748–1799*, 4 vols. (Boston, 1925), 1: 5–6; "Report of the Journey of Francis Louis Michel, from Berne, Switzerland, to Virginia, October 2, 1701 — December 1, 1702," *Virginia Magazine of History and Biography* 24 (January 1916): 39. See *Itinerarium*, 191.

61. Kathleen M. Brown, *Good Wives, Nasty Wenches, and Anxious Patriarchs: Gender, Race, and Power in Colonial Virginia* (Chapel Hill, 1996), chapter 8; Mary Beth Norton, *Liberty's Daughters: The Revolutionary Experience of American Women, 1750–1800* (Boston, 1980); Linda Kerber, *Women of the Republic: Intellect and Ideology in Revolutionary America* (Chapel Hill, 1980); Ruth Bloch, "The Gendered Meaning of Virtue," *Signs* 13 (Autumn 1987): 37–58.

62. See Merritt Ierley, "The Bathroom: An Epic" in *American Heritage*, May–June 1999, 78–79, for the effort to classify human waste as outdoor filth. See also *BG*, no. 282, April 26, 1725; *BG*, no. 1260, May 6, 1746. Chamber pots were made of pewter, earthenware, or redware and were used by men and women. See Winterthur, 55.126.1, April 4, 1751, for the inventory of twenty-five pewter chamber pots in the stores of Joseph Paxton, merchant. See also imported earthenware chamber pot, 1770–1820, object id. 1978.6022, Winterthur; imported porcelain chamber pot, 1720–1740, object id. 1983.0063A B, Winterthur; maple chestnut close stool, 1740–1750, object id. 1956.0094, Winterthur; "close stul," Rev. Jacob Bacon, April 7, 1788, Rowley, Mass., collection 61, Inventories and Vendues, box 14, 77x206, WL. See Lois K. Stabler, ed. *Very Poor and of a Lo Make: The Journal of Abner Sanger* (Portsmouth, N.H., 1986), 514–515, for Sanger's purchase of a member mug discounted for being cracked. See also Jane Nylander, *Our Own Snug Fireside: Images of the New England Home, 1760–1860* (New York, 1993), 132.

63. Shields, *Civil Tongues and Polite Letters*. See also Thomas Tryon, *A treatise of cleanness in meats and drinks of the preparation of food, the excellency of good airs and the benefits of clean sweet beds; also of the generation of bugs and their cure* (London, 1682).

64. John Gregory, *A Father's Legacy to His Daughters* (London, 1774); Jonathan Swift, *Gulliver's Travels* (London, 1726). See also *BG*, no. 774, November 4, 1734, for the reprint of the humorous will left by a man who bequeathed "cleanliness" to married women and the same quality, along with the utmost decency of behavior, to their husbands.

65. L. H. Butterfield, ed., *Diary and Autobiography of John Adams* (Cambridge, Mass., 1961) 1: 194.

66. I am indebted to Sally Mason for this citation; Charles Carroll to William Graves, August 27, 1767, Charles Carroll of Carrollton Family Papers, Maryland Historical Society.

67. Sarah N. Randolph, *Domestic Life of Thomas Jefferson* (New York, 1871), 71, December 22, 1783. Hamilton took note of a daughter of Mrs. Blackater, as "a pretty buxom girl in a gay tawdry deshabille, having on a robe de chambre of cherry coloured silk laced with silver round the sleeves and skirts and neither hoop nor stays." Upon seeing both Blackater daughters together he reiterated, "They are both pritty ladys, gay and airy. They appear generally att home in a loose deshabille which, in a manner, half hides and half displays their charms, notwithstanding which they are clean and neat." *Itinerarium*, 276, 278. See also *Weekly Museum*, New York, March 16, 1763; *VG*, no. 60, February 20, 1752.

68. "The Journal of Madam Knight," in Martin, *Colonial American Travel Narratives*, 37; Boyd, *Byrd's Histories*, 33; Thomas, "Cleanliness and Godliness," 72.

69. Boyd, *Byrd's Histories*, 313–315.

70. *Itinerarium*, 245; Boyd, *Byrd's Histories*, 163, 77; "Journal of Madam Knight," 62; Fitzpatrick, *Diaries of George Washington*, 1: 8, March 26, 1748.

71. Boyd, *Byrd's Histories*, 317; "Journal of Madam Knight," 67. Travelers' comments about bedding were consistent with the consumer priorities Gloria Main found in early Maryland households. See Main, *Tobacco Colony: Life in Early Maryland* (Princeton, N.J., 1982), 254.

72. Boydston, *Home and Work*; Laurel Thatcher Ulrich, "Wheels, Looms, and the Gender Division of Labor in Eighteenth Century New England," *WMQ* 3rd ser., 55 (January 1998): 3–38; Stabler, *Very Poor and of a Lo Make*, 47; Riley, *Journal of John Harrower*, 121, for the first recorded cloth production on the Daingerfield plantation in 1775; *BG*, no. 523, December 1, 1729. See *Itinerarium*, 298, for a pun about an old woman being homely "both as to mein, make, and dress that ever I saw" because she was "clothed in the coarsest home spun cloth." For Boston's experiment with a linen manufactory to employ poor women and children spinning in 1753, see Laurel Thatcher Ulrich, *The Age of Homespun: Objects and Stories in the Creation of an American Myth* (New York, 2001), 159–166, and for New England homespun, 103–105. See also Adrian Hood, *The Weaver's Craft: Cloth, Commerce, and Industry in Early Pennsylvania* (Philadelphia, 2003).

73. Eleazar Moody, *The School of Good Manners* (Boston, 1769), 8–10, 12.

74. Richard Saunders [Benjamin Franklin], *Poor Richard Improved: . . . Being an almanac . . . for . . . 1763* (Philadelphia, 1763), NYPL copy. Ulrich, *Good Wives*, 80. Fitzpatrick, *Diaries of George Washington*, 1: 5. Peabody diary, June 16, July 9–11, 27, August 1, 29, November 18–27, December 1, 1767; January 5, February 27, March 12, April 12, 1768; Stephen Peabody Diary, 1777–1778, AAS Manuscript, October 22, October 27, October 31, November 2, November 4, November 11, November 20, November 21, November 23, November 24, November 25, November 26, November 30, December 31, 1777; Masur, *Autobiography of Benjamin Franklin*, 49; John C. Fitzpatrick, ed., *The Writings of George Washington from the Original Manuscript Sources* 37 vols. (Washington, D.C., 1931–1944) 1: 31–32, 94, 173, 395; Stabler, *Very Poor and of a Lo Make*, 19, 24, 71. Dr. Hamilton, meanwhile, took pains over a "great hole in the lappet of my coat, to hide which employed so much of my thoughts in company that, for want of attention, I could not give a pertinent answer when I was spoke to." *Itinerarium*, 276. See also Riley, *Journal of John Harrower*, 156.

75. *Itinerarium*, 186–187. In Southhold, Conn, at a Mrs. More's, the house was crowded with "a company of patchd coats and tattered jackets, and consequently the conversation consisted chiefly in "damne ye, Jack," and "Here's to you, Tom"; ibid., 246. See also Hamilton and company mistaken for peddlers because they had pormanteaus; ibid., 254.

76. Ibid., 204. Hamilton was similarly taken aback by the Boston don who wore a weather-beaten wig, greasy gloves, and old leather splatter dashes. Upon forgetting his gloves, the man rode back to get them even though "They were fit for nothing but to be wore

by itchified persons under a course of sulpher"; ibid., 236–237. In Philadelphia, Hamilton saw "a great many men in the meeting with linnen nightcaps, and indecent and unbecoming dress, which is too much wore in all the churches and meetings in America that I have been in, unless it be those of Boston where they are more decent and polite in their dress tho more fantasticall in their doctrines"; ibid., 319–320.

77. Ibid., 240.

78. Soap manufacturers constituted a most interesting exception to the rule that contact with polluting substances had an adverse affect on one's ability to embody gentility. In transforming a dirty substance, the tallow from slaughtered animals, into a substance capable of cleaning fabric, they emphasized the process of refinement and the soap's ability to confer gentility, but they did not try to hide the fact that soap was a by-product of tallow. Thus a 1766 ad for "Fine" and "superfine" soaps noted briefly in closing that the manufacturer was willing to give "Ready Money for Butchers good Fat and Tallow." See *PG*, February 13, 1766.

79. *BG*, no. 28 June 27, 1720.

80. "Journal of Madam Knight," 65–66.

81. Ibid., 60.

82. *Itinerarium*, 216. Breen, *Marketplace of Revolution*, has demonstrated the aesthetic significance of small luxuries for the lives of ordinary Anglo-North Americans.

83. Masur, *Autobiography of Benjamin Franklin*, 46. Crane, *Diary of Elizabeth Drinker*, 1: 31. See Thomas, "Cleanliness and Godliness," 64, for early Quaker experiments with ignoring conventions for filth avoidance.

84. John Wesley to Mr. S., Armagh, April 24, 1769, in *The Works of John Wesley*, 3rd ed., 14 vols. (Grand Rapids, Mich., 2002), 12: 247–249. See also 11: 466–477, 5: 132–34). I am grateful to Niki Eustace for these citations. Richard P. Heitzenrater, *Wesley and the People Called Methodists* (Nashville, 1995), 217, 237. John Wesley, *Primitive Physic* (Philadelphia, 1789), xviii.

85. See Carla Pestana, *Quakers and Baptists in Colonial Massachusetts* (New York, 1991), 50; Christine Leigh Heyrman, *Southern Cross: The Beginnings of the Bible Belt* (New York, 1997), 20; Janet Lindman, "Acting the Manly Christian: White Evangelical Masculinity in Revolutionary Virginia," *WMQ*, 3rd ser., 57 (April 2000): 393–417; Rhys Isaac, *The Transformation of Virginia* (Chapel Hill, 1982); Susan Juster, *Disorderly Women: Sexual Politics and Evangelicism in Revolutionary New England* (Ithaca, N.Y., 1994).

86. "Journal of Madam Knight," 69; *Itinerarium*, 229–230. See also Schama, *Embarrassment of Riches*.

87. *Itinerarium*, 276, 273.

88. Jean-Pierre Goubert, *The Conquest of Water: The Advent of Health in the Industrial Age* (Princeton, N.J., 1986), 24, 86; Smith, "Cleanliness."

89. See Benjamin Rush, "An Account of the Manners of the German Inhabitants of Pennsylvania," in Michael Meranze, ed., *Essays—Literary, Moral, and Philosophical* (Schenectady, N.Y., 1988). Franklin quoted in Stephanie Grauman Wolf, *Urban Village: Population, Community, and Family Structure in Germantown, Pennsylvania, 1683–1800* (Princeton, N.J., 1976), 139; and his letter to Peter Collinson, May 9, 1753, *Papers*

of Benjamin Franklin, www.franklinpapers.org (Yale University and American Philosophical Society, 2002–2008), 4: 477.

90. *BG,* no. 518, October 27, 1729; Boyd, *Byrd's Histories,* 305.

91. P. E. H. Hair, Adam Jones, and Robin Law, eds., *Barbot on Guinea: The Writings of Jean Barbot on West Africa, 1678–1712,* 2 vols. (London, 1992), quotations on 84, 92n, 87.

92. Ibid., 779, 780–781.

93. Sean Quinlan, "Colonial Bodies, Hygiene, and Abolitionist Politics in Eighteenth-Century France," in Tony Ballantyne and Antoinette Burton, eds., *Bodies in Contact: Rethinking Colonial Encounters in World History* (Durham, N.C., 2005), 106–121.

94. Gregory A. Stiverson and Patrick H. Butler II, eds., "Virginia in 1732: The Travel Journal of William Hugh Grove," *Virginia Magazine of History and Biography* 85 (1977): 31.

95. Brown, *Good Wives,* 300; Andrews, *Journal of a Lady,* 111; Paul Edwards, ed., *The Life of Olaudah Equiano, or Gustavus Vassa, the African* (Essex, England, 1988); Shannon Lee Dawdy, "Proper Caresses and Prudent Distance: A How-to Manual from Colonial Louisiana," in Ann Laura Stoler, ed., *Haunted by Empire: Geographies of Intimacy in North American History* (Durham, N.C., 2006). 140–162.

96. Andrews, *Journal of a Lady,* 104, 107, 112, 204, and for the reference to "women," 108; "Journal of Madam Knight," 64.

97. John Lawson, *A New Voyage to Carolina,* ed. Hugh Talmagelefler (Chapel Hill, 1967), 180, 193.

98. George Morgan diary, 100, 125, quotation on 207, HSP; Thomas Gist diary, 53, HSP. For similar treatment of visitors by Caddo Indians, see Juliana Barr, *Peace Came in the Form of a Woman: Indians and Spaniards in the Texas Borderlands* (Chapel Hill, 2007), 53.

99. *Itinerarium,* 259. See also Boyd, *Byrd's Histories,* 115; Joyce Chaplin, *Subject Matter: Technology, the Body, and Science on the Anglo-American Frontier, 1500–1676* (Cambridge, Mass., 2001), esp. 157–198.

100. Boyd, *Byrd's Histories,* 123. Byrd alleged that curiosity about the bodies of "these sad-colour'd Ladys" rather than sexual desire made one of his men "try the difference between then & other Women, to the disobligation of his Ruffles, which betray'd what he had been doing"; ibid., 115.

101. "Journal of Madam Knight," 60; Annette Kolodny, ed., "The Travel Diary of Elizabeth House Trist: Philadelphia to Natchez, 1783–84," in William L. Andrews, ed., *Journeys in New Worlds: Early American Women's Narratives* (Madison, Wis., 1990), 214, 223–224.

102. Kolodny, "Travel Diary of Elizabeth House Trist," 204, 205; Hamilton, *Itinerarium,* 183.

103. Kolodny, "Travel Diary of Elizabeth House Trist," 206–207. Trist and Polly thus dressed behind one of the worsted bed curtains; ibid., 209. Trist was capable of acknowledging generous hospitality even as she condemned the accommodations as substandard. "Mrs. Elliot was so kind as to part beds from her husband, on our account," she admitted before commenting, "she wedged me in with her self and child in a miserable dirty place, she having resign'd her birth to Mr. Fowler"; ibid., 210.

6. VIRTUE

1. All references to Sherburne's narrative are from *Memoirs of Andrew Sherburne: A Pensioner of the Navy of the Revolution*, 2nd ed. (Providence, R.I., 1831). Quotations in this and the next two paragraphs are from 119–120.

2. Wolfe quoted in James Kirby Martin and Mark Edward Lender, *A Respectable Army: The Military Origins of the Republic, 1763–1789* (Arlington Heights, Ill., 1982), 19; Burton quoted in Fred Anderson, *A People's Army: Massachusetts Soldiers and Society in the Seven Years' War* (Chapel Hill, 1984), 95. For the differences between regular militias and provincial armies that fought the battles outside their colonies, see John Shy, "A New Look at the Colonial Militia," in *A People Numerous and Armed: Reflections on the Military Struggle for American Independence* (Ann Arbor, 1990), 29–41; Lawrence Delbert Cress, *Citizens in Arms: The Army and Militia in American Society to 1812* (Chapel Hill, 1982), 58–60; Martin and Lender, *A Respectable Army*, 17–20. Anderson, *A People's Army*, 26–27, in contrast, emphasizes the differences separating British regulars, whose lower-class position was permanent, with New England recruits, who were temporarily available for the most dangerous military service because of their youth. For the class differences separating revolutionary officers from enlisted men and militias from the Continental Army see Cress, *Citizens in Arms*; Shy, *A People Numerous and Armed*; Martin and Lender, *A Respectable Army*; Edward C. Papenfuse and Gregory A. Stiverson, "General Smallwood's Recruits: The Peacetime Career of the Revolutionary War Private," *WMQ*, 3rd ser., 30 (January 1973): 116–132; Steven Rosswurm, *Arms, Country, and Class: The Philadelphia Militia and the "Lower Sort" during the American Revolution* (New Brunswick, N.J., 1999); Charles Patrick Neimeyer, *America Goes to War: A Social History of the Continental Army* (New York, 1996); Gregory T. Knouff, *The Soldiers' Revolution: Pennsylvanians in Arms and the Forging of Early American Identity* (University Park, Pa., 2004). See also Wayne Bodle, *The Valley Forge Winter: Civilians and Soldiers* (University Park, Pa., 2002).

3. See Bruce Burgett, *Sentimental Bodies: Sex, Gender, and Citizenship in the Early Republic* (Princeton, N.J., 1998); Dana D. Nelson, *National Manhood: Capitalist Citizenship and the Imagined Fraternity of White Men* (Durham, N.C., 1998); and John Resch, *Suffering Soldiers: Revolutionary War Veterans, Moral Sentiment, and Political Culture in the Early Republic* (Amherst, Mass., 1999). See also Carroll Smith-Rosenberg, "Dis-covering the Subject of the 'Great Constitutional Discussion,'" *JAH* 79 (December 1992): 841–873.

4. See for example, T. Simes, *The Military Guide for Young Officers*, 2 vols. (London, rpt. Philadelphia, 1776).

5. Washington quoted in Martin and Lender, *A Respectable Army*, 45.

6. William H. Guthman, ed., *The Correspondence of Captain Nathan and Lois Peters, April 25, 1775–February 5, 1777* (Hartford, Conn., 1980). See also Seth Oak orderly book, 1775, AAS; Isaac Nichols orderly book, September 17, 1775, AAS; Ephraim Doolittle orderly book, July 6, 1775, AAS; Samuel Ward orderly book, 1775, AAS; Ebenezer Learned orderly book, August 29, 1775, AAS; *Caleb Haskell's Diary* (Newburyport, Mass., 1881); James Frye orderly book, July 5, 1775, AAS; Nathaniel Goodwin, Plymouth, Mass., to the

Honorable Committee of supplies, July 31, 1775, Sol Feinstone Collection, reel 1, no. 389, DL; E. Wayne Carp, *To Starve the Army at Pleasure: Continental Army Administration and American Political Culture, 1775–1783* (Chapel Hill, 1984), 20–32.

7. *Rules and Regulations for the Massachusetts Army* (Cambridge, Mass., 1775); Frye orderly book, June 30, 1775.

8. Nichols Orderly Book, November 12, 1775; Learned orderly book, October 9, 1775; Doolittle orderly book, July 6, 1775, general orders.

9. Doolittle orderly book, April 22, April 25–July 14, July 24, 1775; Oak orderly book, 1775; Martin and Lender, *A Respectable Army*, 47.

10. Elizabeth A. Fenn, *Pox Americana: The Great Smallpox Epidemic of 1775–82* (New York, 2001), 46–47; Learned orderly book, 10; December 4, 1775, n.p; Jedediah Huntington to Jabez Huntington, December 4, 1775, Roxbury Camp, reel 2, no. 588, Feinstone Collection; diary of Dr. John Warren, May 17, 1776, MHS; Dr. Samuel Adams to Sally Preston Adams, March 26, 1776, Boston; October 5, October 8, 1776, Fort George; June 7, 1778, Springfield, Mass., reel 1, nos. 20–22, 27, Feinstone Collection.

11. Doolittle orderly book, April 22, July 14, 1775.

12. Frye orderly book, August 1775; Doolittle orderly book, August 7, 1775. Learned orderly book, August 1, 1775, copied "Character," while the slightly less literate Frye copied "Coughtor." See also Nichols orderly book, September 19, 1775.

13. Doolittle orderly book, June 22, 1775; court-martial, July 5, 1775; August 4, 1775. Learned orderly book, July 29, 1775, p. 1; Frye orderly book, August 11, 18, 21, September 6, 1775, p. 68; Anthony Wayne, *Orderly Book of the Northern Army* (Albany, N.Y., 1859), appendix 1, p. 95.

14. Doolittle orderly book, July 23, 24, August 7, 1775; Learned orderly book, October 28, December 11, 1775; Mattatuck Historical Society, *The Orderly Book of Phineas Porter, 1776* (Waterbury, Conn., 1928), July 24, 1776, p. 19.

15. Learned orderly book, January 5, 1776.

16. *Orderly Book of Phineas Porter*, July 11, 1776, p. 31; Learned orderly book, September 18, November 22, 1775; January 5, 1776.

17. Learned orderly book, January 3, 1776; *Orderly Book of Phineas Porter*, brigade orders, July 16, 28, 1776, pp. 32, 35.

18. Colonel Johnston to Anthony Wayne, February 26, 1776, Anthony Wayne Papers, 1: 29, HSP; Fred Anderson Berg, *Encyclopedia of Continental Army Units: Battalions, Regiments, and Independent Corps* (Harrisburg, Pa., 1972), 97; *Orderly Book of Phineas Porter*; Jedediah Huntington to Jabez Huntington, July 29, 1776, Camp New York, no. 593, reel 2, Feinstone Collection; Anthony Wayne from Fort Ticonderoga, April 14, 1777, Wayne Papers, vol. 3. On the problems with supplying the army from 1777 to 1780, see Carp, *To Starve the Army at Pleasure*, 35–51.

19. *Orderly Book of Phineas Porter*, July 16, 1776, p. 33; William Shainline Middleton, "Medicine at Valley Forge," *Annals of Medical History*, 3rd ser., 3 (November 1941): 463. Colonel Israel Angell's Rhode Island regiment began to suffer from shortages of clothing by August 1777. See *Diary of Colonel Israel Angell*, ed. Edward Field (1899; New York, 1971), xi–xii. See also George Duane, ed., *Extracts from the Diary of Christopher Marshall, kept in Philadelphia and Lancaster, during the American Revolution* (Albany,

N.Y., 1877), November, December 1777, pp. 146, 152. By late 1777 vital stores of food began to be in short supply. In addition, the Continental Army was also seriously short of soap, a need which the command attempted to remedy by issuing orders in early January 1778 for collecting "dirty Tallow" and saving ashes for making their own. See *Valley Forge Orderly Book of General George Weedon* (New York, 1902), January 12, 1778, p. 190, and for other shortages, March 19, 1778, p. 265. Bad food continued to be a problem throughout the war, as Christopher Marshall's diary entry from 1780 attests: the men complained that the meat "stinks so badly that they cannot eat it," *Diary of Christopher Marshall*, August 1780, p. 261.

20. Oak orderly book, August 22, 1775, p. 108. In Colonel James Frye's version, "Ladies of the best fashion" in the neighborhood became "Ladies of the first pasion in the nabourhood"; see Frye orderly book.

21. Knouff, *The Soldiers' Revolution*, 93; Learned orderly book, January 6, 1776; Loammi Baldwin Inventory, June 10, 1776, no. 73, Feinstone Collection. See also Mark Mayo Boatner, *Encyclopedia of the American Revolution* (New York, 1966), 55; "Valley Forge, 1777–1778, Diary of Surgeon Albigence Waldo, of the Connecticut Line," *PMHB* 21 (October 1897): 317–318.

22. Paul David Nelson, *Anthony Wayne, Soldier of the Early Republic* (Bloomington, Ind., 1985), 3, 26, quotations on 71, 168; May 26, 1776, p. 65; Colonel Nicholas Hansegger to Anthony Wayne, March 29, 1776, Wayne Papers, 1: 40. See also Berg, *Encyclopedia*, 47; Wayne Papers, 1: 53; Benjamin Rush to Anthony Wayne, June 5, 1777, ibid., 3: 91; Major Ryan to Anthony Wayne, July 12, 1777, ibid., 3: 110.

23. "Revolutionary Diary kept by George Norton of Ipswich, 1777–1778," Essex Institute Historical Collections 74 (1938): 339–340.

24. Holly A. Mayer, *Belonging to the Army: Camp Followers and Community during the American Revolution* (Columbia, S.C., 1996), 140–142. See also Linda Grant De Pauw, "Women in Combat: The Revolutionary War Experience," *Armed Forces and Society* 7 (Winter 1980): 209–226; Anderson, *A People's Army*, 96–97.

25. Charles Royster, *A Revolutionary People at War: The Continental Army and American Character, 1775–1783* (Chapel Hill, 1979), 59; Mayer, *Belonging to the Army*, 64–65; *Pennsylvania Packet*, May 13, 1778; Guthman, *Correspondence*; Dr. Samuel Adams to Sally Preston Adams, May 6, 15, December 2, 1779, nos. 33, 34, 38, reel 1, Feinstone Collection; Absalom Baird, *Copies of Authentic Letters* (Pittsburgh, 1909), 7–15.

26. Broadside, pub. John Dunlap, April 17, 1777, AAS; Royster, *A Revolutionary People at War*, 59; Mayer, *Belonging to the Army*, 59, 64–65, 133, 141; *Pennsylvania Packet*, May 13, 1778; Guthman, *Correspondence*; Martin and Lender, *A Respectable Army*, 92–93; Linda Kerber, *Women of the Republic: Intellect and Ideology in Revolutionary America* (Chapel Hill, 1980), 60.

27. Frye orderly book, June 30, 1775; William Barton to ?, November 17, 1778, no. 82, reel 1, Feinstone Collection.

28. Richard Godbeer, *Sexual Revolution in Early America* (Baltimore, 2002); Albigence Waldo diary photostat, December 21, 1777, MHS; Alexander Hamilton to Elizabeth Schuyler Hamilton, September 3, 1780, Feinstone Collection; Guthman, *Correspondence*, 36.

29. *Caleb Haskell's Diary*, 6; Wayne, *Orderly Book of the Northern Army*, 116. In contrast, women who agreed to do the wash would be gratefully supplied with wood and water for that purpose; Wayne, *Orderly Book of the Northern Army*, 128. See also Mayer, *Belonging to the Army*, 141, for Colonel Walter Stewart's attempt to deny women rations unless they helped to keep the men of the 2nd Pennsylvania clean.

30. Early in the war, soap rations would have made laundering clothes possible with some regularity: in 1775 Ezra Doolittle reported eight pounds of hard soap issued per hundred men per week.

31. Angell to governor of Rhode Island, August 27, 1777, in *Diary of Colonel Israel Angell*, xi–xii; Royster, *Revolutionary People at War*, 59.

32. Middleton, "Medicine at Valley Forge," 463. See also Herbert Thoms, "Albigence Waldo, Surgeon: His Diary Written at Valley Forge," *Annals of Medical History* 10 (December 1928): 488; "Valley Forge, 1777–1778," 307.

33. Quoted in Middleton, "Medicine at Valley Forge," 465, 467.

34. Colonel Winds to General Gates, Ticonderoga, October 9, 1776, in Wayne, *Orderly Book of the Northern Army*, appendix 1, p. 176. See also Middleton, "Medicine at Valley Forge," 463; Thoms, "Albigence Waldo, Surgeon," 488; "Valley Forge, 1777–1778," 307; *Diary of Colonel Israel Angell*, January 8, 1779, p. 39. John Goodwin recorded in his journal in 1777 that when three men afflicted with "the itch" received the traditional smelly ointment as treatment, "It overcame them that we Thought they would a Died in the Night." See "Military Journal kept in 1777, during the Rhode Island Expedition, by John Goodwin of Marblehead, Mass.," Essex Institute Historical Collections, Salem, Mass., 45 (July 1909), 208; Middleton, "Medicine at Valley Forge," 467.

35. Wayne Papers, June 3, 1777, 3: 89.

36. *Diary of Colonel Israel Angell*, xi–xii.

37. Martin and Lender, *A Respectable Army*, 90, 91–92. Neimeyer, *America Goes to War*, 82–88, notes that African Americans accounted for one out of sixty Continental Army soldiers but reasons that their actual presence might have been greater because white men tended to serve for fewer years in the army and more time in the militias. See also Knouff, *The Soldiers' Revolution*, 85–86, on the small presence of African Americans and Indians in the Pennsylvania Line. One of these men, Nathan Clap, of Colonel Buel's regiment, described himself as a "poor black Indan" but an "honest and faithfull solder." His ordeal suggests the difficulties facing poor soldiers who found that military service did not alleviate the poverty that had motivated their enlistment, as well as those facing men of color, who were subject to the cruelties of their fellow soldiers and the summary justice of commanding officers who thought little of their character. Anthony Wayne to Wood, April 2, 1777, Wayne Papers, 3: 43.

38. James C. Riley, *The Eighteenth-Century Campaign to Avoid Disease* (New York, 1987), 132. See for example, Thomas Hale to his parents, September 13, 1776, no. 451, reel 1, Feinstone Collection, about his illness at the camp in New York.

39. Guthman, *Peters Correspondence*, 42, 45; Dyers journal, 1763–1805, entries for August 11, 23, 1777, p. 91, HSP.

40. Robert Johnston reported to Anthony Wayne that the eastern lads were ready to bolt in April 1777 when two men appeared to have smallpox: Wayne Papers, 3: 58; Colonel

Winds to General Gates, October 9, 1776, Wayne, *Orderly Book,* 176. See also Fenn, *Pox Americana,* 93–102.

41. Anderson, *A People's Army,* 90–91, 97–98; Oak orderly book, July 5, 1775; Learned orderly book, August 1, 14, 1775, January 5, 1776; Ward orderly book, July 27, 1775; Brigade Major Harper standing orders, August 12, 1777, Revolutionary War order books, HSP.

42. Revolutionary War order books, April 14–May 1777, August–October 1777, HSP; orders for August 12, 20, 1777, headquarters, August 12, 1777.

43. Middleton, "Medicine at Valley Forge," 467; *Valley Forge Orderly Book of General George Weedon,* 242–243, 251, 254, 255 (emphasis added); Mayer, *Belonging to the Army,* 133.

44. Elisabeth Donaghy Garrett, *At Home: The American Family, 1750–1870* (New York, 1990), 88–89, 102, 134–135; Jane Nylander, *Our Own Snug Fireside: Images of the New England Home, 1760–1860* (New York, 1993), 114–116; Lawrence Grow, *Country Architecture: Old-Fashioned Designs for Gazebos, Summerhouses, Springhouses, Smokehouses, Stables, Greenhouses, Carriage Houses, Outhouses, Icehouses, Barns, Doghouses, Sheds, and Other Outbuildings* (Pittstown, N.J., 1985), 40–43. See also Lois K. Stabler, ed., *Very Poor and of a Lo Make: The Journal of Abner Sanger* (Portsmouth, N.H., 1986), November 19, 1778, for Sanger's report that he constructed a "shit house" (219) and for evidence of the use of member mugs (514–515). See also *Connecticut Journal,* June 4, 1773, for ads for urinals; pewter commode, 1750–1800, object id. 1983.0064, Winterthur; wood commode, 1770–1800, object id. 1959.0150, Winterthur; Britannia or pewter bedpan, 1775–1820, object id. 1968.0601, Winterthur; mahogany, pine, brass close stool, 1788–1805, object id. 1997.0015A, Winterthur.

45. Middleton, "Medicine at Valley Forge," 463; *Diary of Colonel Israel Angell,* xi–xii; Martin and Lender, *A Respectable Army,* 128–129.

46. "Valley Forge, 1777–1778," 306–307. See also Middleton, "Medicine at Valley Forge," 462.

47. Waldo diary photostat, December 31, 1777.

48. "Valley Forge, 1777–1778," 309. William B. Lapham, ed., *Elijah Fisher's Journal while in the War for Independence and Continued Two Years after He Came to Maine, 1775–1784* (Augusta, Maine, 1880), February 23, 1781, p. 17.

49. Wayne, *Orderly Book of the Northern Army,* October 25–December 7, 1776, pp. 26–114.

50. See also Wayne Papers, 3: 102, for a similar statement in a letter addressed "Dear Sir," dated June 17, 1777.

51. Wayne issued this order to the Second Pennsylvania Continental Line in late March 1778: "As there is no Greater or surer mark of discipline than Cleanliness, so there is nothing more conducive to health and spirit; it introduces a laudable pride which is a substitute for almost every virtue; the Genl. therefore, in the most pointed terms, desires the officers to oblige their men to appear clean & decent at all times and upon all occasions. Even punishing that Soldier that appears dirty whether on duty or not"; Middleton, "Medicine at Valley Forge," 480.

52. Martin and Lender, *A Respectable Army,* 93; *Pennsylvania Packet,* April 22, 1777.

53. Donald Monro, *An Account of the Diseases . . . An essay on the means of preserving . . .*

(London, 1764), emphasized the importance of the hygiene of the men and the camp. He prescribed bathing, offered advice to prevent the spread of infections, including the proper treatment of patients, the need to wash hands, face, and feet when dirty, and the use of fires, smoke, and vinegar as purifying agents. See also Donald Monro, *Observations on the Means of Preserving the Health of Soldiers*, 2 vols., 2nd ed. (London, 1780), which drew upon the British army's experience during the Seven Years' War. Benjamin Rush's own *Sermons to the Rich and Studious* (London, 1764), 57–58, urged readers to bathe, stressed the importance of bodily cleanliness, and extolled the habits of Jews and of Hollanders. In the *Pennsylvania Packet* article under the heading "DRESS," Rush noted with regret the practice of clothing American soldiers in linen, which, he explained, collected perspiration from the body. When activated by rain, the soiled linen would form "miasmata," which current medical theory held to be the source of fevers. Rush recommended flannel shirts, such as those used by the Romans and the British, to protect soldiers from illness. In similar fashion, Rush decried long, uncombed hair, which, in accumulating perspiration from the head, was "apt to becom[e] putrid" and produce disease. To preserve the health, men should either comb and dress the hair every day, a difficult matter for most soldiers, or, preferably, wear it short and thin about the neck.

54. L. H. Butterfield, ed. *Letters of Benjamin Rush*, 2 vols. (Philadelphia, 1951), 1: 155, 158–159, 163–165, 168–169, 180–182.

55. *Pennsylvania Packet*, April 29, 1777.

56. *Continental Journal*, May 15, 1777; *Connecticut Gazette*, May 23, 1777.

57. See the entry on John Dunlap in Allen Johnson and Dumas Malone, eds., *Dictionary of American Biography* (New York, 1937) 5: 514–515. John Gill was the former radical publisher of the *Boston Gazette*; see ibid., 7: 284.

58. See "Instructions for Soldiers in the Service of the United States, Concerning the Means of Preserving Health," in Stanhope Bayne-Jones, *The Evolution of Preventive Medicine in the United States Army, 1607–1939* (Washington, D.C., 1968), chapter 3. I am indebted to Rachel Moskowitz for uncovering the W. broadside.

59. Stephen Dodd, ed., *Revolutionary Memorials Embracing Poems by the Reverend Wheeler Case, Published in 1778* (New York, 1852), 40–47; Timothy Dwight, *The Conquest of Canaan: A Poem, in Eleven Books* (Hartford, Conn., 1785).

60. Royster, *Revolutionary People at War*, 213–254.

61. *The Journal of Lieut. William Feltman of the First Pennsylvania Regiment, 1781–82* (Philadelphia, 1853), 3, 6–7, 25. Feltman recorded numerous occasions when the troops were allowed to wash and refresh themselves, noting, for example, that the regiment "continued on the same ground in order for the men to wash and clean their linen and furbish their arms, &c." In honor of the victory at Yorktown, Wayne provided new clothes for all the officers so that they might look their best during the celebratory marches and parades; journal of Captain John Davis, May 30, July 25, 1781, HSP.

62. Lapham, *Elijah Fisher's Journal*, April 29, 1782; Mayer, *Belonging to the Army*, 68.

63. Thomas Grosvenor, Inspector of Arms, October 4, 1779, no. 437, reel 1, Feinstone Collection; John Durkee to John Sumner, April 5, 1779, no. 300, reel 1, ibid.; George Washington to Anthony Wayne, December 28, 1780, no. 1742, reel 3, ibid. See also Mary Beth

Norton, *Liberty's Daughters: The Revolutionary Experience of American Women, 1750–1800* (Boston, 1980), 178–188. Carp, *To Starve the Army at Pleasure*; Lapham, *Elijah Fisher's Journal*, July 14, 1779, p. 14; Neimeyer, *America Goes to War*, 125.

64. For an example of how humane treatment was described in 1788, see David Humphreys, *An Essay on the Life of the Honorable Major-General Israel Putnam* (New York, 1977), 72–73.

65. Both the *Connecticut Gazette* and the *Continental Journal* reported atrocities in British prisons in the months before the public discussion of the need for cleanliness in Continental Army camps. *Connecticut Gazette*, February 28, 1777; *Continental Journal*, March 13, 1777. See *Pennsylvania Packet*, rpt. from *Connecticut Gazette*, July 23, 1778, which detailed unhealthy air and barbarous conditions.

66. Paul Edwards, ed., *The Life of Olaudah Equiano, or Gustavus Vassa, the African* (Essex, England, 1988).

67. *Memoirs of Andrew Sherburne*, 126–127. One wonders whether his sisters attempted to salvage his clothes. The father of fellow prisoner Jack Robinson told Sherburne that they had put their son's clothes out in the garden and were unsure whether he would ever wear them again.

68. Butterfield, *Letters of Benjamin Rush*, 1: 359. Sherburne handled this issue very differently from Rush. In his narrative, the soldier's return to domestic cleanliness and civility did not result in a loss of manly hardiness but rather exposed the weakness of those who had not served in the war. Having survived the ordeal of imprisonment, Sherburne returned to domestic life to take responsibility for his own cleanliness by washing himself, an act that only reinforced British accountability for his previous lousy, dirty condition and the strength of the self-empowered male citizen.

69. Richard L. Bushman, *The Refinement of America: Persons, Houses, Cities* (New York, 1992). In one satiric poem, the author complained that, unlike London fops, who were authentic, Philadelphia's dandies were merely uncultured wannabes; Buzz Bumblery, *Ephemera, or the History of Cockney Dandies* (Philadelphia, 1819).

70. Rush, *Sermons to the Rich and Studious*, 19.

71. Benjamin Rush, "An Account of the Vices Peculiar to the Indians of North America," in Michael Meranze, ed., *Essays—Literary, Moral, and Philosophical* (Schenectady, N.Y., 1988), 151.

PART III. TRANSFORMING BODY WORK

1. [Mary Hunt Palmer Tyler,] *The Maternal Physician: A Treatise on the Nurture and Management of Infants, from the Birth until Two Years Old. Being the Result of Sixteen Years' Experience in the Nursery. Illustrated by Extracts from the Most Approved Medical Authors* (New York, 1811), 174–175; *The Maternal Physician* (Philadelphia, 1818). For attribution to Tyler, see Frederick Tupper and Helen Tyler Brown, eds., *Grandmother Tyler's Book: The Recollections of Mary Palmer Tyler (Mrs. Royall Tyler), 1775–1866* (New York, 1925), xiv. Abraham P. Brower, Inventories and Vendues, 54.67.32, September 22, 1819, Joseph Downs Collection 61, WL, listed two copies of *The Maternal Physician* selling for one dollar a piece. Subsequent references to *The Maternal Physician*

are from the 1811 edition and appear parenthetically in the text. Lydia Maria Child, *The Family Nurse* (Boston, 1837), 36. See also Megan Marshall, *The Peabody Sisters: Three Women Who Ignited American Romanticism* (Boston, 2005), for Royall Tyler's seduction of Mary Palmer's mother.

2. For female-written medical advice books, see Mary Cole's advice for a healthy diet, contained in *Lady's Complete Guide; or cookery and confectionary . . . also the family physician* (London, 1789); the recipes of E. Bullman, *The Family Physician* (London, 1789).

3. William Buchan, *Domestic Medicine* (London, 1784). The first North American edition was published in 1772. S. A. Tissot, *Advice to the People in General, with Regard to Their Health* (London, 1767); Bernhard Christophe Faust, *A Catechism of Health: Selected from the German of Dr. Faust* (New York, 1798).

4. J. Worth Estes and Billy G. Smith, eds., *A Melancholy Scene of Devastation: The Public Response to the 1793 Philadelphia Yellow Fever Epidemic* (Canton, Mass., 1997). See Margaret Humphreys, *Yellow Fever and the South* (New Brunswick, N.J., 1992), 9, for the disease's impact on the professional standing of doctors.

5. See Felicity Nussbaum, *Torrid Zones: Maternity, Sexuality, and Empire in Eighteenth-Century English Narratives* (Baltimore, 1995), 9, 24–25, 53, 95. Nussbaum charts the dual emergence of the imperial mother, who has domesticated her sexual desires, and the savage mother of the torrid zones, whose unfettered sexual passion obstructs civilization and political freedom.

7 · REIMAGINING SICKNESS AND HEALTH

1. See Billy G. Smith, Comment, "Disease and Community," in J. Worth Estes and Billy G. Smith, eds., *A Melancholy Scene of Devastation: The Public Response to the 1793 Philadelphia Yellow Fever Epidemic* (Canton, Mass., 1997), 148; Susan E. Klepp, appendix 1, "How Many Precious Souls Are Fled?": The Magnitude of the 1793 Yellow Fever Epidemic," ibid., 171–176; Jacquelyn C. Miller, "Passions and Politics: The Multiple Meanings of Benjamin Rush's Treatment for Yellow Fever," ibid., 79–95; Margaret Humphreys, appendix 2, "Yellow Fever since 1793: History and Historiography," ibid., 183–198.

2. James C. Riley, *The Eighteenth-Century Campaign to Avoid Disease* (New York, 1987), 9–30, 44, 141–151; J. Worth Estes, Introduction, "The Yellow Fever Syndrome and Its Treatment in Philadelphia, 1793," in Estes and Smith, *A Melancholy Scene of Devastation*, 9.

3. Riley, *Campaign to Avoid Disease*, 16. See also J. H. Powell, *Bring Out Your Dead: The Great Plague of Yellow Fever in Philadelphia in 1793* (1949; rpt. Philadelphia, 1993); Smith, Comment, 149.

4. Riley, *Campaign to Avoid Disease*, 142. See Michal McMahon, "Beyond Therapeutics: Technology and the Question of Public Health in Late-Eighteenth-Century Philadelphia," in Estes and Smith, *A Melancholy Scene of Devastation*, 103–104, for the unwavering belief of Philadelphia's city officials and their peers in Europe and North America in the relationship between disease and the environment.

5. Powell, *Bring Out Your Dead*, 22, 54.

6. Ibid., 22–24; Humphreys, Appendix 2, 194.

7. Powell, *Bring Out Your Dead*, 43, 46; McMahon, "Beyond Therapeutics," 100.

8. Alexander Hamilton to Abraham Yates, September 26, 1793, no. 502, Sol Feinstone Collection, DL. People commonly distinguished between contagion-bearing commodities, like feathers, rags, and carpets, which they subjected to quarantine and purification, and harmless items like liquor, molasses, and wood. See the Boston quarantine regulations, 1821, and Boston City Council Ordinances, 1824, AAS.

9. Klepp, Appendix 1, 167, 169–170; Phillip Lapansky, "'Abigail, a Negress': The Role and the Legacy of African Americans in the Yellow Fever Epidemic," in Estes and Smith, *A Melancholy Scene of Devastation*, 63.

10. Lapansky, "'Abigail, A Negress,'" 67–68; Klepp, Appendix 1, 166, 168.

11. Margaret Humphreys, *Yellow Fever and the South* (New Brunswick, N.J., 1992). See also Michel Foucault, "The Politics of Health in the Eighteenth Century," in *Power/Knowledge: Selected Interviews and Other Writings, 1972–1977*, ed. Colin Gordon (New York, 1980), 166–182.

12. John Vaughan, medical diary no. 3, 1797–1802, Joseph Downs Collection, WL.

13. Ibid.

14. See Boston City Council ordinances, 1824, AAS. In New York, meanwhile, hogs still roamed freely during the 1830s; David Clapp travel journal, 1831–1843, McKinstry Collection, WL; Hendrik Hartog, "Pigs and Positivism," *Wisconsin Law Review*, no. 4 (1985): 899–935.

15. McMahon, "Beyond Therapeutics," 106–107. See Elaine Forman Crane, ed., *The Diary of Elizabeth Drinker*, 3 vols. (Boston, 1991), 2: 1061, August 1, 1798, for William's trip to the bath on Race Street kept by a "French" man. Harold Donaldson Eberlein, "When Society First Took a Bath," in Judith Walzer Leavitt and Ronald L. Numbers, eds., *Sickness and Health in America: Readings in the History of Medicine and Public Health* (Madison, Wis., 1978), 338. For similar developments in France, see Jean-Pierre Goubert, *The Conquest of Water: The Advent of Health in the Industrial Age* (Princeton, N.J., 1986), 35–47.

16. Benjamin Rush, *Directions for the Use of the Mineral Water and Cold Bath, at Harrogate, near Philadelphia* (Philadelphia, 1786), AAS pamphlet, 7, 9, 12. See also James Parkinson, *Town and Country Friend* (Philadelphia, 1803), 96. In Rush's *Essays, Literary, Moral, and Philosophical* (Philadelphia, 1806), he advocated hot- and cold-water shower baths as treatments for the insane.

17. Falconer is discussed in Virginia Smith, "Cleanliness: The Development of Idea and Practice in Britain, 1770–1850," Ph.D. diss., University of London, 1985, 181.

18. A. F. M. Willich, *Lectures on Diet and Regimen: being a systematic inquiry into the most rational means of preserving health and prolonging life*, 2nd ed. (London, 1799); William Buchan, *Advice to Mothers, on the Subject of their own health; and on the means of promoting the health, strength, and beauty of their offspring* (Charleston, S.C., 1807), 37–41; Smith, "Cleanliness," 179–194, 253.

19. John M. Breese Journal, 1802–1803, Joseph Downs Collection, WL.

20. James H. Cassedy, *Medicine in America: A Short History* (Baltimore, 1991), 35.

21. Richard L. Bushman and Claudia L. Bushman, "The Early History of Cleanliness in America," *JAH* 74 (March 1988): 1215, 1217–1225.

22. Inventory of John Penn, May 22, 1788, Collection 61, Inventories and Vendues, box 16, 55.512; Lansdowne inventory, Collection 61, Inventories and Vendues, box 16, 55.511; sale of John Penn's household goods, June 9, 1795, Collection 61, Inventories and Vendues, box 16, 55.511; all in Joseph Downs Collection, WL; Eberlein, "When Society First Took a Bath," 337, 338; Collection 361, miscellaneous letters, 82x171, October 27, 1801, Joseph Downs Collection, WL; inventory of John P. Gerrard, September 22, 1807, New York, New York, 54.67.96, Joseph Downs Collection, WL; bathing tub listed in inventory of Captain Henry Rogers, April 6, 1811, New York, Collection 61, Inventories and Vendues, box 17, 54.106.70, Joseph Downs Collection, WL; bathing tub listed in inventory of John Brunstrom, pewterer, December 1793, Collection 61, Inventories and Vendues, box 16 56.14.2, Joseph Downs Collection, WL.

23. Crane, *Diary of Elizabeth Drinker,* 2: 1058–1061, 1185.

24. Eberlein, "When Society First Took a Bath," 338. See Crane, *Diary of Elizabeth Drinker,* 3: 1664, July 8, 1803; 3: 1674, August 1, 1803; 3: 1765, September 4, 1804; 3: 1948, July 18, 1806, for Henry and William's use of the Frenchman's bath that summer. See also McMahon, "Beyond Therapeutics," 108.

25. Charles Wilson Peale, *Epistle to a Friend on the Means of Preserving Health, Promoting Happiness, and Prolonging the Life of Man to its Natural Period* (Philadelphia, 1803), 40. For concerns about inner hygiene and constipation as a disease of civilization, see James C. Horton, *Inner Hygiene: Constipation and the Pursuit of Health in Modern Society* (New York, 2000), vii–54.

26. Peale, *Epistle to a Friend,* 38–39.

27. Ibid., 38–39, 44. See also Martin Melosi, *The Sanitary City: Urban Infrastructure in America from Colonial Times to the Present* (Baltimore, 2000), 85–87; experiments with sand filters began in 1830 but were not used on major water systems until the 1880s.

28. John Stevens Cogdell diary, p. 19, Downs Collection, Winterthur; Thomas G. Morton and Frank Woodbury, *The History of the Pennsylvania Hospital, 1751–1895* (1895; rpt. New York, 1973), 78; Eberlein, "When Society First Took a Bath," 336; Marilyn Thornton Williams, *Washing "The Great Unwashed:" Public Baths in Urban America, 1840–1920* (Columbus, Ohio, 1991), 11.

29. George Cheyne, *An Essay on Health and Long Life* (London, 1724).

30. Henry Wilson Lockette, "An Inaugural Dissertation on the Warm Bath," M.D. diss., University of Pennsylvania, 1801, 23–24, 52.

31. Samuel K. Jennings, *A Plain, Elementary Explanation of the Nature and Cure of Disease Predicated upon Facts and Experience: Presenting a View of that Train of Thinking Which led to the Invention of the Patent, Portable Warm and Hot Bath* (Washington City, 1814). See also *Herbert's Air Pump Vapour Bath* (Philadelphia, 1802), a device designed to reduce the atmospheric pressure on a limb diseased with gout, palsy, or rheumatism; *Ten Chapters on the Bath* (London, 1829), CP from the library of the physician John Bell.

32. Eberlein, "When Society First Took a Bath," 339; Crane, *Diary of Elizabeth Drinker,* 3: 1674, August 10, 1803; 3: 1955, August 7, 1806.

33. *Portfolio,* n.s. 5 (June 1811): 473. For the significance of Bristol Springs and other colonial natural baths, see Carl Bridenbaugh, "Baths and Watering Places of Colonial America," *WMQ,* 3rd ser., 3 (April 1946): 151–181.

34. William Dewees, *The Mother's Own Book; or, the Physical and Medical Treatment of Children, for the Prevention and Cure of All Diseases* (London, 1829), 260. The content of the London edition is identical to the first Philadelphia edition, published in 1825, although the pagination differs.

8. HEALING HOUSEWORK

1. Margaret Humphreys makes a strong argument in *Yellow Fever and the South* (New Brunswick, N.J, 1992) and elsewhere for the crucial influence of yellow fever upon public health policy. It shaped the agendas of boards of health in southern cities before the Civil War, she contends, and subsequently directed the shape of federal public health policy.
2. Elizabeth Cranch Norton diary, August 11, September 25, December 23. 1797, MHS. Norton also reported making suits of clothing for her children, threading stockings, mending, making gowns, washing and putting up curtains, and working a patchwork quilt. She paid women to help with laundry and to make gowns and butter. In addition to these duties, she prepared bottles for medicinal metheglin (a spiced mead that she might have made herself).
3. See Kevin J. Hayes, *A Colonial Woman's Bookshelf* (Knoxville, Tenn., 1996), 83–100; Rebecca Tannenbaum, *The Healer's Calling: Women and Medicine in Early New England* (Ithaca, N.Y., 2002), 14–20.
4. Elizabeth Coates Paschall receipt book, CP. See Ellen Gartrell, "Women Healers and Domestic Remedies in 18th Century America: The Recipe Book of Elizabeth Coates Paschall," *New York State Journal of Medicine* 87 (1987): 23–39. Tannenbaum, *The Healer's Calling*, 19; See also Caroline J. Keith journal, MHS, 1797–1819.
5. Paschall receipt book, 7. In at least one case, she included a "sympathetic" remedy for fever and ague: secretly notching a stick without the patient's knowledge. From the second edition of Robert Boyle's posthumous three volume *Philosophical Works*, which appeared in 1738, she extracted a cure for the stone that Boyle had culled from Richard Ligon's *History of Barbadoes*. John Quincy's *Compleat English Dispensatory*, published in 1718, furnished several recipes for healing plasters and salves. See Robert Boyle, *The Philosophical Works of the Honourable Robert Boyle, abridged, methodized, and disposed under the general heads of physics, statics, pneumatics, natural history, chymistry, and medicine*, 3 vols., 2nd ed. corr. (London, 1738), 3: 661. See also Tannenbaum, *The Healer's Calling*, 17.
6. Most of the doctors mentioned in Paschall's text fit this final category and appear in her pages as nameless failures. Only those with remedies of proven value—that is to say, those whose cures made it into her book—were dignified with last names.
7. Hannah W. Heath diary, March 14, 1808, Heath Family Papers, MHS.
8. When Charles's health again became a concern, Heath called in Aunt Susannah White and then a doctor. In this instance, the doctor confirmed Heath's tentative diagnosis of a cold and provided remedies the household could not. White's remedies were made of ingredients found in the home medical cabinet and kitchen garden: rhubarb, an imported drug used widely in North America, water, and onions. The latter two

would have been used in meal preparation. The doctor, in contrast, left powders and an emetic with instructions for their use.

Elizabeth Craft White was Heath's aunt-in-law. She lived next door to Heath with her widowed sister. Hannah Heath had seven children at the time of the button incident. Charles, who was six, had two younger siblings, aged three years and six months, and four older siblings ranging in age from eight to sixteen.

9. Elizabeth Bancroft of Pepperell, Mass., noted Monday washdays in her diary for 1795. See Elizabeth Bancroft diary, AAS. Elizabeth Cranch Norton similarly recorded doing laundry almost every Monday during the late 1790s. See Elizabeth Cranch Norton diaries, August 11, September 25, 1797, MHS.

10. Elisabeth Donaghy Garrett, *At Home: The American Family, 1750–1870* (New York, 1990), 165–170. Anne Emlen book of extracts, HSP, analogized spiritual cleanliness to a clean garment. Thanks to Nicole Eustace for this citation.

11. For the Englishman's turn to the cravat, see C. Willett Cunnington and Phillis Cunnington, *The History of Underclothes* (London, 1951), 102, 123–125. See also Elizabeth Ewing, *Everyday Dress, 1650–1900* (London, 1984), 54, 56–57.

12. "The Washing Day," in *The Blackbird* (New York, 1828), 27–28. On the impossibility of returning to the "old-fashioned monthly wash," see the American edition of the London author Mrs. William Parkes's *Domestic Duties; or, Instructions to young married ladies, on the management of their households, and the regulation of their conduct in the various relations and duties of married life,* 3rd American ed. (New York, 1831), 162.

13. Susan Strasser, *Never Done: A History of American Housework* (New York, 1982); Faye Dudden, *Serving Women: Household Service in Nineteenth-Century America* (Middletown, Conn., 1983). But see also Bruce Dorsey, *Reforming Men and Women: Gender in the Antebellum City* (Ithaca, N.Y., 2002), for his claim that Thursday was Philadelphia's laundry day. Ruth Schwartz Cowan, *More Work for Mother: The Ironies of Household Technology from the Open Hearth to the Microwave* (New York, 1983). Alexis McCrossen, *Holy Day, Holiday: The American Sunday* (Ithaca, N.Y., 2000) 122–127.

14. Eliza Leslie, *The House Book; or, a Manual of Domestic Economy,* 8th ed. (Philadelphia, 1845), 7.

15. Ewing, *Everyday Dress,* 95, notes the persistence of a monthly washing week in England until the end of the eighteenth century. Leslie left England in 1799 at the age of twenty-two, perhaps before this transition had occurred fully in that country. See also Virginia Smith, *Clean: A History of Personal Hygiene and Purity* (New York, 2007), 232.

16. Elizabeth Cranch Norton diaries, MHS. Mangle in the inventory of James Barry, November 25, 1811, New York, Collection 61, Inventories and Vendues, box 1, 54.67.12, Joseph Downs Collection, WL. Washing machines can be found in the following inventories in Inventories and Vendues, Collection 61, Joseph Downs Collection, WL: Captain Thomas Buswell, December 3, 1808, Canterbury, Conn., box 14, 76x403, 1–4; Lodowick Fosdick, May 10, 1819, New York, box 3, 54.67.90; Jacob Hallock, March 27, 1813, New York, box 4, 54.83.86; Dr. John Baker, June 17, 1797, New York, box 16, 54.83.37.

17. Anna Thaxter Cushing diary, June 8, July 18, 1846, AAS.

18. *The Freemason's Magazine and General Miscellany,* 1811, p. 69.

19. When Bascom noted her twentieth birthday in December 1792, she also proudly reported her daily output of linen thread and wool fabric. The following year, Bascom interspersed reports on cotton and linen spun with records of cloth purchased for special uses. Ruth Henshaw Bascom diaries, March 19, April 2, June 5, 8, 1793, AAS. By the 1820s she manufactured less cloth. See Lois S. Avigad, "Ruth Henshaw Bascom: A Youthful Viewpoint," *The Clarion: Museum of American Folk Art, New York City* 12, no. 4 (1987): 35–41. See also Park family papers, AAS, Elizabeth Cranch Norton diaries, MHS. Evidence of cloth production can be found in the following inventories, in Inventories and Vendues, Collection 61, Joseph Downs Collection, WL: spinning wheel and reel, Margaret Shuy, widow, Berks County, Pa., August 4, 1810, box 12, 71x185.1–4; spinning wheels and bucking tub, Susanna Wenhold, Bucks County, Pa., February 11, 1808, box 19, 94x76.4; spinning wheel, Eleanor Sackett, December 23, 1822, box 20, 93x106.21; great wheels and linen wheels, Thomas Buswell, December 3, 1808, Canterbury, Conn., box 14, 76x403.2–4; spinning wheel, Hildah Anderson, Philadelphia, January 19, 1826, box 15, 81x240.1; small spinning wheel, large wheel, Casper Loat, 1796, New York, box 16, 54.37.13; linen wheel, woolen wheel, goods given to Matilda Brown by Samuel Chase, January 1817, box 19, 93x9.

20. George Wright, *The Lady's Miscellany; or, Pleasing Essays, Poems, Stories, and Examples, for the Instruction and Entertainment of the Female Sex in General, in Every Station of Life* (Boston, 1797), 13.

21. Hannah Heath diary, Heath family papers, MHS; Elizabeth Smith, *The Compleat Housewife* (Williamsburg, 1742), 227–228, bound with *Every Man his Own Doctor*, AAS; Stephen Peabody diary, AAS photostat from diary in MHS, August 13, 1767; Nancy Tomes, *The Gospel of Germs: Men, Women, and the Microbe in American Life* (Cambridge, Mass., 1998).

22. Hannah Heath diary, November 9, 1805, October 4, 1806, May 2, 1808.

23. See also Caroline Keith journal, MHS.

24. When "Old Sara" was "dreadfull sick," Aunt White had a "sober time" taking care of her. Heath administered a puke to her daughter but left it to Aunt White to give her a powder in the evening. After Ebenezer Heath was taken with a violent pain in his stomach, Heath first called in a young doctor, but when the medicine he prescribed did not work, she summoned a trusted older doctor, who gave Ebenezer pills that provided relief. Aunt White and another female relative took over his care at that point, bathing him to alleviate the pain and speed the cure.

25. Aunt White's duties suggest that she was valued for particular skills rather than simply as another pair of hands; she was never among the women who assisted with laundry, even on those Mondays after Heath had given birth.

26. Frederick Tupper and Helen Tyler Brown, eds., *Grandmother Tyler's Book: The Recollections of Mary Palmer Tyler (Mrs. Royall Tyler), 1775–1866* (New York, 1925), 130, 135.

27. Royall Tyler had been engaged to the daughter of Abigail and John Adams, but the match broke up over his scandalous reputation. He relocated to New York City, where he wrote *The Contrast*, one of the earliest American comedies produced by a professional company of players.

28. Laurel Thatcher Ulrich, "Wheels, Looms, and the Gender Division of Labor in Eighteenth Century New England," *WMQ* 3rd ser., 55 (January 1998): 3–38.

29. Ruth Perry, "Colonizing the Breast: Sexuality and Maternity in Eighteenth-Century England," *Journal of the History of Sexuality* 2 (March 1991): 204–234. On the dedication page of the *Maternal Physician*, Tyler explicitly connected her own mother's relationship with her helpless child (the author herself) and women's duties to nurture the new nation.

30. William Buchan, *Advice to Mothers, on the Subject of their own health; and on the means of promoting the health, strength, and beauty of their offspring* (Charleston, S.C., 1807). Alexander Hamilton, *The Family Female Physician; or, a Treatise on the Management of Female Complaints* (Worcester, Mass., 1793), 263, warned against confining clothes. See also Virginia Smith, "Cleanliness: The Development of Idea and Practice in Britain, 1770–1850," Ph.D. diss., University of London, 1985, 156, for her discussion of Struve.

31. Bernhard Christoph Faust, *The Catechism of Health; Selected from the German of Dr. Faust* (New York, 1798); A. F. M. Willich, *Lectures on Diet and Regimen: Being a systematic inquiry into the most rational means of preserving health and prolonging life*, 2nd ed. (London, 1799); Michael Underwood, *Treatise on the Diseases of Children, and Management of Infants From the Birth* (Boston, 1806). Hamilton, *Family Female Physician*, recommended bathing, 261, 262; James Parkinson, *Town and Country Friend*, (Philadelphia, 1803). See also Smith, "Cleanliness," 102, for her discussion of George Armstrong's instructions on dandling infants to remove toxins on the skin in *Essay on the Diseases most fatal to infants* (London, 1769).

32. Michel Foucault, *The History of Sexuality*, vol. 3, *The Care of the Self*, trans. Robert Hurley (New York, 1986).

33. *A New Guide to Health compiled from the Catechism of Dr. Faust; with additions and improvements, selected from the writings of medical men of eminence* (Newburyport, Mass., 1810). Unlike the first American edition of Faust cited above, this adaptation eschewed religious and biblical justifications to focus on the state's need for a robust citizenry. See also Charles Rosenberg, "Catechisms of Health: The Body in the Prebellum Classroom," *Bulletin of the History of Medicine* 69 (1995): 175–197.

34. More than simply seeking reinforcement and corroboration, Tyler vetted the competing advice of some of the best-known medical advice book authors of the day and tried to craft a consensus within her text about a mother's best course of action.

35. Appearing in print just four years after her controversial *Appeal in Favor of That Class of Americans Called Africans*, Child's *Family Nurse* was a commercial failure. Child's text remains useful nonetheless for its depiction of nursing and academic medicine. See also Jeanne Boydston, *Home and Work: Housework, Wages, and the Ideology of Labor in the Early Republic* (New York, 1990).

36. Lydia Maria Child, *The Family Nurse* (Boston, 1837), 3.

37. Ibid., 8.

38. Jean Silver-Eisenstadt, *Shameless: The Visionary Life of Mary Gove Nichols* (Baltimore, 2002), 135.

9. REDEMPTION

1. Alexander Hamilton, *The Family Female Physician; or, a Treatise on the Management of Female Complaints, and of Children in Early Infancy* (Worcester, Mass., 1793; first London ed. published as *A Treatise of Midwifery*, 1780), 269. A ninth revised and expanded edition was published in Edinburgh in 1824.

2. William P. Dewees, *A Treatise on the Diseases of Females* (Philadelphia, 1826), 104–105, 114, quotation on 128.

3. [William E. Horner,] *The Home Book of Health and Medicine: A popular treatise on the means of avoiding and curing diseases, and of preserving the health and vigour of the body to the latest period* (Philadelphia, 1835), 100. William A. Alcott, *The Young Mother; or, Management of Children in regard to health* (Boston, 1836), 257–261. Alcott's reformist convictions about the virtues of temperance and self-discipline led him to be more skeptical of the virtues of rural life. He doubted whether rural people were necessarily healthier as a consequence of all the vigorous exercise taken outdoors, which he viewed as a potentially unhealthy overstimulation of animal appetites. John M. Breese journal, December 19, 1802, Joseph Downs Collection, WL. On the British advice about the need for fresh air, see Virginia Smith, "Cleanliness: The Development of Idea and Practice in Britain, 1770–1850," Ph.D. diss., University of London, 1985, 117–132.

4. William Alcott, *The House I Live In; or, The Human Body* (Boston, 1837), 235; Horner, *Home Book of Health*, 101.

5. Horner, *Home Book of Health*, 171–172.

6. William Dewees, *The Mother's Own Book* (London, 1829), 115, 113. See also M. Day, *The Girl's Book* (New York, 1830), 5, for the street vendor's cry to sell sand:

> SAND O!
> "S-A-N-D! Here's your nice white S-A-N-D!
> Sand, O! white Sand, O!
> Buy sand for your floor;
> For so cleanly it looks
> When strewn at your door."

7. Horner, *Home Book of Health*, 102.

8. Suellen Hoy, *Chasing Dirt: The American Pursuit of Cleanliness* (New York, 1995), 10–11. *The Ladies Magazine* 1, no. 2 (1828): 57–58.

9. Frances H. Green, *The Housekeeper's Book, Comprising Advice on the conduct of household affairs in general* (Philadelphia, 1837) 17, 21–35.

10. Ruth Henshaw Bascom papers, May 24, 1840, AAS.

11. Virginia Smith, *Clean: A History of Personal Hygiene and Purity* (New York, 2007), 232.

12. E. T. Salisbury to Stephen Salisbury II, June 20, August 2, 1814; November 3, 1813; July 18, 20, 1815; April 20, 1814, Salisbury Family Letters, AAS. Thanks to Laura K. Mills for calling this correspondence to my attention and for generously sharing her notes with me.

13. Stephen Stowe, *Intimacy and Power in the Old South: Ritual in the Lives of the Planters* (Baltimore, 1987) 193–194.

14. *Portfolio*, 4th ser., 5 (January 1816): 22–25; Thomas Ewell, *The Ladies Medical Companion, Containing, in a Series of Letters, an Account of the Latest Improvements and Most Successful Means of preserving their Beauty and Health . . .* (Philadelphia, 1818), 18–19; inventory of Claudius Fortin, merchant, New York, June 26, 1810, Joseph Downs Collection of Manuscripts and Printed Ephemera, box 1, 54.37.54, WL; DeRosset family papers, 1813, SHC; Laurens papers, June 1, 1827, SHC; Stowe, *Intimacy and Power*, 193–194.

15. "A Mirror for the Petit Maîtres," *Freemason's Magazine and General Miscellany* 1 (1811): 40–41; Buzz Bumblery, *Ephemera; or, The History of Cockney Dandies* (Philadelphia, 1819), mocked Philadelphia's dandies as inauthentic and unnatural.

16. Alcott, *The Young Mother*, 88–89, 91–92.

17. "On the proper management of children depends not only their health and usefulness in life, but likewise the safety and prosperity of the state to which they belong. Effeminacy will ever prove the ruin of any state where it prevails; and when its foundations are laid in infancy, it can never afterwards be wholly eradicated. Parents who love their offspring, and wish well to their country, ought therefore, in the management of their children, to avoid every thing that may have a tendency to render them weak or effeminate"; *A New Guide to Health compiled from the Catechism of Dr. Faust* (Newburyport, Mass., 1810), 13, 25. Dewees, *The Mother's Own Book*, 251.

18. Mrs. William Parkes, *Domestic Duties; or, Instructions to Young Married Ladies on the Management of their Households, and the Regulation of Their Conduct in Various Relations and Duties of Married Life* (New York, 1831), 227.

19. [Ann Taylor Gilbert,] *Rhymes for the Nursery* (Hartford, 1813), 21, 29–30.

20. *Rhymes for the Nursery* (Boston, 1837).

21. Enos Hitchcock, *The Farmer's Friend; or, the History of Mr. Charles Worthy* (Boston, 1793), 85; George Wright, *The Lady's Miscellany* (Boston, 1797), 13, 22, 91–92; "The Sluttish Wife," *Freemason's Magazine* 1, no. 3 (1811): 207–208.

22. Hamilton, *Family Female Physician*, 82, 102–104.

23. Ewell, *Ladies Medical Companion*, 34.

24. Dewees, *Treatise on the Diseases of Females* (1826); Alcott, *The Young Mother*, 95; William A. Alcott, *The Young Wife* (Boston, 1837), 82, 113–120, 248–251. for an early British essay on this topic, see James Graham, *The Guardian Goddess of health; or, the whole art of preserving and curing diseases* (London, 1782), discussed in Smith, "Cleanliness," 109.

25. Eliza W. Farrar, *The Young Lady's Friend* (Boston, 1838), 161. Thanks to Charles Rosenberg for calling this material to my attention. Farrar's book was originally published in 1833 and attributed to "A Lady," and in subsequent editions to her husband, John Farrar. See William Cushing, *Initials and Pseudonyms: A Dictionary of Literary Disguises* (New York, 1888). See also Elizabeth Bancroft Schlesinger, "Two Early Harvard Wives," *New England Quarterly* 38, no. 2 (1965): 147–167.

26. Farrar, *The Young Lady's Friend*, 161. Sixty years earlier, John Armstrong had warned against body odor, but in the context of urging readers to change their linens; see Smith, "Cleanliness," 130. Until 1821 in England, recommendations to use soap fell short of insisting on its use. See A. F. M. Willich, *Lectures on Diet and Regimen: being a system-*

atic inquiry into the most rational means of preserving health and prolonging life, 2nd ed. (London, 1799); William Buchan, *Advice to Mothers, on the Subject of their own health; and on the means of promoting the health, strength, and beauty of their offspring* (Charleston, S.C., 1807); and James Jennings's *Family Cyclopaedia*, cited in David J. Eveleigh, *Bogs, Baths, and Basins: The Story of Domestic Sanitation* (Stroud, Gloucestershire, 2002), 63. Jane Swisshelm, in "Letters to Country Girls," an advice column written during the late 1840s and 1850s, directed a similar message about personal hygiene to farm women, who, she claimed, "do not wash." Despite their assiduous housecleaning and attentiveness to wearing clean clothes, infrequent bathers were simply dirty. Thanks to Renee Sentilles for calling this text to my attention. See also Sylvia D. Hoffert, *Jane Grey Swisshelm: An Unconventional Life, 1815, 1884* (Chapel Hill, 2004), 162–165.

27. Farrar, *The Young Lady's Friend*, 164.

28. Ibid., 163–164. Examples of private washing paraphernalia from the nineteenth century abound in Winterthur's collections. See, for example, the walnut washstand, 1800–1840, object id. 1957.1006; earthenware washbowl, 1830–1860, object id. 1965.1202.

29. Emily Thornwell, *The Lady's Guide to Perfect Gentility, in Manners, Dress, and Conversation, in the Family, in Company, at the Piano Forte, the Table, in the Street, and in Gentlemen's Society* (New York, 1856), 12–14.

30. Ibid., 14–15. See Smith, *Clean*, 208, on the rising sensitivity to smell in Britain.

31. See Catharine Beecher, *A Treatise on Domestic Economy* (1841; rpt. New York, 1977), 100–105.

32. Mrs. L. G. Abell, *The Skillful Housewife's Book* (New York, 1852), 36, 72, 73; *The Family Manual: Containing Several Hundred Valuable Receipts for Cooking well at a Moderate Expense* (Cincinnati, 1856), AAS pamphlet.

33. Accounts of girls growing up in the early nineteenth century depict the mother as the role model for and enforcer of personal hygiene. This trend seems not have been confined to the north. See Laura Cole Smith papers, p. 12, SHC.

34. J. Ross Dix, "Saturday Evening," *Godey's Lady's Book*, November 1846.

10. LABORERS

1. Roberts was hardly the first author to try to make a profit by offering household advice. He had an important predecessor in Amelia Simmons, a young domestic whose niche was cooking: *American Cookery, or the art of Dressing Viands, Fish, Poultry, and Vegetables, and the Best Modes of Making Pasties, Puffs, Pies, Tarts, Puddings, Custards, and Preserves, and all kinds of Cakes, from the Imperial* PLUMB *to Plain Cake Adapted to this Country and all grades of life* (Hartford, 1796). See also Janet Theophano, *Eat My Words: Reading Women's Lives through the Cookbooks They Wrote* (New York, 2002), 233–241, esp. 234–235.

2. Robert Roberts, *The House Servant's Directory; or, a Monitor for Private Families: Comprising Hints on the Arrangement and Performance of Servants' Work*, (Armonk, N.Y., 1998,), lxi. All references to Roberts's text are from this edition.

3. Walter Johnson, *Soul By Soul: Inside the Antebellum Slave Market* (Cambridge, Mass.,

2001); Joanne Pope Melish, *Disowning Slavery: Gradual Emancipation and "Race" in New England, 1780–1860* (Ithaca, N.Y., 1998); John Wood Sweet, *Bodies Politic: The Colonial Origins of the American North, 1730–1830* (Baltimore, 2003); Richard L. Bushman, *The Refinement of America: Persons, Houses, Cities* (New York, 1992); Faye E. Dudden, *Serving Women: Household Service in Nineteenth-Century America* (Middletown, Conn., 1983), 33, 63.

4. Leonore Davidoff, "Mastered for Life: Servant and Wife in Victorian and Edwardian England," *Journal of Social History* 7 (Summer 1974), 406–428; Leonore Davidoff, "Class and Gender in Victorian England," in Judith L. Newton, Mary P. Ryan, and Judith R. Walkowitz, eds., *Sex and Class in Women's History* (London, 1983), 17–71.

5. Carol Lasser, "The Domestic Balance of Power: Power Relations between Mistress and Maid in Nineteenth-Century New England," in Thomas Dublin and Katherine Sklar, eds., *Women and Power in American History*, 2nd ed. (New York, 2002), 127–139; Christine Stansell, *City of Women: Sex and Class in New York, 1789–1860* (New York, 1986), 160.

6. Catherine E. Kelly, *In the New England Fashion: Reshaping Women's Lives in the Nineteenth Century* (Ithaca, N.Y., 1999), 41, notes that by the 1830s even provincial women had "narrowed the range of employments that a woman might pursue and still lay claim to a measure of gentility." See also Dudden, *Serving Women*, 42–47, 60.

7. Dudden, *Serving Women*; Lasser, "Domestic Balance of Power"; Stansell, *City of Women*.

8. Sarah E. Lawrence diaries and account book, 14 vols., Amos A. Lawrence papers, MHS.

9. Noel Ignatiev, *How the Irish Became White* (New York, 1995), deals mainly with this development in public culture.

10. My discussion of Roberts leans heavily on Graham Russell Hodges's Introduction" to *The House Servant's Directory*, xi–xlii. Appleton was one of Boston's wealthiest and most influential merchant investors. He traveled abroad to England and the Continent between 1810 and 1812, possibly with Roberts in tow. Soon after his return, he joined a group of Boston investors who financed the textile mills in Lowell, Massachusetts.

11. Roberts's subsequent career as an activist against slavery and on behalf of African-American civil rights compels us to consider that he, too, might have had reasons for leaving Appleton's employ. Roberts may also have realized that Gore's patronage could enable him to achieve economic independence, making the cultivation of intimacy a worthwhile endeavor. See Hodges, Introduction, xx–xxiv.

12. Roberts, *The House Servant's Directory*, 3, 4.

13. Dudden, *Serving Women*, 105; Roberts, *The House Servant's Directory*, 3, 4, 28.

14. Roberts, *The House Servant's Directory*, 62–63. See also Bushman, *The Refinement of America*; Peter Stallybrass and Allon White, *The Politics and Poetics of Transgression* (Ithaca, N.Y., 1986), esp. on the repression of smell, 139–140; Mikhail Bakhtin, *Rabelais and His World*, trans. Helene Iswolsky (Bloomington, Ind., 1984).

15. Roberts, *The House Servant's Directory*, 63.

16. Ibid., 99, 100–101.

17. See Stallybrass and White, *Politics and Poetics of Transgression*, on the use of the body as a metaphor to map spaces and rank people in the social order.

18. Roberts, *The House Servant's Directory*, lviii–lx.

19. Darlene Clark Hine, "Rape and the Inner Lives of Black Women in the Middle West: Preliminary Thoughts on a Culture of Dissemblance," *Signs* 14 (Summer 1989); James C. Scott, *Domination and the Arts of Resistance: Hidden Transcripts* (New Haven, 1990).

20. Mrs. William Parkes, *Domestic Duties; or, Instructions to Young Married Ladies on the Management of their Households, and the Regulation of Their Conduct in the Various Relations and Duties of Married Life*, 3rd U.S. ed. from the 3rd London ed., with notes and alterations adapted to the American reader (New York, 1831), 55. This book reached its tenth American edition by 1846.

21. Eliza Leslie, *The House Book; or, a Manual of Domestic Economy*, 8th ed. (Philadelphia, 1845), 194; Catherine Clinton, ed., *Frances Kemble's Journal* (Cambridge, Mass., 2000), 61, December 31, 1832.

22. Leslie, *The House Book*, 255, 259; Clinton, *Frances Kemble's Journal*, 42.

23. Leslie, *The House Book*, 254; Catharine Sedgwick, *Home* (Boston, 1835), 48.

24. Frances H. Green, *The Housekeeper's Book, Comprising Advice on the conduct of household affairs in general, and particular directions for the preservation of furniture, bedding, &c; for the laying in and preserving of provisions, with a complete collection of receipts for economical domestic cookery. The whole carefully prepared for the use of American housekeepers By a lady* (Philadelphia, 1837), 29.

25. Dudden, *Serving Women*, 47, notes that the category "servant" arose as mothers withdrew their daughters from housework. See also Jane Hunter, *How Young Ladies Became Girls: The Victorian Origins of American Girlhood* (New Haven, 2002), 11–37.

26. Leslie, *The House Book*, 3, 4; Kelly, *In the New England Fashion*.

27. Leslie, *The House Book* 3–4; Beecher, *A Treatise on Domestic Economy*, 21, 26, 27; Hunter, *How Young Ladies Became Girls*, 11–37.

28. John Cole, Cole's Music Store, Broomseller's jingle, 1827–1828, Joseph Downs Collection, WL.

29. Leslie, *The House Book*, 199, 231, 138, 201, 228.

30. Ibid., 105, 106, 108, 156, 173–175, 178, 181, 185.

31. Ibid., 223; Beecher, *A Treatise on Domestic Economy*, 367.

32. Leslie, *The House Book*, 230; Green, *The Housekeeper's Book*, 23–24; *PI*, July 6, 1840. See also Linen plainweave Shaker washcloths, 1830–1880, object id. 1970 0226, 0227, Winterthur.

33. Anna Quincy Thaxter Cushing papers, February 12, 28, March 3, 4, 1848, AAS.

34. Emeline Draper Rice to Sophia White, March 27, 1849, Draper-Rice Family papers, AAS. Cushing, for example, changed her sweeping day from Friday to Thursday in April 1850. She also delayed the spring cleaning of her parlor until July 28, 1853. The unavailability of help on washday compelled her to make other arrangements. On Friday, March 8, 1850, she brought Edward's nightshirts to the washerwoman Mrs. Hensey. When another washerwoman, Mrs. Holland, was not able to help her on Monday, March 25, 1850, she postponed her Monday wash. Anna Quincy Thaxter Cushing papers, AAS.

35. Beecher, *A Treatise on Domestic Economy*, 149; Leslie, *The House Book*, 7, 8; Leigh Eric

Schmidt, "A Church-Going People Are a Dress-Loving People: Clothes, Communication, and Religious Culture in Early America," *Church History* 58 (1989): 36–51.

36. Mildred Coles Cameron diary, October 31, 1839, p. 1, Cameron family papers, SHC.

37. Beecher, *A Treatise on Domestic Economy*, 308; Leslie, *The House Book*, 8.

38. Leslie, *The House Book*, 229.

39. Green, *The Housekeeper's Book*; Anna Quincy Thaxter Cushing diary, May 6, 1850, AAS. Improved Shaker Washing Machine; Designed Particularly for Hospitals, Hotels, Laundries &c, patented January 26, 1858, by David Parker, Shaker Village, Concord New Hampshire, 1858, Edward Deming Andrews Memorial Shaker Collection, 85, WL. Diagram of a washing machine, John Stevens Cogdell diary, 1800, 32, Joseph Downs Collection, 64x8.1, WL. The washboard was more conventional equipment; see Tin washboard, 1800–1900, object id. 1965.1762, WL.

40. See Carol Turbin, "Fashioning the American Man: The Arrow Collar Man, 1907–1931," *Gender and History* 14 (November 2002): 470–491. My thanks to Rachel Moskowitz for finding this citation. See also "Clothing and Dress," 79x246, Davis and Jones, New York, June 1, 1847, for a new type of cravat; 77x497.1, E. P. Hill and Co., Nashua, New Hampshire, June 1851, lists collars, bosoms, linens, and cravats; Ransom Williams and Joel Hubbard, manufacturers, New York, June 1842, sold collars, bosoms, cotton and woolen undershirts, and drawers; all in Joseph Downs Collection, box 1, WL.

41. Maureen Ogle, *All the Modern Conveniences* (Baltimore, 1996).

42. Kathleen M. Brown, *Good Wives, Nasty Wenches, and Anxious Patriarchs: Gender, Race, and Power in Colonial Virginia* (Chapel Hill, 1996); Stephanie McCurry, *Masters of Small Worlds: Yeoman Households, Gender Relations, and the Political Culture of the South Carolina Low Country* (New York, 1995).

43. Louisa Jane Trumbell diary, October 31, 1836, AAS.

44. Beecher, *A Treatise on Domestic Economy*, 308; Leslie, *The House Book*, 13.

45. Beecher, *A Treatise on Domestic Economy*, 138.

46. Dudden, *Serving Women*, 107.

47. Sedgwick, *Home*, 72; Beecher, *A Treatise on Domestic Economy*, quotation on 200.

48. Dudden, *Serving Women*, 36; Beecher, *A Treatise on Domestic Economy*, 200–201.

49. Dudden, *Serving Women*, 60–71. David M. Katzman, *Seven Days a Week: Women and Domestic Service in Industrializing America* (New York, 1978), discusses the ethnic and racial dimensions of domestic labor for the period after 1870.

50. Parkes, *Domestic Duties*, 138, 145, 148.

51. Green, *The Housekeeper's Book*, 26.

52. Dudden, *Serving Women*, 54; Stansell, *City of Women*, 155–163.

53. Leslie, *The Housebook*, 261, 230, 107.

54. Beecher, *A Treatise on Domestic Economy*, 356, 202: "An employer, then, is bound to exercise a parental care over them, in these respects." See also 199.

55. Dudden, *Serving Women*, 65–67; *Harper's* quoted on 65.

56. Lydia Maria Child, *The Frugal Housewife*, 16. Dudden, *Serving Women*, argues that there was a social reality behind comments that Irish women were dirty and inexperienced housekeepers, a point I largely accept, but with the qualification that American criticism of Irish women reflected an emerging regime of fastidiousness. One hundred

years earlier, the gap between Irish domestics and their American employers would not have been so great.

57. Only rarely do we find firsthand accounts by hired laborers that contain their own evaluations of their working conditions. See Lorenza Stevens Berbineau journal, August 19, 1851, Francis Cabot Lowell II papers, MHS. Berbineau carefully calculated the value of her own labor in numbers of muslins ironed, in personal service provided to Mrs. Lowell, including helping to wash her body in the morning, and in the wages she received.

58. Louisa Waterhouse diary, 102, MHS.

59. Ibid., 103.

60. Ibid., 146.

61. Anna Quincy Thaxter Cushing papers, June 17, 1846; October 12, 1848; July 18, 28, 1853; January 16, 19, 1854, AAS.

62. JADL, January 23, 1840. Emeline Draper Rice to Sophia White, May 28, 1847; February 27, 1850, Draper-Rice Family Papers, AAS.

63. Rice to White, June 4, 1851; February 27, 1850; Hunter, *How Young Ladies Became Girls*, 11–37.

64. Rice to White, July 20, 1853.

65. Rice to White, December 27, February 6, 1853. Sophia soon discovered that her employee Sarah was not immune to the attractions of better situations. After congratulating her sister on procuring American help, she announced, "*I am doing my own work.*" Sophia White to Emeline Draper Rice, February 2, 1854, AAS.

66. Rice to White, February 16, March 20, 1854.

67. Sarah Elizabeth Appleton was twenty years old when she married Amos A. Lawrence, a man eight years her senior. Appleton was the daughter of the shipping merchant William Appleton and niece of Roberts's former employer, Nathan Appleton. Indeed, it is likely that she and Roberts crossed paths when she was a small child and he worked in her uncle's household. Amos Adams Lawrence's land speculations led to his financing Lawrence University in Appleton, Wisconsin (the town was named after Sarah), and the University of Kansas in Lawrence.

68. Stallybrass and White, *Politics and Poetics of Transgression*, 20.

69. On at least one occasion, Lawrence noted her expectation that a healthy chambermaid would relieve her of child care; see Sarah E. Lawrence diary, January 5, 1851, Amos A. Lawrence papers, MHS. See also Dudden, *Serving Women*, 51.

70. Carol Lasser, "Domestic Balance of Power."

71. The birth of her fifth child in 1852 marked Lawrence's third use of a wet nurse. Lawrence set her sights on an "English girl," Hannah Brockway, whose baby was only two weeks old. A month into Brockway's employ, her child suddenly died. Both Lawrence and Mrs. Moulton went to see the dead baby. Brockway remained as wet nurse for the Lawrences until the following October, earning the following notation in Lawrence's book: "Left & lived as chambermaid at several places: turned out well"; Sarah E. Lawrence account book, Amos A. Lawerence papers, MHS.

72. *Selections from the Diaries of William Appleton, 1786–1862* (Boston, 1922), 150, 225;

Amos Lawrence, *Life of Amos A. Lawrence; with Extracts from his Diary and Correspondence* (Boston, 1888), 272.

73. Margaret Cameron correspondence, Cameron family papers, SHC.

74. Louisa Jane Trumbell diary, December 25, 1833, AAS; Dudden, *Serving Women*, 60–71; Stansell, *City of Women*.

75. Eliza Leslie, "The Truant," in *The Mirror; or, Eighteen Juvenile Tales and Dialogues* by a lady of Philadelphia (Boston, 1828), 164–181.

76. *Godey's Lady's Book*, July 1832. Recourse to God's judgment appeared in many publications about cholera; see, for example, *An Appeal on the Subject of Cholera* (New York, 1832), 8: "If the pestilence visit us, shall it not then be seen what Christian faith can do for its subjects?"

77. Charles Rosenberg, *The Cholera Years: The United States in 1832, 1849, and 1866* (Chicago, 1987), 107, 120, 130.

78. *The Two Homes Compared; or, the Advantages of Cleanliness* (Philadelphia, 1850), 6.

79. Ibid., 15–16.

80. Even household almanacs, known more for their pragmatic assemblage of advice than for genteel pretensions, devoted greater attention to these issues. *Turner's Improved House-Keeper's Almanac and Family Recipe Book* (1845) provided advice on removing the unpleasant smell of new paint, water closets, and night chairs by using lime water, soap suds, and the scent from burning pastiles.

81. *The Family Messenger and National Gleaner*, January 10, 1849.

82. For the American Sunday School Union, see Anne M. Boylan, *Sunday School: The Formation of an American Institution, 1790–1880* (New Haven, 1988), esp. 60–100.

83. *The Parlour and Kitchen; or, The Story of Ann Connover* (Philadelphia, 1860), esp. 74–78.

84. Kelly, *In the New England Fashion*; Stansell, *City of Women*, 161–162.

11. IMMERSION

1. *PI*, July 8, 1840.

2. Georges Vigarello, *Concepts of Cleanliness: Changing Attitudes in France since the Middle Ages* (Cambridge, 1988); Jean-Pierre Joubert, *Conquest of Water: The Advent of Health in the Industrial Age* (Princeton, N.J., 1986).

3. David Clapp travel journal, 1831–1843, p. 49, McKinstry collection, WL. See *PI*, February 4, 1831, for the *Charleston Courier's* ranking of that city as second to Boston, followed by Baltimore, New York, and Philadelphia. See also Joseph Andrews diary, Joseph Downs collection, WL, 29; Charles Rosenberg, *The Cholera Years: The United States in 1832, 1849, and 1866* (Chicago, 1987), 16–17.

4. Clapp travel journal, 57. See also Hendrik Hartog, "Pigs and Positivism," *Wisconsin Law Review*, no. 4 (1985): 899–935.

5. Clapp travel journal, 8, 28. See also Rosenberg, *Cholera Years*; Christine Stansell, *City of Women: Sex and Class in New York, 1789–1860* (New York, 1986).

6. Clapp travel journal, 26–27, 36–37.

7. Ibid., 10. See Joseph Andrews diary, Joseph Downs Collection, WL, for his comparisons of London and Boston. For the larger intellectual shift to dematerialized thinking about individual identity, see Jeffrey Sklansky, *The Soul's Economy: Market Society and Selfhood in American Thought, 1820–1920* (Chapel Hill, 2002).

8. Rosenberg, *Cholera Years*, 2; NYEP, July 6, 21, 1832.

9. NYEP, July 2, 3, 1832.

10. NYEP, July 3, 21, 26, 1832; George Shattuck diary, December 17, 1834, MHS.

11. NYEP, July 6, 7, 1832; *Godey's Lady's Book*, July 1832; Hone quoted in Rosenberg, *Cholera Years*, 107.

12. NYEP, May 2, 1832, July 1, July 26, 1832. See Stephen Nissenbaum, *Sex, Diet, and Debility in Jacksonian America: Sylvester Graham and Health Reform* (Westport, Conn., 1980); *PI*, Feb. 2, 1831.

13. Margaret Humphreys, *Yellow Fever and the South* (New Brunswick, N.J., 1992); *PI*, October 2, 1840. Philadelphia newspapers reported fifteen dead from cholera and eleven from yellow fever in New Orleans for September 1850; *PI*, October 7, 1850.

14. NODP, December 27, 1839, March 17, 1842. See also Andrea Tone, *Devices and Desires: A History of Contraceptives in the United States* (New York, 2001).

15. NYEP, January 6, 1832; *PI*, July 7, 1840; Tone, *Devices and Desires*.

16. NODP, January 18, 1838.

17. NODP, December 27, 1839; NYEP, July 9, 1832; *PI*, October 7, 1850; Kathy Peiss, *Hope in a Jar: The Making of America's Beauty Culture* (New York, 1998), 22–31; Karen Halttunen, *Confidence Men and Painted Women: A Study of Middle-Class Culture in America, 1830–1870* (New Haven, 1982), 88–89.

18. Catharine Beecher, *A Treatise on Domestic Economy* (1841; rpt. ed. New York, 1977), 105. Her instructions for tooth care appeared in a section labeled "Cleanliness." *Godey's Lady's Book*, December 1833, November 1846; NYEP, January 3, 1832.

19. NODP, March 17, 1842; *PI*, July 1, 1840; NYEP, February 7, 1832.

20. John Harley Warner, "The Idea of Southern Medical Distinctiveness: Medical Knowledge and Practice in the Old South," in Judith Walzer Leavitt and Ronald L. Numbers, eds., *Sickness and Health in America: Readings in the History of Medicine and Public Health* (Madison, Wis., 1978), 53–65. An American newspaper in 1832 noted that different climates in England and America produced different aging processes: "The same man in the climate of England would have been more round and rosy with better teeth, perhaps, for they decay in this country sooner than there, with fewer wrinkles." He reassured his American readers that the benefits to the Englishman were deceptive, however, for "he was, after all, no younger in constitution, and no further from the close of life." See NYEP, March 1, 1832. A water cure journal from 1850 debunked the notion that "the exquisite bloom on the cheeks of American girls fades in the matron much sooner than in England" simply because of the "softness of the English climate," insisted rather that the difference could be traced to the lack of significant exercise. See the *New Graefenberg Water-Cure Reporter* 2 (April 1850): 109; Ker family papers, May 24, 1850, SHC; William Holcombe diary, SHC.

21. Joseph Andrews diary, 1835–1836, May 16, 26, 1835; July 20–21, 1836, pp. 2, 7, 137.

22. Caroline Olivia Laurens diary, October 11, 1827, SHC; Joseph Andrews diary, 139.

23. Frederick Law Olmstead, *The Cotton Kingdom: A Traveller's Observations on Cotton and Slavery in the American Slave States*, ed. Arthur M. Schlesinger (New York, 1984), 177; Thomas Bennehan to Rebecca Bennehan, October 26, May 6, 1800, Cameron family papers, SHC. The place had not improved in Bennehan's view by May 11, 1801, when he described it to his mother as a "dirty, confused, and disagreeable place," especially compared with Richmond; Cameron family papers. Margaret Anderson to Duncan Cameron, Hillsborough, North Carolina, January 21, 1801, Cameron family papers.

24. Mary Phillips, Mount Prospect, North Carolina, to Rebecca Cameron, September 10, 1813, Cameron family papers.

25. *Selections from the Diaries of William Appleton, 1786–1862* (Boston, 1922), 6.

26. Caroline Olivia Laurens diary, April 11, May 8, 1827, May 2?, 1827, SHC.

27. *Appleton Diaries*, 65, 73, 158–159.

28. Mildred Coles Cameron diary, December 2, 1839, p. 24; January 4, 5, 6, 1840, pp. 56, 58, Cameron family papers, SHC.

29. Ibid., December 30, 1839, p. 51. See also Susan Burns to James Burns, 1849, p. 5, Burns family papers, 3861, SHC.

30. Account Book of Mildred Coles Cameron, May 30, 1840, Cameron family papers, SHC.

31. Charlene M. Boyer Lewis, *Ladies and Gentlemen on Display: Planter Society at the Virginia Springs, 1790–1860* (Charlottesville, Va., 2001); Mildred Coles Cameron diary, November 20, 1839, p. 17; February 24, 1840, p. 94.

32. William Cameron to Duncan Cameron, July 7, 1813, Cameron family papers, SHC; William Cameron to Duncan Cameron?, April 23, 1817, Cameron Family Papers, SHC.

33. Ann Stanley to Miss Mary Hollock, Elizabethtown, New Jersey, October 18, 1801, Cameron family papers, SHC; Davis Ker to Mother, April 9, 1850; Susan Ker Butler to Mother, May 24, 1850, folder 34, Ker family papers, SHC; Margaret Bain Mordecai to Paul Cameron, Raleigh, North Carolina, June 20, 1854, Cameron family papers, SHC; Lizzie Jones to Cousin Becca, October 2, 1855, Cameron family papers, SHC.

34. Lewis, *Ladies and Gentlemen on Display*, 101, 107.

35. Ker begged her mother "not [to] let anyone see this letter, for I would not have any one know I had written about such a scandalous thing," but she proudly noted "my calling the old black thing 'Auntie' so often was too good to be lost"; Mary Ker to Mother, Galt House, Louisville, July 1, 1855, Ker family papers, SHC.

36. *Appleton Diaries*, 65; Sarah Weeks Curtis diary, July 2, July 20, 1858, Walter G. Curtis papers, SHC. Weeks appears to have been born in Massachusetts, where she met her husband, the physician Walter G. Curtis, who eventually relocated to the South to practice medicine.

37. *NODP*, May 21, 1842; *NYEP*, June 1832.

38. *PI*, July 7, 1840; *NODP*, September 1, 1843. See also Art Wrobel, "The Pursuit of Pleasure (and Health) at Mid-Nineteenth Century Mineral Springs in Kentucky and West Virginia," *Border States: Journal of the Kentucky-Tennessee American Studies Association*, no. 12 (1999).

39. *NODP*, March 17, 1842; *PI*, July 9, 1840; Sarah Ker Butler to Mother, June 1, 1851, Ker family papers, SHC.

40. Joshua Wright to Paul Cameron, July 30, 1854, Cameron family papers, SHC; Lewis, *Ladies and Gentlemen on Display*, 160–161; *NODP*, September 17, 1843.

41. Jean-Didier Urbain, *At the Beach*, trans. Catherine Porter (Minneapolis, 2003), 67–94, distinguishes between the recreational bather's pursuit of pleasure and the patient's pursuit of health, a difference in motive that is less clear in the sources I have used here. Virginia Smith, *Clean: A History of Personal Hygiene and Purity* (New York, 2007), 244–246, describes the rise of ocean resorts in England and Europe.

42. Burns family papers, 1849, p. 5, SHC; Sarah Ker Butler to Mother, May 25, 1851, Ker family papers, SHC.

43. Louisa Clap Trumbell diary, December 1, 1839; July 22, 1841, AAS.

44. *PI*, July 3–4, 1840. See Alexis McCrossen, *Holy Day, Holiday: The American Sunday* (Ithaca, N.Y., 2000), 82, for the significance of Sunday at the beach in transforming Sunday from a day of rest to a day of leisure.

45. Sarah E. Lawrence diary, entries for July, August, and September 1846–1851, MHS. In addition to ocean bathing and experimenting with the water cure, Lawrence also made use of a midwife during the 1840s, when midwifery underwent a brief resurgence in popularity in the Boston area; *Appleton Diaries*, 127.

46. Sarah Ker Butler to Mother, July 27, August 8, 1854, folder 34, no. 1467, Ker family papers, SHC.

47. Mary Ker to Mother, July 15, 1855; Mary Ker to Brother, August 18, 1855, Ker family papers, SHC.

48. William Swift diaries, May 6, 1822, MHS.

49. Virginia Smith, "Cleanliness: The Development of Idea and Practice in Britain, 1770–1850," Ph.D. diss., University of London, 1985, 261–268. See, for example, E. S. Farson of Philadelphia, sale of shower baths, water coolers, and filterers, 73x394, 74x394.2, 74x394.3, printed bills, collection 71, Joseph Downs collection, WL; Richard L. Bushman and Claudia L. Bushman, "The Early History of Cleanliness in America," *JAH* 74 (March 1988): 1225. *PI*, January 8, 1831, notes that New Orleans was getting a supply of pure water so that private cisterns could be turned into bathing houses. Maureen Ogle, *All the Modern Conveniences: American Household Plumbing, 1840–1890* (Baltimore, 1996), 4, 67; Suellen Hoy, *Chasing Dirt: The American Pursuit of Cleanliness* (New York, 1995), 14.

50. *PI*, October 11, 1850. See also iron and brass bathtub, dated 1842–1857, manuf. Boston, object id. 1983.0088; Ironstone bathtub, dated 1833–1870, object id. 1987.0035, Winterthur; Mary Dyer, 1852, two bathtubs, 93x17.19, inventories and vendues, collection 61, box 19, Joseph Downs collection, WL.

51. Catharine Sedgwick, *Home* (Boston, 1835), 8; Andrew Combe, *The Principles of Physiology Applied to the Preservation of Health* (Edinburgh, 1833), discussed in Smith, "Cleanliness," 213; *Godey's Lady's Book*, September 1833. A year later the popular women's magazine recommended a warm bath as a good remedy for a long, hot day and reassured readers that it was not at all debilitating; *Godey's*, June 1834. For the rising

number of bathtubs in England, see David J. Eveleigh, *Bogs, Baths, and Basins: The Story of Domestic Sanitation* (Stroud, Gloucestershire, 2002), 61–81.

52. Hoy, *Chasing Dirt*, 14; Frances Burgess diary, May 9, 1864, Joseph Andrews diary, 28, Joseph Downs Collection, WL; Lorenza Stephens Berbineau journal, October 24, 1853, Francis Cabot Lowell II papers, MHS; Stephan Scott, "Faith and Family in the Old South," Ph.D. diss., Indiana University, 2001, 280; John Hammond Moore, ed., *A Plantation Mistress on the Eve of the Civil War: The Diary of Keziah Goodwyn Brevard, 1860–61* (Columbia, S.C., 1993), 111.

53. George Shattuck diary, December 20, 1834, MHS; Philadelphia City Directory, 1839; *NYEP*, July 3, 1832; New York City Directory, 1853–1854; Directory of the City of Boston, George Adams, 1850.

54. *NYEP*, March 27, July 3, 1832. "The Peel testimonial will, it is stated, be in the form of baths and wash houses, that being considered by the committee to combine the greatest amount of public good"; *PI*, October 10, 1850. In smaller cities, however, public baths seem to have gotten less support: Louisa Jane Trumbell of Worcester observed, "Emma & U set out for a ride. We went out to the Tide Mill in Worcester to take a salt bath but the bathing house was destroyed so we drove on"; June 14, 1835, Louisa Jane Trumbell diary, AAS.

55. *PI*, October 1, 1840; Margaret Bain Cameron Mordecai listed bath tickets along with her washing among her expenses in Philadelphia for November 1856; *PI*, October 9, 1850.

56. *NODP*, May 21, May 29, 1842; Holcombe diary, March 14, April 16, June 12, 1855, SHC, for his purchase of a shave, shampoo, and "bathing operations" at a French barbering establishment.

57. *Godey's Lady's Book* included model cottage designs with space for water closets in the September and October issues of 1846.

58. See, for example, the ads for James Chapters, Neale and Tatum, and Jacob W. Clark, in *PI*, October 7, 1850. See also *NODP*, January 4, 1856.

59. Hoy, *Chasing Dirt*, 24; foot bath, dated 1815–1842, object id. 1966.0561, Winterthur; John Burdell, *Tobacco and Health Almanac for 1849* (New York, 1848), 28.

60. Sarah Evelina Ker diary, June 1841, Ker family papers, SHC; Holcombe diary, May 1, 1855, SHC.

61. Bushman and Bushman, "Early History," 1234; Hoy, *Chasing Dirt*, 14; *NODP*, May 21, 1842; September 1, 14, 1843; Vigarello, *Concept of Cleanliness*; Joseph Andrews diary, 29, McKinstry collection, WL; "Hotels," box 3, Joseph Downs collection, WL; Harold Donaldson Eberlein, "When Society First Took a Bath," in Leavitt and Numbers, *Sickness and Health in America*, 340.

62. Lewis, *Ladies and Gentlemen on Display*; Holcombe diary, January 22, 1855, SHC. *Godey's Lady's Book*, February 1834, warned mothers not to give medicine to healthy children as a preventive, advice that spoke to the often harmful effects of allopathic medicines. William Cameron to Duncan Cameron, October 12, 1813, Cameron family papers, SHC; Susan E. Cayleff, *Wash and Be Healed: The Water-Cure Movement and Women's Health* (Philadelphia, 1987); Jane D. Donegan, "Hydropathic Highway to

Health": Women and the Water Cure in Antebellum America (New York, 1986); *New Graefenberg Water-Cure Reporter* 1 (January 1849): 13.

63. *New Graefenberg Water-Cure Reporter* 1 (January 1849): 14; *Tobacco and Health Almanac for 1849*, 29.

64. *New Graefenberg Water-Cure Reporter* 1 (January 1849): 21; *Water-Cure Journal and Teacher of Health* 1 (March 1845): 68.

65. *New Graefenberg Water-Cure Reporter* 1 (December 1849): 373, 380; *Water-Cure Journal and Teacher of Health* 1 (January 1845): 46; 1 (February 1845): 54; 1 (March 1845): 67; 1 (December 1845): 30; *PI*, November 9, 1830; February 3, 1831.

66. *Water-Cure Journal and Teacher of Health* 1 (March 1845): 70, for the quotation from Alcott on the importance of cleanliness 1 (May 1845), for the quotation from William Penn's letter to Dr. Bayard on Native American bathing (101), and reprint from the *Boston Post* on how bathing can remove decayed animal matter from the skin (111); *New Graefenberg Water-Cure Reporter* 2 (May 1850): 157.

67. *Water-Cure Journal and Teacher of Health* 1 (April 1845).

68. Ibid., 1 (November 1844): 11, 14; *New Graefenberg Water-Cure Reporter* 2 (March 1850): 74; 2 (January 1850): 17–18.

69. *Water-Cure Journal and Teacher of Health* 1 (December 1844): 26.

70. *Water-Cure Journal and Teacher of Health* 1 (November 1844): 10.

71. Sarah E. Lawrence Diary, December 22, 1850, MHS; Cayleff, *Wash and Be Healed*, 64–65, and 195, n. 63; Anna Quincy Thaxter Cushing papers, February 3, 1854, AAS; Holcombe diary, June 10, 1855, SHC.

72. Emeline Draper Rice to Sophia Draper White, March 12, 1851, Draper-Rice family papers, AAS.

73. Emeline Draper Rice to Sophia Draper White, March 27, 1849; January 18, 1851.

74. Sophia Draper White to Emeline Draper Rice, New York, June 2, 1851, Draper-Rice family papers, AAS.

75. Ibid.

76. Emeline Draper Rice to Sophia Draper White, February 6, 1853; Sophia Draper White to Emeline Draper Rice, March 21, 1853.

77. Emeline Draper Rice to Sophia Draper White, January 4, 1853.

78. Sophia Draper White to Emeline Draper Rice, June 27, 1853.

79. Emeline Draper Rice to Sophia Draper White, July 20, 1853.

80. Emeline Draper Rice to Sophia Draper White, December 27, 1853; February 16, 1854; Sophia Draper White to Emeline Draper Rice, August 4, December 6, 1853; June 14, 1854; New York City Directory, 1853–1854, 12th ed., Charles R. Rode.

81. Sophia Draper White to Lucy Draper, August 17, 1865, Draper-Rice family papers, AAS.

82. Margaret Baines Cameron Mordecai to Mr. Mordecai, November 21, December 16, 1855; January 25, 5, February 1, July 30, 1856, Cameron family papers, SHC.

12. MISSION

1. *Little Bill at the Pump* (Philadelphia, 1850), AAS pamphlet.
2. Ibid.
3. Bruce Dorsey, *Reforming Men and Women: Gender in the Antebellum City* (Ithaca, N.Y., 2002), 52–89.
4. Suellen Hoy, *Chasing Dirt: the American Pursuit of Cleanliness* (New York, 1995), 26–27; Christine Stansell, *City of Women: Sex and Class in New York, 1789–1860* (New York, 1986), 200.
5. Stansell, *City of Women*, 200–216.
6. For the new prominence of cleanliness in English public discourse, see Virginia Smith, *Clean: A History of Personal Hygiene and Purity* (New York, 2007), 284–285.
7. Ann Stoler, "Tense and Tender Ties: The Politics of Comparison in North American History and (Post) Colonial Studies," *JAH* 88 (December 2001): 829–865; Ann Stoler, *Race and the Education of Desire: Foucault's History of Sexuality and the Colonial Order of Things* (Durham, N.C., 1995); Ann Stoler, ed., *Haunted by Empire: Geographies of Intimacy in North American History* (Durham, N.C., 2006).
8. Walter Johnson, *Soul by Soul: Life inside the Antebellum Slave Market* (Cambridge, Mass., 1999).
9. *American Sunday School Union Select Poetry for Children*, (Philadelphia, 1857), 38–39.
10. Ibid., 70–71.
11. Henry Barnard, *School Architecture; or, Contributions to the Improvement of School-Houses in the United States*, 2nd ed. (New York, 1848), 20.
12. *New Graefenberg Water-Cure Reporter* 1 (January 1849): 27. Other features in the same journal argued for the importance of proper ventilation; see1 (December 1849): 380; 2 (January 1850): 16.
13. *Tobacco and Health Almanac for 1849* (New York, 1848), 28.
14. Frances Anne Kemble, *Journal of a Residence on a Georgian Plantation in 1838–1839*, ed. John A. Scott (Athens, Ga., 1984), 13.
15. See, for example, *Godey's Lady's Book*, March 1836.
16. Louisa Clapp Trumbell diary, January 5, 1840, AAS; Susan Weeks Curtis diary, vol. 5, January 1859, Walter G. Curtis papers, no. 22, SHC; Sarah Ker Butler to Mother, August 9, 1853, Ker family papers, SHC.
17. William A. Alcott, *Essay on the Construction of School-Houses, to which was awarded the prize offered by the American Institute of Instruction, August 1831* (Boston, 1832), 7.
18. Barnard, *School Architecture*, 20.
19. Ibid., 163, excerpt from William Hosking, *A Guide to the Proper Regulation of Buildings in Towns as a means of promoting and securing the health, comfort, and safety of the inhabitants* (1848).
20. Ibid., 47, 36. See also James Whorton, *Inner Hygiene: Constipation and the Pursuit of Health in Modern Society* (New York, 2000).
21. Barnard, *School Architecture*, 230; William Holcombe diary, June 18, 1855, SHC.
22. *The Two Homes Compared; or, the Advantages of Cleanliness* (Philadelphia, 1850).
23. Ibid., 11.

24. Ibid., 17.

25. Ibid., 27.

26. Ibid., 28.

27. Ibid., 29.

28. Ibid., 30.

29. Ibid., 39, 31.

30. Ibid., 33.

31. Christine Jacobson Carter, ed., *The Diary of Dolly Lunt Burge, 1848–1879* (Athens, Ga., 1997), April 1, 1849, p. 37; January 13, 1850, pp. 50–51.

32. Horatio Alger, *Ragged Dick, and Mark the Match Boy* (1868; New York, 1962), 40, 57; Katherine Ashenburg, *The Dirt on Clean: An Unsanitized History* (New York, 2007), 172.

33. Alger, *Ragged Dick*, 57.

34. Ibid., 58.

35. Anne McClintock, *Imperial Leather: Race, Gender, and Sexuality in the Colonial Conquest* (New York, 1995); Timothy Burke, *Lifebuoy Men, Lux Women: Commodification, Consumption, and Cleanliness in Modern Zimbabwe* (Durham, N.C., 1996).

36. Eric Lott, *Love and Theft: Blackface Minstrelsy and the American Working Class* (New York, 1993); Thomas Holt, "Marking: Race, Race-Making, and the Writing of History," *AHR* 100 (February 1995): 1–17.

37. *The Slaves' Friend*, 1, no. 8 (1836): 5–6.

38. J. Hume Simons, *The Planter's Guide and Family Book of Medicine; for the instruction and use of planters, families, country people and all others who may be out of the reach of physicians or unable to employ them*, 3rd ed. (Charleston, S.C., 1848), 207–210. Guides to slave health written for Caribbean planters were also popular among North American planters: see Dr. Collins, *Practical Rules for the management and medical treatment of Negro slaves, in the sugar colonies* (London, 1803), 51–73, 120–131, 231–266. See also Todd Savitt, *Medicine and Slavery: The Diseases and Health Care of Blacks in Antebellum Virginia* (Chicago, 1978), for diseases resulting from poor plantation sanitation, 57–73; Johnson, *Soul by Soul*; Ariela Gross, *Double Character: Slavery and Mastery in the Antebellum South Courtroom* (Princeton, N.J., 2000); Sharla Fett, *Working Cures: Healing, Health, and Power on Southern Slave Plantations* (Chapel Hill, 2002); John Harley Warner, "The Idea of Southern Medical Distinctiveness: Medical Knowledge and Practice in the Old South," in Judith Walzer Leavitt and Ronald L. Numbers, eds., *Sickness and Health in America: Readings in the History of Medicine and Public Health* (Madison, Wis., 1978), 53–65.

39. Margaret Humphreys, *Yellow Fever in the South* (New Brunswick, N.J., 1992), 21–25; Jo Ann Carrigan, "Yellow Fever: Scourge of the South," in Todd L. Savitt and James Harvey Young, eds., *Disease and Distinctiveness in the American South* (Knoxville, Tenn., 1988), 55–78, esp. 62–63; Sally G. McMillen, *Motherhood in the Old South: Pregnancy, Childbirth, and Infant Rearing* (Baton Rouge, La., 1990), 16–17.

40. John Hammond Moore, ed., *A Plantation Mistress on the Eve of the Civil War: The Diary of Keziah Goodwyn Hopkins Brevard, 1860–1861* (Columbia, S.C., 1993), 43, 69, 70.

41. Kemble, *Journal of a Residence*, 10.

42. Moore, *Plantation Mistress*, 95, 100.

43. Burns family papers, no. 3861, p. 11, SHC.

44. Ibid., 11–12.

45. Ibid., 11, 14; Kemble, *Journal of a Residence*, 20.

46. Eliza Anne Marsh Robertson diary, November 5, 6, 7, 9, 1854; April 17, 1856, SHC; Moore, *Plantation Mistress*, 93.

47. Robertson diary, March 13, July 16, 1855; November 25, 1854; March 2, April 4, 1855.

48. Cornelia Peake McDonald, *A Woman's Civil War: A Diary with Reminiscences of the War from March 1862*, ed. Minrose C. Gwin (Madison, Wis., 1992), June 11, 1863, p. 154.

49. Ella Gertrude Clanton Thomas, *The Secret Eye: The Journal of Ella Gertrude Clanton Thomas, 1848–1889*, ed. Virginia Ingraham Burr (Chapel Hill, 1990), April 27, 1855, p. 125.

50. Robertson diary, March 21, 1856; Kemble, *Journal of a Residence*, 168.

51. Kemble, *Journal of Residence*, 168, 177–178.

52. See for example, ibid., 11, 17, 24–25, 28, 34, 45; Catherine Clinton, ed., *Fanny Kemble's Journals* (Cambridge, Mass., 2000), 50, 55; Stoler, *Haunted by Empire*.

53. Kemble, *Journal of a Residence*, 61.

54. Ibid.

55. Ibid., 61–62; Sean Quinlan, "Colonial Bodies, Hygiene, and Abolitionist Politics in Eighteenth-Century France," in Tony Ballantyne and Antoinette Burton, eds., *Bodies in Contact: Rethinking Colonial Encounters in World History* (Durham, N.C., 2005), 106–121.

56. Kemble, *Journal of a Residence*, 67–68.

57. Ibid., 69.

57. Ibid., 71, 98, 100.

58. Ibid., 88, 77, 98, 69.

60. Ibid., 134, 173.

61. Ibid., 173, 185.

62. Ibid., 220.

63. Ibid., 182, 188.

64. Ibid., 105, 129.

65. Frederick Law Olmsted, *The Cotton Kingdom: A Traveller's Observations on Cotton and Slavery in the American Slave States*, ed., Arthur M. Schlesinger (New York, 1984), 177, 519.

66. Ibid., 519.

67. Ibid., 520.

68. Stansell, *City of Women*, 212–213; Stoler, *Haunted by Empire*.

AFTERWORD

1. *A New Guide to Health compiled from the Catechism of Dr. Faust* (Newburyport, Mass., 1810).

2. Michel Foucault, "The Politics of Health in the Eighteenth Century," in *Power/Knowledge: Selected Interviews and Other Writings, 1972–1977*, ed. Colin Gordon (New York,

1980), 166–182, offers a sharp analysis of this transformation but fails to explain how and why women might have been its main protagonists.

3. David Barnes, *The Great Stink of Paris and the Nineteenth-Century Struggle against Filth and Germs* (Baltimore, 2006).

4. *Harper's Weekly*, September 27, 1862, p. 624. Thanks to Melissa Naulin for this reference.

5. Leslie Schwalm, *"A Hard Fight for We": Women's Transition from Slavery to Freedom in South Carolina* (Urbana, Ill., 1997); Margaret Humphreys, *Yellow Fever and the South* (New Brunswick, N.J., 1992), 1–3, 19, 27; Margaret Humphreys, Appendix 2, "Yellow Fever since 1793: History and Historiography," in J. Worth Estes and Billy G. Smith, eds., *A Melancholy Scene of Devastation: The Public Response to the 1793 Yellow Fever Epidemic* (Canton, Mass., 1997), 183–198; Suellen Hoy, *Chasing Dirt: The American Pursuit of Cleanliness* (New York, 1995).

6. *Harper's Weekly*, August 24, 1861, "Rules for Preserving the Health of the Soldier."

7. Nancy Tomes, *The Gospel of Germs: Men, Women, and the Microbe in American Life* (Cambridge, Mass., 1998), 5–6, 10; Hoy, *Chasing Dirt*.

BIBLIOGRAPHIC ESSAY

The primary sources for this study are wide-ranging and eclectic. Popular medical guides, conduct-of-life (manners) books, newspapers, religious tracts, magazines, and didactic fiction all contain evidence of Anglo–North American cleanliness standards. Such sources are useful for tracking changing ideas about cleanliness but are less helpful in illuminating how people actually cared for their bodies. Diaries, travel narratives, and advice books that reveal individual personal experience provide a helpful corrective. But these personal accounts provide much better documentation of what Jacqueline S. Wilkie ("Submerged Sensuality: Technology and Perceptions of Bathing," *Journal of Social History*, 1986) has described as "middle class purpose," than of "lower class practice," overemphasizing purposeful care of the body by the literate, who were often the children or wives of doctors, and underemphasizing recreation—most notably, swimming—which was motivated as much by sociability and pleasure as by medical theories about the functions of the body.

No single theorist enables us to untangle the complicated history of cleanliness. Norbert Elias, Michel Foucault, Mikhail Bakhtin, and the sociologist Pierre Bourdieu direct us to the body and its habits to discover the rise of modern sensibilities. Elias's *The Civilizing Process* (1939, 1994), perhaps the most influential Western history of the body, traces a centuries-long dispersion of politeness from the court to the middle class, with modernity emerging from rising thresholds of embarrassment. This polite body supplanted the early modern body portrayed by Bakhtin in *Rabelais and His World* (1968) as "grotesque," unruly, and unconstrained. Foucault dates modernity to the moment when incarceration replaced public spectacles of punishment (*Discipline and Punish*, 1979), and efforts to classify sexual desire created normative standards for behavior (*History of Sexuality*, 1990). Foucault's "The Politics of Health in the Eighteenth Century" (1980) points to the state's interest in the family's growing role in health care. Bourgeois methods of body care, including scrutiny of the child's body, accompanied these developments—part of what Foucault describes as an "epistemic shift" that produced the modern body and impinged on its exploration of pleasure. But we never learn from Foucault what middle-class women's motives might be for defining and participating in new standards. Bourdieu (*The Logic of Practice*, 1990; *Distinction*, 1984) emphasizes the impact of contemporary society's changing expectations for deportment on the body's own sensibilities, noting how new social and economic arrangements usher in new ways of inhabiting the body. Peter Stallybrass and Allon White (*The Politics and Poetics of Transgression*, 1986) analyze how the lower body serves a metaphor for the working class and their neighborhoods. In sharp contrast, the anthropologist Mary Douglas (*Purity and Danger*, 1966) sets aside questions of modernity to find cleanliness at the root of almost all social classification, in both modern and so-called "primitive" cultures, as society deals both metaphorically and practically with "matter out of place." William Ian Miller's *Anatomy of Disgust* (1997) provides a sophisticated interdisciplinary analysis of disgust and how it orders society, morality, and politics.

These sophisticated studies leave a number of questions unanswered. None of these studies accounts for women's central role in producing the modern body. Efforts to avoid disease also get short shrift in all of these accounts, which emphasize instead the social and symbolic meanings of cleanliness. In fact, as I have argued, health concerns were never wholly distinct from cultural symbols and social imperatives; rather, techniques for ensuring long life often overlapped in important ways with the pursuit of beauty and refinement. Furthermore, all of these theorists focus on Europe, paying little attention to the impact of a wider world. Douglas offers an intriguing analysis of the larger meaning of filth taboos but gives little guidance about how to interpret concerns with smell. Foucault places too much importance on the sexed body, slighting the nonsexual meanings of "decency" at the center of bourgeois culture. Bourdieu helps us to understand the relationship between calculated efforts at distinction and involuntary revulsion, although he, too, slights health concerns.

Other scholars point to a global context for manners, medical theories, and forms of body care. The anthropologist Ann Stoler (*Race and the Education of Desire*, 1995) gives Foucault's body-centered theory an imperial geography. Sexual modernity in the Foucauldian sense becomes for Stoler a consequence of imperialism's penetration of the intimate lives of colonized peoples. Her approach can also help us to reframe Elias's classic account of politeness: Europeans expanded into the Atlantic basin as courtly manners began to spread, and they judged indigenous peoples according to this new standard. As the historian Anna Bryson (*From Courtesy to Civility: Changing Codes of Conduct in Early Modern England*, 1998) observes, English encounters with New World indigenous peoples stimulated a collective European sense of cultural superiority over the Irish and Native Americans, contained in judgments of civility and savagery. Beyond this claim, however, she does not explore how the concept of civility might have arisen from specific Euro-indigenous encounters, but focuses instead on establishing a detailed English context. "Civility," Bryson explains, "is both a static model of well-ordered humanity and a technique of self-orientation in a complex social world" (96).

I have been influenced by several other excellent studies of body care. Georges Vigarello (*The Concept of Cleanliness*, 1988) provides perhaps the most sophisticated cultural history of the decline and resurgence of bathing and the importance of linen for bodily cleanliness. Lawrence Wright's *Clean and Decent* (1960) is a witty tour of cleanliness through the ages. Harold Eberlein, "When Society First Took a Bath" (1943), presents an older but still useful account of the rising American interest in bathing, the establishment of public baths, and the ownership of bathtubs in the early nineteenth century. Richard L. Bushman and Claudia Bushman, "The Early History of Cleanliness" (1988), trace the gradual turn to bathing in hot soapy water, late in the nineteenth century, from the more casual use of water—washing hands and face in basins—earlier in the century, a shift they attribute to growing interest in appearance as a manifestation of morality. Jean-Pierre Goubert, *The Conquest of Water* (1986), recounts the increasing presence of water as a necessity of French life during the nineteenth century, a process he claims transformed urban architecture, landscapes, public health, and ways of caring for the body. Maureen Ogle, *All the Modern Conveniences* (1996), documents a similar process in the United States, reminding readers that even before the availability of water from commercial suppliers, people from all walks of life used cisterns and local sources for domestic purposes.

Several essential works specifically address the history of the body in North America. Joyce Chaplin (*Subject Matter*, 2001) claims that an initial English admiration for Indian bodies and technology soon gave way to indictments of the artifice believed to be responsible for indigenous vulnerability to disease. Richard Bushman, *The Refinement of America* (1992), argues that the middling order appropriated aristocratic manners and material culture during the eighteenth century in an effort to bolster its own class authority, and continued to pursue gentility despite the emerging contradictions between genteel ways and republican ideals. C. Dallett Hemphill, *Bowing to Necessities* (1999), argues, contra Bushman, that advice aimed at the middling order proliferated during the eighteenth century, a sign of the rising political importance of these groups in the flattened social hierarchy of British North America. Conduct-of-life authors did not simply appropriate advice formerly intended for aristocrats as a means of seizing class authority, she claims, but transformed it, placing more emphasis on correct behavior with peers and achieving gentility than on distinguishing themselves from the lower orders. Jane Donegan, *"Hydropathic Highway to Health": Women and Water-Cure in Antebellum America* (1986), and Susan Cayleff, *Wash and Be Healed: The Water-Cure Movement and Women's Health* (1987), provide complementary accounts of the water cure in the antebellum United States.

Several historians examine linen production and consumption. Eric Kerridge, *Textile Manufactures in Early Modern England* (1985), provides an indispensable and encyclopedic account of England's textile industries, while W. H. Crawford, *The Impact of the Domestic Linen Industry in Ulster* (2005), looks at Irish linen production. C. Willett Cunnington and Phillis Cunnington, *The History of Underclothes* (1951), provide the classic account of changing fashions in English undergarments. Elizabeth Ewing, *Everyday Dress* (1984), surveys changing fashions in Britain before 1900. Beverly Lemire, *Dress, Culture, and Commerce* (1997), presents multifaceted cultural and economic analysis of changing English clothing markets. I have been especially influenced by the work of Robert DuPlessis.

There are several excellent studies of the changing medical perspectives reflected in cleanliness. Two of the most important were unpublished dissertations. Virginia Smith ("Cleanliness: The Development of Idea and Practice in Britain, 1770–1850," 1985) stresses health as an important motive for cleanliness. Her recent book, *Clean* (2007), sets this study in a broad context from prehistory to the present. Mark Jenner ("Early Modern English Conceptions of Cleanliness and Dirt" [1991]) attempts to unite a history of medicine with the history of the built environment. He analyzes London's seventeenth-century environmental regulations, noting the importance of smell as an indication of cleanliness, and the significance of changes to urban spaces, like sidewalks.

Also essential are three works by Charles Rosenberg: *The Cholera Years* (1962), the still unsurpassed account of cholera epidemics in the nineteenth century United States; "Medical Text and Social Context: Explaining William Buchan's *Domestic Medicine*" (1983), which examines the significance of William Buchan's brand of domestic advice; and "Catechisms of Health: The Body in the Prebellum Classroom" (1995), which looks at the presentation of the body in antebellum health primers. James C. Riley, *The Eighteenth-Century Campaign to*

Avoid Disease (1987), explains the eighteenth-century attribution of disease to environmental causes and the eventual incorporation of contagion into this model as yet one more airborne environmental agent that could infect the body through respiration. Nancy Tomes (*The Gospel of Germs*, 1998) presents a compelling history of the American popular reception of the germ theory. She finds the American housewife preoccupied with preventing disease during the 1870s, even before the germ theory saddled her with the responsibility for maintaining a healthy home.

Five essential histories discuss this transformation in women's domestic labor during the nineteenth century. Ruth Schwartz Cowan, *More Work for Mother* (1983), documents the rising standards that accompanied so-called labor saving devices, arguing that, by century's end, men and boys were the ones who reaped the savings in labor, leaving the housewife to perform most of her work alone. Faye Dudden, *Serving Women* (1983), argues for a shift in hired domestic labor, from the hired girl of the eighteenth century, to the domestic of the nineteenth. Jeanne Boydston's *Home and Work* (1990) reveals how larger economic changes effectively diminished the perceived value and visibility of women's domestic labor. Of the few accounts that actually deal centrally with cleanliness, Suellen Hoy's *Chasing Dirt* (1995) charts the American obsession with cleanliness from the early nineteenth century to the mid-twentieth century, noting its increasing importance as an expression of national identity and a means of Americanizing immigrants. Finally, Katherine Ashenburg's *The Dirt on Clean* (2007) presents a lively synthesis of the existing literature on cleanliness that captures many of the key transformations in Western standards and practice.

INDEX

Odor (*continued*)
erences to, 122; as a sign of moral corruption, 1–3, 341; as a source of illness, 10,
124, 175–177, 196–198, 199–200, 295; unpleasant, 158, 242–243, 285–290, 295,
350; wholesome, 139. *See also* Air; Contagion; Miasma; Perfume
Olmstead, Frederick Law, *The Cotton
Kingdom*, 302, 353, 365
Onesimus, 128. *See also* Inoculation
Oviedus, Gonzalus Ferdinandus, 54–55

Parkes, Mrs. William (Frances Byerly), *Do-
mestic Duties*, 239, 259, 272
Paschall, Elizabeth Coates, 112, 133, 139,
146, 214–215, 222, 229, 231, 232
Peabody, Stephen, 95–97, 133, 139, 147
Peale, Charles Wilson, *Epistle to a Friend
on the Means of Preserving Health*, 207–
208
Peale's Museum (New York), 294, 295–296
Pechey, John, *General Treatise of the Dis-
eases of Infants and Children*, 139
Penelope, 28
Penn, John, Jr., 206
Pennsylvania Packet, 178–182
Pepys, Samuel, 23, 26
Perfume, 1, 10, 33
Perspiration, 10, 23, 243
Peters, Lois, 162, 171, 174; Nathan, 162
Philadelphia, 123–125, 133, 147, 193, 195–
211, 212, 297, 314; reputation of, for clean-
liness, 262–263, 269–270, 297; Watering
Commission, 201, 206
Physicians, 192–193, 213–214, 222, 224–232,
297
Pigs, 39, 295
Pilgrims, 70–73, 75–77
Plague, 10, 20–21, 31–32, 127
Plumbing supplies, 268, 315
Plymouth, 70–73, 75–77
Politeness, 33–34, 120–121
Pollution, the body as a source of, 8

Poor people, 38, 128, 130–131, 148, 149–150,
171, 182, 196, 244, 283–286, 292, 297–298,
313, 326–327, 331, 339, 349, 353, 355
Poor Richard's Almanack, 139, 146
Priscilla, (Maine servant), 76
Prisons, 159, 183–184, 189, 235
Privacy, 4, 93, 158, 244–246, 253, 327, 367
Privies, 176, 315, 343
Prostitution, 17, 19–22, 143, 169, 296
Protestants, 17, 23–24
Public culture, 4
Puritans, 23–24, 58–60, 70–89, 92

Quakers, 122, 138, 206, 150, 364. *See also*
Drinker, Elizabeth Sandwith; Paschall,
Elizabeth Coates
Quarantine, 126, 128–130, 196–197, 198

Rabelais, *Pantagruel*, 10
Racial difference, cultural expressions of,
42–51, 93, 341–343, 351–352; hardening
categories of, 184; interpretations of,
347–353; significance of cleanliness for,
345–350; significance of skin color for,
42–44, 341–343. *See also* Blackamoor;
Ethiopians; Whiteness
Read, Joseph, Jr., 110
Receipt books, 213–215, 222–223, 226, 229
Refinement, 119; aspirations to, 11, 109, 155,
254; cleanliness as an indication of, 236–
238, 327; conflicted relationship of, with
masculinity, 185–189, 247; heightened
sensitivity resulting from, 246, 349; ideal
of, 116, 157, 193; material manifestations
of, 107, 152, 237; as reflected in appearance, 2, 108, 111, 269, 328, 341; reputations for, 152; and sympathy, 184
Reformers, 189, 191, 291–292, 294, 315–355
Regimen: cool, 60–61, 89–92, 234; hot,
dangers of, 89–92, 235
Religious conversion, 9
Republican motherhood, 192, 212, 224, 225
Resorts, seaside, 293, 294, 309–311; Cape